C000225005

New Testament Commentary

Exposition
of the
Epistles of Peter
and of the
Epistle of Jude

Simon J. Kistemaker

 EVANGELICAL PRESS

EVANGELICAL PRESS
16/18 High Street, Welwyn, Hertfordshire, AL6 9EQ,
England.

© Baker Book House 1987

First published by Evangelical Press 1987

ISBN 0 85234 246 2

Printed and bound in Great Britain by the Bath Press, Avon.

Contents

Contents

Abbreviations

ASV	American Standard Version
Bauer	Walter Bauer, W. F. Arndt, F. W. Gingrich, and F. W. Danker, *A Greek-English Lexicon of the New Testament,* 2d ed.
BS	*Bibliotheca Sacra*
BibTrans	*Biblical Translator*
BibZeit	*Biblische Zeitschrift*
I Clem.	First Epistle of Clement
EDT	*Evangelical Dictionary of Theology*
ExpT	*Expository Times*
GNB	Good News Bible
Interp	*Interpretation*
ISBE	*The International Standard Bible Encyclopedia,* rev. ed.
JB	Jerusalem Bible
JBL	*Journal of Biblical Literature*
JETS	*Journal of the Evangelical Theological Society*
JTS	*Journal of Theological Studies*
KJV	King James Version
LCL	Loeb Classical Library edition
LXX	Septuagint
MLB	Modern Language Bible
Moffatt	The Bible: A New Translation by James Moffatt
NAB	New American Bible
NASB	New American Standard Bible
NEB	New English Bible
NedThT	*Nederlands Theologisch Tijdschrift*
Nes-Aland	Eberhard Nestle; Kurt Aland, rev.; *Novum Testamentum Graece,* 26th ed.
NIDNTT	*New International Dictionary of New Testament Theology*
NIV	New International Version
NKJV	New King James Version
NovT	*Novum Testamentum*
NTS	*New Testament Studies*

Abbreviations

Phillips	The New Testament in Modern English
RSV	Revised Standard Version
RV	Revised Version
SB	H. L. Strack and P. Billerbeck, *Kommentar zum Neuen Testament aus Talmud und Midrasch*
SEB	Simple English Bible
SWJournTheol	*Southwest Journal of Theology*
Talmud	The Babylonian Talmud
TDNT	*Theological Dictionary of the New Testament*
Thayer	Joseph H. Thayer, *Greek-English Lexicon of the New Testament*
TR	Textus Receptus: *The Greek New Testament According to the Majority Text*
TynB	*Tyndale Bulletin*
WTJ	*Westminster Theological Journal*
ZNW	*Zeitschrift für die Neutestamentliche Wissenschaft*
ZPEB	*Zondervan Pictorial Encyclopedia of the Bible*

Exposition
of the
Epistles of Peter

Introduction

The First Epistle of Peter

Outline

A. Author
B. Source
C. Theology
D. Readers
E. Date and Place
F. Structure
G. Outline of I Peter

I n most translations, the title of this letter is simply I Peter. Some versions, however, expand this title to "The First Epistle of Peter" (NASB, NKJV) or "The First General Epistle of Peter" (MLB). The expression *general* means that the letter belongs to the category *general Epistles* which comprises Hebrews, James, I Peter, II Peter, John's epistles, and Jude.

Scribes (presumably in the second century) added titles to the individual books of the New Testament. The earliest Greek manuscripts have the unadorned title *First Peter*. But later manuscripts reveal that scribes expanded the superscription to include the terms *epistle* and *general*. Some even added the words *the apostle Peter*. Avoiding embellishment, we adopt the shortest reading of the title and call the letter First Peter.

A. Author

According to the address, Peter sent this epistle to Christians who were "scattered throughout Pontus, Galatia, Cappadocia, Asia and Bithynia" (1:1). These names refer to regions that cover most of Asia Minor (modern Turkey) and indicate that the letter was read in numerous places. Was it known in the first few centuries? The church fathers affirm that they were acquainted with Peter's epistle.

1. External Evidence

About A.D. 95, Clement of Rome wrote a letter, I Clement, to the church in Corinth. In it he provided some parallels to First Peter. The first example in Clement's epistle is the greeting, which is remarkably similar to that of Peter's letter:

> To those who are called and sanctified by the will of God through our Lord Jesus Christ. Grace and peace from God Almighty be multiplied to you through Jesus Christ.[1]

In Greek, Peter uses the same vocabulary: called, sanctified, grace and peace, be multiplied (1:2). Next, Clement writes, "Let us fix our gaze on the Blood of Christ, and let us know that it is precious to his Father."[2] The

---

1. I Clem. Salutation (LCL).
2. I Clem. 7:4 (LCL).

5

allusion to Peter's words, "the precious blood of Christ" (1:19), is unmistakable. Third, Clement's vocabulary features a number of words that occur only in Peter's epistles. And last, two of the Old Testament quotations (Prov. 10:12; 3:34) in First Peter also appear in the letter of Clement (4:8 and I Clem. 49:5; 5:5 and I Clem. 30:2).[3]

In the first half of the second century, Polycarp composed a letter to the church in Philippi. This letter has a number of quotations from First Peter; for example, "[Jesus Christ] in whom, though you did not see him, you believed in unspeakable and glorified joy" (1:3 and I Peter 1:8).[4] Even though Polycarp fails to mention Peter's name, the source of the quotations is Peter's epistle.

Toward the end of the second century (A.D. 185), Irenaeus not only quotes I Peter 1:8 but also introduces the quotation with the words "and Peter says in his Epistle."[5] In the next century, Clement of Alexandria and Tertullian quote Peter's epistle and refer to the apostle by name. Church historian Eusebius notes that Papias, who was bishop in Asia Minor (about A.D. 125), "used quotations from the first Epistle of John, and likewise also from that of Peter."[6] In short, external evidence shows that the church received this epistle as authentic and apostolic.

2. Internal Evidence

Peter's epistles bear testimony that the apostle is the author, for in the greeting the writer identifies himself as "Peter, an apostle of Jesus Christ" (1:1). The author also speaks with authority and notes that he is an eyewitness of Jesus' sufferings (5:1). Then, in the second epistle, the writer states, "Dear friends, this is now my second letter to you" (3:1). And last, Peter mentions Silas and Mark, and thus refers to apostolic helpers whose names were well known in the early church (see Acts 15:22, 37; 12:12).

Another source of internal evidence is Acts, where Luke has recorded some of Peter's sermons in summary form. Peter preached to the crowd gathered in Jerusalem for the Pentecost celebrations (Acts 2:14–40). He addressed the people who came to Solomon's Colonnade (Acts 3:11–26). Peter spoke before the Sanhedrin (Acts 4:9–12; 5:29–32). He preached in the house of Cornelius (Acts 10:34–43). And Peter counseled the Assembly of Jerusalem (Acts 15:7–11). The parallels between Peter's sermons and his

---

3. Consult Charles Bigg, *A Critical and Exegetical Commentary on the Epistles of St. Peter and St. Jude,* International Critical Commentary series (1901; Edinburgh: Clark, 1961), p. 8.

4. This is a list of the quotations in Polycarp's Epistle to the Philippians: 1:3—I Peter 1:8; 2:1—I Peter 1:13, 21; 2:2—I Peter 3:9; 5:3—I Peter 2:11; 7:2—I Peter 4:7; 8:1—I Peter 2:22, 24; 10:2—I Peter 2:12.

5. Irenaeus *Against Heresies* 4.9.2. In *The Apostolic Fathers,* vol. 1 of *The Ante-Nicene Fathers,* ed. Alexander Roberts and James Donaldson (1885; Grand Rapids: Eerdmans, 1962), p. 472. Also see *Against Heresies* 4.16.5; 5.7.2.

6. Eusebius *Ecclesiastical History* 3.39.17 (LCL).

epistle are striking. E. G. Selwyn observes, "Few would suggest that the parallels of thought and phrase between the speeches and I Peter are based upon S[ain]t Luke's reading of the Epistle."[7] Evidence, both external and internal, supports the apostolic authorship of First Peter.

3. Objections

Nevertheless, some scholars object to acknowledging Peter as author of the first epistle. They claim that they encounter a number of difficulties. Here are a few of the major objections.

History

Critics say that if Peter is the author of this letter, we should have expected him to include numerous personal reminiscences.[8] However, Peter wrote his epistle not as a historical recollection of his discipleship training with Jesus but as a letter of exhortation and encouragement addressed to suffering Christians. A second objection is this: The sufferings mentioned in the epistle cannot be a result of the persecutions Nero directed against Christians. Some scholars assume that the Neronian persecutions seemed to have been limited to the imperial city and did not spread to the provinces (where the readers of the epistles lived). Therefore, say those who doubt apostolic authorship, the epistle was written not during the reign of Emperor Nero but later, during the rule of Domitian or Trajan.[9] According to this view, Peter is not the author of the epistle that bears his name, because he died in the time of Nero.

However, the evidence is scarce to prove that a general persecution occurred in the Roman provinces during the reign of Domitian.[10] Although Domitian was a persecutor who victimized Christians, there is no indication that he instigated a persecution that affected residents in all the provinces. In addition, the evidence is insufficient to prove that Trajan adopted and executed newly declared measures against Christians. Moreover, the assertion that Neronian persecutions were limited to Rome and failed to extend to the provinces remains doubtful. If the necessary facts to establish a point in history are absent, scholars do well to avoid making dogmatic statements.

The content of First Peter reveals that the readers are first-generation converts, for "there is no hint of second-generation Christianity."[11] The

---

7. E. G. Selwyn, *The First Epistle of St. Peter: The Greek Text with Introduction, Notes, and Essays* (London: Macmillan, 1946), p. 36.

8. Refer to Ernest Best, *I Peter,* New Century Bible series (London: Oliphants, 1971), p. 52.

9. Consult Francis Wright Beare, *The First Epistle of Peter: The Greek Text with Introduction and Notes,* 2d ed. (Oxford: Blackwell, 1961), p. 13.

10. See Donald Guthrie, *New Testament Introduction,* rev. ed. (Downers Grove: Inter-Varsity, 1971), pp. 781–83.

11. J. N. D. Kelly, *A Commentary on the Epistles of Peter and Jude,* Thornapple Commentaries series (1969; Grand Rapids: Baker, 1981), p. 30.

internal evidence of the epistle, then, seems to point to the time of Nero, not to the reign of either Domitian or Trajan.

A third objection pertains to the respective missionary fields of Peter and Paul. Critics argue that Peter could not have written a letter to churches which Paul had founded. But both Acts and Paul's epistles furnish no proof that Paul the apostle to the Gentiles established churches in Pontus, Cappadocia, and Bithynia. The contrary is true, for Luke reports that the Spirit of Jesus did not allow Paul and his companions to enter Bithynia (Acts 16:7). Besides, the argument of the critics loses its force when we consider Peter's visit to the Corinthian church—a church founded by Paul (see I Cor. 1:12; 9:5).

Style

Scholars who object to Petrine authorship assert that an unschooled fisherman from an obscure village along the Lake of Galilee would be incapable of composing a letter in excellent Greek. As evidence they refer to Acts 4:13 where Luke observes that the members of the Sanhedrin took note of Peter's and John's courage and "realized that they were unschooled, ordinary men." Werner Georg Kümmel states, "The language of I Peter is in impeccable Greek, which uses numerous rhetorical devices: word order (1:23; 3:16); parallel clauses (4:11); series of similar compounds (1:4), etc. . . . And the numerous O[ld] T[estament] quotations and allusions stem without exception from the LXX. Both are inconceivable for the Galilean Peter."[12]

Before we are able to assess the objection, we must take note of a number of points. First, in the eighth century before Christ Isaiah already called Galilee "Galilee of the Gentiles" (Isa. 9:1; also see Matt. 4:15). In the days of Jesus, Galilee was heavily influenced by Greek culture and the people knew the Greek language. For example, both Matthew and James, native Galileans, composed a Gospel and a letter respectively in acceptable Greek.

Next, after Peter left Jerusalem (Acts 12:17), he traveled extensively in areas where Greek was the first language of the population. We know from his speeches recorded in Acts that he was able to express himself well; we assume that he developed his oratorical and writing skills during the years of his apostleship.

Last, Peter informs the reader that he has written his epistle with the help of Silas (5:12). We would do injustice to the text if we interpret it to mean that Silas was only the letter carrier and not the helpful scribe. From Luke's account in Acts, we know that Silas was a leader in the church (15:22), a prophet (15:32), a fellow worker of Paul (15:40), and a Roman citizen (16:37). Paul mentions Silas in three of his epistles (II Cor. 1:19; I Thess. 1:1; II Thess. 1:1). Granted that we have no certainty whether Silas assisted

---

12. Werner Georg Kümmel, *Introduction to the New Testament,* trans. A. J. Mattill, Jr., 14th ed. (Nashville and New York: Abingdon, 1966), p. 297.

Paul in letter writing,[13] we are sure of Silas's help in the composition of First Peter.

We do not have to assume that Silas drafted Peter's epistle,[14] for then we make Silas, not Peter, the author of the epistle. It is more acceptable to state that Peter wrote the letter and Silas assisted him, just as Tertius helped Paul in writing the Epistle to the Romans (see Rom. 16:22).

Let it be sufficient to say that Jews and Christians in the provinces read the Greek Septuagint instead of the Hebrew text. Writing his epistle, Peter used the Septuagint to effectively communicate God's revelation.

Composition

One last objection to Petrine authorship concerns the composition of the epistle. The letter seems to be a composite production because it has two separate conclusions. In 4:11, the critics assert, the author writes a doxology concluded with the word *amen*. The next verse begins with the familiar address, "dear friends," and thus marks the beginning of a second letter. Also, 5:10–11 is a conclusion in the form of a prayer, doxology, and *amen*. The final greetings seem to come from still another writer. However, New Testament writers often intersperse doxologies in their discourses. Take Paul's epistle to the Romans, for example, which has numerous benedictions (1:25; 9:5; 11:36; 15:33; 16:20, 24 [variant reading], 27). Finally, the argument that the address *dear friends* marks the beginning of a letter cannot be applied consistently. Peter uses this expression also in 2:11, where the context simply does not allow a break. In brief, Peter composes his letter and follows the style current in his day.

Inference

On the basis of both external and internal evidence in addition to historical and stylistic considerations, we accept First Peter as an apostolic book written by Peter. And we conclude that this traditional view appears "more reasonable than any other alternative hypothesis."[15]

B. Source

The names *Peter* and *Paul* always appear in this sequence. The order can be attributed to the fact that Peter, not Paul, was one of the original disciples, and with James and John, sons of Zebedee, belonged to the inner circle of Jesus' disciples. After the ascension of Jesus, Peter became the leader of the eleven apostles and of the emerging Jerusalem church. Peter,

---

13. Consult Selwyn for further details. *The First Epistle of St. Peter*, pp. 9–17, 369–84.

14. See Kelly, *Peter and Jude*, p. 215.

15. Guthrie, *New Testament Introduction*, p. 790. Also see Alan M. Stibbs, *The First Epistle General of Peter*, Tyndale New Testament Commentaries series (Grand Rapids: Eerdmans, 1960), p. 23.

accompanied by John, went to Samaria to acknowledge the reception of the Samaritans into the Christian church (Acts 8:14–25). And Peter preached the gospel in the home of Cornelius, a Roman centurion (Acts 10:27–48).

Even though Paul calls himself "the least of the apostles" (I Cor. 15:9), he is better known than Peter. Paul gained prominence because of the thirteen epistles he wrote. Among his letters are the epistle of Christian liberty (Galatians), the charter of Christianity (Romans), and the pastoral epistles to Timothy and Titus. Paul is the theologian of the early church, yet Peter's letter ought not to be overlooked.

Peter, too, is a theologian, as his first epistle clearly shows. He combines theological instruction and advice for practical Christian living, so that his epistle from beginning to end is a didactical document. Granted that already in the sermons that Luke recorded in Acts Peter demonstrates his theological acumen, in his first epistle we encounter Peter as a theologian.

"Probably no document in the N[ew] T[estament] is so theological as 1 Peter, if 'theological' is taken in the strict sense of teaching about God."[16] Peter mentions God's characteristics of holiness, goodness, faithfulness, and grace. He refers to God's work of electing, regenerating, redeeming, and judging his people. And Peter defines his doctrine of Christ by disclosing the divinity, humanity, and sinlessness of Jesus. Furthermore, his Christology features Christ's resurrection and ascension. Peter also points to the ministry of the Holy Spirit, to the early church, and to the end of time.

1. Dependence on Paul

Before we discuss Peter's theology as such, we must ask a few questions. First, is Peter dependent on Paul for his theology? No, because we lack evidence that Peter slavishly copied Paul's epistles. Undoubtedly he was fully acquainted with Paul's writings (see especially II Peter 3:15–16), because the allusions to the Pauline epistles in these letters are numerous.[17] But similarities can be attributed to a mutual interest in and discussion of doctrinal issues. Parallelism of Peter's and Paul's writings, then, can be explained by the mutual respect these two apostles had for one another as well as by the view that the one apostle borrows from the other. That is, these two apostles had a relationship characterized by interdependence. The possibility of personal meetings held in Jerusalem, Asia Minor, Mace-

---

16. Ralph P. Martin, "Peter, First Epistle of," *ISBE*, vol. 3, p. 809. Also see *The Acts, the Letters, the Apocalypse*, vol. 2 of *New Testament Foundations: A Guide for Christian Students*, 2 vols. (Grand Rapids: Eerdmans, 1978), p. 344. And consult W. D. Kirkpatrick, "The Theology of First Peter," *SWJournTheol* 25 (1982): 58–81.

17. From the list of parallels which Bigg provides, I mention only those that are prominent: from Ephesians, 1:21—I Peter 3:22; 5:22–24—I Peter 3:1–6; from Romans, 4:24—I Peter 1:21; 8:18—I Peter 5:1; 8:34—I Peter 3:22; 12:1—I Peter 2:5. *The Epistles of St. Peter and St. Jude*, pp. 16–18.

donia, Greece, or Italy is not unthinkable. In fact, some of these meetings we know about from references in Paul's epistle to the Galatians (1:18; 2:9, 11–14) and in Acts (15:2, 7).

Moreover, because Paul encouraged Christians to read his letters in the churches, Peter was acquainted with their content (II Peter 3:15–16). We should be careful, however, not to suppose that Peter was completely dependent on Paul's epistles. The truth of the matter is that Peter composed his epistle as an independent writer.

2. Dependence on James

Next, is Peter dependent on the Epistle of James? The parallelism between James 4:6–10 and I Peter 5:5–8 is undeniable. Both writers quote Proverbs 3:34, both mention submission and humility, and both refer to the devil. A cursory look at the parallels, however, is sufficient to see a difference: Peter's version is more expansive than that of James. If we adopt the rule of thumb that the shorter reading is likely to be the original, we conclude that Peter was acquainted with the letter of James. He borrowed and expanded the text. Here are the parallels:

James 4:6–7a, 10	*I Peter 5:5–6*
	Young men, in the same way be submissive to those who
Scripture says:	are older . . . because,
"God opposes the proud	"God opposes the proud
but gives grace to the humble."	but gives grace to the humble."
Submit yourselves, then,	
to God. . . . Humble yourselves	Humble yourselves, therefore,
before the Lord,	under God's mighty hand,
and he will lift you up.	that he may lift you up
	in due time.

James 4:7b	*I Peter 5:8*
Resist the devil, and	Your enemy the devil prowls
he will flee from you.	around like a roaring lion
	looking for someone to devour.

Resemblances between James's epistle and First Peter are numerous; see, for example, James 1:1 and I Peter 1:1; James 1:2–3 and I Peter 1:6–7; James 1:10–11, 18 and I Peter 1:23. Because an affinity existed between Peter and James, Peter not only was acquainted with the Epistle of James; he also had established an interdependent relationship with James.

3. Words of Jesus

Last, Peter's epistle includes many words of Jesus, some of which are obvious; others are indicated by synonyms. Here is one distinct parallel:

John 20:29	I Peter 1:8
"Because you have seen me, you have believed; blessed are those who have not seen and yet have believed."	Though you have not seen him, you love him; and even though you do not see him now, you believe in him and are filled with an inexpressible and glorious joy.

In every chapter of this epistle, Peter alludes to the words of Jesus.[18] Robert H. Gundry observes, "Examination of the gospel-passages where [these words of Jesus] appear shows that in most instances the Apostle Peter is a specially active participant in the narrative contexts."[19] Indeed, Peter remembered Jesus' teachings and in addition had taught the gospel for decades when he wrote his epistle.

C. Theology

1. Doctrine of God

Peter clearly teaches the doctrine of the Triune God at the beginning of his epistle. God the Father elects his people according to his foreknowledge, Jesus Christ shed his blood for them, and the Holy Spirit sanctifies them (1:1–2). The three persons of the Trinity take part in redeeming the sinner. Peter refers to God the Father in two other places (1:3, 17). In his epistle, he discloses God's sovereignty. God foreordains (1:2; compare 2:9), he creates (4:19), and he governs by extending his will to the believer's life: conduct (2:15), suffering (3:17; 4:19), and life in general (4:2).

Some of God's attributes that Peter notes are holiness, goodness, faithfulness, and grace. By quoting the Old Testament (Lev. 11:44, 45), Peter teaches that God is a holy God who commands his people to be holy, just as he is holy (1:15–16). He writes that "the Lord is good" (2:3). And he notes God's faithfulness in an exhortation to the believers to "commit themselves to their faithful Creator" (4:19). Moreover, he mentions God's electing grace (2:9–10), God's gift of grace (4:10–11), and the gift of grace "when Jesus Christ is revealed" (1:13).

---

18. For instance, compare 1:22 with John 13:34–35; 2:12 with Matt. 5:6; 3:9 with Luke 6:27–28; 4:7 with Luke 21:31, 34, 36; and 5:8–9 with Luke 22:31–32.

19. Robert H. Gundry, " 'Verba Christi' in I Peter: Their Implications Concerning the Authorship of I Peter and the Authenticity of the Gospel Tradition," *NTS* 13 (1966–67): 350.

Peter reveals that God displays a possessiveness toward his people when he writes, "But you are a chosen people, a royal priesthood, a holy nation, a people belonging to God" (2:9).[20] With a reference to Hosea 2:23, Peter states that the readers who at one time were "no people" now are called "people of God" (2:10). That is, God has given them new birth (1:3), so that they are "born again, not of perishable seed, but of imperishable [seed]" (1:23). God has redeemed his people, says Peter, not with perishable things (silver and gold) but with the precious blood of Jesus Christ (1:18–19). And last, God judges his people on the judgment day, when he begins with the family of God and continues with those who disobey his Word (4:17).

In summary, the doctrine of God is central in Peter's epistle. Writes Francis Wright Beare, "Clearly the thought of this writer is not Christocentric but theocentric; it begins from and returns constantly to the thought of God as Creator, Father, and Judge."[21]

2. Doctrine of Christ

Although Peter does not develop a doctrine of Christ, he implicitly directs attention to Jesus' humanity and divinity. Peter assumes the humanity of Jesus, for he admonishes us to follow in the footsteps of Christ, who is our example (2:21). And he refers to Jesus' body on the tree (2:24), on which Christ died for our sins (3:18). Also, Peter states that Christ suffered in his body (4:1) and that the apostle himself was a witness of Christ's suffering (5:1).

With quotations and allusions from Isaiah's prophecy, Peter teaches the sinlessness of Christ. "He committed no sin, and no deceit was found in his mouth" (2:22; Isa. 53:9). As the sinless Christ he bore our sins on the cross (2:24). Says Peter, "By his wounds you have been healed" (v. 24: Isa. 53:5). Christ, "a lamb without blemish or defect" (1:19; Isa. 53:7), died for the unrighteous (3:18). Peter teaches the doctrine of atonement when he points to the "sprinkling by [Christ's] blood" (1:2), and to the believer's redemption "with the precious blood of Christ" (1:19).

Peter indirectly notes the divinity of Jesus Christ. He does so by placing Jesus on the level of God the Father and mentions them together in at least two verses (1:2, 3). Thus Peter demands belief in Christ's unique sonship.[22] For Peter, Jesus is Lord (1:3; 3:15), just as the Father is Lord (1:25; 3:12).

Does Peter mention the resurrection and the ascension of Christ? Yes, most directly. At the beginning of his letter he writes that God the Father

---

20. Consult Donald Guthrie, *New Testament Theology* (Downers Grove: Inter-Varsity, 1981), p. 635.

21. Beare, *The First Epistle of Peter*, p. 33.

22. Refer to George E. Ladd, *A Theology of the New Testament* (Grand Rapids: Eerdmans, 1974), p. 599.

"has given us new birth into a living hope through the resurrection of Jesus Christ from the dead" (1:3). And when he discusses baptism, he notes that "it saves you by the resurrection of Jesus Christ" (3:21). Even the words of Peter's benediction—"his eternal glory in Christ"—suggest Jesus' resurrection (5:10). Accordingly, Donald Guthrie pointedly asserts:

> If the apostle *Peter* had anything to do with the first epistle that bears his name (and there are strong reasons for maintaining that he did), his testimony to the resurrection of Christ would be invaluable, not simply because of his apostolic office, but especially because as a former disciple of the historical Jesus he had come to accept what he had once declared unthinkable—a suffering and resurrected Messiah.[23]

We must admit that Peter's comments on the ascension are limited to one particular verse. He writes, "Jesus Christ . . . has gone into heaven and is at God's right hand" (3:21–22). Yet this single reference is sufficient, for in harmony with the rest of the New Testament Peter points to Christ's exalted position (see Acts 1:9–11; Heb. 1:3; 4:14; 12:2). Angels, authorities, and powers are subject to him (3:22; Eph. 1:21; 6:12).

3. Holy Spirit

References to the Holy Spirit are few in Peter's epistle (1:2, 11, 12; 4:14). Although they are sparse, their description of the work of the Holy Spirit is broad. That work ranges from sanctifying the elect (1:2) and predicting the sufferings of Christ and "the glories that would follow" (1:11) to guiding "those who have preached the gospel" (1:12). Not only does the Spirit take an active role in the resurrection of Christ (3:18), but also as the Spirit of glory he rests on suffering Christians (4:14).

With the words *the Spirit of Christ,* Peter links the Holy Spirit closely to Jesus Christ (1:11). This choice of words appears in Paul's epistles as well (see Rom. 8:9; Phil. 1:19). Paul also speaks of the Spirit of God's Son (Gal. 4:6). And last, Luke relates that when Paul and his companions tried to enter Bithynia, the Spirit of Jesus would not allow them to do so (Acts 16:7).

4. The Church

Peter employs the term *church* nowhere in his epistle. Yet he uses a variety of expressions to describe God's people. For instance, he depicts the followers of Jesus Christ as "God's elect" and "strangers in the world" (1:1). For Peter, believers are "a chosen people, a royal priesthood, a holy nation, a people belonging to God" (2:9). These terms Peter derives from the Old Testament, so that he sees the members of Christ's church as a continuation of spiritual Israel. The people of Israel, portrayed in the Old Testament, received God's revelation that they were God's chosen people who be-

---

23. Guthrie, *New Testament Theology,* p. 388.

longed to him (see Deut. 10:15; I Sam. 12:22). And the descriptive terms *a royal priesthood, a holy nation* echo God's instruction to Israel at Sinai: "You will be for me a kingdom of priests and a holy nation" (Exod. 19:6; also see Deut. 7:6; Isa. 62:12).

Peter calls Jesus the spiritual Shepherd and Overseer of God's people (2:25). As Jesus is the Chief Shepherd, so Peter and his fellow elders are shepherds responsible to Jesus for the oversight of the flock (5:1–4). Even though Peter identifies himself as an apostle (1:1), he places himself on the level of the elders. Modestly he calls himself "a fellow elder" (5:1) and thus exemplifies what he exhorts the elders to do: "not [to lord] it over those entrusted to you, but [to be] examples to the flock" (5:3).

Last, from the beginning to the end of his epistle, Peter designates both the church and Jesus as chosen by God (1:2; 2:4, 6, 9; 5:13). For this reason, Peter concludes with the words that the readers are "in Christ" (5:14).

5. Eschatology

In view of the intense suffering the readers endured, does Peter give any indication that they are living in the last days during which Jesus' return is imminent? Peter is rather pointed in expressing his expectations. Says he, "The end of all things is near" (4:7). This is an indication that Peter expects Jesus to come soon (compare James 5:9). In other passages, Peter discloses that he and his contemporaries are living in the last days (1:5; 2:12). He encourages suffering Christians by telling them that God will call them from suffering to eternal glory (4:13; 5:10).

The believer's inheritance is not on earth but is kept by God in heaven (1:4). What is heaven, according to Peter? Heaven is the place where Jesus is at God's right hand and where angels, authorities, and powers are subject to him (3:22). Peter describes heaven as an abode of the Holy Spirit (1:12), where angels long to learn about man's salvation.

Peter also speaks about the judgment of believers and those who disobey God. In fact, Peter brings to light that for the family of God the time of judgment is here. "And if it begins with us, what will the outcome be for those who do not obey the gospel of God?" (4:17). To support his words he appeals to an Old Testament passage: "If it is hard for the righteous to be saved, what will become of the ungodly and the sinner?" (v. 18; Prov. 11:31).

6. Will of God

The apostle encourages the Christians to live a life that is commendable so that pagans may acknowledge their good deeds and even glorify God (2:12). Peter's recurring theme is that believers ought to do good (2:15, 20; 3:6, 17). They should live and suffer in obedience to God's will (4:2, 19). Christians know that God's will is determinative in their lives, for he expects them by their behavior to win others for Christ. Peter appeals directly to the example Christ has set and thus he counsels the readers to walk in the steps of Jesus (2:21). In conclusion, the Christian can never act independently of Jesus' example but must always be in Christ.

D. Readers

1. Regions

Who were the recipients of Peter's epistles? From the address we learn that they lived in Asia Minor (modern Turkey)—in its eastern, central, and western regions and in those bordering the Black Sea. Peter writes "to God's elect, strangers in the world, scattered throughout Pontus, Galatia, Cappadocia, Asia and Bithynia" (1:1). We know that residents from these areas were present in Jerusalem on the day of Pentecost (Acts 2:9–11) and heard the gospel proclaimed by the apostles. We assume that some of the three thousand converts to the Christian faith were from Cappadocia, Asia, and Pontus (Acts 2:9, 41). During his missionary journeys, Paul established churches in some of these provinces (see Acts 16:6; 18:23; 19:10, 26).

If we acknowledge that Peter wrote this epistle from Rome, we may expect that he uses the names *Pontus, Galatia, Cappadocia, Asia,* and *Bithynia* to refer to Roman provinces and not to geographic areas. However, Peter mentions Pontus and Bithynia separately, even though Roman administrators had turned these two areas into one province. Note also that the names *Pisidia, Phrygia, Pamphilia,* and *Cilicia,* known because of Paul's travels, are omitted. These names are usually associated with the southern part of the Galatian province. We conclude, then, that Peter addressed his letter to "the whole of Asia Minor that was not evangelized by Paul."[24]

Peter wrote to believers who were members of individual churches. He speaks in general about the elders and their duties (5:1–4). This indicates that the apostolic injunction to appoint elders in every church was in effect.

2. Jews and Gentiles

Were the recipients Jewish, Gentile, or both? The numerous quotations from and allusions to the Old Testament leave the impression that the readers were Jewish. In addition, the address is quite Jewish, especially in the opening words: "To *God's elect, strangers* in the world, *scattered*" (1:1, italics added). These were key words to a Jew living outside Israel: he considered himself one of God's elect, he knew he was a stranger in the world, and he lived in dispersion. Furthermore, whereas Paul was the missionary to the Gentiles, Peter was the apostle to the Jews (Gal. 2:7–9).

However, the distinction between Peter and Paul ought not be made too strictly, because in Acts and in Paul's epistles we read that Paul ministered the Good News to Jews and Gentiles. For example, in his farewell address to the Ephesian elders on the beach at Miletus Paul says, "I have declared to

---

24. Stibbs, *The First Epistle General of Peter,* p. 64.

both Jews and Greeks that they must turn to God in repentance and have faith in our Lord Jesus" (Acts 20:21; also see Rom. 1:16). And on his second missionary journey, while in Corinth, "Paul devoted himself exclusively to preaching, testifying to the Jews that Jesus was the Christ" (Acts 18:5).

Although little is known of Peter's work after he left Jerusalem "for another place" (Acts 12:17), we are sure that he, too, preached to Jews and Gentiles. Earlier Peter himself had entered the house of Cornelius, where he stated, "It is against our law for a Jew to associate with a Gentile or visit him. But God has shown me that I should not call any man impure or unclean" (Acts 10:28). His epistle provides proverbial straws in the wind that indicate some of its readers were Gentiles. Thus Peter reminds his readers that formerly they lived in ignorance (1:14), that they "were redeemed from the empty way of life handed down to [them] from [their] forefathers" (1:18), that "once [they] were not a people, but now [they] are the people of God" (2:10), and that they had "spent enough time in the past doing what the pagans choose to do" (4:3).

Considering the population mixture in the provinces of Asia Minor, we think that both Jews and Gentiles received the gospel of Christ and responded in faith to the call of the apostles. Moreover, some of the people Peter addresses were slaves. We infer that many of these slaves were Gentiles (2:18–20).

Jewish people through their local synagogues in Asia Minor, Macedonia, and Greece evangelized the Gentile population, so that many Gentiles were known as "God-fearers" (Acts 10:2; 13:26, 50; 17:4, 17). God-fearing Gentiles readily accepted the gospel of Christ and became members in the church together with Jewish Christians.[25]

3. Persecutions

In four of the five chapters of his epistle Peter alludes to the persecution of Christians. He implies that believers are living in hard times because as a minority they experience rejection by the rest of the population. Christian slaves endure unjust suffering at the hands of cruel masters (2:18–20), and believers receive abuse from pagans who think it strange that Christians disassociate themselves from riotous living (4:3–4).

The passages in which Peter indirectly refers to persecution are these: 1:6–7; 3:13–17; 4:12–19; 5:9. In the first reference, the word *trial* occurs: "You may have had to suffer grief in all kinds of trials" (1:6). In the second, legal phrases are prominent: "give an answer," "clear conscience," "good behavior," and "slander" (3:15–16). In the third passage, courtroom terminology is again evident: "painful trial," "murderer or thief or any other kind of criminal," and "judgment" (4:12–17). Finally, the suffering which

---

25. Consult Richard R. DeRidder, *The Dispersion of the People of God* (Kampen: Kok, 1971), pp. 88–96.

Christians experienced was widespread: "Your brothers throughout the world are undergoing the same kind of sufferings" (5:9). However, Peter's epistle provides no details on official court proceedings against Christians. Also, in this letter the term *persecution* does not occur. We ought to refrain, then, from reading specific historical facts into the text of this epistle.

Historiographers have recorded information about the persecutions instigated by Roman emperors. Nero, who ruled from A.D. 54 to 68, burned two-thirds of the dwellings and buildings in Rome in July of 64 and blamed the Christians for this deed. Even though Roman historians tell us that Nero burned Christians at the stake in Rome, we cannot prove that the translation *fiery trial* (4:12) must have a literal interpretation. If we take the word *fiery* figuratively, we give it a broader meaning than a single reference to a specific event. Consider, for example, a matter of exegetical consistency. If we adopt the hermeneutical rule to let Scripture be its own interpreter, then we must compare the "fiery trial" of 4:12 with the trials described in 1:6–7. In this passage (1:6–7), Peter explains the concept *trial* with an illustration of gold that is refined by fire. He concludes that this fiery refining process is necessary to prove the genuineness of the believer's faith (1:7). In short, the evidence to link the expression *fiery trial* to incidences of Christians being burned at Nero's behest is not overwhelming.

Christians were persecuted "because of the name of Christ" (4:14). That name in itself was sufficient ground to drag a Christian into court. Jesus predicted as much when he said, "On my account you will be brought before governors and kings as witnesses to them and to the Gentiles" (Matt. 10:18). We should not link the persecutions to which Peter alludes to correspondence of Pliny, governor of Bithynia in A.D. 109–11. Pliny conducted an inquisition against Christians in that province and asked Emperor Trajan whether he could persecute Christians because of "the name itself."[26] However, we have no indication that the inquisition in the time of Trajan was worldwide. All appearances are that we encounter a single incidence of persecution mentioned in the correspondence between Pliny and Trajan but no official persecution that was sponsored by the emperor. We conclude by saying that the persecutions alluded to in Peter's epistle appear to be local harassment generated by people who expressed hatred toward Christians.

E. Date and Place

If we accept the apostolic authorship of First Peter, we rule out a late date for this epistle (either during the reign of Domitian in the early 90s or during Trajan's reign in 110–11). We accept, then, a date of composition before 68, when Nero committed suicide. According to tradition, Peter was crucified outside Rome in the last few years of Nero's rule. Because First

---

26. Pliny *Letters* 10.97 (LCL).

Peter has numerous cross-references to Paul's epistles, we presume that Peter composed his epistle after Paul wrote his. Romans was written in 58 when Paul concluded his third missionary journey. And Paul wrote Ephesians and Colossians when he spent two years (61–63) in Rome under house arrest.[27] Accordingly, we must date First Peter after the composition of these prison Epistles.

A second indication of an early date is the reference to elders and their duties (5:1–4). Peter calls himself a fellow elder and thereby places himself on the same level as the elders who serve in local churches. His instructions to the official leaders in these congregations are in harmony with Paul's instructions to Timothy and Titus concerning the qualifications for elders and deacons (I Tim. 3:1–13; Titus 1:5–9). Paul wrote these two pastoral epistles in approximately 63–64. We know that Peter was acquainted with all the epistles Paul had written and considered them to be Scripture (refer to II Peter 3:16).

Furthermore, the epistle lacks any hint that it is addressed to second-generation Christians, so a date in the sixties seems plausible. "This kind of situation, prevailing in a fair number of communities in Anatolia [modern Turkey] simultaneously, is more likely to have obtained earlier rather than later in our period."[28]

A fourth indication is that Peter exhorts the readers to be submissive to the king and to honor him (2:13, 17). This could hardly be expected of Peter if he wrote his letter after Nero had executed numerous Christians following the burning of Rome in 64.[29] Therefore, we date the composition of First Peter at 63 or the early part of 64.

Peter's reference to Babylon (5:13) is traditionally understood to be a code name for Rome. The secrecy with which Peter conveys greetings reflects not only the perilous times in which he and the readers lived, but also the desire to protect the church from possible harm. Peter writes, "She who is in Babylon, chosen together with you, sends you her greetings" (v. 13). If Peter had meant to say that his wife (I Cor. 9:5) sent her regards, he would have added his own greetings. Moreover, we would have expected him to indicate that he was with her in Babylon. Because Peter's reference to a lady cannot be to his wife, scholars interpret the verse figuratively. They say that the elect church of Jesus Christ is sending greetings to the churches in Asia Minor. New Testament writers often depict the church in female terms.[30]

---

27. These are references in I Peter to Ephesians, Colossians, and Romans: 1:1–3 and Eph. 1:1–3; 1:7 and Eph. 1:14; 1:14 and Rom. 12:2; 1:21 and Rom. 4:24; 2:5 and Rom. 12:1; Eph. 2:21–22; 2:18 and Col. 3:22; 3:1–6 and Eph. 5:22–25.

28. Kelly, *Peter and Jude,* p. 30.

29. Robert W. Thurston asserts that the first part of the epistle (1:1–4:11) was written before the burning of Rome in 64 and the second part (4:11–5:14) after 64 when the persecutions raged and Christians submitted to a "painful trial." "Interpreting First Peter," *JETS* 17 (1974): 176.

30. See, e.g., John 3:29; Eph. 5:25–33; Rev. 19:7–8; 21:2–3; 22:17.

The expression *she* refers to the church in Babylon. But if Peter speaks figuratively, is the term *Babylon* also symbolic? Yes, it is, because we have no evidence that Peter traveled into Babylon to preach the gospel there. Moreover, an attempt to equate Babylon with a Roman military fortress in Egypt seems unlikely. Scholars, therefore, opt for the explanation that the name is a pseudonym for Rome. From Revelation and also from Jewish writings we learn that to call Rome "Babylon" was commonplace.[31] Jewish writers did so because of the similarity between the Babylonians destroying Solomon's temple in 586 B.C. and the Romans destroying Jerusalem in A.D. 70. In Revelation, "Rome is Babylon, not because she has destroyed the Holy City, but because she is the mother of harlots and abominations."[32]

Tradition holds that Peter spent time in the imperial city and in its vicinity met martyrdom. The assumption that Peter wrote this epistle from Rome seems credible, for the evidence from tradition points to Rome as the place of composition. Papias, bishop of Hierapolis (A.D. 125), reports that Mark was Peter's interpreter. And Irenaeus comments that both Peter and Paul had preached in Rome, and that afterward "Mark, the disciple and interpreter of Peter, did also hand down to us in writing what had been preached by Peter."[33] The church fathers unmistakably link Peter to Rome, where the apostle wrote his first epistle.

F. Structure

1. Purpose

What is the purpose of First Peter? Upon first glance, we fail to discover any objective and possibly conclude that the writer states no purpose at all. But that is not the case, for at the end of his epistle Peter formulates a brief explanation of the purpose of his writing: to encourage the readers and to testify to God's true grace (5:12). This brief statement actually summarizes what Peter is telling the readers in other parts of the letter (1:1–2; 4:12–5:14).[34] He encourages suffering Christians to anticipate and accept the difficulties which they encounter because of their faith in Christ. Peter exhorts them to stand firm. He tells them that they share in Christ's sufferings and participate in his glory (4:13–14).

In brief, the purpose for writing this letter is that Peter wishes to convey a message of hope and encouragement. The word *hope* is a key word that occurs five times in First Peter (1:3, 13, 21; 3:5, 15). Peter writes a letter of hope to Christians who experience frequent and intense suffering.

---

31. See Rev. 14:8; 16:19; 17:5; 18:2, 10, 21. Best uses the Jewish sources to suggest that I Peter was written after A.D. 70. *I Peter*, p. 179.

32. Bigg, *The Epistles of St. Peter and St. Jude*, p. 76.

33. Irenaeus *Against Heresies* 3.1.1. Also see Eusebius *Ecclesiastical History* 6.14.6; 2.15.1–2.

34. Consult Leonhard Goppelt, *Der Erste Petrusbrief*, Kritisch-Exegetischer Kommentar über das Neuen Testament, ed. Ferdinand Hahn, 8th ed. (Göttingen: Vandenhoeck und Ruprecht, 1978), vol. 12/1, p. 38.

2. Theme

Although scholars find more than one theme in Peter's epistle, they agree that the theme *suffering* is woven into the fabric of the entire letter. In every chapter Peter discusses this theme. In his first explicit reference, he states that the readers "now for a little while . . . may have had to suffer grief in all kinds of trials" (1:6). In his last statement, he once more speaks of the brevity of suffering: "And the God of all grace, who called you to his eternal glory in Christ, after you have suffered a little while, will himself restore you and make you strong, firm and steadfast" (5:10). In between, Peter mentions suffering in many passages.[35]

Christians endure suffering in a world that is not theirs. They are strangers in the world and therefore are rejected by it. As a result, they receive its scorn and contempt. They experience suffering on account of Christ's name. Note, then, that Peter addresses the readers not as brothers and sisters in the Lord but as "strangers in the world" (1:1). He calls them "aliens and strangers" (2:11). Peter does not advocate retreat from the world. Rather, he exhorts Christians to live commendable lives in the world and to do that which is good (2:12, 15, 20–21; 3:13–17; 4:19).

From the first to the last chapter of his epistle, Peter writes a series of exhortations and instructs the readers to be holy and to avoid evil (1:14–16; 2:1, 11; 3:8–9; 4:1–11). He wants the believers to understand that when they suffer, they are not undergoing a futile exercise but are submitting themselves to a divine test designed to prove their faith (1:7). Suffering in itself is not an abnormality which believers have to endure. Instead, it is the common experience of anyone who lives in communion with Christ (4:13).

Peter addresses slaves who suffer unjustly at the hands of cruel masters (2:18), wives who live with unbelieving husbands (3:1–6), and all others who suffer for the sake of righteousness (3:13–17) and must submit to a "painful trial" (4:12). He informs them that they are in the world to do the will of God. Thus, he exhorts the believing wife that she must seek to convert her husband with her purity and reverence (3:2) and win him not by argument but by conduct. Peter admonishes Christians to show proper respect to the king by honoring him (2:17); yet he uses the pseudonym *Babylon* when he refers to Rome, the imperial capital (5:13). Peter wants the Christians to live honorably in the midst of unbelievers. In the words of Jesus, believers should "be as shrewd as snakes and as innocent as doves" (Matt. 10:16).

The theme of suffering effectively binds the entire epistle together as a literary unit. True, Peter's epistle is a mixture of theology and admonitions for practical Christian living; nevertheless, this particular theme speaks to an actual situation within the early Christian community that experienced oppression and persecution.

---

35. See 2:12, 20–21; 3:14–17; 4:1, 12–19; 5:9.

Another subject Peter discusses at length is submission. He challenges the readers to be obedient to superiors. Here is a list of references: 1:2 ("obedience"); 1:14 ("obedient"); 1:22 ("obeying"); 2:8 ("disobey"); 2:13 ("submit"); 3:1, 5 ("submissive"); 3:6 ("obeyed"); 3:20 ("disobeyed"); 4:17 ("obey"); 5:5 ("submissive").

3. Liturgy

In this relatively short epistle of five chapters, Peter lists twelve quotations from the Old Testament: six are from the prophecy of Isaiah, two from Proverbs, two from the Psalms, one from Exodus, and one from Leviticus.[36] First Peter has proportionately more quotations from and allusions to the Old Testament than any other New Testament epistle has. In quoting these passages, Peter relies both on the Septuagint version and on memory.

In addition to quoting Scripture verses, does the apostle resort to citing fragments of hymns and creeds that were used in the early Christian church? We lack solid evidence, but in a few passages this seems to be the case (see, e.g., 1:18–21; 2:21–25; 3:18–19). If we put 3:18 and 22 in poetic arrangement, we see the rudimentary form of a confessional statement that perhaps was recited in the church:

> Christ died for sins once for all,
> the righteous for the unrighteous,
> to bring you to God.
> He was put to death in the body
> but made alive by the Spirit . . . .
> [Christ] has gone into heaven
> and is at God's right hand—
> with angels, authorities and powers
> in submission to him.

Concludes William Joseph Dalton, "A simple reading of the text. . . strongly supports the idea that 3:18, 22 is hymnic in form, while 3:19–21 is a prose insertion. What is more, v[erse] 22 seems to follow on from v[erse] 18. Hence we may say that 3:18, 22 is part or whole of a christological hymn, while 3:19–21 is a catechetical piece on Baptism."[37] Moreover, because the text begins with the conjunction *for*, scholars are of the opinion that Peter quotes from an early christological hymn. Paul also incorporates the words of a creedal hymn in one of his letters:

---

36. Here is a list of quotations in the sequence of occurrence: 1:16—Lev. 19:2; 1:24–25—Isa. 40:6–8; 2:6—Isa. 28:16 (LXX); 2:7—Ps. 118:22; 2:8—Isa. 8:14; 2:9a—Isa. 43:20 (LXX); 2:9b—Exod. 19:6 (LXX); 2:9c—Isa. 43:21 (LXX); 2:22—Isa. 53:9; 3:10–12—Ps. 34:12–16; 4:18—Prov. 11:31 (LXX); 5:5—Prov. 3:34 (LXX).

37. Compare William Joseph Dalton, *Christ's Proclamation to the Spirits: A Study of 1 Peter 3:18–4:6*, Analecta Biblica 23 (Rome: Pontifical Biblical Institute, 1964), p. 97.

> He appeared in a body,
>> was vindicated by the Spirit,
> was seen by angels,
>> was preached among the nations,
> was believed on in the world,
>> was taken up in glory. [I Tim. 3:16]

Is First Peter a sermon on baptism? Much has been written on this question, especially by scholars who have researched the basic structure of this epistle. Certainly the letter as such may represent sermonic material that Peter himself had preached.[38] To this material he presumably added greetings, an introduction, a benediction, and a conclusion and sent it as a letter to the churches in Asia Minor. First Peter, of course, is not a sermon but an apostolic epistle.

Some scholars have presented a detailed survey of the epistle to show that Peter's epistle from 1:1 to 4:6 is a baptismal sermon which was preached to recent converts and that the segment 4:7 to 5:14 was addressed to the entire congregation.[39]

Others claim that First Peter is a baptismal liturgy related to Easter.[40] However, the evidence that the epistle consists of a liturgy on baptism is doubtful and faces objections.

One objection to the theory is that Peter's epistle speaks explicitly about baptism in only one place, namely, 3:21. Consequently, a scholar who lists implicit references to baptism in First Peter risks the charge of being subjective. He must show convincingly that Peter wishes to convey a baptismal meaning with the expression *new birth* (1:3; also see 1:23; 2:2). But the context of these verses connotes "spiritual regeneration without reference to any external rite . . . [and] without reference to water."[41]

Another objection is the multiplicity of references to suffering which the Christians endure: experiences ranging from a slave suffering at the hand of his cruel master (2:18–20) to believers who face a painful trial (4:12). Indeed, the suffering of these Christians points not to recent converts but to believers of long standing. Therefore, we must conclude that interpreting Peter's epistle as a baptismal liturgy is a theory that has not yet been adequately substantiated.[42]

---

38. Stibbs, *The First Epistle General of Peter*, p. 58.

39. Refer to Hans Windisch and Herbert Preisker, *Die Katholische Briefe*, Lietzmann's *Handbuch zum Neuen Testament*, 3d ed. (Tübingen: Mohr, 1951), pp. 156–58. And see Bo Reicke, *The Epistles of James, Peter, and Jude*, The Anchor Bible, vol. 37 (Garden City, N.Y.: Doubleday, 1964), p. 74.

40. Consult F. L. Cross, *I Peter, A Paschal Liturgy* (London: Mowbray, 1970).

41. Guthrie, *New Testament Introduction*, p. 798.

42. Consult P. E. Robertson, "Is 1 Peter a Sermon?" *Theological Educator* 13 (1982): 35–41. And see T. C. G. Thornton, "I Peter, a Paschal Liturgy?" *JTS* 12 (1961): 14–26. For a general survey on this subject, refer to Martin, "Peter, First Epistle of," pp. 811–12.

4. Unity

Does First Peter consist of two parts (1:1–4:11 and 4:12–5:14)? Defenders of the hypothesis that the first part of the epistle is a baptismal liturgy see a combination of two independent documents. But a few facts support the unity of First Peter. First, these two parts are not at all unrelated, as the similarities in word choice and grammar clearly show. For instance, the word *suffering* occurs throughout the epistle, and the use of the imperative (which in the Greek often appears as a participle) is peculiar to both parts of the epistle.

Next, "if the two specialized parts of I Peter are set side by side, they prove to contain a good deal of the same material."[43] The themes that appear in both parts include suffering for the sake of Christ (2:21; 4:13), undeserved suffering (3:17; 4:16), submission to authority (2:13; 5:5), the short duration of suffering (1:6; 5:10), resistance to evil (4:1; 5:9), and the end of all things (4:7; 4:17).

We conclude that First Peter shows homogeneity because of the Old Testament quotations, fragments from hymns and creeds, and sermonic material. In view of the parallels and resemblances that appear throughout the epistle, we see the unity of the entire epistle rather than the disunity of independent parts.

And last, if we accept the unity of the letter, there is no need to explain why a postscript was added to a baptismal liturgy and why this liturgy was turned into a letter.[44] A rejection of the epistle's unity, of course, raises these and other questions that demand plausible answers. The unity of First Peter is apparent; disunity must be proved.

G. Outline of I Peter

Here is a simple outline of First Peter that can easily be committed to memory:

Introduction	1:1–2
Salvation	1:3–12
Holiness	1:13–2:3
Election	2:4–10
Submission	2:11–3:12
Suffering	3:13–4:19
Conclusion	5:1–14

---

43. C. F. D. Moule, "The Nature and Purpose of I Peter," *NTS* 3 (1956–57): 10.
44. Thornton, "I Peter, a Paschal Liturgy?" p. 26.

Introduction

A complete outline of this epistle is as follows:

Introduction

Commentary
The First Epistle of Peter

1

Introduction

(1:1–2)

Salvation

(1:3–12)

and Holiness, *part 1*

(1:13–25)

Outline

1 1 Peter, an apostle of Jesus Christ,
To God's elect, strangers in the world, scattered throughout Pontus, Galatia, Cappadocia, Asia and Bithynia, 2 who have been chosen according to the foreknowledge of God the Father, through the sanctifying work of the Spirit, for obedience to Jesus Christ and sprinkling by his blood:
Grace and peace be yours in abundance.

I. Introduction
1:1–2

A. Salutation
1:1

First we have the name and title of the sender on the envelope, so to speak. Next we have the address. That is, the writer is sending his letter to addressees who live in various parts of Asia Minor. This envelope with enclosed letter is carried from place to place.

1. Peter, an apostle of Jesus Christ,
To God's elect, strangers in the world, scattered throughout Pontus, Galatia, Cappadocia, Asia and Bithynia.

a. *Name.* Peter is brief and direct in introducing himself. Instead of saying that he is Simon son of Jonah (Matt. 16:17) or Simon son of John (John 1:42; 21:15–17), he uses the name *Peter.* This is the name Jesus gave him when Andrew introduced his brother Simon to the Lord. Jesus said, " 'You are Simon son of John. You will be called Cephas' (which, when translated, is Peter)" (John 1:42). As the footnote in the New International Version explains, "Both *Cephas* (Aramaic) and *Peter* (Greek) mean *rock.*"[1] The name that Simon received from Jesus reflects his character, perhaps not so much during the years of Jesus' ministry, but certainly after Peter's reinstatement (John 21:15–23).

As leader in the Jerusalem church, Simon became known as Peter or Simon Peter (see, for example, the numerous references in Acts). Incidentally, only twice in the New Testament "the more exact Sem[itic] form Symeon is used" (in the Greek, Acts 15:14; II Peter 1:1).[2]

---

1. "You are Peter, and on this rock I will build my church," said Jesus (Matt. 16:18). Paul frequently calls Peter "Cephas" (see I Cor. 1:12; 3:22; 9:5; 15:5; Gal. 1:18; 2:9, 11, 14). In Gal. 2:7 and 8 Paul calls him "Peter."
2. Bastiaan Van Elderen, "Simon Peter," *ZPEB*, vol. 4, p. 733.

b. *Title.* Peter expresses his authority and influence by using the name that Jesus gave him when he became Jesus' disciple. He is the only one who has that name and he is the recognized leader in the church.

Peter also calls himself "an apostle of Jesus Christ." Although he belonged to the inner circle of the twelve disciples during Jesus' earthly ministry, Peter places himself on the same level as all the other disciples. As he puts it, he is *an* apostle and certainly not *the* apostle of Jesus Christ.

Peter does not need to explain or defend his apostleship, as for example Paul has to do in most of his epistles (e.g., Gal. 1:1). Peter merely refers to himself as "an apostle of Jesus Christ." With the other apostles, Peter has received the outpouring of the Holy Spirit on the day of Pentecost and so proclaims the resurrection of Jesus (refer to Acts 2:1–4). Next, he has received his apostleship as a lifetime office. And last, he has received Christ's commission to make disciples of all nations by baptizing them and by teaching them the gospel (Matt. 28:19–20).[3]

The term *apostle* has a broader connotation than the words *the one who has been sent.* Besides being sent, an apostle has received full authority from Jesus Christ. Thus he delivers not his own thoughts but the message of the one who sends him.[4] Conclusively, then, in his epistle Peter writes with the divine authority Jesus Christ has given him.

The double name *Jesus Christ* points first to Jesus' earthly ministry and second to Christ's divine calling, task, and position. Jesus Christ commissions Peter to serve him as apostle and to write this general epistle to the church in Asia Minor, that is, modern Turkey.

c. *Addressees.* Who are the recipients of this letter? Before Peter tells us where they live, he describes them spiritually, socially, and politically. He writes his letter to "God's elect, strangers in the world, scattered throughout Pontus, Galatia, Cappadocia, Asia and Bithynia."

God's elect. In the Greek, the adjective *elect* or *chosen* appears in the plural without the qualifying noun *of God.* Within the context of the epistle (1:2; 2:4, 6, 9), the adjective means that God has chosen the readers. They are his people, separated from the world, experiencing the world's hatred and enduring suffering and persecution. Yet they are the ones whom God favors and loves. Out of the human race, God has chosen his own people. "For many are invited, but few are chosen" (Matt. 22:14). Also, in the broader context of his epistle, Peter teaches the purpose of election: "But you are a chosen people, a royal priesthood, a holy nation, a people belong-

---

3. Refer to Dietrich Müller, *NIDNTT,* vol. 1, p. 131. Also see Karl Heinrich Rengstorf, *TDNT,* vol. 1, pp. 424–43.

4. Consult Uwe Holmer, *Der Erste Brief des Petrus,* in *Die Briefe des Petrus und der Brief des Judas,* Wuppertaler Studienbibel (Wuppertal: Brockhaus, 1976), p. 21. Literature on the subject *apostle* is extensive. I mention only the representative article by Rudolf Schnackenburg, "Apostles Before and During Paul's Time," in *Apostolic History and the Gospel,* ed. W. Ward Gasque and Ralph P. Martin (Exeter: Paternoster, 1970), pp. 287–303.

ing to God, that you may declare the praises of him who called you out of darkness into his wonderful light" (2:9).

Strangers in the world. Christians are resident aliens in this world (Heb. 11:13). They are not at home in this world, for their stay on earth is temporary (I Peter 2:11). Their citizenship is in heaven (Phil. 3:20). Therefore, as God's elect they live on this earth as exiles and temporary residents.[5]

Scattered throughout. The expression *scattered* refers to the exile and its aftermath. The Jewish people were driven from their native land and lived in dispersion (see John 7:35). Moreover, after the death of Stephen, Jewish Christians were scattered and had to reside in foreign countries (Acts 8:1; 11:19; James 1:1).

Is Peter referring to Jewish Christians who were driven from Israel to live in Asia Minor? Perhaps. Or ought the expression to be taken figuratively? The previous expression *strangers in the world* is understood symbolically; thus we should not be too literal in interpreting this part of the text. If we understand the text figuratively, the readers need not be only Jewish Christians; some of them may be Gentile Christians (compare 1:18; 2:10, 25; 4:3–4). The Jewish and Gentile readers live in five districts of Asia Minor: Pontus, Galatia, Cappadocia, Asia, and Bithynia.

d. *Districts.* Where are the districts that Peter mentions in his epistle? The map on page 34 shows the areas that are listed. Note that Peter fails to mention some regions. For instance, he omits the names *Lycia, Phrygia, Pisidia, Pamphylia, Lycaonia,* and *Cilicia.* But these names pertain to the southern part of Asia Minor. Peter addresses his letter to readers in the northern, eastern, central, and western provinces.

We assume that after Peter's release from prison (Acts 12:1–17), he brought the gospel to these areas. At the same time, Paul evangelized parts of Asia Minor, but the Holy Spirit prevented him from preaching in the province of Asia and from entering Bithynia (Acts 16:6–7). Paul would not preach in areas where the gospel was known, for he refused to build "on someone else's foundation" (Rom. 15:20).[6]

Peter lists the five districts in the following order: Pontus, Galatia, Cappadocia, Asia, and Bithynia. The person who delivered the letter, perhaps Silas (5:12), came first to Pontus along the shores of the Black Sea, then followed a circuitous route to Galatia and to Cappadocia. From there he traveled to Asia and concluded his journey in Bithynia.[7]

---

5. Consult Hans Bietenhard, *NIDNTT*, vol. 1, p. 690. Also refer to John Brown, *Expository Discourses on I Peter*, 2 vols. (Edinburgh: Banner of Truth Trust, 1975), vol. 1, p. 16. Brown comments that the word *strangers* "expresses two ideas: not natives of the country in which they are; not settled residents in that foreign country."

6. Refer to E. G. Selwyn, *The First Epistle of St. Peter: The Greek Text with Introduction, Notes, and Essays* (London: Macmillan, 1946), p. 45. And see J. N. D. Kelly, *A Commentary on the Epistles of Peter and Jude*, Thornapple Commentaries series (1969; Grand Rapids: Baker, 1981), p. 3.

7. Consult C. J. Hemer, "The Address of I Peter," *ExpT* 89 (1978): 239–43.

Finally, Peter refers to districts and not to Roman provinces. In 64 B.C., Bithynia and Pontus became one province under Roman rule. Although the name *Galatia* designates a province, it also refers to a district.

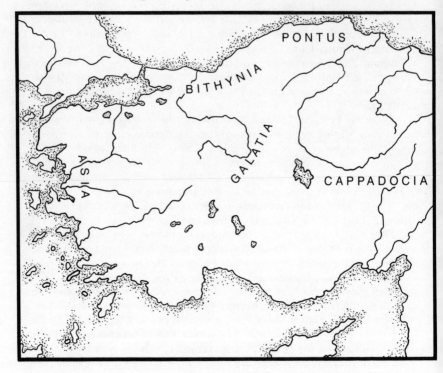

Greek Words, Phrases, and Constructions in 1:1

Πέτρος—all nouns and substantives in the address and greeting (vv. 1–2) lack the definite article. Nevertheless, many of them are definite because of the formal structure of the introduction to the epistle.

ἐκλεκτοῖς παρεπιδήμοις—the adjective *elect* modifies the substantive *strangers*. The adjective is verbal and expresses the passive idea; that is, God is the agent. The compound substantive consists of the prepositions παρά (beside) and ἐπί (upon) and the noun δῆμος (people). The compound means "the people who dwell beside native residents on the land."

διασπορᾶς—from the verb διασπείρω (I scatter abroad), this noun in the genitive singular describes Jewish exiles dispersed among the nations; it also relates to Christians who are "scattered abroad among the Gentiles."[8]

---

8. Thayer, pp. 141–42.

B. Addressees
1:2

2. Who have been chosen according to the foreknowledge of God the Father, through the sanctifying work of the Spirit, for obedience to Jesus Christ and sprinkling by his blood.

In three separate clauses Peter describes three acts of the Triune God. The Father has foreknowledge, the Spirit sanctifies, and Jesus Christ expects obedience from those whom he has cleansed from sin. These three clauses explain the term *elect* (v. 1).

Note the following points:

a. *Foreknowledge*. "According to the foreknowledge of God the Father." Most translators favor linking the word *elect* to the three prepositional clauses:

> according to the foreknowledge of God the Father,
> through the sanctifying work of the Spirit,
> for obedience to Jesus Christ
> and sprinkling by his blood.[9]

A few translations follow the Greek word order verbatim: "Peter, an apostle of Jesus Christ, to the elect who are sojourners of the Dispersion in Pontus, Galatia, Cappadocia, Asia, and Bithynia, according to the foreknowledge of God the Father."[10] But the force of the sentence focuses attention on the expression *elect*, because the concept *foreknowledge* is directly related to election.

What is foreknowledge? It is much more than the ability to predict future events. It includes the absolute sovereignty of God in determining and implementing his decision to save sinful man.[11] The word *foreknowledge* appears in Peter's Pentecost sermon, where he declares to his Jewish audience that Jesus "was handed over to you by God's set purpose and foreknowledge" (Acts 2:23). Peter implies that God worked according to his sovereign plan and purpose which he had made in advance.

Paul also refers to foreknowledge. The verb *foreknow* occurs in Romans 8:29, "For those God foreknew he also predestined to be conformed to the likeness of his Son." Paul indicates that the concepts *foreknowledge* and *predestination* go together. Foreknowledge and predestination were acts of God

---

9. With variations, these translations include KJV, NKJV, NASB, RSV, NAB, NEB, NIV, JB, GNB, MLB, and *Moffatt*.

10. See, e.g., RV, ASV.

11. Lothar Coenen writes that the purpose of election is to show "in the midst of world history God's sovereign acts, his grace, and the seriousness of his demands. The doctrine of election is thus an indissoluble part of the knowledge of God's holiness, uniqueness, and unconditioned sovereignty." *NIDNTT*, vol. 1, p. 538.

before the creation of this world (see Eph. 1:4–5). The prefixes *fore-* and *pre-* in the phrase *foreknew and predestined* (Rom. 8:29) denote as much.

Returning to Peter's first epistle, we note that Peter, writing about Christ, mentions the teaching of election when he says, "He was chosen [foreknown] before the creation of the world" (1:20).

With perfect ease Peter weaves the doctrine of the Trinity into the cloth of his epistle. Within the Christian community, that doctrine was accepted and understood, so that the writers of the New Testament had no need to introduce, explain, or defend it against possible Jewish attacks.[12]

Peter speaks of God the Father, the Spirit, and Jesus Christ (see also Eph. 1:3–14). The order he chooses is arbitrary, for he is interested not in sequence but in the function each person of the Trinity performs. God the Father foreknows and chooses the sinner. By describing God as Father, Peter implies that the people God has chosen and whom Peter calls "elect" are indeed God's children. They are highly privileged because they are parties to the covenant God has made with his people:

> "I will be a Father to you,
>   and you will be my sons and daughters,
>   says the Lord Almighty." [II Cor. 6:18]

Note that God's elect "have been chosen [elected] according to the foreknowledge of God the Father." How is man's election realized? It is effected through the power of the Holy Spirit, who cleanses the elect from sin.

b. *Sanctification.* Peter writes his epistle to the elect "who have been chosen . . . through the sanctifying work of the Spirit." When Peter speaks of the sanctifying work of the Holy Spirit, he delineates the difference between a holy God and a sinful man. The Spirit is at work when he makes man holy and acceptable in the sight of God; sinful man, however, cannot enter the presence of a holy God unless God through his Spirit sanctifies him.

Peter is not alone in teaching the sanctifying work of the Holy Spirit. Paul writes virtually the same thing to the church in Thessalonica: "From the beginning God chose you to be saved through the sanctifying work of the Spirit and through belief in the truth" (II Thess. 2:13).

The original Greek indicates that the sanctifying work of the Spirit is a continuing activity or process rather than a completed act that results in a state of perfected holiness.[13] In this process man does not remain passive

---

12. Donald Guthrie observes that none of the New Testament writers "sees the need to speculate about such a doctrine." *New Testament Theology* (Downers Grove: Inter-Varsity, 1981), p. 112.

13. Refer to D. Edmond Hiebert, *First Peter: An Expositional Commentary* (Chicago: Moody, 1984), p. 38.

while the Spirit is active. Man is also deeply involved. Peter exhorts the believers, "But just as he who called you is holy, so be holy in all you do; for it is written: 'Be holy, because I am holy' " (1:15–16).

c. *Obedience and sprinkling.* Why does the Spirit sanctify the elect? Peter says that it is "for obedience to Jesus Christ and sprinkling by his blood." He repeats his reference to obedience in subsequent verses of this chapter: "As obedient children, do not conform to the evil desires you had when you lived in ignorance" (v. 14); "Now that you have purified yourselves by obeying the truth, so that you have sincere love for your brothers, love one another deeply, from the heart" (v. 22).

In the Greek Peter actually says, "for obedience and sprinkling of the blood of Jesus Christ."[14] With the terms *obedience* and *sprinkling* Peter refers to the confirmation of the covenant that God made with the people of Israel (see Exod. 24:3–8). Moses read the Book of the Covenant to the people. "They responded, 'We will do everything the LORD has said; we will obey' " (v. 7). Then Moses sprinkled blood on the people and said, "This is the blood of the covenant that the LORD has made with you in accordance with all these words" (v. 8). The writer of the Epistle to the Hebrews comments that Jesus shed his blood to take away the sins of God's people (9:18–28; 12:24).[15]

Peter declares that through Jesus' sacrificial death on the cross, he redeemed and purchased the elect (compare 1:18–19). Thus, in summary, the Triune God has given them three distinct privileges: God the Father foreknows them, God the Spirit sanctifies them, and Jesus Christ cleanses them from sin through the sprinkling of his blood. Although the shedding of blood has taken place once for all, its significance has lasting effect and is an enduring process.[16] Jesus Christ continues to cleanse us from sin.

d. *Greeting.* The words "grace and peace be yours in abundance" also appear in II Peter 1:2 (and see Jude 2). The greeting is rather typical of New Testament authors who write letters. With variations, Paul, James, John, Jude, and the writer of Hebrews extend greetings and benedictions at either the beginning or the end of their epistles.[17]

The term *grace* is comprehensive; it encompasses the concepts of mercy, love, and remission of sin. Grace is that which God extends to man. Peace,

---

14. Some translations follow the exact word order of the Greek (KJV, RV, ASV, NKJV). The NEB has the reading "hallowed to his service by the Spirit, and consecrated with the sprinkled blood of Jesus Christ."

15. Consult F. J. A. Hort, *The First Epistle of St. Peter* (London: Macmillan, 1898; Minneapolis: Klock and Klock, 1976), p. 23. Compare Vincent Taylor, *Jesus and His Sacrifice* (London: Macmillan, 1937), p. 137. Also see Selwyn, *The First Epistle of St. Peter*, p. 120; Guthrie, *New Testament Theology*, p. 474.

16. Refer to S. Greijdanus, *De Brieven van de Apostelen Petrus en Johannes, en de Brief van Judas,* Kommentaar op het Nieuwe Testament series (Amsterdam: Van Bottenburg, 1929), p. 33.

17. Consult Bauer, p. 877, and Thayer, p. 666.

by contrast, is a state of internal happiness which the possessor expresses externally to his fellow man. In a sense, the concepts *grace* and *peace* relate to each other as cause and effect. That is, God's gift of grace results in peace.

A literal translation of this greeting is "grace to you and peace be multiplied" (NKJV).

Doctrinal Considerations in 1:1–2

Peter, who was an unschooled fisherman (Acts 4:13) from Galilee and the former leader of the Jerusalem church, now writes a letter to Christians living in Asia Minor. He begins his letter with an address in which he teaches the readers basic Christian truths: the doctrine of election and the doctrine of the Trinity.

Peter addresses his epistle to "God's elect . . . who have been chosen." He reveals that election is God's work, that God wants a people for himself, and that the Triune God cares for his elect.

The doctrine of election provides genuine comfort and enormous encouragement for God's people. By electing his people, God demands a thankful response from them. He expects them to obey his commands and to do his will. Nevertheless, he knows our weaknesses and frailty and realizes that we fall occasionally into sin. Therefore, he has made available the sanctifying power of the Spirit and the lasting effect of the sprinkling of Christ's blood.

> There is a fountain filled with blood,
> Drawn from Immanuel's veins;
> And sinners, plunged beneath that flood,
> Lose all their guilty stains.
> —William Cowper

Greek Words, Phrases, and Constructions in 1:2

πρόγνωσιν θεοῦ πατρός—the genitive is subjective. That is, πρόγνωσις (foreknowledge) belongs to God the Father and in harmony with it he reveals himself to his people.

ἁγιασμῷ πνεύματος—the ending -μος of the noun ἁγιασμός (sanctification) expresses progressive activity. The dative case can either be instrumental or refer to sphere. Scholars prefer the instrumental dative. The case of πνεύματος (Spirit) is the subjective genitive ("the sanctifying power belonging to the Spirit").

ῥαντισμὸν αἵματος—because of the -μος ending, the noun ῥαντισμός (sprinkling) denotes progress. The noun is qualified by the word αἵματος (blood) which points to the genitive case of Ἰησοῦ Χριστοῦ. This genitive is subjective ("of Jesus Christ") and as such relates only to αἵματος and not to ὑπακοήν (obedience). If the genitive of Ἰησοῦ Χριστοῦ is linked to ὑπακοήν, it is objective ("to Jesus Christ"). But a possible occurrence of the subjective and objective genitive in the same clause is difficult to explain. Therefore, I favor the use of the subjective genitive in the last part of this clause.

πληθυνθείν—this is the aorist passive in the optative mood from the verb πληθύνω (I multiply). The use of the passive indicates that God is the implied agent. The aorist is ingressive. And the optative connotes a wish (compare Dan. 4:1 LXX).

---

3 Praise be to the God and Father of our Lord Jesus Christ! In his great mercy he has given us new birth into a living hope through the resurrection of Jesus Christ from the dead, 4 and into an inheritance that can never perish, spoil or fade—kept in heaven for you, 5 who through faith are shielded by God's power until the coming of the salvation that is ready to be revealed in the last time. 6 In this you greatly rejoice, though now for a little while you may have had to suffer grief in all kinds of trials. 7 These have come so that your faith—of greater worth than gold, which perishes even though refined by fire—may be proved genuine and may result in praise, glory and honor when Jesus Christ is revealed. 8 Though you have not seen him, you love him; and even though you do not see him now, you believe in him and are filled with an inexpressible and glorious joy, 9 for you are receiving the goal of your faith, the salvation of your souls.

10 Concerning this salvation, the prophets, who spoke of the grace that was to come to you, searched intently and with the greatest care, 11 trying to find out the time and circumstances to which the Spirit of Christ in them was pointing when he predicted the sufferings of Christ and the glories that would follow. 12 It was revealed to them that they were not serving themselves but you, when they spoke of the things that have now been told you by those who have preached the gospel to you by the Holy Spirit sent from heaven. Even angels long to look into these things.

II. Salvation
1:3–12

A. A Living Hope
1:3

Throughout his epistle, Peter encourages his readers to hope. Hope is based on a living faith in Jesus Christ. It characterizes the believer who patiently waits for the salvation God has promised to his people. "Hoping is disciplined waiting."[18]

3. Praise be to the God and Father of our Lord Jesus Christ! In his great mercy he has given us new birth into a living hope through the resurrection of Jesus Christ from the dead.

Filled to overflowing with spiritual blessings which he wants to convey to his readers, Peter writes one long sentence in Greek (vv. 3–9). In our modern versions, translators have divided this lengthy sentence. Nevertheless, the sentence itself reveals the intensity of the writer and the fullness of his message. In the introductory part of this sentence we observe the following points:

a. "Praise." This word is actually the first word in a doxology, for instance, at the conclusion of many books of the Psalms: "Praise be to the LORD, the God of Israel, from everlasting to everlasting" (Ps. 41:13; and

---

18. Ernst Hoffmann, *NIDNTT*, vol. 2, p. 244.

with variations 72:18; 89:52; 106:48). The word *praise* is common in the New Testament, too. Zechariah begins his song with an exuberant burst of praise: "Praise be to the Lord, the God of Israel, because he has come and has redeemed his people" (Luke 1:68; also see Rom. 1:25b; 9:5).

b. "God and Father." Within the early church, Jewish Christians adapted the benedictions of their forefathers to include Jesus Christ. Note that the doxology in verse 3, "Praise be to the God and Father of our Lord Jesus Christ," is identical to the wording of II Corinthians 1:3 and Ephesians 1:3 (compare also II Cor. 11:31).

God has revealed himself in his Son, the Lord Jesus Christ. Through Jesus, all the elect share in his sonship. Through him they call God their Father, for they are his children. With the church universal, the believer confesses the words of the Apostles' Creed:

> I believe in God the Father Almighty,
> Maker of heaven and earth.

Because of Jesus Christ, we call his Father our Father and his God our God (John 20:17). Fatherhood is one of the essential characteristics of God's being; it is part of his deity. God is first Father of Jesus, and then because of Christ he is Father of the believer.

Peter indicates our relationship to the Father and the Son when he uses the personal pronoun *our* ("God and Father of our Lord Jesus Christ"). Also, in the next sentence, Peter discloses that God is our Father because God "has given us new birth." That is, the Father has begotten us again in giving us spiritual rebirth. The Father has given us rebirth because of our Lord Jesus Christ.

c. "Lord." Verse 3 is the only text in this epistle in which Peter writes the title and names *our Lord Jesus Christ*. With the pronoun *our*, Peter includes himself among the believers who confess the lordship of Jesus Christ. "To call Jesus Lord is to declare that he is God."[19] Moreover, in the early church Christians confessed their faith in the brief statement *Jesus is Lord* (I Cor. 12:3). The name *Jesus* encompasses the earthly ministry of the Son of God, and the name *Christ* refers to his messianic calling. Four times in three verses (vv. 1–3) Peter employs the name *Jesus Christ*.

d. "Mercy." Peter describes our relationship to God the Father by saying, "In his great mercy he has given us new birth." We read almost the same wording in one of Paul's epistles ("God, who is rich in mercy, made us alive with Christ" [Eph. 2:4–5]). Apparently Peter was acquainted with Paul's epistles (see II Peter 3:15–16). Together with the other apostles, Peter presents Christian doctrine on regeneration (e.g., see John 3:3, 5).

---

19. Robert H. Mounce, *A Living Hope: A Commentary on 1 and 2 Peter* (Grand Rapids: Eerdmans, 1982), p. 11.

e. "Birth." Notice that we receive a new spiritual birth from God the Father. Peter writes that God "has given us new birth" (v. 3), and later he continues, "For you have been born again" (v. 23). Just as we are passive in natural birth, so we are in spiritual birth. That is, God is active in the process of begetting us, for he causes us to be born again. With the words *new* and *again* in these two verses, Peter shows the difference between our natural birth and our spiritual birth.

Peter speaks from personal experience, for he remembers when he fell into the sin of denying Jesus. Later, when Jesus restored him to apostleship, he became the recipient of God's great mercy and received new life through restoration. Therefore, he includes himself when he writes, "He has given *us* new birth" (italics added). Incidentally, the passages in which Peter uses the personal pronouns *our* or *us* are few (1:3; 2:24; 4:17). First Peter is an epistle in which the author addresses his readers as "you." The infrequent use of the first person, singular (2:11; 5:1, 12) or plural, is therefore much more significant.

f. "Hope." What is hope? It is something that is personal, living, active, and part of us. In verse 3, it is not something that pertains to the future (compare Col. 1:5; Titus 2:13).[20] Instead, it brings life to God's elect who are waiting with patient discipline for God's revelation in Jesus Christ.

g. "Resurrection." What is the basis for our new life? Peter tells us that "through the resurrection of Jesus Christ from the dead" God has made us alive and has given us living hope. Without the resurrection of Christ, our rebirth would be impossible and our hope would be meaningless. By rising from the dead, Jesus Christ has given us the assurance that we, too, shall rise with him (see Rom. 6:4). Why? As Peter preached on Pentecost, "God raised him from the dead, freeing him from the agony of death, because it was impossible for death to keep its hold on him" (Acts 2:24). Jesus is the first one to break the bonds of death, so that through him we have our rebirth, and in him we have eternal life (I John 5:12).

Peter speaks as an eyewitness, for he had the unique experience of meeting Jesus after he rose from the grave. Peter ate and drank with Jesus and became a witness of Jesus' resurrection (refer to Acts 10:41).

Doctrinal Considerations in 1:3

Twice in this short epistle Peter introduces teaching on the resurrection of Jesus Christ (1:3; 3:21). This teaching, to be sure, is central to the Christian religion. When the eleven apostles came together after Jesus' ascension and prior to Pente-

---

20. Commenting on Col. 1:5, William Hendriksen remarks that hope is "an objective reality, namely, *the thing hoped for.*" *Colossians and Philemon,* New Testament Commentary series (Grand Rapids: Baker, 1964), p. 50.

cost, they chose a successor to Judas Iscariot. Peter, as spokesman, declared that this person had to be a follower of Jesus from the day of his baptism to the time of his ascension, and that he had to be a witness of Jesus' resurrection (Acts 1:22).

As an eyewitness to the resurrection of Jesus, Peter proclaimed this truth in his sermon to the multitude gathered in Jerusalem on Pentecost (Acts 2:31). When he preached to the crowd at Solomon's porch, he said that God raised Jesus from the dead (Acts 3:15; compare 4:2, 33). And last, when Peter spoke in the home of Cornelius at Caesarea, he taught the resurrection of Jesus (Acts 10:40). Peter testified to this truth throughout his ministry of preaching and writing.

Greek Words, Phrases, and Constructions in 1:3

εὐλογητὸς—the verbal adjective ("blessed") reflects the passive mood; that is, God the Father is praised by his people. The clause lacks the verb. Therefore, some scholars insert the verb *to be* in the indicative, others supply it in the optative or imperative, and still others omit the verb altogether.

ὁ θεὸς καὶ πατήρ—note that the definite article governs both nouns, so that two aspects of the same person are stressed.[21]

ὁ . . . ἀναγεννήσας—between the definite article and the aorist active participle stands a prepositional clause beginning with κατά (according to). The participle derives from the compound verb ἀναγεννάω (I beget).

κατά . . . εἰς . . . διά . . . ἐκ—notice the increased use of prepositions, particularly in this verse, but also in the entire passage (1:1–12). This is one of the stylistic features of this epistle that helps in determining the authorship of First Peter.

B. A Safe Inheritance
1:4

4. And into an inheritance that can never perish, spoil or fade—kept in heaven for you.

The key word in this verse is "inheritance." This particular word calls to mind the death of a person who has willed his property to immediate relatives and to charities. The writer of Hebrews puts it succinctly: "In the case of a will, it is necessary to prove the death of the one who made it, because a will is in force only when somebody has died; it never takes effect while the one who made it is living" (9:16–17).

Peter, however, places the word *inheritance* in the context of life. In the preceding verse (v. 3), he mentions the resurrection of Christ and the new birth which we receive through him. Instead of death there is life. Through the resurrection of Christ, we are recipients of the inheritance God has stored for us in heaven. Paul writes, "We are heirs—heirs of God and co-heirs with Christ" (Rom. 8:17).

---

21. Consult A. T. Robertson, *A Grammar of the Greek New Testament in the Light of Historical Research* (Nashville: Broadman, 1934), p. 785.

The Israelites knew the meaning of the word *inheritance*. When they traveled through the Sinai desert, they remembered that Abraham had received the promise of inheriting the land of Canaan (Gen. 15:18; Acts 7:5; Heb. 11:8). In the Promised Land, every Israelite had his own possession, sat under his own fig tree, and enjoyed the fruit of his own vine (I Kings 4:25). "Nothing appeared to the Israelites more desirable than the quiet, prosperous, permanent possession of this land."[22]

Israel's inheritance, however, was never safe and secure. Marauders from the desert would invade the land and plunder the possessions of the inhabitants. By contrast, in New Testament times the word *inheritance* has a totally different meaning (Eph. 1:14, 18; Col. 1:12; 3:24; Heb. 9:15). It refers to the salvation the believers inherit when they leave this earthly scene and obtain eternal glory. The inheritance of the believers is kept in heaven, where God keeps it absolutely safe for us until the appointed time when we receive it.

What do we inherit? Peter is unable to describe in positive terms the inheritance that is waiting for us. Ironically, because of its great value, he can describe it only in negative terms. He chooses three adjectives to tell us what our possession is not, and implies that these words reveal the true nature of the inheritance.

a. *Imperishable.* Our treasure is not subject to death or destruction; it can never perish. Moreover, it is not limited by time, but is eternal.

b. *Undefiled.* It can never be spoiled, corrupted, or polluted. It remains free from any blemish and is pure (compare Rev. 21:27).

c. *Unfading.* It is incapable of fading. When a flower is past its peak, its beauty fades. This can never be said of our inheritance that is kept in heaven for us.

Earthly possessions are subject to constant variation and change, but our eternal inheritance is safely guarded by God in heaven. Not only is our salvation kept safe, but also, Peter declares, we, the possessors of this inheritance, are protected by God's power.

Greek Words, Phrases, and Constructions in 1:4

κληρονομίαν ἄφθαρτον—the noun is a combination of κλῆρος (a lot) and νένομαι (I possess). The noun is qualified by three adjectives that begin with the privative -α, to describe the inheritance.

τετηρημένην—from the verb τηρέω (I keep), this participle expresses continued action with the perfect tense, and with the passive it implicitly describes God as the agent.

οὐρανοῖς—note that in this verse the writer omits the definite articles. The use of the plural ("heavens") is characteristic in the Hebrew language.

---

22. Thayer, p. 349.

εἰς ὑμᾶς—the author changes his address from the first person plural (v. 3) to the second person plural. The presence of εἰς with the accusative, instead of the dative ὑμῖν, reflects an increased use of prepositions in this epistle.

C. A Joyous Salvation
1:5–6

5. Who through faith are shielded by God's power until the coming of the salvation that is ready to be revealed in the last time.

a. "Who through faith are shielded by God's power." In this particular verse every word is significant, yet the important term is "shielded" or "guarded." In the Greek, this verb is a military term that can mean either "to protect someone from danger" or "to prevent someone from escaping." When Paul was trying to escape from Damascus, "the governor . . . had the city of the Damascenes guarded" (II Cor. 11:32). In a spiritual sense, "the peace of God . . . will guard [our] hearts and minds" (Phil. 4:7) so that evil cannot touch us. This is the meaning Peter conveys when he writes that the believers are shielded by God's power. We are being shielded during our brief stay on this earth, for God does not permit Satan to harm us.

We are shielded by God's power through faith. Paul's imagery conveys this truth: "Take up the shield of faith, with which you can extinguish all the flaming arrows of the evil one" (Eph. 6:16). Peter teaches the doctrine of God's providence. When he speaks of faith, he mentions both God's protective power and human responsibility. That is, although God has promised to protect us, we must employ our faith in our fight against the evil one. Faith in God is both objective and subjective. Objective faith means that "God is seen without rather than felt within."[23] But faith has its subjective side, too, as the numerous references to faith in First Peter demonstrate.

b. "Until the coming of the salvation." Why does God shield us? Our salvation which we now have in principle becomes our possession in reality when we enter the portals of heaven. God protects us so that we may receive our full inheritance when it is "revealed in the last time." The expression *salvation* is a synonym of "inheritance" (v. 4). Peter "uses an astonishing variety of expressions for the coming salvation of the end-time" (for example, "a living hope" [1:3], God's "wonderful light" [2:9], "the gracious gift of life" [3:7], "inherit a blessing" [3:9], "crown of glory" [5:4], and "eternal glory" [5:10]).[24] We joyfully look forward to claiming our salvation. Even as we now taste the goodness of God by experiencing salvation in principle, we know that the fullness of our inheritance shall be made known in due time (Heb. 1:14).

---

23. Charles Bigg, *A Critical and Exegetical Commentary on the Epistles of St. Peter and St. Jude,* International Critical Commentary series (1901; Edinburgh: Clark, 1961), p. 101. Guthrie points out the subjective aspect of faith and remarks that I Peter is "particularly rich in references to faith." *New Testament Theology,* p. 600.

24. Werner Foerster, *TDNT,* vol. 7, p. 995.

c. "That is ready to be revealed in the last time." The term *ready* relates to salvation and not to the verb *revealed*. Our salvation has been prepared for us by Christ through his atoning work. It will be revealed in a single moment at God's appointed time. Everyone shall see the inheritance, but only the believers shall possess it. The word *revealed* in the Greek means "to take away the veil or the cover." Jesus will remove the veil when he returns to grant us salvation full and free.

> How vast the benefits divine
> Which we in Christ possess!
> We are redeemed from sin and shame,
> And called to holiness.
> 'Tis not for works that we have done,
> These all to Him we owe;
> But He of His electing love
> Salvation doth bestow.
> —Augustus M. Toplady
> Revised by Dewey Westra

Practical Considerations in 1:4–5

When we learn that our names are mentioned in a will, we know that we have a share in an inheritance described in that will. Often we do not know the value of that inheritance. We have to wait for the death of the testator and for legal transactions and financial settlements. After the period of waiting is over, however, the value of the inheritance often has diminished. Also, the distribution of the inheritance frequently causes jealousy and strife.

By contrast, our eternal inheritance is a constant source of happiness. From the moment of our salvation we are filled with joy. Granted that we possess our inheritance in principle now, we know that when we leave this earthly scene we receive our full inheritance. We are unable to comprehend the value of this inheritance, for "the gift of God is eternal life in Christ Jesus our Lord" (Rom. 6:23). Furthermore, we cherish that gift in perfect harmony with all believers in the presence of our living testator, Jesus Christ.

---

6. In this you greatly rejoice, though now for a little while you may have had to suffer grief in all kinds of trials.

We note these points:

a. *Rejoice.* Peter writes, "In this you greatly rejoice." But what does he mean by the word *this*? We have no fewer than three interpretations.

First, the pronoun *this* has its antecedent in the last words of the preceding verse, "in the last time" (v. 5). But then the pronoun does not match the present tense of the main verb *rejoice*. For this reason, some translators put the verb in the imperative mood, "be glad about this" (GNB), or in the future tense, "you will rejoice then" (*Moffatt*). However, none of the verbs in the first chapter are imperatives, so a single command to rejoice seems to be a little out of place.[25] In the Greek text the present tense, not the future tense, occurs. Consequently, if we adopt the reading of the New International Version, we cannot link the pronoun *this* to the phrase *in the last time*.

Next, we can translate the phrase *in this* as "in whom." Then the masculine form *whom* refers to "the God and Father" of Jesus Christ (v. 3). The objection to this translation is that the pronoun *whom* is too far removed from its antecedent, "God and Father."

In the third interpretation, which we prefer, the pronoun *this* relates to "the experience of rebirth and the anticipation of salvation" (see vv. 3–5).[26] The main verb, accordingly, we understand as a present indicative; that is, as a declarative statement: "In this you greatly rejoice." The gift of salvation is a cause of great rejoicing and for raising shouts of joy. In his first epistle, Peter mentions joy three times. He does this to encourage his readers, who are experiencing suffering and persecution (1:6, 8; 4:13). The sufferings they endure are insignificant when compared with the joy they will experience at the end of time (see II Cor. 4:17).[27]

b. *Endure.* Peter sympathizes with the readers, who are enduring hardships of various kinds. He writes, "Though now for a little while you may have had to suffer grief in all kinds of trials." The wording is an echo of a verse in the Epistle of James: "Consider it pure joy, my brothers, whenever you face trials of many kinds" (1:2).

This is the first time Peter mentions the word *suffer* (compare 4:13; 5:10). In the original, the word means to *"become sad, sorrowful, distressed."*[28] The verb is in the past tense and undoubtedly relates to a particular incident that caused grief and suffering. First, although the exact time and duration of suffering are not known, this period of suffering is brief in relation to eternity. And second, the ordeal of suffering is necessary in accordance with God's purpose. "Peter firmly believed in the reality of God's sovereign presence in the lives of His people."[29]

The trials which the believers experience come from God's hand. These trials, in whatever form they appear, are ordained by God. Note that the word is "trial," not "temptation." God never tempts anyone (see James 1:13), but he tests the believer to strengthen his faith.

---

25. James 1:2 has the imperative *consider it pure joy,* but that entire context demands the imperative mood.

26. Kelly, *Peter and Jude,* p. 53. He calls this interpretation the "likeliest . . . of a verse which contains both syntactical and textual difficulties."

27. Refer to Erich Beyreuther, *NIDNTT,* vol. 2, p. 354.

28. Bauer, p. 481.

29. Hiebert, *First Peter,* p. 56. On the divine necessity of Jesus' suffering, see, e.g., Matt. 16:21; Mark 8:31; Luke 22:37; 24:44; John 3:14.

Greek Words, Phrases, and Constructions in 1:5–6

Verse 5

τοὺς . . . φρουρουμένους—the participle (from the verb φρουρέω, I guard) is in the present tense to stress continued action. The author marks the significance of the prepositional phrase ἐν δυνάμει θεοῦ (by God's power) by placing it between the definite article and the participle. The preposition ἐν (by) is instrumental.

ἀποκαλυφθῆναι—this aorist passive infinitive from ἀποκαλύπτω (I reveal) is an infinitive of purpose. The aorist shows single occurrence and the passive implies that God is the agent. The verb refers to two parts: ἀπό (away) and κάλυμμα (covering).

καιρός—the noun signifies God's appointed time, whereas χρόνος is chronological time.

Verse 6

ἀγαλλιᾶσθε—the verb can be either a present indicative ("you greatly rejoice") or a present imperative ("rejoice greatly"). Scholars favor the present indicative because of contextual evidence.

εἰ δέον ἐστὶν—"if need be." The participle is from the incomplete verb δεῖ (it is necessary). The inclusion of the verb ἐστίν is debatable.

λυπηθέντες—this aorist passive participle from the verb λυπέω (I grieve, am sorrowful) is concessive.

D. A Genuine Faith
1:7

7. These have come so that your faith—of greater worth than gold, which perishes even though refined by fire—may be proved genuine and may result in praise, glory and honor when Jesus Christ is revealed.

Note these features:

a. *Testing.* Peter seems to anticipate the question about why a believer has to experience trials in his life. He replies, "These have come so that your faith . . . may be proved genuine." A literal translation of the Greek has this reading: "So that the testing of your faith . . . may prove to be for praise and glory" (MLB).

God tests the believer to see if his faith is genuine. Thus he asks Abraham to go to Mount Moriah to sacrifice Isaac (Gen. 22:1–19), and does so to prove Abraham's faith. In the case of Job, God permitted Satan to attack the believer (Job 1:6–2:10). Testing is a process that demands time. But after time has elapsed and the process of testing has ended, the result of the test becomes visible, namely, a genuine faith.

Abraham triumphed in faith when he heard the angel of the Lord say, "Now I know that you fear God" (Gen. 22:12). Because of Job's faith, God "blessed the latter part of Job's life more than the first" (Job 42:12). In fact,

God doubled Job's possessions. Note that the word *testing* occurs twice in the New Testament, here and in James 1:3, "The testing of your faith develops perseverance." Each writer uses the word for his own purposes.

b. *Perishing.* Whereas James writes that "the testing of your faith develops perseverance" (1:3), Peter compares this testing to the process by which gold is refined. Throughout the centuries gold has been treasured as a precious and stable commodity. "This highly prized metal is mentioned 385 times in the Bible, more often than any other metal."[30] Gold serves as a standard in determining monetary transactions (see also I Peter 1:18).

Peter states that faith is of greater value than gold; faith excels this universally prized commodity because it originates in heaven and is a gift of God. Faith is everlasting (I Cor. 13:13). By contrast, gold eventually perishes through use or abuse. This precious metal is refined by fire so that all impurities are removed and pure gold of 24 karats remains. Peter, however, observes that even though gold is refined by fire, it perishes. The obvious implication of the comparison is that if perishable gold is purified, how much more should abiding faith be tested in the life of the Christian? The believer expresses true faith by completely trusting God. He knows that "God will meet all [his] needs according to his glorious riches in Christ Jesus" (Phil. 4:19).

c. *Appearing.* What is the result of faith that is tested? Peter answers that it results "in praise, glory and honor when Jesus Christ is revealed." He is not giving this sequence of three responses to embellish a sentence. The believer proclaims his praise to God in prayer, psalm, and hymn. His praise includes gratitude to God for the divine favor given to him through Christ Jesus.

The terms *glory* and *honor* occur in doxologies (refer to I Tim. 1:17; Rev. 4:11). The believer shall share in heavenly glory and honor when at the end of his earthly life he enters the presence of Jesus Christ. Peter says that these three qualities are present "when Jesus Christ is revealed." He does not tell us when Jesus will return, but he refers to the appointed time when every eye shall see Jesus. Then all believers in heaven and on earth will sing praises and attribute honor and glory to the Son of God.

Practical Considerations in 1:7

Gold is the monetary standard among the nations of the world and serves to determine the value of currencies. The value of gold, however, is set by world markets. That is, man determines the price of gold.

By comparison, faith, which is more precious than gold, originates not in the mines of the earth but in heaven. Faith is refined in the crucible of man's trials. Faith is God's gift to man. God, not man, determines the value of faith; and he reveals that the goal of man's faith is his salvation (1:9).

---

30. George A. Turner, "Gold," *ISBE*, vol. 2, p. 520.

Greek Words, Phrases, and Constructions in 1:7

χρυσίου—the genitive case is due to the comparative adjective πολυτιμότερον (more precious).

δέ—this participle is more than a conjunction. It is adversative and means "nevertheless."

εὑρεθῇ—from the verb εὑρίσκω (I find), this form is the aorist passive subjunctive. For the passive, God is the implied agent.

ἀποκαλύψει—the noun signifies the objective revelation of Jesus Christ. The ending of the noun indicates that this revelation is a process.

E. A Glorious Joy
1:8–9

Peter returns to the subjects *joy* (see v. 6) and *faith* (vv. 5, 7). In effect, he is presenting a summary of the preceding paragraph so that his readers may fully understand the significance of the Christian virtues: faith, hope, and love. Note that in verses 3–9 he teaches the meaning of these three virtues.

8. Though you have not seen him, you love him; and even though you do not see him now, you believe in him and are filled with an inexpressible and glorious joy, 9. for you are receiving the goal of your faith, the salvation of your souls.

These two verses depict parallelism and balance. To demonstrate this point, I place the parallel lines in separate columns:

	and even
though you have	though you do
not seen him,	not see him now,
you love him;	you believe in him
and are filled with an	
inexpressible and glorious joy,	
for you are receiving	
the goal of	the salvation of
your faith,	your souls.

a. *Believe.* Peter implies that he has seen the Lord, and that the readers of his epistle have not had this privilege. Notice that Peter uses the first person plural in verse 3: "Our Lord Jesus Christ . . . has given us new birth." But in verse 8 he employs the second person plural *you*: "Though you have not seen him." Also notice the past tense, "have not seen him." He contrasts the past tense with the present tense of the parallel statement, "And even though you do not see him now, you believe in him." All these points imply that Peter has seen the Lord and that he is an eyewitness of Jesus' ministry. Later in the epistle he explicitly calls himself "a witness of Christ's sufferings" (5:1).

Because of time and distance, the recipients of Peter's letter had not seen Jesus; yet, because of the gospel, they love Jesus and believe in him. Indeed, they are a living commentary on the beatitude Jesus spoke to Thomas: "Blessed are those who have not seen and yet have believed" (John 20:29). They love Jesus and put their trust in him, even though they are unable to see him in this earthly life. The recipients do this on the basis of the message spoken by the apostles (compare John 17:20). As Paul put it, "We live by faith, not by sight" (II Cor. 5:7; also see 4:18).

Is it possible that the apostles who saw and heard Jesus were of the opinion that their faith in the Lord was not so great as the faith of those who would believe without seeing Jesus?[31] This possibility is real, first, because Peter was present when Jesus spoke the beatitude to Thomas (John 20:29). Second, Peter resorts twice to the use of concessive clauses that in translation begin with the word *though*—"though you have not seen him" and "though you do not see him now." Third, he stresses the temporal adverb *now*. In brief, Peter commends the readers for their faith in Jesus Christ.

b. *Joy.* "You believe in him and are filled with an inexpressible and glorious joy." Already in this present life believers experience indescribable joy; they do not have to wait until they leave this earthly scene. Even now they are filled with joy that is "inexpressible and glorious."

The emphasis in this part of the verse is on the joy that fills the hearts of Christians. A literal translation conveys this concept in both verb and noun: "You greatly rejoice with joy" (NASB). This is the second time in this first part of his epistle that Peter introduces the subject *joy.* Peter repeats the word he used earlier, "you greatly rejoice" (v. 6). The word depicts shouting for joy that cannot be contained.

Besides, Peter qualifies the noun *joy* with two unusual adjectives: "inexpressible" and "glorious." The first word, "inexpressible," occurs nowhere else in the New Testament. Peter uses it to describe the activity of a person who possesses great joy. That person cannot express his joy in human terms. In fact, he copes with not only an inability but also an impossibility to convey the depth of his joy. The second word, "glorious," signifies that which has been glorified and continues to be glorified. It connotes the presence of heavenly glory that characterizes this particular joy (compare II Cor. 3:10).

c. *Receive.* The writer states the reason for this joy. He says, "For you are receiving the goal of your faith, the salvation of your souls." Although many translators have chosen the verb *to receive* to convey the meaning of the Greek,[32] the word means "to obtain something that is due to a person."

---

31. Consult John Albert Bengel, *Gnomon of the New Testament,* ed. Andrew R. Fausset, trans. William Fletcher, 7th ed., 5 vols. (Edinburgh: Clark, 1877), vol. 5, p. 48.

32. See, e.g., KJV, RV, ASV, NKJV, NIV, GNB.

In this case, the word signifies that through the work of Christ the believer obtains salvation.[33] Already in this life the Christian claims for himself the salvation Christ provides (see I Cor. 1:18).

What do believers obtain? Peter gives them a direct answer. He tells them that they will obtain "the goal of [their] faith," as the New International Version has it. The text actually says, "the end of your faith." However, if we stop at this point, Peter's answer is deficient, for we need to know what the goal of faith is. Peter, however, completes the sentence by adding the explanatory phrase *the salvation of your souls*.

Scripture teaches that salvation belongs to us already in principle. We will have full possession when we are with Christ eternally. The wording of verse 9, "the salvation of your souls," agrees with the teaching of numerous New Testament passages that our salvation in Christ affects our total life.[34] Christ Jesus saves completely, so that every believer can say:

> He has fully paid for all my sins with his precious blood,
> and has set me free from the tyranny of the devil.
> He also watches over me in such a way
> that not a hair can fall from my head
> without the will of my Father in heaven:
> in fact, all things must work together for my salvation.[35]

Doctrinal Considerations in 1:8–9

What is joy? Joy is not only an emotional outburst that lasts momentarily. It is not simply a response to external circumstances that favor and encourage expression of joy. Joy often appears in the midst of hardship, suffering, trials, and persecutions. Joy is a gift that we receive from God, for Scripture shows that God is the giver of joy (see Ps. 16:11; John 16:24; Rom. 15:13). This gift, then, comes to the believer who puts his complete trust in God.

Joy is a gift that must be shared with others. The shepherd who finds his sheep and the woman who finds her coin share their joy with neighbors, while the angels in heaven rejoice over one sinner who repents (Luke 15:4–10). In Scripture, joy is often related to God's almighty acts of saving man. As a result, man expresses his joy by loving God and by obeying his commands (see especially John 15:9–11).[36] And last, joy is the fruit of the Spirit (Gal. 5:22).

---

33. On this verse Bauer writes, "*obtain as an outcome of faith the salvation of souls*" (p. 442). Also see RSV, MLB, NASB, *Moffatt*.
34. For instance, see Luke 21:19; Heb. 10:39; James 1:21; 5:20.
35. Heidelberg Catechism, answer 1.
36. Creath Davis, "Joy," *EDT*, p. 588. Also consult Erich Beyreuther and Günter Finkenrath, *NIDNTT*, vol. 2, pp. 356–61.

Greek Words, Phrases, and Constructions in 1:8–9

Verse 8

ὂν οὐκ ἰδόντες—the relative pronoun ὅν has its antecedent in "Jesus Christ" (v. 7). The aorist active participle (from the verb εἶδον, I saw) is negated by the adverb οὐκ, while the present participle ὁρῶντες (from ὁράω, I see) has the negative adverb μή. The first participle with a negative adverb relates to history; the second refers to present reality. Both participles denote concession—"although."

ἀνεκλάλητος—this is a verbal adjective that is active in a sense.[37] The adjective consists of the privative ἀ- (not), the preposition ἐκ (out of), and a form derived from the verb λαλέω (I speak).

δεδοξασμένη—from the verb δοξάζω (I glorify), this perfect passive participle expresses lasting effect.

Verse 9

κομιζόμενοι—the present middle participle of the verb κομίζομαι (I receive, obtain) has a causal meaning. It gives the reason for inexpressible joy.

ὑμῶν—although one leading manuscript (Codex B) omits the pronoun, others include it. Scholars generally favor its inclusion.

σωτηρίαν ψυχῶν —the absence of the definite article makes these two nouns distinct. The emphasis falls on the concept *the salvation of your souls*.

F. An Intensive Search
1:10–11

10. Concerning this salvation, the prophets, who spoke of the grace that was to come to you, searched intently and with the greatest care, 11. trying to find out the time and circumstances to which the Spirit of Christ in them was pointing when he predicted the sufferings of Christ and the glories that would follow.

What do these two verses teach? In summary, the main points of the passage are these:

1. The Old Testament prophets taught the doctrine of salvation.
2. They researched and investigated this subject.
3. They tried to find out the time and circumstances to which the Spirit pointed.
4. The Spirit predicted Christ's sufferings and glory.

Peter relates the teaching of salvation to the prophecies of the Old Testament. He concludes that the topic *salvation* has been:

---

37. Consult Robertson, *Grammar,* p. 1096.

a. *Prophesied.* "Concerning this salvation, the prophets . . . spoke of the grace that was to come to you." Who are these prophets? Peter mentions no names but has in mind all of the Old Testament prophets, from Moses to Malachi. They are the prophets to whom Luke refers when he records the conversation of Jesus and the two men on the way to Emmaus: " 'Did not the Christ have to suffer these things and then enter his glory?' " Luke adds, "And beginning with Moses and all the Prophets, he explained to them what was said in all the Scriptures concerning himself" (Luke 24:26– 27).

Directed by the Holy Spirit (II Peter 1:21), these prophets taught the "grace that was to come." The expression *grace* is more comprehensive than its synonym *salvation.* It includes God's gracious rule in relation to man's redemption. Here are two examples:

> Jacob on his deathbed says, "The scepter will not depart from Judah, nor the ruler's staff from between his feet, until he comes to whom it belongs and the obedience of the nations is his" (Gen. 49:10).

> Daniel, interpreting Nebuchadnezzar's dream, prophesies, "In the time of those kings, the God of heaven will set up a kingdom that will never be destroyed, . . . it will itself endure forever" (Dan. 2:44).

Did the prophets understand what they were prophesying? Peter states that they "searched intently and with the greatest care."

b. *Searched.* The prophets received God's revelation but did not always understand what their prophecies meant. However, they did not shrug their shoulders when they failed to understand the significance of their words; instead they searched diligently and carefully to determine the meaning of God's Word (compare Isa. 6:11; Dan. 7:15–16; Matt. 13:17; John 12:41). The prophets took their task seriously, for their words concerned the salvation of man. And about this salvation, they wished to know as much as possible. Therefore, they "were trying to find out the time and circumstances" of which the Holy Spirit spoke.

c. *Investigated.* Instead of the reading "[they] were trying to find out the time and circumstances," a few translations have "they inquired what *person* or *time* was indicated" (RSV, italics added).[38] The prophets knew that the Messiah would be coming, but they had no knowledge when he would appear or what the circumstances of his appearance would be. Therefore they inquired about the "when and how" of the Messiah's coming. In general, scholars favor the reading *time and circumstances* to "person or time."[39]

The prophets, of course, received God's revelation about the coming of the Messiah. Isaiah prophesied about his birth (7:14; 9:6; 11:1), his minis-

---

38. Also see NASB, MLB, and the alternate reading of GNB.
39. Hiebert discusses the matter at length. See *First Peter,* pp. 65–66.

try (11:2–5; 35:4–6; 61:1–2), and his suffering and death (52:13–53:12). And Micah predicted the place of his birth: Bethlehem (5:2). When they prophesied, these men were filled with God's Spirit.

d. *Predicted.* Not the prophets but the Holy Spirit "predicted the sufferings of Christ and the glories that would follow." Peter says that it was the Spirit of Christ who was in them (see Acts 16:7). Peter indicates that Christ existed before he came to dwell among men. Through his Spirit Christ directed the prophets and thus inspired their writings.[40]

The wording of the text reveals that a constant interaction between the prophets and the Spirit of Christ took place. That is, the prophets were constantly investigating the meaning of their prophecies, and the Spirit of Christ, working in them, was repeatedly pointing to the time and circumstances disclosed in these prophecies. The Spirit, then, revealed to them by means of predictions what the Christ had to endure. Note that in this passage, Peter unequivocally teaches the preexistence of Christ when he writes, "the Spirit of Christ in them . . . predicted the sufferings of Christ." In the Greek, the present tense of the verb *predict* (as a participle) indicates the repeated nature of this activity. Christ made these predictions centuries before their fulfillment.

Notice that the Spirit of Christ reveals these predictions to the prophets of the Old Testament era. These prophets assumed the task of searching diligently for the meaning of these prophecies. In brief, we draw the conclusion that in this passage Peter teaches the doctrine of verbal inspiration.[41]

The psalmist and the prophets reveal the sufferings of Christ (e.g., Ps. 22:7; Isa. 53:3). Peter writes the term *suffering* in the plural to stress the magnitude and variety of the pain and sorrow Jesus had to endure. However, Peter contrasts Jesus' suffering with the "glories that would follow." Note the use of the plural, "glories." The plural refers to the glory of Jesus' resurrection, the glory of his ascension, and the glory of his return.[42]

Practical Considerations in 1:10–11

An amazing characteristic of Scripture is its clarity, for God speaks to us in simple terms. For that reason, the Reformers of the sixteenth century taught about "the perspicuity of Scripture." What they meant by "perspicuity" is that anyone guided by the Holy Spirit is able to read and understand the Bible because of its clarity. They acknowledged that some passages of Scripture are difficult to interpret; nevertheless they realized that the basic message of the Bible is clear.

---

40. Refer to Kelly, *Peter and Jude,* pp. 60–61. Also see John Calvin, *Commentaries on the Catholic Epistles: The First Epistle of Peter,* ed. and trans. John Owen (Grand Rapids: Eerdmans, 1948), pp. 39–40.

41. Consult Alan M. Stibbs, *The First Epistle General of Peter,* Tyndale New Testament Commentaries series (Grand Rapids: Eerdmans, 1960), p. 82. And see Greijdanus, *De Brieven,* p. 56.

42. Refer to Bengel, *Gnomon of the New Testament,* vol. 5, p. 49.

The Bible is still a best seller, but the people who regularly read it are a minority. Furthermore, persons who search the Scriptures, as the Bereans did in Paul's day (see Acts 17:11), are in a class by themselves; they usually attend a seminary or Bible college. But serious Bible study should not be limited to one particular group of people. The Bible is an open book in which God tells us about the riches of salvation we have in Christ Jesus. Therefore, study the Scriptures to be wise in respect to salvation (II Tim. 3:15).

Greek Words, Phrases, and Constructions in 1:10–11

Verse 10

ἐξεζήτησαν—this compound verb from ἐκ (out of) and ζητέω (I seek) has a perfective meaning: "search intently." The verb is in the aorist, which signifies that the prophets belonged to the Old Testament era.

ἐξηραύνησαν—a verb that occurs only here in the New Testament, it is a compound with a perfective stress: "inquire carefully."

Verse 11

ἐραυνῶντες—the present tense of this participle denotes a continual process. This form is more comprehensive than the compound verb of verse 10.

καιρόν—a fixed time, determined by God and referred to in prophecy.

ἐδήλου—the imperfect tense of the verb δηλόω (I show, point out) indicates repeated action in the past.

G. A Personal Revelation
1:12

Peter is about to conclude his discussion on salvation. He has presented this topic by looking at the three Christian virtues: faith, hope, and love. Furthermore, he has described the joy of the believers, for they are indescribably rich in respect to their spiritual inheritance. And he has reminded them of the teachings of the Old Testament prophets. Now he concludes his reference to these prophets and says:

12. It was revealed to them that they were not serving themselves but you, when they spoke of the things that have now been told you by those who have preached the gospel to you by the Holy Spirit sent from heaven. Even angels long to look into these things.

a. "It was revealed to them that they were not serving themselves but you." Peter does not specify how and when the Old Testament prophets received the information that they were serving future generations. By his use of the past tense, he seems to indicate that this information came in a general way. Here are a few examples taken from the Old and the New Testaments:

55

In his fourth oracle Balaam says, "I see him, but not now; I behold him, but not near. A star will come out of Jacob; a scepter will rise out of Israel" (Num. 24:17).

Moses tells the Israelites, "The LORD your God will raise up for you a prophet like me from among your own brothers. You must listen to him" (Deut. 18:15).

On Pentecost, Peter quotes a psalm of David (Ps. 16:8–11) to illustrate Christ's resurrection. Peter calls David a prophet and says, "Seeing what was ahead, he spoke of the resurrection of the Christ" (Acts 2:31).

In his sermon after he healed the crippled man, Peter quotes Deuteronomy 18:15, applies it to Christ, and adds, "Indeed, all the prophets from Samuel on, as many as have spoken, have foretold these days" (Acts 3:24).[43]

In the Greek, the past tense of the verb *were serving* reveals that the prophets kept on doing so.

b. "When they spoke of the things that have now been told." In this segment of the verse we note, first, that the word *things* is most important. This word refers to the sufferings and glories of Christ (v. 11) and summarizes the content of the gospel. The message of the Old Testament prophets as they prophesied concerning the life, death, and resurrection of Christ was not self-serving. Rather, their prophecies continue to be a ministry to the church of the New Testament era.

Accordingly, we note next that Peter emphasizes the word *now*. He is speaking of the gospel that is being preached in his day. He links the message of the Old Testament with that of the New Testament and thereby implicitly teaches the unity of Scripture.[44] Peter looks at the Old Testament messianic prophecies in the light of their New Testament fulfillment; he confirms that Jesus has fulfilled these prophecies. Lutheran commentator R. C. H. Lenski astutely observes, "The whole New Testament gospel rests on the Spirit's Old Testament testimony that was made through the Old Testament prophets. Cancel that testimony, and you remove the basis of the gospel of Christ."[45]

c. "By those who have preached the gospel to you." The recipients living in Asia Minor (modern Turkey) heard the gospel from missionaries who had come to their area. The statement is too general to determine whether

---

43. Consult Henry Alford, *Alford's Greek Testament: An Exegetical and Critical Commentary*, 5th ed., 4 vols. (1875; Grand Rapids: Guardian, 1976), vol. 4, pt. 2, p. 338.

44. Refer to Kelly, *Peter and Jude*, p. 62.

45. R. C. H. Lenski, *The Interpretation of the Epistles of St. Peter, St. John, and St. Jude* (Columbus: Wartburg, 1945), p. 49. And refer to Stibbs, *The First Epistle General of Peter*, p. 83.

Peter himself was one of these missionaries. The phrase *preached the gospel* alludes to the spiritual darkness in which the recipients were before these missionaries came.

d. "By the Holy Spirit sent from heaven." The Spirit inspired the prophets in Old Testament times. On the day of Pentecost, however, he descended from heaven to guide and direct those who proclaim the gospel. Thus, the Holy Spirit directed the apostles and their helpers and gave them divine power, so that their message was not the word of man but the word of God (I Thess. 2:13).

e. "Even angels long to look into these things." Angels surround the throne of God, are messengers sent by God to serve man who inherits salvation (Heb. 1:14), rejoice when a sinner repents (Luke 15:7, 10), and gather the elect on the judgment day (Matt. 24:31). Nevertheless their knowledge of man's salvation is incomplete, for they long to look into the mystery of salvation.

The verb *look into* in the original actually means "to gaze at with outstretched necks." (In his epistle, James uses the same verb with reference to a mirror, presumably fastened on a table. People would bend their bodies to look into the mirror [1:23–24]).[46] Angels will learn about salvation through the church. As Paul says, "[God's] intent was that now, through the church, the manifold wisdom of God should be made known to the rulers and authorities in the heavenly realms" (Eph. 3:10).

Greek Words, Phrases, and Constructions in 1:12

διηκόνουν—the imperfect active of διακονέω (I serve) signifies continual action in the past. The verb itself refers to general services of any kind.[47]

αὐτά—this pronoun is important because it controls the entire verse. It looks back to the "sufferings of Christ and the glories," and it points ahead to the two relative pronouns ἅ (which) and εἰς ἅ (into which).

ἀποσταλέντι—the aorist passive of ἀποστέλλω (I send) alludes to the outpouring of the Holy Spirit at Pentecost which Peter experienced personally.

παρακύψαι—from παρά (beside) and κύπτω (I bend), this aorist active infinitive denotes that angels have not had the opportunity to come to a full knowledge of salvation.

---

13 Therefore, prepare your minds for action; be self-controlled; set your hope fully on the grace to be given you when Jesus Christ is revealed.   14 As obedient children, do not conform to the evil desires you had when you lived in ignorance.   15 But just as he who called you is holy, so be holy in all you do;   16 for it is written: "Be holy, because I am holy."

---

46. See Luke 24:12; John 20:5, 11. Also consult Thayer, p. 484.
47. Consult Bauer, p. 184.

III. Holiness
1:13–2:3

A. Be Holy
1:13–16

As the Old Testament prophets searched God's revelation in an effort to understand its meaning, so the recipients of Peter's letter ought to take the Word of God no less seriously. God has given Christian believers his Word and through it his assurance of their salvation.

13. Therefore, prepare your minds for action; be self-controlled; set your hope fully on the grace to be given you when Jesus Christ is revealed.

Believers, having received the gift of salvation (see v. 9), cannot take this treasure for granted. They are children of God and thus are expected to do the will of their heavenly Father (v. 14). Peter tells them what to do in a series of commands.

a. "Prepare your minds for action." In the Greek, the literal wording is, "Gird up the loins of your mind" (NKJV). The double metaphor *loins* and *mind* is somewhat confusing. But the picture is clear when we think of a first-century person who tucked the folds of his long, flowing garment under his belt so that he was no longer hindered in his walk or work (compare Luke 12:35; I Kings 18:46; Prov. 31:17). Peter then applies that imagery to the mind. He is saying: "Let nothing hinder your mind as you put it to work."

What is the meaning of the term *mind*? It refers to the believer's spiritual consciousness, that is, his conscious relationship to God. The term also means that his mind is ready and able to think actively to promote God's name, will, and kingdom (compare Matt. 6:9–10). The mind ought to be free from any hindrance (for example, fear or worry) to serve the Lord.

b. "Be self-controlled." Three times in this epistle Peter exhorts the readers to be self-controlled (1:13; 4:17; 5:8). He wants us to have clear minds and sound judgment so that we are ready for the return of Jesus Christ.[48] The mind must be free from rashness and confusion; it must reject the temptation to be influenced by intoxicating beverages or drugs. It must remain alert.

The translators of the New English Bible have adopted the reading *perfectly self-controlled*. They have taken the adverb *perfectly* (or *fully*), which can be understood with either the verb *self-controlled* or the verb *hope* (in the next clause), and have placed it with the first verb. The choice is difficult to make, yet scholars generally take the adverb with the verb *hope*. One argu-

---

48. Consult Philip J. Budd, *NIDNTT*, vol. 1, p. 515. And see Otto Bauernfeind, *TDNT*, vol. 4, p. 939.

ment for this choice is that the command to "be self-controlled" needs no modifier, while the injunction "to hope" demands an adverb.[49]

c. "Set your hope fully on the grace to be given you." In the Greek, this clause contains the main verb. The preceding exhortations, in fact, are subsidiary to the primary charge *to hope*. The concept *hope* is prominent in I Peter. In the original Peter uses the word as a noun in 1:3, 21, and 3:15, and as a verb in 1:13 and 3:5.

Peter speaks a word of encouragement to his readers. He realizes that as they experience persecution and hardship their hope is waning. He encourages the believers to look expectantly toward the fulfilling of their salvation, for he wants them to have a living hope with respect to their inheritance (v. 3).

The preposition in the clause "set your hope fully *on* the grace to be given you" (italics added) is significant. Here hope is not in a person but in an object. That object is "the grace to be given." Again, the word *grace* (see v. 10) is the equivalent of the two terms *salvation* (vv. 9–10) and *inheritance* (v. 4). The believers, then, focus their attention on their salvation.

Note that Peter indicates that grace is to be given. The Greek says that grace is being brought, in the sense that it is already on the way. God is the active agent in bringing salvation to the believers, who themselves are passive recipients. They know that grace is brought to them through the work of Jesus Christ and will be made complete when he appears.

d. "When Jesus Christ is revealed." Here we have a repetition of the last part of verse 7. The wording is identical, and therefore the meaning does not vary. That is, the reference to Jesus' appearing cannot be to his first coming but rather to his eventual return (compare I Cor. 1:7). When Jesus returns at the appointed time, he will bring to his followers the fulfillment of their salvation. When he appears, his redemptive work will be realized in all the believers. He grants them full salvation through deliverance from sin, glorification of body and soul, and the knowledge that he will be in their midst forever.

In the next three verses, Peter warns the believers to avoid conformity with the world, urges them to strive for holiness, and confirms his words with a quotation from the Old Testament. Accordingly, we notice three points: a warning, an exhortation, and a confirmation. The first of these is a warning.

A Warning

14. As obedient children, do not conform to the evil desires you had when you lived in ignorance.

---

49. The argument that the verb *be self-controlled* in 4:7 and 5:8 lacks an adverb cannot be regarded as substantial proof. Also, the comment that "it is unusual for an adverb to follow the verb which it qualifies" (Selwyn, *The First Epistle of St. Peter,* p. 140) does not hold true, because Peter often "places the adverb (contrary to the commoner practice) after the word it qualifies" (Kelly, *Peter and Jude,* p. 66).

"As obedient children." Those who receive an inheritance usually are children of the person who has died and has left a last will and testament. We are called children, not by birth but by adoption. Among the Greeks and the Romans of the first century, the practice of adopting was rather common. An adopted son enjoyed the same privileges as the natural son, even to the point of sharing the inheritance.

Parents train their children to be obedient, so that obedience is second nature to children. Obedience is expected from children but not from strangers. Peter literally calls the recipients of his letter "children of obedience." This is a Semitic idiom[50] that in translation becomes "obedient children." Peter, however, uses the word order *children of obedience* to introduce the concept *holiness*. Obedience and holiness are two sides of the same coin (see vv. 2, 22).

"Do not conform to the evil desires you had when you lived in ignorance." Similarity between the writing of Peter and Paul is unmistakable in this verse. Paul tells his readers, "Do not conform any longer to the pattern of this world, but be transformed by the renewing of your mind" (Rom. 12:2). We have no reason to argue that the one writer depended on the other. Rather, both present the truth in similar wording.

The world has its own lifestyle to which believers often are drawn, but Peter warns them not to conform to the evil desires that are prominent in the world. New Testament writers, in their epistles, repeatedly warn the Christians to reject the ways of the world and to live in obedience to God's Word.[51]

Peter refers to the background of some of the original recipients of this letter. They were pagans who lived in ignorance and who were separated from God (compare Eph. 4:18). They were ignorant of the moral law of God and therefore their conduct was governed by evil desires. By contrast, the Jew had received "the very words of God" (Rom. 3:2) and knew that his first duty was to obey God's law (Lev. 18:4–5; Deut. 6:4–9). Peter, then, addresses not only Jewish Christians, but also readers who formerly were pagans (see 2:10).

The negative command *do not conform* (v. 14) is a prohibition, whereas the positive precept *be holy* (v. 15) is an exhortation. Peter knows that the temptation for readers to return to their former conduct is real and that some of them may have succumbed. Therefore, he commands them to stop heeding sinful desires and to yield their lives instead in obedience and holiness to God.

The apostle next writes an exhortation.

---

50. Compare, for example, these references: "children of light" (Eph. 5:8), "man of peace" (Luke 10:6), and "the man of lawlessness" (II Thess. 2:3).

51. Here are a few passages: I Cor. 6:9–11; II Cor. 6:14–18; James 4:4; I John 4:4–6.

An Exhortation

15. But just as he who called you is holy, so be holy in all you do.

The word *but* introduces the positive aspect of this passage. Peter informs the readers that God has called them "out of darkness into his wonderful light" (2:9). They are now the ones who have been called out of the world; they are the elect (1:1–2; 2:9). In his electing love, God effectively calls his people to form a holy nation (2:9). In brief, calling and holiness are cause and effect.

God calls his people to be holy because he is holy. Among God's characteristics, as he has revealed himself, none is more significant than his holiness. Both the Old and New Testaments speak about his holiness more than any other attribute of God.[52] The descriptive adjective *holy* reveals God's absolute purity. This adjective describes the state and action of God's being. God is sinless, cannot be influenced by sin, and in his holiness destroys sin.

Peter takes the concept *holy* and applies it to his readers: "As he who called you is holy, so be holy in all you do." God calls his people out of a world of sin to a life of holiness; and he expects that whatever we do, say, or think is holy. The daily confession of the Christian ought to be:

> So shall no part of day or night
> From sacredness be free.
> —Horatius Bonar

When Peter says, "But just as he who called you is holy, so be holy in all you do," he expects the believers to be imitators of God in respect to holiness. In his Sermon on the Mount, Jesus presents a similar injunction: "Be perfect, therefore, as your heavenly Father is perfect" (Matt. 5:48). And when he preaches elsewhere he says, "Be merciful, just as your Father is merciful" (Luke 6:36).

What is Peter's basis for exhorting the believers to avoid sin and strive for holiness? Peter opens the Scriptures and appeals to the highest authority. He offers confirmation of his teaching with words spoken by God himself.

A Confirmation

16. For it is written: "Be holy, because I am holy."

When Jesus was tempted by Satan, he disarmed the devil with the formula *it is written* and appropriate quotations from Scripture (see Matt. 4:4, 7, 10). Satan acknowledged the authority of God's Word, even to the point of (mis)using it for his own purpose. That authority rendered Satan unable to tempt Jesus. The written word, then, demands respect and obedience.

---

52. Discussing the holiness of God, Everett F. Harrison asserts that "it is no exaggeration to state that this element overshadows all others in the character of the deity." See his article "Holiness; Holy," *ISBE*, vol. 2, p. 725.

Peter takes the written word from Leviticus 11:44–45. He appeals to Leviticus, for it features the theme *holiness*. Leviticus teaches that God's people ought to be holy, because God is holy.[53] In fact, the adjective *holy* appears more often in Leviticus than in any other book of the Bible.

"Be holy, because I am holy." For the believer, holiness does not end with forgiveness and cleansing of sin, but begins with an active life of opposing sin. The believer must strive to live obediently before God and thus demonstrate the meaning of the word *holy*.

Doctrinal Considerations in 1:14–16

In the world, the word *holy* is heard more as an expletive than as a term that evokes reverence and awe. In Christian circles, however, we call Jerusalem the holy city, Scripture the holy Bible, and the sacraments holy baptism and holy communion. When we describe someone or something with the adjective *holy*, we recognize a direct relationship with God in that person or thing.

That which we call holy we dedicate to God, because we deem it pure and in some cases even perfect.[54] But we hesitate to call man holy, for sin has destroyed perfection and man will never reach perfection during his life on earth. Yet the Bible calls us saints; that is, we are made holy through Jesus Christ (e.g., Acts 20:32; 26:18; I Cor. 6:11; Heb. 10:10). As saints we receive God's call to holy living (Eph. 4:22–24; Col. 3:9–10; I Thess. 5:23–24; I John 3:3). Thus, as sanctified children of God we pray the petition, "Our Father in heaven, hallowed be your name" (Matt. 6:9).

Greek Words, Phrases, and Constructions in 1:13–16

Verse 13

ἀναζωσάμενοι—this aorist middle participle is a compound from the preposition ἀνά (up) and ζώννυμι (I gird). The aorist signifies that the action should be a single occurrence. The middle implies that the person does the girding in his own interest. Because of its proximity to the main verb ἐλπίσατε (hope! [aorist imperative]), this participle is also translated as an imperative. In the New Testament, the compound in this form occurs only once.

νήφοντες—notice that this is a present participle in the active, whereas the preceding participle is in the aorist tense. This participle, translated as an imperative, is from the verb νήφω (I am sober; self-controlled).

τελείως ἐλπίσατε—the adverb τελείως (fully) modifies the verb *hope*. The aorist is constative, that is, it is all-inclusive.

φερομένην—the present passive participle from the verb φέρω (I bring, bear) takes an adjectival position in the clause: it stands between the definite article and the noun χάριν (grace). The present tense denotes the process that is linked to the coming of Jesus Christ.

---

53. In addition to Lev. 11:44–45, see 19:2; 20:7, 26; 21:8, 15; 22:9, 16, 32.
54. Consult Bauer, p. 9.

Verse 14

συσχηματιζόμενοι—this is a compound as a present passive participle derived from σύν (with) and σχῆμα (form, shape, external appearance). As a participle it is influenced by the main verb in verse 15 (γενήθητε, be! [aorist imperative]) and is therefore translated as an imperative.

τῇ ἀγνοίᾳ—notice the use of the definite article that denotes the ignorance of the recipients prior to their conversion.

Verse 15

αὐτοί—the personal pronoun referring to the second person plural *you* is used for emphasis.

ἀναστροφῇ—from the verb ἀναστρέφω (I behave, conduct myself), this noun refers to a way of life. This noun occurs thirteen times in the New Testament; six uses are in I Peter (1:15, 18; 2:12; 3:1, 2, 16) and two in II Peter (2:7; 3:11).

γενήθητε—the aorist imperative of γίνομαι (I become) substitutes for the verb εἰμί (I am), which lacks the aorist tense. The translation should be "be holy" and not "become holy." The aorist is all-inclusive.

Verse 16

διότι—this is a causal conjunction that looks forward to that which follows.

γέγραπται—the perfect passive from γράφω (I write) is a perfect of resultant state. The perfect indicates lasting effect.

ἔσεσθε—the future tense of the verb εἰμί (I am) is equivalent to a present imperative.

---

17 Since you call on a Father who judges each man's work impartially, live your lives as strangers here in reverent fear.   18 For you know that it was not with perishable things such as silver or gold that you were redeemed from the empty way of life handed down to you from your forefathers,   19 but with the precious blood of Christ, a lamb without blemish or defect.   20 He was chosen before the creation of the world, but was revealed in these last times for your sake.   21 Through him you believe in God, who raised him from the dead and glorified him, and so your faith and hope are in God.

B. Live in Reverent Fear
1:17-21

Peter teaches, exhorts, and counsels his readers how they should live. He mentions again the relationship they have as God's children to God the Father, who is holy and just.

17. Since you call on a Father who judges each man's work impartially, live your lives as strangers here in reverent fear.

Every word in this text is important and filled with meaning. Note that this verse is an introduction to the next four verses (vv. 18–21).

a. "Since you call on a Father." The translators of the New International Version have correctly captured the thought of this verse with the word

63

since. A literal translation of the Greek is, "And if you call on a Father." However, the conditional sentence expresses the reality of a long-standing practice, so that the words *and if* can mean "since."

In the Greek, the word *Father* stands before the verb *call on* to receive special emphasis. Although the noun *Father* is without a definite article, in its absolute form it refers to God the Father. In other words, Peter indicates that he does not have in mind any father other than God the Father. Already in Old Testament times people called upon God as Father (Ps. 89:26; Jer. 3:19; Mal. 1:6). But the New Testament reveals that Jesus teaches us to pray intimately to the Father in the Lord's Prayer (Matt. 6:9; Luke 11:2). Paul writes that we cry, "Abba, Father" (Rom. 8:15; Gal. 4:6).

When we call God our Father because we are his children, we should expect him to be our judge as well. Peter adds that the Father "judges each man's work impartially." God does not favor anyone, whether he is rich or poor (James 2:1–9), Jew or Gentile (Rom. 2:11), slave or master (Eph. 6:9; also see Col. 3:25).[55] The text says that God judges without looking at man's face (compare I Sam. 16:7) and that God the Father is already judging the works of each man. No one is going to be excluded from judgment, for God will judge impartially man's every deed. Accordingly, when we invoke the Father's name, we face an impartial judge.

What is the purpose of knowing that God is our Father and our judge? Peter continues, "Live your lives as strangers here in reverent fear." The Christian should consciously live in the presence of God. He knows that God's eye is constantly upon him. Moreover, he also realizes that the non-Christian is carefully observing him in regard to the words he speaks and the deeds he performs. Therefore, he must be a true child of God, so that in the child the virtues of the Father are reflected.[56]

The New International Version has rightly translated the word *fear* by qualifying it with the adjective *reverent.* The relationship between God and his child is not one of dread but of respect. God wants his child to live as a stranger on the earth. That is, the child of God has his citizenship in heaven (Phil. 3:20; Heb. 11:9). He is a stranger in the world (v. 1; 2:11) for the duration of the time God has given him (compare II Cor. 5:1, 6). He is a pilgrim who seeks to please God in his daily conduct, who has deep reverence for God and his Word, and who knows that he has been bought with the price of Jesus' blood (vv. 18–19).

Next we read a paragraph of four verses in which Peter sets forth a short summary of the Christian faith. These verses teach the doctrines of redemption, revelation, and Christ's resurrection.

---

55. Consult Eduard Lohse, *TDNT,* vol. 6, p. 780.
56. Refer to Kenneth S. Wuest, *Peter I,* vol. 6 of *Word Studies in the Greek New Testament,* 16 vols. (Grand Rapids: Eerdmans, 1942), p. 41.

Redemption

18. For you know that it was not with perishable things such as silver or gold that you were redeemed from the empty way of life handed down to you from your forefathers, 19. but with the precious blood of Christ, a lamb without blemish or defect.

Note, then, the first doctrinal point.

a. *Redemption*. This passage has a negative and a positive aspect. To put it differently, items that are perishable (silver and gold) are compared to Christ, whose blood has eternal significance.

1. "For you know that it was not with perishable things such as silver or gold that you were redeemed." Here is a gentle reminder of what the readers know about their salvation: their knowledge of salvation has filled them with "an inexpressible and glorious joy" (v. 8). They know that God, through Christ, has redeemed them at an enormous cost.

Peter rates the cost of redemption first in terms of created things; they, of course, are subject to change and decay. He mentions two precious metals (silver and gold) that comparatively speaking are least perishable. First he specifies silver. But silver, when exposed to any sulphur compounds in the air, tarnishes, corrodes, and loses its value. Next Peter cites gold, which is more durable than silver. Even this precious metal is subject to decay. In brief, earthly possessions do not qualify as payment to redeem the believers (see Isa. 52:3).

When we use the word *redeem* today, we think of it in a reflexive sense: "I have redeemed myself." We mean that we have regained our former standing. We also use the word when we exchange trading stamps for commodities at a redemption center. Last, we can redeem something by buying it back or by fulfilling financial obligations (e.g., by repaying a loan).

What does Scripture say? In the Old Testament, God redeemed his people from the yoke of slavery in Egypt (Exod. 6:6). He accomplished this by sending ten plagues on Israel's oppressors. In the ancient world, slaves obtained freedom with a sum of money paid either by themselves or by someone else.

In the New Testament, the focus shifts to Christ. We read that "Christ redeemed us from the curse of the law by becoming a curse for us" (Gal. 3:13).[57] Paul says that Christ Jesus "gave himself for us to redeem us from all wickedness and to purify for himself a people that are his very own, eager to do what is good" (Titus 2:14; also compare Ps. 130:8). Peter, too, uses the word *redeem* to refer to Christ's death and our deliverance from sin (1:18–19).[58]

---

57. Refer to Robert D. Knudsen, "Redeemer, Redemption," *ZPEB*, vol. 5, p. 50. Also see John Murray, *Redemption: Accomplished and Applied* (Grand Rapids: Eerdmans, 1955), p. 47.
58. Colin Brown, *NIDNTT*, vol. 3, p. 200.

2. "From the empty way of life handed down to you from your fore-fathers." The phrase *empty way of life* describes a lifestyle that is without purpose, unfruitful, and useless. The text provides no information whether Peter is referring to the forefathers of the Jews who lived by tradition instead of God's Word (Jesus rebuked the Jews for observing the traditions of the elders and setting aside the commands of God [Mark 7:5–13]). Another possibility is that Peter thinks of the pagan forefathers of the Gentile readers; in his epistles Paul comments on the futile life of the Gentiles (Rom. 1:21; Eph. 4:17). A third option is that Peter means the forefathers of both the Jews and the Gentiles.

3. "But with the precious blood of Christ, a lamb without blemish or defect." Here is the positive aspect of our redemption. Peter speaks as a Jew who is fully steeped in the Passover history and ritual. The Jewish people were set free from slavery when each family took a lamb without defect, slaughtered it at twilight on the fourteenth of the month Nisan, put the blood on the sides and tops of the doorframes of their homes (Exod. 12:1–11), and ate the Passover.

The writers of the New Testament teach that Christ is that Passover lamb. John the Baptist points to Jesus and says, "Look, the Lamb of God, who takes away the sin of the world!" (John 1:29). Paul comments that our redemption has been accomplished through Christ Jesus because "God presented him as a sacrifice of atonement" (Rom. 3:25). The writer of Hebrews declares that Christ did not enter the Most Holy Place by means of the blood of goats and calves but entered "once for all by his own blood, having obtained eternal redemption" (9:12). And John in Revelation has recorded a new song that the saints in heaven sing to Christ: "You are worthy to take the scroll and to open its seals, because you were slain, and with your blood you purchased men for God from every tribe and language and people and nation" (5:9).

The New Testament unfolds the teaching that Christ Jesus is our redeemer. In our Christian vocabulary, unfortunately, the word *redeemer* is not so common as the word *savior*. We readily acknowledge that Jesus Christ has saved us from the power and destruction of sin. Of even greater significance, however, is the truth that he has purchased us by shedding his precious blood on Calvary's cross. Of the two terms, therefore, the expression *redeemer* deserves more prominence than the word *savior*.[59]

With Philip P. Bliss every believer gratefully and joyfully sings:

> I will sing of my Redeemer;
> And His wondrous love to me;
> On the cruel cross He suffered,
> From the curse to set me free.

---

59. Consult Everett F. Harrison, "Redeemer, Redemption," *EDT*, p. 918.

Revelation

20. He was chosen before the creation of the world, but was revealed in these last times for your sake.

In this verse Peter formulates his second doctrinal theme:

b. *Revelation.* Notice that this text consists of two clauses that are balanced. For instance, the phrases *before the creation of the world* and *in these last times* are perfect counterparts. We note, first, that Christ Jesus was chosen.

1. *In eternity.* The New International Version has, "He was chosen." Many translators opt for a literal version of the Greek: "he was foreknown."[60] The meaning of the Greek word is much more comprehensive than knowing something in advance. The word in context reveals God's divine purpose in election—compare the wording of verse 2, where the teachings of election and foreknowledge are combined (see Eph. 1:4). For this reason, other translators prefer to give the term *foreknown* (v. 20) a meaning that includes the concept *destined* or *chosen.*[61] They see that God has assigned a predestined role to Christ in eternity.[62]

Peter puts the reference to time in terms we are able to understand. He writes, "[Christ] was chosen before the creation of the world." Creation relates to the beginning of history, but Christ was chosen before that time. God did not create the world and then decide to choose Christ to assume his redemptive task. God appointed him in eternity, "before the creation of the world."

2. *In these last times.* The contrast between eternity and time is clear. Christ was chosen in eternity, but was revealed in time. The verb *revealed* is passive and implies that God is the agent. To be precise, the term points to the birth of Jesus (see John 1:14; I Tim. 3:16). Through conception and birth, Jesus entered this sinful world. He came for the purpose of saving the elect in a period which Peter describes as "these last times." Peter means not merely the days of Jesus' life on earth; rather, the entire period from Jesus' birth to his eventual return comprises "these last times" (refer to Acts 2:17; I Tim. 4:1; II Tim. 3:1; Heb. 1:2; I John 2:18). The plural *times* indicates the totality of time. However, Peter singles out the *last* part of it as that period in which the history of the world will come to an end. In this period the Lord Jesus Christ has been revealed (refer especially to Rom. 16:25–26; II Tim. 1:9–10).

The appointment of Christ in eternity and his appearance in time serve only one purpose: to redeem the believers. Peter writes to his readers that this happened for their sakes. Believers, whether Jew or Gentile, are highly privileged persons, for God loves them so much that he has given his only

---

60. E.g., see KJV, NKJV, RV, ASV, NASB, and MLB.
61. RSV, NEB, NAB, GNB, NIV, and *Moffatt.*
62. Refer to Guthrie, *New Testament Theology,* p. 78. And Kelly observes that for Peter "God's foreknowledge includes His creative will and determination." *Peter and Jude,* p. 76.

Son for their redemption, "that whoever believes in him shall not perish but have eternal life" (John 3:16).

Resurrection

21. Through him you believe in God, who raised him from the dead and glorified him, and so your faith and hope are in God.

Here is the last part of this doctrinal section. These four verses (vv. 18–21) appear to have belonged to an early Christian hymn or a doctrinal formulation.[63] In this last part, the doctrine of the resurrection is prominent.

c. *Resurrection.* The readers have never seen Jesus, yet they believe in him (v. 8). Peter actually tells them that Jesus has given them faith so that they believe in God. Through Jesus Christ the believers come to know God the Father (compare John 1:18; 14:6). Notice that the believers have faith in God, even though Christianity emphasizes a Christocentric approach to God. Yet faith in Christ is always in the context of the Trinity, so that Christians believe in the Triune God.[64]

Why do we believe in God? Because he raised Jesus from the dead! From the teachings of the New Testament we have learned that the cardinal doctrine of the Christian faith is belief in the resurrection of Jesus Christ (Acts 2:24; Rom. 4:24; 10:9). Moreover, God raised Jesus from the dead and glorified him. That is, God perfected him (Heb. 2:9) and exalted him by giving him a name that is above everything God has made (Phil. 2:9). God, who predestined Christ in eternity to be our redeemer, could not leave him prey to death. Christ could not be held in the power of death, for God raised him on the third day.

"And so your faith and hope are in God." The implication is that in Jesus' resurrection, the believer has the assurance that he, too, will be raised from the dead. The basis of our faith is the resurrection of Jesus. Says Paul, "If there is no resurrection of the dead, then not even Christ has been raised. And if Christ has not been raised, our preaching is useless and so is your faith" (I Cor. 15:13–14). Faith and hope are intimately linked (vv. 3, 5, 7, 9, 13). The one virtue strengthens the other. The glory Jesus now possesses will be our glory at the moment of our resurrection. That is the hope that supports our faith in the Triune God.

Doctrinal Considerations in 1:18–21

Verses 18–19

When terrorists take hostages or kidnapers hold someone captive, they demand a ransom before they are willing to release their victims. In the New Testament the expression *ransom* also occurs. Jesus says, "The Son of Man did not come to be served, but to serve, and to give his life as a ransom for many" (Matt. 20:28; Mark

---

63. See especially Kelly, *Peter and Jude,* p. 75.
64. Refer to Selwyn, *The First Epistle of St. Peter,* p. 148.

10:45). And Paul writes, "For there is one God and one mediator between God and men, the man Christ Jesus, who gave himself as a ransom for all men—the testimony given in its proper time" (I Tim. 2:5–6). Furthermore, the saying "you were bought at a price" occurs twice in Paul's epistles (I Cor. 6:20; 7:23; also see Acts 20:28; Rev. 5:9; 14:4).

The biblical focus is on the price that is paid and the effects of deliverance; it is not on the one who demands or receives the ransom. Christ shed his precious blood on the cross. The effect of his death is the deliverance of his people. His people are set free from the curse of the law (Gal. 3:13), from sin (Eph. 1:7), and from death (Rom. 8:2).

To whom did Christ pay the ransom? Scripture gives no answer to this question and therefore we do well not to raise it. Christ did not pay Satan, because Christ defeated him. If God were demanding a ransom, he would be holding his own people hostage. Scripture tells us that God presented Christ as a sacrifice to demonstrate God's justice (Rom. 3:25). Obviously, then, the question *who receives the ransom?* ought not to be asked.

Christ Jesus has met the demands of the law, has removed the curse that was upon us, and through his death has acquitted us. We have been redeemed by his precious blood.

Verses 20–21

Scripture teaches that Christ's appointment to redeem sinners took place in eternity and that Adam and Eve fell into sin sometime after they were created. The sequence of these two events appears unusual to our reasoning, because it does not follow the customary course of cause and effect. Normally the remedy comes after the disease has been diagnosed. That is, first Adam and Eve fall into sin, and then God appoints Christ to redeem them.

Sixteenth-century Reformer John Calvin comments that we should see God's foreknowledge, wisdom, and goodness in Christ's election and man's redemption. "For herein shines forth more fully the unspeakable goodness of God, that he anticipated our disease by the remedy of his grace, and provided a restoration to life before the first man had fallen into death."[65]

Greek Words, Phrases, and Constructions in 1:17–21

Verse 17

ἀπροσωπολήμπτως—this is a compound adverb derived from the privative ἀ (not), the noun πρόσωπον (face), and the verb λαμβάνω (I receive). In this form it occurs only here in the entire New Testament. Without the privative it appears once as a verb (James 2:9) and five times as a noun (Acts 10:34; Rom. 2:11; Eph. 6:9; Col. 3:25; James 2:1).

τὸν ἀπροσωπολήμπτως κρίνοντα—the present active participle from κρίνω (I judge) with the definite article modifies the noun πατέρα (father). The present tense denotes continued action.

τὸν χρόνον—note that this word signifies duration of time, not point of time as in καιρός.

---

65. Calvin, *The First Epistle of Peter*, p. 52.

Verse 18

τῆς ματαίας ἀναστροφῆς—the definite article in this context means "the *well-known* empty way of life." Note the lack of definite articles in this section (vv. 18–21).

πατροπαραδότου—this compound occurs only once in the New Testament. It is a verbal adjective which is passive and expresses capability.

Verse 19

ἀλλά—a strong adversative that stresses the positive over against the negative statement of the preceding verse.

αἵματι—the noun relates to Χριστοῦ, and not to ἀμνοῦ (lamb). Notice that five words begin with the vowel ἀ. The lack of the definite article and the use of assonance strengthen the supposition that these lines are part of an early Christian hymn.

Verse 20

προεγνωσμένου—the perfect passive participle from the verb προγινώσκω (I foreknow) is in the genitive case because of Χριστοῦ. The prefix πρό reveals the preexistence of Christ.

φανερωθέντος—the aorist passive participle of the verb φανερόω (I reveal) contrasts with the tense of the preceding perfect passive participle. The contrast is heightened with the use of μέν and δέ.

Verse 21

πιστούς—manuscript evidence favors the reading πιστεύοντας (present active participle). However, scribes would more readily change the adjective πιστούς to the participle form than vice versa. The more difficult reading, therefore, is the adjective πιστούς.

ὥστε—this conjunction introduces the result clause ("so that"). One definite article governs the two nouns πίστιν and ἐλπίδα.

---

22 Now that you have purified yourselves by obeying the truth so that you have sincere love for your brothers, love one another deeply, from the heart. 23 For you have been born again, not of perishable seed, but of imperishable, through the living and enduring word of God. 24 For,

> "All men are like grass
>   and all their glory is like the flowers of the field;
> the grass withers and the flowers fall,
> 25   but the word of the Lord stands forever."

And this is the word that was preached to you.

C. Love One Another
1:22–25

As a next step in their spiritual walk, Peter urges his readers to demonstrate their holiness by loving their fellow man. He wants them to live by the truth of the Word of God to implement Jesus' teaching: "Love one another" (John 13:34; also see I John 3:23).

22. Now that you have purified yourselves by obeying the truth so that you have sincere love for your brothers, love one another deeply, from the heart.

Note these observations:

a. *State.* "Now that you have purified yourselves." Peter writes that the believers have cleansed themselves morally. He does not mean that they have washed their bodies or have undergone ceremonial cleansings to participate in a religious feast (compare John 11:55; Acts 21:24, 26; 24:18). In fact, the New Testament is devoid of ceremonial regulations—except for the decree to abstain from eating sacrificial food, blood, or the meat of strangled animals, and from sexual immorality (Acts 15:28–29). We assume that the Gentile readers of Peter's epistle would be unacquainted with ceremonial cleansings.[66] The readers understood the verb *purify* in terms of moral purity. They themselves have been and are personally involved in purifying themselves (see James 4:8; I John 3:3).

b. *Means.* How do believers attain purity? Peter explains, "By obeying the truth." He means that the believers are obedient to the truth of God's Word; when they live obediently in that sphere, they are pure. The sphere of obedience is God's revelation in Jesus Christ (v. 12). Peter implies that the readers have accepted the teachings of the gospel in faith. In a different and earlier context, when he addressed the Council of Jerusalem, Peter spoke in behalf of Gentile Christians and said, "[God] made no distinction between us and them, for he purified their hearts by faith" (Acts 15:9).

c. *Result.* "So that you have sincere love for your brothers." When we obey the Word of God, we express our love not only to God but also to our neighbor (Matt. 22:37–39). In the New Testament the words *neighbor* and *brother* have equal standing in respect to the command to love one's fellow man. Nevertheless, in the context of the New Testament epistles the word *brother* has a spiritual meaning; it refers to brothers and sisters in Christ.[67] This brotherly love must be sincere (II Cor. 6:6).

d. *Command.* The emphasis falls on the main verb, purposely placed in the last part of the verse: "Love one another deeply, from the heart." Peter precludes the possibility that members of the Christian community will have only a liking for one another without deeply loving each other from the heart. Peter repeats the command first given by Jesus on the night of his betrayal (John 13:34) and taught by the apostles Paul (I Thess. 3:12; 4:9; II Thess. 1:3), Peter (I Peter 1:22; 2:17; 3:8; 4:8), and John (I John 3:23).

---

66. Consult Heinrich Baltensweiler, *NIDNTT,* vol. 3, p. 101.

67. See Rom. 12:10; I Thess. 4:9–10; Heb. 13:1; I Peter 1:22; II Peter 1:7. Consult Leonhard Goppelt, *Der Erste Petrusbrief,* Kritisch-Exegetischer Kommentar über das Neuen Testament, ed. Ferdinand Hahn, 8th ed. (Göttingen: Vandenhoeck und Ruprecht, 1978), vol. 12/1, p. 130.

Peter qualifies the command to love with two adverbial expressions: "deeply" and "from the heart." These expressions convey the extent and the seriousness of love. When such love is present, it erases tension, abolishes enmity, and banishes hatred.

23. For you have been born again, not of perishable seed, but of imperishable, through the living and enduring word of God.

Why should we love one another? Says Peter, "Because you have been born again." Note that in the process of rebirth, the believers are passive. That is, God brings them through spiritual birth into this world. Once they are born again, the believers are active in the process of purifying themselves (v. 22).

When Nicodemus asks, "How can a man be born when he is old?" (John 3:4), Jesus teaches him about spiritual birth. In the first chapter of his epistle, Peter mentions spiritual birth twice (vv. 3, 23). The verb *born again* means that God has given us spiritual life that is new. Without this new life, we are unable to enter the kingdom of God (John 3:3, 5). We demonstrate that we possess this new life through faith in God's Son, Jesus Christ (John 3:36; I John 5:11). Moreover, the Greek text indicates that our spiritual rebirth occurred in the past and has lasting significance for the present and the future.

"Born again, not of perishable seed, but of imperishable." Peter describes rebirth first in negative and then in positive terms.

a. *Negative.* One of the characteristics of seed is that it is designed to die; that is, seed loses its own form in the process of generating life. Jesus put it graphically to Philip and the Greeks: "Unless a kernel of wheat falls to the ground and dies, it remains only a single seed. But if it dies, it produces many seeds" (John 12:24).

b. *Positive.* Interpreting the parable of the sower for the benefit of his disciples, Jesus said, "This is the meaning of the parable: The seed is the word of God" (Luke 8:11). The Word of God is imperishable; it regenerates, gives life, and nurtures, yet in the process remains unchanged. God provides the imperishable seed through his Word (compare John 1:13; James 1:18). In his first epistle, John mentions that after spiritual birth (being born of God) has taken place, God's seed endures. He writes, "No one who is born of God will continue to sin, because God's seed remains in him" (3:9). The seed is God's divine nature that resides within the child of God. Peter links the imperishable seed to the Word of God, which is living and enduring.

"Through the living and enduring word of God." Because of the position of the adjectives *living* and *enduring,* the Greek text can be translated in two ways. Here is another version: the "word of the living and eternal God" (jb).[68] This version not only is grammatically correct, but also has a parallel

---

68. jb follows the Vulgate; also see *Phillips.* In his commentary on *The First Epistle of Peter,* Calvin prefers the translation *the word of the living God* and adds that this "reading is less forced" (p. 57).

in Daniel 6:26, "For he is the living God and he endures forever." Nonetheless, scholars favor the first translation. They point out that the two adjectives describe the noun *word* better than the noun *God* (compare Heb. 4:12), especially when Peter supports this text with the quotation "but the word of our God stands forever" (Isa. 40:8). With these adjectives Peter calls attention not to God but to his Word.

24. For,
> **"All men are like grass,**
>> **and all their glory is like the flowers of the field;**
> **the grass withers and the flowers fall,**
> **25a.**   **but the word of the Lord stands forever."**

Peter appeals to the Old Testament Scriptures to substantiate his teachings. Admittedly, he does not introduce the quotation from Isaiah's prophecy with the formula *it is written* (v. 16) or *in Scripture it says* (2:6). Yet the conjunction *for* is sufficient to demonstrate that the quotation is from the Old Testament Scriptures. Throughout his epistle Peter repeatedly quotes them. He seems to have a preference for the prophecy of Isaiah, because he cites it more than any other book.[69]

The wording of this quotation differs slightly from the text in Isaiah. Peter omits the lines "because the breath of the LORD blows on them. Surely the people are grass" (Isa. 40:7). And in the line "but the word of our God stands forever" (Isa. 40:8), he has changed the words *our God* to "Lord."

"All men are like grass." The term *all* excludes no one. Furthermore, man is frail, as the literal translation of the text shows: "All flesh is like grass." Man's frailty is compared with grass that is here today and gone tomorrow (Ps. 103:15; and see Matt. 6:30).

"And all their glory is like the flowers of the field; the grass withers and the flowers fall." The beauty of a flower is short-lived, especially in a tropical or subtropical climate; so is the glory that man radiates because of his talents, achievements, or riches (see James 1:11). The winds of change blow and quickly remove all glory and honor. Peter gives no reason for the passing of man's glory. He uses the illustration of the grass and the flowers only to stress the contrast between temporal man and the abiding Word of God.

"But the word of the Lord stands forever." Even if we should forget everything else in this quotation, its concluding sentence is etched in our memories. In the Greek, the term *word* differs from its earlier use in verse 23, "the living and enduring word of God." In verse 25 it can mean "utter-

---

69. Peter quotes the prophecy of Isaiah six times: 1:24–25—Isa. 40:6–8; 2:6—Isa. 28:16 (LXX); 2:8—Isa. 8:14; 2:9a—Isa. 43:20 (LXX); 2:9c—Isa. 43:21 (LXX); 2:22—Isa. 53:9. By contrast, he cites the Psalms twice: 2:7—Ps. 118:22; 3:10–12—Ps. 34:12–16; and Proverbs twice: 4:18—Prov. 11:31 (LXX); 5:5—Prov. 3:34 (LXX). Last, he has one quotation from Exodus: 2:9b—Exod. 19:6 (LXX); and one from Leviticus: 1:16—Lev. 19:2.

ance." However, because Peter may have intended to do no more than use a synonym, we ought not to be dogmatic in our translation (e.g., see Acts 10:36–37, which gives one translation for these two different words in Greek).[70]

Peter's change from the wording "but the word of our God" to "but the word of the Lord" is deliberate. In the Old Testament, the word LORD signifies "the self-disclosed name of the covenant-God of Israel, Yahweh, 'Jehovah.' In the New Testament it is a standard designation for Jesus Christ."[71] With the term *Lord* Peter highlights Jesus' divinity; he shows that the word of God is identical with the word of the Lord Jesus. For that reason, Peter concludes this section in these words:

25b. And this is the word that was preached to you.

The word the apostles preached was the gospel of Jesus. God revealed himself in Jesus Christ, whose gospel the apostles proclaimed to Jew and Gentile. This abiding word of God's revelation in his Son also was brought to the recipients of Peter's letter, for they themselves had heard the authoritative message of Jesus' gospel (see v. 12). In fact, a literal translation of verse 25b is, "This word is the gospel that was preached to you."

Doctrinal Considerations in 1:22–25

Verses 22–23

The news media have given the term *born again* a degree of prominence which it had never attained in earlier times. Yet with all the publicity, countless people still do not understand the term. What does the Bible say about rebirth?

The New Testament teaches that rebirth is an act of God in the heart of man. In the process of birth man is passive, but as soon as he is born again man is active. The effects of his rebirth are evident in respect to his intellect, his emotions, and his moral disposition. God gives new life to man and man immediately demonstrates this new life in thought, word, and deed.

How do I know that I am born again? Here are three telltale marks. First, if I am born again, I have morally purified myself and with my new heart I strive to obey God's Word. Next, I dedicate my new life to obeying God by loving him and my fellow man. And finally, because of my rebirth, I have innumerable spiritual brothers and sisters.

Verses 24–25

Verses 24 and 25 demonstrate the unity of Scripture (as well as other doctrines). The readers of Peter's epistle received the Old Testament as the Word of God. When the apostles and their helpers preached the gospel of Jesus to them, they accepted it also as God's Word. For them both the Old Testament and Christ's gospel had equal authority and validity.

---

70. Consult KJV, ASV, NASB, RSV, NKJV.
71. Hiebert, *First Peter*, p. 107.

Greek Words, Phrases, and Constructions in 1:22–25

Verse 22

ἡγνικότες—from the verb ἁγνίζω (I purify), this active participle is in the perfect tense to show complete action in the past with lasting significance for the present.

τῆς ἀληθείας—this is an objective genitive ("to the truth"). The use of the definite article indicates that this is the truth of God.

διὰ πνεύματος—absent from many "early and good witnesses," this phrase appears "to be a theological expansion introduced by a copyist."[72]

ἐκ [καθαρᾶς] καρδίας—the inclusion or exclusion of the adjective καθαρᾶς (pure) is difficult to determine. However, scholars favor inclusion on the basis of stronger manuscript evidence.

ἀγαπήσατε—this is the main verb in verses 22 and 23 and thus receives emphasis. It is the aorist active imperative of ἀγαπάω (I love). The aorist is ingressive.

Verse 23

ἐκ σπορᾶς—from the verb σπείρω (I sow), this noun can mean either the act of sowing or the seed that is sown. The context favors the second meaning.

ζῶντος—together with μένοντος it modifies λόγου, not θεοῦ. If it described θεοῦ, it would follow it.

μένοντος—some translators include the phrase εἰς τὸν αἰῶνα (see v. 25) in the text. It is easier to explain the insertion than the omission. Manuscript evidence supports omission.

Verse 24

αὐτῆς—the Textus Receptus and the Majority Text have the reading ἀνθρώπου to agree with the Septuagint wording of Isaiah 40:6.

ἐξηράνθη—from ξηραίνω (I wither), this verb is an aorist passive.

ἐξέπεσεν—from ἐκπίπτω (I fall off), the form is aorist active. The aorists are timeless and therefore are translated in the present tense.

Verse 25

μένει—although the verb is present, it looks to the future.

εὐαγγελισθέν—as an aorist passive neuter singular participle from εὐαγγελίζομαι (I proclaim the gospel), the aorist points to past action.

Summary of Chapter 1

After writing the address and greeting, Peter expresses his gratitude to God for the new life God has given us. This new life is an incorruptible inheritance, is kept in heaven for us, and will be revealed fully at the end of

---

72. Bruce M. Metzger, *A Textual Commentary on the Greek New Testament*, 3d corrected ed. (London and New York: United Bible Societies, 1975), p. 688.

time. Although we endure all kinds of trials, we nevertheless are filled with great joy. We know that these trials are given to us so that our faith may be proved to the praise and glory of Jesus Christ. Even though we have not seen Jesus, yet we love him, have faith in him, and rejoice in the gift of our salvation.

The teaching of salvation did not originate recently, for the ancient prophets, guided by God's Spirit, already were searching and trying to understand when Christ would suffer and be crowned with glory. Even angels long to look into these matters.

With many exhortations, Peter admonishes us to action, self-control, obedience, and holiness. In view of our redemption, Peter exhorts us to live as strangers on this earth. He notes that with his precious blood Christ redeemed us from an empty way of life. And he teaches that God appointed Christ as our mediator before the creation of this world but revealed him in our times.

Peter exhorts us to love one another from a heart that is pure through the truth of God. This truth is the everlasting Word of God that has been preached to us.

2

Holiness, *part 2*

(2:1–3)

Election

(2:4–10)

and Submission, *part 1*

(2:11–25)

Outline (continued)

2   1 Therefore, rid yourself of all malice and all deceit, hypocrisy, envy, and slander of every kind.   2 Like newborn babies, crave pure spiritual milk, so that by it you may grow up in your salvation,   3 now that you have tasted that the Lord is good.

D. Grow Spiritually
2:1–3

Peter comes to the last exhortations that relate to the subject *holiness*—a subject he introduces and explains in the preceding chapter (1:13–25). He encourages the readers to divest themselves of negative attitudes and he urges them to express their need for spiritual food, so that they may mature in faith and knowledge.

1. Therefore, rid yourselves of all malice and all deceit, hypocrisy, envy, and slander of every kind.

The first word in the sentence is "therefore." On the basis of what Peter said in the last section of the previous chapter (1:22–25), he now draws a conclusion. That is, reborn children of God ought to exhibit their new life in their daily conduct.

When someone is born again (1:23), we expect to see the evidence in his personal behavior. In fact, we are looking for demeanor that is distinctively Christian.

How are the recipients to live a Christian life? Peter instructs, "Rid yourselves of all malice." In the Greek, he uses a verb that expresses the imagery of removing garments, for he says, "Put off all malice." (Paul also uses this same metaphor: "Put off your old self" [Eph. 4:22; and see Col. 3:9].) Peter figuratively tells the readers to take off the garments of malice, deceit, hypocrisy, envy, and slander.

a. "All malice." This is the first evil in a catalogue of sins. Note that the word *all* is comprehensive and allows no exceptions. In his list of sins Peter writes the term *all* three times. The word *malice* signifies ill will that originates in our sinful nature.[1] If we allow this evil to express itself in our relations with others, love for our neighbor vanishes. In brief, malice is a desire to inflict pain, harm, or injury on our fellow man.

---

1. Compare R. C. Trench, *Synonyms of the New Testament* (1854; Grand Rapids: Eerdmans, 1953), pp. 37–38. Also see Ernst Achilles, *NIDNTT*, vol. 1, p. 563. And consult Thayer, p. 320.

b. "All deceit." Once again Peter uses the adjective *all* to include everything that is deceitful. He alludes to a number of actions that are covered by the phrase *all deceit:* falsehood, craft, seduction, slander, and treachery. The concept *deceit* comes to expression, for example, in Paul's description of the sorcerer Elymas on the island Cyprus. Paul calls him "a child of the devil and an enemy of everything that is right." Then he adds, "You are full of all kinds of deceit and trickery" (Acts 13:10).[2] Deceit takes on the appearance of truth so that the unwary may be tricked. Therefore, deceit and hypocrisy are twins: by deceit a person is wronged and by hypocrisy he is deceived.[3]

c. "Hypocrisy, envy." These two words appear in the plural in Greek. The hypocritical person pretends to be what he is not; he is a man with a double heart and a lying tongue. For instance, Jesus rebuked the Pharisees and teachers of the law for their hypocrisy when he said, "You hypocrites! Isaiah was right when he prophesied about you: 'These people honor me with their lips, but their hearts are far from me' " (Matt. 15:7–8; Isa. 29:13). Envy is an attitude expressed in a desire to possess what belongs to someone else. Envy often leads to holding a grudge.

d. "And slander of every kind." Although the New International Version does not indicate this, the Greek puts the words *slander* and *of every kind* (that is, *all*) in the plural and literally says, "all evil speakings" (KJV). Also, for the third time in this catalogue of vices Peter uses the adjective *all*. He implies that the tongue is a ready and willing instrument to talk about our neighbor behind his back (compare Rom. 1:30; II Cor. 12:20; James 4:11). Slander occurs in numerous ways and the misuse of the tongue gives impetus to other sins.

Peter does not tell his readers to fight against these evils but to lay them aside as a garment and to get rid of them. We put off our old nature and cherish our new life in Christ by craving spiritual nourishment and growing in our salvation.

2. Like newborn babies, crave pure spiritual milk, so that by it you may grow up in your salvation, 3. now that you have tasted that the Lord is good.

a. "Like newborn babies." Is Peter intimating that the readers are recent converts? Not necessarily. Possibly he uses the phrase *like newborn babies* figuratively to give the readers of his letter the mental picture of infants craving nourishment. Parents know how newborn babies vocally and ardently express their desire to be fed regularly. In fact, newborn babies act as if their life depends on the next feeding. Likewise, believers must show their longing for the Word of God. Peter encourages his readers to crave

---

2. Also compare these verses: Matt. 26:4; Mark 7:22; 14:1; John 1:47; Rom. 1:29; II Cor. 12:16; I Thess. 2:3; I Peter 2:22; 3:10; Rev. 14:5.

3. Consult John Albert Bengel, *Gnomon of the New Testament,* ed. Andrew R. Fausset, trans. William Fletcher, 7th ed., 5 vols. (Edinburgh: Clark, 1877), vol. 5, p. 53.

the milk of God's Word. He does not chide them (see, e.g., I Cor. 3:2; Heb. 5:12–13) but wants them to crave spiritual nourishment.

b. "Crave pure spiritual milk." The verb *crave* in the Greek must be understood favorably, not unfavorably. For example, Paul uses this verb approvingly when he expresses his longing to see the believers to whom he writes his epistles.[4] Similarly, Peter exhorts the readers to crave spiritual food, just as newborn babies long for milk at feeding time.

Peter describes the word *milk* with the adjectives *pure* and *spiritual*. He does not say that the readers eventually will receive solid food when they mature, but that their nourishment is pure and spiritual. Only here in the entire New Testament the Greek adjective *pure* occurs. It denotes an absence of fraud and deceit (see John 1:47).[5] The term *spiritual* in this context points to the Word of God. Notice that in 1:23, Peter tells the readers that they are born again through the Word of God (also consult 1:25). In the Greek, the term translated "spiritual" comes from the same root as the expression *word*. Because this particular term occurs only once more in the New Testament (Rom. 12:1, where Paul speaks of spiritual worship) it is difficult to translate. In English we lack derivatives and therefore furnish the reading *spiritual*. We rely on the context, which clearly indicates that Peter has the Word of God in mind. The spiritual food the believers consume comes to them verbally through the Word of God.

c. "So that by it you may grow up in your salvation." The main verb in this clause is "grow." The result of consuming the milk of God's Word ought to be the spiritual growth of the believers. As a mother constantly looks for evidence of growth in her child, so God wants to see continued spiritual growth in his children. The verb *to grow* literally refers to physical growth in children.[6] Interestingly, Peter makes no distinction between babies and adults, milk and solid food. Instead he indicates that all believers continue to be babies whose constant diet is the milk of God's Word.

Once again Peter introduces the concept *salvation*. In fact, we observe a parallel between the first chapter, where the writer teaches that we experience rebirth that leads to salvation (see 1:3, 5, 9), and the second chapter, where he says that we grow up in our salvation (2:2).[7]

d. "Now that you have tasted that the Lord is good." Although most translations do not indicate that this verse resembles Psalm 34:8, the similarity is clear. David says, "Taste and see that the LORD is good."

We mark three points. First we note that Peter indicates a lapse of time since the readers initially became acquainted with the Word of God. They

---

4. The verb appears nine times in the New Testament, seven of which occur in Paul's epistles (Rom. 1:11; II Cor. 5:2; 9:14; Phil. 1:8; 2:26; I Thess. 3:6; II Tim. 1:4), one in James 4:5, and one in I Peter 2:2.

5. Compare Trench, *Synonyms of the New Testament*, p. 209.

6. Consult Bauer, p. 121.

7. Refer to Bengel, *Gnomon of the New Testament*, p. 53.

have tasted it and now Peter wants them to continue to receive the nourishment of that Word. He encourages them to "crave pure spiritual milk" with the intensity of newborn babies who demand nourishing milk. Once babies taste nourishment, they do not stop craving it until they are satisfied. Likewise the believers, now that they have tasted God's Word, must crave it until they are filled.

The second point is that the word *Lord* in Peter's epistle relates to Jesus, but in the psalm (Ps. 34:8) it relates to the Lord God of Israel. Peter indirectly teaches the divinity of Jesus by placing him on an equal level with God.

And the last item is the word *good*. This Greek word is also translated "kind" and serves as a synonym of "gracious."[8] Peter wants to say that when the believer reads the Bible, he meets his personal God in Jesus Christ, who grants him numerous blessings. The child of God, then, joyfully exclaims that the Lord is good and kind.

Practical Considerations in 2:2

Do you have family devotions? You would like to say yes, but your answer is really no. There are too many conflicts and interruptions for regular family devotions. You have tried, but you cannot get the whole family together. Perhaps you have given up. However, there are times when the family is together.

Mealtime is family time, and family time should include prayer and Bible reading. The Christian family comes together at mealtime, not only to enjoy each other's company, but also to express thanks to God and to read his Word. Families should look forward to mealtime and make it devotional. We need spiritual food just as much as other food, with the same regularity.

Family devotions ought to be for the entire family, and each member should be urged to participate. We should let the children each read some Bible verses, ask them to present their prayer requests to God, and teach them the practice of regularly reading God's Word. Consistent family devotions are a spiritual blessing to all members of the family, especially if each one participates. Moreover, the home is the training ground for life, for in the family circle lifelong patterns are set.

Family devotions are exercises in the practice of holiness, because in prayer and the reading of Scripture we enter the holiness of God. Therefore, devotions should never be rushed, conducted thoughtlessly, or skipped altogether. God wants us to come to him with regularity and reverence. As we eat regularly, so we read Scripture and pray regularly. The old cliché is worth repeating: "The family that prays together stays together." And last, God wants his children to grow spiritually in the grace and knowledge of Jesus Christ (II Peter 3:18).

---

8. Consult Donald Guthrie, *New Testament Theology* (Downers Grove: Inter-Varsity, 1981), p. 108. Also see Konrad Weiss, *TDNT*, vol. 9, pp. 487–88.

Greek Words, Phrases, and Constructions in 2:1–3

Verse 1

ἀποθέμενοι—this aorist middle participle from the verb ἀποτίθημι (I lay aside) depends on the main verb *to crave*, which is imperative. Therefore, the participle has imperative force.

πᾶσαν—Peter employs this adjective three times: twice in the singular and once in the plural.

ὑποκρίσεις, φθόνους, καταλαλιάς—these three nouns are idiomatic plurals. "This use of the plural of abstract substantives does indeed lay stress on the separate acts."[9]

Verse 2

λογικόν—the adjective has its origin in the noun λόγος (word). Also, ἄδολον γάλα (pure milk) probably was a common expression.[10]

ἐπιποθήσατε—the preposition ἐπί (on, for, toward) makes this compound perfective and stresses the intensity of the action. The aorist tense of this imperative verb is constative.

εἰς σωτηρίαν—the Majority Text omits these two words (as do the KJV and NKJV). Bruce M. Metzger thinks that they were deleted "either through an oversight in copying or because the idea of 'growing into salvation' was theologically unacceptable."[11]

Verse 3

ἐγεύσασθε—the aorist tense of this verb denotes past experience (see Heb. 6:4, 5).

χρηστός—this adjective comes from the verb χράομαι (I employ; *treat a person in a certain way*).[12]

---

4 As you come to him, the living Stone—rejected by men but chosen by God and precious to him—   5 you also, like living stones, are being built into a spiritual house to be a holy priesthood, offering spiritual sacrifices acceptable to God through Jesus Christ.   6 For in Scripture it says:

> "See, I lay a stone in Zion,
>   a chosen and precious cornerstone,
> and the one who trusts in him
>   will never be put to shame."

---

9. A. T. Robertson, *A Grammar of the Greek New Testament in the Light of Historical Research* (Nashville: Broadman, 1934), p. 408.

10. Friedrich Blass and Albert Debrunner, *A Greek Grammar of the New Testament and Other Early Christian Literature,* trans. and rev. Robert Funk (Chicago: University of Chicago Press, 1961), sec. 269.5.

11. Bruce M. Metzger, *A Textual Commentary on the Greek New Testament,* 3d corrected ed. (London and New York: United Bible Societies, 1975), p. 689.

12. Bauer, p. 884 (italics in original).

7 Now to you who believe, this stone is precious. But to those who do not believe,

"The stone the builders rejected
has become the capstone,"

8 and,

"A stone that causes men to stumble
and a rock that makes them fall."

They stumble because they disobey the message—which is also what they were destined for.
9 But you are a chosen people, a royal priesthood, a holy nation, a people belonging to God, that you may declare the praises of him who called you out of darkness into his wonderful light.   10 Once you were not a people, but now you are the people of God; once you had not received mercy, but now you have received mercy.

IV. Election
2:4–10

A. Living Stones
2:4–8

Peter colors his epistle with imagery that portrays life: newborn babies craving milk (2:2), stones to build a house (2:5), and a capstone rejected by the builders (2:7). All these images, however, are figurative. They convey a spiritual message, as is obvious from the expression *living stone*.

1. Chosen
2:4

4. As you come to him, the living Stone—rejected by men but chosen by God and precious to him.

Some scholars are of the opinion that in this verse Peter again alludes to Psalm 34, as he did in the preceding verse (v. 3). The Septuagint has this reading: "Come to him and be enlightened" (Ps. 34:5 [33:6 LXX]).[13] The words *to him* obviously refer to Jesus, whom Peter mentions in verse 3. Moreover, the act of coming to Jesus is an act of faith that occurs not once but continuously.

The phrase *the living Stone* appears to be a paradox: a stone has no life. Yet in Scripture the term *stone* sometimes has a figurative meaning (Ps. 118:22; Isa. 8:14; 28:16; Matt. 21:42; Mark 12:10–11; Luke 20:17; Acts 4:11; Rom. 9:33). Peter himself used this imagery when he addressed the Sanhedrin and portrayed Jesus Christ as "the stone you builders rejected, which has become the capstone" (Acts 4:11; Ps. 118:22).

---

13. See, e.g., J. N. D. Kelly, *A Commentary on the Epistles of Peter and Jude,* Thornapple Commentaries series (1969; Grand Rapids: Baker, 1981), p. 87. With reference to Psalm 34, Charles Bigg comments, "Indeed the whole Psalm was present to St. Peter's mind throughout the Epistle." See *A Critical and Exegetical Commentary on the Epistles of St. Peter and St. Jude,* International Critical Commentary series (1901; Edinburgh: Clark, 1961), p. 128.

Especially when Peter qualifies the word *stone* with the descriptive adjective *living*, he is no longer speaking of a stone but of a person. Notice first that Peter is not using his own name *Petros/petra* (rock, Matt. 16:18) as a play on words. The word is "stone," not "rock." Next, when Jesus asked the disciples to identify him, Peter confessed: "You are the Christ, the Son of the living God" (Matt. 16:16). During his ministry, Jesus taught the Samaritan woman about living water (John 4:10–11; also see 7:38) and living bread (John 6:51). Third, the adjective *living* (see 1:3, 23; 2:5) not only shows that the stone lives, but also describes Christ, the giver of life. The image of a stone is furthermore a reminder of God's judgment. Even though Christ is a firm foundation for anyone who puts his faith in him, he is a crushing stone to those who reject him.[14]

Before Peter continues with the rest of the sentence, he presents an interpretive comment with a built-in contrast. He says that the living Stone has been "rejected by men but chosen by God and [is] precious to him." The contrast is in the verbs *rejected* and *chosen* and in the nouns *men* and *God*. Peter contrasts unbelieving people who have rejected Jesus, and continue to do so, with God for whom Jesus is elect and precious. Peter repeats the theme of election, for he calls the recipients of his epistle "God's elect" (1:1) and "a chosen people" (2:9). Also, in his sermons recorded by Luke in Acts, Peter repeats the theme that Jesus is rejected by men but chosen by God (Acts 2:22–36; 3:13–15; 4:10–11; 10:39–42). "The factor of election might well be seen as permeating and determining of the thought of I P[eter] as a whole."[15] Conclusively, with Jesus the believers share in God's electing love.

Greek Words, Phrases, and Constructions in 2:4

λίθον—without the definite article, this noun stresses the noun in the absolute sense: Jesus is *the* living Stone.

μὲν . . . δέ—in this brief parenthetical sentence, contrast is prominent.

ἀποδεδοκιμασμένον—this perfect passive participle from ἀποδοκιμάζω (I reject) shows lasting effect.

---

2. *Built*
2:5–6

5. You also, like living stones, are being built into a spiritual house to be a holy priesthood, offering spiritual sacrifices acceptable to God through Jesus Christ.

a. *Translations.* The main verb in verse 5 is "you are being built." The

---

14. Consult S. Greijdanus, *De Brieven van de Apostelen Petrus en Johannes, en de Brief van Judas,* Kommentaar op het Nieuwe Testament series (Amsterdam: Van Bottenburg, 1929), p. 91.
15. John Hall Elliott, *The Elect and the Holy,* supplements to *Novum Testamentum,* vol. 12 (Leiden: Brill, 1966), p. 147.

translators of the New International Version, with translators of other versions, have taken the verb in the indicative mood and in the passive voice.[16] That is, the verb is descriptive of the process of building God's spiritual house: believers are seen as stones that are put in place by God.

Other translators, however, take the verb in the imperative mood in the passive voice. Here is a representative translation: "Come, and let yourselves be built" (NEB).[17] Still another possible translation is to render the verb in the imperative mood but with a reflexive connotation: "Build yourselves up."[18]

Translators generally agree that the verb is in the passive, so that God is the agent who builds the spiritual house. They are divided, however, on the proper mood. Some point to Peter's frequent use of the imperative in the preceding section (1:13–2:3).[19] But others argue correctly that a new section with a doctrinal theme need not follow the pattern set by a series of exhortations in the previous section.[20] In other words, the context supports the use of the indicative mood. Hence, we have good reason to hold to the indicative mood in verse 5 (NIV), for it provides a description of the life of the church.

b. *Illustrations.* Peter resorts to illustrations that with increasing clarity depict worship: living stones, spiritual house, holy priesthood, spiritual sacrifices.

Living stones. Peter describes Jesus as "the living Stone" (v. 4) and the believers as "living stones." Believers derive the life-giving principle from Jesus. In the form of stones they are the building blocks of God's house. Incidentally, Peter furnishes a parallel of a spiritual house and spiritual sacrifices.[21]

Spiritual house. Peter speaks metaphorically, because not the stones but the individual members form the household of God (Eph. 2:19–22; I Tim. 3:15; Heb. 3:6; 10:21). This metaphor conveys the idea of a community of believers who as a holy priesthood present living sacrifices.[22]

Holy priesthood. This expression, commonly phrased as "the priesthood of all believers," refers to the community of priests and means that every true Christian is a priest in the household of God (see v. 9). "It is a singular honour, that God should not only consecrate us as a temple to himself, in which he dwells and is worshipped, but that he should also make us

---

16. See KJV, NKJV, RV, ASV, NAB.

17. Also see RSV, MLB, GNB, *Phillips.*

18. Bauer, p. 558. The JB has, "so that you too, . . . may be living stones making a spiritual house."

19. Refer especially to Bigg, *The Epistles of St. Peter and St. Jude,* p. 128.

20. Consult, e.g., E. G. Selwyn, *The First Epistle of St. Peter: The Greek Text with Introduction, Notes, and Essays* (London: Macmillan, 1946), p. 159.

21. For a complete list of parallels, consult Elliott, *The Elect and the Holy,* pp. 17–18.

22. Compare Guthrie, *New Testament Theology,* pp. 782–83.

priests."[23] The adjective *holy* signifies that the priesthood is dedicated to God and separated from the world.

Spiritual sacrifices. What is the task of the priest? He has no need to offer sacrifices to remove sin and guilt, for "Christ was sacrificed once to take away the sins of many people" (Heb. 9:28). A member of the priesthood of all believers, then, offers sacrifices of gratitude to God for the redemptive work of Christ.[24] That is, he presents to God "a sacrifice of praise—the fruit of lips that confess his name" (Heb. 13:15). Furthermore, the priest seeks to reflect God's holiness in harmony with his command: "Be holy, because I am holy" (1:16). And last, he offers his body as a living sacrifice in thankful service to God (Rom. 12:1). These spiritual sacrifices can be presented to God only through Jesus Christ, for without Christ our righteous deeds are nothing but filthy rags (Isa. 64:6).

6. For in Scripture it says:

> **"See, I lay a stone in Zion,**
> **a chosen and precious cornerstone,**
> **and the one who trusts in him**
> **will never be put to shame."**

This is the first of three quotations from the Old Testament and a number of allusions on which Peter bases the entire doctrinal paragraph (2:4–10). Note that with the clause *for in Scripture it says*, Peter bases his doctrinal teaching on the Old Testament Scriptures. He first quotes from Isaiah 28:16 in verse 6, then he cites Psalm 118:22 in verse 7, and last he has a quotation from Isaiah 8:14 in verse 8. Also, in verses 9 and 10 he alludes to some Old Testament passages: Exodus 19:6 and Isaiah 43:20–21 in verse 9 and Hosea 1:6, 9; 2:3, 25 in verse 10.

"See, I lay a stone in Zion, a chosen and precious cornerstone." We perceive that in verses 4 and 5 Peter borrows the wording from Isaiah 28:16 and Psalm 118:22. We know from the Gospels that in teaching the parable of the tenants, Jesus applied the imagery of Psalm 118:22 to himself (see, e.g., Matt. 21:42). And we know from Romans 9:33 that in discussing Israel's unbelief, Paul quotes Isaiah 28:16 to indicate that Jesus rejec_d by the Jews is the "stone in Zion."

In Peter's quotation the word *cornerstone* is important. Although this word may mean the keystone that was placed in the center of an arch, it can also refer to a foundation stone.[25] For instance, Peter interprets the word *cornerstone* as "a capstone" in verse 7 and as "a stone that causes men to

23. John Calvin, *Commentaries on the Catholic Epistles: The First Epistle of Peter,* ed. and trans. John Owen (Grand Rapids: Eerdmans, 1948), p. 65.

24. See Philip Edgcumbe Hughes, "Priesthood," *EDT,* p. 876.

25. Consult Joachim Jeremias, *TDNT,* vol. 1, p. 792; vol. 4, pp. 271–80. And see Wilhelm Mundle, *NIDNTT,* vol. 3, pp. 389–90. Also refer to R. J. McKelvey, "Christ the Cornerstone," *NTS* 8 (1961–62): 352–59.

stumble and a rock that makes them fall" in verse 8. In Isaiah 28:16, the word depicts the stone that was laid at the foundation of a building. Figuratively, the house of God is "built on the foundation of the apostles and prophets, with Christ Jesus himself as the chief cornerstone" (Eph. 2:20).

An anonymous poet of the seventh century captured the scriptural teaching on the stone in the form of a hymn. In the nineteenth century, John Mason Neale translated this hymn into English:

> Christ is made the sure Foundation,
> Christ the Head and Cornerstone,
> Chosen of the Lord and precious,
> Binding all the church in one;
> Holy Zion's help for ever,
> And her confidence alone.

"And the one who trusts in him will never be put to shame." Not the location of the stone but its function is significant. The imagery of the stone describes Jesus, who calls upon every believer to trust in him. Jesus Christ, the object of our faith, will honor our dependence on him. He will never let us down; that is, he will not allow us to lose face.

Greek Words, Phrases, and Constructions in 2:5–6

Verse 5

οἰκοδομεῖσθε—in the light of the immediate context, I take this verb as a present passive indicative.

εἰς—this preposition is omitted in the Majority Text (also see KJV, NKJV), but is strongly supported by leading manuscripts.

Verse 6

περιέχει—from the verb περιέχω (I contain), this word describes the content of a book or letter: "it is contained in Scripture."[26]

ἐν γραφῇ—as in the English idiom *in Scripture*, so in Greek the definite article is superfluous. "The article is not necessary to make the noun definite in a prepositional phrase."[27]

---

3. Rejected
2:7

With the well-known quotation from Psalm 118:22, Peter brings to a climax the contrast between believers and unbelievers. This is the quotation

---

26. See C. F. D. Moule, *An Idiom-Book of New Testament Greek*, 2d ed. (Cambridge: Cambridge University Press, 1960), p. 28.
27. Robert Hanna, *A Grammatical Aid to the Greek New Testament* (Grand Rapids: Baker, 1983), p. 424.

Jesus applied to himself (see Matt. 21:42 and parallels) and is the one Peter cited when he addressed the members of the Sanhedrin (Acts 4:11).

7. Now to you who believe, this stone is precious. But to those who do not believe,

> **"The stone the builders rejected**
> **has become the capstone."**

In this pair of sentences, Peter emphasizes the believers, so that in the Greek he says, "you, you who continue believing." He strengthens the readers of his letter and encourages them to place their confidence in Jesus.

"Now to you who believe, this stone is precious." Even though the Greek text does not have the words *this stone,* translators have taken these words from the quotation to provide the contrast Peter intends.[28] Others are of the opinion that Peter has Jesus in mind and writes, "To you therefore who believe, he is precious."[29] And still other translators prefer a literal translation of the Greek: "For you therefore which believe is the preciousness."[30]

The key to verse 7a lies in the word *preciousness,* which actually means "respect" or "honor."[31] The believers are honored by God because of Christ, who is precious to him (vv. 4, 6). If Christ is the cause of their honor, they in turn ascribe honor and respect to him. As Peter indicates, believers honor the stone while unbelievers reject it (compare II Cor. 2:16).

In the quotation from Psalm 118:22, the psalmist borrows a figure from the building trade. Stones used in the construction of buildings had to be regular in size. They were cut with the aid of a hammer or a chisel or even a saw (I Kings 7:9). Stones that did not pass inspection were rejected by the builders. The builders figuratively represent the unbelievers who reject the stone that is Christ. God, the chief architect, takes this reject and puts it down as capstone. He honors Christ by giving him the preeminent position in the building, that is, God's household. For "capstone" the Greek has the words *the head of the corner.* Christ, then, is the keystone or the chief cornerstone.

Greek Words, Phrases, and Constructions in 2:7

τιμή—this noun signifies honor or respect. In an active sense, it can mean that one is showing honor to someone. Here it is in the passive sense: one receives honor.[32]

ἀπιστοῦσιν—from ἀπιστέω (I refuse to believe), this verb is the exact opposite of the preceding πιστεύουσιν (present active participle, dative plural) and thus points

---

28. See, e.g., JB, NAB, NIV, GNB.
29. RSV, KJV, NKJV, *Phillips.*
30. See RV, ASV, and with variations NASB, NEB.
31. Consult Bauer, p. 817.
32. Ibid.

out the sharp contrast Peter intends to portray.[33] The reading ἀπιστοῦσιν enjoys stronger textual support than the variant ἀπειθοῦσιν.

---

4. Destined
2:8

8. And,

**"A stone that causes men to stumble
and a rock that makes them fall."**

They stumble because they disobey the message—which is also what they were destined for.

a. *Scripture.* The stone rejected by the builders and elevated to be the capstone has another function. Peter quotes Isaiah 8:14, "A stone that causes men to stumble and a rock that makes them fall." He implies that the stone causes embarrassment, offense, and hurt for all who refuse to believe. What is Peter saying? Simply put, he says that we either put our faith in Jesus, the foundation stone, or we dash our foot against it.

Unbelievers stumble and fall because of Jesus' message (compare Luke 2:34); they experience that Jesus is "a rock that makes them fall." Paul also writes about Israel's unwillingness to believe the message of Jesus; he combines quotes from Isaiah 8:14 and 28:16 to illustrate that unbelievers "stumbled over the 'stumbling stone' " (Rom. 9:32).

b. *Message.* "They stumble because they disobey the message." The reason for their stumbling is that they have chosen to disobey the Word of God. Their disobedience arises from a heart that is filled with unbelief. In other words, the sequence which Peter delineates is unbelief, disobedience, and downfall which eventually leads to ruin. Unbelievers, then, meet God in Christ as their enemy because they have chosen to be a friend of the world (James 4:4). Moreover, they can never say that they have not received the message of Christ. Figuratively, they touch it with their foot when they stumble and fall.

c. *Destiny.* "Which is also what they were destined for." This last sentence in verse 8 is emphatic in its conclusion. The word *also* and the verb *destined for* provide emphasis. Note the sequence Peter gives in verses 7 and 8. First, he contrasts the attitudes of believers and unbelievers (v. 7a). Next, he discloses that unbelievers reject Jesus Christ, the stone (v. 7b). Third, because they disobey the message of Christ, the unbelievers stumble (v. 8a). And last, the unbelievers were destined for their fall (v. 8b).

Notice also that, except for verse 8b, every verb is in the present tense and is active; the unbelievers continue to reject Jesus and they continue to stumble. The last verb in verse 8b, however, is in the past tense and is passive:

---

33. Refer to Robertson, *Grammar,* p. 418.

"they were destined for" this stumbling. Peter writes from man's point of view when he says that disobedient unbelievers are appointed to stumble because of their disobedience to the Word of God; therefore they themselves pay the penalty for their refusal to believe and to obey. Peter implies that God has destined these disobedient people to eternal destruction.

No believer can say that because he decided to accept Christ as his Savior he has secured salvation. Scripture teaches that God elects man and saves him (Rom. 9:15–16); in the process of salvation, God is first and man is second. Likewise, no unbeliever ought to think that his stubborn unbelief gives him independence from God and freedom to ignore him. God is in control. He holds the unbeliever accountable and tells him that because of his unbelief he is destined for eternal damnation.

The use of the passive voice in the clause *what they were destined for* results from the "Jewish reverential dislike of the use of God's name." Therefore, "the third person plural passive is often used in the N[ew] T[estament] where we would attribute the action directly to God."[34]

Greek Words, Phrases, and Constructions in 2:8

προσκόπτουσιν—derived from the verb προσκόπτω (I stumble), this present active verb can take τῷ λόγῳ (the word) as a direct object. However, translators prefer to link this object to the present active participle ἀπειθοῦντες (disobey). The participle has its roots in the negative ἀ (not) and the verb πείθω (I persuade). Disobedient people, then, do not want to be persuaded by the Word of God.

B. Chosen People
2:9–10

Peter addresses believers and communicates to them the glad tidings that they are God's people who possess tremendous privileges. In fact, this passage is one of the most precious verses of the entire epistle.

9. But you are a chosen people, a royal priesthood, a holy nation, a people belonging to God, that you may declare the praises of him who called you out of darkness into his wonderful light.

The contrast is evident; the term *but* marks the difference between disobedient unbelievers and God's chosen people. In ascending order, Peter enumerates the glorious riches of the believers in terms that approach incredulity. From the Greek we learn that he addresses them personally and emphatically with the plural pronoun *you*. How does Peter describe the believers? Here are the words:

a. "A chosen people." Peter writes to people who lived before the destruction of the Jerusalem temple. Himself a Jew, Peter addresses numerous

---

34. Ernest Best, *I Peter*, New Century Bible series (London: Oliphants, 1971), p. 106.

Jewish Christians and Christians of Gentile descent. Moreover, he speaks to all believers of every age and place who read his epistle. Fully acquainted with the Old Testament, Peter applies its wording to his readers because he views them as God's chosen people. He borrows from the prophecy of Isaiah, who records the words of the Lord: "My people, my chosen, the people I formed for myself that they may proclaim my praise" (Isa. 43:20–21). Peter, then, views the believers as the body of Christ, that is, the church.

Other translations have the term *race* instead of "people." Members of a race have a common ancestor and through that ancestor are related to one another. For instance, Abraham is the father of the Jewish race. Christians through Jesus Christ call God their Father, and they are related to each other as brothers and sisters. Furthermore, because Jesus has been chosen by God (vv. 4, 6), they also are designated God's chosen people (see 1:1; compare Deut. 10:15; I Sam. 12:22).

b. "A royal priesthood." Peter continues to describe the glorious riches the believers possess. He calls them "a royal priesthood." In verse 5 he speaks of a holy priesthood, a phrase which is meaningful in the light of the command to be holy (1:15–16). The descriptive adjective *royal*, however, adds the dimension of kingdom and king. In the kingdom of priests (compare Exod. 19:6), there is a king. In fact, the Messiah is both priest and king, as Zechariah prophesied: "He will be clothed with majesty and will sit and rule on his throne. And he will be a priest on his throne" (6:13; also see Heb. 7:14–17; Rev. 1:5–6). Whereas Zechariah prophetically portrays the Messiah as the royal priest, Peter reveals that believers are priests in a royal priesthood.[35]

c. "A holy nation." Again Peter relies on Old Testament phraseology. He borrows the language of Exodus 19:6 (also see Deut. 7:6; Isa. 62:12).[36] Peter resorts to using national and political terminology, but wants his readers to understand these terms in a nonpolitical manner.[37] For this reason he qualifies the word *nation* with the adjective *holy*.

A nation consists of citizens who reside in a given locale, obey rules and regulations, and strive for the well-being of their society. Citizens of a "holy nation," however, have common characteristics through Jesus Christ. Peter portrays God's people as a holy nation, which means that the citizens have been set apart for service to God.

d. "A people belonging to God." Throughout the ages God has claimed for himself his own people (see Mal. 3:17; Acts 20:28; Titus 2:14). These

---

35. Although we apply the rule "let Scripture be its own interpreter," we admit that Peter does not teach participation of the believers "in the royalty and priesthood of Jesus Christ." Consult Elliott, *The Elect and the Holy*, p. 170.

36. Elliott asserts that the adjective *royal* is a substantive that signifies "the king's house." Ibid., pp. 149–54.

37. Refer to Guthrie, *New Testament Theology*, p. 783.

people, who differ from the nations of the world, are his prized possession. They are independent of nationalistic ties because they have a special relationship to God.[38] They belong to God, who has bought them with the blood of Jesus Christ.

e. "Declare the praises." Peter points to the task of God's special people. As a skilled pastor, Peter addresses his readers personally. He says, "that you may declare the praises of him who called you out of darkness into his wonderful light" (compare Isa. 43:21). Everywhere they should vocally proclaim God's praiseworthy virtues, deeds, power, glory, wisdom, grace, mercy, love, and holiness. By their conduct, they must testify that they are children of the light and not of darkness (Acts 26:18; I Thess. 5:4).

Peter implies that in earlier days his readers lived in spiritual darkness. God called them to repentance and faith in Jesus Christ and redeemed them from the powers of darkness. Through the gospel of Christ, God called them into the kingdom of his Son (Col. 1:13).

10. Once you were not a people, but now you are the people of God; once you had not received mercy, but now you have received mercy.

Once again Peter relies on Old Testament imagery. He alludes to the prophecy of Hosea where the Lord addresses the prophet when Gomer gave birth to her second son: "Call him Lo-Ammi [not my people], for you are not my people, and I am not your God" (1:9; and see 2:23). The second part of verse 10 also is an allusion to Hosea's prophecy. Gomer gave birth to a daughter and the Lord tells Hosea, "Call her Lo-Ruhamah [no mercy; or, not loved], for I will no longer show love [mercy] to the house of Israel" (1:6).

"Once you were not a people [useful to God], but now you are the people of God." Here is an obvious reference to the past of these recipients. They were Gentiles and Jews who through the preaching of the Word of God had been converted (1:12). God saved them through the redemptive work of his Son and now these same persons are part of the body of believers known as "the people of God." They are God's special people, whom Peter designates "a people belonging to God" (v. 9).

"Once you had not received mercy, but now you have received mercy." The Greek wording indicates that the recipients had lived without God for a long time, during which they had tried but failed to obtain mercy for themselves. Peter contrasts the past of these people with their present: "now you have received mercy." That is, they have received remission of sin and rejoice in the love and the grace of God.

The prophet Hosea contrasts the unfaithfulness of his contemporaries in ancient Israel with the electing love of their covenant God (Hos. 1:1–2:23). In the New Testament, Paul applies the prophecy of Hosea to the Gentiles (Rom. 9:25–26). Moreover, he regarded as Gentiles the Jewish people

---

38. Consult Hermann Strathmann, *TDNT,* vol. 4, p. 54.

who had broken God's covenant. Yet God takes Gentiles and converted Jews into a covenant relationship with himself. Peter affirms this same truth when he addresses both Jewish and Gentile Christians in his epistle: "You are . . . a people belonging to God."

Doctrinal Considerations in 2:9–10

In these two verses, the New International Version uses the word *people* four times: "a chosen people"; "a people belonging to God"; "not a people"; and "the people of God." Peter intimates that we are most precious in the sight of God. He indicates that we are God's treasured possession, for we have been chosen through Christ. In his own way, Peter reflects God's claim: "I will walk among you and be your God, and you will be my people."[39]

God's claim is a biblical truth that is woven through the fabric of Scripture as a golden thread. God's people are his own possession. In turn, we always should be mindful of our status, for Peter pictures us as chosen by God, royal, and holy.

Greek Words, Phrases, and Constructions in 2:9–10

Verse 9

περιποίησιν—from the verb περιποιέομαι (I preserve for myself), this noun with the -σις ending denotes the continuing activity of claiming one's own possession.

ὑμᾶς—mark the position of this personal pronoun in the sentence. Between a prepositional phrase and a participle, it receives emphasis.

αὐτοῦ—this possessive pronoun occupies an emphatic position in the last part of the sentence.

Verse 10

οὐ λαός—the significance of this noun lies in its use: in this sentence λαός refers to God's special people.

ἠλεημένοι—from ἐλεέω (I have mercy), this perfect middle participle denotes lasting activity in the past and an attempt to obtain mercy for oneself.

ἐλεηθέντες—the aorist passive participle indicates single occurrence in the past with the implied agent, namely, God, who has extended mercy to his people.

11 Dear friends, I urge you, as aliens and strangers in the world, to abstain from sinful desires, which war against your soul. 12 Live such good lives among the pagans that, though they accuse you of doing wrong, they may see your good deeds and glorify God on the day he visits us.

39. This covenantal teaching appears in both the Old and New Testaments (Lev. 26:12; Jer. 7:23; 11:4; 24:7; 30:22; 31:1, 33; 32:38; Ezek. 36:28; 37:27; Zech. 13:9; II Cor. 6:16; Heb. 8:10; Rev. 21:3).

V. Submission
2:11–3:12

A. An Appeal
2:11–12

Here is the second pastoral section. In the first section Peter exhorts his people to holiness (1:13–2:3); in the second he appeals to the readers to submit to authorities (rulers, masters, husbands). He begins with an appeal in which he urges them to live as aliens in the world.

11. Dear friends, I urge you, as aliens and strangers in the world, to abstain from sinful desires, which war against your soul.

a. *Address.* The New International Version presents a typical contemporary translation, "dear friends" (see 4:12).[40] Yet this address indicates much more than an amicable relationship. The Greek word literally means "beloved." This address has its origin in the verb *to love* (given in the summary of the law; see, e.g., Matt. 22:37–40). In the broader context of his epistle, Peter exhorts the readers to love one another (1:22).

The term *beloved*, in the Greek, accentuates two aspects: first, the passive implies that the recipients are loved by God and by the writer of this epistle. And second, the term reveals not only what is taking place, but also what must occur. In other words, the term conveys a sense of obligation. God not only has adopted his people, whom he regards as his elect. He also loves them and calls them the people of God (vv. 9–10; Hos. 1:9–10; 2:23; Rom. 9:25–26).

b. *Appeal.* "I urge you, as aliens and strangers in the world." As pastor and counselor, Peter uses the first person singular "I" (also see 5:1, 12) to speak directly to the readers. He uses the verb *to urge* to express encouragement; he knows that they are able to do what he requests. Peter calls the believers "aliens," which is the designation for persons who live in a foreign country but who keep their own citizenship (1:1). They do not possess the same privileges and rights as the citizens of the country in which they live (Gen. 23:4; Ps. 39:12; Heb. 11:9, 13; I Peter 1:17). They are "strangers" in a world that is foreign to them; they live on this earth for only a brief period; they know that their citizenship is in heaven (Phil. 3:20).

c. *Abstain.* Peter, however, does not exhort the readers to separate themselves from the world. Rather, he urges them to "abstain from sinful desires" and to look into their own souls. That is the place where desire originates. Desire in itself is not wrong, except when it leads to evil. Evil

---

40. The word *beloved* occurs sixty-one times in the New Testament. Except for nine occurrences in the Gospels and one in Acts, all appear in the Epistles (twenty-seven in Paul's epistles; one in Hebrews; three in James; two in I Peter; six in II Peter; five in I John; four in III John; three in Jude).

desire conceives and "gives birth to sin, and sin, when it is full-grown, gives birth to death" (James 1:15). Sinful desires conduct warfare against the soul, says Peter (compare Gal. 5:16–17, 24). Notice that Peter does not say that these desires fight against man's soul but that they wage a war against his soul with the purpose of destroying it.

What are these sinful desires? Peter answers this question in another context; they are "living in debauchery, lust, drunkenness, orgies, carousing and detestable idolatry" (4:3).[41] These desires give a person temporary physical satisfaction but in reality wage decisive warfare against his soul. Fully aware of the dangers of this warfare, however, the believer abstains from these desires. By his conduct and good deeds, he shows unbelievers the way to God.

12. Live such good lives among the pagans that, though they accuse you of doing wrong, they may see your good deeds and glorify God on the day he visits us.

d. *Conduct.* God calls us to be his people in the society in which we live. He wants us to be living testimonies of his love and mercy toward sinners because through our lives he calls others to himself. Our conduct and confession, then, ought never to be stumbling blocks for our unbelieving neighbors.

"Live such good lives." Our lifestyle should be distinctively Christian so that it serves to encourage others to follow our example. The word *good* occurs twice in this verse: "good lives" and "good deeds." It denotes that which is praiseworthy, noble, and morally good in the sight of our fellow man (compare James 3:13).

"Among the pagans." Christians are living in glass houses; they are on display. Their conduct, deeds, and words are evaluated constantly by non-Christians who want to see if Christians indeed live up to what they profess.

e. *Accuse.* "Though they accuse you of doing wrong." The verb that Peter uses means "to slander" (see Rom. 1:30). Christians should strive for such exemplary conduct that slanderous accusations of unbelievers remain groundless (3:16). When they are vilified as criminals, the record of their Christian conduct should reveal good works and an absence of faults and vices. By doing good, the Christian will "silence the ignorant talk of foolish men" (2:15).

In the middle of the first century, Christians were a distinct minority and often were the object of slander and subsequent persecution. For example, because of their refusal to participate in emperor worship, they faced false accusations that often resulted in suffering and death. To suppress the rumor that he himself had put the city to the torch, Nero blamed the Christians for the burning of Rome. He made Christians scapegoats by slandering and persecuting them.[42]

---

41. See Guthrie, *New Testament Theology*, p. 931.
42. Consult Tacitus *The Annals of Tacitus* 15.44 (LCL); Suetonius *Nero* in *The Lives of the Caesars* 6.16.2 (LCL).

f. *Glorify.* Non-Christians ceaselessly scrutinize the conduct of believers. Regularly they have observed the good deeds of the believers and have become accustomed to the exemplary conduct of Christians. Their accusations have proved to be false in light of the good deeds done by the Christians. Now Peter indicates that the time is coming when unbelievers will "glorify God in the day he visits us."

The startling conclusion of verse 12 is open to various interpretations (see Isa. 10:3; Luke 19:44). Scholars try to determine when and how unbelievers glorify God. First, some say that the phrase *the day he visits us* refers to the last day of this age when God judges everyone. But we can hardly expect unbelievers to glorify God on that day when they receive their condemnation. Next, other scholars are of the opinion that Peter thinks of a trial before earthly magistrates. Still others believe that God's visitation is one of grace and mercy whereby non-Christians accept the offer of salvation and glorify God in thankfulness. This view seems to offer the best interpretation, for then the expression *glorify God* is meaningful (Matt. 5:16).[43]

Greek Words, Phrases, and Constructions in 2:11–12

Verse 11

ἀγαπητοί—a verbal adjective that conveys a passive voice in the vocative case. The passive implies that God is the agent. Moreover, the adjective expresses obligation.

παροίκους—derived from the verb παροικέω (I dwell beside someone in a foreign land), this substantivized adjective is synonymous with παρεπιδήμους (stranger; compare 1:1).

ἀπέχεσθαι—the present middle infinitive ("to abstain") governs the genitive case of ἐπιθυμιῶν (desires) because the verb relates to the act of ceasing or abstaining. Some early and major Greek manuscripts have the present middle imperative ἀπέχεσθε.

σαρκικῶν—this adjective with the -ικός ending, in distinction from the -ινος ending (σάρκινος; see, e.g., Rom. 7:14; I Cor. 3:1), has an ethical connotation. It refers to a person "who lives according to the flesh."[44] The -ινος ending denotes "made of," as in σάρκινος (made of flesh).

αἵτινες—the indefinite relative pronoun is causal in meaning and can be translated "because they. . . . "

Verse 12

ἔχοντες—this present active participle of ἔχω (I have) is the nominative plural. It presents a break with the preceding verse by modifying the accusative plural of παροίκους (aliens), provided the present middle infinitive ἀπέχεσθαι is the correct reading. The present participle is translated as an imperative.

---

43. Compare D. Edmond Hiebert, *First Peter: An Expositional Commentary* (Chicago: Moody, 1984), p. 149. Also see Kelly, *Peter and Jude*, p. 106.

44. Robertson, *Grammar*, p. 158.

καλήν—note that the adjective occupies a peculiar position in the sentence; separated from the definite article and the noun, it receives special emphasis.

ἐκ—in this prepositional clause ἐκ denotes cause ("because of, on the basis of").

ἐποπτεύοντες—from the verb ἐποπτεύω (I view attentively), this participle occurs only twice in the New Testament (I Peter 2:12; 3:2). The noun ἐπόπτης (eyewitness) appears once (II Peter 1:16).

---

13 Submit yourselves for the Lord's sake to every authority instituted among men: whether to the king, as the supreme authority,   14 or to governors, who are sent by him to punish those who do wrong and to commend those who do right.   15 For it is God's will that by doing good you should silence the ignorant talk of foolish men.   16 Live as free men, but do not use your freedom as a cover-up for evil; live as servants of God.   17 Show proper respect to everyone: Love the brotherhood of believers, fear God, honor the king.

B. Instituted Authority
2:13–17

1. Obedience
2:13–15

After making an appeal for Christian conduct, Peter directs our attention to instituted authority and to those appointed to rule the people. He implies that the first demonstration of the Christian's personal behavior is his conduct toward government. He urges the believers to honor the persons who have been appointed to rule them (v. 17). Peter virtually reiterates the message that Paul wrote to the church in Rome, for Paul teaches that legitimate authorities are instituted by God for the well-being of the people (Rom. 13:1–7; see also Titus 3:1–2). And Peter asserts that Christians must submit to authority "for the Lord's sake." That is, the law of the land must be upheld as long as it does not force the Christian to disobey God's law (compare Acts 4:19; 5:29).

13. Submit yourselves for the Lord's sake to every authority instituted among men: whether to the king, as the supreme authority,   14. or to governors, who are sent by him to punish those who do wrong and to commend those who do right.

Here Peter introduces the verb *to submit,* which is a key word in this passage.[45] The verb itself can be translated "be subject" (in the passive sense) or "submit yourselves" (in the reflexive sense). The word basically means "to place under; to subordinate," and in this passage is a synonym of the verb *to obey.* The implication is not that a person who submits to authority loses his dignity, but that he recognizes authority that God has instituted.

Peter begins by mentioning authorities in general. Thereafter he specifies and refers to kings and to governors.

---

45. The verb *to submit* appears six times in I Peter (2:13, 18; 3:1, 5, 22; 5:5).

a. "To every authority." If the Christians in Peter's day had refused to obey Roman law, they would have given their opponents the necessary evidence to accuse them of lawlessness.[46] Even though they desire freedom from Roman servitude, Peter admonishes his readers to obey the magistrates "for the Lord's sake." With this phrase he implies that God is sovereign in every area of life and in full control of every situation. Therefore, Peter encourages Christians to submit to instituted authority and to fulfill God's purposes in the world. Unfortunately, text and context are of little help in determining whether Peter understands "Lord" to mean "God" or "Christ." Because God has established governing authorities (Rom. 13:1), the reference to God seems quite appropriate.

What is the meaning of the clause "to every authority instituted among men"? Literally the Greek text has, "to every human creation." The term *creation*, however, refers to an "act by which an authoritative or governmental body is created."[47] It denotes, then, the creative act of instituting authority, presumably by a legislative body. Peter speaks in general terms to avoid the charge that he prefers one type of government to another.

Furthermore, human efforts to build a structured society do not run counter to, but are in harmony with, God's creative plan. Kings and queens, presidents and prime ministers, dictators and despots rule by the grace of God (see Prov. 8:15; Dan. 2:21; Rev. 1:5).

b. "To the king." Peter wrote his epistle in the last few years of Emperor Nero's wicked rule. Nero came to power in A.D. 54 at the age of seventeen and committed suicide fourteen years later. During the reign of this emperor, Peter himself met martyrdom outside Rome. Yet the apostle tells the readers to submit themselves to the king [emperor], "as the supreme authority." The title *king* was often used for "emperor" in the Mediterranean world of the first century (e.g., Luke 23:2; Acts 17:7). Because of his conduct Nero was not worthy of the highest office in the Roman Empire. Nevertheless, Peter recognizes him as supreme authority and exhorts the Christians to obey him.

c. "To governors." The New Testament lists the names of three governors of Judea: Pilate, Felix, and Festus. These three governors were appointed by the Roman emperor and were directly responsible to him. They governed in behalf of Rome. Peter writes that the governors "are sent by him" and thus indicates that the emperor repeatedly commissioned governors. However, Peter uses the term rather loosely. He makes no distinctions between governors who were sent out by the Roman senate and governors who were appointed by the emperor for an indefinite period of time. Governors commissioned by the Roman senate served for a stated interval as "legates" or "proconsuls" (Quirinius [Luke 2:2]; Sergius Paulus [Acts

---

46. Refer to Calvin, *The First Epistle of Peter*, p. 80.
47. Bauer, p. 456.

13:6]; Gallio [Acts 18:12]). Governors sent out by the emperor usually served in troublesome areas. However, Peter is not interested in the rank of governors but in their function.

The task of governors is "to punish those who do wrong and to commend those who do right" (v. 14; compare Rom. 13:3). As the representative of Roman authority the governor had the power to inflict punishment on condemned criminals. The governor received this power from the emperor and the emperor received it from God. Thus Jesus said to Pilate, "You would have no power over me if it were not given to you from above" (John 19:11). Paul parallels Peter's teaching on the role of government, for he points out that rebelling "against the authority is rebelling against what God has instituted" (Rom. 13:2). Paul adds that the one in authority is "God's servant to do you good" and "an agent of wrath to bring punishment on the wrongdoer" (Rom. 13:4). The role of the magistrate, then, is to restrain evil, maintain law and order, and promote the welfare of the people.

Whether Christians received words of praise from Roman governors is inconsequential. Christians were a despised and persecuted minority. They tried to advance the cause of Christ, not their own name and interests. Indeed, the possibility is not remote that the words "to punish those who do wrong and to commend those who do right" are instructions a civil magistrate received for keeping order in society.[48] Whatever the source may be, Peter exhorts the Christians to do that which is good and right because this is the will of God.

15. For it is God's will that by doing good you should silence the ignorant talk of foolish men.

The first word *for* is causal. In the Greek, the next term is "so" or "thus," but many translators have omitted it. This term, however, either looks back to Peter's exhortation to submit to authorities or looks ahead to silencing foolish men who ignorantly oppose the believers.[49]

"It is God's will." In his epistle, Peter frequently teaches the readers to live by the will of God (3:17; 4:2, 19). The believers ought to set their lives in harmony with the petition *your will be done* (Matt. 6:10). The will of God is that they continue to do good, for then they are able to muzzle those who accuse them. The word Peter uses for "silence" is a term used for muzzling an animal (see I Tim. 5:18). Figuratively it means to reduce someone to silence (compare Matt. 22:12, 34).

Who are the Christian's opponents? Peter calls them foolish men who utter ignorant talk. They are a specific group of people who refuse to accept the evidence Christians are presenting by their moral behavior and good deeds. In fact, Peter resorts to using the word *ignorant*. This word

---

48. Refer to Francis Wright Beare, *The First Epistle of Peter: The Greek Text with Introduction and Notes*, 2d ed. (Oxford: Blackwell, 1961), p. 117.

49. Among others, the RSV, NEB, NIV, and GNB omit the word *so*. Also refer to Hiebert, *First Peter*, pp. 156–57.

signifies "a failure to know in the sense of a disobedient closing of the mind to the revealing word of God" (see Acts 13:27; Rom. 10:3).[50] In other words, ignorance and disobedience have joined forces against incontestable evidence. For this reason Peter calls these people foolish, because their ignorance is inexcusable.

Greek Words, Phrases, and Constructions in 2:13–15

Verse 13

ὑποτάγητε—the aorist passive imperative (from the verb ὑποτάσσω, I submit) should be taken in the reflexive sense: submit yourselves. The aorist is constative because it is inclusive.

πᾶσα . . . κτίσις—the adjective πᾶσα conveys the meaning *every* and the noun κτίσις means either "creature" or "creation." The second translation is preferred because of the implication of a governing institution.

Verse 15

φιμοῦν—this is the present active infinitive of the verb φιμόω (I muzzle).

ἀγνωσίαν—as a synonym of ἀγνοία (ignorance, 1:14), this noun denotes not only lack of knowledge but also lack of religious experience.

2. Freedom
2:16–17

16. Live as free men, but do not use your freedom as a cover-up for evil; live as servants of God. 17. Show proper respect to everyone: Love the brotherhood of believers, fear God, honor the king.

a. "Free men." Peter concludes his discussion on submission to governmental authorities by telling the Christians how to conduct themselves in society: "Live as free men." Although translators supply the verb *to live* to complete the sentence, Peter wants to stress the concept *free*. He realizes that people who suffer oppression and persecution long for freedom. Now he tells them: "Be free!" That is, he wants the readers to know that the Christian is free indeed because he has been set free from the power of sin (see, e.g., John 8:32, 36; Rom. 8:2; II Cor. 3:17; Gal. 5:1, 13).

b. "Freedom." Martin Luther explained the concept *freedom* in his characteristic pithy style: "A Christian is a perfectly free lord of all, subject to none. A Christian is a perfectly dutiful servant of all, subject to all."[51] The Christian is free from enslavement that promotes evil; instead he uses his

---

50. Eduard Schütz, *NIDNTT,* vol. 2, p. 407.

51. Consult J. Dillenberger, ed., *Martin Luther: Selections from His Writings* (Garden City, N.Y.: Doubleday, 1961), p. 53. Also see Jürgen Blunck, *NIDNTT,* vol. 1, p. 720. And consult Lester DeKoster, "Christian Liberty," *EDT,* pp. 638–39.

freedom to serve his God and to love his fellow man. The more he demonstrates his willingness to serve, the more he experiences true freedom (compare James 1:25; 2:12). The Christian conducts himself in public life as
God's elect. He is free, without any fear, as long as he serves God in absolute obedience.

Peter adds a warning: "Do not use your freedom as a cover-up for evil."
He knows that the Christian is tempted to abuse his freedom. As soon as the
Christian employs freedom to advance his own cause, he no longer obeys
the law of love; in fact, he fails to serve God. "True liberty, then, is that
which harms or injures no one."[52] For this reason, Peter admonishes the
believers to remain faithful servants of God.

c. "Servants." The last exhortation in verse 16 is, "Live as servants of God."
The word *servant* in the Greek actually means "slave." The expression *servants of God* appears a few times in the New Testament. For example, the
slave girl in Philippi called Paul and his companions "servants of the Most
High God" (Acts 16:17). Paul calls himself "a servant of God" (Titus 1:1); so
does James in his epistle (1:1; also see Rev. 7:3; 15:3). The apostles demonstrate their complete freedom by wholeheartedly serving God.

d. "Respect." Peter sums up the duty of God's servants: "Show proper
respect to everyone." The word *everyone* is all-inclusive, for it ranges from
kings and governors to all others who have been entrusted with authority.
The servant of God honors all men who are appointed to rule (see vv. 13–14).

How is the first sentence in verse 17, "Show proper respect to everyone,"
related to the rest of the verse? Some translations make this sentence the
heading for the next three clauses: "Love the brotherhood of believers, fear
God, honor the king."[53] The objections to this arrangement are weighty.
First, these three clauses fail to show balance. The only feature that binds
them together is the present tense in the Greek, which can be best communicated with the term *continue:* the readers must continue to love the brothers
and sisters in the Christian community, continue to fear God, and continue
to have respect for the king. Next, the command to "fear God" is more
important than the other two injunctions. And third, the last two clauses
allude to Proverbs 24:21, "Fear the Lord and the king."[54]

How do we read and understand verse 17? We see that it consists of a
configuration that is two lines with two parts each.

Honor everyone	Love the brotherhood
Fear God	*Honor* the king

Note that the first clause and the fourth clause have the same verb, even
though in the Greek the tense differs (aorist and present). In addition, the

---

52. Calvin, *The First Epistle of Peter*, p. 84.
53. See, for instance, NEB and NIV.
54. Also consult Ernst Bammel, "The Commands in I Peter ii.17," *NTS* 11 (1965): 279–81.

first line shows balance in its two parts; so does the second line. The first line is general, because it includes everything and all those who are brothers in Christ. The second line specifies: God and king. Peter puts God first and then the king. Christians should honor the king by first revering God. "The king must be honoured in such a way, that the love of the brotherhood, and the fear of God, be not violated."[55]

Practical Considerations in 2:13–17

When Paul was under house arrest in Rome (Acts 28:30), he taught the gospel to all who came to visit him. Even the soldiers who guarded him received the Good News. In fact, in his epistle to the Philippians he mentions the progress of the gospel in connection with the whole palace guard (1:13). The gospel affected the palace of Emperor Nero, for Paul writes that the believers in Rome, especially those who belong to Caesar's household, send greetings (Phil. 4:22).

The teachings of the Word of God ought to penetrate every area of life, including government. Pharaoh placed Joseph second in command in ruling Egypt (Gen. 41:39–40), and Daniel filled a similar position during the reigns of Darius and Cyrus (Dan. 6:3, 28). Wherever possible, Christians should seek to give leadership at every level of government and apply the principles which Scripture teaches. Although they are not of the world, they are nevertheless in the world. "If the church wishes to exert an influence for good upon the State, it should not take recourse to separation but should try spiritual infiltration."[56]

Greek Words, Phrases, and Constructions in 2:17

τιμήσατε—the aorist active imperative from the verb τιμάω (I honor) expresses the constative idea. By contrast, three verbs in the present active imperative show continuity: ἀγαπᾶτε, φοβεῖσθε, τιμᾶτε.

---

18 Slaves, submit yourselves to your masters with all respect, not only to those who are good and considerate, but also to those who are harsh.   19 For it is commendable if a man bears up under the pain of unjust suffering because he is conscious of God.   20 But how is it to your credit if you receive a beating for doing wrong and endure it? But if you suffer for doing good and you endure it, this is commendable before God.

C. Commendable Behavior
2:18–20

In his continuing discussion on submission, Peter moves from the sphere of government to that of society. He counsels the readers to respect instituted authority and servants to be submissive to their masters.

---

55. Bengel, *Gnomon of the New Testament*, vol. 5, p. 59.
56. William Hendriksen, *Romans*, New Testament Commentary series (Grand Rapids: Baker, 1980), p. 447.

18. Slaves, submit yourselves to your masters with all respect, not only to those who are good and considerate, but also to those who are harsh.

a. *Slaves.* In our present-day society we are unacquainted with slavery, but when we open the Scriptures we read about slaves or servants. Because of our unfamiliarity with this subject, we often form an incomplete picture of living conditions of slaves, especially those whom Peter addresses. The word *slave* in the text actually means "house servant." Arthur A. Rupprecht presents a lucid description of the life and status of a slave in the Roman Empire:

> The living conditions of many slaves were better than those of free men who often slept in the streets of the city or lived in very cheap rooms. There is considerable evidence to suggest that the slaves lived within the confines of their master's house. They usually lived on the top floor of their owner's city house or country villa (Cil. Phil. 2.67; Colum. Rust. 1.63). In Pliny's Laurentian villa the quarters for the slaves and freedmen were in [a] separate section of the house, but were considered attractive enough to be used for the entertainment of overnight guests (Plin. Ep. 2.17.22).
>
> The slave was not inferior to the free men of similar skills in regard to food and clothing. That most slaves in Rome were as well dressed as free men is indicated in an unusual way. Seneca stated that legislation was introduced in the Senate that slaves should be required to wear a type of clothing that would distinguish them from free men (Sen. *de Clementia* 1.24.1).[57]

Peter exhorts the slaves to submit to their masters with all respect. He echoes the words of Paul, who in his letters repeatedly advises slaves to obey their masters respectfully (Eph. 6:5; I Tim. 6:1; and see Col. 3:22; Titus 2:9). Peter does not explain the term *respect,* but the context indicates that the slaves are Christians whereas their masters are not. Peter intimates that the slaves ought to respect their superiors and thus fear God (see also 1:17; 3:2, 15).

b. *Masters.* Peter uses the word for "master" in Greek, from which we have the English derivative *despot.* The term implies the unlimited power and authority of a lord. It "denotes the lord as owner and master in the spheres of family and public life, where lordship sometimes entails harshness and caprice."[58] This is the message Peter imparts to the slaves. Some of them served masters who were good and considerate, but others had to endure the whims of unjust and unscrupulous masters. The New International Version describes the masters as "harsh," but in the Greek the word actually means "crooked." Peter is fully aware of the unjust suffering nu-

---

57. Arthur A. Rupprecht, "Slave, Slavery," *ZPEB,* vol. 5, p. 460.
58. Hans Bietenhard, *NIDNTT,* vol. 2, p. 508. Also see Karl Heinrich Rengstorf, *TDNT,* vol. 2, p. 48; Trench, *Synonyms of the New Testament,* p. 96.

merous slaves had to endure. Therefore, he continues his exhortation and writes:

19. For it is commendable if a man bears up under the pain of unjust suffering because he is conscious of God.

Here are a few observations:

a. Although Peter is conscious of the suffering that defenseless slaves have to endure from perverse masters, he now broadens his scope and includes anyone who experiences the pain of unjust suffering. For this reason Peter writes the indefinite term *anyone,* which is translated in the New International Version as "a man." In other words, Peter no longer addresses only slaves but all the readers of his epistle.

b. Peter reveals the influence Jesus' teaching has had on him, for he uses the same idiom in evaluating human suffering that Jesus used. Jesus always questioned a person's motives for showing love to someone, doing good to him, or lending something to him.

Peter asserts that "it is commendable" to suffer pain unjustly. In the Greek, the same word is used for "commendable" and "credit." Jesus asks the rhetorical question, "If you love those who love you, what *credit* is that to you?" (Luke 6:32, italics added; and see vv. 33–34). Three times Jesus poses the question "What credit is that to you?" with reference to doing something to others who are able to repay in kind. But he advocates doing such things to those who cannot repay. "Then your reward will be great, and you will be sons of the Most High, because he is kind to the ungrateful and wicked" (6:35).

In a modified form Peter employs the same principle Jesus teaches. In verse 19 of the second chapter of his epistle, Peter does not stress the virtue of doing good but rather that of receiving evil. Confidently Peter asserts that unjust suffering is commendable as long as the believer is conscious of God.

c. When the Christian endures the pain of unjust suffering, he must know that he is fulfilling God's will. When a believer is conscious of God, Peter implies, God gives him the necessary strength to bear the pain, extends to him grace and mercy, and is fully in control of every situation.

The translations *conscious of God* (NIV), *mindful of God* (RSV), and *awareness of God's presence* (NAB) altogether describe the believer's relationship to God. Because of his awareness of God, the Christian is able to endure the pain of unjust suffering.[59] He has insight into the realities of life, especially when he knows that he is suffering unjustly. However, he also knows that suffering justly as a result of wrongdoing has no merit.

20. But how is it to your credit if you receive a beating for doing wrong and endure it? But if you suffer for doing good and you endure it, this is commendable before God.

a. *Retribution.* Here is the conclusion to the argument on suffering that

---

59. Consult Raymond Opperwall, "Conscience," *ISBE,* vol. 1, p. 764.

Peter develops. First he states the negative, and then the positive. The negative part he puts in the form of an inverse conditional sentence. The last clause of this sentence he places at the beginning so that it receives emphasis: "But how is it to your credit?" In the original, this particular word for "credit" differs from the term *commendable*. The word *credit* has its root in the verb *to call*. Whatever is reported favorably about someone is to a person's credit; that is, he receives praise and honor.

The conditional clause in the sentence depicts indisputable reality. "If you receive a beating for doing wrong and endure it," why should you receive praise? Peter describes the situation of a slave whose master beats him with blows of a fist because the slave transgressed. Presumably the slave knew the instructions his master had given him. He chose to ignore them, however, and now being caught he has to endure his punishment. He deserves no sympathy and certainly no praise.

b. *Reward.* The original readers of Peter's letter appear to have suffered pain unjustly. They have been trying to do that which is good, and yet have received physical blows for doing so. "But if you suffer for doing good and endure it, this is commendable before God." Peter repeats this theme a few times in his epistle (see 2:19; 3:14, 17; 4:13–16). Furthermore, in the second half of the verse Peter echoes Jesus' words: "And if you do good to those who are good to you, what credit is that to you?" (Luke 6:33).

When the Christian slave does his work in harmony with the will of his master, he generally does so in harmony with the will of God.[60] If the slave performs his duties well, but his perverse master beats him nevertheless, then he suffers unjustly.

Whenever possible, we should avoid seeking undeserved punishment. If we solicit punishment for the sake of glory, we are defeating ourselves. But when suffering is unavoidable, we should endure it patiently without complaint, for then we know that we are doing God's will and receive his commendation. Such suffering, says Peter, who repeats the words of verse 19, "is commendable before God." Moreover, although unjust suffering may arouse sympathy among men, in the sight of God the sufferer receives praise and commendation.

> Blessed are you when people insult you, persecute you and falsely say all kinds of evil against you because of me. Rejoice and be glad, because great is your reward in heaven. [Matt. 5:11–12]

Practical Considerations in 2:18–20

Verse 18

We who live in free countries know about slavery from history books but are unacquainted with the living conditions of a slave. Although times have changed,

---

60. Refer to Best, *I Peter*, p. 119.

the scriptural teachings Peter expounds apply as well to the present labor relations of employers and employees, management and unions as to the master-slave relations of former times. The Bible teaches that in our workaday world we ought to apply and uphold the principles of justice and righteousness, of honesty and integrity, of thoughtfulness and consideration. In disputes, both employers and employees should settle their differences through arbitration and conciliation. Management is entitled to a full day's work from the laborer, and the laborer is entitled to full pay for diligent and competent work (compare II Thess. 3:10; Col. 4:1).

Verse 20

Even though in our society slavery belongs to history, numerous persons can testify that oppression nevertheless takes place today. They experience nonphysical oppression in the form of either verbal abuse or unethical rules and dishonest practices in their place of work. Quite often they cannot voice their grievances for fear of losing their source of income. Furthermore, oppression that is nonphysical usually is subtle and elusive, and generally cannot be proved. To all those who silently suffer in their place of employment Peter says, "If you suffer for doing good and endure it, this is commendable before God."

Greek Words, Phrases, and Constructions in 2:18-20

Verse 18

οἱ οἰκέται—the definite article with the noun connotes categories of people addressed as in the vocative case (see 3:1, 7; Eph. 5:22, 25; 6:1, 4, 5; Col. 3:18, 21, 22; 4:1). The noun οἰκέται derives from οἶκος (house) and signifies "house slave."

ὑποτασσόμενοι—this present middle participle takes the place of the imperative (compare 3:1).[61] The present tense expresses progressive action.

Verse 19

χάρις—occurring in this verse and the next (v. 20), the noun χάρις (grace) denotes *"that which brings someone* (God's) *favor."*[62]

Verse 20

ποῖον—this interrogative pronoun conveys a qualitative force: how?[63]

κλέος—derived from the verb καλέω (I call), this noun occurs only once in the New Testament and means "good report, praise."

εἰ—as in the preceding verse (v. 19) and twice in this verse, the particle εἰ introduces a simple-fact conditional sentence that expresses reality.

κολαφιζόμενοι—from the verb κολαφίζω (I strike with the fist), the present passive participle is related to the noun κόλαφος (a cuff on the cheek).

---

61. Refer to Robertson, *Grammar*, p. 946. Also see H. E. Dana and Julius R. Mantey, *A Manual Grammar of the Greek New Testament* (1927; New York: Macmillan, 1967), p. 229.

62. Bauer, p. 877.

63. See Robertson, *Grammar*, p. 740.

21 To this you were called, because Christ suffered for you, leaving you an example, that you should follow in his steps.

22 "He committed no sin,
and no deceit was found in his mouth."

23 When they hurled their insults at him, he did not retaliate; when he suffered, he made no threats. Instead, he entrusted himself to him who judges justly. 24 He himself bore our sins in his body on the tree, so that we might die to sins and live for righteousness; by his wounds you have been healed. 25 For you were like sheep going astray, but now you have returned to the Shepherd and Overseer of your souls.

D. Shepherd and Overseer
2:21–25

1. Suffered
2:21–23

Peter directs the attention of the Christian who suffers unjustly in this world to the sufferings of Christ. He points to Christ, who, fulfilling the Old Testament prophecy of Isaiah 53, is the supreme example of unselfish submission to suffering.[64]

21. To this you were called, because Christ suffered for you, leaving you an example, that you should follow in his steps.

In his discourse, Peter changes the course of his discussion by mentioning the suffering of Christ. He wants the Christian who suffers unjustly to look to Jesus from whom the believer receives new strength for body and soul. Looking to Jesus, the Christian experiences a renewal of attitude and disposition. With clear vision he sees that God is calling him to become more like Jesus in his daily conduct. Therefore, the Christian is able to sing the words of Charles H. Gabriel:

> More like the Master I would ever be,
> More of His meekness, more humility;
> More zeal to labor, more courage to be true,
> More consecration for work He bids me do.

Peter tells his readers that they have been called by God to the situation in which they endure suffering. In other words, they must realize both that God knows the injustice which they patiently endure and that he has called them to face injustice.

---

64. Some scholars (e.g., Hans Windisch, Rudolf Bultmann) think that the last five verses of this chapter (2:21–25) constitute a christological hymn which Peter adapted to his discussion on suffering. Thomas P. Osborne disputes this assertion because Peter makes use of citations from and allusions to Isaiah 53. See "Guide Lines for Christian Suffering: A Source-Critical and Theological Study of 1 Peter 2, 21–25," *Biblica* 64 (1983): 381–408.

Why does God call us to experience suffering? Peter answers, "Because Christ suffered for you, leaving you an example, that you should follow in his steps." No servant is greater than his master (John 13:16; 15:20), Jesus told his disciples. If the master suffers and sets the example for his servants, they are not exempt from persecution.[65] In fact, this is how Paul puts it: "For it has been granted to you on behalf of Christ not only to believe on him, but also to suffer for him" (Phil. 1:29).

We acknowledge that Christ suffered and died in our behalf, but we do not understand in what way he is our example. We are unable to perform the mighty miracles Jesus performed and we cannot suffer the same agony he endured in Gethsemane and at Calvary. We follow Christ not in the degree of anguish and pain but in the manner in which he endured suffering. Note that Peter confirms this interpretation by quoting repeatedly from Isaiah 53 in the next few verses.

Peter borrows the word *example* from the educational world. In education this term relates to the training a child receives in school. The word refers to "the faint outlines of letters which were traced over by pupils learning to write, then also of the sets of letters written at the top of a page or other piece of writing material to be copied by the learner on the rest of the page."[66] Peter uses the noun in a figurative sense. As a child traces letters on a page, so the Christian traces the path of Christ. In this verse, Peter exhorts the reader to follow in Christ's footsteps (compare Rom. 4:12; II Cor. 12:18). The path that Christ has cut is marked by patience, meekness, integrity, and honesty.

22. "He committed no sin, and no deceit was found in his mouth."

This is the first direct quote from the messianic prophecy of Isaiah 53:9.[67] In the early church, the so-called suffering servant passage was well known because nearly all the New Testament writers either quote from it or allude to it. The wording of Isaiah 53:9 differs slightly from Peter's citation; we assume that the apostle quoted from memory. The passage from Isaiah has these words: "though he had done no violence, nor was any deceit in his mouth." Instead of the word *violence* Peter writes the expression *sin*, which better suits the general context of his discussion (e.g., see v. 20 [doing wrong] and v. 24 [sin]).

Why does Peter cite this passage from Isaiah? To indicate the sinlessness of Jesus. The one criminal on the cross rebuked the other who insulted Jesus, and said: "We are punished justly, for we are getting what our deeds

---

65. Consult Guthrie, *New Testament Theology,* p. 636.
66. F. F. Bruce, *NIDNTT,* vol. 2, p. 291.
67. Here is a list of the direct quotations in I Peter 2:21–25 from Isa. 53 (LXX): 2:22—Isa. 53:9; 2:24a—Isa. 53:12; 2:24b—Isa. 53:5; 2:25—Isa. 53:6.

deserve. But this man has done nothing wrong" (Luke 23:41; also compare John 7:18; 8:46; II Cor. 5:21; Heb. 4:15; I Peter 1:19; 3:18; I John 3:5).

Jesus personifies sinlessness and innocence. Because of this innocence, his suffering is completely unjust. The contrast between Jesus and his followers is, therefore, so much the greater; no one can rightly object to suffering when he looks at the example Jesus has set.[68] Furthermore, no one can ever claim perfection here on earth, for "if anyone is never at fault in what he says, he is a perfect man, able to keep his whole body in check" (James 3:2). In brief, Isaiah's prophecy applies only to Jesus: "No deceit was found in his mouth."

23. When they hurled their insults at him, he did not retaliate; when he suffered, he made no threats. Instead, he entrusted himself to him who judges justly.

As a disciple of Jesus, Peter personally can testify to the suffering of Jesus. He was present in the courtyard of the high priest when Jesus was tried by the Sanhedrin (see Matt. 26:57–75; Mark 14:53–73; Luke 22:54–62). Peter was fully acquainted with the trial before Pontius Pilate; the chief priests and elders accused Jesus of many things but he made no reply (refer to Matt. 27:12–14). And Peter knew that when Jesus hung on the cross he suffered without complaint (Matt. 27:34–44). The content of verse 23 is such "as we might have expected to be written by an eyewitness" who reflected on the prophecy of Isaiah 53:7–9 (also see 5:1).[69]

Peter depicts the patience and endurance of Jesus and suggests that we follow Jesus' example. However, the tendency to retaliate when we are insulted is always present. For instance, Paul reacted instantaneously to the command of the high priest Ananias, who ordered "those standing near Paul to strike him on the mouth" (Acts 23:2). Paul invoked the judgment of God: "God will strike you, you whitewashed wall" (v. 3). By contrast, Jesus prayed for his enemies: "Father, forgive them, for they do not know what they are doing" (Luke 23:34; and see Acts 7:60).

In the last part of verse 23 Peter states the reason for Jesus' meekness. Writes Peter, "Instead, he entrusted himself to him who judges justly." That is, Jesus did not invoke God's wrath upon his persecutors and demand retaliation. Jesus knew that his suffering was divinely ordained. He had to take upon himself the curse that was resting on the human race in consequence of man's sin. Jesus was fully aware of God's righteous judgment against sin (see II Cor. 5:21).[70] For this reason, Jesus entrusted himself and his cause to God, the righteous judge.

---

68. Consult Calvin, *The First Epistle of Peter*, p. 90.
69. Selwyn, *The First Epistle of St. Peter*, p. 180.
70. Consult Alan M. Stibbs, *The First Epistle General of Peter*, Tyndale New Testament Commentaries series (Grand Rapids: Eerdmans, 1960), p. 119.

Greek Words, Phrases, and Constructions in 2:21

ὑπέρ—as a preposition it signifies "for, in behalf of man." It is a preposition that in the New Testament "was chosen for no other reason than its ref[erence] to the redeeming death of Christ."[71]

ὑπολιμπάνων—this present active participle derives from a variant form of the verb ὑπολείπω (I leave behind).

ἐπακολουθήσητε—this is the aorist active subjunctive of the compound verb ἐπακολουθέω (I follow after). The aorist is ingressive, the subjunctive expresses purpose, and the compound is directive.

---

2. Died
2:24

24. He himself bore our sins in his body on the tree, so that we might die to sins and live for righteousness; by his wounds you have been healed.

We observe these points:

a. *Manner.* The first item we notice is the similarity between this verse and the prophecy of Isaiah 53. Peter follows the wording of the Septuagint, but even in English we see the resemblance. Here are three lines from chapter 53:

> He took up our infirmities (v. 4).
> He will bear their iniquities (v. 11).
> He bore the sin of many (v. 12).

Next, we point out that Peter sees this prophecy fulfilled by Jesus Christ. Thus he places the verse within the setting of Jesus' earthly life. He refers to Jesus' death on the cross. For the word *cross* he uses the expression *tree*, which is an idiom borrowed from the Old Testament (see Acts 5:30; 10:39; 13:29). The law explicitly states,

> If a man guilty of a capital offense is put to death and his body is hung on a tree, you must not leave his body on the tree overnight. Be sure to bury him that same day, because anyone who is hung on a tree is under God's curse. [Deut. 21:22–23; also see Gal. 3:13]

Peter implies that Jesus endured God's curse when he suffered and died on the cross. He teaches that Christ gave his body as a sacrifice for our sins (compare John 1:29; Heb. 9:28; 10:10). That is, Jesus the sinless One became a substitute for us who are burdened by sin. Voluntarily he took

---

71. Bauer, p. 838.

upon himself the curse that was pronounced upon us and by his death removed it.

b. *Significance.* What is the purpose of Christ's sacrificial death? Peter answers, "So that we might die to sins and live for righteousness." Literally Peter says, "That we might be utterly alienated from our sins."[72] By his death, Jesus has set us free from the bondage of sin, so that we are dead to sin and alive to God in Christ (consult Rom. 6:2–13; II Cor. 5:15; Gal. 2:20). We appropriate our freedom from sin's tyranny when we come to God in repentance and faith. And we demonstrate our life in Christ when we obediently submit to God and do his will.[73]

c. *Consequence.* Peter concludes this verse with a quotation from Isaiah 53:5, "By his wounds we are healed." Because he is addressing the readers, Peter changes the first person plural to the second person plural: "By his wounds you have been healed." Although the translation has the plural noun *wounds*, the Greek has the singular form, which actually means "a wound that is caused by flogging." The slaves who were beaten unjustly by their masters could undoubtedly relate to Peter's description of Jesus' suffering. The expression *healed* means "to be forgiven." Peter is saying that the scourging Jesus received before he was crucified and the wounds inflicted on him when he was crucified were the penalty Jesus paid for the redemption of the believer. The word *healed* has a figurative meaning, for it "denotes the restoration of divine fellowship through the forgiveness of sins, and all the saving benefits which accompany it."[74]

Greek Words, Phrases, and Constructions in 2:24

αὐτός—the pronoun ("himself") is emphatic, especially in view of the relative pronoun ὅς (who) at the beginning of the sentence.

ἀπογενόμενοι—from the compound verb ἀπογίνομαι (I die), which occurs only once in the New Testament, this form is the aorist middle participle.

---

3. Returned
2:25

25. For you were like sheep going astray, but now you have returned to the Shepherd and Overseer of your souls.

In this verse Peter cites the Old Testament prophecy of Isaiah 53:6, "We all, like sheep, have gone astray." Once again Peter changes the wording

---

72. See Thayer, p. 60.
73. Consult Hiebert, *First Peter*, p. 178. Also see R. C. H. Lenski, *The Interpretation of the Epistles of St. Peter, St. John, and St. Jude* (Columbus: Wartburg, 1945), p. 124.
74. Albrecht Oepke, *TDNT*, vol. 3, p. 214.

from the first person plural to the second person plural and applies the text to his readers.

In the agricultural society of ancient Israel, the image evoked by Isaiah 53:6 was quite familiar to the people (see Ps. 119:176; Jer. 50:6; Ezek. 34:4, 5, 6, 16). Moreover, in his teachings Jesus often mentions the wandering sheep and the shepherd who cares for the lost (see, e.g., Luke 15:4–7; John 10:1–18). When a sheep is lost and is cut off from the flock, it becomes bewildered; it lies down, is unwilling to move, and will wait until the shepherd comes to take it back to the flock.[75] Intelligence is not one of the sheep's characteristics; a sheep depends completely on the daily care of the shepherd.

Peter writes, "But now you have returned to the Shepherd and Overseer of your souls." First, he compares the readers with sheep who have wandered from the flock and the shepherd, that is, from the church and Christ. Next, he speaks figuratively of the conversion experience the readers have had when they returned to the Shepherd. Does Peter indicate that the readers turned to Christ on their own power? Hardly. In an earlier context he writes that God had chosen them and had called them out of the darkness of sin into his marvelous light (2:9–10). When we turn to the Shepherd and Overseer of our souls, Christ already has found us.

Peter calls Jesus the Shepherd and Overseer of souls; in the fifth chapter of this epistle he characterizes Jesus as the Chief Shepherd (5:4). He obviously thinks of the words of Jesus, who in the Gospel refers to himself as "the good shepherd" (John 10:11, 14). Peter implicitly applies the concepts *shepherd* and *sheep* to the community of believers, that is, the church. Christ Jesus is the Overseer of the church. As the shepherd watches over every sheep in the flock, so Jesus watches over every member of the church. Jesus is the example to his spiritual followers: he suffered and died for his people; and he keeps a close watch over his church.

> Jesus, My Shepherd, Guardian, Friend!
> My Prophet, Priest, and King!
> My Lord, my Life, my Way, my End!
> Accept the praise I bring.
> —John Newton

Practical Considerations in 2:21–25

Of all the religions in the world only Christianity teaches freedom from sin and guilt. The gospel of Christ offers relief to everyone shackled by sin but ready to listen and respond in faith. The gospel proclaims the joyful message: "Christ sets us

---

75. Refer to Simon J. Kistemaker, *The Parables of Jesus,* 2d ed. (Grand Rapids: Baker, 1980), p. 207.

free from all our sins." Christ breaks the bonds of sin that fetter the sexual offender, the drug addict, the alcoholic, the gambler, the murderer, the robber, and the perjurer. Christ releases the sinner from the bondage of sin.

Before his conversion, Paul tried to destroy the church of Jesus Christ. He persecuted Christians, brought them to trial, and consented to their deaths. Afterward, when Paul as an apostle of Christ reflected on his former life, he openly declared:

> Here is a trustworthy saying that deserves full acceptance: Christ Jesus came into the world to save sinners—of whom I am the worst. [I Tim. 1:15]

Greek Words, Phrases, and Constructions in 2:25

πλανώμενοι—observe that the present tense of this passive participle (from πλανάω, I lead astray) indicates continued action.

ἐπεστράφητε—the aorist passive with a middle connotation (from the verb ἐπιστρέφω, I turn). The recipients of this epistle "were headed in the wrong direction, away from God, but they were arrested and turned about."[76]

Summary of Chapter 2

Peter exhorts the readers of his letter to lay aside their sinful nature and to nourish their new life with the pure spiritual milk of God's Word. Because of this nourishment they will grow in their salvation.

The apostle teaches his readers that they are living stones of the house of God and are precious in God's sight. In this spiritual house they form a holy priesthood and offer spiritual sacrifices. And of this house, Christ is the cornerstone which was rejected by men but placed there by God. This stone is precious for the believers but an offense to unbelievers. The believers are the elect people of God who have been called out of darkness to live in his marvelous light. They are the recipients of God's mercy.

Peter admonishes the readers to live without reproach to the glory of God. He tells them to submit to governing authorities and to show proper respect to God and to the king. Furthermore, he counsels slaves to submit to their masters even when they are suffering unjust punishment. He directs their attention to Christ and urges them to follow the example of Jesus' patience and endurance. He consoles them by reminding them of the benefits they receive as a result of their conversion.

76. Hiebert, *First Peter*, p. 179.

3

Submission, *part 2*

(3:1–12)

and Suffering, *part 1*

(3:13–22)

Outline (continued)

3 1 Wives, in the same way be submissive to your husbands so that, if any of them do not believe the word, they may be won over without words by the behavior of their wives, 2 when they see the purity and reverence of your lives. 3 Your beauty should not come from outward adornment, such as braided hair and the wearing of gold jewelry and fine clothes. 4 Instead, it should be that of your inner self, the unfading beauty of a gentle and quiet spirit, which is of great worth in God's sight. 5 For this is the way the holy women of the past who put their hope in God used to make themselves beautiful. They were submissive to their own husbands, 6 like Sarah, who obeyed Abraham and called him her master. You are her daughters if you do what is right and do not give way to fear.

7 Husbands, in the same way be considerate as you live with your wives, and treat them with respect as the weaker partner and as heirs with you of the gracious gift of life, so that nothing will hinder your prayers.

E. Wives and Husbands
3:1–7

1. Conduct
3:1–2

In their epistles Paul and Peter spend much time writing instructions for wives and husbands. They know that the individual family units are the building blocks in the structure of society, and that a healthy relationship between husband and wife is the cement that holds the family together.[1]

1. Wives, in the same way be submissive to your husbands so that, if any of them do not believe the word, they may be won over without words by the behavior of their wives, 2. when they see the purity and reverence of your lives.

Observe the following points:

a. *Admonition.* Peter continues his discussion on submission. After admonishing the readers to be submissive to authorities and telling the slaves to obey their masters, he exhorts the wives to submit to their husbands. Peter adds the phrase *in the same way.* He is not saying that wives should compare themselves to slaves. Rather, Peter enumerates categories of people: first, the readers (2:13); then, the slaves (2:18); next, the wives (3:1); afterward, the husbands (3:7); and last, "all of you" (3:8). The phrase *in the same way* is equivalent to the connective adverb *also.* By addressing the wives as a class

---

1. See I Cor. 7; 11:3–16; 14:33b–35; Eph. 5:22–33; Col. 3:18–19; I Tim. 2:9–15; Titus 2:3–5.

of people, Peter indicates that he speaks in general terms. Thus he averts any potential accusation of being offensive.

In this passage (3:1–7), Peter enumerates the duties of wives and husbands and teaches the equality of the husband and wife. Nowhere does he imply that wives are inferior to their spouses; instead he stresses the roles which each gender ought to fulfill. Peter has more to say to the woman than to the man because he addresses her in her own circumstances.

In the middle of the first century, a wife was expected to profess the religion of her husband. If the husband adopted the Christian faith, his spouse would have to do so, too. But if the wife became a Christian, her husband would consider her unfaithful to him and his pagan religion.[2] This caused tension in the home. Peter therefore counsels these wives to submit to their spouses, even if their husbands make life miserable for them because of their Christian commitment.[3] He fully realizes the predicament of Christian women whose husbands refuse to listen to the gospel.

b. *Action.* A wife who has become a recent convert readily talks about Jesus Christ from the abundant joy in her heart. The case may be, however, that she encounters her husband's indifference or direct opposition to the Christian religion.

Peter counsels believing wives to submit to their own husbands so that by their exemplary conduct they may lead their spouses to Christ. In the Greek, Peter adds the adjective *own* to emphasize the bond of marriage. He confines his discussion to the family unit and does not apply it to society.[4] Peter teaches that within the bonds of matrimony, the husband has authority to which his wife is expected to submit. He gives no indication that one partner is superior to the other; he intimates only that by submitting to her husband, the wife "shows her respect for the divine ordering of human relationships."[5] That is, neither Peter nor Paul formulates rules for husband and wife; God himself has established marital norms (see, e.g., Gen. 3:16; I Cor. 11:3; Eph. 5:22; Col. 3:18).

c. *Attention.* We do not always have to resort to words when we evangelize people around us. Often by our behavior we are able to influence them and point to Christ. Peter tells Christian women that they ought to witness "without words" to their husbands. He knows that their husbands are not persuaded of the truth of the gospel and thus are disobedient to the call of

---

2. Consult Francis Wright Beare, *The First Epistle of Peter: The Greek Text with Introduction and Notes,* 2d ed. (Oxford: Blackwell, 1961), p. 127.

3. See James B. Hurley, *Man and Woman in Biblical Perspective* (Grand Rapids: Zondervan, 1981), p. 152.

4. Consult E. G. Selwyn, *The First Epistle of St. Peter: The Greek Text with Introduction, Notes, and Essays* (London: Macmillan, 1946), p. 182. Selwyn writes that "subordination is one of function, within the intimate circle of the home."

5. Robert H. Mounce, *A Living Hope: A Commentary on 1 and 2 Peter* (Grand Rapids: Eerdmans, 1982), p. 40.

Jesus. Says Peter, "When [your husbands] see the purity and reverence of your lives" (v. 2), then "they may be won over." Another translation of this verse is, "when they see your holy behavior with respect (toward your husbands)."[6] God calls the Christian wife to show obedient love to her unbelieving husband so that he is able to see in her a picture of Christ's love for the church. Moreover, guided by the Word of God, she should demonstrate to her husband moral purity that is exemplary.

Practical Considerations in 3:1–2

When God made us, he gave us numerous talents. Within the family structure, a husband displays and uses the talents God has given him; his wife uses hers. The husband and wife mutually complement each other with their natural abilities, proficiencies, and gifts. They are expected to use their talents for the advancement of God's kingdom in the family, society, and church. Thus they observe the divine command to love their neighbor as themselves.

In married life, a husband is expected to give leadership, exercise authority, and obey God. He should understand that God has given him authority which he must use lovingly for the well-being of his wife. His wife should strive to uphold her husband and help him in his task. With her talents and abilities, she is God's servant in fulfilling her role as her husband's helper.

In conclusion, therefore, within the family we observe that a husband and his wife practice equality as human beings, but that they define and display their differences in their respective functions and roles.

Greek Words, Phrases, and Constructions in 3:1

ὑποτασσόμεναι—this is the present middle participle of the verb ὑποτάσσω (I subject) which is used in the imperatival sense (see 2:18; see also the broader context, beginning with 2:13).[7] In this epistle, Peter has a penchant for using the participle as an imperative (see, e.g., 2:12; 3:7, 9; 4:8, 9).

ἰδίοις—the adjective signifies "one's own" and denotes emphasis within the structure of the sentence (see v. 5).

καὶ εἰ—the particle introduces a conditional clause that expresses reality. Peter indicates that there are unbelieving husbands. The use of καὶ is emphatic.

2. Dress

3:3–4

3. Your beauty should not come from outward adornment, such as braided hair and the wearing of gold jewelry and fine clothes.

---

6. Dennis Sylva, "Translating and Interpreting 1 Peter 3:2," *BibTrans* 34 (1983): 147.

7. Refer to A. T. Robertson, *Grammar of the Greek New Testament in the Light of Historical Research* (Nashville: Broadman, 1934), p. 946. Also consult H. E. Dana and Julius R. Mantey, *A Manual Grammar of the Greek New Testament* (1927; New York: Macmillan, 1967), p. 229.

4. Instead, it should be that of your inner self, the unfading beauty of a gentle and quiet spirit, which is of great worth in God's sight.

"Beauty is only skin deep," says the well-known proverb. Note that in counseling the married women of his time, Peter grasps the meaning of this proverb. He is not so much concerned about their outward beauty as about their inner charm.

a. "Your beauty should not come from outward adornment." We ought to read verses 3 and 4 as a unit and see the comparison Peter makes. He compares the outward beauty of a woman with her inner grace. And he teaches that the latter is much more important than the former.

Peter does not say that a woman should refrain from adorning herself. He writes no prohibition against using cosmetics or wearing attractive apparel. "Peter's emphasis is not on prohibition but on a proper sense of values."[8]

b. "Such as braided hair and the wearing of gold jewelry and fine clothes." Peter provides three examples of outward adornment: hair, jewelry, and clothes. He is not saying that women should neglect their outward appearance; he does not intend that they have unkempt hair, or wear no ornaments, or dress in shabby clothes. Like Isaiah in the Old Testament period (Isa. 3:18–24), Peter objects to the excesses of make-up and dress that were common among the wealthy ladies in the church and society of his day (see also I Tim. 2:9). J. N. D. Kelly comments, "The elaboration in hair-styles, make-up, dress and personal jewellery in the [first] and [second] cent[urie]s is eloquently attested by the literature and art of the period."[9]

If we paraphrase Peter's words to capture the intent of the Greek, we hear him say, "I object to the work of elaborately braiding your hair, the ostentatious wearing of gold ornaments, and the undue effort of dressing yourself in expensive clothes." Peter does not address slave women who lacked the means to wear expensive garments and gold jewelry. On the contrary, he admonishes the wealthy ladies in the Christian community not to stress outward appearance but to develop the inward beauty of a gentle spirit. He says,

c. "Instead, it should be that of your inner self." The contrast is clear. In place of "outward adornment" Peter stresses "the inner self." A literal translation of the Greek is "the hidden person of the heart." Whereas hairstyles, jewelry, and expensive clothes are meant for display, the inner self is hidden from view (compare I Cor. 14:25; Eph. 3:16). Peter gives the reader a description of this inner self:

---

8. Edwin A. Blum, *1 Peter*, in *Hebrews–Revelation*, vol. 12 of *The Expositor's Bible Commentary*, ed. Frank E. Gaebelein, 12 vols. (Grand Rapids: Zondervan, 1981), p. 237.

9. J. N. D. Kelly, *A Commentary on the Epistles of Peter and Jude*, Thornapple Commentaries series (1969; Grand Rapids: Baker, 1981), p. 129. Also see Charles Bigg, *A Critical and Exegetical Commentary on the Epistles of St. Peter and St. Jude*, International Critical Commentary series (1901; Edinburgh: Clark, 1961), p. 152.

d. "The unfading beauty of a gentle and quiet spirit." The translators of the New International Version have supplied the word *beauty*, which is needed to complete the sentence.[10] The descriptive phrase *unfading beauty* contrasts with ever-changing hairstyles, jewelry, and clothes. The beauty of the inner self does not lose its luster but is lasting and stable because of "a gentle and quiet spirit." The Greek word which is translated "gentle" occurs only four times in the New Testament; two instances are self-descriptions of Jesus (Matt. 11:29; 21:5); one is a beatitude spoken by Jesus ("Blessed are the meek [gentle]," Matt. 5:5); and the last one is Peter's exhortation in 3:4. Peter exhorts the female readers to display the same gentle spirit Jesus had during his earthly ministry.

Furthermore, the Christian woman must have a "quiet" spirit.[11] A woman with a meek and quiet spirit ought never to be underestimated, for meekness is not the same as weakness, and quietness is not synonymous with dullness. The most effective women are those who possess the inner qualities of gentleness and quietness. Because of these qualities, Christian women receive favor in God's sight.

e. "Which is of great worth in God's sight." Not man's evaluation of a meek and quiet spirit counts, but God's. Peter employs the term *of great worth* when he mentions the inner qualities of a gentle and quiet spirit. This term is the same Greek word Paul uses to describe "expensive" clothes (I Tim. 2:9). God, then, highly values these qualities in God-fearing women.

Greek Words, Phrases, and Constructions in 3:3

ὁ . . . κόσμος—note the separation of the definite article from the noun. This construction compares favorably with that of classical Greek.

περιθέσεως—from the verb περιτίθημι (I place around), the noun περίθεσις displays a process (indicated by the -σις ending).

ἐνδύσεως—this noun in the genitive singular (from ἔνδυσις, a putting on) denotes prolonged activity (as the -σις ending shows).

---

3. Dignity
3:5–6

For standards of conduct, Peter resorts to examples from the ancient past. He consults the Old Testament and in particular mentions Sarah, the wife of Abraham.

5. For this is the way the holy women of the past who put their hope in

---

10. All translations supply an appropriate noun, e.g., "apparel" (RV, ASV), "ornament" (KJV, NKJV, JB, NEB), "quality" (NASB), "qualities" (MLB), "jewel" (RSV), "loveliness" (*Phillips*), or "beauty" (NAB, GNB, *Moffatt*).

11. In his epistles, Paul exhorts Christians "to lead a quiet life" (I Thess. 4:11; I Tim. 2:2).

God used to make themselves beautiful. They were submissive to their own husbands, 6. like Sarah, who obeyed Abraham and called him her master. You are her daughters if you do what is right and do not give way to fear.

In this passage we observe three characteristics:

a. *Pattern.* Peter resorts to the Old Testament to prove that he is not the only one who tells women how they should live with their husbands. He appeals to a pattern, set in Old Testament times, that stresses spiritual values. When he calls the women of the past "holy," Peter does not mean that they were perfect; he refers to their relationship with God, for their gentle and quiet spirits were precious in God's sight.

What made these women holy? First, they "put their hope in God." The unnamed ladies of earlier centuries had one thing in common: their hope in God (see I Tim. 5:5). "Hope in God is true holiness."[12] They knew that God would never fail them, whatever their circumstances were.

Next, these women "used to make themselves beautiful" by cultivating the virtues of gentleness and quietness that are precious to God. Throughout the Old Testament era they set the pattern for holy living and invited succeeding generations to follow their example.

Third, wives of the ancient past "were submissive to their own husbands." When Peter exhorts the female readers of this epistle to submit to their husbands, he bases his advice on a long-standing tradition. He knows that the women in ancient times demonstrated their submission with inner qualities that are highly favored in the sight of God.

b. *Example.* If Abraham is the father of believers, Sarah is their mother. Therefore, Peter mentions Sarah's name as an example to married women of his day. Peter writes, "Sarah . . . obeyed Abraham and called him her master" (compare Gen. 18:12).[13]

In our culture, no married woman calls her husband "master." If she did, she and her husband would be the laughingstock of society. Is Peter telling wives to address their husbands as "master"? No, he is not. Peter is describing the culture of a bygone era in which a woman respectfully addressed her spouse as "master." Customs vary from area to area and from culture to culture. Here is a biblical example: When Jesus' mother approached him about the lack of wine at the wedding in Cana, he said: "Woman, what does your concern have to do with Me?" (John 2:4 [NKJV]). No impoliteness was intended by Jesus; he followed the custom of his day.

And here is a modern example: In the southern part of the United States of America, a son respectfully addresses his father as "sir" and his mother as "ma'am." He will answer his father's questions with a polite "yes, sir" or

---

12. John Albert Bengel, *Gnomon of the New Testament*, ed. Andrew R. Fausset, trans. William Fletcher, 7th ed., 5 vols. (Edinburgh: Clark, 1877), vol. 5, p. 63.

13. Refer to SB, vol. 3, p. 764. Also see Kelly, *Peter and Jude*, p. 131.

"no, sir." He shows deference, not in slavish subjection, but because his surrounding culture demands it.

Married women ought to observe the customary rules of address in their own culture. They also should make a distinction between principle and application of that principle. The principle is to be submissive; the application varies according to place, time, and culture. Thus, within the setting of her culture, Sarah applied this principle and called Abraham her "master."

c. *Practice.* Peter uses Sarah as an example. More than that, he indicates that she is the mother of all the women who fear God. "You are her daughters if you do what is right and do not give way to fear."

Sarah is the spiritual mother of all Christian women, just as Abraham is the father of all believers (compare Isa. 51:1–2; Rom. 4:11–12; Gal. 3:7–9, 14, 16, 18, 29; Heb. 2:16). Here Peter states a fact: Christian wives *are*, not *shall become*, daughters of Sarah. And he implies the truth of the proverb: "Like mother, like daughter."

The apostle expects two things of Sarah's daughters: that they continue to do good deeds (see 2:14, 20) and to dispel fear. If they do, they are worthy indeed to stand next to Sarah. Peter does not elaborate how Sarah did good deeds or how she subdued fear. Instead he seems to allude to a few lines from Proverbs:

> Have no fear of sudden disaster
>   or of the ruin that overtakes the wicked,
> for the LORD will be your confidence
>   and will keep your foot from being snared.
> Do not withhold good from those who deserve it,
>   when it is in your power to act. [Prov. 3:25–27]

Christian women ought to put their trust in God and thus confidently and calmly meet fear and disaster. When unbelieving husbands mistreat them, God himself will shield them from harm and danger.

Greek Words, Phrases, and Constructions in 3:6

ἐγενήθητε—as an aorist passive indicative from the verb γίνομαι (I become, am), this verb is a timeless aorist.

πτόησιν—from the verb πτοέω (I terrify), the word occurs once in the New Testament. The nominative πτόησις with the -σις ending describes continued action.

---

4. Consideration
3:7

7. Husbands, in the same way be considerate as you live with your wives, and treat them with respect as the weaker partner and as heirs with you of the gracious gift of life, so that nothing will hinder your prayers.

In this verse Peter gives husbands three exhortations: be considerate, show respect, and have unimpeded prayers.

a. *Be considerate.* After he addresses the wives as a group, Peter speaks to their husbands. The phrase *in the same way* means no more than the adverb *next* (see v. 1). Notice that Peter omits the verb *to submit* in his remarks to the husbands; this shows that he departs slightly from the topic of the preceding passage, in which he discusses submission. Yet he maintains continuity of thought, because he is still discussing the relationship between wives and husbands. (In passing, however, notice that after exhorting the slaves Peter does not address the masters.)

Although the apostle is elaborate in his discussion on the duties of the wife and relatively brief in his instructions to the husband, the significance of his exhortations to the husband ought not to be taken lightly. As is evident from his remarks on prayer, Peter addresses believers. Christian husbands must realize that if their marriage is built on a "foundation of love," their mutual husband-wife relationship will flourish.[14]

Peter tells the husbands: "Be considerate as you live with your wives." Here are two literal translations: "Dwell with them according to knowledge" (KJV) and "Live with your wives in an understanding way" (NASB). Because Peter addresses believers, Peter wants the husbands to love their wives in a Christian manner. That is, husbands ought to live with their spouses in accordance with Christian knowledge (compare Eph. 5:25–33; Col. 3:19).[15] In their marriage, they should demonstrate the love of Jesus that is revealed in the Scriptures and thus be considerate and understanding. Husbands must love and respect their wives in harmony with God's Word.

b. *Show respect.* Peter tells the husbands: "Treat [your wives] with respect as the weaker partner." How can Christian husbands be respectful of their wives? Peter replies, "By honoring them" (compare 2:17). A husband ought to praise his wife of noble character and call her blessed. With the writer of Proverbs he honors his spouse and says, "Many women do noble things, but you surpass them all" (31:29).

The first reason for husbands to honor their wives stems from the knowledge that the wives are the weaker partner in the marriage. The word *weaker* refers to physical stamina and not to intellectual abilities, moral courage, or spiritual strength. The adjective *weaker* is comparative and implies that husbands are physically stronger. Therefore, as the stronger of the two marriage partners, the husband ought to shoulder the heavier burdens, protect his wife, and provide for her according to her needs. Although the husband claims authority, he nevertheless honors, sustains,

---

14. Bengel, *Gnomon of the New Testament*, vol. 5, p. 63.
15. Bauer, p. 163. Also see Rudolf Bultmann, *TDNT*, vol. 1, p. 708; Ernst Dieter Schmitz, *NIDNTT*, vol. 2, p. 400.

and loves his wife. We detect an apparent contradiction: the physically weaker wife submits to her husband's authority, yet she receives his honor and respect. We conclude that the wife who understands her submissive role according to the scriptural norms finds complete fulfillment in her husband.[16]

The second reason for husbands to honor their wives is that Christian husbands and wives should consider each other equals. Peter says that together they are "heirs . . . of the gracious gift of life." The New English Bible has, "You share together in the grace of God which gives you life." Husbands and wives are equal heirs of God's grace for their daily lives; spiritually as male and female they are one in Christ (Gal. 3:28).

c. *Pray*. Peter brings verse 7 to a climax by focusing on the devotional life of the husband and wife as they present their prayers to God: "So that nothing will hinder your prayers." Indeed, this is a touching statement in Peter's epistle, for the apostle indicates that he is fully acquainted with married life; he speaks from experience (I Cor. 9:5).

When a husband fails to live with his wife according to Scripture and does not respect her, he finds that he is unable to pray with her. Similarly, when a wife refuses to accept her husband's authority, she experiences an inability to pray with her spouse.

God does not accept prayers that husband and wife offer in an atmosphere of strife and contention. He wants them to be reconciled so that they are able to pray together in peace and harmony and thus enjoy untold divine blessings.

Practical Considerations in 3:7

If the husband is to be considerate of his wife, does this mean that he must speak a word of correction to her whenever this is necessary? Yes, indeed. Suppose that the wife accepts a certain doctrine that is contrary to the teaching of Scripture, should her husband instruct her "according to knowledge" (KJV)? Certainly. He is responsible to help her in understanding the message and the application of God's Word.

Even though husband and wife are one (Gen. 2:24), the husband is not responsible for the sins of the wife, nor can she be held accountable for his sins.[17] Nevertheless, both husband and wife have a responsibility to help each other withstand temptation, grow spiritually, love God, and serve him in church and society. The husband should give spiritual leadership in the home so that all the members of the family are able to develop their gifts harmoniously in the context of a Christian home.

---

16. Consult Uwe Holmer, *Der Erste Brief des Petrus*, in *Die Briefe des Petrus und der Brief des Judas*, Wuppertaler Studienbibel (Wuppertal: Brockhaus, 1976), p. 114.
17. Consult Susan T. Foh, *Women and the Word of God: A Response to Biblical Feminism* (Nutley, N.J.: Presbyterian and Reformed, 1979), p. 208.

Greek Words, Phrases, and Constructions in 3:7

συνοικοῦντες—because of the broader context, this present active participle of the compound verb συνοικέω (I dwell together) becomes an imperative in translation. The same thing is true for ἀπονέμοντες (from ἀπονέμω, I show, pay).

σκεύει—this noun in the dative singular literally means "vessel, jar, dish." Figuratively it refers to a person's physical body or to a man's wife (compare I Thess. 4:4).[18] In the context of this verse, we ought to understand the word σκεῦος as "marriage partner."[19]

συγκληρονόμοις—not the nominative plural but the dative plural has the stronger manuscript support. The dative case relates to the wives, the nominative to the husbands.[20]

---

8 Finally, all of you, live in harmony with one another; be sympathetic, love as brothers, be compassionate and humble. 9 Do not repay evil with evil or insult with insult, but with blessing, because to this you were called so that you may inherit a blessing. 10 For,

"Whoever would love life
  and see good days
must keep his tongue from evil
  and his lips from deceitful speech.
11 He must turn from evil and do good;
  he must seek peace and pursue it.
12 For the eyes of the Lord are on the righteous
  and his ears are attentive to their prayer,
but the face of the Lord is against those who do evil.

F. Unity in Christ
3:8–12

1. Harmony
3:8

Here is Peter's conclusion to the topic *submission,* which he introduced in 2:13. In this conclusion he delineates how Christians ought to live; therefore, he gives them a pattern for Christian conduct.[21]

Notice that at both the beginning and the conclusion of this topic Peter addresses all the readers. To leave no doubt that he is bringing this particular discussion to a close, he writes,

---

18. See Bauer, p. 754. And consult Christian Maurer, *TDNT*, vol. 7, p. 367.

19. Kelly suggests the translation *member of the household. Peter and Jude*, p. 133.

20. See Bruce M. Metzger, *A Textual Commentary on the Greek New Testament*, 3d corrected ed. (London and New York: United Bible Societies, 1975), pp. 690–91.

21. Consult Donald Guthrie, *New Testament Theology* (Downers Grove: Inter-Varsity, 1981), p. 930.

8. Finally, all of you, live in harmony with one another; be sympathetic, love as brothers, be compassionate and humble.

Peter's concluding exhortations are for all the recipients of his letter. Thus he admonishes everyone to follow his instructions. In this verse, Peter writes five admonitions that, when heeded, present "an ideal portrait of the church."[22]

a. "Live in harmony with one another." In the Greek, the text has the reading [be] *like-minded.* Does Peter mean that all Christians have to think in the same manner? No, not quite. Paul focuses attention on the same question in his letter to the Philippians: "And if on some point you think differently, that too God will make clear to you" (3:15). In view of the variety of gifts and talents God has given his people, differences of opinion exist. Peter, however, wants Christians to be governed by the mind of Christ, so that differences do not divide but rather enrich the church. Therefore, he exhorts the believers to "live in harmony with one another" (compare Rom. 12:16; 15:5; Phil. 2:2).

b. "Be sympathetic." Christians should demonstrate their concern for and interest in their neighbor, especially in times of joy or sorrow. They are to "rejoice with those who rejoice; [and] mourn with those who mourn" (Rom. 12:15; also see I Cor. 12:26).

c. "Love as brothers." Peter repeats what he has already written, for already in his first chapter he observes that the readers "have sincere love for [the] brothers" (v. 22). The Greek term Peter uses is general, so it includes both brothers and sisters in God's household (refer to Rom. 12:10; I Thess. 4:9–10; Heb. 13:1).[23]

d. "Be compassionate." In the Greek, the word translated "compassionate" is far more descriptive. It depicts feelings that appear to come from our inner parts (literally, our intestines), especially when we observe the suffering which another person endures. Translators usually associate the Greek word with the heart and thus render it "tenderhearted." The term *compassion* is one that appears in a list of Christian virtues (Col. 3:12).

e. "[Be] humble." Humility is a virtue Jesus taught when he washed the feet of his disciples (John 13:4–17). Jesus set the example of selfless service by his willingness to be the least in the company of his disciples and to be the servant of all. In the fifth chapter of his epistle, Peter repeats his admonition to be humble when he addresses young men: "Clothe yourselves with humility toward one another" (5:5; also see Eph. 4:2; Phil. 2:6–8).

These virtues reflect the glory of the church when brothers and sisters live harmoniously. Spiritual brothers and sisters exemplify these virtues when together they acknowledge God as their Father and know Christ as

---

22. D. Edmond Hiebert, *First Peter: An Expositional Commentary* (Chicago: Moody, 1984), p. 198.

23. Consult Colin Brown, *NIDNTT,* vol. 2, p. 549.

their brother (Heb. 2:11). Then, as the body of Christ, believers indeed experience God's marvelous blessings.

Greek Words, Phrases, and Constructions in 3:8

ὁμόφρονες—from ὁμός (together) and φρήν (understanding), this adjective and the four adjectives that follow need a form of the verb *to be* in the imperative mood to complete the sentence.

---

2. Inheritance
3:9

9. Do not repay evil with evil or insult with insult, but with blessing, because to this you were called so that you may inherit a blessing.

Are Christians interested only in fellow believers? No, they also demonstrate their love toward people who abuse and insult them. Christians follow the teachings of Christ: "Love your enemies and pray for those who persecute you" (Matt. 5:44; Luke 6:27).

In the early church the apostles formulated Christ's teaching in their own words. Thus in his letter to the Romans Paul writes, "Do not repay anyone evil for evil" (12:17), and in his first epistle to the church at Thessalonica, he teaches, "Make sure that nobody pays back wrong for wrong" (5:15). In his epistle Peter writes a similar admonition.

Peter indicates that the readers are trying to settle injuries and insults on their own terms. He tells them to stop retaliating; repaying evil for evil and insult for insult has no place in the Christian religion. In verses 10 and 11 Peter strengthens his teaching with a quote from Psalm 34:12–16 in which the word *evil* occurs three times.

The apostle instructs the readers to bless their opponents rather than to repay them in kind (compare Luke 6:28). If they do so, they imitate God himself and are his children. God causes the sun to rise and the rain to fall even on unrighteous and evil persons (refer to Matt. 5:45). What is the meaning of the term *bless*? It means that we pray for our enemies, be kind to them in word and deed, and seek to promote their well-being.[24]

"Because to this you were called," writes Peter. But to what does the word *this* refer? It can refer either to the duty of blessing one's adversaries or to the prospect of inheriting a blessing.

The believer does not earn a blessing; he inherits it. Thus Peter writes, "So that you may inherit a blessing." The concept *inherit* stems from patriarchal times when, for example, Isaac blessed his sons and gave them the inheritance of the land (Gen. 27:27–29, 39–40). "An inheritance is never

---

24. Refer to Selwyn, *The First Epistle of St. Peter,* p. 190. And see Hans-Georg Link, *NIDNTT,* vol. 1, p. 215.

earned; it is received as a gift. The inheritance which our writer has in mind is salvation, final salvation rather than its present enjoyment."[25]

Greek Words, Phrases, and Constructions in 3:9

ἀποδιδόντες—preceded by the negative particle μή (not), this present active participle (from ἀποδίδωμι, I pay back) assumes the function of a present imperative. A prohibition in the present tense "demands the cessation of some act that is already in progress."[26]

---

3. Peace
3:10–12

The apostle knows the Old Testament Scriptures, so that throughout his epistle he quotes from them to substantiate his teachings. Peter appears to have a penchant for quoting from Psalm 34. He alludes to verse 9 of that psalm in verse 2:9 and he quotes verses 12–16a in 3:10–12.

10. For,

> **"Whoever would love life**
> **and see good days**
> **must keep his tongue from evil**
> **and his lips from deceitful speech.**
> **11. He must turn from evil and do good;**
> **he must speak peace and pursue it.**
> **12. For the eyes of the Lord are on the righteous**
> **and his ears are attentive to their prayer,**
> **but the face of the Lord is against those who do evil."**

The difference in wording between the quotation and Psalm 34 may stem from the use of the psalm in the early Christian church.[27] Peter introduces the words of this quotation with the word *for* to tell his readers that God's Word is authoritative.

a. "Whoever would love life and see good days." Although many of the recipients of his letter experience hardship and misery, Peter looks positively at life and with the psalmist speaks about loving it. Life is a gift from God and so are good days. Christians whose hearts are attuned to God and his Word participate now in the fullness of life here on earth and afterward with Christ in eternity.

b. "[He] must keep his tongue from evil." Note the expression *evil*, which in the quotation refers to the spoken word. It serves to reinforce Peter's

---

25. Ernest Best, *I Peter*, New Century Bible series (London: Oliphants, 1971), p. 130.
26. Dana and Mantey, *Manual Grammar*, p. 302.
27. Consult, for example, Selwyn, *The First Epistle of St. Peter*, pp. 190, 413.

admonition not to repay evil with evil. The tongue is like a world of evil (James 3:6) that without proper restraint corrupts and destroys the speaker and the listener. A Christian must be true to his word, so that his fellow man can trust him (Matt. 5:37; James 5:12). When the heart of the Christian is free from falsehood and deceit (2:1), he follows the example Christ set (2:22), loves life, and enjoys "good days" on this earth.

c. "He must turn from evil and do good." Once again the term *evil* is prominent. Not only in word but also in deed a Christian must avoid even the appearance of evil (see I Thess. 5:22). The Greek says that he must lean away from evil and instead do that which is good (Ps. 37:27; Isa. 1:16; III John 11).

Together with David (Ps. 34:14) Peter encourages the believer to seek peace and pursue it. Because peace itself is fragile and elusive, we can never take it for granted but must actively pursue freedom from strife and discord. The New Testament repeatedly exhorts us to live in peace with all men (see Rom. 12:18; 14:19; II Cor. 13:11; I Thess. 5:13; II Tim. 2:22; Heb. 12:14). Jesus himself pronounced the beatitude, "Blessed are the peacemakers, for they will be called sons of God" (Matt. 5:9).

d. "The eyes of the Lord are on the righteous." God sees the people who do that which is right. When they pray to him, he hears their prayers. This comforting word means that God's favor rests upon all who fear him (Ps. 33:18), that nothing escapes his attention, and that he answers prayer.

e. "The face of the Lord is against those who do evil." The contrast is clear, for as God sees the works of righteous people so he sees those of people who practice evil. Nothing escapes his view. And no one should think that God does not care. Those who delight in doing evil do not have God as their friend but as their adversary. He is against them. Peter is not interested in explaining what God does to his adversaries. In fact, he does not finish the quotation from Psalm 34:16, which describes the end of God's adversaries. The desire is to give the evildoer time and opportunity to repent and establish a living relationship with God.

Practical Considerations in 3:12

The building in which I spend my working hours has a reflective covering on the windows to shield the inside of the building from the heat of the sun. The effect of this reflective covering is that I am able to look outside and see everything, but people outside the building are unable to look in. I can see them but they cannot see me.

When Scripture tells us that God's eyes are upon us, we know that God sees us even though we cannot see him. Yet we often act as if we are behind reflective windows and God is unable to notice us. We should know, however, that God is always observing us and that nothing escapes his attention.

God sees us and hears us. He is patiently waiting for us to come to him with our prayers and petitions. As David says, "The eyes of the LORD are on the righteous and his ears are attentive to their cries" (Ps. 34:15). Even though we cannot see God, we know he sees us. And even though we do not hear an angelic voice from heaven, we know that God answers our prayers.

Greek Words, Phrases, and Constructions in 3:10–12

Verse 10

ἰδεῖν—this aorist infinitive from ὁράω (I see) is ingressive. The verb *to see* in this verse is comprehensive and means "to enjoy and experience life."

τοῦ μὴ λαλῆσαι—the infinitive preceded by the definite article in the genitive case expresses purpose. The negative particle μή makes the phrase a prohibition.

Verse 12

ἐπί—used twice in this verse, this preposition has a favorable connotation in the first occurrence ("on") and an unfavorable one in the second ("against").[28]

---

13 Who is going to harm you if you are eager to do good?   14 But even if you should suffer for what is right, you are blessed. "Do not fear what they fear; do not be frightened."

VI. Suffering
3:13–4:19

A. Deliverance
3:13–14

Peter returns to the thought of an earlier exhortation. In 2:12, he exhorts the believers to live exemplary lives in society so that adversaries may observe the good works of believers and glorify God. Now Peter places the objective to do good within the context of suffering. He knows that God does not shield the believer from external causes that bring about suffering but that God always stands next to the Christian to support him in doing what is good.

13. Who is going to harm you if you are eager to do good? 14. But even if you should suffer for what is right, you are blessed. "Do not fear what they fear; do not be frightened."

a. "Who is going to harm you?" The question is rhetorical and reminds us of a similar question asked by Paul: "If God is for us, who can be against us?" (Rom. 8:31). Of course, no one. As the sixteenth-century Scottish Reformer John Knox used to say, "With God on his side man is always in the majority."

Peter addresses all Christians when he poses the question "Who is going

---

28. Refer to C. F. D. Moule, *An Idiom-Book of New Testament Greek*, 2d ed. (Cambridge: Cambridge University Press, 1960), p. 49.

to harm you?" He wants them to realize that the person who is intent on harming them is a perpetrator of evil. The apostle is not blind to the possibility of physical or material attacks on Christians who are zealous to do good. He also knows that God does not forsake his children when they do his will.

"Who is going to harm you?" Is Peter then contradicting himself when he asks a rhetorical question which demands a negative answer? No, he is not. In verse 14 he indicates that the possibility of suffering is real. He is teaching the readers that if they suffer physically or mentally for Christ's sake, they will not lose, because God does not forsake them. "If you suffer for doing good and you endure it, this is commendable before God. To this you were called" (2:20–21).

b. "If you are eager to do good." The second part of this rhetorical question is actually a conditional clause. Peter writes, "Who is going to harm you if you are eager to do good?" The implication is that if you do evil and someone harms you, you have only yourself to blame. But if you do good and receive harm, God stands next to you to strengthen you.

The Greek word Peter uses to express the Christian's eagerness to do good can be translated "zealots."[29] This particular word had political overtones in first-century Israel. For example, one of Jesus' disciples, Simon, was a Zealot (Luke 6:15; Acts 1:13).[30] However, Peter is exhorting the readers not to become political extremists but to spend their energy on doing good.

c. "But even if you should suffer for what is right, you are blessed." The first word in this sentence is adversative. The possibility of suffering is real, but at the same time it is rare. In fact, the Greek construction Peter uses affirms that this possibility is remote.

The resemblance between Peter's words and one of the beatitudes of Jesus is striking. Jesus said, "Blessed are those who are persecuted because of righteousness, for theirs is the kingdom of heaven" (Matt. 5:10). What does Peter mean by the term *doing what is right* or *righteousness*? The term describes one of God's characteristics: God is righteous (1:17; Heb. 6:10).[31] The same is true of Christ, for Peter writes: "Christ died for our sins once for all, the righteous for the unrighteous" (3:18). If Christians on occasion should suffer for doing what is right, they suffer for the sake of a righteous God. And God promises that he will bless them.

d. "Do not fear what they fear; do not be frightened." Once again Peter resorts to quoting the Old Testament Scriptures and cites the words of Isaiah 8:12–13 to prove his point. But how are we to understand this verse?

---

29. Of the English translations, only the kjv and nkjv have the reading *followers*, which derives from the Greek word for "mimics." Manuscript support for this reading is weak.
30. Consult Hans-Christoph Hahn, *NIDNTT*, vol. 3, p. 1167. Also see Best, *I Peter*, p. 132.
31. Consult Colin Brown, *NIDNTT*, vol. 3, p. 370.

Peter may be referring to either a subjective fear or an objective fear. When we understand the word *fear* subjectively, we hear Peter warning the readers, "Do not share the same fear others have." If we take the term *fear* objectively, we hear him advising the Christians, "Do not be afraid of them or be intimidated by them." Although the translators of the New International Version have chosen the subjective interpretation, I feel that the general context favors the objective meaning. Hence, Peter is saying to his readers, "In case you suffer persecution, don't be afraid of your adversaries, and don't be disturbed by them" (compare John 14:1, 27). Adversaries may be able to hurt the believers, but they are unable to harm them when Jesus Christ is in their hearts. When Christ is present in the Christian's heart, fear has no place. In short, Christ is their defense.

Greek Words, Phrases, and Constructions in 3:14

εἰ καὶ πάσχοιτε—here is one of the few optative forms that appear in the New Testament. The particle εἰ (if) introduces a conditional sentence with the present optative of πάσχω (I suffer) in the protasis and μακάριοι (blessed) in the apodosis. "The protasis suggests, even intentionally, a concession, but it is a true causal conditional clause."[32]

φόβον αὐτῶν—this noun in the accusative case is a cognate accusative because of the verb φοβηθῆτε. The genitive is objective: *"do not be afraid with fear of them."*[33]

μὴ φοβηθῆτε—the aorist passive subjunctive of the deponent verb φοβέομαι (I am afraid) with the negative particle μή (not) is a prohibition that warns against doing something not yet begun.[34]

---

15 But in your hearts set apart Christ as Lord. Always be prepared to give an answer to everyone who asks you to give the reason for the hope that you have. But do this with gentleness and respect, 16 keeping a clear conscience, so that those who speak maliciously against your good behavior in Christ may be ashamed of their slander.

B. Defense
3:15–16

15a. But in your hearts set apart Christ as Lord. Always be prepared to give an answer to everyone who asks you to give the reason for the hope that you have.

Notice the following points:

a. "Set apart." In poetic form, Carolyn M. Noel captures the thought of

---

32. Robert Hanna, *A Grammatical Aid to the Greek New Testament* (Grand Rapids: Baker, 1983), p. 425.
33. Moule, *Idiom-Book*, p. 40.
34. Consult Dana and Mantey, *Manual Grammar*, p. 302.

the first sentence of verse 15. She exhorts her fellow Christians to acknowledge Jesus as their Lord and King:

> In your hearts enthrone Him,
> There let Him subdue
> All that is not holy,
> All that is not true.

Christians must consecrate Christ Jesus in their hearts. The heart is the central part of man's existence, "for it is the wellspring of life" (Prov. 4:23). When the heart is controlled by Jesus Christ, the believer dedicates his entire life to him. Then the Christian is safe from fear and is able to defend himself against his opponents.

Peter adapted this quotation from Isaiah 8:13, which has, "The LORD Almighty is the one you are to regard as holy." In his day, Isaiah told the people not to fear the invading Assyrian armies but to revere God. In his epistle, Peter has the same encouraging message. However, he changes the wording by honoring Christ as the Lord Almighty, so that he is the Lord Christ. The position of the term *Lord* in the sentence creates two different translations: "sanctify the Lord Christ"[35] or "sanctify Christ as Lord."[36] Although both versions make good sense, I prefer the second translation because it imparts greater emphasis to the word *Lord*.

b. "Be prepared." When Peter exhorts the readers to be ready to witness for the Lord at all times, does he mean that Christians should speak indiscriminately about their faith? No, not at all. Jesus says,

> "Do not give dogs what is sacred; do not throw your pearls to pigs."
> [Matt. 7:6]

Christians, then, must be discreet, "shrewd as snakes and innocent as doves" (Matt. 10:16). They must "know when and how far and to whom it is expedient to speak."[37] Christians should respond to opportunities to speak boldly for the Lord Jesus Christ. When Peter tells the readers to be ready, he means that they not only should be willing but also should have the ability to speak for Christ. Therefore, they must know the teaching of the Bible and Christian doctrine so that they are always ready to give an answer.

c. "Give an answer." The admonition to "give an answer to everyone who asks you" is not limited to times when a Christian must take the stand in a courtroom. In some instances the Christian must defend himself against verbal attacks from hostile unbelievers. At other times he is asked to teach

---

35. See, e.g., KJV, NKJV, JB, and NEB.
36. Refer to RSV, RV, ASV, NASB, MLB, GNB, NIV, and *Moffatt*.
37. John Calvin, *Commentaries on the Catholic Epistles: The First Epistle of Peter*, ed. and trans. John Owen (Grand Rapids: Eerdmans, 1948), p. 108.

the gospel to a neighbor who shows genuine interest in understanding the Christian religion. The term *everyone* is inclusive and relates to all circumstances. When we revere Christ as Lord, we experience that "out of the overflow of the heart [our] mouth speaks" (Matt. 12:34). Accordingly, our verbal expressions should be exemplary, gracious, and wholesome. We should demonstrate an ability to give an answer to everyone who asks us about our faith in Christ (compare Col. 4:6).

d. "Give the reason." What does a Christian have? He has hope, says Peter. Although hope is one of the three Christian virtues (see I Cor. 13:13), faith and love seem to overshadow it. In sermons and discussions we often neglect to talk about hope. Nevertheless, in his epistle Peter mentions hope frequently. In the Greek, the verb occurs in 1:13 and 3:5, and the noun in 1:3, 21, and 3:15. What is the hope that a Christian possesses in his heart? "Hope is a patient, disciplined, confident waiting for and expectation of the Lord as our Saviour."[38] The writer of Hebrews exhorts, "Let us hold unswervingly to the hope we profess" (10:23).

15b. But do this with gentleness and respect,   16. keeping a clear conscience, so that those who speak maliciously against your good behavior in Christ may be ashamed of their slander.

a. "But do this with gentleness and respect." Peter instructs the readers to exercise gentleness, and thus he echoes the words of Jesus ("I am gentle and humble in heart" [Matt. 11:29]), whose example the believer should adopt.

When we sanctify Christ in our hearts, we should exercise gentleness and respect toward all men. In our behavior we exert ourselves to demonstrate gentleness toward persons who are spiritually weak (see Rom. 15:1–2). In our conduct we make every effort to show honor and respect toward God and toward those whom God has placed over us (2:13–17; Rom. 13:1–7).[39] We strive to be living models of the example Christ has set.

b. "Keeping a clear conscience." Christians who have a clear conscience are more easily provoked than those whose conscience is guilty. When as a prisoner in Jerusalem Paul defended himself before the Jewish Sanhedrin, he exclaimed, "My brothers, I have fulfilled my duty to God in all good conscience to this day" (Acts 23:1). That is, before God he had done his missionary work in all sincerity and truth; his conscience was clear.

c. "Those who speak maliciously against your good behavior." To opponents of the Christian faith, a Christian who professes his faith in Christ has already provided sufficient evidence of wrongdoing. Moreover, numerous accusations can be leveled at an innocent Christian.

Notice the similarity with a preceding verse in this epistle. There Peter

---

38. Ernst Hoffmann, *NIDNTT*, vol. 2, p. 243.
39. Consult Bengel, *Gnomon of the New Testament*, vol. 5, p. 67.

writes, "Live such good lives among the pagans that, though they accuse you of doing wrong, they may see your good deeds and glorify God on the day he visits us" (2:12). Translators of at least two versions have adopted the reading of Greek manuscripts that have included the phrase *as evildoers* in 3:16.[40] However, indications are that well-intentioned scribes in earlier centuries inserted this particular phrase by taking it from 2:12. The text itself is sufficiently clear with the words *speak maliciously*.

d. "May be ashamed of their slander." When unbelievers maliciously direct falsehoods against Christians who seek to live by the example Christ has set, truth eventually triumphs. When the evidence shows that the conduct of Christians is blameless, the unbelievers themselves are put to shame by their own slander (compare 2:15).

Practical Considerations in 3:15

The writer of Hebrews tells the readers to leave behind the elementary doctrines about Christ and to move on to maturity (6:1). A Christian must be able to formulate his faith in elementary propositions so that when he is asked about his faith, he is able to speak about the Christian religion. He must be able to lead others to Christ and refute the charges of unbelievers. In evangelizing neighbors, a Christian should have the elementary qualifications to teach others the way of salvation. When he confronts the attacks of the humanist and the atheist, a Christian should have a basic working knowledge of the Scripture to be able to substantiate the phrase *the Bible says*. And when members of sects ring the doorbell, the well-informed Christian should become the teacher to lead these visitors to the Lord Jesus Christ.

Greek Words, Phrases, and Constructions in 3:16

καταλαλεῖσθε—"you are slandered"; this is the present passive indicative construction. A number of leading Greek manuscripts have the present active indicative καταλαλοῦσιν ὑμῶν (they slander you). Identical wording in 2:12 "prompted copyists to modify the shorter reading by adding ὡς κακοποιῶν [as evildoers]."[41]

---

17 It is better, if it is God's will, to suffer for doing good than for doing evil.

C. Undeserved Suffering
3:17

The teaching methodology of Peter is to reiterate basic concepts. In 2:20b he extols the virtue of undeserved suffering that receives God's com-

---

40. See, e.g., KJV, NKJV.
41. Metzger, *Textual Commentary*, p. 692.

mendation. In 3:14a he expresses the same thought in the form of a beatitude. Now once more he concisely states the merits of enduring suffering for doing good.

17. It is better, if it is God's will, to suffer for doing good than for doing evil.

No explanation is needed for the statement that the evildoer will suffer for his deeds. That is expected. By contrast, when a person who is doing good things is subjected to suffering, he has a conscience free from guilt and entrusts himself to God. Peter writes, "if it is God's will." The Christian who suffers unjustly while doing good works knows that God is in control and that in his providence God will guide and direct the Christian's life to its destined end.

This particular text has an implied reference to the judgment day. In the next chapter Peter specifically states, "If you suffer as a Christian, do not be ashamed, but praise God that you bear that name. For it is time for judgment to begin with the family of God; and if it begins with us, what will the outcome be for those who do not obey the gospel of God?" (4:16–17).[42] If God causes Christians to suffer in this life for their spiritual well-being, how much more will he bring judgment on unbelievers in the judgment day!

Verse 17 is a transitional verse that summarizes the preceding section (beginning with 3:14). At the same time this verse is introductory to Peter's discussion about the ministry of Christ (3:18–22).

---

18 For Christ died for sins once for all, the righteous for the unrighteous, to bring you to God. He was put to death in the body but made alive by the Spirit, 19 through whom also he went and preached to the spirits in prison 20 who disobeyed long ago when God waited patiently in the days of Noah while the ark was being built. In it only a few people, eight in all, were saved through water, 21 and this water symbolizes baptism that now saves you also—not the removal of dirt from the body but the pledge of a good conscience toward God. It saves you by the resurrection of Jesus Christ, 22 who has gone into heaven and is at God's right hand—with angels, authorities and powers in submission to him.

D. Ministry of Christ
3:18–22

1. Death and Life
3:18

From verse 18 to the end of the chapter Peter writes about Christ's death, his preaching to the spirits in prison, the water of baptism that symbolizes the salvation of the believer, and last, the resurrection and ascension of

---

42. J. Ramsey Michaels writes, "Christians may be called upon to suffer and die under the judgement of pagan courts, but they have the hope of being vindicated when the tables are turned and the injustice of human tribunals gives way to the perfect justice of God's tribunal." See "Eschatology in I Peter iii.17," *NTS* 13 (1967): 401. Also see Best, *I Peter*, p. 135.

Jesus. Indeed, this passage is one of the most difficult to interpret. Some scholars see in verses 18 and 19 fragments of a hymn or a creed used in the early Christian community.[43] Other scholars express their reservations because they claim that "sheer guesswork" in this matter is of little help.[44] Even if we adopt the theory that Peter borrowed a fragment from existing hymns or creeds circulating in the church, we still must maintain that Peter wrote his own account of Christ's redemptive work. Apart from this question, the difficulties of interpreting the next few verses remain.

18. For Christ died for sins once for all, the righteous for the unrighteous, to bring you to God. He was put to death in the body but made alive by the Spirit.

Mark the following points:

a. *Suffering.* The first word *for* links verse 18 to the preceding passage in which Peter extols the merits of suffering for doing good. In an earlier section, he draws a parallel between his commendation of slaves who suffered unjustly (2:20b) and Christ who suffered for them (2:21). Now once again he places the Christian's suffering next to that of Christ. However, in this case we cannot speak of Christ as serving as an example to the believer, for Christ's suffering is unique.

Most translations have the reading *Christ died for sins.*[45] The translation *Christ suffered for sins*[46] has the support of reliable Greek manuscripts. Within the context of verses 14–17, the translation *suffer* fits in naturally. But the introduction of the word *died* in verse 18 causes a definite break with the preceding section.[47]

In addition to its use in verse 18, the verb *to suffer* occurs eleven times in this epistle and seems to be a favorite expression of the author, whereas the verb *to die* "occurs nowhere else in the epistle."[48] Furthermore, in the early church, the words *Christ died for sins* constituted a theological statement "of first importance" (1 Cor. 15:3), which Paul received and passed on to the church. The possibility is not remote that this creedal declaration gained preference to the reading *Christ suffered for sins.* Although the teaching of verse 18 remains the same whatever reading we adopt, the word *suffered* presents a broader historical perspective than the term *died.*

---

43. Literature on this topic is extensive. For a comprehensive summary see Ralph P. Martin, "Peter, First Epistle of," *ISBE,* vol. 3, pp. 807–15. And consult Leonhard Goppelt, *Der Erste Petrusbrief,* Kritisch-Exegetischer Kommentar über das Neuen Testament, ed. Ferdinand Hahn, 8th ed. (Göttingen: Vandenhoeck und Ruprecht, 1978), vol. 12/1, pp. 239–42.

44. Consult Kelly, *Peter and Jude,* p. 147. Selwyn thinks that "a baptismal hymn to Christ" in 3:18–22 is unlikely. See *The First Epistle of St. Peter,* p. 195.

45. For example, see RSV, NEB, NAB, NIV, JB, GNB, MLB, NASB, SEB, *Moffatt.*

46. See KJV, RV, ASV, NKJV.

47. Consult Beare, *The First Epistle of Peter,* p. 141.

48. Metzger, *Textual Commentary,* p. 692. These are the references for the verb *to suffer:* 2:19, 20, 21, 23; 3:14, 17, [18, variant reading]; 4:1 [twice], 15, 19; 5:10.

Within the church Peter taught the doctrine that Christ suffered for sins once for all. As the high priest entered the Most Holy Place once a year to sprinkle blood as an atonement for the sins of the people (Lev. 16:3–34; Heb. 9:7, 25), so Jesus suffered for the sins of his people once for all (Heb. 7:27; 9:26, 28; 10:10, 14).

b. *Justice.* Christ, who is righteous, took upon himself the sins of unrighteous people. Peter already mentioned the concept *suffering unjustly* in previous verses (see 2:20–24; 3:14, 17). Now he states that Christ suffered not for the righteous but for the unrighteous. Note that in Peter's sermon at the temple in Jerusalem he refers to Jesus as "the Holy and Righteous One" (Acts 3:14; also see 7:52; 22:14; I John 2:1, 29). Jesus is righteous, that is, without sin. Thus, Paul writes, "God made him who had no sin to be sin for us, so that in him we might become the righteousness of God" (II Cor. 5:21). Jesus fulfilled God's demand for justice, paid the penalty that was ours, and offered himself as a sacrifice "to take away the sins of many people" (Heb. 9:28).

c. *Entrance.* The effect of Jesus' sacrificial death is to enable us to enter God's presence. Jesus opens the way to the throne of God, introduces us to the Father, and reestablishes for us an intimate relationship with the Father. By removing sin as the cause of our alienation from God, Jesus provides access to God and makes us acceptable in his sight.

In the Greek, the noun *access* or *approach* occurs three times in the New Testament (Rom. 5:2; Eph. 2:18; 3:12) and connotes a "friendly relation with God whereby we are acceptable to him and have assurance that he is favorably disposed toward us."[49]

d. *Death and resurrection.* Peter writes that Jesus "was put to death in the body but made alive by the Spirit." He presents the contrast in two parallel clauses. The question is whether the term *spirit* in the second clause should be capitalized. See the differences in a few representative translations:

1. "Put to death in the flesh but made alive in the spirit" (RSV, and with variations, NEB, ASV, NASB, JB).
2. "Put to death in the body but made alive by the Spirit" (NIV; with variations, KJV, NKJV, MLB).

The first clause presents no problem because the words describe the verdict pronounced on Jesus and his subsequent death on the cross. In respect to the second part of the sentence, commentators agree that the contrast is not between the human and divine natures of Christ. The spirit is immortal and therefore does not have to be made alive. Scholars are of the opinion that the word *body* signifies Jesus' earthly life so the word *spirit* refers to his

---

49. Thayer, p. 544. Also consult Karl Ludwig Schmidt, *TDNT*, vol. 1, pp. 128–34.

resurrected life.[50] The term *spirit,* then, relates to the spiritual sphere of Christ's postresurrection existence. Indeed, this is a plausible interpretation of a difficult sentence.

At the same time, a reference to the work of the Holy Spirit cannot be ruled out. The resurrection of Jesus is the work of the Triune God, for Jesus himself declared that he possessed the power to lay down his life and to take it up again (John 10:18; see also John 2:19–21; 11:25). Paul teaches that the Father raised Jesus from the dead (Rom. 6:4; Gal. 1:1; Eph. 1:20; also see Acts 2:32). And in Romans 8:11, he mentions that the Holy Spirit was involved in Jesus' resurrection.[51]

Commentators note that to achieve balance in the sentence, "Put to death in the body [flesh] but made alive in the spirit," the two clauses must have the same preposition: "*in* the flesh" and "*in* the spirit." However, we do not have to abide by strict logic. If this were the case the translation of I Timothy 3:16, "He appeared in a body, was vindicated by the Spirit," would also require the same preposition to achieve two perfectly balanced clauses in translation. In the Greek, however, the same preposition occurs in both clauses, but in these two clauses many translations have the reading *in a body* and *by the Spirit.*[52] Consequently, the translation *made alive by the Spirit* has merit and cannot be dismissed simply in the interest of making parallel clauses in translation.

Last, the verb forms *put to death* and *made alive* are in the passive voice. From this we could infer that an agent (someone or something) put Christ to death and made him alive. For the first verb form Peter does not indicate an agent, but for the second he does: the person of the Holy Spirit.

Greek Words, Phrases, and Constructions in 3:18

ἔπαθεν—"he suffered." The manuscript evidence is equally supportive of ἔπαθεν and ἀπέθανεν (he died). "In view of the presence of the expression [for sins] scribes would be more likely to substitute [he died] for [he suffered] than vice versa."[53]

ὑμᾶς—the pronoun ὑμᾶς (you) fits with the use of the second person plural in verses 15 and 16. Translators are divided on whether the text should read "you" or "us."

μέν, δέ—here are two particles that denote contrast in two successsive clauses.

---

50. Compare William Joseph Dalton, *Christ's Proclamation to the Spirits: A Study of 1 Peter 3:18–4:6,* Analecta Biblica 23 (Rome: Pontifical Biblical Institute, 1964), pp. 124–34.

51. Refer to Louis Berkhof, *Systematic Theology,* 2d rev. ed. (Grand Rapids: Eerdmans, 1941), p. 347. And see Calvin, *The First Epistle of Peter,* p. 112.

52. See, e.g., GNB, MLB, NIV, SEB.

53. Metzger, *Textual Commentary,* p. 692.

2. Spirits
3:19–20a

Verse 19 is difficult to interpret, for in this relatively short sentence the meaning of each word varies. D. Edmond Hiebert observes, "Each of the nine words in the original has been differently understood."[54] Accordingly, we cannot expect unanimity in the interpretation of this passage; concurrence eludes us.

Here is the reading of the New International Version:

19. Through whom also he went and preached to the spirits in prison 20a. who disobeyed long ago when God waited patiently in the days of Noah while the ark was being built.

What does this text say? Let us look at the component parts, explain them sequentially, and view the text in its context.

a. "Through whom." The antecedent of the word *whom* is the term *spirit* (either with or without a capital letter). If we take the relative pronoun *whom* to relate to the nearest antecedent, then we understand that it refers to the Holy Spirit (see the preceding verse). Through the instrumentality of the Spirit of God, Jesus Christ after his resurrection "went and preached to the spirits in prison." Note that in his epistle Peter mentions the Spirit a few times: "the sanctifying work of the Spirit" (1:2), "the Spirit of Christ" (1:11), and the preaching of the gospel "by the Holy Spirit" (1:12).

We can also relate the phrase *through whom* to the word *spirit* without the capital letter. If we interpret the phrase in this sense, its meaning actually is "in which" or "in the resurrected state." The relative pronoun, then, relates to the spiritual state of Christ after his resurrection.[55]

Some interpreters suggest the translation *in the course of which*. The antecedent of "which" then seems to be the general context.[56] However, the connection between the relative phrase *through whom* and the nearest term *spirit* is unmistakable and thus preferred.

b. "Also he went and preached." What is meant by the word *also*? Apparently Peter wants us to understand it in the sequence of the verbs *put to death* and *made alive*. The words *he went and preached* follow this sequence in the preceding verse. We understand, then, that after his resurrection Jesus went to preach to the spirits in prison.

In the Greek, the same word ("went") is used in verse 19 as in verse 22 ("who has gone into heaven"). We assume that if Peter speaks about the ascension of Jesus in the one verse, by implication he does so in the other

---

54. Hiebert, *First Peter*, p. 226.

55. Compare R. T. France, "Exegesis in Practice: Two Examples," *New Testament Interpretation, Essays on Principles and Methods*, ed. I. Howard Marshall (Grand Rapids: Eerdmans, 1977), p. 269.

56. See, e.g., Selwyn, *The First Epistle of St. Peter*, p. 197.

(also see Acts 1:10–11).[57] We have no certainty, however, because the word *went* as such is indefinite and means "to go elsewhere."[58] But if we interpret Paul's remark about the "spiritual forces of evil in the heavenly realms" (Eph. 6:12) spatially, then the verb *went* can mean "to go up" and can refer to Christ's ascension. Also, the sequence of verses 18 and 19 indicates that Christ went to preach in his resurrected state.

Does the statement *he went and preached* mean that Jesus descended into hell? No, it does not, because evidence for this assumption is lacking. Scripture nowhere teaches that Christ after his resurrection and prior to his ascension descended into hell. Moreover, we have difficulty in accepting the explanation that Christ in his spirit went to preach to Noah's contemporaries. But before we continue this point, we must ask this question:

What is meant by the word *preached*? The verb stands by itself, so that we are unable to determine the content of preaching. In brief, only the fact of preaching, not the message, is important. That is, we understand the verb *preached* to mean that Christ proclaimed victory over his adversaries. In his brevity, Peter refrains from telling us the context of Christ's proclamation. We would be adding to the text if we should interpret the word *preached* to signify the preaching of the gospel. "Hence we may suppose with reason that it is the victory of Christ over *His* adversaries which is emphasized in 3:19, not the conversion or evangelization of the disobedient spirits."[59]

c. "To the spirits in prison." Do the spirits belong to human beings or to fallen angels or to both? In this passage Peter gives the word *spirit* two qualifications. First, the spirits are kept in prison. In Revelation 20:7 John writes that Satan "will be released from his prison" (see also vv. 1–3). And in his second epistle, Peter writes that God sent angels that sinned "into gloomy dungeons to be held for judgment" (II Peter 2:4; compare Jude 6). Incidentally, Scripture nowhere states that the souls of men are kept in prison.

Next, Peter says that the spirits are those "who disobeyed long ago" (v. 20a). He writes, "the spirits . . . who disobeyed." He does not say, "the spirits of those who disobeyed." If this were the case, Peter could mean the souls of departed men who had been disobedient during their lifetime. However, the word *spirits* as Peter qualifies it refers to supernatural beings. Peter's use of this word agrees with the connotation in the Gospels, where it refers to "evil spirits" (see, e.g., Mark 3:11). This usage also agrees with intertestamental literature, in which the term *spirits* designates angels or demons.[60]

---

57. Compare Dalton, *Christ's Proclamation to the Spirits*, p. 160.

58. Consult Friedrich Hauck and Siegfried Schulz, *TDNT*, vol. 6, p. 577. Günther Ebel comments that the general use of this verb is "variable and many-sided." *NIDNTT*, vol. 3, p. 946.

59. Dalton, *Christ's Proclamation to the Spirits*, p. 155.

60. See, e.g., Bauer, p. 676; consult also Bo Reicke, *The Disobedient Spirits and Christian Baptism: A Study of I Peter III.19 and Its Context* (Copenhagen: Munksgaard, 1946), p. 90; Selwyn, *The First Epistle of St. Peter*, p. 199; Dalton, *Christ's Proclamation to the Spirits*, p. 161; Kelly, *Peter and Jude*, p. 154; Best, *I Peter*, p. 143.

According to the writer of Hebrews, Christ does not help angels (2:16). Rather, he redeems the spiritual descendants of Abraham. Furthermore, if we would interpret the word *spirits* to be those of men, we should realize that Peter's qualification regarding disobedient spirits points to willful rejection of God's authority. Scripture teaches that there is no forgiveness for the sin of deliberate disobedience (Heb. 6:4–6; 10:26). Last, no scriptural doctrine teaches that man has a second chance for repentance after death. When the curtain is drawn between time and eternity, man's destiny is sealed, and the period of grace and repentance has ended (read the parable of the rich man and Lazarus [Luke 16:19–31]). Consequently, I interpret the phrase *the spirits in prison* to refer to supernatural beings and not to the souls of men.

d. "God waited patiently." A literal translation of this part of the verse is, "when the patience of God kept waiting" (NASB). That is, God's forebearance lasted 120 years before he destroyed humanity, eight persons excepted, with the flood. The construction, translated "God waited patiently," stresses the leniency of God before he executed his sentence on the human race (compare Gen. 6:3). From the time of Adam to the day when Noah entered the ark, God exercised patience. Noah's contemporaries were notoriously wicked and served as agents of demonic spirits in their rebellion against God. There is no other time in history in which the contrast between faith and unbelief, obedience and disobedience, was as pronounced as in the days of Noah. The rebellious spirits seemed to control the human race with the exception of Noah and his family.[61]

Greek Words, Phrases, and Constructions in 3:19–20a

Verse 19

ἐν ᾧ καί—in 1902 British New Testament scholar J. Rendel Harris popularized a conjecture that had been suggested by J. Bowyer in 1763. Harris conjectured that the reading of the first part of verse 19 should be ἐν ᾧ καὶ Ἐνώχ (in which Enoch [went and preached]). Although the suggestion proved to be attractive, scholars applied the rule that for a conjecture to be acceptable, it must fulfill two conditions: the text must be incomprehensible without the conjecture and the conjecture must improve our understanding of that text. Examining the evidence, however, they concluded that the conjecture was unable to satisfy these two conditions and therefore had to be dismissed.[62]

ἐν φυλακῇ—although the noun *prison* is not explained in the text, its position is emphatic. The prepositional phrase *in prison* is placed between the definite article *the* and the noun *spirits*.

---

61. The pseudepigraphal book of I Enoch, in chapters 6–11, sheds light on the sins of fallen angels at the time of the flood. Consult R. H. Charles, ed., *The Apocrypha and the Pseudepigrapha of the Old Testament*, 2 vols. (1913; Oxford: Clarendon, 1977), vol. 2, pp. 433–36.

62. See Dalton, *Christ's Proclamation to the Spirits*, pp. 135–36; Metzger, *Textual Commentary*, p. 693.

Verse 20a

ἀπειθήσασιν—this aorist active participle in the neuter dative plural clarifies the noun πνεύμασιν (spirits). The participle derives from the verb ἀπειθέω (I disobey). In the aorist tense it points to sins committed in the past. The position of the participle is predicate. We translate noun and participle as "spirits who disobeyed."[63]

ἀπεξεδέχετο—this compound verb is in the imperfect tense and in the middle (deponent) voice. It expresses continued action in the past tense. Because of the compound, this verb is intensive or perfective. It means "to wait patiently for" or "to wait it out."[64]

κατασκευαζομένης—the present passive participle in the genitive case with κιβωτοῦ (ark) in the same case constitutes the genitive absolute constructon. Note that the use of the present tense denotes duration; from use of the passive voice we infer that a work force was needed to build the ark.

Additional comments on 3:19–20a

Interpretations of this particular text are many. Here are some of them listed in chronological sequence.

a. Clement of Alexandria, about A.D. 200, taught that Christ went to hell in his spirit to proclaim the message of salvation to the souls of sinners who were imprisoned there since the flood (*Stromateis* 6.6).

b. Augustine, about A.D. 400, said that the preexistent Christ proclaimed salvation through Noah to the people who lived before the flood (*Epistolae* 164).

c. In the last half of the sixteenth century, Cardinal Robert Bellarmine introduced a view that has been held by many Roman Catholics: in his spirit Christ went to release the souls of the righteous who repented before the flood and had been kept in Limbo, that is, the place between heaven and hell where, Bellarmine said, the souls of the Old Testament saints were kept (*De Controversiis* 2.4, 13).[65]

d. An interpretation promulgated by Friedrich Spitta in the last decade of the nineteenth century is this: After his death and before his resurrection, Christ preached to fallen angels, also known as "sons of God," who during Noah's time had married "daughters of men" (Gen. 6:2; II Peter 2:4; Jude 6).[66]

---

63. Consult Robertson, *Grammar*, p. 778.

64. Thayer, p. 56.

65. Consult Reicke, *The Disobedient Spirits and Christian Baptism*, pp. 42–43. Also consult Joseph A. Fitzmyer, *The First Epistle of Peter*, in *The Jerome Biblical Commentary*, ed. Raymond E. Brown, Joseph A. Fitzmyer, and Roland E. Murphy, 2 vols. (Englewood Cliffs, N.J.: Prentice-Hall, 1968), vol. 2, pp. 366–67.

66. Consult Friedrich Spitta, *Christi Predigt und die Geister (I Petr. 3, 19ff.): Ein Beitrag zur neuetestamentischen Theologie* (Göttingen: Vandenhoeck und Ruprecht, 1890), pp. 22–24. Reicke expands this view to include the souls of men. *The Disobedient Spirits and Christian Baptism*, pp. 52–59.

e. Contemporary commentators teach that the resurrected Christ, when he ascended into heaven, proclaimed to imprisoned spirits his victory over death.[67]

Although space prevents me from commenting on all the strengths and weaknesses of these views, I select a few of the major objections. And although it is virtually impossible to achieve unanimity in understanding the text, I call attention to the view that many theologians favor.

The first view is the one of Clement of Alexandria. He taught that Christ went to hell in his spirit to proclaim the message of salvation to the souls of sinners who were imprisoned there since the flood. Two basic objections can be voiced against Clement's interpretation: one, Scripture is silent on imprisonment of souls condemned by God, and two, Augustine's doctrine that there is no conversion after death repudiates Clement's view.

Next, Augustine said that the preexistent Christ proclaimed salvation through Noah to the people who lived before the flood. No one disputes the fact that the Spirit of Christ was active in the time between Adam's fall into sin and the birth of Jesus (see Peter's comment in 1:11). The objection to Augustine's view is that he departs from the wording of I Peter 3:19. Augustine speaks of the pre-incarnate Christ and not of the Christ who "was put to death in the body but made alive by the Spirit." Augustine's interpretation dominated the theological scene for centuries until the doctrinal view of Bellarmine displaced it in the Roman Catholic Church.

Third, Bellarmine taught that even though Christ's body died on the cross, his soul remained alive. Thus in his spirit Christ went to release the souls of the righteous who repented before the flood and were in Limbo. Bellarmine's interpretation has been rejected by Protestants, because they point out that Scripture teaches that the Old Testament saints are in heaven (see, e.g., Heb. 11:5, 16, 40; 12:23).[68]

Then there is the interpretation of Spitta. He said that Christ after his death and before his resurrection preached to fallen angels who during Noah's time had married "daughters of men." But this view faces a serious objection. Answering the Sadducees who asked him about the resurrection, Jesus asserted that angels neither marry nor are given in marriage (Matt. 22:30). We have difficulty understanding how fallen angels, who are spirits, can have sexual relations with women.

Last, recent commentators teach that the resurrected Christ, during his ascension to heaven, proclaimed to imprisoned spirits his victory over death. The exalted Christ passed through the realm where the fallen angels are kept and proclaimed his triumph over them (Eph. 6:12; Col. 2:15). This interpretation has met favorable response in Protestant and Roman Catho-

---

67. Refer to Dalton, *Christ's Proclamation to the Spirits,* pp. 38–39, for literature.
68. Consult Simon J. Kistemaker, *Hebrews,* New Testament Commentary series (Grand Rapids: Baker, 1984), p. 394.

lic circles and is in harmony with the teaching of the Petrine passage and the rest of Scripture.

---

3. Baptism
3:20b–21a

At this point Peter changes the topic, introduces symbolism, and develops the theme *baptism*. The flood represents baptism and baptism characterizes salvation. The division of the text, unfortunately, is awkward in many translations. We do well to mark this division with a separate sentence, as the translators of the New International Version have done.

20b. In it only a few people, eight in all, were saved through water, 21a. and this water symbolizes baptism that now saves you also—not the removal of dirt from the body but the pledge of a good conscience toward God.

We make these observations:

a. *History*. The building of the ark in the days of Noah took a considerable period of time, but when the day of the flood came only a few people entered the ark. Peter is specific and mentions that only eight persons (Noah and his wife, three sons and their wives) were saved.

The paucity of persons who actually entered the ark and were saved from the destructive waters of the flood stands in stark contrast to the masses who drowned. Even though we have no scriptural evidence, we assume that of the people who drowned, many helped Noah build the ark. Of the multitudes who had heard Noah, "a preacher of righteousness" (II Peter 2:5), and who had seen the slow but steady progress of constructing the ark, not one was saved. However, Peter stresses not the negative but the positive side: "eight in all were saved" (Gen. 7:13, 23). The verb with the following prepositional phrase literally says, "were saved by going through the water."

The phrase *through water* raises some questions. For example, how were the eight survivors saved by going through the water if the flood had a destructive effect? One observation is that the waters of the flood drowned the masses but caused the ark to float.[69] More to the point, however, we see that the household of Noah went into the ark and left behind a world of iniquity. After going through the waters of the flood for more than a year, Noah's family left the ark and knew that God had saved them from being drowned by an ocean of human corruption. Note that the believers were only eight in number. Before the flood of wickedness could sweep away the members of Noah's household, God saved them and continued the human race.

In his second epistle, Peter draws a parallel between Noah and Lot. Both men were tortured by the lawlessness of their times. But observe that Peter concludes the parallel on Noah and Lot by saying, "And if [God] rescued

---

69. Consult Lenski, *Interpretation of the Epistles*, p. 169.

Lot, a righteous man, who was distressed by the filthy lives of lawless men, . . . then the Lord knows how to rescue godly men from trials" (II Peter 2:7–9).[70]

b. *Symbol.* Peter continues, "And this water symbolizes baptism that now saves you also." These words have caused much debate among scholars in respect to the significance of baptism. The expression *this water* looks backward to the waters of the flood and forward to the water of baptism. "Noah's deliverance through the waters of the flood is seen as a prefiguration and type of the saving event of baptism."[71]

What does Peter mean when he introduces the term *symbol*? Are the waters of the flood the original and is baptism a symbol of the flood? No, not really. We should not make any comparison between something great (the flood waters) and something small (the water of baptism), because Peter is only indicating likeness or correspondence.[72] The text allows for a resemblance between the flood and baptism. That is, as the flood waters cleansed the earth of man's wickedness, so the water of baptism indicates man's cleansing from sin. As the flood separated Noah and his family from the wicked world of their day, so baptism separates believers from the evil world of our day. Baptism, then, is the counterpart of the flood.[73]

Peter tells the readers of his epistle that "baptism now saves you." What precisely does he mean? Does baptism itself save a person? Before we answer these questions, let us examine Scripture, which teaches in the Old and the New Testaments that sins are washed away. For example, look at these passages:

> David prays, "Wash away all my iniquity and cleanse me from my sin" (Ps. 51:2).

> God says to Israel, "I will sprinkle clean water on you, and you will be clean; I will cleanse you from all your impurities and from all your idols" (Ezek. 36:25).

> Ananias instructs Paul to "get up, be baptized and wash your sins away" (Acts 22:16).

> Paul writes, "[God] saved us through the washing of rebirth and renewal by the Holy Spirit" (Titus 3:5).

---

70. Refer to Dalton, *Christ's Proclamation to the Spirits,* p. 210.

71. Heinrich Müller, *NIDNTT,* vol. 3, p. 906.

72. Consult Calvin, *The First Epistle of Peter,* p. 117.

73. Refer to Leonhard Goppelt, *TDNT,* vol. 8, p. 253. Bauer observes, "The saving of Noah fr[om] the flood is a . . . 'foreshadowing,' and baptism corresponds to it" (p. 76). Reicke remarks that Noah experienced baptism in a metaphorical sense. *The Disobedient Spirits and Christian Baptism,* p. 145.

Baptism is a symbol for cleansing the believer from sin, but Scripture does not teach that baptismal water saves a person. Rather, a believer is saved because of Christ's atoning death on the cross and his resurrection from the grave (Rom. 6:4). Baptism is a symbol of the shed blood of Christ that cleanses the believer from sin.

c. *Reality.* Peter explains how baptism saves the believer. By explaining baptism first negatively and then positively, Peter writes that baptism is "not the removal of dirt from the body but the pledge of a good conscience toward God." When we wash dirt from the body, we cannot compare this action to baptism. Baptism is a sacrament Christ instituted and which we administer by the washing with water. But the sacrament of baptism alone is not effective in obtaining salvation. Baptism that saves a person must be expressed by the outward ceremony of this sacrament and through the "pledge of a good conscience toward God" that comes from the believer's heart.

Some commentators see a connection between the Old Testament rite of circumcision and the New Testament sacrament of baptism. They are of the opinion that in the wording "removal of dirt from the body," Peter may imply that he is thinking about the rite of circumcision. If this is so, then this passage indicates a link between circumcision and baptism (compare Col. 2:11–12).[74]

After saying that baptism is not "the removal of dirt from the body," Peter states the positive side of the sacrament and adds that baptism denotes "the pledge of a good conscience toward God." Mark the word *pledge.* This is a crucial word that is also translated "request" or "*appeal to God for a clear conscience.*"[75]

Here, then, are the differences in translation. Does the believer make a "pledge [with] a good conscience toward God"? In this version, we look at baptism from our point of view and express ourselves subjectively. The other translation is that the believer "appeals to God for a clear conscience." When we ask God to help us, we see the importance of baptism objectively. Without God's aid we are unable to make a pledge to serve him.

Although translators present numerous variations in their versions, they lean more toward the subjective than the objective reading of this part of the text.[76] If we take the subjective translation of the text, the term *pledge* signifies "response." In short, the believer receives not only the sign of baptism with water; he also responds by "keeping a clear conscience" (see v. 16). The person in charge of the baptismal ceremony asks the candidate

---

74. Consult Selwyn, *The First Epistle of St. Peter,* p. 205; Dalton, *Christ's Proclamation to the Spirits,* pp. 215–24.

75. Bauer, p. 285. Also consult Heinrich Greeven, *TDNT,* vol. 2, p. 688; Gervais T. D. Angel, *NIDNTT,* vol. 2, p. 881.

76. These translations have the subjective reading: KJV, NKJV, RV, ASV, NEB, *Phillips,* GNB, JB, NAB, NIV. Those that have the objective reading are RSV, MLB, NASB, SEB, *Moffatt.*

for his response to becoming a member of the church. When the candidate is baptized, he pledges to serve the Lord with a good conscience.[77] If the water of baptism symbolizes the washing away of sins, then the believer's response to God is to live conscientiously to his honor and glory.

Greek Words, Phrases, and Constructions in 3:20b–21a

Verse 20b

διεσώθησαν—in the aorist passive, this verb from διασῴζω (I rescue) expresses more the directive than the perfective use of the compound. Note that the preposition διά (through) is repeated, that the passive voice denotes an implied agent (God), and that the aorist tense signifies a single occurrence.

Verse 21a

ὅ—as a relative pronoun in the neuter singular, this word refers to the previous sentence.[78] The reading ὑμᾶς (you) is preferred to ἡμᾶς (us) because of manuscript support and the context of the passage.

---

4. Ascension
3:21b–22

This is the last part of a lengthy paragraph in which the writer discusses the ministry of Christ. He concludes his remarks about baptism with a reference to Christ's ascension, session at God's right hand, and royal rule.

21b. It saves you by the resurrection of Jesus Christ,   22. who has gone into heaven and is at God's right hand—with angels, authorities and powers in submission to him.

The doctrine of Christ's resurrection is basic to the Christian faith to which Peter already testified in the introductory verses of this epistle (see 1:3; and compare 3:18). "If Christ has not been raised," Paul writes, "our preaching is useless" (I Cor. 15:14). And in respect to baptism we wish to say that without the resurrection of Christ, baptism is worthless and of no avail. "His resurrection is the ground of righteousness and guarantee of victory."[79]

In verse 22, Peter recites a doctrinal statement of the Christian faith: "[Christ] has gone into heaven." Even though Peter writes the same verb in the Greek ("he went" in verse 19 and "he has gone" in verse 22 [NIV]), some

---

77. Refer to Reicke, *The Disobedient Spirits and Christian Baptism,* p. 185; Dalton, *Christ's Proclamation to the Spirits,* p. 225; J. H. Moulton and G. Milligan, *The Vocabulary of the Greek Testament Illustrated from the Papyri and Other Non-Literary Sources,* 3 vols. (London: Hodder and Stoughton, 1929), vol. 3, pp. 231–32.

78. Consult Robertson, *Grammar,* p. 714.

79. Hiebert, *First Peter,* p. 236.

translations do not convey the original meaning in these two verses. By adding the phrase *into heaven,* Peter recalls the account of Jesus' ascension (Luke 24:50–51; Acts 1:9–11; also see Mark 16:19; John 6:62; I Tim. 3:16).

The next clause, "and is at God's right hand," is a well-known article of faith; we read these words verbatim (in Greek) in Romans 8:34 (see also Eph. 1:20; Heb. 1:3; 10:12; 12:2). The difference between being and sitting at God's right hand presents no doctrinal difficulties. The point is that Christ has received the greatest honor imaginable: he is next to God.

The last part of the verse is interesting. Peter mentions that "angels, authorities and powers" are subject to Christ. What does Peter mean? The term *angels* includes good and evil spirits. Both angels and demons are subject to Christ. The expressions *authorities* and *powers* indicate rulers and functionaries in the angelic world. For example, Paul writes that at the end of time, Christ "hands over the kingdom to God the Father after he has destroyed all dominion, authority and power" (I Cor. 15:24). That is, all spiritual forces inimical to him will be destroyed (compare Eph. 6:12; Col. 2:15).[80] All created spiritual authorities and powers are subject to Jesus Christ. As the writer of Hebrews explains, the Son of God is the Creator of the angelic world and therefore angels, principalities, authorities, and powers in heavenly places submit to him.

In the general context of this chapter, Peter seems to imply that when Christ ascended to heaven, he proclaimed victory over the spiritual forces that were at enmity with him.[81] The spiritual enemies of Christ are Satan and his cohorts. As Paul puts it, Satan is "the ruler of the kingdom of the air, the spirit who is now at work in those who are disobedient" (Eph. 2:2; and see 6:12). Having disarmed these evil forces, Christ defeated them and proclaimed his triumph over them (Col. 2:15). In Psalm 110:1, which Jesus applied to himself (Matt. 22:41–46), we read that upon his enthronement Christ triumphs over his enemies:

> The LORD says to my Lord:
> "Sit at my right hand
> until I make your enemies
> a footstool for your feet."

Greek Words, Phrases, and Constructions in 3:22

θεοῦ—the Vulgate inserts the following addition: "swallowing up death that we might be made heirs of eternal life." This addition probably results from a Latin translation of a Greek gloss.[82]

---

80. Consult Bauer, p. 278. Also compare Eph. 1:21; 3:10; Col. 2:10.

81. France comments, "We may be sure that Peter's readers, who were facing the very real onslaught of evil powers through their persecutors, could find real courage from these words." See "Exegesis in Practice: Two Samples," p. 276.

82. Refer to Metzger, *Textual Commentary,* pp. 693–94.

ὑποταγέντων—the second aorist passive participle (from ὑποτάσσω, I subject) together with three nouns in the genitive case forms the genitive absolute construction. Notice that the nouns lack the definite articles to stress the qualitative aspect of their function.

Summary of Chapter 3

Peter encourages wives to be submissive to their husbands, to stress not external adornment but the inner beauty of a quiet and gentle spirit, and to imitate holy women of the past. He mentions Sarah by name and calls women who seek to do that which is right her daughters. Peter exhorts husbands to live thoughtfully and respectfully with their wives.

The author admonishes all recipients to be harmonious, sympathetic, compassionate, and humble toward one another. He supports his exhortation with a lengthy quotation from Psalm 34:12–16. If they avoid evil and do good, they receive God's indispensable blessing.

Some believers suffer for doing what is right. Peter calls these people blessed. He tells the readers to be able to give a reason for the hope that they have, to keep a clear conscience, and to be willing to suffer for doing good. He directs their attention to the suffering, death, and resurrection of Christ. Peter illustrates salvation with a reference to Noah and his household, who survived the flood. The waters of the flood symbolize baptism. Baptism points to Jesus Christ; his death and resurrection provide the cleansing that baptism signifies. Christ ascended to heaven, sits in majesty at God's right hand, and rules over the spiritual world of angels, authorities, and powers.

4

Suffering, *part 2*

(4:1–19)

Outline (continued)

4 1 Therefore, since Christ suffered in his body, arm yourselves also with the same attitude, because he who has suffered in his body is done with sin. 2 As a result, he does not live the rest of his earthly life for evil human desires, but rather for the will of God. 3 For you have spent enough time in the past doing what pagans choose to do—living in debauchery, lust, drunkenness, orgies, carousing and detestable idolatry. 4 They think it strange that you do not plunge with them into the same flood of dissipation, and they heap abuse on you. 5 But they will have to give account to him who is ready to judge the living and the dead. 6 For this is the reason the gospel was preached even to those who are now dead, so that they might be judged according to men in regard to the body, but live according to God in regard to the spirit.

E. Examination
4:1–6

1. The Will of God
4:1–2

The author of this epistle calls the readers to examine their lifestyles by looking to the sufferings of Christ. In these verses, Peter returns to the subject of Christ's suffering and prepares the believers for the suffering that they must endure.

1. Therefore, since Christ suffered in his body, arm yourselves also with the same attitude, because he who has suffered in his body is done with sin.

We make these observations:

a. *Example.* The first word in this verse is "therefore." It has no connection with the last verse of the preceding chapter, but rather serves as a conclusion to the thought expressed in 3:18. This means that verses 19–22 of the previous chapter are a parenthetical comment. Peter, then, repeats the basic thought of 3:18 and exhorts the readers to have the mind of Christ.

In his epistle Peter mentions the subject *suffering* a number of times, usually in relation to Jesus Christ, who serves as an example. In 2:20 he tells slaves that if they suffer for doing that which is good, they receive God's commendation. He links this observation to the suffering of Christ (2:21) and encourages slaves to follow Christ's example. In the next chapter Peter repeats the same remark and addresses all the readers: "It is better, if it is God's will, to suffer for doing good than for doing evil" (3:17). He contin-

155

ues his discourse by speaking about the reason for Christ's death (v. 18). In this respect the readers are not able to follow Christ's example, because Christ died for their sins, as "the righteous for the unrighteous." In the words of Paul, "The death he died, he died to sin once for all" (Rom. 6:10).

Peter resumes his discussion on the suffering of Christ, for in a rather brief statement he says, "Christ suffered in his body." This is a reference to all of Christ's suffering that culminated in his death on the cross. Jesus endured his martyrdom in behalf of his people. For this reason, some Greek manuscripts have the reading *Christ suffered for us.*[1] The words *for us* seem to have been added by copyists who wished to conform the manuscripts to the wording of 2:21 and 3:18. Nevertheless, the association of Christ with his people is evident in the text. Here Peter expresses the need to identify Christ with the Christians.

b. *Action.* "Arm yourselves also with the same attitude." The verb *arm yourselves,* which Peter uses to spur the believers to action, is a military term which refers to a soldier putting on his weapons to fight the enemy (see Rom. 13:12; II Cor. 6:7; 10:4; Eph. 6:11). Notice that Peter identifies the believers with Christ: the word *also* unites them. However, the Christian arms himself not for physical warfare but for a spiritual conflict. He utters a daily prayer:

> May the mind of Christ my Saviour,
> Live in me from day to day,
> By His love and pow'r controlling
> All I do and say.
> —Kate B. Wilkinson

Peter then adds the concluding part of the sentence, which in one sense is explanatory of the preceding part, but in another way raises some difficult issues. First we examine the sentence and then consider the issues.

c. *Result.* Says Peter, "Because he who has suffered in his body is done with sin." Most translations and commentators maintain the causal conjunction *because* at the beginning of the clause. They assert that the conjunction expresses the reason for imitating Christ. However, we can also interpret this last part of the sentence as an explanation of the phrase *attitude of Christ.* Then we eliminate the conjunction altogether. For instance, consider the following translation: "Christ suffered in the flesh; therefore arm yourselves with his same mentality. He who has suffered in the flesh has broken with sin" (NAB). The meaning of the phrase *mentality of Christ* lies in the last part of the sentence. Before we discuss that part, however, we must look at the parallelism of this passage. In view of the verbatim repetition, the phrase "he who has suffered in his body" first describes Christ and then the believer.

---

1. See KJV and NKJV for the additional phrase *for us.*

In explaining this text we encounter many difficulties. For example, if we apply the last clause to Christ, do we imply that Christ at one time was a sinner? Certainly not, for he is without sin (Heb. 4:15). The comparison does not have to correspond in every detail. "It is then enough that we should in a measure be made conformable to the death of Christ."[2] He bore the wrath of God for the sins of his people. As Paul writes, "God made him who had no sin to be sin for us" (II Cor. 5:21). By quoting Isaiah 53:9, Peter teaches that Christ himself committed no sin (2:22). And he comments that Christ "bore our sins in his body on the tree, so that we might die to sins" (2:24).

When the believer identifies completely with Christ, he knows that he "is done with sin." This means that the last few words of verse 1 apply to the Christian whose life is firmly established in Christ (Rom. 6:18; I John 3:9). The follower of Christ has abandoned a life of sin, because the ruling power of sin has been broken. Granted that he is unable to live a perfect life, the believer is free from the dominance of sin.

In Greek, Peter chooses the perfect tense in the verb form *has broken with*. The perfect tense indicates that the action occurred in the past and has lasting effect for the present and the future.

Should every Christian who identifies with Christ desire physical suffering to break with sin? Certainly not! First, remember that the act of breaking with sin happened as a past event. Next, the verb form *has broken with* can be interpreted in the passive voice, as the Greek text indicates. Literally we read, "he has been released" from sin. This means that God is the implied agent. In other words, God has stopped man from living in continual sin. This liberating act, then, is a work of God and not of man.

Why does Peter repeat the phrase *suffered in his body* if suffering does not necessarily relate to the act of breaking with sin? Some commentators are of the opinion that Peter quotes a proverbial saying that illustrates the purpose of Christ's suffering and death, and the resulting freedom from sin for the believer (compare Rom. 6:7).[3] The saying conveys the exhortation for the Christian to arm himself with the mind of Christ.

2. As a result, he does not live the rest of his earthly life for evil human desires, but rather for the will of God.

The message Peter delivers to his readers is that they who have armed themselves with the mind of Christ have been set free from their earlier life of sin.[4] They no longer live for themselves but for God.

---

2. John Calvin, *Commentaries on the Catholic Epistles: The First Epistle of Peter,* ed. and trans. John Owen (Grand Rapids: Eerdmans, 1948), p. 122.

3. Refer to Francis Wright Beare, *The First Epistle of Peter: The Greek Text with Introduction and Notes,* 2d ed. (Oxford: Blackwell, 1961), p. 153. And see Robert H. Mounce, *A Living Hope: A Commentary on 1 and 2 Peter* (Grand Rapids: Eerdmans, 1982), p. 62; Leonhard Goppelt, *Der Erste Petrusbrief,* Kritisch-Exegetischer Kommentar über das Neuen Testament, ed. Ferdinand Hahn, 8th ed. (Göttingen: Vandenhoeck und Ruprecht, 1978), vol. 13/1, p. 269.

4. Consult George E. Ladd, *A Theology of the New Testament* (Grand Rapids: Eerdmans, 1974), p. 598.

"He does not live the rest of his earthly life." At first glance, this wording appears foreboding, as if death will soon overtake the reader. This is exactly the purpose of the writer: to remind man of the brevity of life. In general, man measures his lifespan in double digits and sometimes not even that.

"For evil human desires." How does man redeemed by Christ live his daily life? The verb *to live* actually means "to conduct life" (compare I Tim. 2:2), and relates to man's behavior that can reflect either the ways of the world or faithful obedience to the will of God. Already Peter has exhorted the readers not to conform to the evil desires they had when they lived in ignorance of God's law (1:14; also see 2:11; 4:3). Once more he reminds them of their past and directs their attention to obedience to God. The contrast between "evil human desires" and "the will of God" is startling: it is an either-or proposition. And the believers should know that they cannot have both (compare Rom. 6:2, 6–7; I John 2:16–17).

Doctrinal Considerations in 4:1

The Christian who identifies with Christ must be prepared to endure physical suffering. Peter and the rest of the New Testament writers see an inseparable link between Christ and his followers in respect to suffering (I Peter 4:1, 13, 16; Rom. 8:17; II Cor. 11:23–29; Phil. 3:10; Heb. 10:32–34; Rev. 2:10).

Throughout his first epistle, Peter develops a theology of suffering which centers on Jesus Christ. Christ suffered vicariously for his people, as the prophets in the Old Testament period foretold (1:11; see also.Luke 24:46; Acts 3:18). He suffered to set the sinner free (2:24–25). Because of Christ's suffering, his followers participate in his sufferings (4:13; compare Col. 1:24). To suffer for Christ is a privilege (1:6, 8) and a cause for joy (4:13). Moreover, the Christian's identification with Christ is an invitation not only to be like-minded but also to suffer in the body on his behalf (4:1).[5]

Greek Words, Phrases, and Constructions in 4:1

παθόντος—from πάσχω (I suffer), this aorist active participle with the noun *Christ* in the genitive case forms the genitive absolute construction. The participle denotes cause.

σαρκί—the dative case has a metaphorically local use that signifies "anyone who has suffered physically" (as contrasted to τῷ πνεύματι, spiritually).[6]

---

5. See Burkhard Gärtner, *NIDNTT,* vol. 3, p. 724. Also consult Bastiaan Van Elderen, "Peter, First Epistle," *ZPEB,* vol. 4, p. 725; Gordon R. Lewis, "Suffering and Anguish," *ZPEB,* vol. 5, p. 531.
6. Consult C. F. D. Moule, *An Idiom-Book of New Testament Greek,* 2d ed. (Cambridge: Cambridge University Press, 1960), p. 44. And refer to Robert Hanna, *A Grammatical Aid to the Greek New Testament* (Grand Rapids: Baker, 1983), p. 426.

πέπαυται—the perfect indicative from παύω (I stop) is either the middle ("to desist") or the passive ("to be stopped"). The implied agent of the passive is God.

---

2. Life of Sin
4:3–4

Peter recalls that the readers have spent considerable time living in sin. He identifies the people he addresses as former Gentiles who are now set free from "the empty way of life handed down to [them] from [their] forefathers" (1:18).

3. For you have spent enough time in the past doing what pagans choose to do—living in debauchery, lust, drunkenness, orgies, carousing and detestable idolatry.

The apostle does not condone the sinful past of the believers (see Acts 17:30). Rather, he only mentions the time in which the readers lived as worldly people, and now reminds them of the brevity of time. The period of living apart from God belongs to the past. Peter is fully aware that the world and its pressures constantly surround the Christians. He recalls their former lifestyle with which they have broken once for all.

The readers no longer go along with their Gentile neighbors who choose to live a life that is contrary to the will of God (see Rom. 1:18–32; 13:13; Eph. 2:2; 4:17–19). What is that life? Peter describes it with a series of nouns that in the original are in the plural but appear in translation as singular.

Living in debauchery. In the Greek, the plural form *debaucheries* indicates multiple acts of unbridled lust and lawlessness; that is, the Gentiles demonstrate a complete disregard for any restraint. This introductory word conveys a general meaning; Peter goes on to list specific sins relating to immorality and drunkenness.

Lust. In the New Testament, this term occurs numerous times and is almost always "used in a bad sense of evil desire."[7] Often it relates to immorality. In only three or four instances does the noun have a good or neutral connotation.[8]

Drunkenness. In the original this expression means "overflowing with wine." It points to the excess consumption of wine that characterizes a drunkard.

Orgies. Here is a telling definition of the term *orgies:* "A nocturnal and riotous procession of half-drunken and frolicsome fellows who after supper parade through the streets with torches and music in honor of Bacchus

---

7. Hans Schönweiss, *NIDNTT*, vol. 1, p. 457. Also see Friedrich Büchsel, *TDNT*, vol. 3, p. 170.
8. "In the Greek, the noun is found in a neutral or good sense only in Lk. 22:15; Phil. 1:23; 1 Thess. 2:17 and perhaps Rev. 18:14." Schönweiss, ibid.

or some other deity, and sing and play before the houses of their male and female friends."[9]

Carousing. The Greek word translated "carousing" signifies a drinking party, "not of necessity excessive, but giving opportunity to excess."[10]

Detestable idolatry. By worshiping the creature instead of the Creator, the sinner transgresses God's command not to have other gods before him (Exod. 20:3; Deut. 5:7). With respect to this sin, John Albert Bengel observes that "the most sacred law of God is violated."[11] Moreover, in that time idol worship resulted in immorality and intemperance. For this reason Peter calls idolatry detestable.

Peter provides a detailed list of sins; these sins are mentioned in other New Testament passages as well (Rom. 13–14; Gal. 5:20–21). He describes the life of worldly persons, who consider Christians strange and out of step with society.

4. They think it strange that you do not plunge with them into the same flood of dissipation, and they heap abuse on you.

a. "They think it strange." In a world of sin, Christians are strangers, especially if they were formerly part of that world. They do not feel at home anymore in an environment that is alien to them. The consequence is that the world is shocked by the strange behavior of the Christians (compare Acts 17:20). Because of the Christians' conduct, the world reacts and takes offense.

b. "You do not plunge with them." The Greek has the verb form *you do not run*, which in the New International Version is translated "plunge." This translation hinges on the phrase *into the same flood* that completes the sentence. The text expresses the thought of associating with bad companions (see the parallel in Ps. 50:18). The Greek verb in this clause is in the present tense, which indicates that the readers are not going along with the world. They seek to do God's will.

c. "Flood of dissipation." The word *flood* indicates an overflowing or pouring out of a substance that springs up and flows down as lava from the crater of a volcano. The term translated "dissipation" actually means "incorrigibility."

d. "They heap abuse on you." The estrangement between the people of the world and the Christian results in a campaign of insult and slander against the believer. As Peter comments, "[They] speak maliciously against your good behavior in Christ" (3:16; also compare James 2:7). Friendships that Christians had enjoyed before their conversion now have turned into

---

9. Thayer, p. 367. Also consult R. C. Trench, *Synonyms of the New Testament* (1854; Grand Rapids: Eerdmans, 1953), p. 226.

10. Trench, ibid., p. 225.

11. John Albert Bengel, *Gnomon of the New Testament*, ed. Andrew R. Fausset, trans. William Fletcher, 7th ed., 5 vols. (Edinburgh: Clark, 1877), vol. 5, p. 74. And consult E. G. Selwyn, *The First Epistle of St. Peter: The Greek Text with Introduction, Notes, and Essays* (London: Macmillan, 1946), p. 212.

fierce hatred directed against them. Christians, however, take comfort in Jesus' word: "If the world hates you, keep in mind that it hated me first" (John 15:18).

Practical Considerations in 4:3–4

If we move from the first century to our age, from an ancient community to a modern society, nothing changes with respect to the world's hostility toward the Christian. Worldly people are shocked when a Christian abstains while they revel and consume quantities of strong drink. They are offended because, in their opinion, the Christian refuses to be sociable. They do not see anything wrong in viewing perverted movies. They register annoyed surprise when the Christian makes his objections known by refusing to visit theaters that show X-rated films or to watch pornographic films on television. To them the Christian is an object of scorn, ridicule, and laughter. Whenever they have an opportunity to abuse him, they will do so.

However, the worldly person is to be pitied, for he is swept along by the destructive forces of evil. At the end of his life he must stand before his Maker, who is not his redeemer but his judge. The author of Hebrews writes about the unbeliever when he observes, "It is a dreadful thing to fall into the hands of the living God" (10:31).

Greek Words, Phrases, and Constructions in 4:3–4

Verse 3

παρεληλυθώς—the perfect active participle of the verb παρέρχομαι (I pass by) reveals that the time (χρόνος) of ignorance belongs to the past. Note, then, that the perfect tense occurs three times in this verse. Besides the participle see the perfect middle infinitive (κατειργάσθαι) and the perfect middle participle (πεπορευμένους). The perfect indicates a completed process.[12]

ἀσελγείαις—all the nouns in the series are without the definite article to stress their qualitative nature.[13] All of them appear in the plural to indicate that the sinful acts are repeated.

Verse 4

συντρεχόντων—from the verb συντρέχω (I run together), this present active participle is part of the genitive absolute construction. The participle denotes cause ("because you do not run with them").

ἀσωτίας—the negative ἀ (not) precedes the word σωτία, which derives from σῴζω (I save). The word signifies an abandoned life and incorrigibility.

---

12. Refer to H. E. Dana and Julius R. Mantey, *A Manual Grammar of the Greek New Testament* (1927; New York: Macmillan, 1967), p. 203.
13. Consult Friedrich Blass and Albert Debrunner, *A Greek Grammar of the New Testament and Other Early Christian Literature,* trans. and rev. Robert Funk (Chicago: University of Chicago Press, 1961), sec. 460.2.

ἀνάχυσιν—the compound noun from ἀναχέω (I pour forth) has a -σις ending that suggests process.

---

3. Judgment
4:5-6

Throughout his epistle Peter comforts and encourages the people to whom he writes. As a caring pastor, he knows their hardships and is acquainted with the persecutions they endure. He understands their plight and knows their lot as they face harassment and verbal abuse. Peter tells them that their opponents must appear before Christ, who calls the adversaries to give account of their words and deeds.

5. But they will have to give account to him who is ready to judge the living and the dead.

Peter's reference to the judge fits in with his teaching about the end of time and the judgment day. For example, he instructs the readers that salvation "is ready to be revealed in the last time" (1:5). He describes God as Father, "who judges each man's work" (1:17) and who "judges justly" (2:23).[14]

a. "They will have to give account." The wording pertains to the world of bookkeeping and appears frequently in the New Testament. To mention only one instance: Jesus told the Pharisees, "Men will have to give account on the day of judgment for every careless word they have spoken" (Matt. 12:36).[15] Peter writes the verb in the future tense ("will have to give") that expresses necessity. The opponents must appear before the judge and cannot hide.

b. "Ready to judge the living and the dead." Here is a proverbial saying that originated in the early Christian community. Peter incorporates it in his sermon preached in the house of Cornelius (Acts 10:42). Paul employs it in his letter to the Romans (14:9) and in his second epistle to Timothy (4:1).

Who is the judge? In the context of Peter's epistle God is the judge (1:17; 2:23). But in his sermon delivered before Cornelius, Peter designates Christ the judge (Acts 10:42), as does Paul in his epistles (Rom. 14:9; II Tim. 4:1). Accordingly, in view of still more passages (see John 5:22, 27; Acts 17:31), the evidence shows that the Father delegates judgment to Christ.

c. "The living and the dead." Do we interpret these words figuratively or literally? A figurative (or spiritual) interpretation of this text is arbitrary, because the reference is to the judgment day when all people (those who are physically alive and those who have died) will be judged. Therefore, the phrase *the living and the dead* has a literal meaning—that is, it refers specifically to a person's physical state. Also, Peter conveys the message that no one, whether he is living or has died, is able to escape the judge.

---

14. Eschatological references occur in 1:7; 2:12; 4:5, 13, 17; 5:4, 10.
15. See also Luke 16:2; Acts 19:40; Rom. 14:12; Heb. 13:17.

6. For this is the reason the gospel was preached even to those who are now dead, so that they might be judged according to men in regard to the body, but live according to God in regard to the spirit.

This text presents a number of difficulties that have given rise to different interpretations. Let us begin with the first word.

a. "For." Some interpreters link this word to the immediately preceding sentence (v. 5).[16] However, the conjunction *for*, together with the following words *this is the reason*, explains not the clause that Christ will judge the living and the dead. Rather, in view of the broader context, the conjunction relates to Christ's judgment on the adversaries and his justification of the believers.[17] To be exact, the word *for* points forward to the "so that" clause in the last half of verse 6, where Peter mentions judgment and life.

b. "The gospel was preached." By means of the impersonal verb in the Greek ("it was preached"), Peter specifies that he is not interested in the content of the proclamation or even in the persons who preach the gospel. He is interested only in the fact that preaching occurred. Observe that Peter writes the past tense of the verb *to preach* to show that he is speaking of an event that happened in the past. The choice of the past tense is significant because of the next phrase.

c. "Even to those who are now dead." What do these words mean? In the course of time, scholars have provided at least four interpretations for this part of the verse.[18]

First, the word *dead* refers to Christ's descent into hell to preach the gospel to all the dead who either had never heard or had rejected the Good News while they were living. However, in the parable of the rich man and Lazarus Jesus teaches that an unbridgeable chasm has been fixed between heaven and hell (Luke 16:26; also see Heb. 9:27). Scripture nowhere teaches that Christ makes salvation available to a sinner after death. Biblical teaching, therefore, contradicts this interpretation.

Next, the dead are the believers of the Old Testament era, who, because they did not live during New Testament times, had to wait for Christ to proclaim the gospel to them. Proponents of this view see similarities between 3:19 and 4:6. We demur. The word choice in both verses differs considerably, even more in the Greek than in translation. For example, Christ "made his proclamation to the imprisoned spirits" (3:19, NEB), and "the gospel was preached even to those who are now dead" (4:6). Moreover, Scripture indicates that the souls of the Old Testament believers are in heaven (see, e.g., Heb. 11:5, 16, 40; 12:23).

Third, about A.D. 200, Clement of Alexandria suggested that the text

---

16. Consult, e.g., Charles Bigg, *A Critical and Exegetical Commentary on the Epistles of St. Peter and St. Jude,* International Critical Commentary series (1901; Edinburgh: Clark, 1961), p. 170.

17. Consult William Joseph Dalton, *Christ's Proclamation to the Spirits: A Study of 1 Peter 3:18–4:6,* Analecta Biblica 23 (Rome: Pontifical Biblical Institute, 1964), p. 266.

18. See Dalton, *Christ's Proclamation to the Spirits,* pp. 42–54, for details.

refers to the preaching of the gospel to those who are spiritually dead (compare Eph. 2:1; Col. 2:13). This interpretation has given Clement many followers, among whom are Augustine in the early church and Martin Luther during the Reformation. The objection to this exposition comes from the preceding context (v. 5). If Clement's explanation is right, the interpreter would have to prove that Peter uses the word *dead* in two different senses (i.e., to refer to physical and spiritual states) in verses 5 and 6. Peter, however, gives no indication that he intends a shift in meaning. Also, the tense of the verb *preach* is in the past ("was preached"), not in the present. For this explanation, in fact, the interpreter needs the present tense to indicate the continual preaching of the gospel to those who are spiritually dead. The wording of the text, however, gives no support to this interpretation.

Last, contemporary interpreters say that the dead are those Christians who heard and believed the gospel during their lifetime, but afterward died. The translators of the New International Version have inserted the temporal adverb *now* to help the reader to understand the words *to those who are now dead.* In this interpretation, the expression *dead,* referring to persons who have died physically, has the same meaning in both verses 5 and 6. Although the objection can be raised that Peter should have used a word like "those who have fallen asleep" (I Thess. 4:14), we observe that a writer has the freedom to choose his own vocabulary. Of the four interpretations, the last one is the least objectionable and answers most objections. Understandably, numerous commentators have adopted this last and current explanation of the text.[19]

d. "So that they might be judged." Peter gives the reader a perfectly balanced sentence of (Semitic) parallelism:

so that	but
they might be judged	live
according to men	according to God
in regard to	in regard to
the body	the spirit

Let us begin with the words *so that.* This expression introduces a parallel construction that has led commentators to favor one of two interpretations.

First, the wording *so that* reveals that the persons who are to be judged had the gospel preached to them when they were living on earth. The believers knew that although they had accepted the gospel of salvation in faith, they had to face death. From the Scriptures they learned that God had pronounced judgment upon all sinners. But as believers they also knew

---

19. For instance, R. C. H. Lenski, *The Interpretation of the Epistles of St. Peter, St. John, and St. Jude* (Columbus: Wartburg, 1945), p. 186; Selwyn, *The First Epistle of St. Peter,* p. 214; Dalton, *Christ's Proclamation to the Spirits,* p. 267; D. Edmond Hiebert, *First Peter: An Expositional Commentary* (Chicago: Moody, 1984), pp. 250–51.

that they were set free from sin and would inherit eternal life. This includes all those who died in faith, and is a theologically sound interpretation.

Second, in light of the context, we do well to consider the unjust suffering Christians had to endure in the middle of the first century. Christians suffered at the hands of their adversaries; they were slandered and persecuted.

Now mark the difference in the tenses of the verbs Peter uses. He says that believers "might be judged," which is a one-time act, but may "live," which denotes time that lasts eternally. Moreover, Peter adds a contrast by specifying that those who are dead are judged "according to men."[20] What does he mean? The phrase refers to those Christian martyrs who endured intense suffering at the hand of their adversaries. In the sight of their opponents, the believers received their just judgment by suffering physically.

Peter speaks words of encouragement to the readers of his epistle and tells them that they must view life through God's eyes. Peter contrasts the phrase *according to men* with the phrase *according to God*. The adversaries of Christian martyrs were of the opinion that by punishing the believers, perhaps even to the point of death, they were defeating the Christians. But they did not know that in God's sight believers continue to live in the spirit. Fellow believers observing the injustice which these martyrs experienced, however, ought not to be discouraged. In the sight of God, believers continue to live in the spirit, because "the spirit returns to God who gave it" (Eccles. 12:7) and therefore is immortal.

The Christian knows that on the basis of his faith in Christ "[he] will not be condemned; he has crossed over from death to life" (John 5:24). In a book dating from the intertestamental period, a striking parallel occurs. It describes the lot of righteous men who suffer at the hands of the ungodly:

> For though in the sight of men they were punished,
> their hope is full of immortality.
> Having been disciplined a little,
> they will receive great good,
> because God tested them and found them
> worthy of himself. [Wis. 3:4–5, RSV]

In conclusion, the second interpretation of verse 6b has merit because it fits the general context of this epistle in which Peter at length discusses suffering for the sake of Christ.

Greek Words, Phrases, and Constructions in 4:6

ἵνα κριθῶσι—the particle introduces first the aorist passive subjunctive of κρίνω (I judge) and then the present active subjunctive of ζάω (I live). The contrast is particularly vivid because of the use of μέν . . . δέ. C. F. D. Moule paraphrases the

---

20. Selwyn suggests the paraphrase *in men's estimation. The First Epistle of St. Peter*, p. 215.

sentence in these words: "That they might be judged in the eyes of men [as men reckon judgment] physically, but might live as God lives spiritually."[21]

---

7 The end of all things is near. Therefore be clear minded and self-controlled so that you can pray.   8 Above all, love each other deeply, because love covers over a multitude of sins.   9 Offer hospitality to one another without grumbling.   10 Each one should use whatever gift he has received to serve others, faithfully administering God's grace in its various forms.   11 If anyone speaks, he should do it as one speaking the very words of God. If anyone serves, he should do it with the strength God provides, so that in all things God may be praised through Jesus Christ. To him be the glory and the power for ever and ever. Amen.

F. Practical Principles
4:7–11

Translators have to divide the text of this epistle into multiple paragraphs. These divisions indicate the changes the author makes in the subjects he discusses and help the reader in understanding the text. The connection between paragraphs is not always in the form of "and" or "but" (which in verse 7 many translators omit), but sometimes is a sentence that captures the thought of the preceding section. This is the case in the first part of verse 7, which serves as a bridge between verse 6 and the exhortations that follow verse 7a.

7. The end of all things is near. Therefore be clear minded and self-controlled so that you can pray.

Peter encourages the readers to view life in the light of the approaching end. They should wait patiently and fervently for Christ's return. Even though no one knows when the end will come, Christians should live in ardent anticipation of the consummation.

Many writers of the New Testament refer to the end of time. For instance, Paul tells the Romans to understand their time in relation to the end, because, he adds, "Our salvation is nearer now than when we first believed" (Rom. 13:11). The writer of Hebrews exhorts the readers of his epistle to meet together for encouragement; then he notes, "All the more as you see the Day approaching" (Heb. 10:25). James points to the end of time and comforts his oppressed countrymen with these words: "You too, be patient and stand firm, because the Lord's coming is near. . . . The Judge is standing at the door" (James 5:8–9). And last, John alerts his readers to the fact that "this is the last hour" (I John 2:18). In the early church, then, believers expected the imminent return of Jesus.

Waiting for the end of time to come, Christians ought to demonstrate exemplary conduct. Their lives should be marked by the following characteristics:

a. *Prayer.* Peter writes, "Therefore, be clear minded and self-controlled so that you can pray." Notice that in 3:7 he exhorts husbands to be considerate

---

21. Moule, *Idiom-Book*, p. 59.

of their wives so that nothing hinders their prayers. Prayer, then, is an important aspect of the Christian's spiritual life, especially in the context of Christ's return.

Awaiting the end of the world, Christians should be clear minded (1:13; 5:8; and see I Thess. 5:6) and avoid involvement in a frenzy of preparations.[22] Instead the Christian community must pay attention to the signs of the time and wait expectantly for the approaching end. "The proper attitude in this situation is soberness and moderation."[23] That is, Christians must be self-controlled in their endeavor to be clear minded. They must show temperance in eating and drinking, and exhibit the principles of moral conduct (see II Peter 1:6).

The characteristics of being clear minded and self-controlled are essential for unhindered prayer. Prayer requires effort; then the Christian is able to present his praises and petitions earnestly before the throne of God (compare Luke 21:36; Heb. 4:16). Scripture teaches that failure to pray to God is sin (see I Sam. 12:23). Prayer is the basic requirement for a Christian who desires to lead a life that is pleasing to God and man. Through prayer the Christian first establishes a vertical link with God before he fuses a horizontal link with his fellow man.

8. Above all, love each other deeply, because love covers over a multitude of sins.

b. *Love.* Once again Peter instructs the readers to cultivate mutual love, for in a previous chapter he writes, "Have sincere love for your brothers, love one another deeply, from the heart" (1:22; also compare I Thess. 4:9–10; II Peter 1:7). He prefaces his exhortation to love each other with the words *above all.* In other words, Peter alludes to God's law which Jesus taught in the summary: "Love the Lord your God and . . . love your neighbor" (Matt. 22:37–39). Moreover, Peter refers to the well-known command of Jesus, "Love one another" (John 13:34). And three of Jesus' apostles repeat this command in their epistles: Paul (I Thess. 3:12; 4:9; II Thess. 1:3), Peter (I Peter 1:22; 2:17; 3:8; 4:8), and John (I John 3:23).

Peter qualifies the command *to love* with the adverb *deeply.* This adverb conveys the extent of the Christian's love, for love eases tension and breaks hostility. "Love is capable of being commanded because it is not primarily an emotion but a decision of the will leading to action."[24]

The second part of the verse, "Love covers over a multitude of sins," is an allusion to Proverbs 10:12, "Love covers over all wrongs." Because James in his epistle (5:20) has virtually the same words Peter writes, we assume that the saying circulated as a proverb.[25]

---

22. Consult Ulrich Luck, *TDNT*, vol. 7, p. 1102.

23. Ibid.

24. Edwin A. Blum, *1 Peter*, in *Hebrews-Revelation*, vol. 12 of *The Expositor's Bible Commentary*, ed. Frank E. Gaebelein, 12 vols. (Grand Rapids: Zondervan, 1981), p. 246.

25. Also see I Clem. 49:5; II Clem. 16:4.

What is the meaning of this proverbial saying? Whose sins are covered? The saying can be interpreted in the active or the passive sense. A Christian either extends love to his fellow man and covers the sins of his neighbor or he himself experiences God's love by which his sins are forgiven. Although both interpretations are relevant, in the light of the context (which stresses the Christian's relation to his neighbor) the explanation in the active sense appears to be more plausible. God forgives the sinner who comes to him in repentance and faith (Ps. 32:1). He demands that the forgiven sinner show the same forgiving spirit toward his fellow man (compare Matt. 6:14–15; 18:21–22; Eph. 4:32; Col. 3:13).

Practical Considerations in 4:7

From the time of Jesus' earthly ministry to the present, the question concerning the end of time has been on the lips of man. When is the end near? In the early church, Christians expected the return of Christ in their lifetime. During the Reformation, believers thought that the consummation was at hand. And today, because of current international stress and declining moral standards, people frequently raise the question: "When will the end come?"

Jesus instructed his followers to watch for the signs of the time. He told them, "And this gospel of the kingdom will be preached in the whole world as a testimony to all nations, and then the end will come" (Matt. 24:14). True, the gospel of the Lord Jesus Christ is preached throughout the world, but multitudes of people on many continents have as yet not heard the gospel. For example, the teeming millions in India and China must be told about the love of Jesus. When they hear the Good News and turn in faith to Christ, then we know the end is near.

---

9. Offer hospitality to one another without grumbling.

c. *Hospitality.* In the ancient world, travelers would rely on acquaintances, friends, and relatives to provide lodging for the night. In general, inns were unsafe and uncomfortable.[26] Therefore, travelers avoided inns and sought accommodations with private parties. Scripture stresses the virtue of offering hospitality to the wayfarer. "Practice hospitality," writes Paul to the Romans (12:13). He considers this virtue of such importance that he mentions it in the requirements for anyone who desires to be an overseer in the church (I Tim. 3:2; Titus 1:8). He also exhorts a widow in the church to show her good deeds by offering hospitality (I Tim. 5:10).

Peter knows human nature, for he realizes that at times overnight guests take advantage of a host when they prolong their stay or fail to reimburse him. The apostle encourages the hosts to open their homes to overnight guests and adds, "Do it without grumbling." The writer of Hebrews reminds his readers that by welcoming strangers into their homes, "some

---

26. Refer to Robert C. Stone, "Inn," *ZPEB*, vol. 3, p. 280.

people have entertained angels without knowing it" (13:2). Therefore, we must show kindness willingly and cheerfully.[27]

10. Each one should use whatever gift he has received to serve others, faithfully administering God's grace in its various forms.

d. *Gifts.* In Romans, Paul discusses the gifts which the members of the church receive. Says Paul, "We have different gifts, according to the grace given us" (12:6). These gifts include prophesying, serving, teaching, encouraging, giving, governing, and showing mercy (vv. 6–8; see I Cor. 12:7–11; and compare in context Eph. 4:7–8).

Peter also speaks about these gifts. He informs his readers that each member of the Christian community has received gifts (capabilities) from God. A believer cannot create them or claim them, because he receives them from God, who grants them freely to his people. In short, these gifts belong to God and must be used in the interest of his kingdom. "Each one should use whatever gift he has received to serve others." Gifts, then, must be used for each other's benefit within the community and in harmony with God's purpose and design.

In the second part of the verse, Peter tells the readers that they must be engaged in "faithfully administering God's grace in its various forms." Here is a literal translation of verse 10b: "as good stewards of the manifold grace of God" (NKJV). The word *good* actually means "excellent" (compare 2:12). And the term *steward* refers to a manager who is in charge of his master's possessions (e.g., Luke 12:42; 16:1; Gal. 4:2).

In this verse Peter reminds each person who belongs to the body of believers that the gift he has received is "God's grace in its various forms." The gift itself is primarily the gospel of Jesus Christ that is entrusted to the stewards of God.[28] The gift, however, is not restricted to the gospel as such; it also appears in the form of various capabilities and skills. During the first century, the apostles were "entrusted with the secret things of God" (I Cor. 4:1). A contemporary example is the person who serves God as a pastor. He has received a number of talents either in preaching, teaching, counseling, evangelizing, or administering. However, God grants these gifts not only to leaders in the church but also to all members. Each person in the church has received gifts to equip him for building up of the body of Christ (see Eph. 4:12).

Within the church "no one is to be content with one thing and with his own gifts, but every one has need of the help and aid of his brother."[29] Everyone ought to strive to be a good steward of the talents God has given him. In brief, the church is a veritable storehouse of gifts and talents—never locked but always open for service.

---

27. Consult Calvin, *The First Epistle of Peter,* p. 130.
28. See Jürgen Goetzmann, *NIDNTT,* vol. 2, p. 255.
29. Calvin, *The First Epistle of Peter,* p. 130.

11a. If anyone speaks, he should do it as one speaking the very words of God.

e. *Speaking.* How are God's gifts to the believer put to use? Peter singles out an example to which everyone who has witnessed for the Lord can relate. The pastor, teacher, evangelist, instructor, and anyone who has communicated the gospel can testify to the words Jesus spoke to disciples who would even risk arrest: "But when they arrest you, do not worry about what to say or how to say it. At that time you will be given what to say, for it will not be you speaking, but the Spirit of your Father speaking through you" (Matt. 10:19–20; also see Luke 12:11–12).

The power of the Holy Spirit is at work in anyone who speaks the very words of God to edify others. Any preacher or teacher of God's Word can testify to this indwelling power of the Spirit that is at work when he speaks. That is, a spokesman for God cannot substitute his own thoughts and opinions for the "very words of God." He must faithfully deliver the "living words" he has received from God (see Acts 7:38; Rom. 3:2; I Thess. 2:4; I Tim. 1:11). When he faithfully administers God's grace in preaching or teaching the Word, he experiences a miracle taking place: God is speaking through him.

11b. If anyone serves, he should do it with the strength God provides, so that in all things God may be praised through Jesus Christ.

f. *Serving.* Here is the second example. Peter encourages the believer to put his God-given talents to work. The clause *if anyone serves* denotes the activities of the deacons (see the requisites listed in I Tim. 3:8–13). But it includes any Christian who works in the context of the church and who willingly and cheerfully serves the Lord.

The worker is completely dependent, however, on "the strength God provides." In the Greek, the verb *provide* points to someone who defrays the expenses of something, for example, the training of a choir.[30] The verb has the meaning *to supply lavishly.* God, then, abundantly supplies the Christian worker with the necessary strength to accomplish the task.

Because God supplies every need, his name receives the praise in all things. Yet all this is done through Jesus Christ. Paul teaches this doctrine when he concludes his doxology in praise of God with these words:

> For from him and through him and to him are all things.
> To him be the glory forever! Amen. [Rom. 11:36]

11c. To him be the glory and the power for ever and ever. Amen.

g. *Praise.* This doxology is part of our early Christian heritage. With variations it appears in other New Testament writings (e.g., see Rom. 16:27; Phil. 4:20; I Tim. 6:16; Jude 25; Rev. 1:6; 5:13).

Does the phrase *to him* relate to Christ or to God? This is not difficult to

---

30. See Thayer, p. 670, and Bauer, p. 883.

determine, because its immediate antecedent is "Jesus Christ." In 5:11, however, where Peter with a slight variation repeats these words, the reference is to God. This explanation is of little help, because in another passage (Rev. 1:6) Peter's doxology is used verbatim but the words apply to Christ. E. G. Selwyn observes, "It is then the only example in [the] N[ew] T[estament] (if we except Rom. xvi. 27) of glory being ascribed *to* Christ and *through* Christ in the same doxology."[31]

Whether to attribute glory and power to either God or Jesus Christ is not an insurmountable problem. Both interpretations are acceptable. Furthermore, we see that with this wording Peter acknowledges Jesus Christ as God. And last, the phrase "glory and power for ever and ever" are the words every creature in God's creation sings "to him who sits on the throne and to the Lamb" (Rev. 5:13).

Is Peter's doxology put at the correct place in this epistle? We would have expected him to conclude his letter with a doxology; instead he places it here. Indeed, some letters in the New Testament end in a doxology (Rom. 16:27; II Peter 3:18; Jude 25). On the other hand, writers commonly express their feelings by inserting a doxology in the midst of their document (see, for instance, Rom. 9:5; 11:36). The sum of the matter is that Peter adheres to literary practices that were customary in his day.

Practical Considerations in 4:10–11

Persons who have the gift of speaking are always in great demand. Their schedules for speaking engagements in numerous places are constantly filled. Frequently they are unable to meet every request for their services. Often we look at these people with a tinge of envy.

However, we should never permit envy to control our thinking. As we express our love to God and our fellow man, we should instead communicate to God a desire for greater gifts (I Cor. 12:31). Because we belong to the body of Christ, every one of us has some kind of gift (vv. 27–30). In faith we should ask God for additional talents. And God who takes delight in granting us gifts dispenses his grace in various forms.

God owns all gifts even while they are in our possession. He does not grant us his gifts for our personal enjoyment; he gives them for the benefit of the body of Christ. Talented possessors—and that includes all of us—must be faithful stewards who, by continually extending the benefit of these gifts to others, function as channels of God's grace. Moreover, we as talented possessors ought to be humble; we should realize that we possess only some talents, while God has given gifts that we lack to others. All of us in the Christian church, therefore, ought to serve one another so that we can mutually benefit from the variety of riches God has granted his people.

---

31. Selwyn, *The First Epistle of St. Peter*, p. 220.

Greek Words, Phrases, and Constructions in 4:7–11

Verse 7

ἤγγικεν—the perfect tense of ἐγγίζω (I come near) "refers to the near return of Christ and the imminent end of all things."[32]

σωφρονήσατε—from σωφρονέω (I am of sound mind), this is the ingressive aorist active imperative.

προσευχάς—this noun is in the plural to indicate variety and multiplicity of prayer.

Verse 8

ἀγάπην—note the word order designed to emphasize the various elements of the clause. The phrase εἰς ἑαυτούς (for each other) is between the definite article and the noun. The adjective ἐκτενῆ (earnest) follows the noun and is "the equivalent of a relative clause" ("the love which is stretched out").[33] In its context, the definite article can be translated as the possessive pronoun *your*.[34]

ἔχοντες—as with διακονοῦντες (v. 10), this present active participle has an imperatival sense.

Verse 10

καθώς—this adverb means "as" or "*to the degree that* he has received a gift."[35]

διακονοῦντες—because of the general context, this present active participle has imperatival force (see v. 8).

Verse 11

εἰ—introducing a simple-fact condition that expresses reality, this particle is balanced by the phrase *he should do it*, which is lacking but nevertheless understood in the second part of the sentence.

ἰσχύος—the genitive singular noun from ἰσχύς (strength) is feminine and attracts the relative pronoun ἧς (which) in the genitive case.

---

12 Dear friends, do not be surprised at the painful trial you are suffering, as though something strange were happening to you. 13 But rejoice that you participate in the sufferings of Christ, so that you may be overjoyed when his glory is revealed. 14 If you are insulted because of the name of Christ, you are blessed, for the Spirit of glory and of God rests on you. 15 If you suffer, it should not be as a murderer or thief or any other kind of criminal, or even as a meddler. 16 However, if you suffer as a Christian, do not be ashamed, but praise God that you bear that name. 17 For it is time for judgment to begin with the

---

32. Wolfgang Bauder and Hans-Georg Link, *NIDNTT*, vol. 2, p. 55.

33. A. T. Robertson, *A Grammar of the Greek New Testament in the Light of Historical Research* (Nashville: Broadman, 1934), p. 789.

34. Consult Dana and Mantey, *Manual Grammar*, p. 131.

35. Bauer, p. 391.

family of God; and if it begins with us, what will the outcome be for those who do not obey the gospel of God?   18 And,

> "If it is hard for the righteous to be saved,
>   what will become of the ungodly and the sinner?"

19 So then, those who suffer according to God's will should commit themselves to their faithful Creator and continue to do good.

G. Christian Suffering
4:12–19

1. Glory
4:12–14

Throughout the centuries, members of the Jewish nation had become accustomed to persecution. During the course of the first century, Jews who had put their faith in Jesus Christ even withstood the rough edge of harassment from their countrymen (see I Thess. 2:14). But Gentile Christians had not endured persecution, and for them persecution for the sake of Christ was a trying experience. Therefore, Peter addresses an encouraging word to them.

12. Dear friends, do not be surprised at the painful trial you are suffering, as though something strange were happening to you.

As a pastor, Peter figuratively stands next to the Christians who are experiencing persecution. He tenderly addresses them with the words *dear friends,* which in the original means "beloved." Peter expresses his personal love and interest in the readers of his epistle.

a. "Do not be surprised." In the Greek, Peter uses the same verb as in verse 4. There he writes that the pagan world thinks it strange that Christians do not participate in their riotous living; in reaction to this refusal the unbelieving world heaps abuse on the believers. Now Peter says that Christians should not be surprised when they endure persecution. Jesus warns them that the unbelieving world hates his followers (see John 15:18–19; 17:14; and compare I John 3:13). Therefore, having this warning, Christians should not be astonished when they must suffer persecution.

b. "At the painful trial you are suffering." Many translations have the reading *fiery trial* (ordeal or test). This reading comes from the Greek word which refers to the process of burning. Although the term *burning* can be taken in either a literal sense (see Rev. 18:9, 18) or a figurative sense (*Didache* 16:5), Peter indicates with the expression *trial* that he wishes to convey the figurative connotation to his readers. He is not so much interested in portraying the time, circumstances, and occurrences of the painful trial as he is in stressing the purpose of this trial. With an allusion to the smelter's fire, Peter intimates that as gold is refined by fire so the believer's faith is tested through suffering (see 1:6–7). God wants to test the genuineness of the Christian's faith, for faith in God is "of greater worth than gold"

(1:7). The believer, then, should be fully aware of God's purpose in his life and not be surprised.

c. "As though something strange were happening to you." The Christian should not question God's providence when unexpected suffering strikes him. He should not blame God for failing to intervene in his behalf. Certainly God is in control of every situation and has the power to shield a Christian from impending suffering. However, God works out his own purposes to strengthen the believer's faith through suffering.

Christians must understand that God wants to separate true faith from pretense and uses the instrument of suffering to accomplish his purpose. Christians should apply Jesus' words to themselves:

> "Blessed are you when people insult you, persecute you and falsely say all kinds of evil against you because of me. Rejoice and be glad." [Matt. 5:11–12a]

13. But rejoice that you participate in the sufferings of Christ, so that you may be overjoyed when his glory is revealed.

Notice the following points:

a. *Celebrate.* "But rejoice." With the term *but* Peter introduces a contrast. He places the emphasis on the command *rejoice.* Instead of looking negatively at their suffering, Christians need to look positively to Jesus and rejoice in their lot. Peter says, "Rejoice and continue to rejoice." He is fully aware of the apparent contradiction. (Paul remarks that while experiencing numerous hardships in their ministry, he and his fellow servants of God are "sorrowful, yet always rejoicing" [II Cor. 6:10].) Peter tells the readers that when suffering for the sake of Christ is their lot, they should place their affliction in the context of joy. Rejoice! Here is the reason:

b. *Participate.* "You participate in the sufferings of Christ." What a privilege, what an honor for Christians to participate in Christ's sufferings! Especially in the epistles of Paul, the thought of suffering for Christ's sake is prominent.[36] The apostles are not saying that the sufferings of Christ are incomplete until Christians, too, have suffered. Christ's atoning sacrifice is complete and our participation in his suffering has nothing to do with that sacrifice. However, Christ identifies with his people and when they suffer for his cause, he suffers. When they teach and preach the gospel, when they witness for Jesus, and when they encounter affliction for his sake, they participate in the sufferings of Christ. Then, because of their relationship to Christ, they rejoice and are jubilant (compare Acts 5:41).

c. *Jubilate.* "So that you may be overjoyed when his glory is revealed." In the original, Peter writes a combination of two verbs, both of which express the concept *joy.* The resultant translation is "overjoyed."[37]

---

36. See, e.g., Rom. 8:17; II Cor. 1:5, 7; Phil. 1:29; 3:10; Col. 1:24; II Tim. 2:12.

37. With variations in Greek, the combination of two words denoting joy also occurs in 1:8; Matt. 5:12; Luke 1:14.

Why are Christians overjoyed? Once again Peter directs our attention to the imminent coming of Jesus Christ (see I Cor. 1:7). At the return of Christ, the believer will see the glory and splendor of the coming age in its fullness (refer to Matt. 25:31). Christ is the victor and all his followers share in his victory. Together they participate in Christ's glory (Rom. 8:17). Therefore, when we contemplate the glory we shall inherit with Christ, we are unable to refrain from "exulting, jubilating, skipping and bubbling over with shouts of delight."[38]

Charles Wesley has given us a well-known hymn that captures the joy, adoration, and victory we experience when we think of Jesus' return. Thus, we sing:

> Rejoice, the Lord is King:
> Your Lord and King adore;
> Rejoice, give thanks and sing,
> And triumph evermore:
> Lift up your heart, lift up your voice,
> Rejoice, again I say, rejoice.

14. If you are insulted because of the name of Christ, you are blessed, for the Spirit of glory and of God rests on you.

a. *Insults.* In the next few verses, Peter writes a sequence of conditional sentences. He uses the particle *if* to indicate that he is describing reality. With the clause *if you are insulted,* he is pointing to actual insults to which the Christians have to submit. They meet verbal and not physical abuse from unbelievers.

b. *Name.* Why are Christians insulted? Simply put, because of the name of Christ (compare James 2:7). A common theme in the New Testament is that followers of Christ must endure verbal insults because of Jesus Christ.[39] The concept *name of Christ* includes the ministry of preaching, teaching, baptizing, praying, and healing. The apostles spoke in the name of Christ and demonstrated in word and deed that Jesus had delegated his power and authority to them (for example, see Acts 4:7–12). Because Christians confessed the name of Jesus Christ among Jews and Gentiles, they were mercilessly persecuted (see Acts 5:41; 9:16; 15:26). In the early Christian community the single word *name* was synonymous with the Christian religion.[40]

c. *Beatitude.* Twice in this epistle Peter writes, "You are blessed." Both beatitudes are in the context of suffering (3:14; 4:14). Here the beatitude

---

38. Lenski, *Interpretation of the Epistles*, p. 204.
39. See especially Matt. 5:11–12; Luke 6:22; John 15:18–20; Acts 5:41; 9:16; 14:22; 15:26; 21:13; Rom. 8:17; II Cor. 1:5; Phil. 3:10; II Tim. 3:12; Rev. 2:3; 3:8.
40. Refer to Gerald F. Hawthorne, "Name," *ISBE*, vol. 3, p. 482; Walter C. Kaiser, "Name," *ZPEB*, vol. 4, pp. 365–66.

forms the second part of a conditional sentence. If the harsh reality of verbal abuse is the one side of the proverbial coin, the reward of heavenly bliss is the other side. In his Sermon on the Mount, Jesus explains the term *blessed* in these words: "Rejoice and be glad, because great is your reward in heaven" (Matt. 5:12).

d. *Spirit.* This last part of the verse is difficult to explain. First, the text itself shows variations in the New King James Version, which has the reading, "For the Spirit of glory and of God rests upon you. On their part He is blasphemed, but on your part He is glorified" (also see the KJV). All other translations delete the second sentence. The New International Version has this translation: "For the Spirit of glory and of God rests on you." At least two translations have another addition: "the Spirit of glory and power" (*Moffatt* and RSV [margin]). Although this addition has the support of several textual witnesses, translators generally tend to avoid it.

We also face grammatical difficulties in interpreting this part of the text. The literal wording of the text ("the spirit of glory and the Spirit of God rests on you") has a double subject with a verb in the singular. Evidently the context demands that we supply the word *spirit* for the first part, so that we read, "the spirit of glory." But is this spirit of glory different from or identical to the Spirit of God? Explanations of this sentence vary.

e. *Interpretations.* First, note that the last part of verse 14 is a quotation from Isaiah 11:2, "The Spirit of the LORD will rest on him." Because Isaiah prophesies about Christ in this text, some commentators have deduced that Peter is implicitly referring to the Trinity.[41] In other words, the phrase *spirit of glory* points to Christ (compare John 1:14). Thus, both the Spirit of Christ and the Spirit of God rest upon the individual Christian.

Another explanation is that the term *glory* is a reminder of the glory of God filling the tabernacle in the desert (Exod. 40:34–35). Thus the phrase *glory of God* is descriptive of the Spirit of God. A Jewish Christian reader, then, would understand the term as a suitable description of the presence of God.[42]

A third interpretation is to identify the word *spirit* and make its repetition explanatory. This repetition appears either as an expansion, "the Spirit of glory, yes, the Spirit of God, is resting on you" (MLB); or as a relative clause, "that glorious Spirit which is the Spirit of God is resting upon you" (NEB).

In the context of suffering for the name of Christ and the mention of Christ's glory (v. 13), the first explanation has merit indeed. The suffering Christian knows that the Spirit of (the glorious) Christ and of God is resting upon him.[43]

---

41. Lenski writes, "We have the entire Trinity: God—his Spirit—Christ, all are connected with us." *Interpretation of the Epistles,* p. 206. Also see Bengel, *Gnomon of the New Testament,* vol. 5, p. 77.

42. See Selwyn, *The First Epistle of St. Peter,* p. 223.

43. Refer to Gerhard Kittel, *TDNT,* vol. 2, p. 251.

Greek Words, Phrases, and Constructions in 4:12–14

Verse 12

ξενίζεσθε—from the verb ξενίζω (I entertain; surprise), the present passive imperative signifies that the readers are indeed surprised (compare 4:4).

πυρώσει—this noun in the dative singular shows process because of the -σις ending of the nominative πύρωσις (a burning). For emphasis, the prepositional phrase ἐν ὑμῖν (among you) appears between the definite article and the noun.

ξένου—the adjective ξένος (strange; new) is substantivized. It is in the genitive case because of the genitive absolute construction.

Verse 13

τοῦ Χριστοῦ—the genitive is subjective.

ἀγαλλιώμενοι—with the verb χαρῆτε, which is the aorist active subjunctive (from χαίρω, I rejoice), this present middle participle strengthens the verb *to rejoice*.

Verse 14

εἰ—the particle introduces a simple-fact conditional sentence. Peter states a fact and thus describes reality. The apodosis lacks the verb *to be*, which the reader must supply.

τό—both definite articles must be taken with the noun πνεῦμα (spirit).

---

2. Name
4:15–16

Peter expands his teaching on suffering by telling his readers to avoid punishment that the sufferer justly deserves. But if a Christian suffers unjustly because of Jesus' name, he ought not to be ashamed. Hence Peter looks at suffering from two aspects: the guilty party and the innocent party.

15. If you suffer, it should not be as a murderer or thief or any other kind of criminal, or even as a meddler.

a. "If you suffer." In an earlier context Peter teaches that God sends governors to punish those people who do wrong (2:14). Paul, too, teaches that a ruler "does not bear the sword for nothing," but to punish the wrongdoer (Rom. 13:4).

Peter mentions three categories: the murderer, the thief, and the evildoer. He implies that for someone to be so designated he must engage in criminal activities that are punishable by law. He warns that a Christian ought to live such an exemplary life that he can never be classified as a criminal who is guilty before a court of law. Perhaps the warning reflects the earlier life of the Christians to whom he is writing this letter. Now they are no longer part of the world. However, should they suffer for criminal deeds, they would no longer be a testimony for Christ.

177

b. "Or even as a meddler." Peter adds still another category: *meddler*. Because this word appears only once in Greek literature (including the New Testament), scholars are not certain of its meaning.[44] In fact, translations range from "meddler" (NIV, MLB) to "spy" (*Phillips*), "informer" (JB), "revolutionary" (*Moffatt*), and "embezzler."[45] We assume that Peter advises the reader not to be a busybody. By interfering in the lives of others, a meddler disrupts the peace and harmony in the local church and community.

16. However, if you suffer as a Christian, do not be ashamed, but praise God that you bear that name.

a. "As a Christian." The contrast between the preceding verse and this one is marked by the adversative *however*. Peter indicates that the suffering which a Christian at times experiences is not because of criminal activities or misdemeanors. When a Christian suffers persecution, he must have a clear conscience, so that he is able to defend himself without shame.

The name *Christian* occurs three times in the New Testament. During the early years of the fifth decade, believers "were called Christians first at Antioch" (Acts 11:26). They were known as followers of Christ and as the verb *called* indicates, the name did not originate with the believers but with "the unconverted population of Antioch."[46] Before that time, Christians described themselves as "disciples" (e.g., Acts 6:1), "believers" (see Acts 4:32), and those "who belonged to the Way" (Acts 9:2).

Some fifteen years after the name *Christian* was first used in Antioch, Herod Agrippa II asked Paul, "Do you think that in such a short time you can persuade me to be a Christian?" (Acts 26:28). The use of this name seems to have evoked ridicule rather than respect.[47] Moreover, its use spread rapidly throughout the Roman Empire. When Peter wrote his epistle, presumably from Rome, the term *Christian* appears to have been well known among the Gentiles. Peter composed his letter when the persecutions instigated by Nero were at hand and the name *Christian* was an accusation. Two Roman historiographers, Tacitus and Suetonius, report on Nero's cruelties toward Christians after the burning of Rome in A.D. 64. Tacitus writes, "Nero substituted as culprits, and punished with the utmost refinements of cruelty, a class of men . . . whom the crowd styled Christians." Suetonius comments that "punishment was inflicted on the Christians."[48]

---

44. Bauer says that this is "a word whose meaning has not yet been determined w[ith] certainty" (p. 40).

45. Consult J. B. Bauer, "Aut maleficus aut alieni speculator (1 Petr 4, 15)," *BibZeit* 22 (1978): 109–15.

46. John Dickie, "Christian," *ISBE*, vol. 1, p. 657.

47. Refer to Karl Heinrich Rengstorf, *NIDNTT*, vol. 2, p. 343.

48. Tacitus *Annals* 15.44 (LCL); Suetonius *Nero* 16 (LCL); also see E. M. Blaiklock, "Christian," *ZPEB*, vol. 1, p. 803.

Peter exhorts the readers to suffer as Christians and tells them that they ought not to be ashamed of the name by which they are called.

b. "Do not be ashamed." As a wise pastor, Peter knows the heart of man. When a believer meets scorn, ridicule, and contempt because of his faith, shame often prevents him from witnessing for Christ. Accordingly, Peter instructs the reader to overcome shame.

> Ashamed of Jesus! that dear Friend
> On whom my hopes of heaven depend!
> No; when I blush, be this my shame,
> That I no more revere His name.
> —Joseph Grigg

c. "Praise God that you bear that name." The opposite of shame is praise. Shame for Jesus turns a man into a coward, but praise for God makes a man bold. The apostle, who personally had denied Jesus three times in succession (Matt. 26:69–75), now urges his readers to praise God in the face of suffering for Christ (Acts 5:41).

What is the meaning of the term *name*? It refers either to Christ (as is evident from the broader context—"If you are insulted because of the name of Christ" [v. 14]) or to the believer who bears the name *Christian*. Because of the significance of the name *Christian* for the bearer, especially in Peter's day, many scholars prefer this interpretation. A literal reading of the text is, "But in that name let him glorify God" (NASB). The phrase *in that name* can mean "in his capacity as a Christian."[49]

Practical Considerations in 4:16

When the Christian faith permeates society, one of its effects is that the Christian name is a title of respect. At times, politicians seeking votes among their constituents point out that they are church-attending Christians. Many people are of the opinion that if they are known and recognized as a Christian, they improve their status and promote their influence in a Christian community.

But when Christians are a minority group in society, they frequently are the objects of scorn, reproof, attack, and even persecution. They take the brunt of the devil's fury directed against the followers of Christ. In the early church, the bold confession *I am a Christian* was often heard on the lips of martyrs.[50] In their suffering they praised God.

---

49. J. N. D. Kelly, *A Commentary on the Epistles of Peter and Jude,* Thornapple Commentaries series (1969; Grand Rapids: Baker, 1981), p. 191. Based on a variant reading in the Greek, the KJV and the NKJV have the readings *on this behalf* and *in this matter.*

50. See *Martyrdom of Polycarp* 10; Eusebius *Ecclesiastical History* 5.1.19; Robert S. Rayburn, "Christians, Names of," *EDT*, p. 216.

Greek Words, Phrases, and Constructions in 4:16

ἐν τῷ ὀνόματι—the preposition ἐν "probably connotes 'the sphere in which' " the Christian glorifies God.[51] A few Greek manuscripts have the reading μέρει (matter) to replace ὀνόματι (name). However, support for the variant reading is weak.

3. Judgment
4:17–18

17. For it is time for judgment to begin with the family of God; and if it begins with us, what will the outcome be for those who do not obey the gospel of God?

a. *Observation.* In this text Peter echoes the teaching of Scripture concerning God's judgment on his people and on the world. The prophets Jeremiah, Ezekiel, and Amos convey the message to Israel: the people whom God has chosen but who have sinned against him will not go unpunished (Jer. 25:29; Ezek. 9:6; Amos 3:2). Although Peter's statement resembles the Old Testament passages, we detect a distinct difference. The people of Israel refused to listen to God as he spoke to them through his prophets. Eventually the time for judgment came, when God severely punished the house of Israel and the house of Judah.

By contrast, the recipients of Peter's epistle, who also are God's elect (1:1), endure suffering for the sake of Christ. For this reason, Peter calls them blessed (v. 14). These people receive God's judgment not in the form of condemnation but in the name of Christ as exoneration. Peter writes, "For it is time for judgment to begin with the family of God." What does he mean by these words?

First, the Greek has a different preposition; it actually says that judgment begins *from* the family of God. That is, judgment has its point of departure in God's house and then goes to those who are not members of his family.

Next, Peter uses the word *judgment,* not *punishment.* The readers who suffer insult, scorn, and ridicule because of Christ "are a chosen people, a royal priesthood, a holy nation" (2:9). Christ Jesus endured God's wrath, suffered punishment in behalf of God's people, and therefore set them free from God's curse. That is, God will never punish his elect people, because Christ suffered in their place.

Third, God has made it possible for the righteous to escape condemnation through remission of sin.[52] He brings the righteous closer to himself through adversities, and through Christ he leads them into a forgiven and restored relationship with himself. However, the people who refuse to obey

---

51. Moule, *Idiom-Book,* p. 78.
52. Walter Schneider, *NIDNTT,* vol. 2, p. 336.

the gospel face divine condemnation because of their unbelief. God's judgment upon unbelievers results in their exclusion from God's presence (see II Thess. 1:9).

God's judgment comes first to the family of God; afterward it comes inevitably to "those who do not obey the gospel of God." When the judgment day comes, God will be quick to testify against the wicked (see Mal. 3:5). In view of God's judgment on the righteous and the unrighteous, Peter asks his readers a rhetorical question: "If the time of judgment has come for those who suffer for the sake of Christ, what is the lot of unbelievers who eventually will suffer as a result of their disobedience?"

18. And,

> **"If it is hard for the righteous to be saved,**
> **what will become of the ungodly and the sinner?"**

b. *Quotation.* As he does in many other places, Peter strengthens his teaching by quoting from the Old Testament. Here he quotes the Septuagint version of Proverbs 11:31, which differs somewhat from the Hebrew text, "If the righteous receive their due on earth, how much more the ungodly and the sinner!" The intent of the passage, however, is the same.

The first part of the conditional sentence reveals simple-fact reality. Peter uses this statement to point out the difficulty Christians have in obtaining salvation, for he knows that Jesus said, "Small is the gate and narrow the road that leads to life, and only a few find it" (Matt. 7:14). Paul encouraged the Christians in Asia Minor with these words: "We must go through many hardships to enter the kingdom of God" (Acts 14:22).

The key word in this first part is the term *hard.* Another translation is "with difficulty" (NASB). This word appears a few times in Acts, where Luke describes the difficulty Paul and Barnabas encountered in preventing the crowd in Lystra from offering sacrifices to them (Acts 14:18). In another setting, Luke uses the term to relate the difficulty the sailors had in keeping their ship on course (Acts 27:7, 8, 16). The term, then, portrays hard work.

In his epistle to the Philippians, Paul instructs the readers: "Continue to work out your salvation with fear and trembling" (2:12). He adds that "it is God who works in you to will and to act according to his good purpose" (v. 13). That is, man cannot earn his salvation, for it is a gift of God. Man's salvation, however, is a process of spiritual development and growth in knowing Jesus Christ as Savior. In this process man must exert himself to the utmost of his abilities.

"What will become of the ungodly and the sinner?" Here is a saying of Jesus that parallels this verse: "For if men do these things when the tree is green, what will happen when it is dry?" (Luke 23:31).

The writer of this quote employs two terms to describe the unbeliever. He first calls him "ungodly" to indicate that this person neither worships nor loves God, and then "sinner" to show that the wicked man transgresses

God's commands.[53] The quotation ends as a rhetorical question so that the reader can supply the self-evident answer.

Greek Words, Phrases, and Constructions in 4:17–18

Verse 17

καιρός—differing from χρόνος (time in general), this noun expresses "a limited portion of time, with the added notion of suitableness."[54]

τοῦ ἄρξασθαι—the articular infinitive in the genitive case modifies the noun καιρός, "the time is come."[55]

ἀπειθούντων—note the present active tense of this participle derived from ἀπειθέω (I refuse to believe and obey).

Verse 18

φανεῖται—this is the second future passive indicative of φαίνω (I shine; appear). The future is progressive.

---

4. Good
4:19

19. So then, those who suffer according to God's will should commit themselves to their faithful Creator and continue to do good.

c. *Exhortation.* Peter writes his epistle not to unbelievers but to God's people and especially those who experience suffering and hardship. The words *so then* introduce the conclusion to Peter's lengthy discussion on suffering. In other parts of the epistle (2:15; 3:17; 4:2), Peter exhorts Christians to remember that nothing happens without God's will, for God is in control of every situation.[56] In particular the sufferers grapple with the question of injustice to which they have to submit. They ought not to lose sight of God's purpose in their lives, for in his providence he will care for them. Therefore, Peter gives these sufferers an extra word of consolation.

Peter tells his readers to fulfill two obligations. The first one is that they

1. "Should commit themselves to their faithful Creator." The verb *commit* appears in the last saying Jesus uttered from the cross: "Father, into your hands I commit my spirit" (Luke 23:46). Peter exhorts the suffering believers to commit their lives into the hands of their faithful Creator. He describes God as "Creator," a term that appears only here in the entire New Testament. He chooses this word to point to God's creative power. Then he

---

53. Consult Calvin, *The First Epistle of Peter*, p. 141 n. 1. Also see Hiebert, *First Peter*, p. 275.
54. Thayer, p. 319.
55. Hanna, *Grammatical Aid*, p. 427.
56. Refer to Donald Guthrie, *New Testament Theology* (Downers Grove: Inter-Varsity, 1981), p. 147.

qualifies the word *Creator* with the adjective *faithful*. God not only has created man, but also sustains him from moment to moment. To this God the believer can confidently commit himself, for God's word will never fail him. With that knowledge, the Christian should

2. "Continue to do good." This admonition occurs frequently in this epistle (2:15, 20; 3:6, 11, 17).[57] Peter implies that the Christian who commits himself verbally to his faithful God ought to show this commitment in deeds of love and mercy toward his fellow man.

Summary of Chapter 4

Peter, basing his teaching on the example of Christ's suffering, admonishes the believers to not live for evil human desires but rather to obey the will of God. He teaches that those people who choose a life of sin and induce others to follow them will have to give an account to God. The believers who are now dead received the gospel for this reason during their earthly life.

The apostle exhorts the Christians to pursue virtues, including self-control, love, hospitality, and service. The objective is that God may receive the praise through Jesus Christ.

Christians should not be surprised when they experience suffering, because they are participating in the sufferings of Christ. They ought to rejoice whenever they are insulted because of Christ's name. Indeed, they are blessed.

Peter warns the believers that no one should give occasion for suffering as an evildoer. When a believer suffers, he should not be ashamed but should praise God that he is a Christian. God's judgment begins with the family of God and then reaches out severely to those who disobey the gospel of God. Peter exhorts the believers to commit themselves to their faithful God and to serve him by doing good deeds.

---

57. Read W. C. van Unnik, "The Teaching of Good Works in I Peter," *NTS* 1 (1954–55): 92–110.

5

Conclusion

(5:1–14)

Outline

5 1 To the elders among you, I appeal as a fellow elder, a witness of Christ's sufferings and one who also will share in the glory to be revealed: 2 Be shepherds of God's flock that is under your care, serving as overseers—not because you must, but because you are willing, as God wants you to be; not greedy for money, but eager to serve;   3 not lording it over those entrusted to you, but being examples to the flock.   4 And when the Chief Shepherd appears, you will receive the crown of glory that will never fade away.

5 Young men, in the same way be submissive to those who are older. All of you, clothe yourselves with humility toward one another, because,

> "God opposes the proud
> but gives grace to the humble."

6 Humble yourselves, therefore, under God's mighty hand, that he may lift you up in due time.   7 Cast all your anxiety on him because he cares for you.

8 Be self-controlled and alert. Your enemy the devil prowls around like a roaring lion looking for someone to devour.   9 Resist him, standing firm in the faith, because you know that your brothers throughout the world are undergoing the same kind of sufferings.

10 And the God of all grace, who called you to his eternal glory in Christ, after you have suffered a little while, will himself restore you and make you strong, firm and steadfast.

11 To him be the power for ever and ever. Amen.

12 With the help of Silas, whom I regard as a faithful brother, I have written to you briefly, encouraging you and testifying that this is the true grace of God. Stand fast in it.

13 She who is in Babylon, chosen together with you, sends you her greetings, and so does my son Mark.   14 Greet one another with a kiss of love.

Peace to all of you who are in Christ.

VII. Conclusion
5:1–14

A. Duties of Elders
5:1–4

1. Appeal
5:1

The message of the epistle is concluded in chapter 4. The remainder of the epistle consists of admonitions, exhortations, and personal greetings. In fact, in the last chapter of his letter Peter is remarkably personal, for he even relates that he is an eyewitness of Christ's sufferings.

187

1. To the elders among you, I appeal as a fellow elder, a witness of Christ's sufferings and one who also will share in the glory to be revealed.
Note these points:

a. *Elder.* In the Greek, the word *elders* appears without the definite article to stress the function of this office. The word *elder* refers not so much to the age (v. 5) as to the task of the person who holds the position of leader in the church (vv. 2–3).

Following the example of the elders of Israel who ruled in the synagogues, elders in the early church gave leadership to local congregations (Acts 11:30; 21:18). The apostles appointed elders in every church (Acts 14:23), and apostolic helpers were instructed to do likewise (Titus 1:5). The apostles charged the elders to provide spiritual care for the members of the church by teaching and preaching the Word; to guard the purity of the Christian faith by warning God's people against false doctrines; and to promote peace and order in the church by setting examples in their own households (vv. 1–4; Acts 20:28; Eph. 4:11–13; I Tim. 5:17). Paul gives Timothy and Titus a list of qualifications for elders (see I Tim. 3:2–7; Titus 1:7–9).

The term used in 5:1 is *presbyteros* (elder), from which we have the derivative *presbyterian*. Observe that in the New Testament the word *episkopos* (overseer, bishop), which gives us the derivative *episcopal,* also occurs. In some passages, these two terms are interchangeable and therefore have the same meaning (see Acts 20:17, 28; I Tim. 3:2; 5:17, 19; Titus 1:5, 7).[1] Notice that Peter calls himself a fellow elder (v. 1; compare II John 1; III John 1). He reveals that he places himself not above but next to the elders. And thus he indicates that an apostle can also be an elder.

Peter writes, "I appeal [to you] as a fellow elder." He intimates that the elders should set an example in committing themselves to God and in doing good (4:19). He does so by directing the attention of the elders to his previous discussion. A few translations, on the basis of a particle in the Greek text, begin verse 1 with the adverb *therefore.*[2] The adverb links this verse to the last verse of the preceding chapter.

b. *Witness.* The apostle describes himself as a fellow elder and an eyewitness of the sufferings of Christ. He points to Gethsemane and Golgotha, even though the Gospels do not relate whether Peter was present at the crucifixion of Christ. Peter witnessed Jesus' agony in the Garden of Gethsemane, the trial before the high priest, and the condemnation of Jesus that caused him to stand trial in the presence of Pilate. In effect, Peter is an eyewitness.

---

1. Ronald S. Wallace remarks, "The word *presbyteros* denotes rather the status of eldership while *episkopos* denotes the function of at least some elders." "Elder," *EDT,* p. 347.

2. See, e.g., MLB, NASB, RV, ASV. Others have the translation *so* or *now.* Still others either leave the Greek particle untranslated (NIV, SEB) or adhere to the variant reading that deletes the Greek particle (KJV, NKJV).

The term *witness* has a double connotation: to see something take place (in a literal sense; see John 19:35), and to proclaim the message of the occurrence (a figurative sense). This term usually is used in the figurative sense; every believer in effect is a witness for Christ. Some commentators accept only the second interpretation and thereby preclude the authorship of Peter.[3] However, Peter himself formulated the prerequisite of apostleship when Matthias was chosen by lot to take the place of Judas Iscariot:

> "Therefore it is necessary to choose one of the men who have been with us the whole time the Lord Jesus went in and out among us, beginning from John's baptism to the time when Jesus was taken up from us. For one of these must become a witness with us of his resurrection." [Acts 1:21–22]

Peter is one who testifies to the sufferings of Christ (Luke 24:45–48; Acts 1:8). He proclaims the message of salvation because he is an eyewitness of the suffering Jesus experienced in Gethsemane, before the Sanhedrin and Pilate, and at Calvary. The context of verse 1 permits the interpretation that he is not only a fellow elder but even a fellow sufferer for the sake of Christ.[4] Suffering leads to glory in which Peter shares.

c. *Participant.* Peter says that he is "one who also will share in the glory to be revealed." From the day Peter followed Jesus, he had seen his glory during his ministry, especially at the time of Jesus' transfiguration (Matt. 16:27; 17:2; John 1:14; 2:11; also see II Peter 1:17). Although Peter writes the future tense *will share*, he already has indicated that the Spirit of glory is resting on the believers (4:14; compare 1:8). A Christian shares in Christ's glory now, although in part, and afterward fully.

Peter alerts the readers that this glory is about "to be revealed." The time separating us from the revelation of God's glory is short. Moreover, Peter notes that this revelation is not a single event but a continuous act. The unfolding of divine glory is an unbroken process.

Practical Considerations in 5:1

When an athlete consistently scores in a particular game, he receives the adulation of the spectators. He basks in glory because he is the hero of the day. But when in the next game he fails to perform according to the crowd's expectations, his glory disappears as green leaves on the morning of a severe frost. Particularly in sports, the glory of the players is transient.

---

3. For example, consult Francis Wright Beare, *The First Epistle of Peter: The Greek Text with Introduction and Notes*, 2d ed. (Oxford: Blackwell, 1961), pp. 25, 172. And see Ernest Best, *I Peter*, New Century Bible series (London: Oliphants, 1971), pp. 63, 168.

4. Refer to S. Greijdanus, *De Brieven van de Apostelen Petrus en Johannes, en de Brief van Judas*, Kommentaar op het Nieuwe Testament series (Amsterdam: Van Bottenburg, 1929), p. 181. And see J. N. D. Kelly, *A Commentary on the Epistles of Peter and Jude*, Thornapple Commentaries series (1969; Grand Rapids: Baker, 1981), p. 199.

A person's physical appearance can be strikingly beautiful in youth and the early years of adulthood. But when the wrinkles begin to appear, youth's glory vanishes. Achievements, in whatever area these may be, often garner glory and honor. Yet they are temporal and soon forgotten. Therefore the Latin proverb is pertinent: *Sic transit gloria mundi* (So the glory of the world passes on).

Scripture, however, reveals a glory that is heavenly, divine, and eternal. Persons who were permitted to see this glory have seen it only momentarily: the shepherds in Bethlehem's fields witnessed heaven's glory when Jesus was born (Luke 2:8–15); Peter, James, and John were with Jesus at his transfiguration (Matt. 17:1–13); Paul on the way to Damascus was blinded by the heavenly brilliance of Jesus' glory (Acts 9:1–9); and John at Patmos saw Jesus in all his splendor (Rev. 1:9–20).

In his epistle Peter teaches that heavenly glory is abiding.[5] This is what he says: we share in the glory that God will continue to reveal (5:1), we will receive an unfading crown of glory (5:4), and we have been called to God's eternal glory in Christ (5:10). The heavenly glory which we shall share with Christ is eternal.

Greek Words, Phrases, and Constructions in 5:1

ὁ συμπρεσβύτερος καὶ μάρτυς—one definite article describes two functions of the apostle: presbyter and witness. The preposition σύν (here translated "fellow") applies to both nouns.

μελλούσης—this present active participle is a substitute for the future tense.

ἀποκαλύπτεσθαι—the present passive infinitive from ἀποκαλύπτω (I reveal) denotes continuous action. The use of the passive implies that God is the agent.

---

2. Serve
5:2–3

2. Be shepherds of God's flock that is under your care, serving as overseers—not because you must, but because you are willing, as God wants you to be; not greedy for money, but eager to serve; 3. not lording it over those entrusted to you, but being examples to the flock.

a. "Be shepherds of God's flock." The imagery is striking in view of Jesus' words spoken at the time of Peter's restoration: "Feed my lambs," "Take care of my sheep," and "Feed my sheep" (John 21:15–17). Here is a figure of speech that Jesus often used. He applied the saying *I am the good shepherd* (John 10:11, 14) to himself and called the church a flock of sheep. He borrowed the imagery from the Old Testament (see, e.g., Ps. 78:52; Isa. 63:11; Jer. 31:10; Zech. 13:7). As Jesus is the "Chief Shepherd" (v. 4), so the elders should be shepherds working under him and caring for God's people, called "God's flock." Here Peter commands the elders to be shepherds while they serve as overseers. They must feed the flock "by discipline and doctrine."[6]

---

5. The Greek term *glory* occurs ten times in I Peter (1:7, 11, 21, 24; 4:11, 13, 14; 5:1, 4, 10).
6. John Albert Bengel, *Gnomon of the New Testament*, ed. Andrew R. Fausset, trans. William Fletcher, 7th ed., 5 vols. (Edinburgh: Clark, 1877), vol. 5, p. 80.

The expression *flock* appears four times in the New Testament: Jesus uses it to calm his disciples ("Do not be afraid, little flock" [Luke 12:32]); Paul exhorts the Ephesian elders to "keep watch over yourselves and all the flock" and to protect it from savage wolves that "will not spare the flock" (Acts 20:28–29); Peter tells the elders to "be shepherds of God's flock that is under your care" (v. 2) and to be "examples to the flock" (v. 3). The Greek word for "flock" is a diminutive form. It is a term of endearment and means "God's precious flock" that has been bought with the blood of Christ.

b. "Serving as overseers." Elders serve by being overseers of the flock. Peter gives them a number of instructions about how they are to do their work. We have the following scheme, put in parallel form to show the negative and positive directives:

not because you must	but because you are willing, as God wants you to be
not greedy for money	but eager to serve
not lording it over those entrusted to you	but being examples to the flock

First, let us consider the negative statement *not because you must*. In the Greek, the adverbial expression which in the New Testament occurs only here means "by compulsion"[7] or "by force or constraint."[8] The desired attitude is similar to that of the person who donates his gifts: "Each man should give what he has decided in his heart to give, not reluctantly or under compulsion, for God loves a cheerful giver" (II Cor. 9:7).

Positively, an elder must serve willingly and spontaneously to please God (compare Philem. 14). He does so freely, with the sole purpose of doing God's will. By doing so, he demonstrates his love and thankfulness toward God.

Second, the prohibition *not greedy for money* is telling, for this is one of the vices the elders should avoid (see I Tim. 3:3, 8; Titus 1:7, and see 11).[9] During his earthly ministry, Jesus instructed the disciples: "The worker deserves his wages" (Luke 10:7). Paul amplifies this thought when he writes about the material support of the preacher. Says he, "The Lord has commanded that those who preach the gospel should receive their living from the gospel" (I Cor. 9:14). And in the pastoral Epistles Paul indicates that elders received remuneration for their labors in the church. "The elders who direct the affairs of the church well are worthy of double honor, especially those whose work is preaching and teaching" (I Tim. 5:17). In the next verse, Paul quotes Jesus' saying, "The worker deserves his wages,"

---

7. Bauer, p. 52.

8. Thayer, p. 36.

9. Also consult *Didache* 15:1 (LCL); and Polycarp's Epistle to the Philippians 5:2 (LCL).

to show that the term *honor* includes financial support. The elders, however, ought to shun every desire to enrich themselves. Should they yield to this desire, they would commit the sin of greed, "which is idolatry" (Col. 3:5). "What is forbidden is not the desire for fair remuneration, but the *sordid* love of gain."[10]

Peter tells the elders not to be greedy "but eager to serve." He says that they must be filled with enthusiasm in their task of serving God's people. They must find their satisfaction in serving Christ, not in serving Money.

Third, as shepherds of the flock, the elders receive their authority directly from the Chief Shepherd (v. 4) through the Holy Spirit (compare Acts 20:28). However, they are not to misuse this authority; hence the admonition, "not lording it over those entrusted to you." That is, Jesus has given them a charge to serve the people of his flock.

The words *lording it over* "speak of a high-handed autocratic rule over the flock."[11] Although Jesus delegates authority to leaders in the church (see I Tim. 5:17), no elder may abuse the power he has received. When Paul writes to the Christians in Corinth, he advances their spiritual stability. Says he, "Not that we lord it over your faith, but we work with you for your joy, because it is by faith you stand firm" (II Cor. 1:24; also compare Ezek. 34:4).

The apostles Peter and Paul never used their apostolic office for personal advantage. They placed themselves alongside the members of the church to strengthen the weak, heal the sick, and bind up the wounded.

Peter notes that the elders are to serve the people who are entrusted to their care. In the Greek, Peter literally says, "not lording it over the lots." The lots are "the various parts of the congregation which have been assigned as 'portions' to the individual presbyters."[12] Jesus, then, entrusts various parts of his church to the elders and holds them accountable to God for the work they perform (see Heb. 13:17). The elders serve God's people not because of natural leadership capabilities or because Peter ordained them as presbyters. They serve because Jesus the Chief Shepherd called them to this task.[13]

Church leaders must "be examples to the flock." Paul instructs Timothy to be an example to the believers in speech, life, love, faith, and purity (I Tim. 4:12; and see Titus 2:7). The elders must induce the people to imitate them in true obedience to the gospel of Christ. Furthermore, when

---

10. E. G. Selwyn, *The First Epistle of St. Peter: The Greek Text with Introduction, Notes, and Essays* (London: Macmillan, 1946), p. 230.

11. Kenneth S. Wuest, *Peter I*, vol. 6 of *Word Studies in the Greek New Testament*, 16 vols. (Grand Rapids: Eerdmans, 1942), p. 125.

12. Bauer, p. 435. Also see Thayer, p. 349.

13. Compare Selwyn, *The First Epistle of St. Peter*, p. 231. And see John Calvin, *Commentaries on the Catholic Epistles: The First Epistle of Peter*, ed. and trans. John Owen (Grand Rapids: Eerdmans, 1948), p. 146.

these leaders faithfully proclaim the Word and live in accordance with it, they enhance the name of Christ and thus strengthen their authority. In short, for the elders words and deeds must be synonymous (compare I Cor. 11:1; Phil. 3:17).

Practical Considerations in 5:2–3

People are slavish borrowers of expressions they do not have in their own tongue. The result is that words in time assume different shades of meaning. Often the original meaning of a word disappears completely.

One such word is the term *clergy*. Today we use it of ordained pastors. We place it in opposition to the unordained members of the church whom we call "laity." Now notice an interesting development in the history of these two terms. The word *clergy* comes from the Greek *kleeros* (v. 3), which in the original means "lot" or in this verse "an allotment of members of the church." In early ecclesiastical Latin, the expression *clerus* signified a congregation and pointed to a group of unordained members. In later years, however, the Latin term *clericus* became the designation for an ordained person; the rest of the people were called "laity" (from the Greek word *laos* or *laikos,* people).

When Peter wrote verses 2 and 3 and instructed the elders to be shepherds of the people, he told them not to lord it over those who were entrusted to their care. But the Greek term he employed to describe the ones entrusted to the elders now functions as a label for the clergy.

Greek Words, Phrases, and Constructions in 5:2–3

Verse 2

ποιμάνατε—the aorist active imperative of the verb ποιμαίνω (I tend a flock) is a constative aorist without reference to a distinct period of time.[14]

ἐπισκοποῦντες—the present active participle translated "serving as overseers" is absent in important Greek manuscripts. Many translators adopt the reading of these witnesses and omit the participle. Because of the internal evidence from the epistle itself (for example, Peter's penchant for using participles), other translators incorporate the words *serving as overseers* (or an equivalent) in the text.[15]

Verse 3

κατακυριεύοντες—note the compound of this present active participle; it is intensive.

τοῦ ποιμνίου—this is the objective genitive: "models for the flock."

---

14. Refer to Friedrich Blass and Albert Debrunner, *A Greek Grammar of the New Testament and Other Early Christian Literature,* trans. and rev. Robert Funk (Chicago: University of Chicago Press, 1961), sec. 337.2.

15. Consult Bruce M. Metzger, *A Textual Commentary on the Greek New Testament,* 3d corrected ed. (London and New York: United Bible Societies, 1975), pp. 695–96.

3. Receive
5:4

4. And when the Chief Shepherd appears, you will receive the crown of glory that will never fade away.

Pastors should never forget that they are directly responsible to Jesus, who bears the title *Chief Shepherd* in this text. They ought to remember that the church belongs to Jesus, even though they faithfully love and serve God's people. They must acknowledge that they serve the master Shepherd, whom they serve until he returns. As Jesus' undershepherds, they guide his sheep to the green pastures of his Word and feed them spiritual food.

Only here in the New Testament the expression *Chief Shepherd* appears. True, Peter refers to Jesus as "the Shepherd and Overseer of your souls" (2:25). And the writer of Hebrews calls him "the great Shepherd of the sheep" (13:20). But in this verse he tells the readers that this Chief Shepherd will return some day. When that day comes, Jesus will bring his rewards with him (see Rev. 22:12).

When Jesus comes, the undershepherds will receive their prize from him, namely, an unfading crown of glory. They accept this trophy as a recognition of the labors of love they have devoted to the members of the church. Theirs is "the crown of glory that will never fade away" (compare I Cor. 9:25).

The Greek word for "fade away" relates to the amaranth flower, which does not lose its beauty and therefore symbolizes immortality. Skillful hands formed a crown of these flowers; the crown then was given to the victor as a token of his glory.

At the end of his missionary career, while in a Roman prison, Paul says that "there is in store for me the crown of righteousness, which the Lord, the righteous Judge, will award to me on that day" (II Tim. 4:8). James also mentions that the person who perseveres in trials "will receive the crown of life" (1:12; and see Rev. 2:10). Touching is the contrast between the crown of thorns Jesus wore (Mark 15:17; John 19:2, 5) and the unfading crown of glory he gives his people. Jesus bore the crown of humiliation so that we may wear the garland of glory. Conclusively, the victim became the victor who shares his victory with his followers.

Even though the translation *the glorious crown* (GNB) is grammatically acceptable, the structure of the sentence in the original stresses the word *glory.* Furthermore, in the broader context this word is prominent, for Peter mentions that he is "one who also will share in the glory to be revealed" (v. 1); and in his benediction he states that God calls us into "his eternal glory" (v. 10).

Greek Words, Phrases, and Constructions in 5:4

φανερωθέντος—the genitive in this aorist passive verb from φανερόω (I reveal) is part of the genitive absolute construction. Mark that the aorist tense denotes single occurrence and that the passive suggests an implied agent (God).

ἀμαράντινον—pertaining to the amaranth flower, "so called because it never withers or fades, and when plucked off revives if moistened with water; hence it is a symbol of perpetuity and immortality."[16]

τῆς δόξης—the use of the genitive points to the quality of the noun. Scholars call this "the genitive of definition."[17]

B. Exhortations
5:5–9

1. Submission
5:5–7

a. Clothe yourselves
5:5

Once again Peter issues a set of instructions and exhortations (compare 2:13, 18; 3:1, 7, 8). In verse 1 he addresses the elders, in verse 5 the younger men, and in verses 6–9 all the readers. In concluding his epistle, the apostle first instructs the elders and then the next generation.

5. Young men, in the same way be submissive to those who are older. All of you, clothe yourselves with humility toward one another, because,

> **"God opposes the proud**
> **but gives grace to the humble."**

Observe these points:

a. *Subjection.* Peter turns to the young men and writes the phrase *in the same way*. In Peter's epistle this phrase may indicate nothing more than that the writer makes a transition in his discussion (see 3:1 with its explanation). The phrase, then, is more or less equivalent to the connective adverb *also*.[18]

Accordingly, Peter first instructs the elders to demonstrate willingness to serve and to be examples to the believers. Next, he tells the young men to be submissive to those who are older. Is Peter discussing first the office of elder and then an office filled specifically by younger men? Although

---

16. Thayer, p. 30.

17. A. T. Robertson, *A Grammar of the Greek New Testament in the Light of Historical Research* (Nashville: Broadman, 1934), p. 498. Also consult Robert Hanna, *A Grammatical Aid to the Greek New Testament* (Grand Rapids: Baker, 1983), p. 428.

18. Bauer notes that when the Greek connective occurs sequentially, it means "also" (p. 568).

Scripture introduces the office of elder (I Tim. 3:1–7; Titus 1:5–9), it mentions no office for younger men. True, in the early church the younger men performed duties in burial services (Acts 5:6, 10); and Paul instructs Timothy to "treat younger men as brothers" (I Tim. 5:1) and Titus to encourage them to be self-controlled (Titus 2:6). But the New Testament provides no evidence that these young men were serving in any official capacity. Therefore, in view of this lack of evidence we cannot prove that Peter thinks of these young men as deacons.

When we consider this verse, we see the clear lines of subordination. The cultural background is evident. The first-century Jewish writer Philo observes that the sect called the Essenes separated the older men from the younger. On the sabbath in their synagogues, "arranged in rows according to their ages, the younger below the elder, they sit decorously as befits the occasion. . . ."[19]

Does the Greek word for "elders" ("those who are older" [v. 5]) refer to function (see v. 1) or to age? Because Peter mentions no specific office for the younger men in verse 5, we infer that he thinks of age and function. The one interpretation does not rule out the other. A word can convey two meanings when a writer provides indications to that effect. For example, Paul confirms such a shift in meaning for the word *presbyteros* in I Timothy 5:1 ("older man") and in I Timothy 5:17 ("elders").

Peter teaches that in the church the elders are called to positions of leadership; he exhorts the junior men to be submissive to them. And he urges these young men to show respect and deference to those who are more advanced in age. By implication, they learn obedience and humility from their elders and at the same time are trained to assume leadership roles in church and community.

b. *Humility.* For both the older and the younger generation, humility ought to be the hallmark of Christian living. Peter writes, "All of you, clothe yourselves with humility toward one another." Is the word *all* restrictive or comprehensive? In the restrictive sense it applies to the younger men, so that verse 5a and 5b form one unit. But this combination leaves the rest of the sentence grammatically unrelated to the preceding. Most translators, therefore, have opted for the comprehensive meaning of *all*. They have combined verse 5b and 5c, so that 5a forms a separate sentence.[20]

"Clothe yourselves with humility toward one another." The Greek gives an interesting description of the act of putting on humility. The word *clothe* means to tie a piece of clothing to oneself. For example, slaves used to knot a white scarf or apron over their clothing to distinguish themselves from

---

19. Philo *Every Good Man Is Free* 81 (LCL). And see Kelly, *Peter and Jude*, p. 205. Compare I Clem. 1:3; 21:6 (LCL).

20. The JB and MLB translate this verse as one complete sentence. The SEB, however, divides it into three separate sentences. And the KJV and NKJV follow the TR and Majority Text with the reading *be submissive* (NKJV) in v. 5b.

freemen.[21] The suggestion is that Christians ought to tie humility to their conduct so that everyone is able to recognize them. Peter exhorts the readers to fasten humility to themselves once for all. In other words, it stays with them for the rest of their lives.

What is humility? Jesus invites his followers to learn humility from him. He invites all those who are weary and burdened to come to him and learn. For, he says, "I am gentle and humble in heart" (Matt. 11:29). Humility comes to expression when we consider others better than ourselves (Phil. 2:3). Humility is one of the Christian virtues, next to compassion, kindness, gentleness, and patience (Col. 3:12). Scripture also warns against false humility, which has the appearance of wisdom and demonstrates its worthlessness in a show of "self-imposed worship" (Col. 2:18, 23). And last, Peter instructs his readers how to live as Christians by telling them, among other things, to "be compassionate and humble" (3:8).

c. *Authority.* "God opposes the proud but gives grace to the humble." Peter supports his exhortation with an appeal to Scripture. He quotes Proverbs 3:34, which in the Hebrew differs slightly from the Greek in wording but not in meaning: "[God] mocks proud mockers but gives grace to the humble." Perhaps this passage circulated in synagogue and church as a proverbial saying, because James also quotes this verse (4:6).

The believer ought to know that God has provided for him everything he needs. "He possesses nothing he has not received, is nothing but for the grace of God, and, apart from Christ can do nothing."[22] Should he attribute anything to himself, he would not only rob God but also meet him as his adversary. Hence, the Christian lives humbly with his God (Mic. 6:8).

b. Humble yourselves
5:6

6. Humble yourselves, therefore, under God's mighty hand, that he may lift you up in due time.

Here is another exhortation in a series of instructions near the end of Peter's epistle. Verse 6 relates to the preceding verse because of the connective adverb *therefore.* On the basis of the quotation from Proverbs, Peter urges the believers to humble themselves. In the previous verse the apostle instructs the recipients to be humble toward one another. But in verse 6, he encourages them to be humble before God (see James 4:10). As man must love both God and man (Matt. 22:37–39), so he must demonstrate humility toward God and man.

a. "Humble yourselves." What does Peter mean by these words? He wants the readers to subject themselves to God in such a manner that they put their confidence in God alone. They should know that God cares for them

---

21. Consult Thayer, p. 166. And refer to Selwyn, *The First Epistle of St. Peter,* p. 234.
22. R. E. O. White, "Humility," *EDT,* p. 537.

and wants them to be completely dependent on him.[23] In the presence of God, man ought to be fully aware of his own insignificance. Indeed, Jesus teaches that when a person humbles himself like a little child, he is the greatest in the kingdom of heaven (Matt. 18:1–5). Jesus himself demonstrated true humility when he, a king, entered the city of Jerusalem on a donkey. He fulfilled the prophecy, "See, your king comes to you . . . gentle and riding on a donkey" (Zech. 9:9; Matt. 21:5).

b. "Under God's mighty hand." This is Old Testament language that describes God's rule in regard to Israel. God showed his powerful hand in leading the nation Israel out of Egypt (see, e.g., Exod. 3:19; Deut. 3:24; 9:26, 29; 26:8). In the New Testament, too, the mighty hand of God is evident. Mary sings: "He has scattered those who are proud . . . but has lifted up the humble" (Luke 1:51–52; and see the parallel I Sam. 2:7). God's hand disciplines some people and defends others.

c. "That he may lift you up in due time." Because of the trials the readers endure, the danger is real that they may lose courage to persevere. Even though God will not test Christians beyond their endurance, they realize that human fortitude has limits. Therefore, Peter encourages the readers and tells them that God responds to their humility with exaltation. God never forsakes his own, but often in the nick of time he lifts them up and gives them the victory. The believer who puts his trust in the Lord knows that God upholds this world and is in full control of every situation. Accordingly he sings,

> This is my Father's world,
> O let me ne'er forget
> That though the wrong seems oft so strong,
> God is the Ruler yet.
> —Maltbie D. Babcock

Although Peter instructs the believers to pursue humility with the result that God may exalt them, he is not promoting a merit system. Such a system, to be precise, fosters false humility. It means that the believer purposely humbles himself to oblige God to exalt him. Peter tells the Christians to be completely dependent on God and notes that God at the right moment will lift them up. (The expression *in due time* also refers to the return of Christ, as Peter indicates in other passages [1:5; 2:12].) Peter assures the readers that they can fully trust God's word, for he invites them to throw all their cares upon God.

c. Cast away anxiety
5:7

7. Cast all your anxiety on him because he cares for you.
Of all the religions in the world, only the Judeo-Christian religion teaches

---

23. Consult Walter Grundmann, *TDNT*, vol. 8, p. 19. And refer to Hans-Helmut Esser, *NIDNTT*, vol. 2, p. 263.

that God cares for his children. In fact, he cares so much that he bids them bring all their problems to him. The Bible says:

> Commit your way to the LORD;
>   trust in him and he will do this:
> He will make your righteousness shine like the dawn,
>   the justice of your cause like the noonday sun. [Ps. 37:5]

> Cast your cares on the LORD
>   and he will sustain you;
> he will never let the righteous fall. [Ps. 55:22]

> "Therefore I tell you, do not worry about your life, what you will eat or drink; or about your body, what you will wear. . . . For the pagans run after all these things, and your heavenly Father knows that you need them." [Matt. 6:25, 32]

> Do not be anxious about anything, but in everything, by prayer and petition, with thanksgiving, present your requests to God. [Phil. 4:6]

Notice that Peter uses the term *cast*. In the Greek, the tense implies that casting is a single act. In true humility and trust in God, the Christian throws all his anxieties on the Lord. The Greek word for "anxiety" means "to be drawn in different directions."[24] Anxiety has a debilitating effect on our lives and results from our loss of confidence and assurance. If we doubt, we assume the burden of worries and thus demonstrate a lack of faith. Therefore Peter urges us to cast our worries on God and to trust in him.

The verb *to cast* signifies the act of exerting effort to fling something away from ourselves. It describes a deliberate act. Once we have thrown away our anxieties, although not our troubles, we know that God cares for us. In both the Old and New Testaments God's promise to care for his children is sure (see Deut. 31:6; Heb. 13:5).

Practical Considerations in 5:6–7

The world regards humility not as a virtue but as a weakness that man should avoid. Just as he avoids arrogance and pride, so he should abhor humility. Humbleness is understood in the derogatory sense of a weak person who is groveling in the dust. Scripture, however, teaches that meekness is not weakness but moral strength. Moses was known as "a very humble man, more humble than anyone else on the face of the earth" (Num. 12:3), and yet served as the greatest leader and lawgiver Israel ever had.

Scripture exhorts us to be humble before God and man. But in daily life, practice often differs from theory. For example, a pastor longs to be the minister of a large

---

24. Thayer, p. 400.

congregation but never receives a call; a member of a church openly campaigns for a position as elder or deacon but never is elected; someone vies for the editorship of a denominational paper but is not appointed. In these cases, pride and self-interest play a dominant role. A humble person knows that not man but God promotes and appoints people to work in the church. The words of the psalmist are to the point:

> No one from the east or the west
> or from the desert can exalt a man.
> But it is God who judges:
> He brings one down, he exalts another. [Ps. 75:6–7]

Greek Words, Phrases, and Constructions in 5:5–7

Verse 5

ὑποτάγητε—this verb also occurs in 2:13. It is the aorist passive (deponent) imperative from ὑποτάσσω (I submit). Because of the inclusive sense of the verse, the aorist is constative. Although some manuscripts include the present middle participle ὑποτασσόμενοι (see 2:18; 3:1, 5), manuscript support is stronger for omission than for inclusion.

ἐγκομβώσασθε—this verb appears only once in the New Testament; it is the aorist passive imperative from ἐγκομβόομαι (I tie) and has a reflexive connotation ("gird yourselves with humility").[25]

Verse 6

ταπεινώθητε—from the verb ταπεινόω (I bring low), this verb is the aorist passive imperative. The verb can be understood either as a passive ("be humbled") or as a middle ("humble yourselves"). Translators prefer the middle.

ὑπό—C. F. D. Moule interprets the preposition to mean location. This is his translation: "humble yourselves therefore [to a position] beneath the strong hand of God."[26]

Verse 7

ἐπιρίψαντες—this aorist active participle from the verb ἐπιρρίπτω (I throw something on someone) assumes an imperatival sense because it is dependent on the aorist passive imperative ταπεινώθητε of the preceding verse.[27]

μέλει—"it matters." As an impersonal verb, it is followed by περί (about) with the genitive ὑμῶν (you). The context, however, implies that God is the subject.

---

25. Robertson, *Grammar*, p. 808.
26. C. F. D. Moule, *An Idiom-Book of New Testament Greek*, 2d ed. (Cambridge: Cambridge University Press, 1960), p. 65.
27. Consult Robertson, *Grammar*, p. 946.

2. Self-control
5:8

The exhortations in the epilogue of this epistle appear to be loosely related. Peter moves from topic to topic: submission, humility, and self-control. And he seems to lack the time to expand on them. He writes,

8. Be self-controlled and alert. Your enemy the devil prowls around like a roaring lion looking for someone to devour.

Peter exhorts the Christian who puts his confidence in God to be in full control of his senses. In two other places in his epistle he urges the readers to self-control (1:13; 4:7). Moreover, he admonishes the people to be alert, that is, to be fully awake (I Thess. 5:6). The warning is clear and crisp: be sober and alert. Be on your guard!

The sentence *be self-controlled and alert* concentrates on two characteristics: self-control is man's ability to look at reality with a clear mind, and alertness is a state of watchfulness and readiness. The first characteristic describes a person who controls his own disposition, while the second discloses his readiness to respond to outside influences. A Christian must always be on guard against both internal and external forces that are bent on destroying him. These forces originate in man's chief adversary, Satan.

Peter calls Satan "your enemy the devil." He speaks from experience, for he remembers the words of Jesus on the night of the betrayal: "Simon, Simon, Satan has asked to sift you as wheat. But I have prayed for you, Simon, that your faith may not fail" (Luke 22:31–32). That same night Peter denied his Lord when he failed to watch and pray (compare Matt. 26:41).

Satan is the adversary who accuses the Christian in the presence of God. The Old Testament provides a vivid illustration of Satan accusing the high priest Joshua, whose filthy garments God changed for clean ones (Zech. 3:1–5; also see Job 1:6; Rev. 12:10). Satan is the prince of this world (John 12:31; 14:30; 16:11); his residence is on this earth and he restlessly moves from place to place. Satan not only controls the whole world (I John 5:19), but also is a slanderer who turns the truth into a lie. He slanders God and man, pits one person against another, and undermines the believer's faith in God.

"The devil prowls around like a roaring lion." In all of Scripture only Peter portrays Satan as a prowling, roaring lion. His simile reminds one of the psalmist's words: "Roaring lions tearing their prey open their mouths wide against me" (Ps. 22:13; also see Ps. 104:21; Ezek. 22:25).

"Looking for someone to devour." Were it not for God's revelation, this portrayal of Satan would strike terror in the heart of a Christian. The believer would have no protection against this fearful adversary. Should he become Satan's victim he would be ruthlessly destroyed.

A Christian, however, has the protection of spiritual armor (Eph. 6:11–

18). When a Christian is fully equipped, the devil is unable to penetrate this armor. Also, Jesus has taught his followers to pray, "Deliver us from the evil one" (Matt. 6:13). And God declares that Satan's defeat is through the blood of the Lamb (Rev. 12:11). Nevertheless, the Christian must always be on full alert "against the devil's schemes" (Eph. 6:11).

> The prince of darkness grim,
> We tremble not for him;
> His rage we can endure,
> For lo! his doom is sure,
> One little Word shall fell him.
> —Martin Luther

Greek Words, Phrases, and Constructions in 5:8

νήψατε, γρηγορήσατε—two aorist active imperatives are written in the form of clear, distinct commands. Both aorists are constative; "this use of the aorist contemplates the action in its entirety."[28]

τινα καταπιεῖν—Bruce M. Metzger defends this reading as original and states that "the others are scribal attempts to alleviate the difficulty of the absolute use of καταπιεῖν."[29]

---

3. Resistance
5:9

9. Resist him, standing firm in the faith, because you know that your brothers throughout the world are undergoing the same kind of sufferings.

a. "Resist him." The parallel in James 4:7 is striking: "Resist the devil." And Paul urges the Ephesians to "stand against the devil's schemes" (6:11, 13). For Christians the state of being alert must continue unabated.

How do we oppose Satan? Peter says, "[By] standing firm in the faith." The Greek word translated "standing firm" means "solid"; that is, in respect to faith the believer must be solid and unmovable. For example, Paul uses the word *solid* when he writes, "God's solid foundation stands firm" (II Tim. 2:19). The word *faith,* however, can be taken in a subjective sense of one's personal faith and trust in God. It can also be objective faith; that is, the body of Christian doctrine. Although Peter uses the word subjectively in other passages (1:5, 7, 9), here the context favors the objective sense. Peter refers not so much to the faith of the individual as to the faith,

---

28. H. E. Dana and Julius R. Mantey, *A Manual Grammar of the Greek New Testament* (1927; New York: Macmillan, 1967), p. 196.
29. Metzger, *Textual Commentary,* p. 696.

or beliefs, of the worldwide body of believers. Thus the term *faith* relates to the teachings of the Christian church.[30]

b. "Because you know." Peter reminds the readers that the Christian church is universal. For this reason the believers must stand together against Satan. The expression *you know* refers not to knowing how to do something but to knowing (thinking about) somebody. In this case, Peter calls the attention of the readers to fellow Christians in other parts of the world.

c. "That your brothers throughout the world are undergoing the same kind of sufferings." Here is a literal translation of the Greek: "That the same experiences of sufferings are being accomplished by your brethren who are in the world" (NASB). Peter does not say "the same sufferings" but "the same kind of sufferings." Perhaps he wants to point to the exact experience other Christians have to endure and thus put it in emphatic form. He conveys the message that the readers ought to see that their sufferings are only part of Christian martyrdom.

In the Greek, Peter chooses the word *brotherhood* to portray the Christian community of brothers and sisters. Peter is saying, "The same sufferings which happen to your brethren are also undergone by you."[31] Christian men and women throughout the world are suffering for the sake of Christ. Because of the fellowship of these saints, this information should be heartening to the readers and should not surprise them (see 4:12).

d. "Are undergoing." Translations of this Greek verb vary, with some translators giving it an active (middle) connotation and others a passive.[32] As some stress that suffering is an experience, others state that through it the sufferers accomplish God's purpose. In fact, the Christian who suffers because of Christ rejoices when Christ's glory is revealed (4:13–14); the time of suffering is but "a little while" (v. 10). In his epistle Peter mentions suffering and glory in the same breath. "Thus the Christian awaits not the *end* of suffering but its *goal*."[33]

Doctrinal Considerations in 5:8–9

Out of the numerous symbols the Bible uses to portray spiritual truths, I select two that appear in Scripture from Genesis to Revelation. They are the symbols of the snake and of the lion. Both of them are descriptive of both Satan and Jesus Christ. The sign of the snake appears in the account about Adam and Eve in Eden;

---

30. Kelly takes the term subjectively and writes that it is "your positive faith and trust in God." *Peter and Jude*, p. 210.

31. Bengel, *Gnomon of the New Testament*, vol. 5, p. 82.

32. Here are a few versions that have the passive: "are experienced" (NKJV); "are imposed" (MLB); "is required" (RSV). And these have the active (middle) sense: "are going through" (GNB); "is experiencing" (SEB); "is undergoing" (NAB); "are suffering" (JB).

33. Burkhard Gärtner, *NIDNTT*, vol. 3, p. 725.

there it depicts Satan (Gen. 3:1–15). In the last book of the Bible, Satan bears the name *that ancient serpent* (Rev. 12:9; 20:2).

Toward the end of Israel's desert journey, Moses put a bronze snake on a pole so that anyone bitten by a venomous snake might look at it and live (Num. 21:8–9). Note that the symbol of the snake in the desert points to Jesus lifted up on a cross so "that everyone who believes in him may have eternal life" (John 3:15).

Peter portrays Satan as a prowling, roaring lion that seeks to devour anyone in its path. However, the lion is also the symbol of sovereignty; first it refers to the tribe of Judah (Gen. 49:9), and then it represents Judah's greatest descendant, Jesus Christ, "the Lion of the tribe of Judah" (Rev. 5:5).

Greek Words, Phrases, and Constructions in 5:9

τὰ αὐτὰ τῶν παθημάτων—this is a peculiar Greek construction designed to stress "the same 'kinds' of sufferings, rather than the same sufferings."[34] Observe that παθημάτων is plural.

C. Prayer
5:10–11

Peter concludes his epistle with a benediction that is eloquent and at the same time touching. He speaks from the heart and from the personal experience of suffering. He says,

10. And the God of all grace, who called you to his eternal glory in Christ, after you have suffered a little while, will himself restore you and make you strong, firm and steadfast.   11. To him be the power for ever and ever. Amen.

What a beautiful benediction! It sparkles in its simplicity, yet in depth it is profound. Every word is significant in this prayer.

a. "And the God of all grace." The connective particle *and,* which some translators understand as *but* to show contrast with the immediately preceding verse, introduces a fitting prayer at the conclusion to the epilogue. In this prayer Peter calls upon "the God of all grace." The wording occurs only here in the New Testament, with the exception of a parallel in II Corinthians 1:3, where Paul writes, "the God of all comfort." Peter intimates that God is the source, the possessor, and the giver of all grace. He mentions the concept *grace* repeatedly in his epistle.[35] The apostle teaches that God's grace is rich and varied (4:10) and is given to those who are humble (5:5).

b. "Who called you to his eternal glory in Christ." The term *call* is not merely an invitation which a person can accept or reject as he pleases. "It is a divine summons."[36] It is a royal command which the recipient must obey and cannot ignore.

---

34. Robertson, *Grammar,* p. 505.
35. These are the references in the Greek: 1:2, 10, 13; 2:19, 20; 3:7; 4:10; 5:5, 10, 12.
36. Wuest, *Peter I,* p. 130.

Moreover, Peter reveals that God calls us to holiness (1:15), to his wonderful light (2:9), to serve (2:21; 3:9), and to eternal glory (5:10). This calling is
effectual and is the consequence of election, by which God chooses, sanctifies, and summons us to obedience (1:2).

Notice that Peter adds the name of Christ when he says that God called
the recipients of his letter "to his eternal glory." That is, God called them
effectively in Christ. God has chosen them in Christ "before the creation of
the world" (Eph. 1:4) and has called them in him in this present age (Rom.
8:30). The good news is that they will share in God's eternal glory (see 4:13;
5:1, 4).

c. "After you have suffered a little while." Peter specifies that entering
God's eternal glory takes place after the believers have experienced a short
period of suffering. The contrast between the brevity of human suffering
and the eternity of God's glory is clear. For the moment the intensity of
suffering seems severe, but it is both little and of short duration compared
to the glory of eternity (1:6; Rom. 8:18; II Cor. 4:17).

d. "[God] will himself restore you." The basic meaning of the Greek word
for "restore" is to repair that which has been broken so as to make it
complete. Paul urges Christian brothers and sisters to restore gently a person who has fallen into a sin (Gal. 6:1). In his mercy, God takes the fallen
sinner and perfects him; that is, makes him what he ought to be. A commendable translation is this: "[God] will see that all is well again" (JB).

e. "And make you strong, firm and steadfast." The New International
Version has a series of three adjectives, but the Greek has three verbs:
"confirm, strengthen, and establish you" (NASB).[37] God continues the work
of restoring man. Says Peter, God makes the believers strong in their faith.
The apostle remembers the words Jesus spoke to him on the night of the
betrayal: "I have prayed for you, Simon, that your faith may not fail. And
when you have turned back, *strengthen* your brothers" (Luke 22:32, italics
added). In the Greek, Peter uses the same word that Jesus spoke to him.

The next verb, translated "make you firm" (NIV), occurs only here in the
New Testament and all of Greek literature. The last verb, "to make steadfast," literally means "to lay a foundation," and figuratively, "to establish."[38] These verbs are synonymous and serve to emphasize the significance of God's work in us. With this prayer Peter encourages the believers,
who experience untold suffering for Christ, and gives them the assurance
that God stands next to them.

f. "To him be the power for ever and ever. Amen." This is the conclusion
of Peter's prayer. Except for the omission of the word *glory* and in the
Greek the deletion of the verb *to be,* this doxology is a repetition of an

---

37. Some ancient manuscripts have four verbs, translated in the KJV and NKJV as "perfect,
establish, strengthen, and settle you."
38. Bauer, p. 356.

earlier passage (4:11). In a few passages the expression *power* occurs (I Tim. 6:16; I Peter 4:11; 5:11; Jude 25; Rev. 1:6; 5:13). Along with other terms it describes majesty and grandeur.[39] It is a term used as an attribute or title for rulers (kings and emperors) and for God.

A verb must be supplied in this doxology. Thus most translators insert the optative of wish: "To him *be* power." Others choose the indicative mood and write either "is" ("dominion is his" [*Moffatt*]), "holds" ("he holds dominion" [NEB]), "belongs" ("power belongs to him" [SEB]), or "lasts" ("his power lasts" [JB]).

The last word in this doxology is "Amen." That is, so let it be! With this concluding term Peter has ended his formal letter. In the rest of his epistle he writes final greetings and the benediction.

Greek Words, Phrases, and Constructions in 5:10

αὐτοῦ δόξαν—the personal pronoun in the genitive case is emphatic; it strengthens the definite article that precedes the adjective αἰώνιον (eternal).

καταρτίσει—notice that this verb and the three that follow are in the future tense. In the compound verb κατά has a perfective force.[40]

D. Greetings
5:12-14

1. Purpose
5:12

The writer concludes his epistle with a postscript. He states the purpose of his letter and mentions the name of his assistant. He extends the greetings of fellow Christians, and he pronounces his apostolic benediction.

12. With the help of Silas, whom I regard as a faithful brother, I have written to you briefly, encouraging you and testifying that this is the true grace of God. Stand fast in it.

We ask these questions:

a. *Who is Silas?* Is he the same person who accompanies Paul on his second missionary journey?[41] In his epistles Paul mentions Silvanus (II Cor. 1:19; I Thess. 1:1; II Thess. 1:1). Is this name a variant of "Silas"? We know that Silas was a prophet (Acts 15:32) and held Roman citizenship (Acts 16:37). "It is hardly to be doubted that this Silas is the same pers[on] as the *Silvanus* who is mentioned in Paul and 1 P[e]t[er]."[42] This person has either two names or a Greek and a Latin spelling of his name. Peter's comment

---

39. Georg Braumann, *NIDNTT*, vol. 3, p. 718.
40. Consult Robertson, *Grammar*, p. 606.
41. See the following verses: Acts 15:22, 27, 32, 40; 16:19, 25, 29; 17:4, 10, 14, 15; 18:5.
42. Bauer, p. 750.

that he regards Silas as a faithful brother suggests that the recipients of this letter were well acquainted with Silas. The word *brother* signifies a fellow Christian. We assume, therefore, that because of his missionary travels with Paul and Peter, Silas was a respected person in the early Christian church.

b. *Who wrote the letter?* Peter states that he composed the letter "with the help of Silas." Could Silas have been the letter carrier? Certainly. However, the phrase *with the help of* implies more than only delivering the epistle. Did Silas compose the entire letter, to which Peter added a postscript? Hardly. Peter states, "I have written to you briefly." He indicates that he is the author of this epistle and that Silas helped him as a secretary. From letters written before, during, and after the first century of the Christian era, we have learned of the common practice of employing a scribe for writing out messages. A sender would ask a secretary to write a personal message for him and often the sender would add greetings in his own handwriting.[43]

Peter engaged the services of Silas, who was skilled in writing letters in acceptable Greek. As Tertius served Paul as secretary in the writing of Romans (16:22), so Silas was Peter's scribe. Presumably, "as a faithful brother" Silas helped Peter in presenting the readers with a letter written in flowing Greek. The term *faithful* conveys the information that Peter and the recipients of the letter can depend on Silas. And Peter speaks from experience. Nevertheless, not Silas but Peter is the author of this epistle.

c. *What does "briefly" mean?* The writer of Hebrews also makes the qualification that his epistle is "only a short letter" (13:22). The implication is that Peter would like to discuss in greater detail the topics he has mentioned in his letter. Because Silas is a faithful brother, Peter entrusts the discussion of the details to him. In the concluding remarks, Silas sends no greetings to the readers as, for example, Tertius does to the Romans. We infer that Peter commissioned Silas not only to carry but also to explain the epistle.

d. *What is the purpose of the letter?* In a few words Peter states his intention for writing. He says he is "encouraging you and testifying that this is the true grace of God." He confirms that God's grace preached by the apostles and accepted in faith by the believers is genuine. He is telling the Christians that they can fully trust the message they have heard from the apostles. Now they can read it in this epistle. The sufferings they endure are severe; for this reason, they need all the encouragement Peter is able to give them. In a summary statement, then, he testifies that God's grace indeed is true.

Peter's final admonition is, "Stand fast in it." This is a command, just as Paul wrote the church at Corinth: "Be on your guard; stand firm in the faith; be men of courage; be strong" (I Cor. 16:13). As the Christians face cruel oppression because of their faith, Peter exhorts them to stand firm.

---

43. Refer to Richard N. Longenecker, "Ancient Amanuenses and the Pauline Epistles," *New Dimensions in New Testament Study,* ed. Richard N. Longenecker and Merrill C. Tenney (Grand Rapids: Zondervan, 1974), p. 287.

Greek Words, Phrases, and Constructions in 5:12

ὑμῖν—grammarians and translators generally link this personal pronoun as an indirect object to the verb *I have written* and not as a dative of reference to the phrase *a faithful brother*. The definite article in τοῦ πιστοῦ ἀδελφοῦ has possessive qualities and can denote "our."

ἔγραψα—this verb in the aorist "refers to an epistle just finished" (compare Philem. 19; I John 5:13).[44]

εἰς—in New Testament Greek, the preposition εἰς (into) often takes the place of the locative ἐν (in).[45]

στῆτε—the manuscript evidence favors the aorist active imperative. Other manuscripts have the word ἑστήκατε, which is the perfect active indicative with the force of a present tense (from ἵστημι, I stand).

2. Farewell
5:13–14

13. She who is in Babylon, chosen together with you, sends you her greetings, and so does my son Mark.

a. *Wife or church?* The language Peter uses in the final greeting is cryptic. To whom does he refer? To say that Peter's wife, who accompanied him on his journeys (I Cor. 9:5), now sends greetings seems highly unlikely. Scholars, judging on the basis of Peter's use of the verb *chosen together,* are of the opinion that Peter is not writing about his wife but about the Christian church in the place where he resided. If Peter's wife had been with him, he would have said, "She who is in Babylon with me." This is not the case, and thus we conclude that the elect church of Jesus Christ is sending greetings. New Testament writers often describe the church in female terms (see, e.g., John 3:29; Eph. 5:25–33; Rev. 19:7–8; 21:2–3; 22:17). Accordingly, scholars favor the explanation that John in his second epistle addresses not a lady but a church (II John 1, 13).

b. *Babylon or Rome?* The evidence for taking the expression *Babylon* literally appears unconvincing. We have no proof that Peter traveled east to Mesopotamia to establish the church in Babylon. In fact, specific information concerning the church in Babylon during the first century is lacking. Also, the suggestion that Babylon is the name of a fortress in Egypt to which Peter sent his epistle appears to be improbable. Rather, "Babylon" is a cryptic name for Rome. In times of persecution, writers exercised unusual care not to endanger Christians to whom they wrote letters. For instance, when John was banished to Patmos during the persecution insti-

---

44. Robertson, *Grammar*, pp. 845–46.
45. Consult Blass and Debrunner, *Greek Grammar*, sec. 250.

gated by the emperor Domitian, he called Rome "Babylon" (Rev. 14:8; 16:19; 17:5; 18:2, 10, 21).

Peter, who mentions persecution in nearly every chapter of his epistle, died a martyr's death near Rome. According to tradition, he was crucified upside down. In short, Peter wrote this epistle near the end of his life, when he probably stayed in the imperial city.

c. *Son or spiritual son?* If we assume that Peter sends the greetings of his wife in Babylon, then his natural son Mark also sends his regards. However, if Babylon is a code name for the church in Rome, then Mark probably is Peter's spiritual son. Affectionately Peter calls him "my son Mark." Whether Peter was instrumental in the conversion of John Mark, son of Mary (Acts 12:12), is difficult to prove. John Mark accompanied Paul as a fellow helper in the spread of the gospel. He stayed with Paul during the apostle's imprisonments in Rome (Col. 4:10; II Tim. 4:11; Philem. 24).

Tradition indicates that Mark, with the aid of Peter, wrote the Gospel named after him. Papias, bishop of Hierapolis (about A.D. 125), writes that Mark was Peter's interpreter and composed the Gospel.[46] Peter calls Mark his son in the same way Paul names Timothy his son (I Tim. 1:2; II Tim. 1:2).

14a. Greet one another with a kiss of love.

The practice of greeting one another differs from culture to culture. It varies from the bow (in the Orient), the simple handshake, and the warm embrace to the kiss. In the ancient East, the practice of kissing each other prevailed not only in society but also in the synagogue and early church. We know that the kiss of greeting was customary among the Jews (see the references in the New Testament). Simon the Pharisee failed to greet Jesus with a kiss (Luke 7:44–46); the father kissed the prodigal son and welcomed him home (Luke 15:20); and Judas kissed Jesus in the Garden of Gethsemane (Matt. 26:48–49). In the Gentile church, the Ephesian elders embraced Paul and kissed him good-by (Acts 20:37). "The kiss in the ancient world was both a friendly sign of greeting and an emotional token of farewell."[47]

In his epistles Paul exhorts the Christians to greet one another with a holy kiss (Rom. 16:16; I Cor. 16:20; II Cor. 13:12; I Thess. 5:26). The adjective *holy* signifies that all those who are in the church of Jesus Christ regard one another as brothers and sisters. Peter uses a synonymous expression by calling the kiss "a kiss of love."

In the middle of the second century, Justin Martyr writes that the practice of greeting one another with a holy kiss was a customary part of the Christian worship service.[48] Scripture provides no evidence that this prac-

---

46. Refer to Eusebius *Ecclesiastical History* 3.39.15 (LCL).
47. Walther Günther, *NIDNTT*, vol. 2, p. 549.
48. See Justin Martyr *Apology* 1.65.2 (LCL).

tice must be observed in obedience to an apostolic command. In the universal Christian church, the matter is part of local custom (the bow, the handshake, or the embrace).

14b. Peace to all of you who are in Christ.

Peter's benediction is a variant of those Paul gives at the end of his epistles (Rom. 15:33; Eph. 6:23; I Thess. 5:23; also see III John 14). The farewell greeting *peace* encompasses the gospel of salvation, because Jesus himself conveys this message to all who believe in him (John 14:27; 20:19). In Jesus Christ we have peace with God and with one another. Although Peter expresses this prayer as a wish, all Christians have this peace in fellowship with Christ.

Summary of Chapter 5

Peter begins this chapter by exhorting the elders in the church to be shepherds of God's flock, for he also is an elder who is responsible to the Chief Shepherd Jesus Christ. He tells them to serve as overseers, to avoid greed, and to be examples to the members of the church. Then they will receive the crown of glory as their reward.

The apostle continues with a few admonitions: he exhorts young men to be submissive, and all the readers to be humble. Peter encourages the believers to cast their anxieties on God, to be self-controlled, and to resist the devil.

The apostle prays a prayer that is eloquent in its simplicity. In it he assures the readers that God will restore them, make them strong, and establish them. He mentions that Silas has helped in writing the epistle and in summary states the purpose of the letter. With final greetings and a prayer of peace he concludes this first epistle.

Introduction

The Second Epistle of Peter

Outline

A. Who Wrote the Epistle?
B. How Does the Epistle Relate to Other Books?
C. Who Received the Epistle?
D. What Is the Purpose of II Peter?
E. When and Where Was the Epistle Written?
F. What Is the Place of the Epistle in the Canon?
G. How Do We Outline II Peter?

T he heading of this epistle is either "The Second Letter of Peter" (e.g., RSV), "II Peter" (NIV), or "The Second Epistle General of Peter" (KJV). For the translator, the choice depends on the text of Greek manuscripts. If we adopt the rule that the shorter reading probably is the more original, then we favor the title *II Peter*. We know that scribes in ancient times tended to add to the text but abhorred taking anything away from it.

Regardless of the exact wording of the title, the book belongs to the category of eight letters known as the general Epistles (Hebrews, James, I–II Peter, I–III John, Jude) that were addressed to churches and individuals. These epistles circulated among the churches.

Moreover, the epistle bears the name of Peter, who is known from the Gospels and Acts as the spokesman of the twelve apostles. In spite of the self-identification or perhaps because of it, scholars have debated the question of authorship. For centuries, they have asked whether Peter or a person assuming his name had actually written this letter.

A. Who Wrote the Epistle?

1. Name

From a survey of books and articles written in the twentieth century, we conclude that this epistle has suffered from scholarly neglect. This neglect can be attributed to a view, held by many scholars, that the apostle Peter did not write this letter. They affirm that a late first-century or an early second-century writer who assumed the name of Peter composed this epistle. Scholars who accept apostolic authorship also have taken insufficient notice of II Peter. Unfortunately, therefore, "the epistle in our canon that historically has been attributed to the apostle Peter has probably received the least scholarly attention in the twentieth century."[1]

The issue scholars face is that they either hold to apostolic authorship or propose that II Peter was composed by a pseudonymous writer. But before we come to any conclusion on this matter, we want to examine the author's own attestation in the opening greetings and in the rest of the epistle.

The writer identifies himself at the outset of the letter. He calls himself Simon Peter, which in the better Greek manuscripts appears as Simeon

---

1. John Snyder, "A 2 Peter Bibliography," *JETS* 22 (1979): 265.

Peter. This latter combination is peculiar; the only other place where the name *Simeon* is used for Peter is Acts 15:14. In Peter's second epistle, however, both names, Simeon Peter, identify the apostle. The name *Simeon* is typically Hebraic and belongs to the aged Jew who blessed Jesus in the temple (Luke 2:25–35), to one of Jesus' ancestors (Luke 3:30), and to a Jewish prophet/teacher called Simeon Niger in Antioch (Acts 13:1).

Whereas II Peter 1:1 has the combination *Simeon [Simon] Peter*, I Peter 1:1 begins with the single name *Peter*.[2] The combination *Simeon Peter* does not appear elsewhere, not even in postapostolic literature. Nevertheless, from a human point of view the author prefers to use the Hebraic form *Simeon* because that name is precious to him.

2. Function

The author introduces himself as "a servant and apostle." The term *servant* is a general expression that in the context of the church applies to apostles and apostolic helpers. More specifically, the author adds the word *apostle* to indicate that he is one of the twelve disciples of Jesus. That is, as an apostle, Peter has received his authority from Jesus Christ, who sent him forth as his representative. As an apostle, Peter presents the message of his sender, so that in his epistle he speaks with Christ's authority. Jesus Christ delegated his authority to the twelve apostles and to Paul to speak in his name.

Peter's letter is an epistle that finds its origin in the authority that Jesus Christ extended to the apostles. Negatively, the expression *apostle* signifies that this epistle was not written without divine authority. Positively, it means that Peter functions as spokesman for Jesus Christ. This term, then, ought not to be taken lightly, for it has bearing on the authorship of II Peter.[3]

3. Examples

Throughout his epistle Peter alludes to incidents that are known from the Gospels. The precise wording differs considerably from the events recorded in the Gospels. In itself this is no surprise, for Peter did not rely on others to provide him relevant information. He was an eyewitness; he could still hear Jesus' words ringing in his ears, so to speak. In his own words he relates the details of these incidents.

One example is Peter's recollection of Jesus' prediction concerning the apostle's death (1:14). Peter would not have to rely on others to provide the

---

2. The combination *Simon Peter* appears twice in Matthew, once in Mark, twice in Luke, seventeen times in John's Gospel, three times in Acts, and once in II Peter.

3. Literature on the subject *apostle* is extensive. Refer to William Childs Robinson, "Apostle," *ISBE*, vol. 1, pp. 192–95; Karl Heinrich Rengstorf, *TDNT*, vol. 1, pp. 407–45; Donald Guthrie, *New Testament Theology* (Downers Grove: Inter-Varsity, 1981), p. 769.

details of this prediction. In fact, the record in John 21:18 was not written until decades after Peter's death. Peter knew that his departure from this life was imminent, and thus he wrote that his physical body would soon have to be discarded.

Another example of Peter's recollection relates to his presence at the Mount of Transfiguration, where Jesus was glorified in the presence of Moses and Elijah (1:16–18). Peter's account differs from that in the Gospels (Matt. 17:1–8; Mark 9:2–8; Luke 9:28–36). In his epistle Peter does not mention Moses and Elijah. He does not repeat his remark, recorded in the synoptic Gospels, about pitching three tents. In the Greek, the words "this is my Son, whom I love; with him I am well pleased" (1:17) vary from those in the Gospels. And the exhortation *listen to him* (Matt. 17:5) is lacking. Peter recalls the words of God the Father that are written indelibly on his mind. Although the author of II Peter could have received his material from an oral source, "it is much more natural to assume that this account is a genuine eyewitness account."[4]

A third example is Peter's acquaintance with Paul, whom he calls "our dear brother" (3:15). Peter places the epistles of Paul on the same level as the Old Testament and thus calls them Scripture. To Peter, both the writings of the Old Testament prophets (compare 1:21; I Peter 1:11–12) and those of the New Testament apostles are Scripture. Because of his apostleship, Peter implies, his epistles also are inspired and authoritative Scripture. Peter was familiar with the content of Paul's letters and expresses his view about difficulties some people have in interpreting these epistles. Of course, there is no evidence whether Paul was alive. Not Paul but his writings are of importance. Yet the appellation *our dear brother* certainly shows that the readers knew Paul personally. Even if Paul had not evangelized their area, he may have visited them.

4. Objections

On the authorship of II Peter only two views exist, and they color the interpretation of this epistle: either Peter wrote the letter or it comes in pseudonymous form from the hand of a forger or a secretary. Scholars who object to Petrine authorship point to numerous problems in the epistle. These problems are significant and merit serious discussion. Even though some writers are absolutely certain that Peter cannot be the author of this epistle, the evidence they present is unconvincing.[5]

Here are some of the objections which scholars adduce.

---

4. Donald Guthrie, *New Testament Introduction,* rev. ed. (Downers Grove: Inter-Varsity, 1971), p. 831.

5. Consult Richard J. Bauckham, *Jude, 2 Peter,* Word Commentary series, vol. 50 (Waco: Word, 1983), p. 159; J. N. D. Kelly, *A Commentary on the Epistles of Peter and Jude,* Thornapple Commentary series (1969; Grand Rapids: Baker, 1981), p. 235.

Introduction

Name

The combination *Simeon Peter* (1:1) is proof that a forger is at work. A pseudepigraphal writer has chosen this combination to make the letter look authentic. Peter is known either by the name *Simon,* or by his given name *Peter,* or by the Aramaic name *Cephas,* but he is not known as Simeon (apart from Acts 15:14). However, the use of "Simeon Peter" instead of "Simon Peter" is more likely to come from the apostle himself than from a forger. In view of the greeting in I Peter 1:1 ("Peter") and the reference to a first epistle (II Peter 3:1), we would expect a forger to use the simple form *Peter* in place of the combination *Simeon Peter.*

Writings

Some scholars think that the wording of 1:15 represents an effort by a forger to link the Gospel of Mark to Peter. But this is an assumption. The text itself is too vague to determine whether the author is referring to the doctrinal statements he has noted in the preceding verses, to a letter that is now lost, or to a letter that he intended to write, but did not. We are unable to determine the nature of the instrument designed to refresh the reader's memory.

A second point to disprove apostolic authorship is the writer's statement that this letter is the second he has written (3:1). The assumption is that the pseudonymous author wants to link his letter to Peter's first epistle. However, if Peter is the author of both letters, the readers would expect him to make the remark as a matter of course. The argument, then, rather than disproving Peter's authorship of II Peter, appears to affirm it.

A last objection concerns the author's reference to Paul's epistles. These writings, scholars say, were not incorporated into the canon until the last two decades of the first century. Peter died during the reign of Nero and therefore he could not have written II Peter. This is open to question, however. For example, what proof do we have that Paul's epistles were not accepted as Scripture until the last two decades of the first century? Paul himself testifies to the fact that his letters possessed divine authority. He tells the Corinthians that he communicates his message "not in words taught us by human wisdom but in words taught by the Spirit" (I Cor. 2:13). Next, Paul positively answers those Corinthians who demand "proof that Christ is speaking through [him]" (II Cor. 13:3). And he commends the Thessalonians for receiving his teaching "not as the word of men, but as it actually is, the word of God" (I Thess. 2:13). The evidence for accepting Paul's epistles, then, points to an early date instead of a late date.

Date

Debate concerning the origin of II Peter centers on the clause *ever since our fathers died* (3:4). If the expression *our fathers* denotes first-generation Christians who have passed from the scene, then the author is writing in the

216

last quarter of the first century. Because the apostle Peter died in the days of Emperor Nero, that is, before A.D. 68, some scholars consider this verse (3:4) proof positive that the letter is pseudonymous. However, already during Paul's second missionary journey (A.D. 50–53), the Christians in Thessalonica asked Paul what would become of "those who fall asleep" (I Thess. 4:13). Paul responded by saying that "God will bring with Jesus those who have fallen asleep" (v. 14). We assume that the question concerning the passing away of loved ones surfaced repeatedly in the Christian community during the middle of the first century.

If the words *our fathers* mean the same thing as in Acts 3:13, Romans 9:5, and Hebrews 1:1, then they signify the Old Testament fathers. And if this is the correct interpretation, then the matter of accurately dating II Peter no longer relates to the eighties and nineties. It is not inconceivable to date II Peter in the mid-sixties.

Style

Even in translation, the reader of the two Petrine epistles notices a difference in style. In I Peter, the manner of presentation is smooth and polished. This is not true for Peter's second epistle, in which the style is abrupt, the wording stilted, and the meaning of many passages obscure. In the Greek, the usual connecting particles that link sentences and clauses are missing. The use of the definite article is infrequent, the occurrence of words that are found only in II Peter but not in the rest of the New Testament is extensive (fifty-seven words), and the "percentage of out-of-the-way expressions" is unusual.[6]

How do we account for these differences in style? In the first century, people often relied on secretaries to assist them in writing letters or documents. In Paul's epistle to the Romans, Tertius acknowledges that he wrote this letter (Rom. 16:22). Peter informs the readers that Silas (Silvanus) assisted him in the writing of his first epistle (5:12). Granted that Peter refrains from mentioning the name of a scribe in his second letter, the probability that Peter received assistance is not at all implausible.

Church fathers of the first two centuries mention names of persons who assisted Peter in his writings. For instance, Papias, bishop of Hierapolis near Colosse (A.D. 125), who had been a disciple of John, says that Mark became Peter's interpreter.[7] And Clement of Alexandria, who lived from the middle of the second century to the second decade of the third century, mentions one of Peter's scribes whom he calls Glaucias.[8] The difference in

---

6. Joseph B. Mayor, *The Epistle of St. Jude and the Second Epistle of St. Peter: Greek Text with Introduction and Notes* (1907; Grand Rapids: Baker, 1965), p. lxiv.

7. Eusebius *Ecclesiastical History* 3.39.15 (LCL). Also see Irenaeus *Against Heresies* 3.1.1.

8. Clement of Alexandria *Stromata* 7.17 (LCL). Consult Michael Green, *The Second Epistle General of Peter, and the General Epistle of Jude: An Introduction and Commentary,* Tyndale New Testament Commentaries (Grand Rapids: Eerdmans, 1968), p. 17.

the style of the two Petrine epistles may be attributed to two scribes. But because Peter is silent on the use of a secretary for his second epistle, we will never attain certainty in this matter.

Secretary

Some scholars assert that II Peter was written by a secretary decades after the death of the apostle. They base their theory on the time difference they see in 1:13 and 15. They claim that a secretary who speaks in the name of Peter writes, "I think it is right to refresh your memory as long as I live in the tent of this body" (v. 13). Here the scribe is speaking about Peter's active ministry. But in verse 15, Peter's secretary is putting words on Peter's lips to reflect the passing of time: "And I will make every effort to see that after my departure you will always be able to remember these things." In verse 15, therefore, the reference is to Peter's death.

Scholars assume that a secretary is composing a testament for Peter after the apostle's death and that he is speaking on the authority of Peter. Even though the link between Peter and the secretary is explained in view of the time difference in 1:13 and 15, this explanation lacks substantiating proof and "must remain a hypothesis."[9] In the case of Tertius (Rom. 16:22) and Silas (I Peter 5:12), these two scribes worked directly for Paul and Peter respectively. There is no proof that a secretary composed a letter independently of an apostle and published it decades after the apostle died. True, in the first century authors often employed secretaries to write their epistles. But the church accepted their documents as authentic only because they wrote at the request of the apostles. Accordingly, we must conclude that this theory faces the difficult task of avoiding the charge of pseudepigraphy.[10]

Already in New Testament times, the church rejected pseudonymous writings. Paul instructed the church at Thessalonica "not to become easily unsettled or alarmed by some prophecy, report or letter supposed to have come from us" (II Thess. 2:2). He warned the readers not to be deceived in any way. Should a forger compose a letter in the name of an apostle, his epistle would be considered suspect and would be denied canonicity. The church rejected pseudonymous writings bearing Peter's name (for example, the Gospel of Peter, the Acts of Peter, the Teachings of Peter, and the Revelation of Peter) and regarded them as uninspired documents.

The question arises whether the Holy Spirit would inspire an epistle of someone who spoke in the name of Peter, but who would write independently of the apostle. Although a scribe might attempt to represent Peter, he would never be able to justify the use of the word *apostle* (1:1). Moreover, because this person was not an apostle and lacked apostolic authority, the Spirit would withhold inspiration from a secretary's epistle. In the early

---

9. J. Ramsey Michaels, "Peter, Second Epistle of," *ISBE*, vol. 3, p. 818.
10. Refer to Bauckham, *Jude, 2 Peter*, pp. 131–35.

church, numerous documents that were instructive and informative (e.g., *Didache*, I Clement, the Epistle of Barnabas) circulated. Yet these worthwhile manuscripts never became part of Scripture. By contrast, II Peter is an inspired letter that belongs to the New Testament canon.[11]

5. Conclusion

Both sides on the issue of authorship face problems that are difficult to explain. The proponents of the epistle's apostolic authenticity must explain the reason for the alternating use of the present and future tenses. For instance, the author notes that there will be false teachers in the midst of God's people (2:1). But in the course of the discussion he asserts that these teachers are already at work (2:10–12). Is the writer presenting reality and prophecy in the same document? Of course, an author has the freedom to vary his style, including the use of either the present or future tense. Nonetheless, the variations in this epistle remain problematic.

The opponents of Petrine authorship also face numerous problems. They must explain the personal reminiscences and allusions in this epistle. For what purpose does the writer mention his impending death (1:14)? And why would a forger write, "We were eyewitnesses of [Jesus'] majesty" (1:16)? Last, how can a pseudepigraphic author refer to Paul as "our dear brother" (3:15)?

The choice is between apostolic authorship of II Peter or a document written by a forger. Writes Donald Guthrie, "Both obviously present some difficulties, but of the two the former is easier to explain."[12] To explain apostolic authorship of II Peter is easier than to disprove it. For that reason, I conclude that in spite of the problems we encounter in this epistle, accepting Petrine authorship is a viable option.

B. How Does the Epistle Relate to Other Books?

1. I Peter

If the two Petrine epistles are apostolic, what is the relationship between these two letters? Are there any similarities in word choice, Old Testament citations, structure in composition, content, and theology?

The difference in vocabulary between I Peter and II Peter is obvious to anyone who reads the text of these epistles in Greek. To the reader, the vocabulary of I Peter is not insurmountable, but the choice of words in II Peter seems formidable. Even though the language of II Peter is pompous and cumbersome, the style in this composition is not out of harmony with

---

11. Consult Werner de Boor, *Der Zweite Brief des Petrus und der Brief des Judas,* in *Die Briefe des Petrus und der Brief des Judas,* Wuppertaler Studienbibel (Wuppertal: Brockhaus, 1976), p. 189. Refer to Edwin A. Blum, *2 Peter,* in *Hebrews–Revelation,* vol. 12 of *The Expositor's Bible Commentary,* ed. Frank E. Gaebelein, 12 vols. (Grand Rapids: Zondervan, 1981), pp. 260–61.

12. Guthrie, *New Testament Introduction,* p. 847.

that of I Peter. If we view II Peter as the apostle's last address, then we are able to appreciate this document as a "last will and testament" in which Peter exhorts the readers to "grow in the grace and knowledge" of Jesus Christ (3:18).

Moreover, in both epistles the peculiar Hebraic habit of repeating words occurs.[13] From the many examples in Peter's first epistle, here is one illustration: " 'But the word of the Lord stands forever.' And this is the word that was preached to you" (1:25). Here are two examples from II Peter: "[They] will in the destruction of those creatures also be destroyed" (2:12, NASB); "They will be paid back with harm for the harm they have done" (2:13).

In Peter's first epistle, many Old Testament allusions and quotations are from Proverbs. In his second letter, his one and only quotation from the Old Testament is from Proverbs 26:11, "A dog returns to its vomit" (2:22). In addition to the quotations from the Old Testament, we discover a number of parallels in these two epistles:[14]

I Peter		*II Peter*
1:10–12	inspiration of the Old Testament	1:19–21
1:2	doctrine of election	1:10
1:23	doctrine of the new birth	1:4
2:11–12	need for holiness	1:5–9
3:19	sinful angels in prison	2:4
3:20	Noah and his family protected	2:5
4:2–4	immorality and judgment	2:10–22
4:7–11	exhortation to Christian living	3:14–18
4:11	doxology	3:18

A structural similarity between the two Petrine epistles is undeniable and supports the probability that one author composed these two letters. The material presented in both documents provides substantial evidence to indicate that these letters are the product of one author.

The subject matter in Peter's two epistles is different. In his second epistle, the writer develops an eschatological theme of divine judgment, the destruction of the world, and the promise of a new heaven and a new earth. Especially in the third chapter of this second letter he frequently refers to the day of the Lord, which is a day of judgment and a day of God (vv. 7, 8, 10, 12). By contrast, I Peter has only one distinct allusion to the judgment day (2:12).

---

13. For a comprehensive list, refer to Charles Bigg, *A Critical and Exegetical Commentary on the Epistles of St. Peter and St. Jude,* International Critical Commentary series (1901; Edinburgh: Clark, 1961), pp. 225–26.

14. Refer to E. M. B. [Michael] Green, *2 Peter Reconsidered* (London: Tyndale, 1961), pp. 22–23. Also see William Joseph Dalton, "The Interpretation of 1 Peter 3,19 and 4,6: Light from 2 Peter," *Biblica* 60 (1979): 550–51.

In general, the teaching concerning Christ hardly differs in the two epistles. Christ is called "God" in the opening verse of II Peter (1:1) and the doxology is addressed to Christ (3:18). The writer of this second epistle interchanges the words *Lord* and *God* and thereby indicates the divinity of Christ (3:8, 9, 10). In I Peter the author likewise uses the term *Lord* for both Jesus and God (1:3, 3:15; 1:25, 3:12 respectively). Whereas the theme of Christ's suffering, death, resurrection, and ascension appears in Peter's first epistle, in his second letter the emphasis is on Jesus' transfiguration. One last observation on the Christology of II Peter is that the writer has a penchant for using the term *Savior* to refer to Jesus (1:1, 11; 2:20; 3:2, 18).

We conclude that the relationship between the two epistles of Peter is not insignificant. Apart from Peter's personal greetings (1:1), his reminiscences of the transfiguration of Jesus (1:16–18), and his expression of warm regards for Paul (3:15), the internal evidence in II Peter confirms apostolic authorship. In both epistles, Peter's emphasis on the inspiration of Scripture is telling. He states that the Holy Spirit moved men to speak, so that the human writers did not publish their own views but God's revelation. For Peter, the Old Testament and the epistles of Paul are Scripture. By implication, Peter's letters (composed by an apostle of Jesus Christ) also belong to Scripture.

We find similarities in the Petrine epistles, but in comparing II Peter and Jude we see direct parallels. With respect to these parallels, the question of priority arises. Did the writer of II Peter rely on Jude's epistle or did Jude borrow from Peter's second epistle? Or are both letters dependent on a common source?

2. Jude

Here are the three possibilities.

Dependence on Jude

A quick glance at the second chapter of II Peter and the Epistle of Jude proves to any reader the parallelism of these writings. Jude's letter totals twenty-five verses; nineteen of these are paralleled in II Peter. This parallelism includes not only words and phrases; also the order of presentation is virtually the same.

What arguments are we able to marshal in favor of the priority of Jude? First, we apply the basic rule that the shorter text is more likely to be the original. That is, writers are more apt to add to a text than to reduce its size. We ask, why would a writer present a shorter edition (Jude) of a text (II Peter) that already was in circulation? Therefore, because the Epistle of Jude is shorter than II Peter, we think it reasonable to accept the priority of Jude's epistle.

Next, if we accept apostolic authorship of the Petrine epistles, we see that Peter copies passages from the Epistle of James. James wrote his letter about two decades before Peter composed his first epistle. In the fifth chapter of his first epistle, Peter borrows from James and expands this material to suit his own presentation. Similarly, Peter uses the Epistle of Jude as the source for his second letter and develops it in greater detail for his own use. Peter, then, is indebted to both James and Jude, who were brothers (Jude 1). The fact that Peter receives his material from other writers has no bearing on apostolic authorship.

Third, in his epistle Jude has incorporated a reference (v. 9) to the Assumption of Moses and a quotation (vv. 14–15) from I Enoch. These are apocryphal books which in Jewish circles and also in many Christian communities were rejected. Because Jude included apocryphal material in his epistle, the church hesitated to accept it as canonical. Scholars assume that Peter deliberately omitted the apocryphal references from his source to remove any cause for offense. A close examination of the text of II Peter 2:11 reveals a break at the place where Peter deleted the reference to the apocryphal book. In fact, the verse itself presents exegetical difficulties and must be understood with the help of Jude 9. Conclusively, this text shows that the source of II Peter is Jude's epistle.

Dependence on II Peter

Some writers defend the view that Jude depended on the second epistle of Peter for his material. They prefer the priority of II Peter for a number of reasons. Their first observation is that it is more likely that a lesser writer borrows from a greater writer than vice versa. They maintain that Jude, who is not an apostle, would borrow from the head of the apostles, Peter. They have difficulty believing that Peter relied on Jude, who is hardly known in the Christian church. However, this argument has its own problems. For example, the danger of subjectivism is apparent when we rule that Peter could not have borrowed passages from Jude and say that Jude had to consult II Peter. Furthermore, we do not know how much influence Jude may have had in the development of the church at large in the middle of the first century. The significance of his relation as a half-brother to Jesus and a full brother to James ought not to be underestimated.[15]

Next, the writer of II Peter improves the style of Jude in at least one passage. Jude 12b–13 has the wording, "They are clouds without rain, blown along by the wind; . . . wandering stars, for whom blackest darkness has been reserved forever." But the text of II Peter 2:17 is clearer: "These men are springs without water and mists driven by a storm. Blackest darkness is reserved for them."[16]

Also, the reading of Jude 4, "for certain men whose condemnation was written about long ago," is a possible reference to Peter's second epistle,

---

15. Refer to J. W. C. Wand, *The General Epistles of St. Peter and St. Jude*, Westminster Commentaries series (London: Methuen, 1934), p. 132.

16. Consult Ralph P. Martin, *The Acts, the Letters, the Apocalypse*, vol. 2 of *New Testament Foundations: A Guide for Christian Students*, 2 vols. (Grand Rapids: Eerdmans, 1978), p. 385.

provided we give Jude's letter a late date. This holds true, too, for Jude 17, "But, dear friends, remember what the apostles of our Lord Jesus Christ foretold." Both passages appear to indicate a time lapse of many years. Even though the expression *long ago* is weighty, we face the objection that proof for making Jude 4 refer to II Peter is lacking. And we must admit that the plural *apostles* (v. 17) seems out of place when we know that II Peter was written by one apostle.

Last, the use of the future tense in II Peter 2:1–3 and 3:3 appears predictive. In Jude 4 and 17–18 the writer employs the present tense to indicate that the prediction has been fulfilled. The conclusion that we draw is that II Peter precedes the Epistle of Jude. However, in his second letter Peter alternates between present and future tenses when he refers to the false teachers and the scoffers.[17] And this fact weakens the argument considerably.

In general, the evidence which has been given seems to favor the priority of Jude; that is, Jude is the source for II Peter. Another solution to the problem lies in the theory that both authors relied on a common source.

Dependence on a Common Document

This theory proposes that both Peter and Jude were acquainted with a document written in Hebrew and Aramaic, and that both translated and used it for their respective epistles.[18] The probability that tracts circulated in the early Christian communities cannot be denied. For instance, Paul refers to prophecies, reports, and letters that reached the Thessalonian church (II Thess. 2:2). However, we must conclude that although it is possible that both authors relied on a common source, we lack evidence. Attractive as it is, this theory remains a hypothesis.

One last comment must be made. In respect to the writing of the synoptic Gospels, scholars use the term *interdependence* for showing that Luke and Mark, who served Paul as fellow workers, shared their information and documents in writing their Gospels. Perhaps the term *interdependence* also can be used if we assume that Peter and Jude worked together in approximately the same area.

C. Who Received the Epistle?

From the letter itself, we are unable to answer this question directly. In the greeting, the author states his name (Simon Peter) and function (a servant and apostle of Jesus Christ), but he refrains from identifying the recipients of his epistle. Notice that in I Peter, the author mentions the readers and their place of residence. He identifies them as "God's elect, strangers in the world, scattered throughout Pontus, Galatia, Cappadocia,

---

17. See especially the changes of tense in 2:1–3, 12–14, 17–19; 3:3–4, 5.
18. G. de Ru, "De Authenticiteit van II Petrus," *NedThT* 24 (1969–70): 8. Also see Bauckham, *Jude, 2 Peter*, pp. 141–43.

Asia and Bithynia" (1:1). But in II Peter, the writer only says, "To those who through the righteousness of our God and Savior Jesus Christ have received a faith as precious as ours" (1:1). Peter's second epistle appears to be a general epistle that is not addressed to any particular group.

In II Peter, however, the writer addresses the readers personally. He states that "this is now my second letter to you" (3:1). If we interpret these words to refer to I Peter, we are able to conclude that the readers reside in Pontus, Galatia, Cappadocia, Asia, and Bithynia. Moreover, the readers are acquainted with the epistles of Paul (see 3:15–16), because some of Paul's letters were written to Christians residing in Asia Minor.

Not every scholar interprets the phrase *my second letter* as a reference to I Peter. Some commentators are of the opinion that this phrase points to another letter Peter composed but which is no longer extant. This assumption leads them to conclude that II Peter provides no information about the readers. We must point out, however, that we should resort to the use of a hypothesis concerning the "second letter" only when all other attempts to explain the phrase have failed.

Who are the people Peter addresses in his letter? As in I Peter, we assume that the recipients of II Peter were both Jewish Christians and Gentile Christians. On the basis of the content of II Peter, we are unable to distinguish between Christians of Jewish or Gentile origin. For instance, in II Peter we detect a use and reliance on the Old Testament that is also evident in I Peter. In both epistles the writer quotes from and alludes to the Old Testament; in both letters he mentions the flood from which Noah and his family were protected; and in both documents he teaches the doctrine of divine inspiration.

Notice the similarities between I Peter and II Peter. In both letters the writer rouses the readers from spiritual lethargy (see I Peter 1:13; 4:7; II Peter 1:5, 10; 3:17). In these two epistles, Peter exhorts the readers to be mindful of the judgment day (compare I Peter 2:12; II Peter 3:12). And in these writings, the author exhorts the recipients to follow the example of Jesus Christ. Accordingly, Peter's admonitions apply not only to the Jewish Christian but also to the Gentile Christian. We do not encounter any phrases that are applicable to Christians of Jewish persuasion only and not to Christians of Gentile background. Nowhere does the author distinguish between one or the other group, for he directs his exhortations to all believers. We conclude, then, that the original readers of II Peter are probably those who earlier had received Peter's first epistle.

D. What Is the Purpose of II Peter?

Paul writes two letters to the church in Thessalonica and two to the Corinthians. Likewise, Peter addresses two epistles to the Christians in Asia Minor. As Paul displays his spiritual interest in and concern for the believers in Thessalonica and Corinth by sending them successive epistles, so Peter functions as the spiritual father to his readers. He completes his literary work by composing a second epistle in which he alerts the believers to the dangers of false teachers who have infiltrated the Christian communities.

1. Purpose and Unity

Peter's second epistle has three distinct parts: an exhortation for the believers to grow spiritually (chap. 1), instructions for them to oppose the doctrines and lifestyle of false teachers (chap. 2), and teachings that prepare them for the end of the world, the judgment, and the day of the Lord (chap. 3).

Peter realizes that the end of his life is near. Before he departs from this earthly scene, he wants to give his readers spiritual directives so that they are able to reject heresies and mature spiritually in the knowledge of Christ. He rouses the readers from spiritual lethargy and urges them to add to faith the virtues of goodness, knowledge, self-control, perseverance, godliness, brotherly kindness, and love (1:5–7). Peter urges them to develop spiritual qualities, to remain firmly established in the truth, to listen attentively to Christ's gospel proclaimed by eyewitnesses, and to pay attention to the inspired Scriptures (1:12–21).

At first glance, chapter 2 appears to be an entirely different document. In fact, some scholars maintain that this chapter stands by itself as a parallel to Jude's epistle.[19] But such is not the case, for the apostle encourages and admonishes the Christians to grow spiritually. He strengthens them in their faith so that they are able to appreciate his warnings against the false teachers. Peter warns the readers of false prophets who appear among them with destructive heresies and who live corrupt lives (vv. 1–2, 13–14). He assures them that these lawless people will be punished when they meet swift destruction (vv. 3–4). The author bolsters his observation by citing examples from the ancient past, when judgment came to fallen angels, to the contemporaries of Noah, and to the fellow citizens of Lot (vv. 4–8). Peter compares the false teachers with Balaam, who was rebuked by a donkey (vv. 15–16). He notes that these heretics are determined to lead new Christians astray by promising them freedom; instead they turn them into slaves of corruption (vv. 17–22).

In chapter 3, Peter continues his teachings from the first two chapters. He directs the attention of the readers to the day of the Lord, which is a day of reckoning and destruction for the scoffers (vv. 3–7). Peter also develops his doctrine concerning the end of time by revealing how the present heaven and earth will come to an end (vv. 10–13). He concludes his epistle by exhorting the Christians to "make every effort to be found spotless, blameless and at peace with [God]" (v. 14). He urges them to grow in the grace and knowledge of Jesus Christ (v. 18).

---

19. Consult Ernst Käsemann, "An Apologia for Primitive Christian Eschatology," in *Essays on New Testament Themes,* Studies in Biblical Theology, no. 41 (London: SCM, 1964), p. 191.

The entire epistle displays unity from beginning to end. In the seventeenth century, the Dutch scholar Hugo Grotius suggested that the first two chapters formed one letter and chapter 3 the second letter. With slight variations this theory has survived the centuries. It provides an easy explanation for the sentence "this is now my second letter" (3:1). But this explanation is unable to meet the valid criticism that the style of II Peter displays continuity in all three chapters. Hence, the style of this epistle nullifies the argument that favors discontinuity.[20]

2. Theology

Even though the second epistle of Peter is short, the theological emphases are distinct. For example, in the opening verse (1:1), Peter describes Jesus Christ as divine. He writes, "the righteousness of our God and Savior Jesus Christ." That is, he calls him God and Savior. We observe that Peter does this purposely to stress the divinity of Christ, for in the next verse (1:2) he clearly distinguishes between God and Christ: "the knowledge of God and of Jesus our Lord." For Peter, Jesus is not only divine, but also Lord and Savior (1:11; 2:20; 3:2, 18). Furthermore, Peter encourages the believers to increase their "knowledge of Jesus our Lord" (1:2, 3, 8; 2:20; 3:18). And he tells them about the coming of the Lord (1:16) and the day of the Lord (3:10, 12 [God]).[21]

In his second epistle, Peter reveals that heaven and earth will be destroyed by fire and the elements will melt (3:10, 12). In fact, no other New Testament book has the explicit detail that Peter provides on the end of the universe. With other writers, however, Peter teaches the promise of a new heaven and a new earth (3:13; Isa. 65:17; 66:22; Rev. 21:1). Peter describes the new earth as "the home of righteousness" (3:13). After the complete destruction of heaven and earth, sin has lost its place and righteousness finds a home in God's new creation.

Christians already participate in the divine nature and have escaped the corruption of the world (1:4), yet they must wait for and anticipate "a rich welcome into [Jesus'] eternal kingdom" (1:11). Christians, then, experience the tension of the "already" and the "not yet," the "now" and the "then" in their life of faith.[22]

A Christian encounters this tension in Peter's letter, for he learns that God has given him everything, even to the point of permitting the believer to participate in the divine nature (1:4). That is, a Christian is elect, yet he must strive to make his calling and election sure (1:11). He must do so by

---

20. For a comprehensive discussion, consult Guthrie, *New Testament Introduction*, p. 852.

21. Käsemann discredits christological doctrine in this epistle when he asserts that the "eschatology [of II Peter] lacks any vestige of Christological orientation." See "An Apologia for Primitive Christian Eschatology," p. 178.

22. Compare Green, *2 Peter Reconsidered*, p. 18. And see George E. Ladd, *A Theology of the New Testament* (Grand Rapids: Eerdmans, 1974), p. 604

cultivating the spiritual qualities of faith, goodness, knowledge, self-control, perseverance, godliness, brotherly kindness, and love (1:5–7). Comments Guthrie, "In no clearer way could Peter bring out the human responsibility side of his doctrine of election."[23]

Because believers are elect, they are told to cultivate Christian virtues. Thus, being firmly established in the truth, they will never fall (see 1:10, 12). Nevertheless, they are facing the destructive heresies of false teachers who live among them (2:1). Is it possible, then, that believers lose their salvation? Peter reassures the readers of God's protecting care. He illustrates this truth by teaching the believers that God protected Noah, the preacher of righteousness, from the waters of the flood and that God rescued righteous Lot from the city of Sodom (2:5–8). Peter concludes by observing, "If this is so, then the Lord knows how to rescue godly men from trials" (v. 9).

However, one particular passage in Peter's epistle can be interpreted to mean that Christians can fall away from grace. Peter writes,

> If they have escaped the corruption of the world by knowing our Lord and Savior Jesus Christ and are again entangled in it and overcome, they are worse off at the end than they were at the beginning. It would have been better for them not to have known the way of righteousness, than to have known it and then to turn their backs on the sacred command that was passed on to them. [2:20–21; consult the commentary]

Who is the subject of this passage? The flow of chapter 2 seems to point to the false teachers who at one time gained intellectual knowledge of Jesus Christ but failed in their commitment to him. It is significant that in these verses the words *faith* and *believe* are absent. Also, by using the third person, Peter refers to the individuals who are the subject of this section. Thereby he indicates a separation between these people and the Christian church. We conclude that not the true believers but the false teachers have entangled themselves in sin and have turned away from Jesus Christ. Peter teaches the readers of his epistle that "[God] is patient with you, not wanting anyone to perish, but everyone to come to repentance" (3:9). Note that in this verse he employs the second person *you*. He addresses the Christian community. Conversely, he writes that the day of the Lord is "the day of judgment and destruction of ungodly men" (3:7). God protects his people but rejects the scoffers.

3. False Teachers

Although Peter mentions the false teachers in chapter 2 and the scoffers in chapter 3, he actually refers to only one group of people. Peter identifies the scoffers as persons who, "following their own evil desires" (3:3), ques-

---

23. Guthrie, *New Testament Theology*, p. 636.

tion the return of Christ. And he describes the false teachers as people "who follow the corrupt desire of a sinful nature" (2:10; and see v. 18). In short, we are unable to find any striking differences between these two groups.

Already in the first chapter, Peter indirectly points to the doctrines of these false teachers. He informs his readers that the apostles "did not follow cleverly invented stories when [they] told you about the power and coming of our Lord Jesus Christ" (v. 16). Then, in warning the readers about the pernicious influence of these teachers, he states that they "will exploit you with stories they have made up" (2:3). And he reveals that these scoffers ask, "Where is this 'coming' he promised?" (3:4). He also affirms that the prophecy of Scripture does not originate by private interpretation but by the Holy Spirit (1:20–21). Peter firmly teaches the doctrine of inspiration before he discusses the heresies of the false teachers. Near the conclusion of his letter he returns to the doctrine of Scripture when he asserts that ignorant people distort the meaning of Scripture "to their own destruction" (3:16).

Who are these false teachers? In former times they were members of the church, but they had broken with the Christian faith (2:1, 20–21). Now they continue to mingle with the believers for the purpose of teaching them destructive heresies. Peter mentions their teachings and describes their lifestyle. In summary form I list them:

1. They reject Jesus Christ and his gospel (2:1).
2. They repudiate Christian conduct (2:2).
3. They despise authority (2:10a).
4. Arrogantly they "slander celestial beings" (2:10b).
5. Their lives are characterized by immorality (2:13–14).
6. Although they teach freedom, they are slaves of depravity (2:19).
7. They ridicule the doctrine of Christ's return (3:4).
8. They refuse to acknowledge the coming judgment (3:5–7).
9. They distort the teachings in Paul's epistles and live in sin (3:16).

Are we able to identify the false teachers as members of any particular group that was known in the early church? For scholars who favor a late date for the composition of II Peter, identification of the false teachers with the Gnostics appears a ready solution.[24] But by comparing the tenets of second-century Gnosticism with the doctrines of the false teachers, we discover that many elements that ought to have been discussed are missing. For instance, a reference to the demiurge as the creator of the world would have been essential to Gnosticism of the second century. Yet in the second

---

24. See Käsemann, "An Apologia for Primitive Christian Eschatology," p. 171.

and third chapters of II Peter references to this essential part are absent.[25] The content of Peter's epistle, therefore, fails to reflect a setting that is one hundred years removed from that of the apostles.

Scholars who opt for an early date of II Peter point out that the description of the false teachers' life and doctrine adequately portrays conditions in the middle of the first century. For example, the immorality of the Corinthians was proverbial when Paul and Peter visited Corinth during the fifties. Among the Corinthians were those who desecrated the love feasts of the Christians (I Cor. 11:21; II Peter 2:13). Paul had to devote an entire chapter (I Cor. 15) to refuting errors concerning the doctrine of Christ's resurrection and return.[26] At Thessalonica, the believers raised questions concerning the coming of Christ and the end of the world. Paul instructed them about the "secret power of lawlessness" already at work (II Thess. 2:7).

Every detail of Peter's discussion of the false teachers has a link to the middle of the first century. The only item that has an echo of Gnosticism is Peter's emphasis on knowledge (see, e.g., 1:2, 3, 5, 6, 8). Perhaps this emphasis was in reaction to heretics who were precursors of second-century Gnostics (compare, e.g., Col. 2:2–3, 18). False teachers roamed the countryside when Paul wrote his letter to the church at Colosse. By all appearances, then, II Peter seems to date from the last years of Peter's life.

E. When and Where Was the Epistle Written?

The date of II Peter is directly linked to the authorship of this epistle. If the apostle is the author, then the date must be placed before the death of Peter. But if he is not the writer, then any date in the late first century or early second century can be suggested. Scholars assign either an early date (66–67), a late first-century date (80), or a second-century date (125) to II Peter.

1. Early Date

From the first chapter of his epistle we learn that Peter wrote this letter shortly before his death. In this chapter Peter alludes to his imminent departure from this life (vv. 13–14). He wishes to take the opportunity to strengthen the believers in their faith, to warn them against the teachings of heretics, and to direct their attention to the coming of a new heaven and a new earth. In other words, Peter is writing a kind of last will or testament in which he expresses his parting admonitions.

Do we know when Peter passed away? We have no knowledge of the exact date, even though the church historian Eusebius puts Peter's death

---

25. Consult Green, *2 Peter Reconsidered*, p. 26. For additional arguments, see Bauckham, *Jude, 2 Peter*, p. 156.
26. See especially Green, *The Second Epistle General of Peter*, p. 39.

during the Neronian persecutions (A.D. 64–68).[27] If we date the composition of I Peter at A.D. 63 or 64, then we should allow some time for developments in the Christian community that necessitated the writing of an additional letter. Hence we assume that Peter wrote his second epistle shortly before A.D. 68.

2. Late First-century Date

Other scholars think that a disciple of Peter wrote the epistle after Peter had died. This writer, then, composed the letter in the name of Peter perhaps twenty years after the apostle's death. These scholars opt for a late first-century date because they maintain that the letter discloses a Christology that reflects a later date. Moreover, the phrase *participate in the divine nature* (1:4) appears to have its origin in the Hellenistic Judaism of the last two decades of the first century. And last, they see a response to heresy within the church that points "to a relatively late date."[28] The use of the future tense instead of the present tense (e.g., "in the last day scoffers will come" [3:3]) seems to favor a date of A.D. 80. Scholars who interpret the clause *since our fathers died* (3:4) to signify Christian fathers also favor a late first-century date.

3. Second-century Date

The dates assigned to II Peter by scholars who view the epistle as a second-century manuscript range from A.D. 100 to 150. Those who place the letter in the middle of the second century see a cultural and religious setting in which heretics, excluded from the church, actively seek converts among the believers. They declare that the writing of II Peter is dependent on the Epistle of Jude, which they claim was written probably in A.D. 100.[29] Concerning the date of the composition of II Peter, every scholar has to resort to a hypothesis. But scholars who dispute the apostolic authorship of II Peter face a dearth of historical facts and therefore are forced to choose an arbitrary date somewhere in the first half of the second century.

4. Place

Where was II Peter composed? The epistle itself presents no information about the place of origin. Assuming that the name *Babylon* in I Peter 5:13 is pseudonymous for Rome, we place the origin of I Peter in that city and are inclined to locate the origin of II Peter there, too. We know that Peter spent some time in Rome before his death, so that the imperial city appears to be a likely place. We also know that Peter traveled and visited churches elsewhere, for instance, in Corinth. Nevertheless, we must conclude that be-

---

27. Refer to Eusebius *Ecclesiastical History*, 2.25.5.
28. Bauckham, *Jude, 2 Peter*, p. 158. Consult Martin, *The Acts, the Letters, the Apocalypse*, p. 386.
29. Consult Helmut Koester, *History and Literature of Early Christianity*, vol. 2 of *Introduction to the New Testament*, 2 vols. (Philadelphia: Fortress, 1982), p. 56.

cause of the absence of factual material we are unable to determine the place of origin.

F. What Is the Place of the Epistle in the Canon?

How was II Peter received in the early Christian church? The external evidence for direct recognition of this epistle in the second century is virtually nonexistent. We are able to detect some allusions or resemblances to Peter's second epistle in the writings of Clement of Rome and in the Shepherd of Hermas. However, the Epistle of Barnabas, which dates from the end of the first century or the first part of the second century, has a phrase that echoes II Peter 3:8, "With the Lord a day is like a thousand years, and a thousand years are like a day." The author of Barnabas 15.4 writes, "Lo, the day of the Lord shall be as a thousand years." In the middle of the second century, Justin Martyr writes these same words (*Dialogue* 81). This is also true of Irenaeus, who in about A.D. 185 says, "A day of the Lord is as a thousand years." Yet both First and Second Peter are absent from the Muratorian Canon (A.D. 175).

In the beginning of the third century, Origen is the first writer who, by quoting II Peter six times, calls the epistle Scripture. Church historian Eusebius discloses that Origen expressed some reservation when he said, "Peter . . . has left one acknowledged epistle, and, it may be, a second also; for it is doubted."[30] His teacher Clement of Alexandria, who died approximately A.D. 216, wrote commentaries on all the general Epistles, according to Eusebius. We assume that the term *general Epistles* includes II Peter. Clement alludes to verses in Peter's second epistle, but does not quote it anywhere in any of his extant writings.[31]

About A.D. 325, Eusebius classified II Peter with the so-called controversial writings and refused to put the epistle in the canon. He reflected the thinking of others in that century. Toward the end of the fourth century, Jerome acknowledged that Simon Peter composed two epistles that are called general. But, he added, many people doubted the authenticity of II Peter because of the variation in style with I Peter. However, the universal church acknowledged II Peter as canonical. The Council of Laodicea (A.D. 360), the Council of Hippo Regius (A.D. 393), and the Council of Carthage (A.D. 397) placed II Peter among the canonical books. Nevertheless, when the fourth-century church accepted the second epistle of Peter as canonical, doubts still lingered.

During the Reformation, John Calvin voiced his misgivings on Petrine authorship. To be exact, he questioned the authorship of the epistle, but not its canonical significance:

---

30. Eusebius *Ecclesiastical History* 6.25.8 (LCL).
31. For detailed information, refer to Bigg, *The Epistles of St. Peter and St. Jude*, p. 202.

And yet, when I examine all things more narrowly, it seems to me more probable that this Epistle was composed by another, according to what Peter communicated, than that it was written by himself, for Peter himself would have never spoken thus.[32]

Martin Luther accepted II Peter as part of the canon and placed it among the numbered books in his New Testament list.

G. How Do We Outline II Peter?

The main points of this short epistle can readily be committed to memory chapter by chapter. These are the headings:

Introduction	1:1–2
Promises and Virtues	1:3–11
Divine Revelation	1:12–21
False Teachers	2:1–22
The Day of the Lord	3:1–13
Exhortations	3:14–18

Here is a more detailed outline of II Peter:

I. 1:1–2	Introduction	
A. 1:1	Greetings	
B. 1:2	Salutation	
II. 1:3–11	Promises and Virtues	
A. 1:3–4	Promises	
B. 1:5–7	Virtues	
	1. Faith, Goodness, and Knowledge	1:5
	2. Self-control, Perseverance, and Godliness	1:6
	3. Brotherly Kindness and Love	1:7
C. 1:8–9	Growth	
D. 1:10–11	Assurance	
III. 1:12–21	Divine Revelation	
A. 1:12–15	Memory	
B. 1:16–18	Eyewitnesses	
	1. Christ's Coming	1:16
	2. Christ's Glory	1:17
	3. Christ's Companions	1:18
C. 1:19–21	Prophecy	
	1. Certainty	1:19

---

32. John Calvin, *Commentaries on the Catholic Epistles: The Second Epistle of Peter*, ed. and trans. John Owen (Grand Rapids: Eerdmans, 1948), p. 423.

Commentary
The Second Epistle of Peter

1

Introduction

(1:1–2)

Promises and Virtues

(1:3–11)

and Divine Revelation

(1:12–21)

Outline

1 1 Simon Peter, a servant and apostle of Jesus Christ,
To those who through the righteousness of our God and Savior Jesus Christ have received a faith as precious as ours:
2 Grace and peace be yours in abundance through the knowledge of God and of Jesus our Lord.

I. Introduction
1:1–2

A. Greetings
1:1

In the first verse of this epistle the author tells us something about himself by revealing his name and status. And in his address, he describes the recipients of the epistle in terms of righteousness and faith, which are spiritual qualities that come to them from God and Jesus Christ.

1. Simon Peter, a servant and apostle of Jesus Christ,
To those who through the righteousness of our God and Savior Jesus Christ have received a faith as precious as ours.

a. *Name.* This self-identification of Peter is a point of debate among scholars who defend apostolic authorship of this epistle[1] and those who question it.[2] If Peter is the author, why does he not identify himself as "Peter, an apostle of Jesus Christ" (I Peter 1:1)? Instead, he introduces himself as Simon Peter, which many early manuscripts have as Simeon Peter.[3] The name *Simeon* is a variant of *Simon* and occurs in the address that James delivered at the Council of Jerusalem (Acts 15:14). Moreover, the name *Simeon* belongs to the head of one of Israel's tribes (Rev. 7:7). It is also the name of an elderly man who, filled with the Holy Spirit, uttered a hymn while holding the baby Jesus (Luke 2:25–28, 34). One of Jesus' ancestors bore the name *Simeon* (Luke 3:30) and so did Simeon Niger (Acts 13:1). In

---

1. For example, see Charles Bigg, *A Critical and Exegetical Commentary on the Epistles of St. Peter and St. Jude,* International Critical Commentary series (1901; Edinburgh: Clark, 1961), pp. 246–47. And consult Edwin A. Blum, *2 Peter,* in *Hebrews-Revelation,* vol. 12 of *The Expositor's Bible Commentary,* ed. Frank E. Gaebelein, 12 vols. (Grand Rapids: Zondervan, 1981), pp. 257–61.
2. Among others, refer to Richard J. Bauckham, *Jude, 2 Peter,* Word Commentary series, vol. 50 (Waco: Word, 1983), pp. 166–67.
3. A number of translations have the reading *Simeon* (NAB, NEB, JB, and *Moffatt* [Symeon]).

short, the name occurs rather frequently in Scripture and perhaps was a preferred pronunciation among some Jews.

The name *Simon* in Hebrew is a diminutive form of "Samuel," which means "God has heard." Simon's parents gave him this name at birth. But when Jesus called Simon to be his follower, he gave him the name *Peter* (rock), which in the Aramaic language is "Cephas." Simon Peter is not the only one with this name, for in the New Testament at least nine different persons bear the name *Simon*.[4]

The combination *Simon Peter* occurs numerous times in all four Gospels and in Acts. In the early church, among Gentile Christians who spoke Greek, Peter apparently was known by his double name. For example, when Luke describes Peter's visit to the house of Cornelius the Roman centurion, he uses the double form (Acts 10:5, 18, 32; 11:13). Likewise, John, who presumably wrote his Gospel in Asia Minor, almost exclusively uses the double name *Simon Peter*. Of the twenty-two times that John mentions the apostle, seventeen are the combination form—the other five instances either introduce Simon (1:41, 42) or indicate the special circumstance of Simon's reinstatement as an apostle (21:15, 16, 17).[5] When reinstating Simon after his denial, Jesus refrained from calling him "Peter" (rock) because the significance of that name was inappropriate at that moment.

b. *Function.* Peter calls himself "a servant and apostle of Jesus Christ." The word *servant* also occurs in the greetings of the epistles of James (1:1) and Jude (1). Both James and Jude refrain from using the double title *servant and apostle*. Peter uses this combination to indicate that as a servant he stands next to any other servant of Jesus Christ. He is ready to accept, obey, and fulfill the orders of his Lord. Peter applies the term *servant* to all believers (see I Peter 2:16). Peter adds that he is "an apostle of Jesus Christ." Although he served as leader of the twelve apostles and head of the Jerusalem church, he places himself not above but next to the other apostles. Peter writes that he is *an* apostle and not *the* apostle of Jesus Christ.

Note that Paul also introduces himself as "a servant of Christ Jesus, called to be an apostle" (Rom. 1:1; also see Gal. 1:1; Phil. 1:1; Titus 1:1; Rev. 1:1). With the other apostles, Peter is a servant and an apostle of his Sender, Jesus Christ. As an apostle, he seeks to make disciples of all nations by baptizing them and by teaching them the gospel (Matt. 28:19–20).[6] The term *apostle* means not only that someone is sent out, but also that he has received full authority from Jesus Christ. In his preaching and in his writ-

---

4. They are Simon Peter (Matt. 4:18), Simon the Zealot (Matt. 10:4), Simon the brother of Jesus (Matt. 13:55), Simon of Cyrene (Matt. 27:32), Simon the leper (Mark 14:3), Simon the Pharisee (Luke 7:36–40), Simon the father of Judas Iscariot (John 6:71), Simon the sorcerer (Acts 8:9), and Simon the tanner (Acts 9:43).

5. See John 1:41; 6:8, 68; 13:6, 9, 24, 36; 18:10, 15, 25; 20:2, 6; 21:2, 3, 7, 11, 15.

6. Refer to Dietrich Müller, *NIDNTT*, vol. 1, p. 131. Also see Karl Heinrich Rengstorf, *TDNT*, vol. 1, pp. 424–43.

ing, Peter delivers not his own message but that of the Lord (compare I Peter 1:1; Gal. 1:1). Therefore, Peter writes his second epistle on behalf of Christ, who confers his authority upon this letter. Peter writes his epistle in the capacity of an apostle of Jesus Christ, and he expects its recipients to acknowledge it as an apostolic document (see Luke 10:16).[7]

c. *Addressees.* In his first epistle, Peter lists the places where the addressees reside. He does not list them in his second letter. Peter writes "to those who through the righteousness of our God and Savior Jesus Christ have received a faith as precious as ours." Peter is not interested in locations but in spiritual possessions which the readers have in common with the apostle.

Peter addresses people "who . . . have received a faith as precious as ours." First, let us consider the meaning of the Greek verb *to receive.* It suggests that someone obtains something by casting lots (refer to Luke 1:9; John 19:24) or by the will of God (consult the Greek text of Acts 1:17).[8] Peter uses this verb to indicate that man receives his faith from God in accordance with God's will. He reminds his readers that faith does not originate in themselves but is a gift from God.

Second, how do we understand the term *faith?* Faith, which both the readers and Peter have in common, can be either objective or subjective. Objective faith refers to a body of Christian truths formulated, for example, in a creed. Subjective faith is the trust a believer places in God. Scholars are unable to agree on the interpretation of the word *faith.* Some interpret it in the objective sense and others in the subjective sense. However, the context points to the subjective meaning: first, because God grants subjective faith and, second, because in this context subjective faith is closely linked to the concept *righteousness.* God imparts righteousness to the believer.

Next, Peter notes that the recipients of his letter share the same faith with him. "[You] have received a faith as precious as ours." He stresses equality and with this choice of words he seems to point to his unassuming self-identification, "*a* servant." In the Christian community every believer receives the same precious gift of faith from God. Peter uses the plural pronoun *our* in this text to demonstrate that the faith of the apostles is the same as that of the readers. In other words, the apostles are on the same spiritual level as all the other Christians. The word *our* should not be interpreted to refer to a distinction between Jewish Christians and Gentile Christians, because the epistle itself fails to support such a distinction.

Fourth, what is the meaning of the prepositional phrase "through the righteousness of our God"? The expression *righteousness* refers to God's justice in respect to man.[9] In fact, some translators have the reading "the

---

7. Consult S. Greijdanus, *De Brieven van de Apostelen Petrus en Johannes, en de Brief van Judas,* Kommentaar op het Nieuwe Testament series (Amsterdam: Van Bottenburg, 1929), pp. 232–33.

8. Refer to Bauer, p. 462; Thayer, p. 367.

9. Gottlob Schrenk, *TDNT,* vol. 2, p. 198.

justifying power of our God" (NAB; also see NEB). The concepts *righteousness* and *faith* are closely linked in Scripture, especially in the epistles of Paul. "For the gospel reveals how God puts people right with himself: it is through faith from beginning to end" (Rom. 1:17, GNB). Here are two observations: In the relation of faith and righteousness, faith is a personal trust in God; righteousness originates with God and "through Christ it flows down to us."[10]

Last, scholars differ in their interpretation of the words *our God and Savior Jesus Christ*. Is Peter writing about God and Jesus Christ or is he saying that Jesus Christ is God? With variations some translators present this reading: "the righteousness of our God and of our Savior, Jesus Christ" (SEB).[11] However, numerous translators and commentators prefer the translation "the righteousness of our God and Savior Jesus Christ." They base their preference on the Greek in which one definite article links the two nouns *God* and *Savior*.

Notice, then, that at the beginning of his epistle Peter emphasizes the divinity of Jesus Christ. Calling Jesus "our God" is not at all unusual, for one week after Jesus' resurrection Thomas said to Jesus, "My Lord and my God!" (John 20:28). New Testament writers stress the divinity of Christ. Paul writes, "For in Christ all the fullness of the Deity lives in bodily form" (Col. 2:9; also see Rom. 9:5; Titus 2:13; Heb. 1:8).

Jesus Christ is both God and Savior. Of course, the name *Jesus* itself signifies salvation. The angel told Joseph to give Mary's Son "the name Jesus, because he will save his people from their sins" (Matt. 1:21). The word *Savior* does not occur in Peter's first epistle, but in his second it appears five times (1:1, 11; 2:20; 3:2, 18). Except for the first instance (1:1), all these verses have the familiar expression *Lord and Savior*. Because Jesus is God and Lord, he is able to set us free from sin, to make us righteous, and to restore us completely. Therefore, in response we joyfully and thankfully sing,

> Hallelujah! what a Saviour!
> Hallelujah! what a Friend!
> Saving, helping, keeping, loving,
> He is with me to the end.
> —J. Wilbur Chapman

Greek Words, Phrases, and Constructions in 1:1

λαχοῦσιν—the second aorist active participle is derived from the verb λαγχάνω (I receive by lot). See its use in Acts 1:17.

---

10. John Calvin, *Commentaries on the Catholic Epistles: The Second Epistle of Peter*, ed. and trans. John Owen (Grand Rapids: Eerdmans, 1948), p. 367.
11. Also see KJV, RSV margin, and *Phillips*.

τοῦ θεοῦ ἡμῶν καὶ σωτῆρος—when one definite article "connects two nouns of the same case," it relates to the same person.[12] In at least four instances, Peter adheres to this rule when he writes the combination *Lord and Savior* (1:11; 2:20; 3:2, 18).

B. Salutation
1:2

At the beginning of this epistle, Peter follows the conventional rules of letter-writing. He identifies himself, describes the addressees, and greets them with an apostolic salutation.

2. Grace and peace be yours in abundance through the knowledge of God and of Jesus our Lord.

The words *grace and peace* are part of a fixed formula that appears in many epistles.[13] In the two letters of Peter, the formula has the verb *be in abundance* (NIV), which literally means "be multiplied" (also see Jude 2). How do we multiply grace and peace? We are unable to comprehend how abstract qualities can be increased in number. The source of grace is God, who also grants peace. Furthermore, the Greek verb is in the passive voice that appears in the form of a wish. Peter's prayer is that God will send us an increasing quantity of both grace and peace. Although the term *grace* is used as a greeting, the term itself implies the qualities of mercy, love, and pardon that God extends to man. Peace flows forth from grace and is man's internal happiness which he desires to share with his fellow man. The concepts *grace* and *peace* are like two sides of the same coin.

Peter adds the phrase "through the knowledge of God and of Jesus our Lord." In a sense, this is the theme of Peter's letter, because the concept *knowledge* occurs repeatedly.[14] Here Peter writes the noun in compound form to express acknowledgment. He conveys the thought that knowledge is not merely an ability to recite facts but an experience that promotes fellowship. The believer who is the recipient of God's grace and peace experiences these gifts through intimate fellowship with God (see vv. 3, 8; 2:20–21). By increasing his knowledge of God and Jesus Christ, he acknowledges that grace and peace are multiplied for him.

Peter expands the reference to the believer's knowledge of God by adding a comment about the knowledge of the Lord Jesus. He reaffirms the words of Jesus: "No one knows the Son except the Father, and no one

---

12. H. E. Dana and Julius R. Mantey, *A Manual Grammar of the Greek New Testament* (1927; New York: Macmillan, 1967), p. 147. Also see C. F. D. Moule, *An Idiom-Book of New Testament Greek*, 2d ed. (Cambridge: Cambridge University Press, 1960), pp. 109–10.

13. Rom. 1:7; I Cor. 1:3; II Cor. 1:2; Gal. 1:3; Eph. 1:2; Phil. 1:2; Col. 1:2; I Thess. 1:1; II Thess. 1:2; Titus 1:4 (without "you"); Philem. 3; I Peter 1:2; II Peter 1:2; Rev. 1:4.

14. In the Greek, the simple verb as a participle appears in 1:20 and 3:3; the compound verb in 2:21 (twice); the simple noun in 1:5, 6; and the compound noun in 1:2, 3, 8; 2:20.

knows the Father except the Son and those to whom the Son chooses to reveal him" (Matt. 11:27).

Throughout this epistle Peter urges the readers to increase their knowledge of the Lord Jesus Christ (refer to v. 8; 2:20; 3:18).[15] This is Peter's main concern in writing his epistle. He urges his readers to increase their personal knowledge of Jesus Christ, their Lord and Savior. He begins his epistle with a prayerful wish for grace and peace through knowledge of God and of Jesus Christ. He concludes his letter with an exhortation to "grow in the grace and knowledge of our Lord and Savior Jesus Christ" (3:18).

Practical Considerations in 1:2

If I wish to know Jesus Christ as my Savior, I must have an intellectual and an experiential knowledge of him. By reading the Scriptures I learn about his birth, ministry, suffering, death, resurrection, ascension, and the promise of his return. From reading the Bible I come to know Jesus Christ, the Son of God, my Savior. Jesus wants me to study the Scriptures, for they testify about him (John 5:39).

However, I must also know Jesus Christ through the personal experiences of answered prayer, the strengthening of faith, the evident blessings of the Lord, and the assurance that I am doing the will of God. I walk and talk with Jesus, because he is my friend (John 15:15), my brother (Heb. 2:11), and my adviser. Like Enoch, who daily walked with God, I confide in Jesus and thus know him more and more.

Greek Words, Phrases, and Constructions in 1:2

πληθυνθείη—only here and in I Peter 1:2 and Jude 2 this particular verb occurs in the aorist passive optative. The passive voice implies that God is the agent. The aorist is constative, because it encompasses the entire action without regard to time. And the optative expresses a wish.

3 His divine power has given us everything we need for life and godliness through our knowledge of him who called us by his own glory and goodness. 4 Through these he has given us his very great and precious promises, so that through them you may participate in the divine nature and escape the corruption in the world caused by evil desires.

5 For this very reason, make every effort to add to your faith goodness; and to goodness, knowledge; 6 and to knowledge, self-control; and to self-control, perseverance; and to perseverance, godliness; 7 and to godliness, brotherly kindness; and to brotherly kindness, love. 8 For if you possess these qualities in increasing measure, they will keep you from being ineffective and unproductive in your knowledge of our Lord Jesus Christ. 9 But if anyone does not have them, he is nearsighted and blind, and has forgotten that he has been cleansed from his past sins.

15. The JB, which reflects some of the readings of Latin versions, has an abbreviated ending of v. 2: "as you come to know our Lord." *Moffatt* has the reading *the knowledge of our Lord.*

10 Therefore, my brothers, be all the more eager to make your calling and election sure. For if you do these things, you will never fall, 11 and you will receive a rich welcome into the eternal kingdom of our Lord and Savior Jesus Christ.

II. Promises and Virtues
1:3–11

A. Promises
1:3–4

The transition from the preceding verse (v. 2) to these two verses is abrupt. The word *knowledge* gives the passage continuity, but the construction of verse 3 causes a break with the salutation. Perhaps the writer deleted a clause that would make the transition smooth between the two verses. Deletion of a clause is not uncommon in Greek manuscripts. If we include such a clause, we can bridge the gap between verses 2 and 3. For example, "We are receiving God's grace and peace, [*because*] *his divine power has given us everything we need*."[16]

An alternative is to take verse 2 as the salutation and the next verse as the beginning of the letter proper, and indicate a definite break between them. Then we accept verses 3 and 4 as part of a lengthy thought with verses 5–7. But the words *for this very reason* (v. 5) do not lend themselves as a natural transition. Taking the simple rule of thumb, "Take Greek as it comes," I prefer to see verse 3 as a continuation of the message that the salutation conveys and thus supply a short clause to introduce verse 3.

3. His divine power has given us everything we need for life and godliness through our knowledge of him who called us by his own glory and goodness.

Some translations, including the New International Version, omit the first Greek word in this verse. The versions that translate this word have the reading *according as* (KJV), *seeing that* (NASB), *as* (NKJV), or *for* (MLB). These translators use it as a bridge between the salutation (v. 2) and this verse.

a. "His divine power has given us everything we need." To whom is Peter referring when he writes, "his divine power"? Commentators have different opinions. Some say that this is a reference to God, but that the pronouns *him* ("knowledge of him") and *his* ("his own glory") relate to Christ.[17] Others say that Peter is thinking of Christ; first, because Jesus is mentioned in the preceding text, and second, because the entire epistle is an exposition

---

16. Compare Robert H. Mounce, *A Living Hope: A Commentary on 1 and 2 Peter* (Grand Rapids: Eerdmans, 1982), p. 105.

17. See C. E. B. Cranfield, *I and II Peter and Jude: Introduction and Commentary*, Torch Bible Commentaries series (London: SCM, 1960), p. 174. And consult J. N. D. Kelly, *A Commentary on the Epistles of Peter and Jude*, Thornapple Commentaries series (1969; Grand Rapids: Baker, 1981), p. 300.

of Jesus' deity (e.g., see v. 1).[18] Perhaps we can say that in this verse Peter fails to present a clear distinction between God and Jesus and, therefore, that we ought to refrain from being dogmatic.

The words *divine power* describe "the godhead and everything that belongs to it."[19] They are an example of the Hebrew fondness for using a circumlocution to avoid mentioning the name of God. Because of his divine power, God has given us everything we need. This is an amazing statement! In fact, in this introductory verse of the epistle we encounter a wonderful cheerfulness.[20] Peter exclaims that he and the readers are the recipients of untold blessings; the word *everything* sums up this idea.

b. "For life and godliness." Observe that God has granted and continues to grant us "everything for life and godliness." He wants us to live in harmony with his Word by honoring, loving, and serving him. Eternal life is not an ideal that becomes reality when we depart from this earthly scene. On the contrary, we possess eternal life through our daily exercise of living for God and our fellow man. By obeying God's will in our lives we practice godliness and experience the possession of eternal life.

c. "Through our knowledge of him who called us." Peter tells the readers of his epistle that God grants them everything they need to enjoy life in his service. He indicates that God grants his gifts liberally "through our knowledge of him." Once again Peter speaks of knowledge (see v. 2) and informs us that God makes his gifts available to us when we come to know him. *Knowledge* is a basic concept in Peter's epistle.

The question is whether the phrase *knowledge of him* applies to God or to Christ. If we understand the pronoun to refer to Christ, then we have to conclude that the word *us* refers to the apostles. But the pronoun *us* in the first part of verse 3 is all-inclusive, for Peter speaks of himself and the readers. Should we interpret the pronoun to apply only to the apostles and not to the readers, we would negate the statements on equality within the church, which Peter teaches by implication in the first two verses of this epistle. We expect, however, that Peter is consistent in the use of this pronoun. Accordingly, we understand the word *him* to point to God and not to Christ. John Calvin observes that Peter "makes God the author of this knowledge, because we never go to him except when called."[21] God has called us, through Christ, to salvation (compare Rom. 8:28, 30; I Peter 1:15; 2:9; 5:10). And last, in the broader context of this chapter, Peter once

---

18. For instance, consult Michael Green, *The Second Epistle General of Peter, and the General Epistle of Jude: An Introduction and Commentary,* Tyndale New Testament Commentaries (Grand Rapids: Eerdmans, 1968), p. 63. And see R. C. H. Lenski, *The Interpretation of the Epistles of St. Peter, St. John, and St. Jude* (Columbus: Wartburg, 1945), p. 257.

19. Bauer, p. 353.

20. John Albert Bengel, *Gnomon of the New Testament,* ed. Andrew R. Fausset, trans. William Fletcher, 7th ed., 5 vols. (Edinburgh: Clark, 1877), vol. 5, p. 85.

21. Calvin, *The Second Epistle of Peter,* p. 369.

more mentions the calling of the readers; he writes, "Therefore, my brothers, be all the more eager to make your calling and election sure" (v. 10).

d. "By his own glory and goodness." The act of calling us is a demonstration of God's own glory and goodness. These two characteristics are highly personal; the adjective *own* modifies both terms. Moreover, the two terms, although in a sense synonymous,[22] differ. We are able to observe glory with our eyes (compare John 1:14), and we become aware of goodness (praise) with our minds and hearts. Conclusively, God reveals his essential being through visible glory and he displays his goodness in his deeds.

4. Through these he has given us his very great and precious promises, so that through them you may participate in the divine nature and escape the corruption in the world caused by evil desires.

We see a correlation between verses 3 and 4 whereby the author is clarifying his message. Here is the parallel:

Verse 3	*Verse 4*
His divine power	Through these
has given us	he has given us
everything we need	his very great and precious
for life and godliness	promises,
through our knowledge	so that through them
of him who called us by his	you may participate
own glory and goodness.	in the divine nature
	and escape the corruption
	in the world caused by
	evil desires.

Note also the cross-shaped configuration of some of the parts: "his divine power" (v. 3) corresponds with "in the divine nature" (v. 4), and "glory and goodness" (v. 3) is the antecedent of "through these" (v. 4). From another point of view, the conclusion of verse 4 contrasts with the last line of the preceding verse: "the corruption in the world" is the opposite of "glory," and "evil desires" is antithetical to "goodness."

a. "Through these he has given us his very great and precious promises." To whom does the pronoun *he* refer—to God or to Christ? Scripture teaches that God has given his people numerous promises, but also Christ has promised his followers that he will return (1:16; 3:4, 9). Because Peter is not specific in distinguishing between God and Christ, we ought to refrain from restricting the meaning of the pronoun.

The promises themselves are an important part of this verse, for Peter describes them as "very great and precious." Observe that he uses the superlative form to depict these promises. With the perfect tense *he has given*, he implies that God not only has given these promises to us but also has fulfilled them in the person and work of Christ.

---

22. Consult Bauckham, *Jude, 2 Peter*, p. 179.

b. "So that through them you may participate in the divine nature." Peter needs an additional clause to tell us what God's purpose is in giving us these promises (compare I Peter 2:9). He informs us that through these promises we share God's nature. Although this statement lends itself to many interpretations, we ought to notice how precisely Peter has chosen his words. He says that we participate in God's nature, not in God's being. He has chosen the term *nature* because it indicates growth, development, and character. The expression *being,* by contrast, points to essence and substance. We can never participate in God's essence, for we are and remain human beings who have been created by God. What Peter discloses is that we share God's holiness, which we experience through the indwelling of the Holy Spirit in our hearts (see I Cor. 6:19). What, then, is God's purpose in making us share in his nature? In the words of Calvin, "Let us then mark, that the end of the gospel is, to render us eventually conformable to God, and, if we may so speak, to deify us."[23]

Peter borrows the term *divine nature* from the philosophical vocabulary of the Greeks. To refute his opponents (see 2:1) he employs their terminology but gives the words a Christian meaning. Greek philosophers taught that man who is living in a corrupt world of physical pleasure must become like the gods. They advised their followers to share the divine nature. Peter resorts to using the same expression, "participate in the divine nature." But whereas the philosophers took their point of departure in man and claimed for him a share in the nature of the gods, Peter views our sharing of God's nature in the light of God's promises. "There is a world of difference between these two concepts. The first is humanistic and reflects the vaulted self-appraisal of natural man. The other is Christian and exalts the gracious provision of God."[24]

Through the promises in Christ, we obtain God's holiness. God has called us into the sphere of holiness in which we have fellowship with the Father and his Son Jesus Christ (I John 1:3). By fixing our thoughts on Jesus, we share in the heavenly calling and in Christ himself (Heb. 3:1, 14).

c. "And escape the corruption in the world caused by evil desires." Already in his life, the believer participates in God's divine nature by reflecting his virtues. He shuns sin and evil because he knows that he belongs not to the world but to God (John 17:14–18; also compare I Thess. 5:22; James 1:27). Surely, when he leaves this earthly scene and participates in eternal glory, he fully displays God's nature. While on earth, he lives in the world even though he is not of the world. He has "put on the new self, created to be like God in true righteousness and holiness" (Eph. 4:24; also see Col. 3:10; Heb. 12:10; and I John 3:2).

---

23. Calvin, *The Second Epistle of Peter,* p. 371.
24. Mounce, *A Living Hope,* p. 107.

Doctrinal Considerations in 1:4

A skilled communicator expresses himself in the language of the people he addresses; he uses their vocabulary and idioms to identify with his audience. But as he employs their terminology, he is completely free to proclaim his own message.

Peter selects a phrase that was current in the Hellenistic world of his day: "participate in the divine nature." Even though Peter avails himself of Hellenistic terminology, he does not teach a Hellenistic view of man, which advocated escape from this material world because of its corruption. "Peter is careful to define the nature of the corruption he has in mind, *i.e.* corruption that is in (*en*) the world because of (*en*) passion. There is a deliberate avoidance of the concept that the material world is itself evil."[25] Peter, therefore, teaches not the doctrine of Hellenistic philosophers who reason from man's perspective. Instead, he presents God's revelation, in which God calls man to have fellowship with him. In short, not man but God takes the initiative.

Greek Words, Phrases, and Constructions in 1:3–4

Verse 3

ὡς—omitted in some translations, this particle performs the functions of introducing a genitive absolute construction: δυνάμεως (power) and δεδωρημένης (perfect middle participle from δωρέομαι [I give, present, bestow]). Verse 3, however, lacks a main verb, which perhaps has been deleted in the transition from verse 2 to verse 3. Notice that the perfect tense of the participle indicates a past action that has lasting effect for the present.

θείας—this adjective, meaning "divine," occurs also in verse 4 and in Acts 17:29, where Paul uses it in his address to Athenian philosophers. It appears frequently in Hellenistic writings, "probably because its very broad usage gave it a polytheistic or pantheistic flavor."[26] We assume that both Paul and Peter accommodated themselves to the vocabulary used by their audiences. Jewish Christians who lived in a Hellenistic environment were acquainted with this word.[27]

ἰδίᾳ δόξῃ—the Majority Text and Textus Receptus have the reading διὰ δόξης (through glory), which has the support of some ancient manuscripts. Bruce M. Metzger comments that the majority of the Editorial Committee of the United Bible Societies edition preferred the reading ἰδίᾳ δόξῃ because it is "more likely that διά would have been written by mistake for ἰδίᾳ than vice versa; and ἴδιος is a favorite word with the author of 2 Peter, occurring six other times in three chapters."[28]

---

25. Donald Guthrie, *New Testament Theology* (Downers Grove: Inter-Varsity, 1981), p. 185.

26. Bauckham, *Jude, 2 Peter,* p. 177.

27. Refer to Werner de Boor, *Der Zweite Brief des Petrus und der Brief des Judas,* in *Die Briefe des Petrus und der Brief des Judas,* Wuppertaler Studienbibel (Wuppertal: Brockhaus, 1976), p. 198.

28. Bruce M. Metzger, *A Textual Commentary on the Greek New Testament,* 3d corrected ed. (London and New York: United Bible Societies, 1975), p. 699.

Verse 4

μέγιστα—as an adjective in the superlative degree, it is emphatic in the sense of "very" or "exceedingly."[29]

γένησθε—the aorist subjunctive from the verb γίνομαι (I become, am) expresses the process that occurs in regard to a believer's sanctification. The aorist is constative.

ἀποφυγόντες—from the verb ἀποφεύγω (I escape), this active participle in the aorist tense denotes single occurrence. As a compound, the participle governs the genitive case without a preposition.

B. Virtues
1:5–7

1. Faith, Goodness, and Knowledge
1:5

The apostle specifies how a Christian ought to live virtuously by claiming God's promises and avoiding the corruption of the world. He lists the qualities the Christian must have to lead a spiritually productive and effective life. He exhorts the believer to possess a number of virtues; faith heads the list.

5. For this very reason, make every effort to add to your faith goodness; and to goodness, knowledge.

Peter reiterates the idea of the preceding verses in the words *for this very reason.* He has alluded to God's work in saving us; now he stresses our work in the process of salvation. In a sense, he says the same thing Paul wrote in one of his epistles: "Continue to work out your salvation with fear and trembling, for it is God who works in you" (Phil. 2:12–13). God has given us his promises and, true to his word, fulfills them. Now God expects us to do our part. Therefore, Peter writes,

"Make every effort to add." The Greek for this particular phrase is interesting indeed. Peter uses the noun *effort,* then the verb *to apply,* and last the verb *to add.* Peter writes the noun first to give it emphasis. The noun itself means "diligence" and even conveys the idea of haste. That is, when God calls a person, he wants him to put forth every possible effort to obey this divine call and to do so without delay. The verb *to apply* signifies that we must bring our diligence into God's presence and place it next to what God does for us. Even though the initiative in salvation comes from God, he works out our sanctification by putting us to work.

The verb *to add* is meaningful in the Greek. The word comes from the Greek world of stage and drama. The director of a play not only coached the cast. Together with the state, he also paid the expenses the members

---

29. Refer to A. T. Robertson, *A Grammar of the Greek New Testament in the Light of Historical Research* (Nashville: Broadman, 1934), p. 670. And see Dana and Mantey, *Manual Grammar,* p. 121.

incurred for giving a performance on stage. In other words, the choir-master added his financial contribution to the amount the state supplied.[30] This verb *to add,* then, signifies that the believer contributes lavishly to the work of his salvation.

Peter presents a list of eight virtues, of which faith is the first and love the last (compare Gal. 5:6, 22). These are the first three virtues:

Faith. Faith is the personal reliance of the believer (see also v. 1). It is his subjective trust in his Lord and Savior and therefore is the basis of his spiritual life. Faith is the root of all the other virtues Peter mentions. Peter exhorts the readers of his letter to add the seven following virtues to faith. "These other virtues are unattainable until the step of faith has been taken."[31] Moreover, because of our trust in Jesus, our faith has its source in him (e.g., see Mark 9:24).

Goodness. Of the seven virtues that are directly related to faith, Peter mentions goodness first. It relates to one of God's characteristics (see v. 3). Because it is a divine attribute, we ought to reflect this virtue in our lives. Our daily conduct should be a demonstration of moral excellence. Faith and excellence support one another.

Knowledge. The next virtue that flows from faith is knowledge. The Greek word implies that we use our minds, have correct insight in all circumstances, and know the moral quality of the people we meet. We put our knowledge to work by using common sense in everything we say, do, and think. Furthermore, knowledge and faith go hand in hand, for faith is strengthened through knowledge and the increase of knowledge is rooted in trust.

2. Self-control, Perseverance, and Godliness
1:6

6. And to knowledge, self-control; and to self-control, perseverance; and to perseverance, godliness.

The next three qualities that contribute to the believer's sanctification are:

Self-control. In the Hellenistic world of Peter's day, this word pertained to sports. As Paul puts it, "Everyone who competes in the games *goes into strict training*" (I Cor. 9:25; the italicized words convey the concept *self-control*). The athletes in preparation for the games "abstained from un-wholesome food, wine, and sexual indulgence."[32] A Christian must exercise self-discipline in all circumstances and should do so by placing his trust in God. The apostles, however, refrain from issuing a detailed command on

---

30. Consult Bigg, *The Epistles of St. Peter and St. Jude,* p. 257; Green, *The Second Epistle General of Peter,* pp. 66–67.
31. Guthrie, *New Testament Theology,* p. 600.
32. Thayer, p. 167.

self-control that covers every situation. They mention self-control as a virtue the believer must practice (I Cor. 7:9; Gal. 5:23; Titus 1:8). Martin Luther aptly remarks, "People are not alike. One is strong, another is weak by nature, and no one is always as fit in every respect as the other person is."[33] A Christian ought to maintain his self-control in complete reliance on God.

Perseverance. A momentary lack of self-discipline leads to failure and a loss of self-respect. Therefore, Peter adds the New Testament concept *perseverance.* This word means "to remain under" a particular conflict. Perseverance is defined as "the characteristic of a man who is unswerved from his deliberate purpose and his loyalty to faith and piety by even the greatest trials and sufferings."[34] The word appears repeatedly in the New Testament (see, e.g., Rom. 5:3–4; I Tim. 6:11; Heb. 12:2; James 1:3; I Peter 2:20; Rev. 2:19). Perseverance is related to faith as daughter to mother. It originates in faith, for the believer knows that God is in complete control of every situation. Accordingly, Zacharius Ursinus explained the combination of perseverance and trust in these words:

> We can be patient when things go against us,
>   thankful when things go well,
>   and for the future we can have
>   good confidence in our faithful God and Father.[35]

Godliness. Peter tells us to add godliness to perseverance. This is the second time he introduces the expression *godliness* (see v. 3). He also mentions it in the context of Christ's return (3:11, where it is translated "godly lives"). As Noah and Lot, whom Peter calls "righteous" (2:5, 7), lived among ungodly people, so the Christian today pursues godliness in a sinful world. A Christian practices godliness when he is fully conscious of God's presence in every circumstance, so that his life is guided by the motto of the Genevan Reformer John Calvin: *Coram Deo* (in the presence of God).

3. Brotherly Kindness and Love
1:7

7. And to godliness, brotherly kindness; and to brotherly kindness, love.

The last two virtues are significant, because both of them express love. Notice that when we show brotherly affection and love, we fulfill the summary of the Ten Commandments:

> " 'Love the Lord your God with all your heart and with all your soul and with all your mind.' This is the first and greatest commandment. And the second is like it: 'Love your neighbor as yourself.' " [Matt. 22:37–39]

---

33. Martin Luther, *The Catholic Epistles*, vol. 30 of *Luther's Works*, ed. Jaroslav Pelikan and Walter A. Hansen (St. Louis: Concordia, 1967), p. 156.

34. Thayer, p. 644. Also consult R. C. Trench, *Synonyms of the New Testament* (1854; Grand Rapids: Eerdmans, 1953), p. 197.

35. Heidelberg Catechism, answer 28.

Transliterated from the Greek, the term *brotherly kindness* is *philadelphia* (see Rom. 12:10). The term implies that we express our love to the brothers and sisters in the church and that we "love one another deeply, from the heart" (I Peter 1:22).

Peter writes, "[Add] to brotherly kindness, love." He seems redundant in his emphasis on love. But Peter does not want us to restrict our love to the members of the church. He knows the teaching of Jesus, "Love your enemies" (Matt. 5:44). Love is a debt we owe our fellow man (Rom. 13:8) without exception. In other words, whereas we can limit the application of brotherly kindness to the Christian community, we are unable to restrict the practice of love. "God is love," writes John. "Whoever lives in love lives in God, and God in him" (I John 4:16). Love, which Peter mentions as the last characteristic in the series of eight virtues, is the fruit of faith in God.

C. Growth
1:8–9

What are we doing with the virtues Peter enumerates in the preceding verses? He exhorts us to apply them so that we may reap an abundant harvest in knowing Jesus Christ. A neglect of these virtues results in spiritual loss and deprivation. Peter states the matter first positively (v. 8) and then negatively (v. 9) to show the purpose of these virtues and the consequence of lacking them.

8. For if you possess these qualities in increasing measure, they will keep you from being ineffective and unproductive in your knowledge of our Lord Jesus Christ.

a. *Translations*. This verse lends itself to two possible translations because of the word order in the Greek. The lengthy prepositional phrase "in your knowledge of our Lord Jesus Christ" can be taken either with the adjectives *ineffective and unproductive* (NIV and other versions) or with the Greek verb *to bring*. This is the first translation: "If you have a generous supply of these [virtues], . . . they will bring you to a real knowledge of our Lord Jesus Christ" (JB). However, the other translation is preferred, because the verb *to bring* also has the meaning *to make*, which with the adjective *ineffective* appears to be an idiom. Most translators favor this combination and present the reading, "and make you not useless and unproductive in your knowledge of our Lord Jesus Christ."

b. *Meaning*. If we possess these eight virtues, says Peter, and if they continue to increase, we are reaping an abundant harvest. Peter is not indicating that we must take the virtues successively, as if the one depends on the other. Rather, he means that we must cultivate all of them at the same time and see them grow and develop (see I Thess. 3:12). The consequence of this development is that we are not ineffective and unproductive in our spiritual lives (refer to Gal. 6:10). We are busy applying these virtues and thus witness their visible results. When we are ineffective, we are idle; and when we fail to be productive, we are useless in society (compare Mark

4:19). Such is not the case when all our virtues increase and bear fruit, especially with reference to our knowledge of Christ. Peter unfolds a favorite theme in this epistle: "Grow in the knowledge of Jesus Christ our Lord" (1:2, 3, 8; 3:18). As·parents want to see their infants gain weight, so Peter desires our spiritual growth in knowing Jesus more and more.

> More about Jesus would I know,
> More of his grace to others show;
> More of his saving fullness see,
> More of his love who died for me.
> —Eliza E. Hewitt

9. But if anyone does not have them, he is nearsighted and blind, and has forgotten that he has been cleansed from his past sins.

Here is the reverse, namely, the negative side of the previous statement (v. 8). We consider the following points: deficient, blind, forgetful.

a. *Deficient.* The first word in this verse presents a contrast: "but." That is, if there is a person in the Christian community who lacks the eight virtues that range from faith to love, he is ineffective and unproductive. In this verse, Peter uses the word *anyone* and no longer the pronoun *you.* He is not accusing the readers. He only states a fact. To illustrate his point, Peter uses the metaphor of a person who is nearsighted and blind.

b. *Blind.* The New International Version has the reading *nearsighted and blind,* but the Greek text has the inverse order. A blind person cannot be nearsighted, but a nearsighted person can eventually become blind. However, the two adjectives are in effect synonymous.[36] The term *nearsighted,* which in transliterated form from the Greek is *myōpazōn* (myopic), means "to close the eyes," that is, to squint. The intent, therefore, is to say that a person without spiritual virtues is as blind as someone who contracts his eyelids. With this illustration, Peter wishes to say that a person who neglects the cultivation of spiritual values is blind to the truth of God's Word. Such a man is able to see earthly things that are nearby but unable to see heavenly things that are far away. He is spiritually blind. In his first epistle, John describes the man who claims to be in the light but hates his brother as a person who stumbles in the darkness "because the darkness has blinded him" (2:11).

c. *Forgetful.* From the illustration of blindness, Peter proceeds to the point at issue: "[This person] has forgotten that he has been cleansed from his past sins." Forgetfulness is detrimental to one's spiritual life. It shuts out the past and blocks the memory of Christ's forgiving grace and love. "This forgetfulness is itself an example of failure in the knowledge of Christ."[37]

---

36. Refer to Bauckham, *Jude, 2 Peter,* p. 189. The word *nearsighted* occurs once in the New Testament. Green suggests that Peter borrowed a line from a poem or popular song. *The Second Epistle General of Peter,* p. 73.

37. Joseph B. Mayor, *The Epistle of St. Jude and the Second Epistle of St. Peter: Greek Text with Introduction and Notes* (1907; Grand Rapids: Baker, 1965), p. 96.

On the other hand, anyone who looks to Jesus in gratitude for his salvation and who continues to develop in his personal relationship with the Lord always remembers his conversion and time of baptism.

Peter's statement *he has been cleansed* has bearing on baptism. It harmonizes with Paul's remark concerning the church: "Christ loved the church and gave himself up for her to make her holy, cleansing her by the washing with water through the word" (Eph. 5:25–26; also see I Peter 3:21). Baptism is the symbol of this cleansing, and Jesus' sacrificial death on the cross is a reality.

With the term *past* Peter indicates that someone who lived in sin was converted and baptized. Perhaps this person failed to realize the significance of his cleansing and therefore did not break with his past but mingled his worldly life with Christian living. Perhaps he gradually drifted from his commitment to Christ by forgetting the significance of his baptism and returning to his former sinful life.[38]

Doctrinal Considerations in 1:8–9

Verse 8

For Peter, faith is a basic virtue. He mentions it in his address: "To those who . . . have received a faith as precious as ours" (v. 1). In verse 5, he places faith at the head of the list of virtues. Faith is the mother of all the spiritual qualities he enumerates. Therefore, we should not view these virtues in a descending order of importance but as equally significant in relation to faith.

Verse 9

Is it possible for a believer to sing the hymn "Blessed Assurance, Jesus Is Mine" and forget his baptism? Hardly. By itself, baptism is no guarantee that a person is saved. Baptism is an external ceremony that must have its counterpart in an internal commitment to Christ. But if true faith is lacking in the heart of a person who has been baptized, all the other virtues that Peter mentions also are absent. John writes about people who in his day had left the church: "They went out from us, but they did not really belong to us. For if they had belonged to us, they would have remained with us; but their going showed that none of them belonged to us" (I John 2:19).

Greek Words, Phrases, and Constructions in 1:8–9

Verse 8

ὑπάρχοντα—from the verb ὑπάρχω (I am present), this present active participle in the nominative plural neuter denotes a conditional statement of simple fact. With

---

38. Consult de Boor, *Die Zweite Brief des Petrus*, p. 204.

the pronoun ὑμῖν (you), which is a dative of possession, the participle is translated with the verb *to have*, "If you have these qualities."

καθίστησιν—as a present active indicative third person singular, the verb can mean either "it brings" or "it makes." With the adjectives ἀργούς and ἀκάρπους, the preferred reading is "it makes." The preposition εἰς, then, means "in respect to" instead of "into."

Verse 9

ᾧ—because of the dative case of this pronoun and the verb *to be* in the compound πάρεστιν (it is present), here is a dative of possession (see v. 8). Note that the verb πάρεστιν, which is present active indicative, is negated by the participle μή (not).[39]

μυωπάζων—this present active participle is a contraction of the words μύειν τοὺς ὦπας (to shut the eyes).[40]

D. Assurance
1:10–11

Here is the conclusion to Peter's exhortation in the section about promises and virtues. Peter encourages his readers to gain certainty in regard to their salvation. He writes,

10. Therefore, my brothers, be all the more eager to make your calling and election sure. For if you do these things, you will never fall.

Observe three aspects in this verse:

a. *Eagerness.* With the adverb *therefore*, Peter summarizes what he has been saying in the preceding verses. The adverb encompasses the assurance of verse 8 and the warning of verse 9. With the personal address *my brothers*, Peter speaks to the people described in verse 8 and separates himself from the persons mentioned in verse 9.

The tender address *my brothers* occurs only here in the two epistles of Peter. But the term *dear friends* is common in both letters.[41] By addressing the recipients pastorally, Peter stresses the importance of their spiritual well-being.

"Be all the more eager." In a sense Peter is using the same exhortation in verse 5. Now he is saying, "Put forth every effort you can muster." The Greek verb also includes the notion of urgency (compare 1:15; 3:14). In fact, Peter commands the readers to act immediately without delay. They must continue to do this by making it part of their daily routine and thus show diligence.

b. *Election.* "Make your calling and election sure." These two nouns are synonymous, for in the Greek they share one definite article. Although God elects and calls a person, and although from a divine aspect the chronological order should be that election is followed by calling, Peter indicates

---

39. Consult Robertson, *Grammar*, p. 962.
40. Thayer, p. 420.
41. See I Peter 2:11; 4:12; II Peter 3:1, 8, 14, 17.

that in this verse he views calling and election from man's perspective. In the Greek word order, the expression *sure* follows the verb *be eager,* and because it precedes the combination *calling and election,* the expression is emphatic. Peter wants the readers to realize that God calls them in their lifetime, but that they must exert themselves diligently in ascertaining and appropriating their calling and election (for a parallel, see Phil. 2:12–13). Peter stresses man's responsibility in regard to salvation.

Election and calling are and remain God's redemptive acts. God elects man in eternity (Eph. 1:4) but calls him in time (Rom. 8:30). Man does not elect or call himself, for Paul writes, "God's gifts and his call are irrevocable" (Rom. 11:29). Hence, God alone decrees man's election and calling. The task for man is to appropriate his salvation, so that he is absolutely certain of the calling with which God has called him and can live in the knowledge that he is God's child (II Tim. 1:9).[42]

Calling is not merely an invitation; it is a royal command which man must obey. And election is evidence of God's grace and love toward man.[43] Man, then, must take possession of his election by exercising the virtues Peter outlines in verses 5–7.

c. *Established.* The purpose of the believer's exertion is that he is able to stand. Says Peter, "If you do these things, you will never fall." In the Greek, the expression *never* is emphatic and indicates that the believer's fall cannot happen when he is "all the more eager to make [his] calling and election sure." The believer is firmly established, unmoved, and absolutely sure of his salvation because he knows that he cannot lose it (see Ps. 15:5; 37:24; Jude 24).

11. And you will receive a rich welcome into the eternal kingdom of our Lord and Savior Jesus Christ.

A literal translation of the beginning of this text is, "for in this way" (NASB). That is, by personally affirming his calling and election, the believer enters Christ's kingdom.

a. *Rewards.* God responds to man's faithfulness and richly provides for him an entrance into the kingdom. Note that Peter employs the word *rich* to describe not the manner but the event of the believer's entrance into heaven. When God welcomes the believer to his heavenly abode, he considers the believer his child. Therefore, God lavishes gifts upon him to make him a rich person who enters heaven as a victor. John Albert Bengel writes, "You may be able to enter, not as having escaped from a shipwreck, or from fire, but as it were in triumph."[44] (Incidentally, contrast the text "If it is hard for the righteous to be saved, what will become of the ungodly and the sinner?" [I Peter 4:18] with this text. Obviously, the contexts of these two verses call for a difference in expression.)

---

42. Also see I Cor. 1:26; 7:20; Eph. 1:18; 4:1, 4; Phil. 3:14; II Thess. 1:11; Heb. 3:1.
43. Refer to Acts 9:15; Rom. 9:11; 11:5, 7, 28; I Thess. 1:4.
44. Bengel, *Gnomon of the New Testament,* vol. 5, p. 90.

Peter uses the personal pronoun *you* and tells the readers, "You will receive a rich welcome." The meaning of the verb *to receive,* which is the same Greek verb translated "to add" in verse 5, implies that God will bless abundantly all those who cultivate spiritual virtues.

b. *Place.* Only in this verse the adjective *eternal* is used to describe the kingdom (compare Ps. 145:13; and see II Tim. 4:18, "heavenly kingdom"). Christ's kingdom is eternal because he himself is eternal. In other words, the kingdom of Jesus is not subject to limitations of cosmic time; it exists forever. In this kingdom, Christ is king. As Jesus clearly teaches, God rules through his Son, Jesus Christ (Matt. 28:18).

Peter is fond of calling Jesus Christ "our Lord and Savior" (see 2:20; 3:2, 18). In verse 1 he calls Jesus "God and Savior" to emphasize his divinity.

c. *Significance.* Because the recipients of this epistle know the Lord as their Savior, Peter is not teaching that they will enter either the church or the kingdom of Christ here on earth. The future tense causes us to look expectantly to the coming of Christ's eternal kingdom. We do not simply identify the kingdom with heaven, even though believers when they die enter this kingdom. The broader perspective, in Peter's own words, is that "we are looking forward to a new heaven and a new earth, the home of righteousness" (3:13).

Doctrinal Considerations in 1:10–11

How do I know that I am a child of God? When I search my spiritual life, I know that the certainty of salvation does not come to me through dreams, visions, and revelations. I have assurance of salvation because God has given me his Word, has revealed himself in Jesus Christ, and has worked and continues to work in my heart through the Holy Spirit. God has created faith in my soul so that I put my complete confidence and trust in him.

> I know not how this saving faith
> To me he did impart,
> Nor how believing in his Word
> Wrought peace within my heart.
> But "I know whom I have believed,
> and am persuaded that he is able
> To keep that which I've committed
> Unto him against that day." [II Tim. 1:12, KJV]
> —Daniel W. Whittle

What is the effect of this gift of faith? When I obediently listen to God's call and do his will, when I experience God's nearness in my soul, then I begin to understand that God's calling and election are an unspeakable source of comfort to me. I realize that as long as I reflect God's virtues in my life, I shall never fall. I know that God is able to keep me from falling and to present me faultless before him in love and with great joy (Jude 24).

Greek Words, Phrases, and Constructions in 1:10–11

Verse 10

τὴν κλῆσιν καὶ ἐκλογήν—here are two nouns introduced by one definite article. The nouns are considered synonyms in this construction.[45]

ποιεῖσθαι—the use of the present middle (reflexive) infinitive shows that Peter instructs every believer to make his own calling and election sure.

ποιοῦντες—the present active participle denotes both a continuing activity and a condition: "If you keep on doing these things."

οὐ μὴ πταίσητε—this is the only time in Peter's epistles that the double negative occurs. The use of this combination signifies emphasis. Also, the aorist subjunctive indicates single occurrence.

Verse 11

ἐπιχορηγηθήσεται—see verse 5, where the same verb appears in the aorist active. Here it is in the future passive. The future is definite. Notice that the adverb πλουσίως (richly) precedes the main verb and is in a position of emphasis.

τοῦ κυρίου ἡμῶν καὶ σωτῆρος—see verse 1. When one definite article governs two nouns, the construction shows that the writer refers to one person.

---

12 So I will always remind you of these things, even though you know them and are firmly established in the truth you now have. 13 I think it is right to refresh your memory as long as I live in the tent of this body, 14 because I know that I will soon put it aside, as our Lord Jesus Christ has made clear to me. 15 And I will make every effort to see that after my departure you will always be able to remember these things.

16 We did not follow cleverly invented stories when we told you about the power and coming of our Lord Jesus Christ, but we were eyewitnesses of his majesty. 17 For he received honor and glory from God the Father when the voice came to him from the Majestic Glory, saying, "This is my Son, whom I love; with him I am well pleased." 18 We ourselves heard this voice that came from heaven when we were with him on the sacred mountain.

19 And we have the word of the prophets made more certain, and you will do well to pay attention to it, as to a light shining in a dark place, until the day dawns and the morning star rises in your hearts. 20 Above all, you must understand that no prophecy of Scripture came about by the prophet's own interpretation. 21 For prophecy never had its origin in the will of man, but men spoke from God as they were carried along by the Holy Spirit.

III. Divine Revelation
1:12–21

A. Memory
1:12–15

Peter informs his readers that he himself is about to leave his physical body and thus enter the eternal kingdom of Jesus Christ. But before he departs this earthly scene, he wants to be absolutely sure that his readers know the truth. He gives them an additional reminder.

---

45. Consult Robertson, *Grammar*, p. 787.

12. So I will always remind you of these things, even though you know them and are firmly established in the truth you now have.

From his perspective as an apostle of Jesus Christ, Peter expresses his interest in and concern for the spiritual well-being of the church. He views the life of the church in relation to the truth of God's Word.

a. "So I will always remind you of these things." Even though Christians have a basic knowledge of the truth, Peter sees the necessity of reminding them. The Greek, at this point, causes some difficulties for translators. In effect, the Greek verb translated "I will" in the New International Version is a double future. Here is a version that has captured the thought best: "That is why I am continually recalling the same truths to you" (JB).[46]

Whenever and wherever the believers read this epistle, they are reminded of the words Peter has written. The content of this letter, then, serves as a reminder of the truth of God's revelation. For this reason Peter qualifies his statement with the adverb *always*. Not merely the spoken word of an apostle but the written word of God's revelation will continually remind the people of the truth. Peter knows that although his earthly life will come to an end, his epistle will remain as a constant reminder. Paul and John, in their epistles, also remind the readers of the truth they have taught. Says Paul, "I have written you quite boldly on some points, as if to remind you of them again" (Rom. 15:15); "It is no trouble for me to write the same things to you again, and it is a safeguard for you" (Phil. 3:1). And John testifies, "I do not write to you because you do not know the truth, but because you do know it" (I John 2:21). They leave written documents that are God's inspired Word.

b. "Even though you know them and are firmly established in the truth you now have." What are the things that the readers know? Certainly they are the truths Peter has written in the first part of this chapter. These truths, then, are not new teachings for the recipients of this letter. They have known them ever since they heard the gospel proclaimed (compare Jude 5). Peter is descriptive when he says, "[You] are firmly established in the truth" (compare I Peter 5:10). He is not addressing recent converts, but Christians who have been fully indoctrinated in the truths of the gospel. Perhaps Peter chooses the words *firmly established* because of his own lack of commitment when he disowned Jesus in the high priest's courtyard (Matt. 26:69–75). Granted that the believers have the truth of God now, they readily forget and need someone to refresh their memories.

13. I think it is right to refresh your memory as long as I live in the tent of this body,   14. because I know that I will soon put it aside, as our Lord Jesus Christ has made clear to me.

Notice that Peter speaks pastorally in a personal manner and with apos-

---

46. Other translations have the reading *I will not hesitate* (NEB), *I intend* (NAB, RSV), *I shall be ready* (RV, ASV, NASB), or *I will not be negligent* (NKJV, KJV, following a variant Greek text). Others present a simple future tense: "I will" (NIV, SEB, GNB, MLB).

tolic authority. He is convinced of his duty to help the people recall what they have learned. He regards this work as his pastoral task of preaching and teaching the Word of God.

The Greek verb *to refresh* means "to wake up, to rouse." The human mind is apt to take a rest and readily becomes sleepy. Peter is not referring to normal nighttime sleep but to a lack of attentiveness. Too often we rest on the laurels of past achievements and fail to be alert. We are lulled asleep, as if we are living in peace while the spiritual warfare against Satan and his cohorts is raging all around us. The time to awaken our minds comes at least once a week on the Lord's Day when God, through his servants, addresses us in the worship service.

Peter rouses his readers by refreshing their memories in a way that builds their faith in God and avoids offense. He does this pastorally and tactfully; yet at the same time he expresses the urgency of his duty. Calvin observes, "We are also taught by the example of Peter, that the shorter term of life remains to us, the more diligent ought we to be in executing our office."[47]

Peter resorts to using a metaphor when he speaks of his physical body. He designates it a tent, much the same as Paul calls it "an earthly tent" (II Cor. 5:1, 4). The illustration is telling, because a house provides a sense of permanence, but a tent is a temporary dwelling. Peter gives no indication that he despises the body and glorifies the soul. On the contrary, his figure of speech conveys the idea of temporality. The time allotted for Peter's earthly ministry is brief. Because of the brevity of the time that still remains, Peter wants to make his readers conscious of the authority and importance of his teachings. Therefore, as long as he is physically capable, he devotes his time to refreshing the memories of the believers.

Peter knows that his physical "tent" will be taken down in the near future. He writes, "I know that I will soon put it aside." We are not told exactly when Peter died, for then we would be able to determine when Peter composed this epistle. If Peter suffered a martyr's death in the last few years of Nero's reign, according to tradition, we aver that Peter died in the mid-sixties. Nero committed suicide on the ninth of June A.D. 68.

Using the expression *soon,* Peter indicates that the end of his life will come suddenly. The Greek adjective *soon* appears only once more in the New Testament, in 2:1 ("swift," NIV). There it conveys the thought of suddenness, "bringing swift destruction." He anticipates not a lingering illness which eventually ends in death, but a swift, unexpected execution that terminates his earthly life. He speaks of his impending death as if he removes a piece of clothing. He says of his body, "I will soon put it aside" (see also Eph. 4:22; Col. 3:9). Peter is not afraid of death, for he will enter eternal glory with Jesus Christ (I Peter 5:10).

"As our Lord Jesus Christ has made clear to me." Peter is guided not by

---

47. Calvin, *The Second Epistle of Peter,* p. 379.

premonitions but by a clear revelation given to him by Jesus Christ. The scriptural reference to this prophecy is Jesus' word recorded by John in the last chapter of his Gospel: "I tell you the truth, when you were younger you dressed yourself and went where you wanted; but when you are old you will stretch out your hands, and someone else will dress you and lead you where you do not want to go" (21:18). These words predict that Peter will become an old man, but they do not say anything about a sudden death. We assume, then, that Jesus' saying "was widely known in the early Church, as a prophecy of Peter's martyrdom."[48]

15. And I will make every effort to see that after my departure you will always be able to remember these things.

Observe these matters:

First, Peter writes the pronoun *I* repeatedly in his letters. In his first epistle, this personal pronoun appears in the last chapter (5:1, 12). In his second letter, he uses the first person singular in the first and third chapters (1:12, 13, 14, 15; 3:1, 2). Peter addresses the readers to demonstrate his personal interest in them.

Next, Peter has a penchant for repetition. For instance, the command *make every effort* also appears in Greek as a noun in 1:5 and as a verb in 1:10 and in 3:14. In 1:15, he writes the verb in the future tense, as if to make a solemn pledge.

Third, why does Peter use the future tense and not the present? If we take these words at face value, we must conclude that Peter intends to write still another document. Some scholars interpret Peter's declaration to mean that together with Mark he wrote the Gospel of Mark. "Certainly no document would redeem the apostle's promise so well as a gospel; and if a gospel is meant, the reference can hardly be to any other than that of St. Mark."[49] Christian writers in the second and third centuries testify to the fact that Mark composed his Gospel with the help of Peter. About A.D. 125, Papias, who was bishop of Hierapolis in Asia Minor and a former disciple of the apostle John, wrote:

> Mark became Peter's interpreter and wrote accurately all that he remembered, not, indeed, in order, of the things said or done by the Lord. For he had not heard the Lord, nor had he followed him, but later on, as I said, followed Peter, who used to give teaching as necessity demanded.[50]

Some sixty years later, Irenaeus, bishop of the churches in Lyons, also testifies to this fact. Writing about the death of Peter and Paul, he says: "But

---

48. Bauckham, *Jude, 2 Peter*, p. 200. Many interpreters understand John 21:18 to refer to Peter's crucifixion. For example, see William Hendriksen, *The Gospel of John*, New Testament Commentary series, 2 vols. in 1 (Grand Rapids: Baker, 1954), vol. 2, p. 490. Also see Lenski, *Interpretation of the Epistles*, p. 282.

49. Bigg, *Epistles of St. Peter and St. Jude*, p. 265.

50. Eusebius *Ecclesiastical History* 3.39.15 (LCL).

after their death [departure], Mark also, the disciple and interpreter of Peter, himself handed down to us in writing the things which were preached by Peter."[51] Even though the evidence from the early church points in the direction of Mark's Gospel, we can only assume but not prove that Peter is thinking of the Gospel.

Fourth, a key word in verse 15 is "departure." This is a term Peter uses to describe his impending death. Undoubtedly he implicitly teaches that his death is a transition from this earthly life to an unending life with Christ. Therefore, he views his death not as a cessation but as a departure. In the New Testament, this expression occurs in two other places (Luke 9:31 and Heb. 11:22 ["end," NIV]) where it refers to a departure from this life. By using this same word in his remark about Peter's death, Irenaeus indicates that he is familiar with Peter's second epistle. "It is hard to escape the conclusion that Irenaeus knew this passage in 2 Peter, and took the implicit promise to refer to Mark's Gospel."[52]

Practical Considerations in 1:12–15

After Jesus reinstated Peter as an apostle (John 21:15–19), Peter exemplified his total commitment to Jesus even in the face of impending death. For instance, the night preceding Peter's trial before Herod Agrippa I (Acts 12:1–19), "Peter was sleeping between two soldiers, bound with two chains" (v. 6). He was sound asleep, so that the angel who came to release him had to strike him on the side to wake him (v. 7). Peter committed himself completely to the care of his Lord and therefore lived without worry and fear. He slept.

In his second epistle, Peter demonstrates this same trust and confidence in Jesus. He knows that the Lord has informed him about his imminent departure. Thus, he compares the passing from this life with the removal of a garment. He departs to be with Jesus, "which is better by far" (Phil. 1:23).

Greek Words, Phrases, and Constructions in 1:12–15

Verse 12

μελλήσω—the verb μέλλω with an infinitive is equivalent to the future tense: "I am about to." Here the future tense may denote an intended action. The future verb form occurs in one other place (Matt. 24:6). The variant reading given in the Majority Text is ἀμελήσω (from the verb ἀμελέω, I reject).

παρούσῃ—this present active participle in the feminine singular (from πάρειμι, I am present) signifies "to have at one's disposal."

Verse 14

ἀπόθεσις—from ἀποτίθημι (I take off), this noun occurs twice in the New Testament (I Peter 3:21; II Peter 1:14). Here it is a euphemism for death.

---

51. Eusebius *Ecclesiastical History* 5.8.3 (LCL). Also see Irenaeus *Against Heresies* 3.1.1 (Ante-Nicene Fathers).

52. Green, *The Second Epistle General of Peter*, pp. 80–81.

σκηνώματος—a synonym of the more common σκηνή, the New Testament features it three times (twice in vv. 13–14 and once in Acts 7:46). The use of this metaphor is not limited to Hellenistic writers, as its frequent occurrence in the Septuagint shows.

Verse 15

σπουδάσω—the future active indicative from σπουδάζω (I make every effort; see v. 10 and 3:14) is punctiliar.

ποιεῖσθαι—note that the use of the middle in this present infinitive is reflexive.

B. Eyewitnesses
1:16–18

If the recipients wish to keep their spiritual treasures, they must be assured that their possessions are genuine. For this reason, Peter speaks as an eyewitness to testify that he personally saw the majesty of Jesus Christ and the coming of his eternal kingdom.

1. Christ's Coming
1:16

16. We did not follow cleverly invented stories when we told you about the power and coming of our Lord Jesus Christ, but we were eyewitnesses of his majesty.

In this verse Peter presents his message first negatively in terms of a disclaimer and then positively by revealing the privileged status of an eyewitness.

a. "We did not follow cleverly invented stories." Notice the interesting change from the singular *I* to the plural *we*. Peter is not only a pastor who speaks personally to the members of his church; he also belongs to the body of the apostles. With the other apostles, he speaks with authority about the veracity of the gospel. When false prophets seek either to distort the gospel or to teach their own fables and legends, Peter voices his apostolic opposition.

The term *stories* in Greek is "myths." According to Peter, false teachers are teaching the church members "destructive heresies" (2:1) and "stories they have made up" (2:3). They will scoff at Christ's promise to return, Peter adds (3:3–4). These teachers deny the historical basis of the gospel message and instead present their own myths.

What is a myth? A myth is a story which man has formulated to express his own desires without any reference to reality. Because of its man-centered focus, a myth is devoid of redemptive power (see I Tim. 1:4; 4:7; II Tim. 4:4; Titus 1:14).[53] By contrast, Scripture originates with God. The

---

53. Consult Karl Hermann Schelkle, *Die Petrusbriefe, Der Judasbrief*, Herders Theologischer Kommentar zum Neuen Testament series, 5th rev. ed. (Freiburg: Herder, 1980), vol. 13/2, p. 198. Refer to Gustav Stählin, *TDNT*, vol. 4, pp. 785–86.

Bible is divinely inspired, rooted in history, and unquestionably true. And last, the gospel message redeems man from sin and glorifies God.

Peter calls the myths of the false prophets "cleverly invented stories." He says that the apostles refused to follow manmade fables and rejected their alleged authority. In his epistle, Peter does not explain the content of these stories but rather reminds the readers of the content of the gospel.

b. "When we told you about the power and coming of our Lord Jesus Christ." These words must be seen in the context of this passage, for they refer to the transfiguration of Jesus (see Matt. 17:1–8; Mark 9:2–8; Luke 9:28–36). Peter relates the event when he with John and James saw a glimpse of the power and majesty of Jesus Christ coming into his eternal kingdom. He uses the term *coming* to explain the promised return of Christ. In their writings, the apostles often testify to the coming of Christ (e.g., Matt. 24:3; John 14:3; I Cor. 15:23; II Thess. 2:8). When Jesus returns, he manifests his power in defeating the forces of his opponents. Some interpreters understand the terms *power* and *coming* to mean "mighty coming."[54] The appearance of Jesus is a coming that is characterized by power (compare Matt. 24:30; Mark 9:1; 13:26; Luke 21:27). The Greek word *coming* signifies not Jesus' birth but his return to earth. In the context of Peter's epistle, this word plays a significant role in the question of the scoffers: "Where is this 'coming' he promised?" (3:4; also see 3:12). In the New Testament, the Greek term *coming* is never used to describe the first coming of Jesus but always the second. Therefore, we relate this term to the return of Christ and see his coming as a revelation of Jesus' power on the last day. As Peter indicates, the transfiguration of Jesus, which the apostle observed, prefigures this glorious event.

c. "We were eyewitnesses of his majesty." In this clause the emphasis is on the term *eyewitnesses*. In Greek, this term occurs only once in the New Testament.[55] In Hellenistic literature it is used for men who, after their initiation, were permitted to look into the mysteries of a cult. The expression in verse 16, however, does not depend on this Hellenistic usage, because the historical context emphasizes that the three apostles were observers. The account of Jesus' transfiguration has nothing to do with the mystery cults of the Greeks. The apostles were eyewitnesses of Jesus' majesty.

2. Christ's Glory
1:17

17. For he received honor and glory from God the Father when the voice came to him from the Majestic Glory, saying, "This is my Son, whom I love; with him I am well pleased."

a. "For he received honor and glory." Peter declares that the preaching

---

54. See, e.g., GNB.

55. In the Greek, however, Peter uses the verb twice (see I Peter 2:12; 3:2).

of the apostles is absolutely trustworthy because they speak as eyewitnesses of the person and words of Jesus Christ. They personally saw Jesus' glory and honor from the time of his baptism to the day of his ascension. John testifies to this fact. He writes, "We have seen his glory, the glory of the One and Only, who came from the Father, full of grace and truth" (John 1:14).

Here is a reference to the time when Jesus was transfigured on a high mountain and talked with Moses and Elijah while Peter, James, and John observed (Matt. 17:1–8). When Jesus was transfigured, "his face shone like the sun, and his clothes became as white as the light" (v. 2). He received honor when a voice from heaven said, "This is my Son, whom I love; with him I am well pleased. Listen to him!" (v. 5).

For at least two reasons we should not look for a chronological order in the listing of "honor and glory." First, the combination *honor and glory* occurs in reverse order in Psalm 8:5 and Hebrews 2:7, 9.[56] The two nouns, then, are interchangeable in this pair of words. Second, in spite of the fact that the translations do not show a grammatical break at the end of verse 17, the sentence is incomplete. That is, the verse begins with a participle that is translated "having received." But the verb on which this participle depends is missing. Thus, we are unable to determine if the apostle meant to show a chronological sequence in the words *honor and glory*.

Granted that honor and glory are closely related, we can distinguish between the two. Glory is a quality that belongs to God and is shared by Christ. Honor is the recognition of someone who has attained a position through his labors and achievements. Glory is external and visible, but honor is abstract and unknown until it is revealed. Jesus was transfigured in heavenly glory and honorably recognized by God the Father.

b. "From God the Father." In his first epistle, Peter introduces the Trinity at the beginning of his letter and mentions God the Father twice (1:2, 3; also see v. 17). In his second letter, Peter places the phrase *God the Father* in the setting of the transfiguration. In this scene, "the glory of Christ is inseparably linked with the glory of God."[57] And the unity of Father and Son is expressed audibly.

c. "When the voice came to him from the Majestic Glory." Peter reveals his Hebraic roots when he deferentially speaks of the Majestic Glory to avoid using the name of God (see Ps. 145:5). A literal translation of this clause particularly depicts the Jewish fear of transgressing the command not to misuse the name of God (Exod. 20:7; Deut. 5:11). The text actually has the reading, "Such a voice as this was conveyed to him by the Majestic Glory." Nevertheless, the relation of Father and Son is clear because of the message spoken by the voice.

d. " 'This is my Son, whom I love; with him I am well pleased.' " At first

---

56. Also refer to Rom. 2:7, 10; I Tim. 1:17; I Peter 1:7; Rev. 4:9.

57. Guthrie, *New Testament Theology*, p. 91.

sight, this statement appears to be identical with that in the synoptic Gospels (Matt. 17:5; and see Mark 9:7; Luke 9:35). But a close examination reveals a difference. All three synoptic Gospels have the additional command, "Listen to him!" Peter's version comes closest to Matthew's account but differs from it in minor details (in the Greek). Peter had no need to rely on written accounts, for we assume that his memory served him well. The wording of this statement has its source in Isaiah 42:1, "Here is my servant, whom I uphold, my chosen one in whom I delight."

What is the significance of this divine proclamation? First, God the Father reveals that Jesus is his Son. If we acknowledge Jesus as the Son of God, whom the Father has sent, we have eternal life (John 17:3; I John 4:15). Next, God qualifies his statement by adding, "my Son, whom I love." Through his Son Jesus Christ, God the Father loves us.[58] Last, God asserts, "With him I am well pleased." At the time of Jesus' baptism God the Father also spoke these words (Matt. 3:17; and compare Mark 1:11; Luke 3:22). Because of his redemptive work, Jesus is the recipient of God's good pleasure at both his baptism and his transfiguration.

Greek Words, Phrases, and Constructions in 1:17

λαβών—the aorist active participle, which expresses a temporal mode, stands unrelated to a main verb. The sentence, therefore, is incomplete.

φωνῆς ἐνεχθείσης—the genitive absolute construction also stands by itself because of the absence of a main clause. The noun φωνῆς is without the definite article (to indicate deference for God). The aorist ἐνεχθείσης (from φέρω, I bear) denotes single occurrence. The passive with ὑπό points to God as the agent.

μου . . . μου—whereas the Synoptic writers have only one personal pronoun in the genitive singular, Peter has two.

---

3. Christ's Companions
1:18

18. We ourselves heard this voice that came from heaven when we were with him on the sacred mountain.

a. "We ourselves heard this voice . . . from heaven." Note the emphatic use of the intensive pronoun *ourselves*. Peter puts the pronoun in the plural to indicate that he is not the only one who witnessed the transfiguration of Jesus. James and John were with him, too. Although John does not refer to this particular event in his Gospel or in his epistles, he nonetheless states, "We have seen his glory" (John 1:14; also see 2:11; 17:24). Peter virtually repeats the wording of the preceding verse. He again discloses his Jewish reverence for God's name and in an effort to avoid its use he writes, "from

---

58. Consult Calvin, *The Second Epistle of Peter*, p. 384.

heaven." Even though the Gospel account reveals that a voice came from a bright cloud that surrounded them (Matt. 17:5), for Peter this was the voice of God the Father in heaven.

b. "When we were with him." Peter reminds his readers that the main character in the transfiguration is Jesus. The apostles testify to his glorification because, as Peter indicates, "we were with him." They were eyewitnesses of an event that was burned into their memories. Peter with his fellow apostles was with Jesus.

c. "On the sacred mountain." In Peter's mind, the mountain where Jesus was transfigured became holy because God was there. Again this is a typical Jewish expression. Matthew calls Jerusalem "the holy city" (Matt. 4:5; 27:53) and in the Old Testament the common expression *holy mountain* refers to Mount Zion (see, e.g., Ps. 87:1; Isa. 11:9; 56:7). This is not to say that the mount of transfiguration is Mount Zion. In fact, the church has never been able to identify the place of transfiguration. Some scholars are of the opinion that the mountain may be Mount Hermon; others have thought of Mount Tabor. The exact location is not at issue. The point Peter makes is that the revelation of God's glory made the mountain holy for the apostles who witnessed the event.

Doctrinal Considerations in 1:16–18

Of all his recollections of Jesus' ministry, why has Peter selected the transfiguration scene for his discourse in this epistle? The transfiguration of Jesus provides Peter with the knowledge that Jesus Christ will give every believer "a rich welcome into [his] eternal kingdom" (v. 11). Instead of listing numerous details of this memorable event, Peter emphasizes the main points: the power and coming of Jesus Christ, the heavenly honor and glory given to Jesus, and his confirmation by God the Father. As human witnesses, the apostles were permitted to see a glimpse of heaven in which Jesus rules with power, honor, and glory, and in which he is the Son of God who receives his Father's love and approval.

Peter chooses to focus on the transfiguration to show that he can personally vouch for the veracity of Christ's teachings. He asserts that a glorious entry into Christ's kingdom awaits the believer, and that everyone must "be all the more eager to make [his] calling and election sure" (v. 10).

C. Prophecy
1:19–21

This is the third part on the subject *divine revelation*. In the first segment Peter exerts himself to refresh the memory of his readers (vv. 12–15). In the second part he gives his eyewitness account of Jesus' transfiguration (vv. 16–18). And in the third section he reveals the certainty, origin, and source of Scripture (vv. 19–21). For Peter, Scripture is God's revelation to man and not man's description of God. For him the written Word of God is indisputably trustworthy.

1. Certainty
1:19

19. And we have the word of the prophets made more certain, and you will do well to pay attention to it, as to a light shining in a dark place, until the day dawns and the morning star rises in your hearts.

In the preceding section Peter focused on the spoken word of God the Father. In this verse he concentrates on the written Word of prophecy, namely, the Old Testament Scriptures. From a broader perspective, we see a definite connection between the message proclaimed by the apostles and the words of the prophets, that is, the entire Old Testament. The point at issue in this verse is whether the Old Testament Scripture is confirmed by the teaching of the apostles or the apostles' message is confirmed by the Old Testament.

a. *Translations.* Here are two translations to show the difference. The King James Version has the reading, "We have also a more sure word of prophecy." This means that the Old Testament supports the teaching of the apostles. In support of this view, we can say that the Jewish people accepted the unquestionable certainty of the Scriptures. As is evident from the New Testament, the writers appeal to Old Testament prophecies for support. Therefore, the Scriptures do not need to be confirmed.[59] The New American Bible supports this view: "Besides, we possess the prophetic message as something altogether reliable." However, the objection to this translation is that verse 19 appears to diminish rather than strengthen Peter's emphasis on the apostolic eyewitness account (v. 16–18).

Hence, other versions have an alternative translation: "And we have the word of the prophets made more certain."[60] This wording does justice to the sequence of the apostolic message confirmed by the transfiguration and by the Old Testament Scripture. Although translators favor this rendering, they must admit that the Greek for "the word *made* more certain" is not as accurate a translation as "we have a more reliable word." Simply put, the verb *made* is not in the Greek text.

b. *Warning.* Peter writes, "And you do well to pay attention to [this prophetic word]." What is this prophetic word? Some scholars interpret it to refer to the messianic prophecies in the Old Testament. Others explain that it relates to the entire Old Testament (understood as prophecy concerning the coming of the Messiah). And still others say that it points to the prophecies of both the Old and New Testaments.[61] The immediate context seems to indicate that Peter is thinking of the prophecies of Scripture. All the

---

59. Consult Bigg, *The Epistles of St. Peter and St. Jude*, p. 268. And see Green, *The Second Epistle General of Peter*, p. 87.

60. NIV. Also see RSV, NEB, NKJV, JB, ASV, NASB. The MLB puts the text in these words: "So we have the prophetic message reaffirmed," and adds in a footnote, "By the gospel of Christ which the writer has been preaching."

61. For a complete list, see Bauckham, *Jude, 2 Peter*, p. 224.

prophets of the Old Testament era from Moses to the last of the minor prophets speak with one voice (compare I Peter 1:10–12). Furthermore, the expression *the word of the prophets* "is comprehensive enough to include, beside the predictions concerning Christ's Second Coming, all the numerous prophecies fulfilled in connection with His earthly life."[62] Peter urges his readers to pay close attention to the context of this prophetic word.

Peter compares the "word of the prophets" to "a light shining in a dark place." At night, light immediately attracts our eye, for it gives us the ability to see. Light dispels darkness and brings everything into view. We do not stare at the light but use it to look at the objects that become visible (refer to Ps. 119:105; also see John 5:35). Peter writes that the prophetic word keeps on shining into a place that is dark. In New Testament Greek, the term *dark* occurs only here. It evokes an image of the squalid conditions of people who are living in spiritual darkness; upon them the light of God's Word shines.

c. "Until the day dawns and the morning star rises in your hearts." What is the significance of the word *day*? This word should be interpreted in relation to the term *morning star*. Peter points to the day of Christ's return. With the expression *morning star,* which in transliterated Greek is *phōsphoros* (light bringer), he points to Christ and his eventual return. These names are symbolic, for in various settings and forms they appear elsewhere in Scripture. Consider, for example, these verses:

A star will come out of Jacob. [Num. 24:17]

The day is almost here. [Rom. 13:12]

As you see the Day approaching. [Heb. 10:25]

"I am . . . the bright Morning Star." [Rev. 22:16]

Because the words are symbolic, we should not expect Peter to write that the morning star arises before the break of day (as is the natural sequence). Venus, usually known as the morning star, reflects the rays of the sun when daybreak has as yet not appeared. But the terms *day* and *morning star* are both poetic descriptions of the coming of Christ and do not necessarily imply a sequence. Like other writers, Peter exhorts the readers to pay close attention to the prophetic word of Scripture and to do so with reference to Christ's imminent return.

What do the words *in your hearts* mean? The second coming of Christ is an event that every eye shall see. It is not something that takes place secretly in the hearts of believers. Michael Green has proposed an ingenious solution

---

62. D. Edmond Hiebert, "The Prophetic Foundation for the Christian Life: An Exposition of 2 Peter 1:19–21," *BS* 141 (1984): 160.

that would completely remove the difficulty we face in the text. He suggests
that we take the phrase *in your hearts* with verse 20 ("Above all, you must
understand in your hearts").[63] But the Greek word order makes no allow-
ance for this proposal. Hence, we prefer to keep the phrase in this text and
interpret Peter's words to signify that every believer must have subjective
knowledge of Christ and his return. That knowledge the believer keeps in
his heart as he waits for the actual, objective appearance of Jesus Christ.

2. Origin
1:20

**20. Above all, you must understand that no prophecy of Scripture came
about by the prophet's own interpretation.**

Here is an important point of doctrine which Peter introduces with the
words *above all*. Before we study the various interpretations of this verse, we
can accept Peter's remark that the readers must know the use of Scripture.
That is, they ought to know that Scripture did not originate in man's mind.
Peter puts it as follows: "No prophecy of Scripture came about by the
prophet's own interpretation."

a. *Differences.* Observe the difference we encounter in two translations:

> "No prophecy of scripture is a matter of one's own
> interpretation" (RSV; compare KJV, NKJV, NASB, and
> JB).

> "No prophecy of Scripture ever came about by a
> prophet's own ideas" (SEB; compare NIV).[64]

The difference centers on the word *own*. Should the reading be "one's own
interpretation" or "the prophet's own interpretation"? This difference is
profoundly important: the one translation means that a person has no
freedom to interpret Scripture; the other version signifies that Scripture
does not originate from the interpretation of a prophet. In simple terms,
the first translation stresses the use of Scripture, the second its origin.

b. *Explanations.* Commentators who favor the first explanation say that
Scripture ought not to be interpreted privately, for in this epistle Peter
himself says, "Ignorant and unstable people distort [Scripture]" (3:16). A
believer may interpret Scripture as long as he abides by the teachings of the
church, which is guided by the Holy Spirit. But Peter places no restrictions
on the individual believer who reads the Scriptures.

In fact, the Reformers taught that believers are free to interpret Scrip-

---

63. Consult Green, *The Second Epistle General of Peter*, p. 87.

64. The translation "No one can interpret any prophecy of Scripture by himself" (NEB; also
see GNB) is a free rendition of the Greek text, which has the verb *is* or *becomes* but not *can
interpret.*

ture and can do so without ecclesiastical regulations. "The Reformers stressed the perspicuity of Scripture. . . . They did not mean to minimize the importance of the interpretations of the Church in the preaching of the Word. They pointed out that Scripture itself testifies to its perspicuity, where it is declared to be a lamp unto our feet, and a light unto our path."[65] Even though we know that the Holy Spirit directs the church into a clearer understanding of Scripture, we cannot deny that the Spirit also guides individuals in interpreting the Bible. Consequently, we must refrain from reading into the text restrictions that Peter did not write; instead we should listen carefully to what the writer is trying to communicate.

The second view is that "no prophecy of Scripture came about by the prophet's own interpretation." Admittedly, the expression *prophet* is not in the Greek text but has been added by the translator for the purpose of clarifying the passage. Translators ask whether Peter was thinking of the reader when he wrote "one's own interpretation" or if he had the prophet in mind. If he means the prophet, then he is talking about the origin of Scripture. In the last part of verse 20 the Greek expression *to come about* denotes origin. Also, the noun *interpretation* "refer[s] to the activity of the Biblical prophet himself; to what was in his mind as he wrote."[66] Incidentally, in the New Testament the noun *interpretation* occurs only here; the verb appears in only two places (Mark 4:34; Acts 19:39). And last, this verse is a prelude to verse 21.

c. *Conclusion.* Many difficulties remain and no conclusion is without detraction. Yet, in my opinion, the second view harmonizes with the elaborate description of prophetic activity that Peter provides in his first epistle (1:10–12). Furthermore, this view fits the immediate context of verse 20, which speaks of the origin of Scripture. In verses 16–19, Peter discusses the origin of the apostolic message; verse 21, which flows forth from the preceding verse and is closely connected with it, reveals the divine origin of Scripture.

3. *Source*
1:21

21. For prophecy never had its origin in the will of man, but men spoke from God as they were carried along by the Holy Spirit.

Here is a beautifully balanced sentence that expresses a contrast in which man is passive and God is active. It reveals this contrast negatively and positively. By taking the word order in the Greek, we see the following parallel:

---

65. Louis Berkhof, *Introductory Volume to Systematic Theology* (Grand Rapids: Eerdmans, 1932), p. 167. Also see Peter Toon, *The Right of Private Judgment* (Portland, Ore.: Western Conservative Baptist Seminary, 1975), p. 3.

66. Anthony C. Thiselton, *NIDNTT*, vol. 1, p. 578. Also consult Henry Alford, *Alford's Greek Testament: An Exegetical and Critical Commentary*, 5th ed., 4 vols. (1875; Grand Rapids: Guardian, 1976), vol. 4, pt. 2, p. 400.

Passive   *Passive*
for   but
by the will of   by the
man   Holy Spirit
prophecy never   men
was borne   were borne

Active
[men] spoke
from God

Note these points:

a. *Negative.* Peter begins his statement on the origin and source of prophecy by stating that Scripture did not come into being by the will of man. With this opening remark he finds support in the Old Testament, which asserts emphatically that true prophecy never originates with man. For instance, God tells Jeremiah, "Do not listen to what the prophets are prophesying to you; they fill you with false hopes. They speak visions from their own minds, not from the mouth of the LORD" (23:16). And God pronounces woes upon the wicked prophets "who follow their own spirit and have seen nothing" (Ezek. 13:3).

Peter says that the human will did not originate true prophecy. He uses an absolute when he writes the term *never*. At no instance in the formation of Scripture did man's will ever prevail. On the contrary, prophecy comes from God.

b. *Positive.* Thus Peter states that prophecy has come about by the Holy Spirit. Both the Old and the New Testaments declare that the men who spoke and wrote realized that the Holy Spirit was at work in them. So David testifies, "The Spirit of the LORD spoke through me; his word was on my tongue" (II Sam. 23:2). Likewise, Paul calls the Holy Spirit the primary author of prophecy and Isaiah the secondary author (Acts 28:25; also see Heb. 3:7; 10:15).

c. *Passive.* In the parallel (above), the verbs in the two main columns are passive and are derived from the verb *to carry.* In the Greek, the verb *was borne* is in the past tense and indicates that the composition of prophecy by the will of man never happened. By contrast, the verb *were borne* in the second column is a participle in the present tense in Greek. This participle discloses the continual activity of the Holy Spirit, who carried men along in the work of writing Scripture. The figure of speech is borrowed from the nautical vocabulary, in the sense that a sailboat is carried along by the wind.

The Holy Spirit employed men, not instruments, for the composition of Scripture. The Spirit used human beings with their talents and insights, their peculiarities and characteristics, keeping them from sin and error. The Holy Spirit is in control of man. Therefore, the text is clear on this point: in the writing of Scripture, man is passive and the Spirit active.

d. *Active.* The main verb in the last part of the sentence is "spoke." "Men

273

spoke from God."[67] Notice that men are active, not passive, in the formation of Scripture. Granted that Peter uses the verb *speak*, we are confident
that it includes the concept *write*. The Greek, however, discloses that Peter
mentions the act of speaking (and writing) and not the content of what was
said. The content of Scripture originates not in man but in God. Therefore,
Peter says, "Men spoke *from God*" (italics added). The message that man
conveys comes from God, for God is the source of Scripture.

Doctrinal Considerations in 1:20–21

Verse 20

The New Testament is replete with verses that encourage the believer to search
the Scriptures. For example, the Bereans "received the message with great eagerness and examined the Scriptures every day to see if what Paul said was true" (Acts
17:11). But if every believer interprets the Scriptures according to his own insights
and applies it as he sees fit, the explanations of a given passage will be countless and
extremely diverse. As we reject the teaching that only the church has authority to
interpret the Bible, so we see dangers in the exercise of pure individualism.

God has entrusted his revelation to his people as a body, and therefore interpreting the Scriptures should involve the fellowship of believers. Together the Bereans
examined the Scriptures daily to check the teachings of Paul. Let us follow the
example of these early Christians.

Verse 21

This is one of the well-known passages in the Bible that attests directly the inspiration of Scripture. Another text, of course, is II Timothy 3:16, "All Scripture is God-
breathed." Both texts reveal that the origin of Scripture is divine, for the primary
author of the Bible is the Holy Spirit. For this reason, we use the adjective *holy* to
describe the Bible. However, "the stress is laid here, not on the spiritual value of
Scripture (though that, too, is seen in the background), but on the divine trustwor-
thiness of Scripture."[68]

The men who wrote Scripture were moved by the Holy Spirit. He directed them
in their writing, so that their human words conveyed the Word of God and not their
own thoughts. In his epistle, James underscores this same truth when he writes,
"Take the prophets who spoke in the name of the Lord" (5:10). What they said was
authoritative not because of their prophetic office but because of the source of their
revelations: the Lord God.

Greek Words, Phrases, and Constructions in 1:21

ἠνέχθη—from the verb φέρω (I carry), this aorist passive corresponds to the
present passive φερόμαι. The aorist indicates single action, the present continual

---

67. Manuscript evidence for the translation *holy men of God* (KJV, NKJV) is strong. Translators,
however, regard this reading as secondary and refrain from adopting it.
68. B. B. Warfield, "Inspiration," *ISBE*, vol. 2, p. 841.

activity. Also note that the passive of this (compound) verb appears in verses 17 and 18.

ἐλάλησαν ἀπὸ θεοῦ—this can mean either "[they] spoke what was derived from God" or "controlled by God."[69] The preposition ἀπό lacks a passive verb. Therefore, the first interpretation given by C. F. D. Moule is preferred.

Summary of Chapter 1

After identifying himself, Peter greets the readers of his letter with a salutation in which he expresses the wish that they may increase in grace and peace through a knowledge of Jesus Christ. He informs them about the great and precious promises God has given them. He exhorts them to add to their faith seven virtues: goodness, self-control, knowledge, perseverance, godliness, brotherly kindness, and love. He teaches them that they will be effective and productive in their spiritual life if they increase these qualities. He encourages them to ascertain their calling and election, so that they may enter Christ's eternal kingdom.

Peter reminds the readers of the truth they possess. He wishes to refresh their memories, especially because the duration of his earthly life is short. He discloses that Jesus Christ has told him about his impending death. Therefore, he puts forth every effort to have them remember spiritual truths.

With the other apostles, Peter preaches not fables but truths about the power and coming of Jesus Christ. He proves the veracity of the apostolic message by relating his account of the transfiguration. He is able to testify that he heard the voice of God the Father commending the Son. God's revelation is confirmed by the prophetic word of the Scriptures, which have been inspired by the Holy Spirit. Indeed, the prophets were carried along by the Spirit when they spoke the Word of God.

---

69. See Moule, *Idiom-Book*, p. 73.

2

False Teachers

(2:1–22)

Outline

2 1 But there were also false prophets among the people, just as there will be false teachers among you. They will secretly introduce destructive heresies, even denying the sovereign Lord who bought them—bringing swift destruction on themselves. 2 Many will follow their shameful ways and bring the way of truth into disrepute. 3 In their greed these teachers will exploit you with stories they have made up. Their condemnation has long been hanging over them, and their destruction has not been sleeping.

4 For if God did not spare angels when they sinned, but sent them to hell, putting them into gloomy dungeons to be held for judgment; 5 if he did not spare the ancient world when he brought the flood on its ungodly people, but protected Noah, a preacher of righteousness, and seven others; 6 if he condemned the cities of Sodom and Gomorrah by burning them to ashes, and made them an example of what is going to happen to the ungodly; 7 and if he rescued Lot, a righteous man, who was distressed by the filthy lives of lawless men 8 (for that righteous man, living among them day after day, was tormented in his righteous soul by the lawless deeds he saw and heard)— 9 if this is so, then the Lord knows how to rescue godly men from trials and to hold the unrighteous for the day of judgment, while continuing their punishment. 10 This is especially true of those who follow the corrupt desire of the sinful nature and despise authority.

Bold and arrogant, these men are not afraid to slander celestial beings; 11 yet even angels, although they are stronger and more powerful, do not bring slanderous accusations against such beings in the presence of the Lord. 12 But these men blaspheme in matters they do not understand. They are like brute beasts, creatures of instinct, born only to be caught and destroyed, and like beasts they too will perish.

13 They will be paid back with harm for the harm they have done. Their idea of pleasure is to carouse in broad daylight. They are blots and blemishes, reveling in their pleasures while they feast with you. 14 With eyes full of adultery, they never stop sinning; they seduce the unstable; they are experts in greed—an accursed brood! 15 They have left the straight way and wandered off to follow the way of Balaam son of Beor, who loved the wages of wickedness. 16 But he was rebuked for his wrongdoing by a donkey—a beast without speech—who spoke with a man's voice and restrained the prophet's madness.

17 These men are springs without water and mists driven by a storm. Blackest darkness is reserved for them. 18 For they mouth empty, boastful words and, by appealing to the lustful desires of sinful human nature, they entice people who are just escaping from those who live in error. 19 They promise them freedom, while they themselves are slaves of depravity—for a man is a slave to whatever has mastered him. 20 If they have escaped the corruption of the world by knowing our Lord and Savior Jesus Christ and are again entangled in it and overcome, they are worse off at the end than they were at the beginning. 21 It would have been better for them not to have known the way of righteousness, than to have known it and then to turn their backs on the sacred command that was passed on to them. 22 Of them the proverbs are true: "A dog returns to its vomit," and, "A sow that is washed goes back to her wallowing in the mud."

IV. False Teachers
2:1–22

A. Destructive Heresies
2:1

The topic Peter discusses in this chapter appears to be opposite from the theme he develops in the previous chapter. In chapter 1, Peter hints at the pernicious influence of false teachers when he assures the readers that the apostles had not followed "cleverly invented stories" (v. 16). He implies that these stories, perpetrated by teachers who opposed Christ, were circulating within the broader Christian community.

When we consider the false teachings that the early church faced, we can understand Peter's desire to encourage the believers to be strong in their spiritual lives. Peter provides all the necessary ammunition for the Christians so that they may successfully oppose the false teachers and defeat their purposes. He alerts the Christians to the war they must fight and equips them with spiritual armor to resist and dispel the anti-Christian forces.

For Peter, the time has come to depict these enemies of Jesus Christ. In the first three verses of this chapter he portrays the objectives of these false teachers (v. 1), shows the intended result of their activities (vv. 2–3a), and mentions their impending condemnation and destruction (v. 3b).

1a. But there were also false prophets among the people, just as there will be false teachers among you.

Peter marks the contrast between chapters 1 and 2 with the word *but*. He introduces a new subject that is familiar to anyone who knows the history of Israel. By mentioning the term *false prophets,* Peter is able to call to mind the spiritual struggle in which Israel was engaged in earlier years. While true prophets conveyed God's Word to the people of Israel (see 1:19), false prophets introduced their own inventions. Here are a few instances in which God reveals his opposition to false prophets:

1. He instructs the people of Israel to put to death a prophet who preaches rebellion against the Lord God (Deut. 13:5; also see 18:20).
2. He compares the false prophets to Sodom because they "commit adultery and live a lie" (Jer. 23:14; also see 6:13).
3. Among the people upon whom God pours out his wrath are the prophets who utter "false visions and lying divinations" (Ezek. 22:28).

These prophets were false for two reasons: because of their message and their claim to the prophetic office. God condemned them for the lie they taught and lived. Furthermore, they were residing among God's people with the purpose of leading them astray.

Just as there were false prophets in Israel, Peter writes, so "there will be false teachers among you." Notice that he uses the future tense to warn the people about the coming of false teachers. He is aware of their presence and knows that others will come. He is saying that the believers in the Christian era can expect just as many false teachers as God's people encountered in Old Testament times. Peter repeats the warning Jesus gave in the discourse on the signs of the time: "Watch out that no one deceives you. For many will come in my name, claiming, 'I am the Christ,' and will deceive many" (Matt. 24:4–5). This is an apostolic warning; Paul, John, and Jude also utter this same warning.[1]

1b. They will secretly introduce destructive heresies, even denying the sovereign Lord who bought them—bringing swift destruction on themselves.

Mark the following questions:

a. What is the objective of these teachers? Peter uncovers their practices and motives when he reveals that these false teachers "will secretly introduce destructive heresies." Furtively and unlawfully, they enter the Christian community to disseminate their heresies.[2] In the parallel account, Jude has virtually the same wording: "Certain men whose condemnation was written about long ago have secretly slipped in among you" (v. 4).

b. What are heresies? The word *heresies* derives from the Greek verb which signifies to take something for one's self, to choose, or to prefer. It refers to a chosen course of thought or action that an individual takes or that a group of people adopts as an article of faith or way of life. The inevitable result is the act of separation which gives the term *heresy* an unfavorable connotation. Thus, the Pharisees separated themselves from the Jewish people, and the Christians were known as a sect (Acts 24:5, 14; 28:22). In the early church, Paul instructs Titus to "warn a divisive person once, and then warn him a second time. After that, have nothing to do with him" (Titus 3:10; and see Matt. 18:15–17; II John 10).[3]

c. What is the result? Peter leaves no doubt that he uses the term *heresy* in a negative sense, for he says that false teachers "will secretly introduce destructive heresies." The literal reading is, "heresies of [for] destruction." The false teachers, then, slyly entered the Christian community with doctrines designed to destroy the spiritual and moral lives of the Christians. The term *destruction* occurs twice in the last part of this verse. Peter writes that these teachers, because of their anti-Christian activities, bring "swift destruction on themselves." By furtively entering the church for the purpose of destroying its members with false doctrines, these teachers destroy themselves. Indeed, they are on a suicidal mission.

d. Were the false teachers former members of the church? The answer to the question must be affirmative. Peter writes that these teachers are "even denying the sovereign Lord who bought them." Note that Peter emphati-

---

1. See Acts 20:29–30; Gal. 1:6–9; Phil. 3:2; II Thess. 2:1–3; I Tim. 1:3–7; II Tim. 3:1–8; I John 2:18–19; Jude 3–4.
2. Consult Wilhelm Michaelis, *TDNT*, vol. 5, pp. 824–25.
3. See Gerhard Nordholt, *NIDNTT*, vol. 1, p. 535.

cally adds the word *even*. In addition to subverting the believers, these teachers continue to say that they have nothing to do with the sovereign Lord, who bought them. The expression *sovereign Lord* applies equally to God (Luke 2:29; Acts 4:24; Rev. 6:10) and Christ (Jude 4). To Jesus has been given all authority and power in heaven and on earth (Matt. 28:18). In the Greek, the word is *despotēs,* from which we have the derivative *despot.* It is closely connected with the verb *to buy.* In the New Testament, this Greek verb occurs twenty-five times in a commercial setting, "but on five other occasions it describes the 'buying' of Christians. This clearly reflects the contemporary terminology of the slave-market" (see I Cor. 6:20; 7:23; II Peter 2:1; Rev. 5:9; 14:3 [redeemed]).[4] With his blood Christ has bought his people that they may do his will. But these false teachers who refuse to obey him demonstrate the height of insolence toward the sovereign Lord.

Just as a master has bought slaves from whom he expects obedience, so Jesus as sovereign Lord has bought his servants and demands obedience. But instead of obeying Jesus, these servants continue to reject him (compare Heb. 10:29). They are "apostate Christians who have disowned their Master."[5] In due time, therefore, Jesus will swiftly destroy them.

Doctrinal Considerations in 2:1

The clause *who bought them* presents difficulties for the interpreter. Can those whom Christ has redeemed ever be lost? Did the false teachers lose their salvation? Some commentators assert that "Christ bought them at the tremendous price of his blood to be his own forever."[6] But the fact that the teachers faced swift destruction contradicts this interpretation.

Commenting on this clause, Henry Alford confidently states, "No assertion of universal redemption can be plainer than this."[7] But if Jesus had given these teachers eternal life, they would never have fallen away. Scripture clearly teaches that those people to whom Jesus has given eternal life "shall never perish" (John 10:28; also see Rom. 8:29–30, 32–35; Eph. 1:3–14).

Although Christ's death was sufficient to redeem the whole world, its efficiency comes to light only in God's chosen people. Were the false teachers recipients of God's saving grace? Apparently not, for they repudiated Christ. If we look at the words "denying the sovereign Lord who bought them" in the light of the broader context, we discover a clue. We notice that at one time these false teachers professed the name of Christ, for they said that they knew him and the way of righteousness (2:20–21). They made it known that Jesus had bought them, but they eventually

---

4. David H. Field, *NIDNTT,* vol. 1, p. 268.

5. Richard J. Bauckham, *Jude, 2 Peter,* Word Commentary series, vol. 50 (Waco: Word, 1983), p. 240.

6. R. C. H. Lenski, *The Interpretation of the Epistles of St. Peter, St. John, and St. Jude* (Columbus: Wartburg, 1945), p. 305.

7. Henry Alford, *Alford's Greek Testament: An Exegetical and Critical Commentary,* 5th ed., 4 vols. (1875; Grand Rapids: Guardian, 1976), vol. 4, pt. 2, p. 402. Also consult D. Edmond Hiebert, "A Portrayal of False Teachers: An Exposition of 2 Peter 2:1–3," *BS* 141 (1984): 260.

rejected Christ and left the Christian community. As John writes, "They went out from us, but they did not really belong to us" (I John 2:19; and see Heb. 6:4–6; 10:26–29). Hence, their denial of Christ showed that they were not redeemed.

B. Shameful Ways
2:2–3

Peter reveals to what conditions adherence to false teaching leads. He presents a graphic description of the lot of gullible Christians who follow false teachers. He shows that their example serves as a grim warning.

2. Many will follow their shameful ways and will bring the way of truth into disrepute.

The effect of this infiltration into the Christian community is detrimental, for "many will follow" these false teachers. In spite of apostolic teaching and admonition, numerous Christians are ready to listen to "cleverly invented stories" (1:16). Jesus pointedly warns, "Watch out for false prophets. They come to you in sheep's clothing, but inwardly they are ferocious wolves" (Matt. 7:15). Unfortunately, however, many Christians will eagerly adopt the teachings and the lifestyle of these heretics (observe that the same verb occurs in 1:16). Instead of shunning their evil practices, gullible Christians "follow their shameful ways."

What are these shameful ways? In the Greek, Peter uses the expression again when he describes the sexually immoral residents of Sodom and Gomorrah. He writes, "[God] rescued Lot, a righteous man, who was distressed by the *filthy lives* of lawless men" (v. 7, italics added). The words in italics are a translation of that same Greek term. Accordingly, we understand the term to mean sexual excesses and extremes.

Teaching and conduct go together. What the false teachers taught, they also practiced, with the inevitable result that Christians who followed them brought the Christian way of life into disrepute.

A Christian lives in a glass house, so to speak, because unbelieving neighbors are always observing the Christian's conduct. By accepting false doctrine and falling into immorality, these Christians were bringing shame upon "the way of truth." Mark that Peter borrows the expression *way of truth* from Psalm 119:30 ("I have chosen the way of truth"). Also, he has a fondness for using the term *way:* "the way of truth" (v. 2), "the straight way" (v. 15), "the way of righteousness" (v. 21). These phrases are synonymous and reflect the idiom *the Way* that designates Christianity in its early stages (Acts 9:2; 19:9, 23; 24:14, 22). In his first epistle, Peter tells the believers to "live such good lives among the pagans that, though they accuse you of doing wrong, they may see your good deeds and glorify God" (2:12; and see 3:16; 4:15). Christianity is not merely a way of life. Christianity is guided by the truth of the gospel. "True doctrine must issue in true living."[8]

---

8. Edwin A. Blum, *2 Peter,* in *Hebrews-Revelation,* vol. 12 of *The Expositor's Bible Commentary,* ed. Frank E. Gaebelein, 12 vols. (Grand Rapids: Zondervan, 1981), p. 277.

3. In their greed these teachers will exploit you with stories they have made up. Their condemnation has long been hanging over them, and their destruction has not been sleeping.

Observe two points:

a. *Purpose.* What is the motive of these false teachers? Peter's answer is brief: greed. They are interested in money that Christians have. When they achieve their purpose, they discover that greed impels them to get more. Greed spawns greed. The false teachers, Peter says, "are experts in greed" (v. 14). In his epistles, Paul warns against this sin. He identifies greed with idolatry (Col. 3:5). People who have fallen into the sin of greed exclude themselves from the kingdom of God, for they have severed the bond between God and the creature (Rom. 1:29; I Cor. 5:10; 6:10; Eph. 5:3). They worship money instead of God.

The false teachers, Peter warns his readers, "will exploit you with stories they have made up." They enter the Christian community with fabricated stories that unsuspicious believers accept as gospel. Paul also is acquainted with such unscrupulous peddlers who are interested in not the souls but the possessions of the people. He writes, "Unlike so many, we do not peddle the word of God for profit" (II Cor. 2:17).

Peter employs the word *exploit* to portray the activities of these teachers. This is a term borrowed from the marketplace, where the merchant is interested in making a profit. The unwary buyer becomes an object of exploitation. Notice that Peter writes the personal pronoun *you* to tell the believers about the perfidious scheme of these peddlers.

b. *Punishment.* What is the destiny of these false teachers? God is in control of every situation and he has assigned them to doom and destruction. "Their condemnation has long been hanging over them, and their destruction has not been sleeping." Peter's statement appears as typical Hebrew parallelism. The second clause supports the first one, for the nouns and verbs of these clauses correspond.

God pronounced a verdict upon these people long ago (see Jude 4). What is the significance of the term *long ago*? Peter explains this term in the succeeding context where he describes the destiny of fallen angels, the destruction of ungodly people in the days of the flood, and the condemnation of Sodom and Gomorrah (vv. 4–9). In short, the phrase points to similar incidents in the past.

The words Peter adopts are derived from the courtroom. God is the Judge who hands down the verdict. The verdict that God has rendered is ultimate destruction of the guilty party. Already Peter has stated that this destruction will be swift (v. 1; and see 3:7). These teachers who have received God's verdict are like prisoners on death row; their condemnation is hanging over them. Literally the Greek says, "Their judgment has not been idle" (NKJV). Peter personifies the word *destruction* by describing it as not sleeping. Judgment and destruction are two forces that are at work and awake to fulfill their mandate in obedience to God. God will not permit these wicked men to escape their punishment.

Greek Words, Phrases, and Constructions in 2:3

πλαστοῖς—the adjective in the dative case (dative of means) describes the words that are spoken. It derives from the verb πλάσσω (I form; see I Tim. 2:13), and connotes fabrication or pretense.

ἐμπορεύσονται—this compound verb signifies "to travel for business" (intransitive, see James 4:13) or "to trade for profit" (transitive). It occurs twice in the New Testament.[9] Here the direct object of the verb is the unassuming Christian.

κρίμα—from the verb κρίνω (I judge), this noun with the -μα ending denotes the result of the process of judging, that is, the verdict.

C. Condemnation
2:4–10a

1. Angels
2:4

Peter provides three illustrations from the past to show that God judges those who oppose him and protects those who love him. The first example concerns the fallen angels (v. 4), the second is a portrayal of the flood (v. 5), and the third refers to the doom of Sodom and Gomorrah (v. 6). Here is the first illustration:

4. For if God did not spare angels when they sinned, but sent them to hell, putting them into gloomy dungeons to be held for judgment.

This is the beginning of one lengthy sentence that introduces the repetitive first parts of a condition. The recurring *if* clause in verses 4, 5, 6, 7, and 9 (in the NIV) finally has its conclusion in verse 9. In this lengthy discourse, Peter presents examples from history.

a. "For if God did not spare angels." Peter reminds the readers that the example he gives is based on historical fact, which he uses to prove his point. He writes, "If God did not spare angels." This clause is not so much a condition as a statement of fact, because the punishment of angels has actually taken place.

Peter chooses his first illustration from the angelic world in which the angels are next to God and surround his throne. But numerous angels sinned against God and no longer appear before him. When did the angels fall into sin? Scripture provides little information. The Bible is God's revela-

---

9. Consult A. T. Robertson, *A Grammar of the Greek New Testament in the Light of Historical Research* (Nashville: Broadman, 1934), p. 474. And see Friedrich Blass and Albert Debrunner, *A Greek Grammar of the New Testament and Other Early Christian Literature,* trans. and rev. Robert Funk (Chicago: University of Chicago Press, 1961), sec. 148.1.

tion about the creation, fall, and redemption of man but not about angels. The angelic world is mentioned only tangentially in Scripture.

God's Word teaches us that many of the angels rebelled against God, yet we do not know the nature of their sin. Therefore, we ought not to speculate and say that angels sinned when they, "the sons of God," married "the daughters of men" (Gen. 6:2). Angels are spiritual beings without physical bodies and are incapable of procreation. In fact, Jesus explains that at the resurrection, people, like the angels in heaven, "will neither marry nor be given in marriage" (Matt. 22:30).

b. "When they sinned, but sent them to hell." Peter states only that angels sinned but omits the details of their sin. These details are not important for his discussion. We infer that the angels who followed Satan fell into sin before Satan tempted Adam and Eve in Paradise. We have no information on God's decision to put some of them into "gloomy dungeons" while others were permitted to afflict mankind. In his first epistle Peter writes about the "spirits in prison who disobeyed long ago" (3:19–20). And in Jude's parallel account, the writer says that these angels "did not keep their positions of authority but abandoned their own home" (v. 6).

God sent the fallen angels to hell, Peter writes. He borrows the word *hell* from Greek mythology, which designated a place called Tartarus an abode for the wicked. Peter uses this term not to teach or approve of Greek mythology but to speak the language of his readers. They understood the term to describe that part of hell where the worst offenders were kept. "Just as Paul could quote an apt verse of the pagan poet Aratus (Acts xvii. 28), so could Peter make use of this Homeric imagery."[10] Within the Christian community, the term *Tartarus* was not unfamiliar, as is evident from Jewish-Greek literature in the first century.

c. "Putting them into gloomy dungeons to be held for judgment." Because of a variant reading in the Greek, another translation has these words: "delivered them into chains of darkness" (NKJV).[11] That is, due to the variation of one letter in the Greek word in question, one translation has the term *dungeons* and the other *chains*. Scholars are unable to decide their translation on the basis of manuscript evidence, for both readings have equal support. However, in view of the context that features the term *hell*, most translators favor the reading *dungeons*. On the other hand, in apocryphal literature we encounter this text: "For with one chain of darkness they all were bound" (Wis. 17:17, RSV). Indeed, the choice is difficult.

The evil angels remain in hell awaiting the judgment of God. This does not mean that on the day of judgment they will be set free. Certainly not!

---

10. Michael Green, *The Second Epistle General of Peter and the General Epistle of Jude: An Introduction and Commentary*, Tyndale New Testament Commentaries (Grand Rapids: Eerdmans, 1968), p. 99.

11. Also see SEB, GNB, and the Greek texts of United Bible Societies, Nes-Aland, and the Majority Text.

The evidence is being gathered so that when God pronounces the verdict on that fearful day, they "will be tormented day and night for ever and ever" (Rev. 20:10).

By implication, the conclusion to this verse results in an argument from the greater to the lesser. If God did not spare the angels who beheld his glory in heaven but cast them into hell, will he not punish teachers who are bent on leading his people astray? To ask the question is to answer it.

Greek Words, Phrases, and Constructions in 2:4

εἰ—the introductory particle of the simple-fact condition stands at the head of one lengthy sentence (vv. 4–10) that forms the protasis. The apodosis appears in verse 9.

θεὸς ἀγγέλων—these two nouns stand next to each other to express contrast. The aorist active participle ἁμαρτησάντων (from ἁμαρτάνω, I sin) denotes single action in the past and states the cause for God's anger toward the evil angels.

ταρταρώσας—this is the aorist active participle from the verb ταρταρόω (I hold captive in Tartarus).

---

2. Flood
2:5

Of the three examples Peter gives to support his claim that the false teachers face doom and destruction, the first one relates to the fallen angels. Whereas the first example reveals only God's wrath and eventual judgment for these angels, the second illustration reveals both divine wrath and divine protectiveness. God destroys the ungodly world with the flood but protects Noah and his family.

5. If he did not spare the ancient world when he brought the flood on its ungodly people, but protected Noah, a preacher of righteousness, and seven others.

Note the following points:

a. *Ancient world.* In both his epistles, Peter uses the theme of the flood to depict the disobedience of the ungodly and the salvation of the righteous. In his first epistle he writes, "The spirits in prison . . . disobeyed long ago when God waited patiently in the days of Noah while the ark was being built. In it only a few people, eight in all, were saved through water" (3:19–20). He refers to the evil spirits who successfully led the entire ancient world into disobedience, except for Noah and the seven members of his family. Once again he mentions the ancient world and the destructive power of the flood when he says in his second epistle, "By these waters also the world of that time was deluged and destroyed" (3:6).

Who were these ungodly people of the ancient world? In Genesis we read that "every inclination of the thoughts of [man's] heart was only evil all the time" (6:5), and the earth was corrupt and full of violence (vv. 11–12). In many respects, we see a parallel to modern times in which news reporters daily feature the sad accounts of crime and corruption in our society. They remind us that we are living in an increasingly violent world and even predict that the human race will destroy itself someday. Jesus compares the days that precede his return to the time when Noah was building the ark (see Matt. 24:37–39).

b. *Flood.* Scripture reminds us that the flood was God's judgment upon the ungodly world in the time of Noah. God destroyed the human race and the animals, except for the eight persons and the pairs of animals he protected in the ark. Whether the flood was universal or local is not relevant at this point. Of importance is that God pronounced judgment upon the ungodly world and destroyed it with the waters of the flood (Gen. 6:5–8:19).

c. *Noah.* Peter calls Noah "a preacher of righteousness." The writer of the Epistle to the Hebrews confirms this observation. He says that when Noah built an ark to save his family, "he condemned the world and became heir of the righteousness that comes by faith" (Heb. 11:7). The construction of a boat on dry ground afforded numerous opportunities to preach righteousness to the wicked inhabitants of the world. For 120 years Noah built the ark and exhorted the people to repent. Yet no one accepted his teaching, for everyone perished.

In addition to his emphasis on the destruction of the world, Peter stresses the protection of Noah and his family. Of those whom God spared from the raging flood, Noah was the eighth, as the Greek text literally indicates. Translators convey the meaning of this phrase by saying that God protected Noah and seven others. The seven included Noah's wife, three sons, and their wives. God spared their lives because they were righteous in his sight. These eight people continued the human race.

If God did not spare the ancient world in the days of Noah, how much less can he be expected to spare the false teachers in Peter's day? Yet as God protected believing Noah and his household, so he will spare believers who remain true to the teaching of Scripture. In other words, Peter's message is designed to exhort and encourage the readers of his epistle.

3. Cities
2:6–8

The third example that Peter cites depicts the destruction of Sodom and Gomorrah (Gen. 19:24–29). From the devastation of the flood, he turns to the burning of two cities. And as eight people were saved from the deluge, so only three escaped the burning salt and sulfur that rained down upon the cities in the plain of the Jordan. Even Lot's wife turned into a pillar of salt (Gen. 19:26). Only Lot and his two daughters survived.

6. If he condemned the cities of Sodom and Gomorrah by burning them to ashes, and made them an example of what is going to happen to the ungodly.

a. *Places.* Peter mentions only the cities of Sodom and Gomorrah as representative places. The other cities were Admah, Zeboiim, and Bela, also known as Zoar (Gen. 14:2). When Lot chose to dwell near Sodom, "the whole plain of the Jordan was well watered, like the garden of the LORD, like the land of Egypt" (Gen. 13:10). Even in those days Sodom and Gomorrah were chief cities known for the wickedness and especially for the homosexuality of their inhabitants (Gen. 19:4–5). The sin of these people was so grievous that God determined to destroy the entire plain of the Jordan. By means of natural causes he permanently devastated this area. "In all likelihood—since volcanic eruption is geologically improbable—it was an earthquake accompanied by the explosive ejection of gas, bitumen and rock salt that wrought destruction to Sodom and Gomorrah."[12] God destroyed all living beings in the plain of Jordan with burning sulphur (Gen. 19:24).

b. *Example*. Jewish people were thoroughly familiar with the history of Sodom and Gomorrah. Through his prophets, God reminded them of the sin, condemnation, and destruction of these city dwellers. For example, Moses refers to the fierce anger of the Lord that caused the total devastation of Sodom, Gomorrah, Admah, and Zeboiim (Deut. 29:23). He uses this calamity as an example of what God will do to the Israelites if they disobey the Lord. The prophets Isaiah, Jeremiah, Ezekiel, Hosea, and Amos also cite the destruction of Sodom and Gomorrah as an example of God's anger against sin.[13] Even Jesus compares the destiny of these two cities to the doom that awaits the unbeliever (Matt. 10:15; 11:23–24; and see Rom. 9:29).

In his parallel account, Jude specifies the sin of these condemned cities. He writes, "In a similar way, Sodom and Gomorrah and the surrounding towns gave themselves up to sexual immorality and perversion. They serve as an example of those who suffer the punishment of eternal fire" (v. 7).

7. And if he rescued Lot, a righteous man, who was distressed by the filthy lives of lawless men   8. (for that righteous man, living among them day after day, was tormented in his righteous soul by the lawless deeds he saw and heard).

a. *Rescued*. The second illustration of the flood is paralleled by the third illustration of the cities. Both examples contrast the destruction of the wicked with the rescue of the righteous. In the third example, Lot is the counterpart of Noah. However, the difference between Noah and Lot is that God protected the one and rescued the other. This difference in wording is not merely stylistic. Rather, Peter accurately describes the historical circumstances of Lot's life in Sodom. Lot hesitated to leave the city. Indeed, the angels had to grasp his hand and the hands of his wife and daughters to lead them to safety (Gen. 19:16). Through his angels, God literally rescued Lot and his daughters. But Lot's wife perished when she disobediently looked back at the burning of Sodom.

---

12. Gordon R. Lewthwaite, "Dead Sea," *ZPEB*, vol. 2, p. 50.
13. See Isa. 1:9; 13:19; Jer. 50:40; Ezek. 16:49; Hos. 11:8; Amos 4:11.

b. *Righteous.* Notice that both Noah and Lot are described as righteous men, even though the life of Lot (portrayed in Genesis) is not commendable. When the Sodomites surrounded Lot's house and demanded that he deliver his two guests to them, "so that we can have sex with them" (Gen. 19:5), Lot offered his two virgin daughters to these lecherous men. "His reasoning seems to have been that it would be better that they satisfy their uncontrollable sexual cravings through natural acts than by grossly unnatural excess."[14] We cannot excuse Lot's reasoning and conclude that he was morally weak. Moreover, Lot's drunken stupor which brought the sin of incest into his own family put a permanent stain on his personal morality (Gen. 19:30–38).

Abraham, however, considered Lot a righteous man, because he pleaded with God not to destroy the cities if there were only ten righteous people living there (Gen. 18:32). Jesus mentions Lot in his discourse on the the the end of time (Luke 17:28). And in apocryphal literature Lot is called a righteous man (Wis. 10:6; 19:17). Observe that Peter emphatically describes Lot three times with the adjective *righteous:*

> "A righteous man" (v. 7);
> "That righteous man" (v. 8a);
> "His righteous soul" (v. 8b).

We should understand Lot's righteousness against the background of God's mercy (Gen. 19:16). In his mercy God rescued Lot, and he also knows how to rescue us from trials (v. 9). Peter portrays Lot as a man whose righteous soul was distressed by the immoral practices of the Sodomites. As a believer, Lot objected to the sins of the people among whom he lived day after day, for he "was tormented in his righteous soul by the lawless deeds he saw and heard." Lot and his family were not swallowed up by the tide of immorality that had swept through the cities of the plain. Like Noah and his household in earlier days, so Lot and his family withstood the onslaught of sin. In brief, Lot's soul was not numbed by the lawless deeds that he saw daily.

c. *Tormented.* We should not take this word, which in the Greek is in the imperfect tense to indicate continuous action in the past, too lightly. In this verse the word connotes Lot's state of mind; the lawless deeds of the Sodomites affected Lot's soul.

If we assume that Lot preached to his fellow citizens, even though he is not known as "a preacher of righteousness" (v. 5), we place him next to Noah. However, Lot chose to live in Jordan's fertile valley not for evangelistic reasons but because of economic considerations (Gen. 13:10–11). Accordingly, Lot lost all his material possessions when he had to flee for his life.

---

14. Gerhard Charles Aalders, *Genesis,* trans. William Heynen, Bible Student's Commentary series, 2 vols. (Grand Rapids: Zondervan, 1981), vol. 2, p. 16.

Perhaps we should translate the participle *living* in verse 8 as either cause or concession. That is, we translate the verse either "because he lived among them . . ." or "although he lived among them day after day, he was tormented."[15] The phrase *day after day* shows that Lot persisted in his opposition to the sinful acts of his neighbors. For this reason, Peter writes that Lot's righteous soul was tormented by lawless deeds. What Lot saw and heard came from people who lived without the law of God. They either knew the law of God but purposely lived in disobedience or were completely ignorant of divine law. Whatever the case, these people daily tormented Lot's righteous soul until God in his mercy rescued him.

Doctrinal Considerations in 2:7-8

God loves the sinner but abhors sin. He loves the homosexual person but detests his sinful acts. In the Scriptures God repeatedly reveals his love toward man (e.g., see John 3:16). But in these Scriptures he also expresses his abhorrence of sin. In clear language, the Old Testament condemns the acts of a homosexual as repulsive to God (see, e.g., Lev. 18:22; 20:13). And in the New Testament, Paul states unequivocally that "neither the sexually immoral nor idolaters nor adulterers nor male prostitutes nor homosexual offenders . . . will inherit the kingdom of God. And that is what some of you were. But you were washed, you were sanctified, you were justified in the name of the Lord Jesus Christ and by the Spirit of our God" (I Cor. 6:9-11). God pronounces his divine judgment on the sexually perverse acts of these persons. Hence Paul writes,

> Because of this, God gave them over to shameful lusts. Even their women exchanged natural relations for unnatural ones. In the same way the men also abandoned natural relations with women and were inflamed with lust for one another. Men committed indecent acts with other men, and received in themselves the due penalty for their perversion. [Rom. 1:26-27]

However, what should be the reaction of a Christian to homosexuality? He must distinguish carefully between condition and conduct.[16] He ought to express Christian love toward the homosexual person, but disapprove of his homosexual acts. A Christian must regard unnatural sexual behavior as a sin against his fellow human beings and a defiance of God's law. Nevertheless, he ought to extend compassion to the homosexual person and understand that he needs social acceptance. Therefore, guided by the teachings of God's Word, he must love the sinner but condemn sin. He should direct him to Jesus Christ, who invites sinners to come to God.

---

15. Consult S. Greijdanus, *De Brieven van de Apostelen Petrus en Johannes, en de Brief van Judas,* Kommentaar op het Nieuwe Testament series (Amsterdam: Van Bottenburg, 1929), p. 300.
16. Refer to R. E. O. White, "Homosexuality," *EDT,* p. 530. Also consult Armand M. Nicholi II, "Homosexualism and Homosexuality," in *Baker's Dictionary of Christian Ethics,* ed. Carl F. H. Henry (Grand Rapids: Baker, 1973), pp. 295-97.

Come ye needy, come and welcome,
God's free bounty glorify;
True belief and true repentance,
Ev'ry grace that brings you nigh,
Without money, without money,
Without money,
Come to Jesus Christ and buy.

—Joseph Hart

Greek Words, Phrases, and Constructions in 2:6-8

Verse 6

τεφρώσας—the aorist active participle from τεφρόω (I reduce to ashes, I cover with ashes) occurs only here.

καταστροφῇ—with the aorist active indicative κατέκρινεν (he condemned to destruction), the noun describes the ruin of Sodom. The dative is instrumental. Some manuscripts omit this noun, perhaps due to an oversight in transcription.

ἀσεβέσιν—this noun occurs three times in the second epistle of Peter (2:5, 6; 3:7) and means "ungodly men." Here it is in the dative plural as an indirect object. A variant reading is the present active infinitive ἀσεβεῖν, which has strong textual support. However, "from the point of view of intrinsic probability, the noun gives better sense ('an example [or warning] to ungodly persons or things in store for them') than the verb ('an example [or warning] to those about to do wrong [act impiously]')."[17]

Verse 8

ἐγκατοικῶν—this present active participle occurs once in the New Testament. It denotes either cause or concession.

ἐβασάνιζεν—the imperfect active from βασανίζω (I torment) expresses continuous activity. This verb is also used by demons who shout to Jesus, "Have you come here to torture us before the appointed time?" (Matt. 8:29).

---

4. Sin
2:9-10a

After giving examples of fallen angels, Noah's contemporaries, and the inhabitants of Sodom and Gomorrah, Peter is ready to formulate his conclusion. He informs his readers how the truth stated earlier applies to them and their godless companions. In this conclusion, he speaks a word of encouragement to the righteous, but for the wicked he reveals God's continuing punishment.

9. If this is so, then the Lord knows how to rescue godly men from trials

---

17. Bruce M. Metzger, *A Textual Commentary on the Greek New Testament,* 3d corrected ed. (London and New York: United Bible Societies, 1975), p. 702.

and to hold the unrighteous for the day of judgment, while continuing their punishment.

In his conclusion to the section on the ruin of the ungodly and the protection of the believer, Peter speaks as a pastor who encourages the members of his flock. He first addresses the believers with a message of encouragement and then discloses the future of the unbelievers. His words also sound a warning to those people who are drifting from the truth of God's Word.

a. "The Lord knows how to rescue godly men from trials." The New International Version has added a short statement ("if this is so") that summarizes the essence of the preceding verses. With the addition of this clause, the sentence itself has a proposition and a conclusion. What is the point of presenting three illustrations? In one word, assurance. Peter wants his readers to know that God is in control of every situation and that they have this assurance. As Paul puts it, "God is faithful; he will not let you be tempted beyond what you can bear" (I Cor. 10:13). The readers experienced the pernicious influence of the false teachers who infiltrated the Christian church. They saw the evidence of the erroneous doctrines in the shameful conduct of these teachers. And they undoubtedly asked why God allowed his people to be harassed by evil men.

John Calvin formulates a question that disheartened Christians usually ask: "If the Lord would have his own to be safe, why does he not gather them all into some corner of the earth, that they may mutually stimulate one another to holiness? Why does he mingle them with the wicked by whom they may be defiled?"[18]

In his role as pastor, Peter knows that despondency is apt to appear. Peter says that the Lord knows how to rescue. He probably chooses the expression *Lord* either as a variation of the word *God* (with which he began the series of examples [v. 4]) or as a name that conveys the grace and mercy of the Lord. God's mercy is linked to the verb *rescue* (v. 7) in the case of Lot (Gen. 19:16). The Lord has shown in numerous instances how he rescues godly men from difficult circumstances. The examples of Noah and Lot are cases in point. If God is able to protect Noah's family from a perverse humanity and rescue Lot and his daughters from a godless society, he knows how to deliver Christians from immoral and corrupt people today.

The language Peter uses at this point is reminiscent of the last petition in the Lord's Prayer: "And lead us not into temptation [trial], but deliver [rescue] us from the evil one" (Matt. 6:13). God tested Noah when he told him to build the ark. And God permitted Lot to enter into temptation when Lot chose to live near Sodom. But as God delivered both of these men from an evil world in ancient times, so he will rescue godly people from trials and temptations today (compare II Tim. 4:18; Rev. 3:10).

---

18. John Calvin, *Commentaries on the Catholic Epistles: The Second Epistle of Peter*, ed. and trans. John Owen (Grand Rapids: Eerdmans, 1948), p. 399.

b. "And to hold the unrighteous for the day of judgment, while continuing their punishment." In the second half of verse 9, Peter reveals what is happening to people who revel in sin. Because they willfully violate God's law, God keeps them in custody for the day of judgment. Jesus speaks of this day, for example, when he refers to the judgment on Sodom and Gomorrah (Matt. 10:15).[19] And Peter discloses that "the present heavens and earth are reserved for fire, being kept for the day of judgment and destruction of ungodly men" (3:7).

What will happen on that judgment day? The ungodly who refuse to turn away from their sinful life will receive everlasting punishment. They will be thrown "into the lake of fire. The lake of fire is the second death" (Rev. 20:14).

As prisoners are held in custody until the day they appear in court, so God keeps the ungodly for the judgment day. However, Peter adds the clause *while continuing their punishment.* We can interpret this clause with either a present or a future connotation. Here is a representative translation that clearly expresses the present tense: "The Lord, indeed, knows . . . how to continue the punishment of the wicked up to the day of judgment" (NAB). And in the following version the future tense is evident: "The Lord knoweth how to . . . reserve the unjust unto the day of judgment to be punished" (KJV). Although both translations are current, I favor the first one, because the Greek has a present participle "to which we cannot easily attribute a future tense."[20] Moreover, in the parable of the rich man and Lazarus, Jesus teaches that the ungodly suffer while waiting for the day of judgment (Luke 16:19–31). Granted that we have no indication that the false teachers at the time of Peter's writing endured divine punishment, we know that by their conduct they were advancing their own destruction.

10a. This is especially true of those who follow the corrupt desire of the sinful nature and despise authority.

Modern translations divide this text into two parts. The first part of verse 10 forms a conclusion to the preceding context, while the second part is an introduction to the verses that follow.

This first part, then, summarizes what Peter has said about the false teachers and their ultimate ruin. He mentions two characteristics of these godless people: they are sexually corrupt and they are spiritual anarchists. The phrase *this is especially true* puts the present situation of the readers in sharp focus. The false teachers engaged in shameful ways, Peter writes (v. 2), and they introduced "destructive heresies" (v. 1).

Even though Peter resorts to euphemism in his description of these ungodly practices, the message is sufficiently clear: "[They] follow the corrupt

---

19. Here are additional references: Matt. 11:22, 24; 12:36; also see I John 4:17.

20. J. N. D. Kelly, *A Commentary on the Epistles of Peter and John,* Thornapple Commentaries series (1969; Grand Rapids: Baker, 1981), p. 335. Also consult Bauckham, *2 Peter, Jude,* p. 254, for additional information.

desire of the sinful nature [literally, flesh]." In his parallel, Jude gives a similar report: "These dreamers pollute their own bodies, reject authority and slander celestial beings" (v. 8). Both Peter and Jude intimate that these godless people are engaging in homosexual practices similar to those pursued by the Sodomites (Gen. 19:5). The result of their practices will be utter destruction.

The wording of this text indicates that these sexually immoral people are slaves to their corrupt desires. "They are not leaders, but travel or trail along" and follow their sinful nature which poses as their leader (compare 3:3; Jude 16, 18).[21] Instead of shunning defilement, these false teachers take great pleasure in moral impurity. A literal translation, therefore, has the reading "those who walk . . . in the lust of uncleanness" (NKJV). The Greek word translated "uncleanness" refers to the act of polluting oneself and others. It is preceded by the term *lust* and forms the phrase *lust of uncleanness*. The phrase means a "hankering after unlawful and polluting use of the flesh."[22]

The doctrines espoused by these teachers lead to deliberate rejection of divine authority. Peter says only, "[They] despise authority." These words communicate that these teachers scorned the authority of Jesus Christ (refer to v. 1). The verb *despise* in the Greek signifies that a person expresses his hatred toward Christ through ridicule and contempt (Matt. 6:24; Luke 16:13). The false teachers hate Jesus Christ.

Greek Words, Phrases, and Constructions in 2:9–10a

Verse 9

ῥύεσθαι—this present middle infinitive expresses God's constant care for his people.

ἡμέραν κρισέως—note the lack of the definite article to express the absolute character of this awesome day.

κολαζομένους—the present passive participle from the verb κολάζω (I punish) implies a divine agent. The present tense denotes continuous activity.

Verse 10a

ἐπιθυμίᾳ μιασμοῦ—the lack of the definite article emphasizes the nature of the persons who "lust for pollution." The genitive is either objective or descriptive.

πορευομένους—the present tense of this middle participle and the present tense of the active participle καταφρονοῦντας describe the daily activities of the false teachers.

---

21. Lenski, *Interpretation of the Epistles*, p. 316.
22. Alford, *Alford's Greek Testament*, vol. 4, pt. 2, p. 406.

D. Flagrant Misconduct
2:10b–16

1. Slander
2:10b–11

Some translators see this passage as a continuation of the preceding section. Others introduce verse 10b as the beginning of a new paragraph and regard this verse as an introduction to the following segment. In it Peter vividly describes the conduct of these arrogant men who are unafraid to slander angels.

10b. Bold and arrogant, these men are not afraid to slander celestial beings; 11. yet even angels, although they are stronger and more powerful, do not bring slanderous accusations against such beings in the presence of the Lord.

Note these observations:

a. *Attitudes.* Peter calls these false teachers "bold and arrogant." They are bold in the sense of being rashly insolent and so adhere to the well-known saying, "Fools rush in where angels fear to tread." The term *bold* in this verse points to presumptuous and conceited individuals whose pursuits in life are self-gratification and physical pleasures. Moreover, they are self-willed to the extent of being arrogant.

b. *Angels.* To what extent are these teachers bold and arrogant? They are unafraid to slander angels. Here we encounter an exegetical difficulty in the Greek text which centers on one word and which, because of its brevity, is hard to explain. In the Greek the word *glories* appears, which translators have tried to render in one of two ways, literal or interpretive. For instance, the New International Version (among others) translates the expression *glories* "celestial beings."[23]

Even if we take the Greek text literally, we still must indicate who the glorious beings are. Some interpreters apply the word *glories* to those human dignitaries who give leadership either in the church or in civic matters.[24] But the succeeding context (v. 11) seems to speak not of church or civil authorities but of angels (also see Jude 8). If we interpret the term *glories* to refer to angels, the question arises whether they are fallen angels or good angels. We readily identify the good angels as glorious beings, for they surround God's throne, share in God's glory, and serve as his messengers.

However, verse 11 clearly indicates that angels, "although they are

---

23. Two categories of translation are possible: literal, as in JB, RSV ("glorious ones"); GNB, MLB, SEB ("glorious beings"); *Moffatt* ("angelic Glories"); and interpretive, as in KJV, RV, ASV ("dignities"); NKJV ("dignitaries"); NASB ("angelic majesties"); NAB, NEB ("celestial beings").

24. For example, see Charles Bigg, *A Critical and Exegetical Commentary on the Epistles of St. Peter and St. Jude,* International Critical Commentary series (1901; Edinburgh: Clark, 1961), p. 279.

stronger and more powerful, do not bring slanderous accusations against such beings in the presence of the Lord." The tacit implication is that not the good angels but the evil angels "merit condemnation."[25] Granted that the text (v. 11) appears to suggest this interpretation, numerous questions remain. Here are two of them. Why are fallen angels called "glorious" when obviously they are condemned? What were the accusations that were hurled against Satan and his followers? We are unable to answer these questions because the text itself provides no further clues.

c. *Accusations.* Peter reveals that the angels refrain from accusing fallen angels in the presence of the Lord. He uses a comparative clause to describe the angels by describing them as "stronger and more powerful." With whom is Peter comparing the angels? The comparison could be with the false teachers or the celestial beings. Within the structure of verse 11, the juxtaposition of the celestial beings to the angels makes the devils a point of comparison. The angels who are upright have reason to accuse those who at one time belonged to their ranks but have since fallen away from God. Nevertheless, God's faithful angels carefully avoid raising accusations against Satan and his cohorts (compare Zech. 3:2; Jude 9), but leave the matter of judging the devils in the hands of God.

Conversely, we think that the comparison is between the angels and the false teachers. Note that the dominant subject in this section is not that of the celestial beings but that of the heretics. These people are bold and arrogant; they are unafraid to slander celestial beings; they blaspheme even the devils and in their arrogance transgress the limits God has set. Writes Peter H. Davids, "The devil himself is not to be the object of insult. The N[ew] T[estament] looks on such mockery as gross presumption, a pride based on a false claim to knowledge and power (Jude 8–10; II Pet. 2:10–12)."[26] These people, then, are devoid of any sense of propriety and show no hesitation in hurling insults at the devils.

In their arrogance, the apostates are of the opinion that they are stronger than demons. They repudiate the power and might of these fallen angels and think that they can insult them by bringing slanderous accusations against them. But notice that God's angels, who stand in the presence of God, do not dare to accuse demons. By contrast, Satan and his followers are denied a place in heaven. They lost the battle against the archangel Michael and his forces, were thrown out of heaven, and were hurled to the earth (Rev. 12:7–9). In short, devils now find their place among men. Bold and arrogant apostates, however, fail to realize the might and power of Satan's forces on earth. With their slanderous accusations they seal their own destruction, as Peter explains in the next verse.

---

25. Kelly, p. 337. Also refer to Blum, *2 Peter*, p. 280.
26. Peter H. Davids, "Blasphemy," *EDT*, p. 161.

Greek Words, Phrases, and Constructions in 2:10b–11

Verse 10b

αὐθάδεις—this adjective in plural form derives from the pronoun αὐτός (self) and the verb ἥδομαι (I am pleased with). See Titus 1:7.

βλασφημοῦντες—the present active participle ("slandering") is supplementary to the main verb τρέμουσιν (they tremble) and is therefore equivalent to the present infinitive, "These men are not afraid to slander."[27]

Verse 11

ὅπου—figuratively as a particle, this word introduces a conditional statement that is translated "insofar as."[28]

μείζονες—the comparative adjective from μέγας (great), even though it appears without an object of comparison, functions as a true comparative.[29]

---

2. Blasphemy
2:12

12. But these men blaspheme in matters they do not understand. They are like brute beasts, creatures of instinct, born only to be caught and destroyed, and like beasts they too will perish.

What a denunciation! Peter minces no words in describing the heretics. These people claim to have knowledge but in effect live and act in abysmal ignorance that inevitably leads to their own destruction. They have rejected wisdom that God grants to all who ask him (James 1:5) and are teaching "destructive heresies" instead (v. 1; also see vv. 3, 18).

Three times in as many verses (vv. 10–12) Peter mentions the slander and blasphemy of these teachers. He notes that they sin in self-willed ignorance, while they parade as teachers of religion.

Implicitly, Peter calls attention to two kinds of knowledge: spiritual and natural. The heretics have spurned spiritual knowledge, for in their ignorance they slander "celestial beings." They possess only natural knowledge, which brute beasts also possess. Such knowledge eventually leads to destruction.[30]

In his epistle, Jude writes a parallel to this verse: "Yet these men speak abusively against whatever they do not understand; and what things they

---

27. Compare Blass and Debrunner, *Greek Grammar*, sec. 415.
28. See Thayer, p. 450.
29. Refer to Robert Hanna, *A Grammatical Aid to the Greek New Testament* (Grand Rapids: Baker, 1983), p. 430. And see Robertson, *Grammar*, p. 665.
30. Refer to Joseph B. Mayor, *The Epistle of St. Jude and the Second Epistle of St. Peter: Greek Text with Introduction and Notes* (1907; Grand Rapids: Baker, 1965), p. 131.

do understand by instinct, like unreasoning animals—these are the very things that destroy them" (v. 10). Even though the two texts in Peter's and Jude's epistles present the same message, Peter's wording is more descriptive than that of Jude. Both writers refer to the ignorance and slander of the false teachers, but Peter compares this ignorance to that of animals. He describes animals as "creatures of instinct."

"They are like brute beasts, creatures of instinct." Animals lack the power of reasoning that man possesses and thus rely on created instinct for meeting the necessities of daily existence. Although this innate quality guides and directs them, they nevertheless run the risk of being caught and destroyed by man or beast.

"[They are] born only to be caught and destroyed." Peter uses this illustration to imply that man was not born to be captured and killed, but rather to live in freedom and with spiritual knowledge, in full reliance on God.[31] But these men who have deliberately departed from God are like the beasts of the field. They live by instinct and because of their spiritual ignorance they will soon perish (Ps. 49:12).

"Like beasts they too will perish." A generally accepted interpretation of commentators is that these false teachers meet a sudden and violent death, much the same as animals that are hunted and killed by men.[32] Another translation puts the emphasis on the destructive work which the false teachers do: "[They] shall in their destroying surely be destroyed" (ASV; also see JB). In the context of the passage, this translation has merit.

Practical Considerations in 2:10b–12

The sin of cursing and swearing is a blight on mankind. Countless people not only misuse the names of God and Christ, but also resort to using the words *hell* and *damn* in numerous connections. But in their cursing, these people reveal their absolute ignorance of spiritual matters. In fact, calloused by the frequency of its use, they are virtually unaware of the profanity they utter. They show their ignorance especially when they are asked about the existence, power, and influence of the devil. For them, Satan is a figment of the imagination whom cartoonists have portrayed as a goat with a tail that ends in an arrow. They do not think that the devil pictured with a three-pronged spear in his hand has any power over them. They are of the opinion that any reference to the devil is made in jest. They imagine that they are in control of their lives and thus they can even taunt Satan to tempt them. They do not know that Jesus calls Satan "the prince of this world" (John 12:31; 14:30; 16:11), and that the apostle John writes, "The whole world is under the control of the evil one" (I John 5:19).

The sad fact, however, is that Satan is tempting them with the mortal goal of

---

31. Consult John Albert Bengel, *Gnomon of the New Testament*, ed. Andrew R. Fausset, trans. William Fletcher, 7th ed., 5 vols. (Edinburgh: Clark, 1877), vol. 5, p. 99.

32. See among others Kelly, *Peter and Jude*, p. 339.

destroying them. Satan's authority is awesome indeed and his power of deception is unrivaled (II Cor. 11:14). Only the person who in faith prays the sixth petition of the Lord's Prayer, "And lead us not into temptation, but deliver us from the evil one" (Matt. 6:13), is able to resist the might and power of the devil. Fully aware of the spiritual battle that we fight, Paul exhorts us to "put on the full armor of God, so that when the day of evil comes, you may be able stand your ground, and after you have done everything, to stand" (Eph. 6:13).

Greek Words, Phrases, and Constructions in 2:12

φθοράν—from the verb φθείρω (I destroy), this noun can be translated in an active form ("is destroying") or as a passive ("to be destroyed").

αὐτῶν—translators generally understand this pronoun to refer to the noun *beasts.*

---

3. Adultery
2:13–14

We face a question of paragraph division at this juncture. Some translators place a comma after verse 12, and then continue with verse 13. Others see a definite break and begin a new sentence or paragraph with verse 13. Unfortunately, the ancient manuscripts of the Greek New Testament are of little help at this point, for they provide no indication of a break. The New International Version marks a division and presents verse 13 as the beginning of a new paragraph.

13. They will be paid back with harm for the harm they have done. Their idea of pleasure is to carouse in broad daylight. They are blots and blemishes, reveling in their pleasures while they feast with you.

In the first sentence, the Greek has a play on words that Peter has chosen intentionally. Literally translated it means "suffering wrong as the wages of doing wrong" (NASB). But the verb *suffering wrong* with the phrase *the wages of doing wrong* can also be translated "being cheated of the profits of their wrong-doing."[33] A number of Greek manuscripts, however, have another verb at this point, which a few translations have adopted as the better reading: "[But these] will receive the wages of unrighteousness" (NKJV; also see KJV, JB). However, it is likely that Peter introduced a play on words and that scribes in the first few centuries altered the text. Therefore, translators favor the reading with verbal witticism.

The intent of Peter's message is to point out the truth of the adage, "A man reaps what he sows" (Gal. 6:7; also compare Prov. 22:8; Hos. 10:12–13; II Cor. 9:6). That is, the false teachers will be paid in full for the wrongs they have perpetrated. What, then, is the harm these apostates have done?

---

33. C. E. B. Cranfield, *I and II Peter and Jude: Introduction and Commentary,* Torch Bible Commentaries series (London: SCM, 1960), p. 184. Also see Bauer, who writes, "damaged in respect to (i.e. cheated out of) the reward of unrighteousness" (p. 17).

In verses 13 through 15 Peter presents a catalogue of evils. Here are the first two:

a. "Their idea of pleasure is to carouse in broad daylight." The object of this sentence is not to imply that carousing at night is acceptable. Sin is usually committed under cover of darkness (refer to John 3:19); for instance, Paul writes, "Those who get drunk, get drunk at night" (I Thess. 5:7; also compare Rom. 12:11–13). But these people scorn all norms of behavior and carouse even during the day. Apparently the heretics have no desire to be gainfully employed, are idle during the day, and spend their time in drunken revelry (see Isa. 5:11).[34] Apart from the verb *to carouse,* the sentence itself conveys a positive message, for pleasure and broad daylight are delightful gifts of God. But the verb changes the entire message: pleasure and daylight are pressed into the service of sin. These people are slaves of Satan.

b. "They are blots and blemishes, reveling in their pleasures while they feast with you." The words *blots* and *blemishes* are the reverse of Peter's description of the believers. He urges them to "make every effort to be found spotless, blameless and at peace with [the Lord]" (3:14). In describing Jesus Christ, Peter portrays him as "a lamb without blemish or defect" (I Peter 1:19). The people described in this text, however, are the exact opposite of Christ and his church. They enter the homes of church members and partake of the food and drink which the host provides.

How is it possible for these revelers to have table fellowship with the believers? The parallel verse in Jude 12 has, "These men are blemishes at your love feasts." The better manuscripts of Peter's epistle do not have the reading *love feasts,* but rather a noun that has a primary meaning *deceptions* and a secondary meaning *pleasures.* Many versions have chosen the primary translation, but the secondary reading fits perfectly. Peter perhaps seeks to avoid the explicit use of the term *love feast.* What was this feast?

> [It] was a meal at which not only bread and wine but all kinds of viands were used, a meal which had the double purpose of satisfying hunger and thirst and giving expression to the sense of Christian brotherhood. At the end of this feast, bread and wine were taken according to the Lord's command. . . . The agape [love feast] was thus related to the eucharist as Christ's last Passover to the Christian rite which He grafted upon it.[35]

Perhaps already in Peter's time, the communal meal was separated from the Lord's Supper. The love feast stressed the brotherhood of the participants; the eucharist marked the unity the believers have in Christ. Paul instructs the Corinthian Christians to make a distinction between these two celebrations when he asks, "Don't you have homes to eat and drink in?"

---

34. Consult Greijdanus, *De Brieven,* p. 313.

35. J. C. Lambert, "Agape," *ISBE,* vol. 1, p. 66.

(I Cor. 11:22). Whether the revelers defiled the Lord's table in Peter's day, the text does not say. Peter, however, indicates that they were feasting to the point of being "blots and blemishes" in the Christian community.

14. With eyes full of adultery, they never stop sinning; they seduce the unstable; they are experts in greed—an accursed brood!

In a series of short clauses Peter continues his enumeration of vices. In a company of revelers, the consumption of alcohol often leads to lust and sexual abuse. Hence Peter provides this graphic description:

a. "With eyes full of adultery, they never stop sinning." The literal reading of the term *adultery* is "adulteress." In this sentence the word refers to "eyes that are full of (desire for) an adulteress, always looking for a woman with whom to commit adultery."[36] Peter's descriptive language echoes the words of Jesus: "Anyone who looks at a woman lustfully has already committed adultery with her in his heart" (Matt. 5:28).

Translators have connected the two clauses that are dependent on each other in forming one sentence. Peter portrays these teachers as adulterers who because of their lustful looking at women never stop sinning. What a degrading view of the opposite sex! In the eyes of these men, a woman is not a person but a tool designed to fulfill their sexual craving.[37]

b. "They seduce the unstable." Peter borrows a word from the fisherman who casts out a lure to catch an unwary fish (v. 18; James 1:14). These teachers try to ensnare men and women, especially those Christians who are unstable in their faith, into sexual sins. They look for church members who have neglected to put on the armor of God (Eph. 6:13) and who have not heeded Peter's admonition to be "firmly established in the truth" (1:12). They are persons who, because of instability, distort the Scriptures (3:16) and thus become an easy prey for the devil and his henchmen.

c. "They are experts in greed." Once again Peter resorts to imagery. He borrows from the world of gymnastics and says that the false teachers have been exercising (as in a gymnasium) their hearts in greed. The sin of greed is not only a transgression of the tenth commandment of the Decalogue; it is equivalent to idolatry (Col. 3:5). That is, man worships not God but the idol of covetousness. At the beginning of his description of these teachers, Peter warns the believers against the danger of exploitation. He says, "In their greed these teachers will exploit you with stories they have made up" (v. 3). Because they have made money their idol (Matt. 6:24; Luke 16:13), these people receive God's curse.

d. "An accursed brood!" Peter reveals his Hebraic background, for he emphatically exclaims, "Children of a curse!" The expression *children of* is Semitic and occurs in a number of forms: for example, "children [objects]

---

36. Bauer, p. 526.

37. Compare Werner de Boor, *Der Zweite Brief des Petrus und der Brief des Judas,* in *Die Briefe des Petrus und der Brief des Judas,* Wuppertaler Studienbibel (Wuppertal: Brockhaus, 1976), p. 228 n. 74.

of wrath" (Eph. 2:3), "children of light" (Eph. 5:8), and "children of obedience [obedient children]" (I Peter 1:14). It is similar to the phrase *sons of disobedience* (Eph. 2:2; 5:6, NKJV).

What is the result of God's curse upon man? A curse is the opposite of a blessing. When a curse is pronounced upon someone or something, blessings are withheld and disaster ensues. Thus, the curse pronounced upon anyone rebuilding Jericho (Josh. 6:26) became effective when, during the reign of King Ahab, Hiel of Bethel rebuilt Jericho. Hiel lost two sons in consequence of the curse that Joshua had uttered centuries earlier.

Peter refrains from placing a curse on the false teachers, for Scripture teaches that Christians should not curse their fellow man but rather bless him (see Matt. 5:44; Luke 6:28; Rom. 12:14, 19). Peter observes and describes the people who deliberately and constantly sin and therefore are recipients of God's wrath and condemnation.[38]

Greek Words, Phrases, and Constructions in 2:13–14

Verse 13

ἀδικούμενοι . . . ἀδικίας—"suffering the injustice of the wages of injustice." Although this combination "involves a very rare construction, . . . the author seems to have tolerated the unusual grammatical construction in the interest of contriving a play on [these two] words."[39]

τὴν . . . τρυφήν—the definite article precedes the noun ("revelry") to specify the distinctive nature of involvement. Also see the close connections of the noun with the compound present participle ἐντρυφῶντες (carousing).

ἀπάταις—in Jude 12 the reading is ἀγάπαις (love feasts). Some leading manuscripts have the same reading in Peter's letter. However, the word ἀπάταις (deceptions; pleasures) probably is original; it is free from the claim of assimilation to the text of Jude 12.

Verse 14

ἀκαταπαύστους—from the compound form ἀ (not), κατά (down), and the verb παύω (I stop), this verbal adjective occurs once in the New Testament and is translated "restless."

ψυχάς—this word means "persons" (compare I Peter 3:20).

γεγυμνασμένην—as a perfect passive participle from γυμνάζω (I train), this term has the derivative *gymnasium* in English. The perfect tense denotes action that began in the past with obvious effect in the present.

4. Wickedness
2:15–16

15. They have left the straight way and wandered off to follow the way of Balaam son of Beor, who loved the wages of wickedness.

38. Refer to Green, *The Second Epistle General of Peter*, p. 112.
39. Metzger, *Textual Commentary*, p. 703.

We consider two points:

a. *Observation*. Peter continues to describe the apostates of his day and observes that they have forsaken the path of obedience. He says, "They have left the straight way." The Greek text signifies that because these false teachers left the straight way they began to wander. With the other writers of the Bible, Peter speaks metaphorically. The phrase *the straight way* is an idiom that points to the path the children of God must walk in accordance with his Word.[40]

By implication, Peter indicates that the heretics at one time pursued the straight way but subsequently left it. As a consequence of this decision, Peter comments, they now wander in darkness. These were the people of whom the apostle John says that "if they had belonged to us, they would have remained with us; but their going showed that none of them belonged to us" (I John 2:19; also compare Heb. 6:4–6). These people are following the path that leads to death and destruction.

b. *Illustration*. "[They] follow the way of Balaam son of Beor, who loved the wages of wickedness." In the parallel passage Jude cites three Old Testament examples: Cain's hatred, Balaam's greed, and Korah's rebellion (v. 11). Peter, however, uses the example of Balaam (Num. 22–24). He wanted to curse the Israelites but through the Spirit of the Lord was forced to bless them (compare Deut. 23:4). Peter sees a reflection of the false teachers in the life and circumstances of Balaam. In the historical setting of Balaam and the people of Moab, he observes the sexual immorality of the Moabites, who in alliance with Balaam tried to seduce the Israelites (see especially Num. 25:1–9; 31:16; Rev. 2:14). Next, Peter is aware of Balaam's interest in personal honor and material gain at the expense of God's people. And last, Balak king of Moab wanted Balaam to curse, not bless, the Israelites.

The similarities are obvious. The heretics of Peter's day are trying to lure the believers into revelry and immorality; their greediness is evident to everyone in the community; and they teach destructive heresies designed to cause the believers to deviate from the way of truth. Indeed, they are an accursed brood.

Peter states that Balaam "loved the wages of wickedness." Balaam, although driven by greed, was fully aware that the Israelites were God's chosen people whom God himself protected. But because he joined forces with God's enemies, he received "the wages of wickedness." Balaam was driven by a love for material rewards, not by a love for God and his people. Within a short period of time, Israel's army killed Balaam in the battle against the Midianites (Num. 31:8).

With this historical illustration Peter reveals the motives of the false teach-

---

40. The expression *straight way* occurs repeatedly in the Old Testament (e.g., Ps. 27:11 [straight path]; 107:7) and in the New Testament (Acts 13:10 [right ways]).

ers. He describes them as followers of Balaam and intimates that they shall have their reward. "Their condemnation has long been hanging over them, and their destruction has not been sleeping" (v. 3). Their reward is the same as that of Balaam.

16. But he was rebuked for his wrongdoing by a donkey—a beast without speech—who spoke with a man's voice and restrained the prophet's madness.

This verse actually is an indirect word of encouragement for the readers of Peter's epistle. They see the "blots and blemishes" of the heretics within the Christian community, they know that the express purpose of these people is to seek the destruction of the church, and they realize that God "knows how to rescue [them] from trials" (v. 9). If the donkey of Balaam rebuked the erring prophet, then believers are able to reprove the false teachers with the teachings of God's Word.

Balaam's donkey, seeing the angel of the Lord with a drawn sword, tried to avoid inevitable disaster (Num. 22:21–28). Even when God gave the donkey the facility of human speech, Balaam still did not realize the danger confronting him. In his mercy, God opened Balaam's eyes so that he could see the angel of the Lord with a sword poised to kill him.

Why does Peter relate the account of the talking donkey? For a number of reasons: to compare Balaam's insensitivity with that of the false teachers; to show that as Balaam proceeded blindly on the path of destruction so the heretics are doomed; to reveal God's intervention in causing Balaam to bless Israel; and to give the believers of Peter's day the assurance that God protects them.

Peter calls Balaam a prophet, not to indicate that he was a true prophet, but that God used him in spite of his madness. If he had been a true servant of God, his conduct would never have been characterized by madness. His obstinacy caused his downfall and death.

Doctrinal Considerations in 2:15–16

Critics of the Christian faith discredit the accounts of miracles that are recorded in the Old and New Testaments. They consider these stories to be legends and myths whose content must be discarded in the light of modern science. And they regard anyone who accepts these miracles in faith as someone who fails to use his reasoning powers. They portray the Christian as a gullible person who would believe the Bible whether it said that Jonah swallowed the whale or that the whale swallowed Jonah.

The believer, however, looks at all the miracles in the Bible and sees the hand of God. He knows that God performs miracles either in response to the faith of his people or to instill and strengthen faith in the believers.

Among the numerous miracles in Scripture, Balaam's talking donkey is not an exceptional case. This incident occurred during a moment of crisis in the history of Israel when hostile forces wanted to see Israel cursed. God intervened and not only caused Balaam's donkey to speak, but also caused Balaam to bless instead of curse God's people. A miracle, therefore, is an act of God. And because of this act of God, the Christian believes.

Is the Christian gullible? For him the greatest miracle God performed is that of Christ's resurrection. All other miracles are secondary. If we do not believe the physical resurrection of Christ, then the message of the gospel is worthless and our faith is useless (I Cor. 15:14).

Greek Words, Phrases, and Constructions in 2:15–16

Verse 15

καταλείποντες—some manuscripts have καταλιπόντες (aorist active) instead of the present active. The difference is that the present tense shows simultaneous action with that of the main verb, while the aorist tense indicates preceding action. Basically the effect is the same. The participle denotes cause.

ἐπλανήθησαν—from the verb πλανάω (I cause to wander), the aorist signifies ingressive action; the passive voice ("to be misled") points to an implied agent.

Verse 16

ἰδίας παρανομίας—the use of the adjective ἰδίας is emphatic: "his own." The noun appears only here in the New Testament. It derives from the preposition παρά (from the side of) and νόμος (law) and means "wrongdoing."

E. Inevitable Doom
2:17–22

1. Description
2:17–19

Peter paints a telling portrait of his adversaries by using striking colors and detailed sketches. With his verbal brush, he describes these people with images borrowed from nature and daily life. He avoids exaggeration and strives for accuracy so that his readers are able to recognize the false teachers without any difficulty.

Nature

17. These men are springs without water and mists driven by a storm. Blackest darkness is reserved for them.

What a picture! Jude has an expanded description in which only the first and the last lines are similar to Peter's version. Here are the lines from Jude 12–13:

> They are clouds without rain, blown along by the wind; autumn trees, without fruit and uprooted—twice dead. They are wild waves of the sea, foaming up their shame; wandering stars, for whom blackest darkness has been reserved forever.

We readily adopt the rule that the shorter version of a text is generally the original reading, because copyists tend to expand, not shorten, a text. If we apply this rule to the text in Jude, we must allow for the possibility that Jude had the text of Peter's letter in his possession. However, we also may assume that Peter and Jude knew each other as fellow workers in the church and that together they discussed problems which the church in the second half of the first century faced. They shared what they discussed and wrote, so that their documents display interdependence.

But let us return to Peter's description of the apostates. He borrows images from nature and in three short clauses discloses the true nature of these infidels.

a. "These men are springs without water." This is a picture of a desert in which the traveler looks for a spring. But when he has discovered the water hole, he finds to his dismay that it is dry. Similarly, the false teachers have nothing to offer the members of the Christian community: they are like dry wells.

The second illustration is equally fitting:

b. "Mists driven by a storm." What a disappointment to people who, having endured a drought, finally see storm clouds from which they expect abundant rain. But the storm pushes along swirling clouds that are waterless. So the heretics cause excitement in the community but offer nothing that is substantial and worthwhile. In a sense, they bring dejection.

c. "Blackest darkness is reserved for them." Near the end of the first century John writes, "God is light" (I John 1:5). The opposite of light is absolute darkness. Whereas God's children share in his light, the children of the devil walk around in the darkness they have chosen. For them God's judgment, which Peter describes as "blackest darkness," is reserved.[41] In the Greek, Peter uses the word *blackest,* which is the same as the term *gloomy* in verse 4 ("God did not spare angels when they sinned, but sent them to hell, putting them into gloomy dungeons to be held for judgment").

Design

18. For they mouth empty, boastful words and, by appealing to the lustful desires of sinful human nature, they entice people who are just escaping from those who live in error.

From the metaphors which he borrowed from God's creation, Peter moves to a description of the design that these false teachers have drawn. Almost in summary form of what he has said in the earlier part of the chapter, Peter sets forth the methods and aims which the heretics pursue.

a. "For they mouth empty, boastful words." The term *words* has two descriptive adjectives in this translation. The first one, "empty," relates to the content of the words that are uttered. They are futile, void of any

---

41. Compare Hans-Christoph Hahn, *NIDNTT,* vol. 1, p. 425.

meaning, without purpose. The second adjective, "boastful," refers to the form and the sound of these words. These are puffed-up, haughty, and exaggerated utterances. They are meaningless because they lack every semblance of truth and integrity. Yet the false teachers use the words for their own purpose (compare Jude 16).

b. "By appealing to the lustful desires of sinful human nature, they entice people." This is a variation of verse 14: "With eyes full of adultery, they never stop sinning; they seduce the unstable." They utter these empty and boastful words for the purpose of ensnaring unstable people. How do they accomplish their objective? They arouse the sexual desires in man that induce him to lust and sensual gratification. Peter's habit of redundancy is evident once again. He literally writes, "They entice by fleshly desires, by sensuality" (NASB).[42] The Greek expression *lustful desires* is strengthened by the term *sensuality,* which signifies the indecent conduct and sexual excess that prevailed in Sodom and Gomorrah.[43]

c. "They entice people who are just escaping from those who live in error." Like carnivorous animals that prey on the weakest members of a herd, so the false teachers focus their attention on recent converts. Believers who have not had sufficient time to grow in grace and understanding of the Christian faith now have to endure the enticements of apostates. Peter adds the word *just,* which means "barely." Another translation of this section of the verse is this: "They allure . . . the ones who have *actually* escaped from those who live in error" (NKJV, italics added; based on a variant reading).

However, the point of Peter's message appears to be that the false teachers are more likely to be successful in enticing new converts than seasoned Christians who in the past escaped from an evil way of life. Furthermore, a present participle in leading Greek manuscripts indicates that the act of escaping was recent. Peter is referring to a minority in the Christian community, not the entire church. His concern is for the new Christians who still have not had sufficient training in the faith to oppose the evil one. In general, novices in the Christian faith readily can be lured back to the ways of the world.

Translators favor the reading that features the present tense and the adverb *just.* For example, "They . . . trap those who are just beginning to escape from among people who live in error" (GNB).[44] Incidentally, the Latin Vulgate departs from the Greek text by placing the two clauses in apposition: "They who escape little by little, that is, who live in error." The ancient Syriac translations also differ from the Greek reading: "Those who

---

42. Also see 1:5–7, 16–17; 2:13.

43. See the translations *shameful ways* (v. 2) and *filthy lives* (v. 7) for the same Greek term.

44. See D. Hemmerdinger-Iliadou, "*II Pierre,* ii, 18, d'apres l'Ephrem grec," *Revue Biblique* 64 (1957): 399–410.

run away from straight words and those who live in error" or "those who with few words run away from those who live in error." These versions, however, could be mere attempts to improve the Greek text.

Who are "those who live in error"? They can hardly be the false teachers, for if this were true we would expect Peter to be more explicit. The wording is insufficiently clear to hold that these teachers are trying to recapture the new converts who had just escaped from their influence and power. It is better to understand the clause to refer to the Gentile population that continued to live in spiritual darkness.

Bondage

19. They promise them freedom, while they themselves are slaves of depravity—for a man is a slave to whatever has mastered him.

Golden promises! But what an irony to hear the false teachers talk about freedom which they themselves do not possess. They are unable to fulfill their promise of freedom because they are in bondage to sin. Slaves of sin are promising their fellow men freedom.

Peter calls these people "slaves of depravity." The degree of depravity is evident in the distortion of the facts.[45] Peter does not describe these teachers as people who, in ignorance and lacking full knowledge of the gospel, are preaching "the benefits and blessings of Christ."[46] Instead, they purposely distort the truth to undermine the advance of the gospel of Christ.

Freedom in Christ means that we are set free from the burden of sin, that Christ has fulfilled the law for us (Rom. 10:4), and that we obey the law of God to express our gratitude to him. But this is not the freedom the errorists offer the recent converts to the Christian faith. Their so-called freedom is utterly depraved, for it is a license to live apart from God's law.

Peter writes about the promise of freedom in another context. There he acquaints the readers with the precious promises which God has given them, so that they may "escape the corruption in the world caused by evil desires" (1:4).

"For a man is a slave to whatever has mastered him." This sentence is a proverb that appears a few times in early Christian literature.[47] It has a parallel in Paul's observation: "Don't you know that when you offer yourselves to someone to obey him as slaves, you are slaves to the one whom you obey?" (Rom. 6:16; and see John 8:34). Peter opposes the false teachers who have deliberately chosen to obey sin and therefore have become slaves of sin. Sin has completely mastered them. Peter vividly describes them in these words: "With eyes full of adultery, they never stop sinning" (v. 14).

---

45. Consult Donald Guthrie, *New Testament Theology* (Downers Grove: Inter-Varsity, 1981), p. 216.

46. Calvin, *The Second Epistle of Peter*, p. 409.

47. For detailed information, refer to Bauckham, *Jude, 2 Peter*, p. 277.

Doctrinal Considerations in 2:19

What is freedom? As soon as we ask this question, we must specify from what bondage we have been delivered. People who have been enslaved to alcohol or drugs can claim freedom from chemical dependence. Nations that have been liberated from enemy occupation experience freedom from oppression. This creation, which has been placed under the bondage of sin, waits patiently for the day when it "will be liberated from its bondage to decay and brought into the glorious freedom of the children of God" (Rom. 8:21).

Many of the first readers of Peter's epistle knew about slavery and freedom from personal experience. The New Testament teaches that in the early church numerous Christians were slaves (compare Eph. 6:5–8; Col. 3:22–25; I Tim. 6:1–2; Titus 2:9–10; I Peter 2:18). But in the fellowship of the Christian church, the distinction between master and slave disappeared. For example, Paul commends Onesimus as a Christian brother to Philemon. And he teaches the Galatians principles of Christian liberty: "There is neither Jew nor Greek, slave nor free, male nor female, for you are all one in Christ Jesus" (Gal. 3:28). The truth of the gospel liberates a believer from the power of sin.

In the Gentile world of the first century, Athenian philosophers taught that "persons who are legally free but controlled by their vices are really slaves; those who are legally slaves but pursue goodness and truth are really free."[48] Although this is a laudable comment, philosophers are unable to liberate man from the burden and shackles of sin. But through his work and word, Christ Jesus grants true freedom to anyone who comes to him in faith and repentance. Only the Son of God sets the believer free so that he is free indeed (John 8:36).

Greek Words, Phrases, and Constructions in 2:18–19

Verse 18

ματαιότητος—although translations give an adjectival meaning ("empty") to this word, it is a noun that signifies *"emptiness, futility, purposelessness."*[49]

ἀσελγείαις—this is the dative plural of the feminine noun meaning "sensuality." A few Greek manuscripts have the genitive singular of this noun ("to the lustful desires of sensuality"). This reading, however, is needlessly repetitious.

ὀλίγως ἀποφεύγοντας—the adverb strengthens the present active participle, which has an ingressive connotation ("just beginning to escape"). The reading ὄντως (actually) syntactically must be taken with the aorist active ἀποφυγόντες and means "actually have escaped." The better manuscripts support the present participle with ὀλίγως (just).[50]

---

48. F. F. Bruce, "Liberty," *ISBE,* vol. 3, p. 120.

49. Bauer, p. 495.

50. Refer to Metzger, *Textual Commentary,* p. 704.

Verse 19

ἥττηται—from the verb ἡττάω (I make inferior), this perfect passive reveals that an action took place in the past but that the results are relevant for the present (see v. 20). The perfect tense of δεδούλωται (from the verb δουλόω, I enslave) makes the same distinction.

---

2. Doctrine
2:20–22

In the last three verses of this chapter, Peter sums up the final destiny of the false teachers by stressing that they have returned to their former way of life. In effect, they affirm a proverbial truth: as a dog returns to its vomit and a pig to its mud so the apostates revert to their sinful lifestyle.

Condition

20. If they have escaped the corruption of the world by knowing our Lord and Savior Jesus Christ and are again entangled in it and overcome, they are worse off at the end than they were at the beginning.

Who is the subject of this verse? Some writers say: "The false teachers."[51] Other commentators assert: "The new Christians who are led astray."[52] The arguments advanced to defend either position are cogent. For instance, the use of the conjunction *for* (omitted in the NIV) as a first word in verse 20 forms a bridge to the immediately preceding verse (v. 19). Because the two texts form one unit, they have the same subject: the false teachers. On the other hand, the verb *to escape* appears in verses 18 and 20. The subject of this verb appears to be identical in both verses. But the argument on the use of a particular verb must be balanced by the observation that the verb *to master, overcome* in verses 19b and 20 refers to the false teachers. And last, in the light of the preceding verses that feature the apostates as the dominant subject, many commentators apply the last three verses to these teachers. Granted that convincing evidence has been presented by both sides, I am persuaded that in view of the flow of the entire chapter the subject is the false teachers.

a. "If they have escaped the corruption of the world." This is a factual statement, even though it appears in a conditional sentence. The element of probability is missing and the experience of what has happened in the past becomes evident. In the Greek, the verb form indicates that the false teachers on one occasion departed from the corruption of the world. "They had once escaped the world's defilements" (NEB; also see JB). The difference in the verb form (in v. 18) is evident: "[They] have barely begun to

---

51. Consult the commentaries of Alford, Blum, Cranfield, Green, Greijdanus, Mayor, Mounce, Schelkle, Senior, and Wand.
52. See the expositions of Bengel, Bigg, Kelly, Moffatt, and Sidebottom. Also compare Duane A. Dunham, "An Exegetical Study of 2 Peter 2:18–22," *BS* 140 (1983): 40–54.

escape" (NEB). This variation in the use of the verb form shows that Peter was thinking of the new converts who were in the process of breaking with their past. Here in verse 20, however, he is describing the heretics who at one time forsook their world and its corruption. "There can be little doubt that the false teachers had once been orthodox Christians."[53] In the past, these people were members of the church and they became acquainted with the teachings of the Christian faith.

b. "By knowing our Lord and Savior Jesus Christ." Did the false teachers at one time know Jesus Christ as Lord and Savior? The answer is yes. For example, when Jesus commissioned his disciples two by two, he sent out Judas and another disciple. "They went out and preached that people should repent. They drove out many demons and anointed many sick people with oil and healed them" (Mark 6:12–13). Obviously, Judas knew Jesus; in the name of Jesus he preached and performed miracles. Yet Judas betrayed his Master.

The apostates had a knowledge of Jesus Christ, but their knowledge lacked the intimacy that characterizes the relationship of the true believer with Christ. Observe Peter's personal touch in the phrases *our knowledge of him* (1:3) and *your knowledge of our Lord Jesus Christ* (1:8). These people had professed the name of Christ as their Lord and Savior but in time fully disclosed that their knowledge was merely intellectual knowledge (compare Matt. 13:20–21). Also note that Peter refrains from using the terms *faith* and *believer* in this context. The teachers never put their faith and trust in Jesus Christ. Because they lacked a personal relationship with Christ, they fell away.

c. "And are again entangled in it and overcome." The Greek actually indicates that these teachers were again woven into the fabric of the world's corruption. This matter is an accomplished fact: although they left the world momentarily, they returned and defiled themselves again with its sordid sin. The result is that they are no longer free; they are slaves of sin (v. 19). Any resistance to the corruption of the world is out of the question, for they are overcome by sin and serve as slaves.

d. "They are worse off at the end than they were at the beginning." Here is the conclusive statement in Greek that Peter borrows almost verbatim from the teachings of Jesus. About casting out a demon who returns to a former demon-possessed person with seven other spirits, Jesus says, "And the final condition of that man is worse than the first" (Matt. 12:45; Luke 11:26; and compare Matt. 27:64).

Peter writes descriptively about the destiny of the apostates. Yet his words contain an urgent warning to the believers not to follow the path of the heretics that leads to irrevocable and everlasting destruction.

---

53. Green, *The Second Epistle General of Peter*, p. 118.

Doctrinal Considerations in 2:20

Within the church of Jesus Christ are true believers and pseudobelievers. Scripture tells the church members to make a clear distinction between these two groups. They live alongside each other much the same as the wheat and weeds in the same field. When the pseudobelievers depart on their own accord, they demonstrate that they never belonged to the body of Christ. Writers of Scripture, therefore, distinguish between the two groups by using the pronouns *we* and *us* over against *they* and *them*.

Peter differentiates between the members of the church and the false teachers with the use of the personal pronouns. In verse 20, for instance, he refers to the teachers with the plural pronoun *they*. In the last three verses of this chapter (vv. 20–22), he speaks only of the teachers and not of the believers. The exception is that Peter uses the possessive pronoun *our* in the phrase "our Lord and Savior Jesus Christ."

In these verses, then, Peter never calls these teachers believers or children of God. Throughout these verses he describes them as people who deliberately sin against God and his Word. He repeatedly declares that these people face God's judgment and destruction (vv. 3, 9, 12, 17).

Did these false teachers ever know Jesus Christ as Lord and Savior? By listening to the words of Jesus we receive an answer. Jesus says that only the person who obeys his Father in heaven will enter the kingdom. "Many will say to me on that day, 'Lord, Lord, did we not prophesy in your name, and in your name drive out demons and perform many miracles?' Then I will tell them plainly, 'I never knew you. Away from me, you evildoers!' " (Matt. 7:22–23).

Command

21. It would have been better for them not to have known the way of righteousness, than to have known it and then to turn their backs on the sacred command that was passed on to them.

a. *Unfulfilled duty.* What Peter communicates about the false teachers is the opposite of what was expected of them. If their faith had been genuine and their knowledge had been true, they would have developed spiritually to teach others the way of salvation. If they were true Christian teachers, they would have taught others the gospel of Christ. However, they refused to follow "the way of righteousness" and they denied Jesus Christ as sovereign Lord (v. 2; Jude 4). Their lives were contrary to fact.

b. *Apostasy.* "It would have been better for them not to have known the way of righteousness," says Peter. But alas, although they were instructed in the Christian faith, they fell away from God and his Word. Because they deliberately have turned against God, they face eternal judgment. Scripture clearly and repeatedly warns against the danger of apostasy. Here are two passages:

> "That servant who knows his master's will and does not get ready or does not do what his master wants will be beaten with many blows. . . .

313

From everyone who has been given much, much will be demanded; and from the one who has been entrusted with much, much more will be asked." [Luke 12:47–48]

If we deliberately keep on sinning after we have received the knowledge of the truth, no sacrifice for sins is left, but only a fearful expectation of judgment and of raging fire that will consume the enemies of God. [Heb. 10:26; also see Heb. 6:4–6; Prov. 21:16]

At this point we must distinguish between intentional and unintentional sins.[54] The person who deliberately sins against God expresses open rebellion that in Old Testament times resulted in capital punishment (Num. 15:30). The writer of Hebrews, commenting on the destiny of an apostate, says: "It is a dreadful thing to fall into the hands of the living God" (10:31).

c. *Comparison.* If they had not known the way of righteousness, the teachers would have been able to claim ignorance. Not now. They have known "the way of righteousness" that John the Baptist already revealed to the people of Israel in preparation for the coming of Jesus (Matt. 21:32). Moreover, the expression *the Way* served as a synonym for the Christian faith in the first half of the first century.[55]

The false teachers not only have known the Way, but also have turned "their backs on the sacred command that was passed on to them." What is this "sacred command"? It is equivalent to the message of Christ's gospel. In the parallel passage, Jude calls this commandment "the *faith* that was once for all entrusted to the saints" (v. 3, italics added). In other words, the command of Peter and the faith (Christian doctrine) of Jude are the same.

Peter writes that this commandment, namely, the gospel, was passed on to them. The expression *passed on* is a technical term that refers to receiving the gospel for the purpose of teaching it and thus handing it on to the hearers (see especially I Cor. 11:2, 23; 15:3; Jude 3).[56] Peter calls this gospel tradition sacred, which means that it must be kept intact, obeyed, and taught. The false teachers, however, broke the chain of receiving and transmitting the gospel of Christ. They altered its content, rejected its teachings, and perverted its truth (compare vv. 1–3). By doing so they committed the unpardonable sin, that is, the sin of blasphemy against the Holy Spirit (Matt. 12:32; I John 5:16).

Conclusion

22. Of them the proverbs are true: "A dog returns to its vomit," and, "A sow that is washed goes back to her wallowing in the mud."

---

54. Refer to Simon J. Kistemaker, *Hebrews*, New Testament Commentary series (Grand Rapids: Baker, 1984), p. 293.

55. Refer to Acts 9:2; 18:25; 19:9, 23; 22:4; 24:14, 22.

56. Consult Friedrich Büchsel, *TDNT*, vol. 2, p. 171; and see Klaus Wegenast, *NIDNTT*, vol. 3, pp. 773–74.

Peter concludes his descriptive analysis of the false teachers with two proverbs. The first one he takes verbatim from the Old Testament. Proverbs 26:11 has this reading:

> As a dog returns to its vomit,
> so a fool repeats his folly.

The Jews treated dogs with contempt and not as man's best friend. According to the Old and New Testaments, Jews treated dogs as unclean animals.[57] A dog "lived on refuse of all kinds and thus was a potential carrier of many diseases."[58] As a scavenger, a dog would return to its own vomit and thus fulfill the proverb. Peter uses this proverb to compare the natural habit of a dog with the practice of false teachers who return to living in sin.

The second proverb seems to have been a common saying in the ancient world, for it appears in various manuscripts.[59] The truth of this proverb is self-evident. A pig seeks relief from pesky insects and the heat of the sun by wallowing in the mud. Although the sow is washed, by nature the pig returns to the mud from which it has come. It rolls around in slime and grunts contentedly. Once again, the application to the apostates is graphic and descriptive. As the pig enjoys wallowing in the mire, so the heretics take pleasure in revelry and immorality.

Jesus mentions dogs and pigs in the same sentence when he says, "Do not give dogs what is sacred; do not throw your pearls to pigs" (Matt. 7:6). He instructs his disciples to distinguish between people who are receptive to the message of the gospel and those persons who trample underfoot that which is sacred. Such people are similar to dogs and swine.

Here is a conclusive observation: By vomiting, the dog relieves itself of *internal* impurities; the sow, when it is washed, is cleansed from clinging *external* mud. Nevertheless, both animals return to the selfsame filth.

Greek Words, Phrases, and Constructions in 2:20–22

Verse 20

εἰ—the simple-fact condition with the indicative mood in both the protasis and apodosis clauses denotes reality.

ἀποφυγόντες—the aorist active (compare the present tense in v. 18) seems to indicate that Peter wants to designate a group of people different from those mentioned in verse 18.

τοῦ κυρίου—Peter employs one definite article for more than one noun: "Lord" and "Savior" (see 3:2).

ἐμπλακέντες—from ἐμπλέκω (I entangle, involve in), this participle is the aorist

---

57. E.g., refer to I Sam. 17:43; 24:14; II Sam. 9:8; 16:9; II Kings 8:13; Rev. 22:15.
58. George S. Cansdale, "Dog," *ZPEB*, vol. 2, p. 153.
59. For further information, consult Bauckham, *Jude, 2 Peter*, p. 279.

passive. The aorist signifies single occurrence of an action; the aorist also means that it precedes the action of the main verb in the clause. The passive implies an agent, namely, the devil.

ἡττῶνται—Peter uses the present passive form of the verb which appears as the perfect passive in verse 19. The present serves as a perfect.[60]

Verse 21

ἦν—the imperfect indicative is translated as a "potential imperfect." It expresses the idea "of an obligation which comes over from the past and is not lived up to."[61] The particle ἄν is absent.

ἐπεγνωκέναι—as a perfect active infinitive from the verb ἐπιγινώσκω (I learn to know), this perfect tense shows lasting effect. The context of the infinitive reveals, however, that the apostates refused to teach the Christian gospel. The dative plural of the aorist active participle ἐπιγνοῦσιν relates to the pronoun αὐτοῖς (for them).

Verse 22

συμβέβηκεν—the perfect active tense of the compound verb συμβαίνω (I meet, happen, come about) stresses continuity.

κύων—this is an independent nominative featured in a proverbial expression. It is equivalent to a nominative absolute.[62] The word κύων refers not to a house dog, but to a stray dog that is wild.

τό—without the accompanying noun, the definite article in the neuter singular has a substantival sense.[63]

λουσαμένη—from λούω (I wash), this middle aorist participle has a passive meaning.

Summary of Chapter 2

Peter writes this chapter to warn the believers against the pernicious heresies of false teachers who openly deny the sovereignty of Christ and consequently face swift destruction. Peter describes the greed and dishonesty of these teachers and as a warning states that many in the Christian community will follow their immoral ways.

With a number of examples from history, Peter compares the destiny of the false teachers to that of the angels who sinned and were condemned to hell, to the unbelieving contemporaries of Noah who perished in the flood, and to the cities of Sodom and Gomorrah that were reduced to ashes. By contrast, God protected Noah and his family and rescued Lot. Thus, the Lord spares the righteous but punishes the unrighteous on the day of judgment.

---

60. Robertson, *Grammar*, p. 881.
61. Ibid., p. 920.
62. Consult H. E. Dana and Julius R. Mantey, *A Manual Grammar of the Greek New Testament* (1927; New York: Macmillan, 1967), p. 70.
63. Refer to Blass and Debrunner, *Greek Grammar*, sec. 266.3.

The false teachers even slander celestial beings, arrogantly level accusations, behave like animals, and thus face inevitable destruction. In broad daylight they yield to drunkenness and practice adultery. They are greedy and skilled in seduction. Peter uses the illustration of the life and motives of Balaam, whose donkey rebuked him.

Peter's language is picturesque. He resorts to metaphors as he describes the false teachers, whom he depicts as waterless springs and clouds without rain. Once more Peter warns the believers against seduction. The heretics promise freedom, yet they themselves are slaves of sin. Because they have known the way of righteousness, the apostates are accountable for their actions. It would have been better for them had they never known Christ. With two proverbs about a dog and a sow, Peter concludes his lengthy description of these false teachers.

3

The Day of the Lord

(3:1–13)

and Exhortations

(3:14–18)

Outline

3 1 Dear friends, this is now my second letter to you. I have written both of them as reminders to stimulate you to wholesome thinking.   2 I want you to recall the words spoken in the past by the holy prophets and the command given by our Lord and Savior through your apostles.

3 First of all, you must understand that in the last days scoffers will come, scoffing and following their own evil desires.   4 They will say, "Where is this 'coming' he promised? Ever since our fathers died, everything goes on as it has since the beginning of creation."   5 But they deliberately forget that long ago by God's word the heavens existed and the earth was formed out of water and by water.   6 By these waters also the world of that time was deluged and destroyed.   7 By the same word the present heavens and earth are reserved for fire, being kept for the day of judgment and destruction of ungodly men.

8 But do not forget this one thing, dear friends: With the Lord a day is like a thousand years, and a thousand years are like a day.   9 The Lord is not slow in keeping his promise, as some understand slowness. He is patient with you, not wanting anyone to perish, but everyone to come to repentance.

10 But the day of the Lord will come like a thief. The heavens will disappear with a roar; the elements will be destroyed by fire, and the earth and everything in it will be laid bare.

11 Since everything will be destroyed in this way, what kind of people ought you to be? You ought to live holy and godly lives   12 as you look forward to the day of God and speed its coming. That day will bring about the destruction of the heavens by fire, and the elements will melt in the heat.   13 But in keeping with his promise we are looking forward to a new heaven and a new earth, the home of righteousness.

V. The Day of the Lord
3:1–13

A. Reminder
3:1–2

After an interlude in which Peter describes the character, life, and destiny of false teachers, the apostle continues to exhort and encourage the members of the Christian church. In this chapter, Peter writes apocalyptically about the day of the Lord. In his teaching, however, he again directs some of his remarks to scoffers. Presumably these scoffers are the same people as the heretics he describes in the preceding chapter.

1. Dear friends, this is now my second letter to you. I have written both of them as reminders to stimulate you to wholesome thinking.

The address is rather common in this chapter: it occurs four times (vv. 1, 8, 14, 17). Incidentally, except for the greeting *my brothers* (1:10), "dear friends" is the only salutation used in both I and II Peter (see I Peter 2:11;

321

4:12). A literal translation is "beloved," which is a frequent address in the New Testament epistles. Peter wants to make certain that the readers know of his pastoral love and concern for them. The recipients are dear friends and differ from the apostates.

a. "This is now my second letter to you." If this is the second letter, which is the first epistle Peter wrote? Commentators provide a number of answers. Here are some of them:

1. Second Peter is a combination of two epistles: the first two chapters form the first epistle and the last chapter constitutes the second letter. This view, however, faces difficulties, for the three chapters in II Peter are interrelated.

2. Peter wrote another letter which is no longer extant, just as Paul wrote more than two epistles to the Corinthian church. These other letters of Peter and Paul are not part of Scripture (see I Cor. 5:9). We have no problem assuming that the apostles composed more letters than those which the church has placed in the canon. However, we hesitate to adopt the hypothesis that Peter is referring to an epistle that is lost. We accept this hypothesis only when all other explanations fail to prove satisfactory.

3. The first epistle Peter wrote is I Peter. Some scholars see problems in regard to Peter's express purpose stated at the beginning of II Peter 3: "I have written both [letters] as reminders" (v. 1). They point out that in the Greek the term *reminder* appears in II Peter 1:13 but not in I Peter. In respect to the term itself, these scholars are correct.[1] In Peter's first epistle, however, not the term but the concept occurs repeatedly (refer to 1:13–17; 2:11–12; 4:13, 17–19; 5:4). Although scholars raise questions regarding the relationship of I and II Peter, these concerns appear to be insufficient to discount the validity of identifying the two letters. We assume, then, that Peter's remark, "I have written both of them," refers to I Peter.[2]

b. "As reminders to stimulate you to wholesome thinking." Peter intimates that with these two letters he puts the minds of the readers to work (see 1:13). Another version says, "I have been recalling to you what you already know, to rouse you to honest thought" (NEB). What is the meaning of the phrase *wholesome thinking*? Peter means unsullied and pure thinking. The expression *common sense* comes close to conveying what Peter means. He contrasts the thinking of the believers with that of the false teachers; and he implies that Christians should be mentally alert to discern truth from error.

---

1. Refer, e.g., to Michael Green, *The Second Epistle General of Peter, and the General Epistle of Jude: An Introduction and Commentary*, Tyndale New Testament Commentaries (Grand Rapids: Eerdmans, 1968), p. 123.

2. Consult Charles Bigg, *A Critical and Exegetical Commentary on the Epistles of St. Peter and St. Jude*, International Critical Commentary series (1901; Edinburgh: Clark, 1961), pp. 288–89. Also see G. H. Boobyer, "The Indebtedness of II Peter to I Peter," in *New Testament Essays: Studies in Memory of T. W. Manson*, ed. A. J. B. Higgins (Manchester: Manchester University Press, 1959), pp. 36–39.

2. I want you to recall the words spoken in the past by the holy prophets and the command given by our Lord and Savior through your apostles.
Notice the following points:

a. *Prophets.* Peter wants his readers to start recalling the prophecies recorded in the Old Testament. This is the second time in this epistle that Peter calls attention to the "word of the prophets" (1:19; also see I Peter 1:10–12). In the context of this verse, we interpret the expression *words* to mean the Old Testament prophecies that pertain to the "day of the Lord."

In Greek, Peter uses the perfect tense for the word *spoken* to indicate that although these prophecies were uttered in the past they are valid in the present. And who communicated these utterances? Holy prophets spoke "as they were carried along by the Holy Spirit" (1:21). Peter designates them "holy," which seems to have been a common description for the Old Testament prophets. For example, in his song Zechariah says that God spoke "through his holy prophets of long ago" (Luke 1:70). And when Peter preached after the healing of the lame man at the temple, he mentioned that God would "restore everything, as he promised long ago through his holy prophets" (Acts 3:21). The qualification *holy* differentiates the true prophets from those who are false, and it discloses that their prophecies have a divine origin.

b. *Christ.* Peter writes, "And the command given by our Lord and Savior." This is the second time in his epistle that Peter employs the word *command* (2:21). In view of the earlier use and interpretation of this word, it is acceptable to say that the term signifies the gospel of Christ that calls man to repentance and faith.[3] It is also feasible to look at the context of chapter 3 and say that the word refers to the second coming of Christ.[4] Still another view is to relate the expression *command* to Peter's warning about the doctrines of false teachers.[5] However, this last view faces the objection that the command originates not with Peter but with "our Lord and Savior."

The words *Lord and Savior* occur four times in this epistle; in three instances Peter has added the names *Jesus Christ* (1:11; 2:20; 3:18, and v. 2 without the names). By combining the two titles, Peter teaches that "sovereignty includes also salvation."[6] Throughout Peter's epistle, the doctrine concerning Christ receives special attention.

c. *Apostles.* The reading *through your apostles* has caused some interpreters to say that Peter could not have penned these words; instead an author of a

---

3. Refer to S. Greijdanus, *De Brieven van de Apostelen Petrus en Johannes, en de Brief van Judas,* Kommentaar op het Nieuwe Testament series (Amsterdam: Van Bottenburg, 1929), p. 332. Also see John Calvin, *Commentaries on the Catholic Epistles: The Second Epistle of Peter,* ed. and trans. John Owen (Grand Rapids: Eerdmans, 1948), p. 413.

4. Among others, consult Robert H. Mounce, *A Living Hope: A Commentary on 1 and 2 Peter* (Grand Rapids: Eerdmans, 1982), p. 138.

5. See Green, *The Second Epistle General of Peter,* p. 125.

6. Donald Guthrie, *New Testament Theology* (Downers Grove: Inter-Varsity, 1981), p. 300 n. 235.

later date wrote them because he wanted to express his respect for the apostles as a group.[7] But this approach to the text is unnecessary when we consider the development of the New Testament Scriptures in the middle of the first century. The words of Jesus were accorded the same authority as those of the Old Testament. Hence the apostles who taught the gospel of Christ were placed on the same level as the holy prophets who wrote the prophecies. The expression *your apostles,* then, means that Peter speaks as a representative of that group.

Greek Words, Phrases, and Constructions in 3:1–2

Verse 1

ταύτην ... δευτέραν ... ἐπιστολήν—notice the position of each word in the Greek text. Peter wants to emphasize each word individually.

γράφω—although this is the present active indicative, translators look at the word from the recipient's point of view. They put it in the past tense ("I have written").

ὑμῶν—the placement of this personal pronoun is unusual because it modifies not ὑπομνήσει (reminder) but διάνοιαν (mind).[8]

Verse 2

μνησθῆναι—the aorist passive infinitive of μιμνήσκομαι (I remind myself, remember) stands in apposition to the preceding verse (v. 1).[9] The aorist is ingressive.

τῆς τῶν ἀποστόλων—the feature of linking the numerous genitives in this verse is unique. Translators avoid literalism by introducing the concept *agency,* "*by* the holy prophets and the command given *by* our Lord and Savior *through* your apostles" (italics added).

B. Scoffers
3:3–4

Peter describes the New Testament age, which he characterizes as "the last days" (compare II Tim. 3:1; Jude 18). He refers to the entire period from the ascension of Jesus to Christ's eventual return; thus he includes the times in which he himself lives. Peter himself encounters scoffers whom he describes as false teachers (see the preceding chapter).

---

7. E.g., consult J. N. D. Kelly, *A Commentary on the Epistles of Peter and Jude,* Thornapple Commentaries series (1969; Grand Rapids: Baker, 1981), p. 354. And see Richard J. Bauckham, *Jude, 2 Peter,* Word Commentary series, vol. 50 (Waco: Word, 1983), p. 288.

8. Refer to C. F. D. Moule, *An Idiom-Book of New Testament Greek,* 2d ed. (Cambridge: Cambridge University Press, 1960), p. 168.

9. Consult A. T. Robertson, *A Grammar of the Greek New Testament in the Light of Historical Research* (Nashville: Broadman, 1934), p. 1086.

3. First of all, you must understand that in the last days scoffers will come, scoffing and following their own evil desires.

When Peter says "first of all," he is not enumerating a list of items. Rather, he stresses the primary importance of what he is about to teach. He intimates that his readers should be alert to and on guard against the errors of these scoffers (see 3:17). And he teaches the believers to be constantly aware of the fact that they are living in the last days.

The expression *last days* is common in the New Testament. For instance, it appears in the Epistle to the Hebrews, where the writer notes that God has spoken through his Son (1:2); and Peter mentions that in this last period God has revealed Jesus (I Peter 1:20; also consider James 5:3). The implied comparison is that the Old Testament era preceded the coming of Christ. That period is first and the one of the New Testament is last.

"Scoffers will come, scoffing." These people know God's revelation and his impending judgment. Because they are familiar with the Scriptures, they have become habitual mockers of God and his Word. Scoffing should not be confused with jesting. Jesting depicts frivolity, but scoffing is a sin that is deliberate. Scoffing occurs when men show willful contempt for God and his Son.

We understand that the mockers are the false teachers Peter has described in the previous chapter. But we can also hear a prophetic note in the future tense *will come*. Peter is saying that in the years that precede the return of Christ numerous scoffers will ridicule Christians for their faith in God. Scoffers indeed demonstrate that they themselves are apostates in word and deed. Says Peter,

"[They follow] their own evil desires." Having rejected God's revelation, the scoffers take pleasure in following their natural desires. This is the exact opposite of doing the will of God, for they continually seek fulfillment in physical pleasures. When believers observe these people, they have visible evidence that they are living in the last days, during which false prophets are rampant (see Matt. 24:3–5, 11, 23–26).

4. They will say, "Where is this 'coming' he promised? Ever since our fathers died, everything goes on as it has since the beginning of creation."

Here, then, are the words these scoffers speak. Arrogantly they deny that the judgment day will come. They repudiate the message that they must give an account of their words and deeds. They scoff at Jesus' promise that he will return on the last day and contemptuously they ask, "Where is this 'coming' he promised?" Notice that they are not interested in the time of Jesus' return but they ask the question *where*? Hence, they doubt the truthfulness of the written and spoken word of God, much the same as the Jewish people in the days before the exile mockingly asked, "Where is the word of the LORD? Let it now be fulfilled!" (Jer. 17:15; also compare Isa. 5:19; Ezek. 12:22).

In the middle of the first century, Christians asked the apostles about

Christ's return.[10] For them, the second coming was a matter of time. They expected the day of the Lord to come in their day. For this reason, then, the question raised by the scoffers fits that particular time in history.[11]

"Ever since our fathers died, everything goes on as it has since the beginning of creation." If in the middle of the first century Christians queried the apostles about the return of Christ, we can understand that even the unbelievers scoffingly repeated the same question. But the apostates go much further, for in their obstinacy they declare that nothing has changed.

Who are these fathers? Some translations add the possessive pronoun *our* to the word *fathers*, which in the Greek is lacking. Are they the forefathers of the scoffers or are they the Christians who have died? *Phillips* has this reading: "Since the first Christians fell asleep, everything remains exactly as it was."

The scoffers are saying that the coming of Christ has not made any difference in respect to death and dying. They say that the first Christians die just the same as other people. They conclude, therefore, that the gospel is irrelevant. Granted that this conclusion is correct, we still face the question why the scoffers would call the first Christians "fathers," especially when they link the word to creation—"since the beginning of creation"—and not to the birth of Christ. In the New Testament, the expression *our fathers* signifies the Old Testament fathers (compare John 6:31; Acts 3:13; Rom. 9:5). Because this was a standard expression, we are not amiss in asserting that Peter appears to conform to the usage that was current in his day.[12]

" 'Everything goes on as it has since the beginning of creation.' " These scoffers leave out the account of the birth, ministry, death, and resurrection of Christ and then reason that everything remains the same since the day of creation. They intimate that the person and work of Christ are without any validity and have no bearing on the natural order of events. But this is exactly the point: the coming of Christ has changed everything and his eventual return will bring about the consummation. Jesus will return.

Doctrinal Considerations in 3:3–4

Hymn writers have composed many hymns about the return of Christ. John Newton depicts the day of Christ's return in these words:

> Day of judgment! day of wonders!
> Hark! the trumpet's awful sound,

---

10. These are the references: I Cor. 15:52; I Thess. 4:15–17; II Thess. 1:7–9; James 5:8–9.

11. Green observes that the question concerning Jesus' return "supports an early rather than a late date" of Peter's letter. *The Second Epistle General of Peter*, p. 127.

12. Consult Edwin A. Blum, *2 Peter*, in *Hebrews–Revelation*, vol. 12 of *The Expositor's Bible Commentary*, ed. Frank E. Gaebelein, 12 vols. (Grand Rapids: Zondervan, 1981), p. 285.

> Louder than a thousand thunders,
> Shakes the vast creation round.
> How the summons
> Will the sinner's heart confound!

Jesus tells us that when he returns, the people who reject him will be as surprised as Noah's contemporaries were when they perished in the flood (Matt. 24:37–39). They will be like the people of Sodom and Gomorrah who were destroyed by fire and sulfur (Luke 17:28–29). The suddenness of Jesus' return will overtake the scoffers who loudly proclaim that he will not come back. In their writings, Peter, Paul, and John compare the second coming of Christ to the arrival of a thief who suddenly steals someone's possessions (3:10; I Thess. 5:2; Rev. 3:3; 16:15).

The writers of the New Testament consistently teach the doctrine of Jesus' return. "In fact, it is found in every N[ew] T[estament] book except Galatians and the short Philemon, 2 John, and 3 John."[13] Despite the scriptural evidence, some scholars hold that this doctrine is a creation of the Christian church. They even contend that Jesus himself never taught that he would return.[14]

Jesus says that the believer must watch the signs of the times. Some of these signs are the proclamation of the gospel to all nations (Matt. 24:14), the appearance of false Christs and false prophets (Mark 13:22), a period of increased lawlessness (II Thess. 2:7), and the coming of the Antichrist (I John 2:18). By observing the signs, believers are strengthened in their faith that God is at work in directing world history to the glorious day of Christ's return.

Greek Words, Phrases, and Constructions in 3:3–4

Verse 3

γινώσκοντες—this present active participle should have been in the accusative plural instead of the nominative plural. The implied subject ὑμᾶς (you) of the aorist passive infinitive in the preceding verse demands the accusative case. Peter, however, writes the nominative to express the sense of the participle.

ἐμπαιγμονῇ ἐμπαῖκται—"scoffing scoffers"; here is a Semitic idiom that parallels the Hebrew use of "the 'infinitive absolute' of a verb with another part of the same verb so as to express emphasis or frequency."[15]

ἰδίας—this adjective *own* expresses contrast to obedience to the will of God.

Verse 4

ἀφ' ἧς—as an abbreviation, the preposition and relative pronoun means "since." The pronoun has its antecedent in the understood noun ἡμέρας (day).

---

13. Leon Morris, "Parousia," *ISBE*, vol. 3, p. 667.
14. E.g., consult C. H. Dodd, *The Parables of the Kingdom* (1935; rev. ed., New York: Charles Scribner's Sons, 1961).
15. Moule, *Idiom-Book*, p. 178.

διάμενει—grammarians call this present tense either a progressive present[16] or a static present, that is, "a condition which is assumed as perpetually existing."[17]

C. Destruction
3:5–7

Peter answers his opponents by reminding them that they deliberately forget two pertinent facts. One of these facts is the flood; the other is the destruction of the world.

5. But they deliberately forget that long ago by God's word the heavens existed and the earth was formed out of water and by water.

a. "But they deliberately forget."[18] The apostates know the account of the flood, but they have chosen the path of deliberate forgetfulness. Accordingly, Peter reminds them of God's word by which heaven and earth were formed. By that same word the flood destroyed the world. Peter wants his opponents to understand that their arguments are erroneous and misleading in the light of God's revelation. God rules his creation and governs the course of world history.

b. "Long ago by God's word the heavens existed and the earth was formed." Does Peter mean that the heavens are eternal but the earth is created? Certainly not. The words *heavens and earth* must be understood as a pair that is mentioned in one breath. With this expression, he tells the reader to recall the creation account in Genesis. The use of the plural *heavens* unmistakably reveals the hand of a Jew. In Hebrew this word is always plural, and throughout this chapter Peter writes the plural form in Greek (vv. 7, 10, 12, 13).[19]

c. "The earth was formed out of water and by water." Peter reminds the reader of the creation story: "And God said, 'Let the water under the sky be gathered to one place, and let dry ground appear' " (Gen. 1:9). The land itself, then, comes forth out of the water. This interpretation relates more to origin than to substance; that is, the text explains how the earth was formed, and does not disclose the source of matter. Peter also says that the earth was formed by water. Here again he refers to the first chapter of Genesis, where we read that God's creative word "separated the water under the expanse from the water above it" (Gen. 1:7). Not only were the

---

16. Consult Robertson, *Grammar,* p. 880.

17. H. E. Dana and Julius R. Mantey, *A Manual Grammar of the Greek New Testament* (1927; New York: Macmillan, 1967), p. 186.

18. Two versions provide an alternate translation: "In believing this, they do not take into account" (NAB), or "In taking this view, they lose sight of the fact" (NEB).

19. However, Peter uses the singular in 1:18. In I Peter, the word occurs three times: once in the plural (1:4 [in Greek]) and twice in the singular (1:12; 3:22).

water from oceans and lakes and the precipitation from the skies instrumental in shaping the earth, but also rain and dew, snow and ice nourish and sustain the earth.

This verse presents some difficulties in interpretation because of the brevity of this text. Translators have tried to overcome these problems by offering a smooth rendition of the text, but some ambiguity still remains. For instance, the phrase *formed . . . by water* seems to be a repetition of the words *formed out of water*. Is Peter making a distinction between "out of" and "by" or do these two prepositions in the Greek mean the same thing? In the next verse (v. 6) Peter uses the same preposition *by* with the meaning *by means of*. In the interest of consistency, therefore, we assert that the two Greek prepositions in verse 5 are virtually the same in meaning.

6. By these waters also the world of that time was deluged and destroyed.

God, who made the world, also has the power to destroy it. He upholds his creation by his power. However, just as by his divine word the universe came into existence, so at his command he can unleash natural elements in creation to destroy that which he has made. As he formed the earth out of water, so he destroys the world by water.[20] The scoffers of Peter's day saw God's creation but refused to recognize the Creator and his authority.

The translators of the New International Version have given a literal interpretation of the Greek which has the two words *by which*. The pronoun *which* is in the plural and is translated "by these waters." When God commanded the waters to destroy man and beast on the face of the earth, "all the springs of the great deep burst forth, and the floodgates of the heavens were opened" (Gen. 7:11; also see 8:2). Water came from below and from above and covered the earth so that "everything on dry land that had the breath of life in its nostrils died" (7:22). Only Noah and his household, along with the animals he had brought into the ark, survived the raging waters of the flood.

An objection to this interpretation is that water at the time of the flood is the only destructive element and thus should be presented in the singular. Should we adopt an alternate reading in the Greek text for the phrase *by which* (in the singular), we would be able to relate the term *which* to "God's word" (v. 5). Then we can say that at God's command the world came into being and at his command the flood deluged and destroyed the earth. But this variant reading in the Greek appears to be a correction made by a scribe. The more difficult text is the plural of *which*, translated "by these waters" (NIV).[21] This text remains problematic.

What is the meaning of the phrase *world of that time*? Scripture says that all living things on dry land perished (Gen. 7:22), which is more extensive than

---

20. Consult Calvin, *The Second Epistle of Peter*, p. 416.
21. Bauckham lists four interpretations of the phrase *by which*. See *Jude, 2 Peter*, p. 298.

saying only that the wicked human race drowned. God's condemnation struck man and beast; heaven and earth were affected by the deluge.

Notice that Peter draws a parallel (see vv. 6 and 7); he contrasts the ancient world with the present heavens and earth. The world of Noah was destroyed by water; the present world will be burned with fire. The conclusion seems to be that the flood was universal, much the same as the imminent destruction by fire will be universal.

The message Peter leaves for the scoffers is direct: as God destroyed the world with the flood, so he will destroy heaven and earth with fire. God's condemnation is "hanging over [the scoffers], and their destruction has not been sleeping" (2:3).

7. By the same word the present heavens and earth are reserved for fire, being kept for the day of judgment and destruction of ungodly men. Consider the following points:

a. *Word.* God determines the beginning of this universe and the end.[22] He speaks as the Creator in the beginning, with the result that the heavens and the earth are formed. He speaks as the Judge on the last day, with the consequence that heaven and earth will be destroyed by fire. God saved believing Noah and his family while the whole world perished. He also will save believers when the conflagration of the world takes place.

b. *Fire.* "The present heavens and the earth are reserved for fire." A more literal translation of the text is, "[They are] kept in store by the same word, reserved for fire" (NKJV), which comes closer to the Greek text: "have been and are treasured for fire."

The readers of Peter's letter knew about God's destructive fire because of their knowledge of the Old Testament.[23] But in other literature, the doctrine concerning the destruction of the world by fire was also current. It appears in Jewish writings, Qumran documents, apocalyptic literature, apocryphal books, and early Christian and Roman works.[24] In the church universal and the world at large, the teaching of a fiery destruction of the world was not unknown.

The nature of this fire is not revealed. Whether a nuclear holocaust will destroy the heavens and the earth remains to be seen. Three times in this chapter Peter discloses the impending destruction of God's creation (vv. 7, 10, 12). The purpose of this fiery demise of the world is for God to judge the wicked.

c. *Men.* Peter writes, "[Fire is] kept for the day of judgment and destruction of ungodly men." This day of judgment (2:9) or day of the Lord (3:10) not only transforms the present form of God's creation. It also cleanses the earth of the wicked people who inhabit this planet. God exercises patience,

---

22. Consult Guthrie, *New Testament Theology,* p. 148.

23. See, e.g., Ps. 50:3; 97:3; Isa. 30:30; 66:15–16; Dan. 7:9–10; Mic. 1:4; Zeph. 1:18; 3:8; Mal. 4:1.

24. See Kelly, *Peter and Jude,* p. 361.

but when his forbearance has come to an end, he pronounces divine judgment upon the scoffers. Their time for destruction has arrived and consequently they receive their due reward.[25]

Greek Words, Phrases, and Constructions in 3:5–7

Verse 5

τοῦτο—this pronoun can be either nominative or accusative. In the nominative, it is the subject of the main verb: "this eludes their attention because they wish that . . . ." As an accusative, the pronoun is the direct object of the present participle θέλοντας (they wish): "because they want this, it escapes their notice that . . . ." Both versions are grammatically correct, yet translators prefer the first one.

οὐρανοὶ . . . καὶ γῆ—without the definite article, this combination constitutes a pair. In English, "heaven and earth" are also mentioned in the same breath.[26]

Verse 6

δι᾽ ὧν—the relative pronoun in the plural has a number of possible antecedents: word, water, and heavens. The double use of ὕδατος (v. 5) perhaps serves as the plural antecedent, yet the presence of ὕδατι (v. 6) is grammatically redundant.

κατακλυσθείς—from the verb κατακλύζω (I deluge, submerge), this aorist passive participle occurs only here in the New Testament.

Verse 7

τεθησαυρισμένοι—this is the perfect passive participle from the verb θησαυρίζω (I store up, treasure). The perfect denotes an action in the past that has lasting effect in the present.

τηρούμενοι—the present passive of τηρέω (I keep, reserve) conveys the message of continuous activity.

κρίσεως—the genitive is descriptive. However, the genitive case of ἀνθρώπων is objective.

D. Time
3:8–9

The day of the Lord will come as irrevocably as the day of the flood dawned in Noah's day. From God's initial announcement of impending judgment to its final execution when he closed the ark, God extended a period of grace to 120 years (Gen. 6:3). Likewise, the day of the Lord will appear at the time God has appointed. True, some people question the coming of this day. Yet that day will come, and then cosmic time, which God has created, will end. God set cosmic time in motion when he made the

---

25. Refer to George E. Ladd, *A Theology of the New Testament* (Grand Rapids: Eerdmans, 1974), p. 606.
26. Consult Robertson, *Grammar*, p. 794.

universe. But when the day of the Lord dawns, chronological time disappears in eternity.

God regards time from a perspective that differs from ours. In the next two verses, Peter teaches the reader to consider both time and patience from God's point of view.

Relativity

8. But do not forget this one thing, dear friends: With the Lord a day is like a thousand years, and a thousand years are like a day.

a. "Dear friends." Peter now turns his attention to the readers; he exhorts and encourages them by teaching them the significance of time. He addresses them as friends (see vv. 1, 14). The readers are people whom Peter loves and for whom he cares as a pastor. Literally, he addresses them as "beloved."

b. "But do not forget this one thing." After they have learned what the destiny of the scoffers will be, the readers are anxious to know what will become of them on the judgment day. Peter has described that day as a day of destruction for the wicked. What will happen to the believer? When will that day come? Although the readers are anxious to multiply their questions concerning the last day, Peter discusses only time itself. In a single sentence, he discloses the relativity of time. He teaches the readers that they should keep one thing in mind: God views time from a perspective that differs from that of man. Introducing this concept, however, Peter tells the recipients of his letter not to "forget this one thing."

Notice that the verb *to forget* in verse 8 is the same as in verse 5. There Peter writes that the scoffers deliberately forget pertinent facts concerning creation. Here he exhorts believers not to forget one thing. But what is this "one thing"? Peter sums it up in one sentence:

c. "With the Lord a day is like a thousand years, and a thousand years are like a day." Peter echoes a verse from a prayer of Moses (Ps. 90:4):

> For a thousand years in your sight
> are like a day that has just gone by.

Of course, Peter refrains from speculating when the end will come. He knows the word of Jesus on this subject: "No one knows about that day or hour, not even the angels in heaven, nor the Son, but only the Father" (Matt. 24:36). Besides, he knows that God looks at time from the perspective of eternity, and that man, who is conditioned by cosmic time, is unable to comprehend eternity. Peter is not interested in explicating the difference between time and eternity, as Moses does in Psalm 90.[27] Rather, he describes time in relation to the last day.

---

27. Consult John Albert Bengel, *Gnomon of the New Testament*, ed. Andrew R. Fausset, trans. William Fletcher, 7th ed., 5 vols. (Edinburgh: Clark, 1877), vol. 5, p. 106.

The expression *a thousand years* occurs in the New Testament only in this verse (v. 8) and in Revelation 20:2–7. Verse 8 provides no information about a literal millennium. In the first two centuries of the Christian era, however, some writers explained this verse in terms of a thousand-year period. These authors used only the words, "With the Lord a day is like a thousand years," and developed a millennial doctrine. Thus the unknown author of the Epistle of Barnabas writes that "the Lord will make an end of everything in six thousand years, for a day with him means a thousand years."[28] And Irenaeus says, "For the day of the Lord is as a thousand years; and in six days created things were completed: it is evident, therefore, that they will come to an end at the sixth thousand year."[29]

These early Christian writers neglect to recite the second part of verse 8, "and a thousand years are like a day." This cancels out the first part of the verse and, therefore, makes it difficult to develop a millenary theory. Peter is not interested in such theories. He faces the taunts of scoffers who express their doubt about the promise of the Lord's eventual return (compare v. 4).

Patience

9. The Lord is not slow in keeping his promise, as some understand slowness. He is patient with you, not wanting anyone to perish, but everyone to come to repentance.

Because the Christians of the first century expected the imminent return of the Lord and waited patiently, they needed a word of encouragement from Peter.

a. "The Lord is not slow in keeping his promise." The term *Lord* in this verse and the next (v. 10) is a synonym for "God." In other words, Peter refers not to Jesus but rather to God with his use of an Old Testament designation for God. Peter alludes to the Old Testament prophecy of Habakkuk:

> For the revelation awaits an appointed time;
> it speaks of the end
> and will not prove false.
> Though it linger, wait for it;
> it will certainly come and will not delay. [2:3]

The writer of Hebrews, who assures his readers that God will fulfill the promises that he made to them, quotes this same Old Testament prophecy (see Heb. 10:37). Why does God delay the return of Christ? The cause of the delay stems not from indifference or inattentiveness on the part of God.

---

28. The Epistle of Barnabas 15.4 (LCL).

29. Irenaeus *Against Heresies* 5.28.3; also see 5.23.2; and consult Justin Martyr *Dialogue* 81 (Ante-Nicene Fathers). For intertestamental literature, see Jub. 4:30.

It lies in God's grace and mercy toward sinners. He allows them time to repent of their sins. Jesus will return when God's patience has ended, when the time allotted has expired, and when the last believer has accepted Christ as Savior. "Not human sin, but divine forbearance, which cannot be constrained, determines the delay. It is the sovereign God who graciously grants an interval for repentance."[30] God works out his plan and purpose even though man expresses doubts.

b. "As some understand slowness." We understand that the "some" in this verse are not the scoffers (v. 3) but believers who have been influenced by these scoffers. Some Christians are unable to explain the delay of Christ's return and begin to doubt as they listen to the scoffers.[31] They need not doubt, because God is in full control.

c. "He is patient with you." Notice that Peter addresses the readers, not the scoffers, when he writes the pronoun *you*.[32] He indicates that God does not judge his people hastily, but grants them sufficient time to come to repentance (compare I Peter 3:20).

d. "Not wanting anyone to perish." Peter is not teaching universalism in this sentence. In his epistle, he clearly states that the false teachers and the scoffers are condemned and face destruction (see 2:3; 3:7; Rom. 9:22). Does not God want the false teachers to be saved? Yes, but they disregard God's patience toward them, they employ their knowledge of Jesus Christ against him, and they willfully reject God's offer of salvation. They, then, bear full responsibility for their own condemnation.[33]

d. "[God wants] everyone to come to repentance." God provides time for man to repent, but repentance is an act that man must perform. Take the case of Esau, who led a godless life and sold his inheritance rights to his brother Jacob. When he wanted to receive the blessing, Esau was rejected. "He could bring about no change of mind, though he sought the blessing with tears" (Heb. 12:17; also compare Rom. 2:4). Likewise the scoffers in Peter's day refuse to come to repentance, even though God is granting them a period of grace.

Doctrinal Considerations in 3:8–9

"So wonderful is [God's] love towards mankind, that he would have them all to be saved, and is of his own self prepared to bestow salvation on the lost."[34] So writes

---

30. Bauckham, *Jude, 2 Peter*, p. 313. Also see Richard J. Bauckham, "The Delay of the Parousia," *TynB* 31 (1980): 27.

31. Refer to R. C. H. Lenski, *The Interpretation of the Epistles of St. Peter, St. John, and St. Jude* (Columbus: Wartburg, 1945), p. 345.

32. The KJV and NKJV have the reading *toward us*. Based on an alternate Greek reading, the margin of RSV has "on your account," and *Moffatt*, "for your sake."

33. Consult Louis Berkhof, *Systematic Theology*, 2d rev. ed. (Grand Rapids: Eerdmans, 1941), p. 442.

34. Calvin, *The Second Epistle of Peter*, p. 419.

John Calvin on verse 9 and thus touches the doctrine of God's mercy toward sinful man. Here are two examples of this divine love; one is from the Old Testament, the second from the New Testament.

First, God showed his love to Cain when he asked, "If you do what is right, will you not be accepted?" (Gen. 4:7). Yet Cain, filled with anger and jealousy, murdered Abel (v. 8). When God continued to speak to Cain, he did not meet a repentant sinner but a selfish individual who sought protection from an avenger. "Cain went out from the LORD's presence" (v. 16), although God demonstrated mercy by shielding him (v. 15). Cain belonged to the evil one, says the apostle John (I John 3:12). That is, he rejected God's grace and mercy and willfully departed from God.

Second, before Jesus appointed the twelve disciples, he spent a whole night in prayer (Luke 6:12). He called Judas Iscariot to the circle of his immediate followers. After a period of instruction, Jesus commissioned the twelve disciples to preach the gospel, to heal the sick, to raise the dead, to cleanse the lepers, and to drive out demons (Matt. 10:7–8). In his love, Jesus commissioned Judas, too. Even at the last Passover celebration in the upper room, Jesus visibly indicated to Judas that he knew of the betrayal (John 13:26). Yet Judas delivered his Master to the chief priests. Granted that Judas was filled with remorse, he never repented (Matt. 27:3). He never returned to Jesus, but instead committed suicide.

When Paul writes that God "wants all men to be saved and to come to a knowledge of the truth" (I Tim. 2:4; also see Ezek. 18:23, 32), he does not mean that all men are indeed saved. Although God desires the redemption of the entire race, he does not decree universal salvation. Therefore, in respect to the verb *want* or *wish* theologians distinguish between God's desire and God's decree.[35]

God extends his mercy to sinful man. However, when man repudiates God's grace, divine condemnation hangs over him (II Peter 2:3) and he faces the inevitable day of judgment (3:7).

Greek Words, Phrases, and Constructions in 3:9

βραδύνει—"he hesitates"; as a verb of separation, it controls the genitive case of ἐπαγγελίας (promise).[36]

βουλόμενος—the present middle participle from βούλομαι (I wish) denotes cause.[37]

E. Elements
3:10

In the immediately preceding verses, Peter answers his opponents with a reference to God's time and patience. Now he tells them what will happen when the day of the Lord appears.

---

35. Ibid. Compare Blum, *2 Peter*, p. 286.

36. Refer to Friedrich Blass and Albert Debrunner, *A Greek Grammar of the New Testament and Other Early Christian Literature,* trans. and rev. Robert Funk (Chicago: University of Chicago Press, 1961), sec. 180.5.

37. Consult Robertson, *Grammar*, p. 1128.

10. But the day of the Lord will come like a thief. The heavens will disappear with a roar; the elements will be destroyed by fire, and the earth and everything in it will be laid bare.

Observe these two points:

a. *Assurance.* As a contrast to God's patience with the sinner, Peter emphatically states that the day of the Lord will come like a thief (compare v. 12). This is an indisputable fact taught also by the apostle Paul. In response to a question concerning the coming of the Lord, Paul writes, "You know very well that the day of the Lord will come like a thief in the night" (I Thess. 5:2). The coming of this day will be marked by an unexpected suddenness.[38] Both Paul and Peter use the metaphor of a thief. When a thief strikes under cover of darkness, he provides no warning. Similarly, Christ will come unexpectedly.

b. *Events.* Peter describes the events that will take place when Jesus returns.

Heavens. Using a word (translated "roar") that imitates the sound associated with it, Peter declares that "the heavens will disappear with a roar." That is, the atmospheric heavens will vanish, as John describes the events of the last day: "The sky receded like a scroll, rolling up" (Rev. 6:14; see Isa. 34:4). As the sky passes away, a crackling sound as of roaring flames will be heard. Peter further explains this point in verse 12: "That day will bring about the destruction of the heavens by fire, and the elements will melt in the heat."

Elements. What are the elements that will be destroyed by fire? Scholars usually present two interpretations:

1. "The reference to 'the elements' (v. 10) means earth, water and air, of which only the first is named explicitly, the last being understood as 'the heavens.' "[39] An objection to this view is that to identify the elements with heaven and earth is redundant in the context of this verse.

2. Peter relies on an Old Testament prophecy: "All the stars of the heavens will be dissolved and the sky rolled up like a scroll; all the starry host will fall" (Isa. 34:4). The expression *elements* signifies the celestial bodies—the sun, moon, and stars. This prophecy reflects the Jewish belief that in the last day even the stars will be destroyed.[40] Other parts of Scripture also indicate the heavenly bodies will be affected when the day of the Lord appears (e.g., Joel 2:10; Matt. 24:29; Mark 13:24; Rev. 6:12–13). As sun, moon, and stars are mentioned in the creation account (Gen. 1:16), so in the day of consummation these celestial light-bearers will disappear.

Earth. "And the earth and everything in it will be laid bare." Translations

---

38. Refer to Matt. 24:42–44, 50; Luke 21:34; Rev. 3:3; 16:15.

39. Hans-Helmut Esser, *NIDNTT*, vol. 2, p. 452. Also consult Gerhard Delling, *TDNT*, vol. 7, p. 686.

40. See Joseph B. Mayor, *The Epistle of St. Jude and the Second Epistle of St. Peter: Greek Text with Introduction and Notes* (1907; Grand Rapids: Baker, 1965), p. 159.

of this sentence differ because of the variant readings of the Greek manuscripts. Most versions have the translation "And the earth and its works *will be burned up*" (NASB; italics added). Another reading is "will be gone" (SEB). However, the most difficult and oldest Greek reading is "will be laid bare" (NIV). A sound exegetical rule is to accept the hardest reading as the original, for the most perspicuous readings usually are derived from it. In this case, due to its lack of perspecuity the verb itself has given rise to all the other variants, even to the point where some Greek manuscripts have omitted the last line of verse 10 altogether. But because the day of the Lord is seen as the judgment day, the verb *will be laid bare* most likely means that "the earth and all man's works will appear before God's judgment seat."[41] The conclusion must be that the verb in the last line remains problematic.

Greek Words, Phrases, and Constructions in 3:10

εὑρεθήσεται—the future passive indicative from the verb εὑρίσκω (I find), this form is difficult to interpret. Therefore, numerous emendations have been suggested. Here are a few: "the earth and the things in it will be found *useless*"; "the earth and the things in it *will flow*"; ". . . will flow together"; ". . . will be burnt to ashes"; and "will be judged."[42] An emendation is acceptable only when the word in question is devoid of any suitable meaning. This is not true for the translation *will be laid bare* which, as a passive form, implies that God is the agent. God, who created the earth and everything in it, will lay bare this great creation in the judgment day.

F. Consummation
3:11–13

God's revelation about the end of the world ought to make the believer aware of living a life that is pleasing to God. The short time that separates us from the dawning of the last day is short. In fact, Peter even uses the word *speed*.

11. Since everything will be destroyed in this way, what kind of people ought you to be? You ought to live holy and godly lives   12a. as you look forward to the day of God and speed its coming.

a. *Fact.* What impact does the information about the end of the world have upon man? The word *everything* is inclusive, for it refers to all that God has made. Man is part of God's creation and he, too, will perish. When the destruction takes place, man will inevitably meet his creator and judge. Before that day of judgment comes, God grants man a period of grace to reflect upon ethical questions.

---

41. *NIV Study Bible,* p. 1903, explanatory note on 3:10.

42. Bruce M. Metzger, *A Textual Commentary on the Greek New Testament,* 3d corrected ed. (London and New York: United Bible Societies, 1975), p. 706. Also see Bauckham, *Jude, 2 Peter,* pp. 317–19. And consult F. W. Danker's emendation in Bauer, p. 325.

b. *Character.* Peter asks the readers a personal question: "What kind of people ought you to be?" He by-passes the scoffers, who, he says, are kept for the day of judgment and destruction (v. 7). Instead, he challenges the recipients of his letter to examine carefully what their purpose in life is.

The verb *ought* indicates that a divine obligation rests upon the readers; they are to be holy in all that they do (compare I Peter 1:15–16). Peter exhorts them to live in the sphere of God's holiness, so that when that great and awful day appears they continue to live in the presence of God. In the introduction to his first epistle, John encourages the Christians to have "fellowship . . . with the Father and with his Son, Jesus Christ" (1:3). In different wording, Peter says the same thing. Christians must cultivate holy living in full awareness of God's sacred presence, so that they become outstanding people. This is exactly Peter's question: "What kind of people ought you to be?"

c. *Expectation.* Christians must look into the future and expect the return of the Lord. Says Peter, "Live holy and godly lives as you look forward to the day of God." Throughout his letter, Peter frequently fails to distinguish between God and Jesus. For him, "the day of the Lord" and "the day of God" are one and the same.

d. *Interpretation.* Peter adds the clause *and speed its coming.* Another translation is possible: "While you wait and long for the Day of God to come" (JB), or "As you wait eagerly for the day of God to come" (marginal reading in NIV). The first translation, "speed its coming," is active; the second translation, "long for," is reflexive. Some commentators have opted for this second version because they believe that man is unable to change the time God has set for Christ's return.[43] However, the cumulative evidence from Scripture, intertestamental literature, and Jewish sources supports the first translation, "and speed its coming."

This is a startling statement indeed. Peter is saying that we have a vital part in shortening the time set for the coming of God's day. This saying corresponds with the ancient prayer the church has prayed since the first century: *Maranatha,* "Come, O Lord!" (I Cor. 16:22; also see Rev. 22:20). Furthermore, it harmonizes with the petition *your kingdom come* (Matt. 6:10; Luke 11:2). In his discourse on the last day Jesus instructs his followers to proclaim the gospel to all nations, "and then the end will come" (Matt. 24:14). And last, Peter exhorts Christians "to live holy and godly lives" to speed the coming of God's day. When Peter addresses a crowd of people after healing the crippled beggar at the temple, he tells the people to repent in order to hasten the coming of Christ (Acts 3:19–21).

In later Judaism, the teaching is prominent that repentance hastens the coming of the Messiah. For instance, here is a statement from a Jewish

---

43. E.g., see Lenski, *Interpretation of the Epistles,* p. 348; Greijdanus, *De Brieven,* p. 345. Also consult Calvin, who interprets this verse (v. 12a) proverbially: "Hasten slowly." *The Second Epistle of Peter,* p. 421.

rabbi of about A.D. 300: "If the Israelites were to repent for one day, then the Son of David (the Messiah) would come."[44] Peter writes that God delays the coming of the day of the Lord because God wants "everyone" to come to repentance (v. 9). Accordingly, if we wish to speed the coming of God's day, we should evangelize the world. When we bring the last of God's children to faith and repentance so that his house may be full (Luke 14:23), then the end comes.

12b. That day will bring about the destruction of the heavens by fire, and the elements will melt in the heat.

The wording of this text is a repetition of verse 10. However, because the last clause in verse 10 is not repeated, we should regard verse 12b as a refrain. Notice also a difference of purpose in relation to these two texts. In verse 10 Peter presents the manner, that is, how the day of the Lord will come; in verse 12b he indicates the result of this day, namely, "the destruction of the heavens by fire."[45]

In the Old Testament, the prophets frequently mention fire in connection with the final judgment. Here is one description of the day of the Lord: " 'Surely the day is coming; it will burn like a furnace. All the arrogant and every evildoer will be stubble, and that day that is coming will set them on fire' " (Mal. 4:1).[46] In the New Testament John mentions fire in the eschatological setting of the final judgment (see Rev. 8:7–8; 9:17–18; 16:8; 18:8; 20:9).

The words "the elements will melt in the heat" are an echo of Isaiah's prophecy: "All the stars of the heavens will be dissolved" (34:4). Moreover, the Old Testament uses the verb *to melt* of the dissolution of the earth (Ps. 46:6) and the disappearance of mountains (Mic. 1:4). We assume that Peter relied on the wording of these Old Testament prophecies when he wrote this text. This reliance on Scripture is especially evident in the next verse.

13. But in keeping with his promise we are looking forward to a new heaven and a new earth, the home of righteousness.

a. *Promise.* Christians need not fear when they learn that fire will destroy God's creation. Living in God's fellowship, they belong to him and know that he keeps them safe. In addition, they have his promise to reassure them. What is this promise? In the three instances where the word *promise* occurs (vv. 4, 9, 13), Peter puts the term in the context of the day of the Lord. The promise is that "in the beginning God created the heavens and the earth" (Gen. 1:1); at the end of time, he will create a new heaven and a new earth. This Old Testament message is paralleled in the next to the last chapter of the Bible. John writes, "Then I saw a new heaven and a new earth, for the first heaven and the first earth had passed away" (Rev. 21:1).

---

44. SB, vol. 1, p. 164. Consult Bauckham, *Jude, 2 Peter*, p. 325. For intertestamental literature, see 2 Esd. 4:38–39; Sir. 36:8.

45. Refer to Mayor, *Jude and Peter*, p. 162.

46. Also see Isa. 66:15–16; Ezek. 39:6; Zeph. 1:18; 3:8; Zech. 12:6.

b. *Renewal.* Peter writes that "we are looking forward to a new heaven and a new earth." He borrows the wording from the prophecy of Isaiah:

> This is what the sovereign LORD says:
> "Behold, I will create
> 　new heavens and a new earth.
> The former things will not be remembered,
> 　nor will they come to mind." [65:13, 17]

"As the new heavens and the new earth that I make will endure before me," declares the LORD, "so will your name and descendants endure." [66:22]

Peter stresses the adjective *new* in his wording. Literally he says, "new heavens and earth new." With the word *new,* Peter teaches that this new creation comes forth out of the old creation. That is, the old has given birth to the new. "The flood did not annihilate the earth, but changed it; and as the new earth was the consequence of the flood, so the final new heavens and earth shall be of the fire."[47]

Observe also that the nouns *heaven* and *earth* lack definite articles, so that these two form a pair (see v. 10). The term *heaven* refers to the atmospheric heavens and not to the abode of the glorified saints. This abode needs no renewal because it is unaffected by sin.

c. *Home.* Because of sin, God's entire creation has been groaning as in pain, Paul writes (Rom. 8:22). It is eagerly waiting for the day when creation is set free from the shackles of sin to share the glory of God's children. God banishes sin from the new heaven and the new earth and thus liberates his creation from its bondage. Peter calls this new creation "the home of righteousness." He personifies the term *righteousness* and says that it has taken up its permanent abode in heaven and earth. This term brings these two together and makes them one.

Doctrinal Considerations in 3:13

The Bible is a book that teaches us about the creation of man, his fall into sin, his redemption through the atoning work of Jesus Christ, and the promise of complete restoration. When a follower of Christ leaves this earthly scene, he is translated to glory. He joins the countless multitude, dressed in white apparel, that surrounds God's throne (Rev. 7:9).

On the last day when the graves are opened and all the saints receive glorified bodies, they will live on a new earth in holiness and righteousness (see Isa. 60:21; Rev. 21:27). The inhabitants of this new earth will be forever with Jesus, who as the Son of Man will dwell with the saints. For the saints, to be eternally with Jesus is to be

---

47. Henry Alford, *Alford's Greek Testament: An Exegetical and Critical Commentary,* 5th ed., 4 vols. (1857; Grand Rapids: Guardian, 1976), vol. 4, pt. 2, p. 418.

in heaven. They will always be in the light, for Jesus is their source of light (compare Rev. 21:22–24; also refer to Isa. 11:4–5; 61:10–11; Jer. 23:6).

> There they need no sunshine bright,
> In that city four-square;
> For the Lamb is all the light,
> And there is no night there.
>
> God shall wipe away all tears;
> There's no death, no pain, nor fears;
> And they count not time by years;
> For there is no night there.
> —John R. Clements

Greek Words, Phrases, and Constructions in 3:11–13

Verse 11

τούτων . . . λυομένων—this is the genitive absolute construction that has a causal connotation. The present passive participle relates to the future passive indicative λυθήσεται in the preceding verse (v. 10). The adjective πάντων (all) is inclusive.

Verse 12

σπεύδοντας—from the verb σπεύδω (I hasten), this present active participle takes a direct object παρουσίαν (coming). In this context, the participle should not be taken as intransitive: "exert oneself."

τήκεται—in the present passive from τήκω (passive: melt), this verb conveys the future tense.

Verse 13

καινούς—the adjective is used in comparing the new with the old, as in the saying, "The new is better than the old." By contrast, the adjective νέους (new, novel) refers to that "which has recently come into existence."[48]

οὐρανούς—from the Septuagint, this noun is in the plural ("heavens"; a Hebrew usage) instead of the singular.

κατοικεῖ—Peter purposely chooses this compound verb to express permanence. The compound consists of the preposition κατά (down) and the basic verb οἰκέω (I dwell).

---

14 So then, dear friends, since you are looking forward to this, make every effort to be found spotless, blameless and at peace with him.   15 Bear in mind that our Lord's patience means salvation, just as our dear brother Paul also wrote you with the wisdom that God gave him.   16 He writes the same way in all his letters, speaking in them of these matters. His

---

48. R. C. Trench, *Synonyms of the New Testament* (1854; Grand Rapids: Eerdmans, 1953), p. 220.

letters contain some things that are hard to understand, which ignorant and unstable people distort, as they do the other Scriptures, to their own destruction.

17 Therefore, dear friends, since you already know this, be on your guard so that you may not be carried away by the error of lawless men and fall from your secure position. 18 But grow in the grace and knowledge of our Lord and Savior Jesus Christ. To him be glory both now and forever! Amen.

VI. Exhortations
3:14–18

A. Be Blameless
3:14

If the believers look forward to living eternally in a "home of righteousness" on the new earth, then already on this earth they ought to practice righteousness. For this reason, Peter devotes the rest of his epistle to a series of exhortations in which he repeats and summarizes his pastoral concerns.

14. So then, dear friends, since you are looking forward to this, make every effort to be found spotless, blameless and at peace with him.

a. *Desire.* The transition between this verse and the preceding verse (v. 13) is summed up in the expression *so then.* That is, the righteousness that characterizes the sinless environment of the saints in the day of the Lord already must be at work in the hearts and lives of the redeemed. As a loving pastor, Peter addresses the readers with the term *dear friends,* which literally means "beloved" (vv. 1, 8, 17).

Three times in as many verses, Peter uses the verb *to look forward to* (vv. 12, 13, 14). He knows that Christians live by hope, especially in respect to the return of the Lord. "For hope is living and efficacious; therefore it cannot be but that it will attract us to itself."[49]

b. *Work.* Peter directs the attention of the readers to Jesus and thus exhorts them to "make every effort to be found spotless, blameless and at peace with him." Note that Peter is fond of the Greek expression *to make every effort,* which occurs in 1:5, 10 ("be all the more eager"), and 15. This word stresses the responsibility of the individual Christian to exert himself in developing Christian conduct (see Phil. 2:12).[50]

How does the Christian live righteously? Peter says that the believer must be found spotless and blameless. This means that the believer ought to follow the example of Jesus, who himself is "without blemish or defect" (I Peter 1:19). Peter's choice of words is deliberate, for he intimates that the readers are the exact opposite of the false teachers. He portrays these teachers as "blots and blemishes" (2:13). By contrast, Christians should pray Paul's prayer: that they may be "blameless and holy" in God's presence when Jesus returns (I Thess. 3:13; also see Jude 24).

---

49. Calvin, *The Second Epistle of Peter,* p. 422.
50. Paul employs the Greek verb *to make every effort* a number of times (see Gal. 2:10; Eph. 4:3; I Thess. 2:17; II Tim. 2:15; 4:9, 21; Titus 3:12; also notice Heb. 4:11).

c. *Peace.* Here is the conclusion to this verse: "Make every effort to be . . . at peace with [Jesus]." The Christian knows that through Jesus Christ he has been justified by faith and that as a consequence he has peace with God (Rom. 5:1). When the Christian lives in the light of God's Word and has fellowship with the Father and the Son, he is at peace with his Creator and Redeemer. He confesses his sin, receives remission, and is purified from all unrighteousness (I John 1:9).

B. Accept God's Truth
3:15–16

God communicates directly with his people through his Word. He asks them to accept this Word in faith, to claim salvation through Jesus Christ, and to treasure the Scriptures.

Salvation

15a. Bear in mind that our Lord's patience means salvation.

Peter repeats himself for the sake of emphasis. Once more he thinks of the argument of the false teachers who scoff at Christ's return and the judgment day. Peter enjoins the readers to put their minds to work and seriously think about the reason for the delay. He wants them to understand the purpose for the patience God exhibits. For Peter, the reason is clear: "Our Lord's patience means salvation." He exchanges the word *God* for "Lord." God's patience, then, results in granting his people a period of extended grace. God is waiting patiently for the sinner to come to repentance and inherit salvation. God's patience is marvelously displayed in the parable of the prodigal son (Luke 15:11–32). In this parable, the father did not go to that distant land where his son herded pigs for a Gentile farmer. If he had gone there and invited his son to come home, he would have had no guarantee of receiving an affirmative reply. Instead, the father waited patiently for the son to come to his senses, to confess his sins to God, to come home of his own accord, and to be reconciled.[51] The patience of the waiting father was amply rewarded.

Peter calls God's grace that leads to salvation "patience" (see v. 9). Paul puts the same subject in different wording and calls it "kindness." Rhetorically he asks, "Or do you . . . not [realize] that God's kindness leads you toward repentance?" (Rom. 2:4). Yet when the period of grace has come to an end, the door that leads to salvation will be shut.

Wisdom

15b. Just as our dear brother Paul also wrote you with the wisdom that God gave him.

a. *Paul and Peter.* Apart from the incident in Antioch where Paul rebuked

---

51. Simon J. Kistemaker, *The Parables of Jesus,* 2d ed. (Grand Rapids: Baker, 1980), pp. 220–21.

Peter for yielding to Jewish pressure not to eat with Gentile Christians (see Gal. 2:11–14), the relationship between Peter and Paul was harmonious. Paul frequently mentions Peter in the First Epistle to the Corinthians (1:12; 3:22; 9:5; 15:5). He also visited Peter for fifteen days in Jerusalem (Gal. 1:18). Next, he states that Peter is "an apostle to the Jews" (Gal. 2:8) and is a pillar in the church (v. 9). Last, they met each other at the Jerusalem Council where both spoke regarding missions to the Gentiles (Acts 15:6–21).

b. *A dear brother.* Peter holds no grudge against Paul for the correction he received in Antioch and for seeing the incident recorded in Paul's letter to the Galatians. The apostle is not afraid to admit his personal failure. Peter considers Paul a dear brother. In the New Testament, the term *brother* refers to a fellow believer; yet in this verse Peter may be thinking of the apostolic church when he writes the adjective *our* (compare 1:1, 16–19). We receive the distinct impression that a warm relationship existed between Peter and Paul.[52] Also notice that Silas, who was a fellow worker of Paul (Acts 15:40; 16:22–40), serves Peter as a scribe and presumably as his letter carrier (I Peter 5:12).

c. *Paul's letters.* Peter introduces the clause *Paul also wrote you* with the words *just as,* which refer to the previous verse (v. 15a). For this reason, scholars have searched the letters of Paul to find a distinct reference to God's patience and man's salvation.[53] Because Romans 2:4 is a parallel to verse 15a, they have suggested that Paul's letter to the Romans must have been sent to the readers of II Peter. Some scholars glean the indirect information that this letter was an epistle sent to all the churches (see Rom. 16:4).

Although this suggestion has its merits, other scholars think that the recipients of II Peter are the same as those of I Peter. The readers, therefore, are residents of Asia Minor. Since Paul wrote letters to the churches in Asia Minor, one of these epistles (Galatians, Ephesians, Colossians) must be the letter Peter has in mind.[54] However, difficulties remain, because the readers were acquainted with a number of Paul's epistles (see v. 16). Perhaps we should refrain from guesswork and simply admit that we do not know which letter Paul wrote to the readers of II Peter.

d. *God-given wisdom.* Peter recognizes the spiritual gift that Paul had received from God. This gift is demonstrated in the inspired epistles he wrote and which were accepted by Christians as Scripture (see v. 16). For instance, Clement of Rome regards as inspired Paul's first epistle to the Corinthians.[55] In that epistle, Paul relates that he has received wisdom from the

---

52. Consult Mayor, *Jude and Peter,* p. 164.
53. For example, consult Green, *The Second Epistle General of Peter,* p. 145.
54. Refer to Bigg, *The Epistles of St. Peter and St. Jude,* p. 300.
55. See I Clem. 47:1–3 (LCL). And refer to Polycarp's Epistle to the Philippians 3:2 (LCL).

Holy Spirit (2:6–16). He acknowledges that this gift of wisdom has been granted to him by the Spirit (see 12:8).[56] Consciously Paul employed this gift in writing his letters to churches and individuals.

Scriptures

16. He writes the same way in all his letters, speaking in them of these matters. His letters contain some things that are hard to understand, which ignorant and unstable people distort, as they do the other Scriptures, to their own destruction.

We make the following comments:

a. *Write.* "He writes the same way in all his letters." Although a literal translation has the word *speaking*—"as also in all his letters, speaking in them of these things" (NASB)—the sense demands the verb *to write*. Of greater importance is the fact that Peter and Paul are saying the same thing concerning the day of the Lord and God's patience toward the sinner. Peter's remark ("all [Paul's] epistles") can refer to the letters that the church possessed up to that time. We are unable to say how many of Paul's thirteen canonical letters are included; nevertheless we assume that Peter's remark encompasses nearly all of them. From Paul's epistles we learn that he urged the churches to exchange the letters he had written, so that the people might come to know his teachings (see Col. 4:16; I Thess. 5:27). We conclude that in Peter's day the church had a definite collection of Pauline epistles which were accepted as canonical (see v. 16b).

b. *Understand.* "His letters contain some things that are hard to understand." Peter informs the reader that he has difficulties understanding Paul's teachings. (Some passages in Peter's epistles are not all that easy to explain either.) But, to the point, Peter acknowledges that Paul writes about the return of Christ in terms that are not clear. For example. Paul informs the believers in Thessalonica about the coming of Jesus Christ, the revelation concerning the man of lawlessness, and the "one who holds it [the power of lawlessness] back" (II Thess. 2:1–12; see especially vv. 6–7). Paul himself is aware of the difficult content of his letters. Thus he reports what the people in Corinth are saying about him: "His letters are weighty and forceful, but in person he is unimpressive and his speaking amounts to nothing" (II Cor. 10:10). As any reader of the Pauline epistles can testify, numerous passages need further elucidation. But in the light of Peter's epistle, we ought to limit ourselves to the topic at hand, namely, the doctrine concerning the day of the Lord.

c. *Distort.* "Things . . . which ignorant and unstable people distort." Once again Peter takes the false teachers to task. Throughout the history of the church people have distorted Paul's teaching. Peter repeats his remarks concerning the errorists who seduce unstable and uninformed persons

56. Also compare Rom. 12:3; 15:15; I Cor. 3:10; 15:10; Gal. 2:9; Eph. 3:2, 7.

(2:14, 18). Together they twist the meaning of Scripture so that the truth of God's revelation is turned into a lie. As torturers make a victim on the rack say the opposite of the truth, so the false teachers place Scripture on the rack and distort its message.

d. *Destroy.* "As they do the other Scriptures, to their own destruction." False teachers, who have no regard for the holiness of Scripture and who twist its intended meaning, "rush headlong into ruin."[57] Ultimately they face God, who has revealed himself in his Word and who turns Scripture against his adversaries to their own destruction.

From a New Testament perspective, the term *Scripture* applies to the entire Old Testament; it is understood to be God's inspired Word.[58] Hence Jesus and the apostles appealed to the authoritative Scriptures, often with the introductory formula *it is written* (e.g., Matt. 4:4). Peter places the epistles of Paul on the same level as the Old Testament. He expresses not only his personal evaluation of Paul's letters, but also the thinking of the Christian community of that day. Paul himself tells the readers that he is conscious of inspiration and that his epistles are God's revelation. Thus Paul writes that "God has revealed it to us by his Spirit" (I Cor. 2:10). He asserts that "Christ is speaking through me" (II Cor. 13:3). And he observes that the Thessalonians accepted his teaching "not as the word of men, but as it actually is, the word of God" (I Thess. 2:13). Last, Peter himself writes decisively about the production of Scripture as a work of God and man: "Men spoke from God as they were carried along by the Holy Spirit" (1:21). Accordingly, Michael Green asks the rhetorical question, "How can one deny the equal applicability of the term [*Scripture*] to prophetic and apostolic writers when the ultimate authorship of God's Spirit is claimed for both?"[59]

Doctrinal Considerations in 3:16

In the middle of the first century, Christians relied on the Old Testament Scriptures and on the spoken word of the apostles. But when the written Gospels and epistles appeared, the apostles were among the first to acknowledge the inherent divine authority of these writings. A vivid illustration of this point is that Paul states that the elders in the church, "especially those whose work is preaching and teaching," are worthy of double honor (I Tim. 5:17). He proves his point by quoting Scripture from two different sources. The first quotation is from the Old Testament: "Do not muzzle the ox while it is treading out the grain" (Deut. 25:4); the second is from the New Testament: "The worker deserves his wages" (Luke 10:7). By the time Paul writes to Timothy (presumably A.D. 63–65), some parts of the New

---

57. Calvin, *The Second Epistle of Peter*, p. 425.

58. In the New Testament, the term *Scripture* in both the singular and plural "is used exclusively of Holy Scripture." Colin Brown, *NIDNTT*, vol. 3, p. 490.

59. E. M. B. [Michael] Green, *2 Peter Reconsidered* (London: Tyndale, 1961), p. 32.

Testament are in circulation and are considered equal in authority with the Old Testament.

The apostles themselves, then, give leadership in the churches and tell the believers that their epistles are divinely inspired (compare II Tim. 3:16). As Paul informs Timothy that Luke's Gospel is Scripture, so Peter writes that Paul's epistles are on a par with the Old Testament.

Greek Words, Phrases, and Constructions in 3:16

λαλῶν—the tense of the present active participle should not be considered proof that Paul was still alive at the time Peter wrote these words. The present tense applies to the content of Paul's letters and thus indicates that Peter's message has lasting significance.

ἐν αἷς—the antecedent of this relative pronoun in the dative feminine plural lies in the noun ἐπιστολαῖς (letters) and not in the nearer pronoun τουτῶν (these).

C. Reject Error
3:17

Peter is nearly at the end of his epistle. With a dual exhortation he encourages the believers, first, to be on guard against lawless men, and second, to grow spiritually in Jesus Christ. The first exhortation relates to external influences and the second to internal development.

17. Therefore, dear friends, since you already know this, be on your guard so that you may not be carried away by the error of lawless men and fall from your secure position.

The adverb *therefore* forcefully contrasts the distorters of Scripture with the readers of Peter's epistle. The believers Peter addresses are different from the false teachers and their followers. These believers need encouragement and guidance. Note that once again Peter tenderly addresses them with the greeting *dear friends,* that is, "beloved" (see vv. 1, 8, 14).

a. "Since you already know this, be on your guard." Peter points to the experience that believers have had with false teachers who entered the Christian community with the purpose of twisting the meaning of Scripture. Peter tells the readers that because of the trying experiences they have had in their relations with these heretics, they should shun the company of such people. The command in the Greek indicates that the believers are indeed guarding themselves. Nevertheless, Peter deems it necessary to reinforce them by describing the consequences of failing to heed his command.

b. "So that you may not be carried away by the error of lawless men." The believers should always be on guard against error and deceit. By keeping close company with the errorists, they run the risk of being swept away by devious teachings. But teachings are always linked to conduct. In this case, they are able to observe the conduct of men whom Peter calls "lawless." In fact, Peter uses the same expression when he describes the "lawless men" of

347

Sodom and Gomorrah (2:7). These men do everything in their power to "entice people who are just escaping from those who live in error" (2:18). Therefore, "watch out that no one deceives you" (Mark 13:5).

c. "And fall from your secure position." Let no one say that only recent converts fall into the clutches of lawless men. Peter knew from bitter personal experience that Satan attacks those who think they are secure. As spokesman for the disciples Peter told Jesus, "Even if all fall away on account of you, I never will" (Matt. 26:33). Yet within hours of saying these words, he denied his Master three times.

Jesus discloses that Satan had asked to sift all the disciples as wheat (Luke 22:31; the Greek uses the plural *you*), but he had prayed for Peter that his faith might not fail (v. 32). What a comfort to know that Jesus prays for his people! We receive additional comfort from Jesus' eschatological discourse, where he says that false Christs and prophets will come "to deceive even the elect—if that were possible" (Matt. 24:24). Possessing that comfort, the believer must put on his spiritual armor (Eph. 6:11) and strengthen fellow believers to stand firm against Satan's attacks.

D. Grow in Grace
3:18

18. But grow in the grace and knowledge of our Lord and Savior Jesus Christ. To him be glory both now and forever! Amen.

Here is Peter's last exhortation, expressed positively and firmly. The believers are already maturing spiritually, but Peter encourages them to continue to do so because the process of growing is their work. This process is not a passive mode of existence, but one in which the individual believer has an active part.

Peter specifies how the believer must grow spiritually: "in the grace and knowledge of our Lord Jesus Christ." In a sense, Peter reiterates part of the salutation at the beginning of his epistle. There he writes, "Grace and peace be yours in abundance through the knowledge of God and of Jesus our Lord" (1:2). But is Peter saying that believers ought to grow in the grace and knowledge that Jesus grants them or that believers should grow in the grace and in the knowledge that they have about Jesus Christ? Because grace and knowledge originate with God and through Christ are given to the believer, commentators admit that both interpretations are possible. They generally prefer the first explanation: Peter urges the believers to appropriate the spiritual qualities of grace and knowledge that Jesus grants them.[60] "Knowledge *of* Christ and knowledge *about* Christ are, if they keep pace with one another, both the safeguard against heresy and apostasy and also the means of growth in grace."[61] In short, Peter exhorts the Christians

---

60. For the concept *knowledge*, consult 1:2, 3, 5, 6, 8.
61. Green, *The Second Epistle General of Peter*, p. 151.

to become more like the Master by displaying his characteristics in their lives.

Peter concludes his letter with a doxology: "To him be the glory both now and forever! Amen." Here is a doxology directed toward Christ. In other New Testament doxologies God receives the glory (but see Rev. 1:5–6). By ascribing glory to Christ, Peter indicates that Jesus is divine and worthy of praise in the present as well as in eternity. The literal translation of the word *forever* is "to the day of the age [of eternity]." In apocryphal literature a similar phrase, "in the day of eternity" (Sir. 18:10), occurs.

This unique saying appears to be linked to the coming of the day of the Lord when cosmic time dissolves into eternity (v. 8). In harmony with many and varied manuscripts, we read the conclusion of the doxology with the resounding *Amen*.

Summary of Chapter 3

In this second epistle to his readers, Peter exhorts them to think clearly and to recall the teachings of the prophets and the apostles. He alerts them to the danger of the presence of scoffers in their midst, for these false teachers deny the return of Jesus Christ and the coming of the judgment day. Peter reminds the readers of the creation of the universe and the destructive forces of the flood. These facts the scoffers purposely forget. Yet as the world perished in the deluge, so heaven and earth will be destroyed by fire.

Peter teaches the readers about time and eternity when he compares a thousand years with one day in the sight of God. The day of the Lord will be postponed because of God's patience toward sinners. Yet that day will come unexpectedly. When heaven and earth have been destroyed, a new heaven and a new earth will appear; they will be known as the home of righteousness.

God's patience signifies salvation for the sinner. This is the message Paul also conveys in all his epistles. Some unstable people twist the meaning of Scripture. Peter concludes his letter by exhorting the readers to be on guard and not to be dissuaded by the false teachers. He urges the believers to grow in the grace and knowledge of Jesus Christ.

Exposition
of the
Epistle of Jude

Introduction

Outline

A. Authorship
B. Characteristics
C. Purpose
D. Apostates
E. Recipients
F. Date and Place
G. Canonicity
H. Outline of Jude

T his short epistle was not lost in the first few centuries of the Christian era but was providentially preserved. It circulated widely in the church and, although some leaders expressed reservation, the letter was accepted as God's Word. Even if the letter was not written by an apostle, the church gave Jude's epistle canonical status. Church councils fully acknowledged its status in the last decade of the fourth century (e.g., the Council of Carthage in A.D. 397).

Jude does not address his letter to any particular church by name, and therefore in a sense speaks to the church universal. To the recipients, he identifies himself as the "brother of James."

A. Authorship

The author, who designates himself "a servant of Jesus Christ and a brother of James," does not convey to the readers that he is the brother of the Lord (see Matt. 13:55; Mark 6:3). He refrains from calling himself a brother of Jesus. By his use of the double name *Jesus Christ*, he stresses not a physical but a spiritual relationship to him. Like James (see 1:1), he is a servant of Jesus Christ; and he is a brother of James, the well-known leader of the mother church in Jerusalem. From the Book of Acts and from James's epistle, we know that James labored faithfully as a servant of the Lord. Except for Jude's epistle, we have no further information about the work of Jude. His self-designation places him in the light of his brother James. This identification undoubtedly proved to be one of the decisive factors in the early church's acceptance of the epistle as canonical.

According to the list of the twelve disciples (Luke 6:16; Acts 1:13), Judas son of James is an apostle. Except for the record of a question Jude raised in the upper room (John 14:22), the New Testament is silent about this particular person, who is also known as Thaddeus. Should this person have written the letter, we would have expected him to call himself an apostle of Jesus Christ. The writer's exhortation, "But, dear friends, remember what the apostles of our Lord Jesus Christ foretold" (v. 17), also proves that he did not consider himself part of the circle of the twelve apostles. The apostle Judas would have been more personal had he composed the letter.

Even though Judas the apostle is a son of James, he is not the brother of

James and Jesus.[1] All other persons who bear the name *Jude* or *Judas* in the New Testament (see the commentary on v. 1) fail to qualify as possible writers of the epistle. We assume that Jude the brother of James was an itinerant preacher (I Cor. 9:5) who wrote a letter to warn Christians about the insidious teachings of heretics.

B. Characteristics

Jude, like his brother James, was reared in Galilee, where he learned to speak not only the vernacular Aramaic but also Greek, which was the universal language of that day. We have every reason to believe that he himself wrote the letter, even if a scribe assisted him. Scripture informs us that Galilee was known as Galilee of the Gentiles (Isa. 9:1; Matt. 4:15), where the Greek culture and language had greatly influenced the population.

What are the literary characteristics of Jude's epistle?

Jude writes an epistle in acceptable Greek, which is simple and vigorous. His letter "is not the work of a literary artist, but of a passionate Christian prophet."[2]

He relies on the writings of the Old Testament as he admonishes the readers. Enumerating three incidents from biblical history, he calls attention to the unbelieving Israelites in the desert (v. 5), to rebellious angels (v. 6), and to the immoral inhabitants of Sodom and Gomorrah (v. 7). In another listing of three historical events, Jude refers to Cain's lifestyle, to Balaam's error, and to Korah's rebellion (v. 11).

Jude alludes to and quotes from apocryphal literature. He mentions the dispute the archangel Michael had with Satan (v. 9; and see the Assumption of Moses). And he cites from the prophecy of "Enoch, the seventh from Adam" (vv. 14–15; also consult I En.).

Throughout the epistle Jude has a peculiar manner of arranging his material in a threefold pattern. Here are a few examples: the addressees have been called, are loved, and are kept (v. 1); in the salutation Jude enumerates mercy, peace, and love (v. 2); the immoral apostates "pollute their own bodies, reject authority and slander celestial beings" (v. 8); the grumblers and faultfinders "follow their own evil desires; they boast about themselves and flatter others for their own advantage" (v. 16); these are men who divide the Christians, follow mere natural instincts, and lack the Holy Spirit (v. 19); and the doxology lists three periods: before all ages, now, and forevermore (v. 25).

Jude's letter is strikingly similar to Peter's second epistle. Although the parallelism is evident especially in the second chapter of II Peter, an exami-

---

1. The KJV has the reading *brother of James* (Luke 6:16). But this reading has no support from Greek manuscripts. When they listed their genealogy, men identified themselves as the son of someone, not the brother of someone.

2. Donald Guthrie, *New Testament Introduction,* rev. ed. (Downers Grove: Inter-Varsity, 1971), p. 927.

nation reveals that neither of the two writers slavishly copied each other's material.[3] This is a list of parallel passages (the list of topics follows the phrasing of Jude's epistle):

Jude		II Peter
4	godless men who deny the sovereign Lord	2:1
6	angels held in darkness for judgment	2:4
7	Sodom and Gomorrah burned to ashes	2:6
8	these men arrogantly slander celestial beings	2:10
9	Michael did not bring a slanderous accusation	2:11
10	these blasphemers are like brute beasts	2:12
11	they have followed the way of Balaam	2:15
12	clouds without rain, driven by a storm	2:17
13	blackest darkness is reserved for them	2:17
16	they lust, boast, and flatter	2:18
17	the apostles of our Lord foretold	3:2
18	in the last days scoffers will come	3:3

C. Purpose

Why did Jude write his epistle? He informs his readers that he had been eager to tell them about the salvation which they have in common. Instead he instructs them about the body of Christian doctrine, which he calls faith. He urges the believers to contend for that "faith that was once for all entrusted to the saints" (v. 3). Near the end of his epistle he encourages the recipients to build each other up in the "most holy faith" (v. 20). And he exhorts the readers of his epistle to show mercy to those who doubt (v. 22).

Jude's purpose appears to be polemical. In the major part of his epistle (vv. 4–19), he teaches the believers to oppose the apostates who have infiltrated their community. He warns them against the pernicious influence of these godless men and inculcates some cardinal truths.[4] Albeit briefly, he touches on a number of Christian doctrines. These are the election of those who have been called (v. 1); the perseverance of those who contend for the faith (vv. 3, 21); the final judgment of the unbelievers (vv. 4, 6, 7, 11, 15); and the eternal security (vv. 1, 21, 24), salvation (v. 3), and eternal life of the believers (v. 21).

D. Apostates

Who were these heretics? Jude characterizes them in various ways: they have "secretly slipped in" among the believers (v. 4a); they are "godless

---

3. See George Lawrence Lawlor, *Translation and Exposition of the Epistle of Jude*, International Library of Philosophy and Theology series (Nutley, N.J.: Presbyterian and Reformed, 1972), p. 13.

4. Refer to William White, Jr., "Jude, the Epistle of," *ZPEB*, vol. 3, p. 735.

men" (vv. 4b, 14–15, 18); they have accepted God's grace but have perverted it into a license to sin (v. 4c); they deny Jesus Christ as their only Sovereign and Lord (v. 4d).

Moreover, Jude depicts their moral, ethical, and spiritual life. He portrays them as immoral people who pollute their own bodies, who do not recognize any higher authority, and who have the audacity to slander angelic beings (v. 8). They have lowered themselves to the level of animals that live by instinct. Although animals know their limits, these people, when they live by instinct, destroy themselves (v. 10).

In their social life, the apostates have become blemishes at the supper gatherings of the Christians, for they eat their fill without any scruples (v. 12). They are dissatisfied people who grumble and find fault; they seek physical pleasures, brag about themselves, and always look to promote their personal advantage (v. 16). These men who have the set purpose of dividing the church do not have the Spirit (v. 19).

To use a paraphrase: These apostates are in the church but are not of the church. In fact, they have repudiated the Triune God. They accept God's grace of salvation, but think that it gives them a right to sin unrestrictedly (v. 4c). They claim to be followers of Christ, but at the same time deny him and scoff at his return (vv. 4d, 18). They think that they have the Holy Spirit, but their shameful conduct shows that they live by natural instincts instead (v. 19).

These men, however, ought not to be identified with the Gnostic teachers of the second century. The interval between the composition of Jude's epistle and the writings of the second-century Gnostics is too great. Furthermore, we should not understand the few general statements Jude makes about heretical teachings to refer to full-fledged Gnosticism.[5] In short, we know nothing about these heretics beyond what Jude discloses in his epistle. The most we can say is that they were forerunners of later heretics who plagued the church.

Because of the similarity between II Peter and Jude, the temptation to identify the apostates mentioned in Jude's epistle with those described in II Peter is real. However, Jude never uses the terms Peter employs for describing the heretics. Peter calls them "false teachers," but Jude refers to them as "godless men." Peter stresses the concept *teach* (II Peter 2:1–3), but Jude highlights the ungodly words and deeds of these evil men (vv. 4, 14–16, 19). Furthermore, Peter indicates that there will be false teachers among the members of the church (II Peter 2:1). He intimates that these teachers are local people. By contrast, Jude informs his readers that godless men "have secretly slipped in" among the believers (v. 4). They have come from outside the community. We conclude that Peter and Jude portray their

---

5. Consult Richard J. Bauckham, *Jude, 2 Peter,* Word Commentary series, vol. 50 (Waco: Word, 1983), p. 12. And see F. W. Danker, "Jude, Epistle of," *ISBE,* vol. 2, pp. 1153–55.

opponents differently. Therefore we ought to be careful not to identify the two groups. Should we do that, we would have to assume that Peter and Jude address the same readers.

E. Recipients

Who are the original readers of Jude's epistle? Frankly, we do not know where they resided, because the envelope with the address is lost, so to speak. By examining the content of the letter, we are able to make a few observations about these readers.

The recipients of the epistle are well versed in the Old Testament Scriptures, for the author commends them for knowing pertinent facts concerning the exodus (v. 5), angels (v. 6), and Sodom and Gomorrah (v. 7). They know the names of Cain, Balaam, and Korah (v. 11). And they are acquainted with Jewish literature current in the first century (vv. 9, 14). We surmise, therefore, that the recipients were Jewish converts to the Christian faith.

Jude's letter contains no explicit or implicit references to a Gentile audience. The content of this epistle is such that only Jewish people can fully understand the meaning of Jude's writing. However, we should also consider the letter from the writer's point of view: Jude wrote as a Jew and thus reflected his own Jewish background. Perhaps we do well to say that Jude addressed Jewish Christians living in dispersion in any of the large Jewish centers of the Middle East.

From the content of the two epistles of Peter we are able to conclude that these letters were addressed to Jewish and Gentile Christians living in Asia Minor (I Peter 1:1). From the content of Jude's epistle, however, we are unable to determine its place of destination.

F. Date and Place

The content of Jude's epistle provides no indication when Jude composed this document. If we assume that Jude is one of the younger sons of Joseph and Mary (Matt. 13:55; Mark 6:3), then we are not amiss in dating it in the third quarter of the first century.[6]

The question of dating the letter of Jude depends not so much on the age of the writer (e.g., John wrote his works when he was very old) as on the sequence of II Peter and Jude. Scholars who are of the opinion that Jude depended on the text of Peter's second epistle put the date of composition at least a decade after Peter's death. They understand the words "But, dear friends, remember what the apostles of our Lord Jesus Christ foretold" (v. 17) to mean that the apostles had died. But this text does not prove conclu-

---

6. Charles Bigg asserts that Jude was older than Jesus, for "he was the son of Joseph by an earlier marriage." *A Critical and Exegetical Commentary on the Epistles of St. Peter and St. Jude,* International Critical Commentary series (1901; Edinburgh: Clark, 1961), p. 318. However, this view has not gained acceptance among scholars.

sively that the apostolic era had ended. The emphasis in verse 17 is not on the life span of the apostles but on the necessity of remembering their teaching.

Other scholars contend that Peter depended on the Epistle of Jude for the writing of his second letter. On the basis of a detailed study of the parallel passages, they present convincing arguments for the Jude–II Peter sequence (consult the Introduction to II Peter for details). If Jude was first in composing a letter which afterward became a source for II Peter, the date for Jude's epistle must necessarily be early.

A third possibility is that both Peter and Jude borrowed material from a common source.[7] Although this is only a hypothesis, the fact remains that this option also calls for an early date for both epistles. Proponents of either of these last two positions, therefore, argue for a date in the middle sixties.

The epistle gives no indication where Jude composed his letter. We assume that he, as an itinerant preacher, visited Christians in predominantly Jewish communities, but we are unable to say anything about a possible place of origin of the epistle.

G. Canonicity

What is the evidence that the early church accepted Jude's epistle as canonical? Considering the brevity of this document, we are surprised to find allusions to the words of Jude. We realize that these are but straws in the wind, yet together they point in the same direction, namely, a general use of this epistle. Numerous documents that date from the end of the first century and the early part of the second century provide indirect references.[8] The first witness that refers to Jude's epistle by name is the Muratorian Canon (A.D. 175): "Further an epistle of Jude and two with the title John are accepted in the catholic Church."[9]

At the beginning of the third century, Clement of Alexandria (A.D. 200) quotes Jude's epistle a few times and mentions Jude by name. The North African writer Tertullian (A.D. 200) notes, "Enoch possesses a testimony in the Apostle Jude." And his contemporary Origen repeatedly cites the Epistle of Jude. He calls Jude an apostle and refers to the letter as Scripture. A century later (A.D. 300), Eusebius composes his history of the church and summarizes the writings of the New Testament. He says,

> Of the Disputed Books which are nevertheless known to most are the
> Epistle called of James, that of Jude, the second Epistle of Peter, and the

---

7. Consult Michael Green, *The Second Epistle General of Peter, and the General Epistle of Jude: An Introduction and Commentary*, Tyndale New Testament Commentaries (Grand Rapids: Eerdmans, 1968), pp. 54–55.

8. These are some of the documents: *Didache*, Epistle of Barnabas, I Clement, Polycarp's Epistle to the Philippians, and the Martyrdom of Polycarp.

9. E. Hennecke, W. Schneemelcher, and R. Wilson, eds., *New Testament Apocrypha*, 2 vols. (London: Lutterworth, 1963), vol. 1, pp. 44–45.

so-called second and third Epistles of John which may be the work of the evangelist or of some other with the same name.[10]

Near the end of the fourth century, Jerome discloses the reason for placing Jude among the disputed books. Although he himself puts the letter among the New Testament epistles and regards it as Scripture, he reveals that many people reject it because of the quote from I Enoch and the allusion to the Assumption of Moses. Nevertheless, both the church at large and the church at its general council meetings (in the second half of the fourth century) acknowledged the canonicity of Jude's epistle.

In the preface to his New Testament edition of 1522, Martin Luther lists all twenty-seven books by name. The first twenty-three he gives sequential numbers, but the last four are numberless. They are Hebrews, James, Jude, and Revelation. Luther maintains that Jude's epistle is an abstract of II Peter and therefore is unnecessary among the New Testament epistles. Evidently Luther was not impressed with the letter, even though he left it in the canon. His fellow Reformer John Calvin accepted Jude because the early church placed it among the canonical books of the New Testament. He writes,

> Though there was a dispute among the ancients concerning this Epistle, yet as the reading of it is useful, and as it contains nothing inconsistent with the purity of apostolic doctrine, and was received as authentic formerly, by some of the best, I willingly add it to the others.[11]

Here is a valid question: "What does Jude's epistle contribute to the totality of God's written revelation?" As we have seen, the parallels in II Peter adequately present the message of Jude. Nevertheless, the greeting, salutation, exhortations to the readers throughout the letter, and the marvelous doxology at the conclusion are not duplicated in the New Testament. For this reason the church has included the Epistle of Jude. Ultimately, however, we humbly confess that God determines the contents of the canon, because he himself has authorized it. The canon is God's Word.

H. Outline of Jude

I.	1–2	Greeting
II.	3–4	Purpose for Writing
III.	5–7	Examples from History
	A. 5	Unbelieving Israel
	B. 6	Evil Angels
	C. 7	Sodom and Gomorrah

---

10. Eusebius *Ecclesiastical History* 3.25.3 (LCL). In two other passages Eusebius mentions Jude's epistle (2.23.25; 6.13.6).
11. John Calvin, *Commentaries on the Catholic Epistles: The Epistle of Jude,* ed. and trans. John Owen (Grand Rapids: Eerdmans, 1948), p. 427.

Introduction

Commentary

Outline

1 Jude, a servant of Jesus Christ and a brother of James,
To those who have been called, who are loved by God the Father and kept by Jesus Christ:
2 Mercy, peace and love be yours in abundance.

I. Greeting
1–2

Like the other New Testament writers who have composed epistles, Jude first mentions his name. This was a customary procedure, as is evident from recorded letters in Acts (see 15:23; 23:26). Paul, Peter, and James also adhere to this practice. John, however, is the exception; he modestly refrains from calling attention to himself in his three epistles.

Jude's greeting differs from that of the apostles because Jude cannot claim apostleship. He introduces himself as a servant of Jesus Christ. As a further self-designation he says that he is a brother of James, who also identifies himself as "a servant of God and of the Lord Jesus Christ" (James 1:1).

1. Jude, a servant of Jesus Christ and a brother of James,
To those who have been called, who are loved by God the Father and kept by Jesus Christ.

a. *Name.* Jude was a common name. It was first borne by Judah, the son of Jacob and head of the tribe of Judah. The tribal head Judah is listed in Jesus' genealogy (Matt. 1:2–3; Luke 3:33); references to the name and the land of his tribe occur frequently (Matt. 2:6; Luke 2:4; Heb. 7:14; Rev. 5:5; 7:5).

The designation *Jude* is the English variant of "Judas." In English we distinguish Jude, the writer of the epistle, from Judas Iscariot, who betrayed Jesus. However, other persons mentioned in the New Testament have the name *Judas:*

1. Judas, the son of James (Luke 6:16; Acts 1:13). He was one of the twelve disciples. He is also known as Thaddeus (compare Matt. 10:3; Mark 3:18; also see John 14:22).
2. Judas the Galilean (Acts 5:37). He was a revolutionary who was killed because of his subversive activities.
3. Judas Barsabbas, who was present at the Jerusalem Council and served as letter carrier to the Gentile churches (Acts 15:22, 27, 32).
4. Judas, an ancestor of Jesus (Luke 3:33; see also v. 30).
5. Judas, the brother of James and the (half) brother of Jesus (Matt. 13:55; Mark 6:3).

From the self-identification of Judas as the brother of James we conclude that Jude, the (half) brother of Jesus, is the author who wrote the epistle. Notice that he does not call himself an apostle. Were that the case, we would know that the writer was Judas, the son of James. Instead, in his epistle the

365

author separates himself from the apostles when he writes, "Remember what the apostles of our Lord Jesus Christ foretold" (v. 17).

Next, the author identifies himself as the brother of James. Usually a person would mention the name of his father, not his brother. But James had gained preeminence as the leader of the church in Jerusalem and was recognized as the author of an epistle. Both James and Jude introduce themselves not as apostles but as servants of Jesus Christ. Although apostles used the term *servant* to describe their relationship to Jesus and the church, the term itself is not the equivalent of "apostle" (compare Rom. 1:1; II Peter 1:1). Furthermore, James and Jude refrain from calling themselves Jesus' brothers (James 1:1; v. 1). We assume that they do not wish to use their familial relationship to Jesus as a means to gain recognition. For that reason, both James and Jude place themselves on the same level as all other believers. They refer to themselves as servants of Jesus Christ. By their use of this term they indicate that their physical kinship to Jesus does not provide them special privileges (see Matt. 12:46–50). With all believers, they recognize Jesus as their Lord and Master.

But who is James? Jude mentions that James is his brother, but he fails to identify him. In the New Testament, five persons are known as James:

1. James the son of Zebedee (Matt. 10:2);
2. James the son of Alphaeus (Matt. 10:3);[1]
3. James the younger (Mark 15:40);
4. James the father of Judas (Luke 6:16; Acts 1:13);
5. James the (half) brother of the Lord (Matt. 13:55).

Of these five, the last one mentioned is the most likely person to be the brother of Jude. The Gospels tell us that among the sons of Joseph and Mary were James and Jude, the brothers of the Lord (Matt. 13:55; Mark 6:3). The other persons in the list cannot claim this distinction. Further corroboration comes from a second-century Jewish-Christian historian named Hegesippus. He relates that grandsons of Jude ("who is said to have been the brother, according to the flesh, of the Saviour") were summoned before Emperor Domitian.[2] This summons presumably took place in A.D. 96. When the emperor saw their calloused hands and learned of their meager income, he despised them as inferior people and dismissed them.

b. *Address.* Jude writes his epistle to people who have been called and who are loved and kept. Already at the outset of his letter, the writer shows a fondness for expressing his thoughts in three parts. Throughout his work he develops this threefold scheme (e.g., see v. 2, mercy, peace, love).

---

1. John Calvin states that the apostle James (son of Alphaeus) was Jude's brother. *Commentaries on the Catholic Epistles: The Epistle of Jude*, ed. and trans. John Owen (Grand Rapids: Eerdmans, 1948), pp. 428–29.

2. Eusebius *Ecclesiastical History* 3.19.1; 3.20.6 (LCL). Also see Josephus *Antiquities* 20.200 (LCL).

"To those who have been called." Jude fails to mention the epistle's place of destination. In his letter Jude provides no evidence that he functions as a spiritual father to a specific group of people. Nevertheless, he writes to Christians who need counsel and encouragement to oppose the doctrines of false teachers. Jude first describes the spiritual gifts the believers have received. They have been called by God to be his people. That is, those who have been called are Christians. They have left the world of sin and have entered the light of life.[3]

"Who are loved by God the Father."[4] Jude uses language that is similar to Paul's letter to the Romans: "You . . . who are called to belong to Jesus Christ. To all in Rome who are loved by God" (1:6–7). When God calls sinners to himself through Jesus Christ, he as their Father expresses his love to them. He welcomes sinners into the family of believers and the household of God. Through Christ, then, believers experience the continual love of God the Father.

Many translators prefer the reading *beloved* in *God the Father* in place of "loved *by* God the Father."[5] The difference in these two translations is not irreconcilable. Believers are living in the sphere of God's love, and consequently are loved by God. The clause *loved by God* relates to the environment in which God is actively loving his people. God, then, grants his love to his people and at the same time provides for them the sphere in which he expresses his love.[6]

"And kept by Jesus Christ." These words echo the prayer of Jesus concerning his disciples: "While I was with them, I protected them and kept them safe by that name you gave me" (John 17:12). Jesus protects his followers from the evil one. Although the previously mentioned clause is a faithful translation, another version has the reading *kept for Jesus Christ.* This version places the emphasis not on Jesus' constant watchfulness over the believers, but on the believers being kept by God for the day of Jesus Christ. The Father protects the followers of Jesus from the attacks of Satan (John 17:15) and keeps them whole and complete at the coming of Jesus Christ (I Thess. 5:23). We conclude that scriptural support for both translations is strong, for these two strands of teaching were current in the early church. Furthermore, the writers of the New Testament epistles often do not carefully differentiate between the work of the Father and the work of the Son.

---

3. Compare the use of the word *called* in Paul's epistles (Rom. 1:6–7; 8:28; I Cor. 1:2, 24). Refer to Lothar Coenen, *NIDNTT,* vol. 1, p. 275; Karl Ludwig Schmidt, *TDNT,* vol. 3, p. 494.

4. Two translations of this text have the reading *sanctified* instead of "loved" (see KJV, NKJV; also consult the Majority Text). This reading has been influenced by the text of I Cor. 1:2.

5. With individual variations, these translations have the reading *in God the Father:* RV, ASV, NASB, NAB, RSV, GNB.

6. Compare Rom. 9:25; Eph. 1:6; Col. 3:12; I Thess. 1:4; II Thess. 2:13; Rev. 20:9. Also consult S. Greijdanus, *De Brieven van de Apostelen Petrus en Johannes, en de Brief van Judas,* Kommentaar op het Nieuwe Testament series (Amsterdam: Van Bottenburg, 1929), p. 603.

2. Mercy, peace and love be yours in abundance.

Note the following observations:

a. *Translation.* Many translators give the reader a paraphrase of the text. They do so because the literal translation is difficult to comprehend and explain. The exact translation is, "May mercy and peace and love be multiplied to you" (NASB). Since the idea of multiplying abstract qualities is difficult to grasp, translators express Jude's wish in terms of increasing the attributes of mercy, love, and peace.

b. *Parallels.* In his two epistles Peter has an apostolic greeting that features the same ending: "Grace and peace be yours in abundance" (I Peter 1:2; II Peter 1:2). Peter, however, follows the conventional norm of greeting someone with the words *grace and peace.*[7] The greeting *grace, mercy and peace* was customary, too (I Tim. 1:2; II Tim. 1:2; II John 3).

What is mercy? Here is one of many definitions: "From a theological perspective the characteristic of mercy is rooted in God and experienced in relation to God, from whom it may be acquired as a Christian virtue and exercised in relation to fellow human beings."[8]

c. *Results.* God reaches out to sinners in their misery and grants them his blessings. He extends his mercy to evildoers by demonstrating tolerance even when justice demands punishment. In response the offender who receives mercy expresses gratitude to God for his kindness and compassion.

When God grants mercy or when man shows mercy to his neighbor, peace results. Peace is the restoration of broken relationships. And the blessing of peace culminates in spiritual and material prosperity. Peace means an absence of tensions prevalent in periods of conflict. Peace, in turn, results in love. That is, God expresses his love to man and man seeks to love God and his neighbor, according to the law.

Practical Considerations in 2

I remember my elementary-school days when my classmates and I had to learn the "times tables." By constant repetition, the teacher taught us to multiply numbers until we mastered these tables. Later in life, I saw the same concept applied in Jude 2: "May mercy, peace and love be multiplied to you." I noticed that the writer did not say we *must* multiply mercy, but that it *may* be multiplied. Jude expresses a wish and implies that God is the one who multiplies mercy, peace, and love for us.

I began to see that mercy is given to us and multiplied as we approach the throne of God and plead for remission of our sins. The more we come to God with our sins, the more God grants us the gifts of mercy, peace, and love.

Jude could have written, "May mercy, peace, and love be added to you." But by

---

7. See Rom. 1:7; I Cor. 1:3; II Cor. 1:2; Gal. 1:3; Eph. 1:2; Phil. 1:2; Col. 1:2; I Thess. 1:1; II Thess. 1:2; Titus 1:4; Philem. 3.
8. Peter C. Craigie, "Mercy," *EDT*, p. 708. Also see David E. Garland, "Mercy," *ISBE*, vol. 3, pp. 322–23.

using the word *multiplied,* he indicates that God's gifts are doubled, tripled, and even quadrupled. The one gift flows into the other, because mercy leads to peace and peace results in love.

I understood that when God grants us the gifts of mercy, peace, and love, we become multiplication signs. In fact, we are God's multiplication signs when we receive these gifts from God and extend them to our fellow man.

My thoughts drifted back to my school days in math class. I remember that it was easy for me to learn the rules for addition:

$$2 + 2 = 4$$
$$4 + 4 = 8$$
$$8 + 8 = 16$$
$$16 + 16 = 32$$

However, multiplying numbers was a different story:

$$2 \times 2 = 4$$
$$4 \times 4 = 16$$
$$16 \times 16 = 256$$
$$256 \times 256 = 65{,}536$$

These multiplied numbers are actually mind-boggling. In the same way, when God applies the principle of multiplication to his gifts of mercy, peace, and love, we are unable to comprehend the results. God does not expect us to understand this truth in mathematical terms. He wants us to pray, "May mercy, peace, and love be multiplied to you."

Greek Words, Phrases, and Constructions in 1–2

Verse 1

ἐν θεῷ—the preposition with the noun in the dative case is a dative of sphere.[9] "The position of ἐν, if it is intended to go with ᾽Ιησοῦ Χριστοῦ as well as with θεῷ πατρί, is extraordinary."[10]

ἠγαπημένοις—this is the perfect passive participle from the verb ἀγαπάω (I love). The perfect tense describes continuous activity. A number of manuscripts have a variant reading, ἠγιασμένοις, from the verb ἁγιάζω (I make holy). "The latter reading, which is modeled upon 1 Cor. 1.2, was introduced by copyists in order to avoid the difficult and unusual combination ἐν θεῷ πατρὶ ἠγαπημένοις."[11]

---

9. Consult A. T. Robertson, *A Grammar of the Greek New Testament in the Light of Historical Research* (Nashville: Broadman, 1934), p. 588.

10. C. F. D. Moule, *An Idiom-Book of New Testament Greek,* 2d ed. (Cambridge: Cambridge University Press, 1960), p. 47.

11. Bruce M. Metzger, *A Textual Commentary on the Greek New Testament,* 3d corrected ed. (London and New York: United Bible Societies, 1975), p. 723.

Verse 2

πληθυνθείη—here is one of the few New Testament verbs in the optative mood. The form is the aorist passive optative of the verb πληθύνω (I multiply). The passive implies that God is the agent, the aorist is constative, and the optative expresses a wish.

---

3 Dear friends, although I was very eager to write to you about the salvation we share, I felt I had to write and urge you to contend for the faith that was once for all entrusted to the saints.   4 For certain men whose condemnation was written about long ago have secretly slipped in among you. They are godless men, who change the grace of our God into a license for immorality and deny Jesus Christ our only Sovereign and Lord.

II. Purpose for Writing
3–4

In a few words Jude reveals the reason for the composition of his letter: first, he wants to encourage the readers to affirm their faith; next, he alerts them to the danger of immoral people who have slipped in among them; and last, he opens the eyes of the believers to the life and doctrine of their opponents.

3. Dear friends, although I was very eager to write to you about the salvation we share, I felt I had to write and urge you to contend for the faith that was once for all entrusted to the saints.

Observe these points:

a. *Love.* Jude addresses his readers with a common greeting of that day: "dear friends" (also see vv. 17, 20). Literally translated the term means "beloved." He puts this greeting in the context of the address ("to those . . . who are loved by God," v. 1) and the blessing ("mercy, peace and love be yours in abundance," v. 2).

As a pastor, Jude clearly distinguishes between the recipients of his letter and the false teachers. He expresses his love to the readers, but also tells them to be aware of the pernicious teachings of these heretics. The term *beloved* demonstrates his affection for the members of the Christian church, who through Jesus Christ experience the love of God the Father.

b. *Salvation.* Because of his pastoral love, Jude composes his letter and writes, "Although I was very eager to write to you about the salvation we share, I felt I had to write and urge you to contend for the faith." Jude indicates that circumstances caused him to change the content of the letter he was planning to write. We have only a few words about the content of this intended epistle: "the salvation we share." We do well not to speculate what Jude would have written. But what does he mean by the phrase *we share*? The letter itself is too brief to provide any evidence that Jude is addressing both Jewish and Gentile Christians. If we lack support for making a distinction between Christians of Jewish and Gentile backgrounds, we have to look at the purpose of Jude's epistle for an answer to this question.

Writing his letter to strengthen the believers in their faith, Jude refers to the common bond of salvation they possess (compare Titus 1:4; also see Acts 2:44). Moreover, he intimates that this bond helps them withstand the false teachers in their community who do not possess salvation. In verses 3 and 4 a contrast is evident between the salvation the believers share and the condemnation God reserves for the godless men.[12]

c. *Faith.* Jude reveals his personal interest in the spiritual life of the readers. He says, "I felt I had to write." He notes the necessity of exhorting the believers to contend for the faith. Notice that at the beginning and the end of his letter, Jude mentions the same subject. In the opening of his epistle he urges the readers "to contend for the faith that was once for all entrusted to the saints." He concludes his epistle with this exhortation: "But you, dear friends, build yourselves up in your most holy faith and pray in the Holy Spirit" (v. 20).

What is this faith Jude mentions? In view of the context, we understand the word *faith* to mean the body of Christian beliefs. It is the gospel the apostles proclaimed and therefore is equivalent to "the apostles' teaching" (Acts 2:42). Thus, it is not the trust and confidence that the individual believer has in God, for that is subjective faith. In this passage Jude speaks of Christian doctrine, that is, objective faith.

The context in which Jude discusses faith relates to its deposit in the community of the saints. Jude writes about "the faith that was once for all entrusted to the saints." The saints, of course, are the members of the church.[13] They have received God's revelation, just as the Jews, as Paul says, "have been entrusted with the very words of God" (Rom. 3:2). God delivered his truth to Jesus Christ (see John 3:34), and Jesus committed God's truth to the apostles, who in turn entrusted it to the believers.

What is the deposit of faith? The apostles transmitted the gospel to the church, which in turn proclaimed it throughout the world (I Thess. 1:6–8). "The idea of tradition, of the gospel as an authoritative message committed to and handed down in the Church, was integral to Christianity from the start."[14] The apostolic teaching as a body was transmitted once for all to the church (compare Luke 1:2; Rom. 6:17; I Cor. 11:2).

Jude urges his readers "to contend for the faith." He encourages the believers not only to fight for the faith, but also to depend on that faith for spiritual help.[15] The New Testament concept *to contend* is familiar to his

---

12. Consult John Albert Bengel, *Gnomon of the New Testament,* ed. Andrew R. Fausset, trans. William Fletcher, 7th ed., 5 vols. (Edinburgh: Clark, 1877), vol. 5, p. 163.
13. Followers of Jesus Christ bear the name *saints.* See, e.g., Rom. 1:7; II Cor. 1:1; Eph. 1:1.
14. J. N. D. Kelly, *A Commentary on the Epistles of Peter and Jude,* Thornapple Commentaries series (1969; Grand Rapids: Baker, 1981), p. 248. Consult Karl Hermann Schelkle, *Die Petrusbriefe, Der Judasbrief,* Herders Theologischer Kommentar zum Neuen Testament series, 5th rev. ed. (Freiburg: Herder, 1980), vol. 13/2, pp. 149–50.
15. Refer to Bauer, p. 281.

readers. In brief, it means to exert oneself without distraction to attain a
goal. It means self-denial to overcome obstacles, to avoid perils, and if need
be to accept martyrdom.[16] Jude implies that the members of the church
must exert themselves in spreading the gospel and defeating heresy (see II
Tim. 4:7).

> Jesus, with Thy Church abide;
> Be her Savior, Lord and Guide,
> While on earth her faith is tried:
> We beseech Thee, hear us.
>
> May she holy triumphs win,
> Overthrow the hosts of sin,
> Gather all the nations in:
> We beseech Thee, hear us.
> —Thomas Benson Pollock

Practical Considerations in 3

The task of the pastor is first and foremost to feed the people the living Word of
God. On the Lord's Day and on other occasions he must faithfully preach and teach
the Scriptures (II Tim. 4:2). He must proclaim the gospel to strengthen the believer
in his faith and to lead the sinner to conversion. He must call the people to repentance, plead on their behalf for remission of sins, and urge them to be reconciled to
God (II Cor. 5:20). His task is to administer the sacraments of baptism and the
Lord's Supper and to be a leader in prayer (Acts 6:4). He must give leadership in
the work of evangelism and mission to extend the church of Jesus Christ (Matt.
28:19).

The pastor's role is to counsel, exhort, and encourage the people "to contend for
the faith that was once for all entrusted to the saints." The pastor seeks to maintain
order and discipline in the church; he opposes any person who through doctrine
and life wants to lead the believers astray. With appointed leaders, the pastor is a
watchman on the walls of Zion (Ps. 122:7–8). He is to promote the well-being of
God's people.

**4. For certain men whose condemnation was written about long ago
have secretly slipped in among you. They are godless men, who change
the grace of our God into a license for immorality and deny Jesus Christ
our only Sovereign and Lord.**

Why does Jude urge the recipients to contend for the faith? Jude says,
a. "For certain men . . . have secretly slipped in among you." As pastor-
teacher, Jude observes a dangerous development within the church. He

---

16. Consult Ethelbert Stauffer, *TDNT*, vol. 1, pp. 137–38; Karl Heinrich Ringwald, *NIDNTT*,
vol. 1, pp. 646–48.

feels the need to alert the members to be on guard and oppose the men who have slipped into the Christian community. Jude places the term *certain men* over against the greeting *dear friends* (v. 3) and indicates that the believers are facing adversaries to the faith. As Paul warns the Galatians to watch out for "false brothers" (Gal. 2:4), so Jude instructs his readers to oppose "godless men." And Peter tells the readers of his second epistle to beware of "false teachers" who have entered their community and who secretly teach pernicious doctrines (II Peter 2:1).

We make two observations: Jude does not indicate whether these godless men at one time belonged to the Christian community; and these infiltrators are dishonest in their relations with the believers, for they furtively slip into the church. By their secrecy they reveal their motives. Probably they were itinerant teachers who were bent on destroying the church of Jesus Christ. The New Testament presents numerous warnings to the believers to avoid strange teachings from false teachers (Phil. 3:2; Col. 2:8; II Tim. 3:6; I John 3:7; 4:1; II John 7).

b. "[Their] condemnation was written about long ago." There are four different interpretations for this clause, of which at least the first two encounter some difficulties.

1. The translation *was written about* can even be given as "Scriptures," for example, "Long ago the Scriptures predicted the condemnation they have received" (GNB; also see NEB). This reading, however, faces the problem that Jude refers to the Old Testament Scriptures in general and not to a specific passage. Consequently, the expression *Scriptures* is too vague.

2. Some commentators accept the priority of II Peter and assert that Jude borrows his material from the apostle. For them, the translation *Scriptures* in Jude 4 relates to the second and third chapters of II Peter. These scholars cannot use the expression *long ago* in the clause "[their] condemnation was written about long ago," and hence substitute the word *already*. They point out that this rendering is possible, for it appears in the New Testament (Mark 15:44; also see the variant reading of the Greek text in Mark 6:47 [NEB]). This is a plausible interpretation that clarifies verse 4 in Jude's epistle; yet a twofold objection remains. First, not all commentators are persuaded that II Peter predates the Epistle of Jude; next, the usual translation of the Greek word *palai* is not "already" but "long ago."

3. Another possibility is to link the expression *written about* to the prophecy of Enoch (I En. 1:9) recorded in verses 14–15. Enoch predicts the coming of the Lord and the condemnation of the ungodly. Also, the words *long ago* support a reference to Enoch's prophecy.[17] We should not place too much emphasis on the written text of I Enoch. We ought to know that in the early Christian church Jude's quotation from this apocryphal book,

---

17. Consult Joseph B. Mayor, *The Epistle of St. Jude and the Second Epistle of St. Peter: Greek Text with Introduction and Notes* (1907; Grand Rapids: Baker, 1965), p. 24. Also see Bengel, *Gnomon of the New Testament*, vol. 5, p. 164.

instead of a canonical book, caused the believers to hesitate before they received his epistle into the canon.

4. Other scholars have understood the term *written about* metaphorically to refer to a list that is kept in heaven.[18] The term appears in secular Greek writing for keeping a list of either influential people or outlaws. God is keeping a list of the godless who deserve condemnation. These sinners, whose names are on the list, are "men who were marked out for condemnation" (NIV, text note). In the parallel verse (II Peter 2:3) Peter gives credence to this reading. He writes about the false teachers and says, "Their condemnation has long been hanging over them, and their destruction has not been sleeping." In brief, this last interpretation of a difficult clause has merit.

c. "They are godless men, who change the grace of our God into a license for immorality." What are these intruders doing that they deserve divine condemnation? To put it in the words of Paul, "They claim to know God, but by their actions they deny him. They are detestable, disobedient and unfit for doing anything good" (Titus 1:16).

Jude does not say that these men are atheists. He indicates that they slyly enter the Christian church by acknowledging the existence of God; otherwise they would be denied entrance. But their personal conduct betrays godlessness (compare vv. 15, 18), for these men think that God's grace allows them to indulge in unbridled sexual freedom.

The word *grace* signifies God's forgiving love whereby the sinner receives freedom to serve God and to express his gratitude. These false instructors, however, teach the Christians to use that freedom not to honor God but to satisfy their sexual lusts (see Gal. 5:13; I Peter 2:16; II Peter 2:19). These people pervert the teachings of God's Word by engaging in a life of sexual filth. The term *license for immorality* is an expression Peter employs to describe the shameful homosexual conduct of the Sodomites (II Peter 2:7).[19]

d. "They are godless men, who . . . deny Jesus Christ our only Sovereign and Lord." This is the second characteristic of the heretics. Except for describing their conduct, Jude provides no information about how they deny Jesus. The Greek indicates that these godless persons are constantly renouncing the divine authority of Jesus Christ, who has absolute sovereignty in every area of life. The nineteenth-century Dutch theologian Abraham Kuyper pointedly stated, "There is not so much as the breadth of a thumb in every area of life of which Christ has not said: 'It is mine.' "

The expression *Sovereign* usually describes God in the New Testament. But in this verse Jesus is designated Sovereign and Lord. Some Greek manuscripts and at least two translations have the reading "and deny the

---

18. See Gottlob Schrenk, *TDNT*, vol. 1, pp. 771–72; Calvin, *The Epistle of Jude*, p. 432; Kelly, *Peter and Jude*, pp. 250–51.

19. Also see Rom. 13:13; II Cor. 12:21; Gal. 5:19; Eph. 4:19; I Peter 4:3; II Peter 2:2, 18.

only Lord God and our Lord Jesus Christ."[20] This reading maintains unanimity by ascribing sovereignty to both God the Father and Jesus. However, the better manuscripts delete the word *God,* and translators favor the shorter text. We must apply a grammatical rule, because in the Greek only one definite article precedes the nouns *Sovereign* and *Lord.* The rule states that when one article controls two nouns the writer refers to one person.[21] This means that Jude points to one person, not two (also see II Peter 2:1). He designates Jesus Christ our only Sovereign and Lord, and intimates that we cannot have any other master besides Jesus.

Greek Words, Phrases, and Constructions in 3–4

Verse 3

ποιούμενος—the present middle (reflexive) participle from the verb ποιέω (I do, make) has a concessive connotation.

γράφειν—Jude writes the present active infinitive for his intended letter and the aorist infinitive γράψαι for his epistle.

ἐπαγωνίζεσθαι—the preposition ἐπί intensifies the meaning of this compound. The present tense of the infinitive shows continued action.

Verse 4

τινες ἄνθρωποι—note that these words stand in opposition to ἀγαπητοί (dear friends) and convey a measure of derision.

προγεγραμμένοι—this compound participle from the verb προγράφω (I write beforehand) emphasizes the concept *time.* The perfect passive tense denotes an action that occurred in the past but that has bearing on the present. The adverb πάλαι (long ago) stresses time past.

---

5 Though you already know all this, I want to remind you that the Lord delivered his people out of Egypt, but later destroyed those who did not believe.   6 And the angels who did not keep their positions of authority but abandoned their own home—these he has kept in darkness, bound with everlasting chains for judgment on the great Day.   7 In a similar way, Sodom and Gomorrah and the surrounding towns gave themselves up to sexual immorality and perversion. They serve as an example of those who suffer the punishment of eternal fire.

III. Examples from History
5–7

A. Unbelieving Israel
5

Before Jude continues with his description of the false teachers and his announcement of their forthcoming condemnation, he turns to history and

---

20. NKJV; also see KJV, and the marginal reading in NEB, TR, and the Majority Text.

21. Consult H. E. Dana and Julius R. Mantey, *A Manual Grammar of the Greek New Testament* (1927; New York: Macmillan, 1967), p. 147.

provides three examples of divine judgment. Notice that Peter also relies on history for three examples (II Peter 2:4–8), but Jude has a different sequence and even cites another event. Peter presents a chronological order: angels, flood, Sodom and Gomorrah. But Jude has a topical arrangement in which he mentions the unbelieving Israelites in the desert, the fallen angels, and the citizens of Sodom and Gomorrah. In these three instances, Jude stresses the theme of disobedience and rebellion against God that points inevitably to condemnation.

5. Though you already know all this, I want to remind you that the Lord delivered his people out of Egypt, but later destroyed those who did not believe.

a. *Preface.* Jude introduces the three examples with a compliment and a wish to give the readers a reminder. Tactfully he praises the believers for their knowledge of the Old Testament Scriptures. With the use of the verb *know,* he indicates that the readers are acquainted with the historical facts pertaining to the examples Jude plans to give. The New International Version has the reading *already,* which in numerous translations is "once" or "once for all." The Greek manuscripts for this verse present some changes in word order, so that the term *once* appears in a subsequent clause: "How the Lord once rescued the people of Israel" (GNB; also see NEB). Because translators must convey accurately the meaning and place of the term, the translation *already* is plausible (JB, NAB, NIV).

We assume that Jude has instructed the readers on earlier occasions. He writes, "I want to remind you" and seems to refer to apostolic teaching in the form of Christian doctrine "that was once for all entrusted to the saints" (v. 3). In his second epistle, Peter also expresses his desire to remind the believers (see 2:12–15; 3:1). Perhaps both writers have in mind the content of catechetical instruction that new converts received when they became members of the church.

b. *Divine deliverance.* The first example comes from Israel's history, when "the Lord delivered his people out of Egypt." God considered Israel his special people. With many miracles he brought this nation out of Egypt and set his people free from slavery. Once again the Greek text has some variant readings. Translators favor the reading *Lord,* which they have chosen from the variants "Jesus," "God," and even "God Christ."

The question remains, however, whether the expression *Lord* refers to God or to the preexistent Christ.[22] Scripture presents support for both readings. For instance, Paul says that the spiritual rock that accompanied the Israelites in the desert was Christ (I Cor. 10:4).[23] Yet the Old Testament

---

22. Consult Richard J. Bauckham, *Jude, 2 Peter,* Word Commentary series, vol. 50 (Waco: Word, 1983), p. 49.

23. Charles Biggs declares, "By 'the Lord' is no doubt meant Christ." *A Critical and Exegetical Commentary on the Epistles of St. Peter and St. Jude,* International Critical Commentary series (1901; Edinburgh: Clark, 1961), p. 328.

narrative reveals that God destroyed the unbelievers in the desert (Num. 14:29–37; Heb. 3:17–19). If the subject of verse 5 in Jude's epistle is uncertain, verse 6 definitely points to God. Not Jesus but God consigned fallen angels to dark prisons (compare II Peter 2:4). Accordingly, I interpret the term *Lord* in verse 5 to refer to God.

c. *Impressive illustration.* "[The Lord] later destroyed those who did not believe." Jude reminds his readers that all the people who were twenty years of age and older, but did not believe, died in the desert. According to Numbers 1:45–46, all the men who were twenty years old or more numbered 603,550. If we add an equal number of women, then those who died in the desert on the way to Canaan totaled 1,207,100 people. And if we divide that total by the number of days of the thirty-eight-year journey to Canaan after God pronounced the death penalty, we arrive at a staggering total of nearly ninety deaths per day (see Deut. 2:14–15). A highly privileged nation witnessed many astounding miracles that effected their deliverance from slavery. Yet these people refused to trust God's visible leadership. By rejecting the guidance that God offered, they experienced God's wrath. That anger was expressed through severe punishments: Many Israelites perished in the desert and were forsaken by God. What a stern warning not to think lightly of God's judgment!

Greek Words, Phrases, and Constructions in 5

εἰδότας—the perfect active participle with a present meaning (from the verb οἶδα, I know) is concessive in translation.[24] The verb indicates inherent knowledge.

ὁ κύριος—although this reading is not as well attested as the words ὁ Ἰησοῦς, the editors and translators prefer the reading ὁ κύριος "and explained the origins in terms of transcriptional oversight ($\overline{\text{KC}}$ being taken for $\overline{\text{IC}}$)."[25]

B. Evil Angels
6

6. And the angels who did not keep their positions of authority but abandoned their own home—these he has kept in darkness, bound with everlasting chains for judgment on the great Day.

Jude's second example of rebellion against God concerns angels. God did not spare even the mighty creatures whom he had given powerful positions, principalities, and authorities (compare Eph. 1:21; 3:10; Col. 2:10, 15). God also gave them tasks that included serving him as messengers (compare Ps. 104:4; Heb. 1:7). However, when these angels rebelled against him, he punished them with imprisonment.

---

24. Consult Robertson, *Grammar*, p. 1129.
25. Metzger, *Textual Commentary*, p. 724.

a. "And the angels who did not keep their positions of authority." In the parallel passage Peter merely states that the angels sinned (II Peter 2:4). Many commentators are of the opinion that angels left their positions of authority and went to earth to marry women (Gen. 6:2). That is, when angels ("the sons of God") married "the daughters of men," they fathered giants and corrupted the earth (Gen. 6:4). These commentators state that Jude received his material from Jewish and Gentile traditions and especially from the apocryphal book I Enoch.[26]

Other expositors observe that we know little about the "positions of authority" held by angels (see Dan. 10:12–21). Scripture does not reveal how these angels lost their status. We assume that they refused to obey God's command because they wanted to be like him (see Gen. 3:5; Luke 4:6). Nevertheless, we should avoid giving prominence to traditions that link the fall of the angels to the intermarrying of "the sons of God" and "the daughters of men" (Gen. 6:2). As spiritual beings, angels have no physical bodies and therefore are incapable of procreation. In answer to a question from the Sadducees about marriage at the resurrection, Jesus explains that people, like angels in heaven, "will neither marry nor be given in marriage" (Matt. 22:30).[27]

b. "[The angels] abandoned their own home." Note the parallelism in this first part of verse 6.

	And the angels	
who did not keep	but abandoned
their positions	their own
of authority	home

Jude strengthens the negative phrase *did not keep* with the verb *abandoned*. He balances the possessive pronouns, and with the two nouns *authority* and *home* he expresses synonymous concepts. These angels resided in heavenly splendor, but after their rebellion God consigned them to live in darkness. Because of their sin, they were no longer able to keep their domain or sphere of influence and left their own dwelling.[28] At one time they held authority, but now they are prisoners in chains and wait for the day of judgment. Jude provides no details about the location of the domain or dwelling of these angels. He is interested only in the theme that God punishes those who refuse to obey him.

---

26. Refer to Bauckham, *Jude, 2 Peter*, p. 51; Kelly, *Peter and Jude*, pp. 256–57. Also consult Edwin A. Blum, *Jude*, in *Hebrews–Revelation*, vol. 12 of *The Expositor's Bible Commentary*, ed. Frank E. Gaebelein, 12 vols. (Grand Rapids: Zondervan, 1981), p. 390. And see SB, vol. 3, pp. 780–85.

27. R. C. H. Lenski mentions the term *fiction* when he refers to the story of angels and women intermarrying. *The Interpretation of the Epistles of St. Peter, St. John, and St. Jude* (Columbus: Wartburg, 1945), pp. 310, 620.

28. Refer to Bauer, pp. 112, 557.

c. "These he has kept in darkness, bound with everlasting chains for judgment on the great Day." Here is one of Jude's descriptive contrasts: "the angels . . . did not keep their positions of authority," but God "has kept [these angels] in darkness." We should not interpret this text to mean that all the fallen angels are locked up in a certain place. If this were the case, the earth would not be plagued by demons. The picture Jude conveys is that the rebellious angels are living in spiritual darkness and are chained to their sentence of divine judgment from which they can never escape.[29]

Additional Comments on 6

Because Jude quotes directly from the apocryphal book I Enoch in verses 14 and 15, we are not surprised that he alludes to this work in verse 6. Jude and his contemporaries were familiar with the Book of Enoch. And even though the book is not canonical, it presents an account of the fall of the angels. In chapters 6–19 of I Enoch, the writer relates the origin of evil on the earth. He describes how fallen angels lust after the beautiful daughters of men, descend upon Mount Hermon, and commit adultery with them. These fallen angels are responsible for producing offspring, the Nephilim, who are the giants in the earth (Gen. 6:4), and for the multiplication of evil in the world. The result is that God destroys the world with a flood in the days of Noah.

Verbal parallels between I Enoch and the Epistle of Jude demonstrate that Jude was acquainted with the content of this apocryphal book. Here are some of the sentences that show similarity:

I Enoch	*Jude*
[The angels] have abandoned the high heaven, the holy eternal place. (12:4)	And the angels who did not keep their positions of authority but abandoned their own home—(v. 6a)
Bind Azaz'el hand and foot (and) throw him into the darkness! (10:4)	these he has kept in darkness, bound with everlasting chains (v. 6b)
that he may be sent into the fire on the great day of judgment. (10:6)[30]	for judgment on the great Day. (v. 6c)

The writer of I Enoch presents a commentary on Genesis 6:1–4 and explains that the angels fell into sin by committing adultery with women. He writes that these angels corrupted the human race and received God's condemnation. They were put in prison and were bound forever. God

---

29. Consult Calvin, *The Epistle of Jude*, p. 436.

30. E. Isaac, *I (Ethiopic Apocalypse of) Enoch*, in *The Old Testament Pseudepigrapha*, ed. James H. Charlesworth, 2 vols. (Garden City, N. Y.: Doubleday, 1983), vol. 1, pp. 17–19.

destroyed the corrupt human race of Noah's day with the waters of the flood.[31]

Although the language in Jude's epistle resembles the word choice of selected passages in I Enoch, Jude provides no evidence that he wants to equate fallen angels with the "sons of God" who married the "daughters of men" (Gen. 6:2). Jude is acquainted with this interpretation, but we note that he does not endorse this idea in his epistle. Many scholars, however, see a definite connection between verses 6 and 7 in respect to sexual immorality. They read the intent of verse 7 into verse 6 because of the introductory phrase *in a similar way*.[32] They understand this phrase to signify that as the men of Sodom and Gomorrah were driven by lust so the fallen angels were prone to lust. But verse 7 must be seen as the third example of those whom God has condemned for their rebellion.

The three illustrations that describe the concept *condemnation* (v. 4) are the Israelites who died in the desert, the fallen angels, and the immoral citizens of Sodom and Gomorrah. These are the three examples of divine condemnation. And Jude uses them as a contrast to the concept *salvation* (v. 3).

For additional comments on this subject, see the section "Doctrinal Considerations in 6 and 9."

Greek Words, Phrases, and Constructions in 6

τε—this adjunction instead of the conjunction καί (and) binds verses 5 and 6 closely together. Conversely, verse 7 stands next to these two verses and begins with the adverb ὡς (as).

τὴν ἑαυτῶν ἀρχήν—the use of the definite article in this phrase and the parallel τὸ ἴδιον οἰκητήριον (their own home) signifies the place given by God to the angels. The pronoun ἑαυτῶν is balanced by ἴδιον and stresses personal possession. The noun ἀρχήν (authority) points to the exalted position the angels occupied.

τετήρηκεν—the perfect active from τηρέω (I keep) conveys lasting significance. Striking is the contrast with τηρήσαντας (aorist active); that is, the angels did not keep but left their place once for all, yet God keeps them in chains forever.

C. Sodom and Gomorrah
7

7. In a similar way, Sodom and Gomorrah and the surrounding towns gave themselves up to sexual immorality and perversion. They serve as an example of those who suffer the punishment of eternal fire.

---

31. For a comprehensive discussion of the interpretation of Gen. 6:1–4, see Willem A. Van Gemeren, "The Sons of God in Genesis 6:1–4," *WTJ* 43 (1981): 320–48.

32. For instance, see Michael Green, *The Second Epistle General of Peter, and the General Epistle of Jude: An Introduction and Commentary*, Tyndale New Testament Commentaries (Grand Rapids: Eerdmans, 1968), p. 166.

Notice these points:

a. *Comparison.* The third example of rebellion is the most vivid, for throughout the Old and New Testaments the cities of Sodom and Gomorrah stand out as symbols of immorality and are known because of their lasting destruction by fire and brimstone.[33] The surrounding towns are Admah, Zeboiim (Gen. 14:2; Deut. 29:23; Hos. 11:8), and Zoar (Gen. 19:22–23), which God spared.

"In a similar way, . . . [these] towns gave themselves up to sexual immorality and perversion." The New International Version avoids a literal translation and transmits the meaning of the text instead. However, a verbatim translation of the Greek has this reading: "How Sodom and Gomorrah and the cities around them in a similar way to these were indulging in sexual immorality and went after other flesh."

b. *Interpretation.* What is Jude saying? This is the usual explanation: "As the angels fell because of their lust for women, so the Sodomites desired sexual relations with angels."[34] Scholars indicate that Jude's reference is to the Sodomites' homosexual lust for those angels who came to visit Lot (see Gen. 19:4–11). The phrase "in a similar way to these" points to the angels who expressed their lust for the "daughters of men" (Gen. 6:2). And by contrast, the men of Sodom desired to have sexual relations with angels.

The objection to this view is that angels are spiritual beings and do not have bodies. Angels assumed physical bodies when they went to Sodom. In fact, "all the men from every part of the city of Sodom—both young and old" call out to Lot and ask: "Where are the *men* who came to you tonight? Bring them out to us so that we can have sex with them" (Gen. 19:4, 5; italics added). The men of Sodom were setting the example of homosexual practices for all the surrounding towns.

If we look again at the literal translation of verse 7a, we are able to read the text as follows: "How Sodom and Gomorrah (and the cities surrounding them in a similar way to these) were indulging in sexual immorality and went after other flesh." In the context of the verse, the position of the pronoun *these* indicates that Jude refers to the men of Sodom.[35] But what is the meaning of the term *other flesh*? The Greek reveals that in the case of duality (for example, male and female) the word *other* can mean "a second of two" and in the context denote a difference of kind.[36] Therefore, when the men of Sodom were interested in sexual relations with men, they perverted the created order of natural intercourse. That is, the men of Sodom

---

33. Compare, e.g., Gen. 13:10, 13; 18:20, 26; 19:24; Deut. 29:23; Isa. 13:19; Jer. 49:18; 50:40; Matt. 10:15; 11:24; Rom. 9:29; II Peter 2:6; Rev. 11:8.

34. Bauckham, *Jude, 2 Peter,* p. 54. And compare SB, vol. 3, pp. 785–86.

35. Other scholars interpret the word *these* to relate to the angels (v. 6) or to the two previous examples of unbelief and disobedience (the Israelites, v. 5, and the angels, v. 6).

36. Robertson, *Grammar,* p. 748.

did not desire females (see Gen. 19:8–9); instead, these men demanded homosexual relations with the men who visited Lot. The activity of the Sodomites is perversion. This is precisely how translators of the New International Version render the phrase *went after other flesh*.

c. *Punishment*. In verse 7, Jude remarks that the inhabitants of Sodom and Gomorrah "serve as an example of those who suffer the punishment of eternal fire." The literal translation of the verb *serve* is "exposed to public view." The evidence of God's judgment on the cities of the plain has been open to view since the day fire and sulfur destroyed the area. "Sodom never occurs again in the Bible as a living city, but the memory of its sin and consequent destruction was kept alive by Moses, the prophets, Jesus, and the authors of the N[ew] T[estament]. Sodom and Gomorrah have become bywords and tokens of God's wrath on sin."[37]

Jude links the lasting destruction of Sodom and Gomorrah and surrounding towns to "the punishment of eternal fire" that is waiting for the people who refuse to obey God and choose to disobey him. The term *example* signifies not something that we should follow or copy but rather something that we must avoid. In short, the term is a synonym of "warning."

Greek Words, Phrases, and Constructions in 7

ὡς—translated "how," this adverb is equivalent to ὅτι (v. 5) and τε (v. 6). It introduces the third example that Jude lists.

τούτοις—the nearest antecedents of this pronoun are the nouns *Sodom* and *Gomorrah*. Although Jude uses the names of the cities, the reference actually is to the inhabitants. Note that the word order is unique for the phrase τὸν ὅμοιον τρόπον τούτοις. This phrase stands between the noun πόλεις (cities) and the aorist participle feminine plural ἐκπορνεύσασαι. The accusative case in this phrase is the so-called adverbial accusative or the loose use of this case.[38]

---

8 In the very same way, these dreamers pollute their own bodies, reject authority and slander celestial beings.   9 But even the archangel Michael, when he was disputing with the devil about the body of Moses, did not dare to bring a slanderous accusation against him, but said, "The Lord rebuke you!"   10 Yet these men speak abusively against whatever they do not understand; and what things they do understand by instinct, like unreasoning animals—these are the very things that destroy them.

11 Woe to them! They have taken the way of Cain; they have rushed for profit into Balaam's error; they have been destroyed in Korah's rebellion.

---

37. Robert L. Alden, "Sodom," *ZPEB*, vol. 5, p. 466.
38. Consult Robertson, *Grammar*, p. 486.

IV. Application and Examples
8–11

A. Godless Men
8

After giving three examples of rebellion against the will of God and subsequent descriptions of divine judgment, Jude continues to portray the godless men of his day. He already has characterized them as "men who change the grace of our God into a license for immorality" (v. 4). Now he offers more detail: he describes the acts of these men with the three verbs *pollute, reject,* and *slander.* Jude writes,

8. In the very same way, these dreamers pollute their own bodies, reject authority and slander celestial beings.

a. *Pollute.* Jude now depicts the false teachers and compares them to the unbelieving Israelites, the rebellious angels, and the perverted Sodomites. He begins the sentence with the phrase *in the very same way.* Notice that the three evils which Jude lists correspond (in reverse order) with the sins named in the preceding three verses. The sin of polluting matches the homosexual acts mentioned in verse 7; the sin of rebelling echoes the rebellion of angels (v. 6). And the sin of slandering celestial beings is equivalent to the unbelief of the Israelites in the desert (v. 5). The unbelieving Israelites slandered God who had redeemed them from slavery and had cared for them in numerous ways (see especially Num. 14:1–4, 10–11). Their utter rejection of God brought about a display of divine glory by which God expressed his anger to the rebellious people.[39] Accordingly we conclude that Jude's purpose is to show that God's judgment falls on those who rebel. He demonstrates that in spite of the evidence of divine judgment, Jude's contemporaries are unwilling to listen to reason and thus invite eternal punishment.

Jude calls these godless men "dreamers." This term means either that they were mystics who claimed to have access to supernatural revelation or that as a result of their sexual immorality these men spent their time dreaming erotic fantasies. Although scholars are divided on this issue, evidence for either interpretation is strong. In support of the first view, commentators note that the noun *dreamers* is the subject of the three verbs *pollute, reject,* and *slander.* They also refer to Peter's Pentecost sermon in which he quotes the prophecy of Joel: "Your old men will dream dreams" (Acts 2:17; Joel 2:28).[40] By contrast, other expositors point out that Jude portrays these godless men not as false prophets who derive their teachings from dreams and ecstasies, but as men who live immorally and who "follow their own evil desires" (v. 16; also see vv. 4, 18–19).

---

39. Consult Greijdanus, *De Brieven,* p. 624.

40. Refer to J. W. C. Wand, *The General Epistles of St. Peter and St. Jude,* Westminster Commentaries series (London: Methuen, 1934), p. 205.

"These dreamers pollute their own bodies." They indulge in sexual excess that is comparable to the sins committed by the residents of Sodom and Gomorrah. They engage in homosexual acts that defile the land (see Lev. 18:24–28; Rom. 1:27).

b. *Reject.* Jude observes that these godless men reject authority. In the parallel passage Peter expresses the same sentiment when he describes the wicked who are kept for the day of judgment. He says, "This is especially true of those who follow the corrupt desire of the sinful nature and despise authority" (II Peter 2:10a).

The expression *authority,* which in the Greek is *kuriotēs* (lordship), occurs in Paul's epistles as "dominion" and "powers." Paul writes that Christ sits at God's right hand, "far above all rule and authority, power and *dominion*" (Eph. 1:21; italics added for clarification). And he says that Christ created all things, "whether thrones or *powers* or rulers or authorities" (Col. 1:16; italics added). Jude, however, is not focusing attention on angelic authority as such but on the divine authority (lordship) of Jesus Christ.[41]

In all his brevity, Jude refers to the godless men who deliberately reject divine authority. The words *reject authority* mean that these men scorn God's authority over them. The verb *reject* in the Greek specifies that they have set aside divine law; consequently they show their contempt for Christ and his gospel. They want to rule their own lives and want to be free from the lordship of Jesus Christ (see v. 4).

c. *Slander.* The last vice Jude mentions is "slander[ing] celestial beings." Peter says virtually the same thing when he relates that "these men are not afraid to slander celestial beings" (II Peter 2:10b). In the context of his epistle, Jude mentions a dispute that the archangel Michael had with the devil. The writer discloses that even though Michael hesitated to bring a slanderous accusation against Satan (v. 9), these godless men utter slander (v. 10).

Are these "celestial beings" good or evil angels? The answer lies in the Greek word *doxas* (glories) that is translated "celestial beings." This term accurately describes the angels that surround God's throne but does not apply to evil angels. Only God's faithful angels reflect his glory. The New Testament also teaches that the law of God "was put into effect through angels" (Acts 7:53; also see v. 38; Gal. 3:19; Heb. 2:2). That is, at the time God gave the law to the Israelites, angels were his messengers.

Why are these godless men slandering angels? In their desire for complete freedom, the infidels slandered angels and refused to accept the authority of anyone connected with the law. "In other words, their 'slandering' of the angels was a way of detaching the Law from God and interpreting it simply as an evil."[42]

---

41. See Kelly, *Peter and Jude,* p. 262.
42. Bauckham, *Jude, 2 Peter,* p. 59.

Greek Words, Phrases, and Constructions in 8

ὁμοίως μέντοι—*"in the same way, too."*[43] The conjunction μέντοι has the adversative meaning *but* in this context.[44]

μὲν . . . δὲ . . . δὲ . . .—observe Jude's literary skill in employing these particles to create structural balance in verses 8 and 9.

ἐνυπνιαζόμενοι—the middle participle from ἐνυπνιάζω (I dream) is in the present tense to describe the usual conduct of these godless men. The three main verbs in verse 8 are in the present tense; they indicate a continual course of action.

B. Michael and Satan
9–10

In these two verses Jude relies on information that is recorded in the apocryphal book the Testament of Moses or the related work known as the Assumption of Moses.[45] Unfortunately, the ending of this testament is no longer extant, but scholars have been able to reconstruct it from early Christian sources.

Because of this allusion to a noncanonical book and the direct quote from the apocryphal book I Enoch, the church in the first few centuries hesitated to accept the Epistle of Jude as canonical. The fact remains, however, that although Jude uses material from other sources, he does not recognize these books as inspired. He borrows examples from apocryphal literature or from the oral tradition of his day to illustrate and clarify his own teachings.

9. But even the archangel Michael, when he was disputing with the devil over the body of Moses, did not dare to bring a slanderous accusation against him, but said, "The Lord rebuke you!"

a. *Michael.* The name given to the archangel means "who is like God?" and is common in the Old Testament. The name also belongs to ten different persons, all of whom are virtually unknown.[46] In the prophecy of Daniel, the name *Michael* belongs to the angel who is "one of the chief princes" (10:13) and "the great prince who protects" the people Israel (12:1). He opposes and overcomes demons whom Satan has sent to influence the rulers of Persia and Greece (10:13, 20). The term *prince* is equivalent to the word *archangel* (compare I Thess. 4:16).

---

43. Bauer, p. 567.
44. Refer to Friedrich Blass and Albert Debrunner, *A Greek Grammar of the New Testament and Other Early Christian Literature,* trans. and rev. Robert Funk (Chicago: University of Chicago Press, 1961), sec. 450.1. Also refer to Robertson, *Grammar,* pp. 1154, 1188.
45. Refer to J. Priest, *Testament of Moses,* in *The Old Testament Pseudepigrapha,* ed. James H. Charlesworth, 2 vols. (Garden City, N.Y.: Doubleday, 1983), vol. 1, p. 925.
46. Consult Douglas Stuart, "Michael," *ISBE,* vol. 3, p. 347. See, e.g., Num. 13:13; I Chron. 5:13, 14; 6:40; 7:3; 8:16; 12:20–21; 27:18; Ezra 8:8.

Apocryphal literature teaches that there are seven archangels. This information corresponds with John's description of "the seven angels who stand before God" (Rev. 8:2).[47] Four of these have names; they are Michael, Gabriel, Raphael, and Uriel. Michael is the leader of the heavenly armies that fight Satan and his fallen angels and drive them out of heaven (Rev. 12:7–9).

b. *Moses*. "But even the archangel Michael ... was disputing with the devil about the body of Moses." The Old Testament is silent about this dispute between Michael and Satan and only records that God "buried [Moses] in Moab, in the valley opposite Beth Peor, but to this day no one knows where his grave is" (Deut. 34:6). A reconstructed outline of the lost ending of the Testament of Moses gives this account of Moses' burial:

> Joshua accompanied Moses up Mount Nebo, where God showed Moses the land of promise. Moses then sent Joshua back to the people to inform them of Moses' death, and Moses died. God sent the archangel Michael to remove the body of Moses to another place and bury it there, but Samma'el, the devil, opposed him, disputing Moses' right to honorable burial. . . . The devil brought against Moses a charge of murder, because he smote the Egyptian and hid his body in the sand. But this accusation was not better than slander against Moses and Michael, not tolerating the slander, said to the devil, "May the Lord rebuke you, devil!" At that the devil took flight, and Michael removed the body to the place commanded by God, where he buried it with his own hands. Thus no one saw the burial of Moses.[48]

Jude uses this illustration about the dispute between Michael and Satan to demonstrate that even this mighty archangel did not dare to rebuke the devil. Even though Michael ranked high above Satan and from our point of view had every right to reprimand this devil, the archangel avoided uttering a rebuke. God is the judge.

c. *Satan*. "The Lord rebuke you!" This sentence is reminiscent of the account that describes "Joshua the high priest standing before the angel of the LORD, and Satan standing at his right hand to accuse him" (Zech. 3:1). Then the Lord said, "The LORD rebuke you, Satan!" (v. 2). Likewise Michael turned Satan over to God when Satan forced him to argue about the body of Moses. Jude uses the literary device of comparison: the greater versus the lesser. That is, if the mightiest archangel Michael refuses to rebuke Satan, how much more should sinful man refrain from reviling (compare II Peter 2:11–12).

10. Yet these men speak abusively against whatever they do not understand; and what things they do understand by instinct, like unreasoning animals—these are the very things that destroy them.

---

47. See I En. 9:1; 20:1–7; 40:9; Tob. 12:15.
48. Bauckham, *Jude, 2 Peter,* pp. 72–73. The ending of the Testament of Moses is no longer extant, yet the church fathers supply source material for its ending.

In passing we note that Peter provides a parallel that is even clearer than the wording in Jude's epistle. He writes, "But these men blaspheme in matters they do not understand. They are like brute beasts, creatures of instinct, born only to be caught and destroyed, and like beasts they too will perish" (II Peter 2:12).

After illustrating his teaching with an incident that involves Michael and Satan, Jude returns to the subject of his discussion, namely, the godless men, whom he calls dreamers (v. 8). He depicts them as people who lack spiritual discernment and yet speak abusively against anyone and everything. As Jude says elsewhere, "[They] follow mere natural instincts and do not have the Spirit" (v. 19). Indeed, they are devoid of divine wisdom, unable to comprehend spiritual truth and unwilling to admit their foolishness (see especially I Cor. 2:14). David also reflected on the thoughts and deeds of evil men when he composed Psalm 14. This is David's view, presented here in verse:

> The God who sits enthroned on high
> The foolish in their heart deny;
> Not one does good; corrupt in thought,
> Unrighteous works their hands have wrought.
> —Psalter Hymnal

"What things they do understand by instinct, like unreasoning animals— these are the very things that destroy them." What is Jude trying to say? He means that persons without spiritual discernment are abysmally ignorant of reality and depend on instinct. That is, they have lowered themselves to the level of animals and in their sexual pursuits (see v. 8) are guided by instinct. Yet, unlike the animals which abide by the laws of nature, these godless men are destroyed by the very things they fail to understand. When men live by instinct, they abandon even natural law and consequently perish. They place themselves on a par with the animals, but because of their refusal to obey even the laws God has placed in nature, they are destroyed (compare Rom. 1:24).

Doctrinal Considerations in 6 and 9

Do you know how many angels there are? The Bible says that there are myriads (Deut. 33:2), which means that their number is countless. Angels have been created to serve God in classes, orders, and ranks; for example, Michael is one of the chief princes (Dan. 10:13; 12:1); others are cherubim (Gen. 3:24) and seraphs (Isa. 6:2). Together the angels form powerful armies that oppose Satan's forces (Ps. 103:20; Matt. 26:53; Rev. 12:7).

Do you know that angels have individual personalities? They have names (Luke 1:19), they rejoice over the salvation of a sinner (Luke 15:10), and they desire to learn about man's salvation (I Peter 1:12). Conversely, evil angels lie (John 8:44), have faith (James 2:19, "believe that there is one God"), and sin (I John 3:8).

Do you know that men and angels differ in numerous ways? Here are some of the differences:

1. Man has a body and a soul, which together form a unit. The soul without the body is incomplete. On the other hand, an angel is a spirit without a body, yet is complete. He has no physical body, and therefore is an individual being who is unrelated to the other angels.

2. Whereas man is related to fellow human beings by family ties, angels exist without families. Angels, then, do not marry (Matt. 22:30), are immortal (Luke 20:35–36), and are invisible (Col. 1:16). Man belongs to a human family and with his fellow men forms humanity. But angels have no families and therefore are unable to form "angelity," so to speak.[49]

3. Man was formed from the dust of the earth (Gen. 2:7), crowned with glory and honor, and appointed to rule God's creation (Gen. 1:28; Ps. 8:5–8; Heb. 2:7–8). Angels are created spirits and are appointed to minister and serve (Heb. 1:7, 14).

4. Adam fell into sin, but the second Adam has come to redeem him (Rom. 5:12, 19; I Cor. 15:45). Angels fell into sin but are not redeemed by Jesus Christ (Heb. 2:16).

5. And do you know that men, but not the angels, are created in the image of God (Gen. 1:27)? Angels are God's messengers and his servants (Ps. 104:4; Heb. 1:7). Conclusively, Scripture teaches that the difference between men and angels is profound.

Greek Words, Phrases, and Constructions in 9–10

Verse 9

ὁ δέ—this combination indicates a change of subject in the discourse.

διακρινόμενος—the use of this middle participle in the present tense denotes duration of time. The tense of the participle relates to the tense of the main verb.

διελέγετο—from the verb διαλέγομαι (I discuss), this form is in the imperfect middle indicative to show duration in the past tense. The imperfect is descriptive.

Verse 10

οὗτοι δέ—Jude returns to the subject of verse 8. The combination of these two Greek words reveals a change of subject in the discourse.

οἴδασιν—this verb in the perfect tense with a present meaning (from οἶδα, I know) expresses innate knowledge.

C. Cain, Balaam, and Korah
11

Jude mentions three examples of wickedness that are recorded in the Old Testament Scriptures. Notice that once again Jude's penchant for grouping items in triads is evident (compare vv. 1, 2). Moreover, in the triad of Cain,

---

49. Refer to Herman Bavinck, *Gereformeerde Dogmatiek*, 4 vols. (Kampen: Kok, 1928), vol. 2, p. 423.

Balaam, and Korah, Jude achieves a gradual crescendo by mentioning the nouns *way, error,* and *rebellion.*[50]

11. Woe to them! They have taken the way of Cain; they have rushed for profit into Balaam's error; they have been destroyed in Korah's rebellion.

The lamentation *Woe to them!* (with variations) is a typical phrase that the Old Testament prophets uttered repeatedly to condemn persons or nations. Jesus uses the word *woe* to place a curse on Korazin and Bethsaida (Matt. 11:21), and he rebukes the Pharisees with a series of seven woes (Matt. 23). And Paul calls a woe upon himself should he fail to preach the gospel (I Cor. 9:16). Likewise, Jude pronounces woes upon his godless contemporaries and tells them that they are heading for destruction. At the same time his words are a warning to his readers not to permit these godless men to lead them astray.

a. *Cain.* "They have taken the way of Cain." The Scriptures mention Cain in four different books: Genesis 4:2, 5, 15, 25; Hebrews 11:4; Jude 11; and I John 3:12. In these passages Cain is depicted as the first murderer and the first willful unbeliever. God spoke to him when he rejected Cain's offering and instructed Cain to overcome sin (Gen. 4:7). After Cain killed Abel, God protected Cain by placing a mark on him (v. 15). But in spite of God's grace, "Cain went out from the LORD's presence" (v. 1). Hence, Cain not only murdered his brother, but also rejected God. Hardened by unbelief, he deliberately cast his lot with the devil (compare Heb. 11:4; I John 3:12). An early Jewish commentary on Genesis 4:8 puts these words on the lips of Cain: "There is no judgment, no judge, no world to come; no reward will be given to the righteous, and no destruction for the wicked."[51]

What is the "way of Cain" which the godless men have taken? Not only Cain lacked the virtues of faith and love; the godless men of Jude's day also are devoid of these qualities.[52] They lack selflessness and generosity (see v. 16). They nurture the vices of envy and greed; they have hearts filled with hatred toward God and man. And hatred leads to murder, as John points out in his epistle (I John 3:15).

b. *Balaam.* "They have rushed for profit into Balaam's error." A superficial reading of the Old Testament account leaves the impression that Balaam obeyed God by blessing the Israelites.[53] In fact, the Old Testament passages fail to disclose that Balaam indeed received a reward for his prophecies. Nevertheless, Scripture indicates Balaam sought to corrupt the Israelites by enticing them to sexual immorality and idol worship (compare Num. 31:16). When John records Jesus' letter to the church of Pergamum

---

50. For further details consult G. H. Boobyer, "The Verbs in Jude 11," *NTS* 5 (1958): 45–47.
51. Jerusalem Targum (author's translation).
52. See Mayor, *Jude and Peter,* p. 37.
53. Compare Num. 22:1–24:25; Deut. 23:4; Josh. 24:9–10; Neh. 13:2; Mic. 6:5.

he writes, "You have people there who hold to the teaching of Balaam, who taught Balak to entice the Israelites to sin by eating food sacrificed to idols and by committing sexual immorality" (Rev. 2:14). Jesus is referring to Israel's sin at Baal-Peor (Num. 25). Because of this sin, thousands of Israelites died in a plague and thousands of Midianites died on the battlefield. Among the slain Midianites was Balaam (Num. 31:8). Balaam loved not God and his people, but money. And because he loved money, he sold Israel to the king of Moab. Accordingly, Peter reveals that Balaam "loved the wages of wickedness" (II Peter 2:15). As Balaam sought the destruction of Israel, so the godless men desire the downfall of God's people.

We should not understand the term *error* in a passive sense, that is, as if Balaam was led astray and thus erred. Rather, this term has an active meaning—Balaam deceived the Israelites by leading them into sin. Similarly, the objective of Jude's opponents is to deceive the Christian community and to make a profit.

c. *Korah*. "They have been destroyed in Korah's rebellion." The sad account of Korah's rebellion against Moses is recorded in Numbers 16:1–35. Korah, Dathan, and Abiram with their respective families were swallowed up by the earth; 250 leaders were consumed by fire. This happened as a result of their refusal to accept the leadership of Moses and Aaron. God severely punished these people for challenging his administration and teaching.

How does Korah's sin differ from that of Cain and Balaam? Cain broke his relationship with God; Balaam desired to lead God's people into sin for profit; but Korah questioned God's wisdom in appointing Moses and Aaron leaders of Israel. Likewise, Jude's adversaries presumably rejected apostolic leadership and teaching in the Christian church. In comparison with Korah and his followers, the adversaries, too, will perish because of God's judgment. Jude is so positive that he writes the verb *destroy* in the past tense, as if the action already had taken place: "They have been destroyed in Korah's rebellion."

These three examples are not merely interesting historical accounts. Jude employs the three references to show that in his day godless men are bent on destroying God's people.

Greek Words, Phrases, and Constructions in 11

ἐπορεύθησαν—this verb and the other two in verse 11 are constative aorists.[54] The three datives are unique: ὁδῷ (dative of place), πλάνῃ (dative of advantage), and ἀντιλογίᾳ (dative of means).

τοῦ Βαλαὰμ μισθοῦ—although the definite article can be construed either with the personal name *Balaam* or with the noun *profit*, in harmony with the other two parts of this verse I take it with the name *Balaam*.

---

54. Consult Dana and Mantey, *Manual Grammar*, p. 196.

μισθοῦ ἐξεχύθησαν—the genitive μισθοῦ is objective, "for profit," and is classified as a genitive of price.[55] The verb form is the aorist passive from ἐκχέω (I pour out). In the passive it means *"give up* or *abandon oneself."*[56]

---

12 These men are blemishes at your love feasts, eating with you without the slightest qualm—shepherds who feed only themselves. They are clouds without rain, blown along by the wind; autumn trees, without fruit and uprooted—twice dead. 13 They are wild waves of the sea, foaming up their shame; wandering stars, for whom blackest darkness has been reserved forever.

14 Enoch, the seventh from Adam, prophesied about these men: "See, the Lord is coming with thousands upon thousands of his holy ones 15 to judge everyone, and to convict all the ungodly of all the ungodly acts they have done in the ungodly way, and of all the harsh words ungodly sinners have spoken against him." 16 These men are grumblers and faultfinders; they follow their own evil desires; they boast about themselves and flatter others for their own advantage.

V. Descriptions
12–16

A. Contemporaries
12–13

In these two verses Jude resorts to using many figures from nature to portray his godless adversaries. His metaphors are eloquent, colorful, and pointed, and aid the reader in recognizing these men who are perverting God's truth. Here is poetic description at its best.

12. These men are blemishes at your love feasts, eating with you without the slightest qualm—shepherds who feed only themselves. They are clouds without rain, blown along by the wind; autumn trees, without fruit and uprooted—twice dead.

In this verse Jude provides another indication that these apostates are mingling freely with the members of the church (see v. 4). They are brazen in their behavior; they boldly come to the love feasts of the believers.

These men are blemishes. What is the meaning of the word *blemishes*? The term is used to describe spots or stains that cover an object, for example, a body. These spots mar the appearance of the item in question. In the parallel of this text, Peter characterizes the false teachers as "blots and blemishes" at the love feasts of the church (II Peter 2:13). The original meaning of the Greek word is "reefs." The term refers to "a hidden reef" or "a dangerous obstacle" (JB) on which a ship can be wrecked when it is approaching land. This translation, then, points to the heretics who mingle in the Christian community and have not yet been identified as dangerous to the life of the church. The choice between these two translations is

---

55. Consult Moule, *Idiom-Book*, p. 39.
56. Bauer, p. 247.

difficult. Nevertheless, the godless persons who come boldly to the love feasts are anything but secretive in their actions. They live immoral lives, reject authority (v. 8), behave like animals (v. 10), and are divisive in their work (v. 15). Accordingly, many translators prefer the reading *blemishes*. They do so in view of the parallel in II Peter 2:13, where Peter uses a different Greek word which means "spots."

At your love feasts. Without hesitation these intruders come to the love feasts of the Christian community. What is a love feast? It is "a common meal eaten by early Christians in connection w[ith] their church services, for the purpose of fostering and expressing brotherly love."[57] At these feasts the apostates satisfy their physical appetites. They do this without qualm in the presence of the Christians whose unity and harmony they seek to destroy.

Shepherds who feed only themselves. This is an obvious reference to the prophecy of Ezekiel, where God pronounces woes upon the spiritual shepherds of Israel "who only take care of themselves" instead of God's people (34:2; also see vv. 8, 10). Jude's adversaries come to the love feasts to feed themselves (compare I Cor. 11:21, 33). But the text says that they "were shepherding themselves," which points to a spiritual dimension. The concept *shepherd* in the New Testament relates to the church of Jesus Christ that is spiritually fed by faithful shepherds (see, e.g., Acts 20:28; I Cor. 9:7; I Peter 5:2).[58] By contrast, these false teachers are not caring for the members of the church; instead they expect monetary support from these members. They take all and give nothing.

Therefore, Jude describes his adversaries with four metaphors taken from nature: "from the air, the earth, the sea, the heaven."[59] He depicts waterless clouds that symbolize deception, dead fruit trees that symbolize uselessness, foaming waves of the sea that show unruliness, and wandering stars that portray disobedience.

They are clouds without rain. An anxious farmer looks expectantly at approaching clouds. He hopes to receive abundant rain for his parched fields. But much to his dismay, he sees these clouds drift past, blown by the wind. They fail to give him a single drop of rain. He knows that he has been deceived by the appearance of these waterless clouds. Similarly, the heretics are verbose in speech but fail to present anything that is substantive and refreshing.

Autumn trees, without fruit and uprooted—twice dead. Here Jude presents a picture of dead fruit trees which apparently had not produced a harvest during the autumn. To the fruit farmer, these trees were dead, that is, useless, and therefore he had pulled them out of the ground to make

---

57. Bauer, p. 6.
58. Consult Erich Beyreuther, *NIDNTT*, vol. 3, pp. 566–69; Joachim Jeremias, *TDNT*, vol. 6, pp. 490–502.
59. Bengel, *Gnomon of the New Testament*, vol. 5, p. 167.

room for other trees. In their uprooted state, the wood of the trees dried up, so that the farmer rightly could call them "twice dead." Except as firewood, these trees had no value for him.

The spiritual application of this metaphor means that the godless men bear no spiritual fruit in their lives (compare Matt. 7:20). Because they deny Jesus Christ as their Lord and Savior (v. 4), they are spiritually dead. They are the false teachers about whom Peter writes, "If they have escaped the corruption of the world by knowing our Lord and Savior Jesus Christ and are again entangled in it and overcome, they are worse off at the end than they were at the beginning" (II Peter 2:20; also see Heb. 6:4–6). And for this reason, Jude describes them as twice dead.

Another view is that Jude regards the physical destruction of these sinners an accomplished fact (v. 11b), even though they are still living. Moreover, God has condemned them (compare vv. 4a, 7b, 14–15). Because they have "change[d] the grace of . . . God into a license for immorality," they demonstrate that they have died a spiritual death. In Scripture, this phenomenon is known as the second death (Rev. 2:11; 20:6, 14; 21:8). The term *second death* is an apocalyptic phrase that expresses God's condemnation of the wicked.[60] Indeed this view has merit.

13. They are wild waves of the sea, foaming up their shame.

Here is a slightly different metaphor, in which Jude mixes the physical elements of nature (waves) with the moral qualities of man (shame). The Old Testament parallel is Isaiah 57:20, "But the wicked are like the tossing sea, which cannot rest, whose waves cast up mire and mud." In this picture Jude portrays both the fierce brute force of the waves and their instability and unpredictability as they roll toward shore (compare James 1:6). They pick up foam and debris which they scatter abroad.

This picture of the sea depicts the wicked whose evil hearts impel them to engage in shameful acts that affect the people who surround them. The evil they commit is forceful, untamed, unpredictable, and involves any unwary bystander. With this metaphor Jude projects an element of fearfulness. As a person standing along the shore tries to avoid the spray of the waves, so the believer ought to shun the words and deeds of the wicked.

Wandering stars. Jude uses this last metaphor to cause the reader to look at the night sky and see the planets. He knows that a careful observer sees some planets wander through the heavens. They illuminate the darkness but because of their wandering courses, they cannot be relied on for navigational purposes. We should stay with the exact wording of the text and not interpret the words to mean meteors or shooting stars that disappear in the darkness of the night. Jude places the emphasis on the concept *wander,* which aptly applies to the false teachers. In fact, the word *error* (v. 11)

---

60. Consult Israel Abrahams, *Studies in Pharisaism and the Gospels,* 2d series (1924; New York: Ktav, 1967), p. 44. Also see Kelly, *Peter and Jude,* p. 273.

derives from the verb *to wander*. By applying this concept to the heretics, Jude describes them as apostates in whose company no Christian can chart a straight path.[61] Their devious course of life leads to eternal damnation.

For whom blackest darkness has been reserved forever. Jude is no longer speaking about the wandering stars but is applying the last line of verse 13 to the godless men whom God has consigned to hell. Notice the resemblance of their destiny to that of the fallen angels whom God has placed in dark dungeons. "These [angels] he has kept in darkness, bound with everlasting chains for judgment on the great Day" (v. 6). Jude qualifies the term *darkness* with the word *blackest,* which also occurs in the parallel passage, "Blackest darkness is reserved for them" (II Peter 2:17). That is, these wicked men will spend eternity in utter darkness. They exist without hope in absolute oblivion.

Of these four metaphors, the last one reveals the ultimate destiny of the false prophets who pretend to be guiding lights but instead are wandering stars. Jude employs the passive voice in the clause "for whom blackest darkness has been reserved forever." With the passive he indicates that God himself has placed the godless men, together with the fallen angels (v. 6), in everlasting darkness.[62]

Greek Words, Phrases, and Constructions in 12–13

Verse 12

ἀφόβως—this adverb translated "without qualm" modifies either the preceding present middle participle συνευωχούμενοι (feasting together) or the following present active participle ποιμαίνοντες (shepherding). Translators are equally divided and the choice is difficult.

ἀνέμων—Jude uses the plural form of ἄνεμον (wind) to depict the frequent changes of direction.

ἐκριζωθέντα—the compound of the preposition ἐκ (out of) and the verb ῥιζόω (I cause to take root) is both directive and perfective in scope. The passive voice metaphorically points to God as the divine agent.

Verse 13

ἀστέρες πλανῆται—these two nouns stand in apposition to each other. They lack definite articles and are translated "wandering stars," literally, "stars that are planets." To translate these two nouns freely as "shooting stars" is inaccurate.

οἷς—grammatically the nearest antecedent of this masculine plural relative pronoun is πλανῆται. However, the sense of the verse dictates that the antecedent is οὗτοι (these) in verse 12.

---

61. Refer to Walther Günther, *NIDNTT,* vol. 2, p. 459; Herbert Braun, *TDNT,* vol. 6, p. 250.
62. Refer to George Lawrence Lawlor, *Translation and Exposition of the Epistle of Jude,* International Library of Philosophy and Theology series (Nutley, N. J.: Presbyterian and Reformed, 1972), p. 96.

B. Saints and Sinners
14–15

In the next two verses Jude quotes from the apocryphal book I Enoch, which was widely known in the first century of the Christian era. It circulated originally in Aramaic and possibly Hebrew. Archaeologists discovered fragments of this book, written in Aramaic, among the Dead Sea Scrolls. Scholars assume that Jude consulted an Aramaic copy of I Enoch and translated into Greek the verses he needed for his epistle.

14. Enoch, the seventh from Adam, prophesied about these men: "See, the Lord is coming with thousands upon thousands of his holy ones 15. to judge everyone, and to convict all the ungodly of all the ungodly acts they have done in the ungodly way, and of all the harsh words ungodly sinners have spoken against him."

Before I interpret these two verses, a few comments must be made. First, even though Jude cites an apocryphal book, he provides no evidence that he regarded it as Scripture. He used this document because, in the two centuries before and after the birth of Christ, I Enoch was a well-known and highly respected volume of religious writings. Next, upon close examination we learn that this apocryphal document has been responsible for influencing indirectly the language and thought of many New Testament books (see the allusions to I Enoch especially in Matthew, Luke, Romans, Hebrews, and Revelation). Their writers show familiarity with the content of I Enoch. Last, we must ask whether the quotation from I Enoch in its biblical context is authoritative. The answer is affirmative. Divine inspiration takes place when the Holy Spirit fills an author and directs him to write Scripture (see II Peter 1:21). The Holy Spirit is free to inspire borrowed words and make them part of God's Word (see, e.g., Acts 17:28). Also, we know that God himself stands behind his Word to give it absolute authority.

Observe these points:

a. *Enoch*. This godly person is known to us from the genealogy in Genesis 5:18, 21–24. He is the man who "walked with God," which is a phrase used twice (in vv. 22 and 24) to reveal his intimate spiritual life. Because of Enoch's devotion, God took him so that he did not see death. Jude designates him "the seventh from Adam." Beginning with Adam, we have seven names, including Seth, Enosh, Kenan, Mahalalel, Jared, and Enoch (Gen. 5:3–24; I Chron. 1:1–3).[63] To the Jew, the number seven signifies completion or fullness.

"Enoch . . . prophesied about these men." If we assume that the words of Enoch were spoken by the godly person who lived before the flood, then we hear a voice from early antiquity. Listing examples from the past (vv. 5–7),

---

63. I En. 60:8–9 has the reading "[Enoch] the seventh from Adam, the first man whom the Lord of the Spirits created." Isaac, *I (Ethiopic Apocalypse of) Enoch*, pp. 40–41. See also 93:3.

Jude makes no reference to any person living prior to the flood. By contrast, Peter in his parallel account includes Noah and his family (II Peter 2:5). In the place of Noah, Jude mentions Enoch, who prophesied in the days before the flood.[64]

Does Jude mean that the verb *to prophesy* in this text must be understood as referring to inspired prophecy? Hardly. Donald Guthrie writes:

> It seems most likely that [Jude] did not intend the word in this sense, but rather in the sense of 'predicting', since he applies to his own day what purports to come from the antediluvian world. It would have been different if any of the normal citation-formulae had been used, for then there would have been little doubt that Jude was treating the book of Enoch as Scripture. But in the absence of a specific formula, the presumption must be in favour of a more general use of the verb.[65]

Jude makes no appeal to Scripture and omits the common introduction, "it is written," that is used by other New Testament writers. "This much we can at least say without straining, that the designation Scripture as 'scripture' and its citation by the formula 'It is written' attest primarily its indefectible authority."[66]

b. *Return of Christ.* "See, the Lord is coming with thousands upon thousands of his holy ones." Except for a few variations (perhaps because Jude presents his own translation), the text is virtually the same as that of I Enoch 1:9. Here is Enoch's prophecy:

> Behold, he will arrive with ten million of the holy ones in order to execute judgment upon all. He will destroy the wicked ones and censure all flesh on account of everything that they have done, that which the sinners and the wicked ones committed against him.[67]

Note that Jude makes "the Lord" the subject of the sentence. He puts the quotation in the perspective of Christ's return. When Jesus comes back, he will be accompanied by "thousands upon thousands of his holy ones," that is, his angels. In the Gospel Jesus affirms that "when the Son of Man comes in his glory, and all the angels with him, he will sit on his throne in heavenly glory" (Matt. 25:31; see 24:30–31). The text gives no precise number of angels but is merely descriptive of an exceedingly great multitude (compare Deut. 33:2; Dan. 7:10; Zech. 14:5; Heb. 12:22). The Lord returns to pass judgment on all people and to convict the wicked.

c. *Judgment.* "[The Lord is coming] to judge everyone, and to convict all

---

64. Consult Lenski, *Interpretation of the Epistles,* p. 639.

65. Donald Guthrie, *New Testament Theology* (Downers Grove: Inter-Varsity, 1981), p. 978.

66. B. B. Warfield, "Inspiration," *ISBE,* vol. 2, p. 844.

67. Isaac, *I (Ethiopic Apocalypse of) Enoch,* pp. 13–14. Also consult C. D. Osburn, "The Christological Use of I Enoch i. 9 in Jude 14. 15," *NTS* 23 (1977): 334–41.

the ungodly of all the ungodly acts they have done in the ungodly way, and of all harsh words ungodly sinners have spoken against him." John Newton describes Christ's return:

> At His call the dead awaken,
> Rise to life from earth and sea;
> All the powers of nature, shaken
> By His looks, prepare to flee.
> Careless sinner,
> What will then become of thee?

Enoch not only observes the wickedness of his day, but also looks into the future and addresses all godless people, including the adversaries of Jude. Jude, then, notes that the Lord judges everyone, for God has given Jesus the authority to judge the people (see John 5:27–30).

Note the repetition, obviously for emphasis, in this verse (v. 15). Jude uses the comprehensive and inclusive Greek adjective *all* four times (in the NIV "all" [three times] and "everyone" [once]). He also repeats the word *ungodly* (four times). Every human being must stand before the Judge. The righteous will be acquitted through the redeeming work of Christ, but the wicked will receive their just recompense. In the judgment day the unbelievers cannot claim ignorance, for they have received warnings throughout history. In fact, the ungodly deliberately ignore these admonitions and sin regardless. In his terse manner, John Albert Bengel remarks, "*A sinner* is bad; one who sins *without fear,* is worse."[68]

d. *Conviction.* As Jude develops his letter, he explains his earlier comment about God's condemnation of godless men (v. 4). Thus, he discloses that these men live immorally, spurn authority, and "slander celestial beings" (vv. 8, 10). He reveals that they find fault, boast, brag, and flatter (v. 16); they scoff at divine revelation and willfully "follow their own ungodly desires" (v. 18). Applying the prophecy of Enoch, Jude indicates that these men will be convicted because of the evil acts they have committed and the harsh words they have spoken against the Lord. All ungodly persons will be judged and all their ungodly deeds and all their hard words will be held as evidence against them in a court of law (see Mal. 3:13; Matt. 12:36). The writer's emphasis on the terms *all* and *ungodly* is designed to call the attention of these godless men to the seriousness of their sin. They deliberately taunt God, dishonor him, and scorn his Word. In the Greek Jude places the two words *ungodly sinners* last in the sentence for special emphasis. A literal translation of these words reveals the climax of the sentence: "sinners, godless persons."

---

68. Bengel, *Gnomon of the New Testament,* vol. 5, p. 169.

Greek Words, Phrases, and Constructions in 14–15

Verse 14

καί—this conjunction is omitted in many translations.[69] Perhaps this καί is a misplaced conjunction that should have preceded the noun Ἐνώχ.[70]

τούτοις—the difficulties with this demonstrative pronoun are disturbing. First, the lack of a preposition before the dative case is confusing because the dative is not an indirect object. Translators meet the problem by supplying the preposition *about*, that is, "he prophesied about these men." Next, the antecedent of the pronoun appears to be the godless men mentioned earlier in Jude's epistle (vv. 4, 8, 10, 12). But did Enoch by-pass the wicked generation of his own day?

ἦλθεν—the aorist active of ἔρχομαι (I come, go) is used in a prophetic sense and is given a future connotation.

ἐν—the meaning of this preposition "draws close to μετά and σύν in usage."[71]

Verse 15

ποιῆσαι κρίσιν—the aorist infinitive reveals single action in the court case. The noun κρίσιν (the process of judging) refers to the duration of the trial in which every deed and every word is examined.

ἐλάλησαν—this verb refers to not so much the content of the spoken words as the manner in which they were uttered.

C. Grumblers
16

After quoting Enoch's prophecy, Jude applies it to the ungodly men whom he first introduced in verse 4. He demonstrates that these men in effect sin against God in word and deed. He shows that they are godless sinners.

16. These men are grumblers and faultfinders; they follow their own evil desires; they boast about themselves and flatter others for their own advantage.

Jude is completing his description of these heretics; he has portrayed them graphically with a series of four metaphors taken from nature (vv. 12–13). Now he lists at least five of their sinful practices and reprehensible characteristics. He writes,

a. "These men are grumblers." In some situations in life, necessity forces people to utter legitimate complaints. For example, in the Jerusalem church, the Greek-speaking Jews complained against the Aramaic-speaking Jews because their widows were being neglected in respect to the daily food

---

69. For example, GNB, JB, NAB, NEB, NIV, SEB.

70. Refer to Moule, *Idiom-Book*, p. 167.

71. Robertson, *Grammar*, p. 589.

distribution (Acts 6:1). Jude, however, uses the term *grumblers* not with a positive but with a negative meaning. These men, he intimates, give vent to their discontent by complaining not against men but against God. When the Israelites grumbled in the desert, they were killed by God's destroying angel (see Num. 16:41; 17:5, 10; I Cor. 10:10). In Jesus' day, not only the Jews but even the disciples grumbled about the words Jesus spoke (see John 6:41, 43, 61). The term *grumble* denotes dissatisfaction with someone's words or deeds and often leads to condemning the speaker or doer.

b. "Faultfinders." The godless persons in Jude's day went one step further; they were grumblers and faultfinders. These two terms are synonymous. Persons who are faultfinders are "finding fault with [their] lot."[72] They bemoan the place God has given them in life and thus they direct their criticism toward God. They consider God responsible for their adversities, losses, and disappointments. They are the ungodly sinners who speak harsh words against God (v. 15).

c. "They follow their own evil desires." Jude repeats these words in verse 18 ("[they] will follow their own ungodly desires"). By adding the qualifying adjective *evil*, Jude rules out the possibility of interpreting the word *desires* in a favorable sense. He is referring to physical lust that reveals itself in unlawful craving.[73] These ungodly people are enslaved to their evil desires, for daily they pursue them and consequently commit ungodly acts (see v. 15).

d. "They boast about themselves." Literally Jude says, "And their mouth speaks haughty words." They utter arrogant speech which they are unable to confirm. They make boastful comments that are empty, without substance, and baseless. Yet in their arrogance they directed these comments to God.

e. "[They] flatter others for their own advantage." These godless men are showing partiality to gain profits for themselves. The Greek has the expression *to admire faces;* it is best translated "flatter." This expression is actually a Hebrew idiom translated into Greek; it conveys the meaning *to show partiality for the sake of material benefits*. But in the Old Testament God instructed the Israelites, "Do not show partiality to the poor or favoritism to the great, but judge your neighbor fairly" (Lev. 19:15; also compare Deut. 16:19; James 2:1–9). The apostates speak arrogant words to God and flattering words to the rich. With their arrogance they flout God's honor and with their flattery they deceive their fellow men.

---

17 But, dear friends, remember what the apostles of our Lord Jesus Christ foretold. 18 They said to you, "In the last times there will be scoffers who will follow their own ungodly

---

72. Thomas McComiskey, *NIDNTT*, vol. 2, p. 145; Walter Grundmann, *TDNT*, vol. 4, p. 574. The term occurs only here in the New Testament.
73. For a few select passages, compare James 1:14–15; I Peter 1:14; 2:11; 4:2; II Peter 2:10, 18; 3:3.

desires." 19 These are the men who divide you, who follow mere natural instincts and do not have the Spirit.

20 But you, dear friends, build yourselves up in your most holy faith and pray in the Holy Spirit. 21 Keep yourselves in God's love as you wait for the mercy of our Lord Jesus Christ to bring you to eternal life.

22 Be merciful to those who doubt; 23 snatch others from the fire and save them; to others show mercy, mixed with fear—hating even the clothing stained by corrupted flesh.

VI. Exhortations to Believers
17–23

A. Remember the Gospel
17–18

Except for a brief comment on the divisiveness of the godless persons, Jude has concluded the major part of his epistle. He is making the transition from describing the heretics (vv. 5–16) to addressing the Christians (vv. 17–23). In a sense, the main part of his letter is an explanation of his remark about the condemnation of ungodly men (v. 4). But in the concluding part of the epistle, Jude wants to write about the salvation of the believers (v. 3).[74] Accordingly, in the next two verses he exhorts the believers to listen to the teaching of Christ's apostles.

17. But, dear friends, remember what the apostles of our Lord Jesus Christ foretold.   18. They said to you, "In the last times there will be scoffers who will follow their own ungodly desires."

a. *Address.* After writing the lengthy discourse on the conduct of false teachers, Jude once more addresses the original recipients of his epistle. He has warned them about the words and deeds of godless men whom God has condemned (see vv. 4, 7, 13). Now he addresses them tenderly with the expression *dear friends.* He uses this term three times, once at the beginning of his epistle (v. 3) and twice at the end (vv. 17, 20). The readers are loved by God (v. 1) and by their faithful pastor Jude.

b. *Recall.* Notice the close parallel to this text in Peter's second epistle: "I want you to recall the words spoken in the past by the holy prophets and the command given by our Lord and Savior through your apostles" (3:2). Jude gives his readers a command when he says, "Remember." He has spoken encouraging words earlier when he commended them for their knowledge of Old Testament teaching (v. 5). But now a direct command is necessary, for neglect of factual knowledge is detrimental to their salvation. The readers must be able to recall the message of the gospel so that they can defend themselves against the pernicious attacks of the heretics. They must know that they can effectively oppose their adversaries with the gospel which has been preached by Christ's apostles.

---

74. See Greijdanus, *De Brieven,* p. 640.

c. *Apostles.* Who are the apostles? Jude writes, "Remember what the apostles of our Lord Jesus Christ foretold." He implies that he is not one of them. Although Jude mentions no apostolic names, the qualification *of our Lord Jesus Christ* provides the evidence that he means the original twelve apostles and Paul. We know almost nothing about their ministry, except for the missionary labors of Peter and Paul recorded in their epistles and in Acts. Because the New Testament is silent about the labors of the broader circle of apostles, we assume that Jude is thinking of the well-known apostles Peter and Paul.

d. *Message.* The literal text has, "Remember the words which were spoken before by the apostles" (NKJV). That is, the Greek term *rēmatōn* (words) refers not to the entire gospel but rather to individual sayings of the apostles. Perhaps Jude has recorded one of these sayings in the next verse (v. 18). The apostles were conscious of the approaching last days and warned the Christians to expect difficult times. Hence in his farewell message to the Ephesian elders Paul said, "Know that after I leave, savage wolves will come in among you and will not spare the flock" (Acts 20:29).

e. *Saying.* What do the apostles say? "In the last times there will be scoffers who will follow their own ungodly desires." The Greek text reveals that the apostles repeatedly taught the content of this saying. Peter also has recorded it, albeit with slight variations from Jude's wording: "First of all, you must understand that in the last days scoffers will come, scoffing and following their own evil desires" (II Peter 3:3). Teaching orally, the apostles drilled these words into the hearts and minds of the believers. They taught that the early Christians lived in the last days or last times, in which false teachers would undermine the members of the church. From the New Testament epistles we know that this teaching was common (e.g., I Tim. 4:1–2; II Tim. 3:1–5).

In New Testament literature, the expression *last times* applies to the present and the future. This time has its beginning in the first century when Christ came and brought the gospel and lasts until his eventual return. Scripture teaches that during this period, the forces of evil will become increasingly visible and audible. The apostles repeat the warnings of Jesus, who in his discourse on the end of the age repeatedly predicts that false prophets will appear to deceive, if possible, even the elect (Matt. 24:4–5, 11, 23–24, 26). In a similar vein, the apostles warn the believers to watch out for scoffers.

Even though we are aware of the negative work of heretics, we should not forget to stress the positive support that God gives us. The author of the Epistle to the Hebrews writes that in these last days God has spoken to us through his Son (1:2; and compare I Peter 1:20). And God's Word stands forever.

f. *Scoffers.* "Scoffers will come, scoffing" (II Peter 3:3). The people Jude describes are not ignorant of God's Word. On the contrary, they are well informed. Because of their knowledge of divine revelation, they make a

401

continual mockery of that which is holy and sacred. Scoffing is not a light, humorous parody but a serious attack on God, his Word, and his people. Scoffers openly demonstrate their contempt and derision for God by following "their own ungodly desires." They deliberately reject God's judgment and opt for a lifestyle of sin instead.

Jude has described these scoffers as immoral men who "reject authority and slander celestial beings" (v. 8). The apostolic saying, however, relates as much to the future as to the present: "In the last times there *will be* scoffers" (italics added). The apostles, then, predict that as the end of time approaches scoffers will increasingly ridicule Christians. As they deride the Christian faith they display their own spiritual bankruptcy. They are apostates who revel in lust and greed.

g. *Lust.* About these scoffers Jude writes, "[They follow] their own ungodly desires." He restates the words of verse 16 (also see II Peter 3:3). Why does Jude repeat himself? We assume that he wants to summarize his portrayal of these godless men by putting emphasis on the term *ungodly.* The Greek text has the wording "walking after their own lusts of ungodlinesses." Granted that the literal English translation is awkward, in Greek the stress is on the plural form *ungodlinesses.* Jude wishes to tell his readers that the sinful desires of these apostates include all acts of impiety (see especially v. 15) and that these men fulfill Enoch's prophecy.

The attitude of the scoffers is diametrically opposed to that of the believer, who desires to do God's will and to express his gratitude to him. Scoffers purposely transgress the law of God to fill up the measure of their godlessness. For believers the impiety of these godless people is a sign that the end of the world is near.

Practical Considerations in 17

In the days of the apostles, the believers relied on memory for the singing of psalms and hymns in their worship services. They learned by heart numerous messianic passages from the Old Testament and retained the message of the gospel they had heard from the apostles. They were forced to develop their retentive memories because they had only limited access to the written books of Scripture kept in local churches.

In our day we have become accustomed to relying on the written word and therefore fail to exercise our memories. We claim that as long as we are able to refer to something in print, we have no need to memorize it. Our minds, then, are like erasable boards; we retain facts for immediate use but soon replace them with new information.

This mind-set also prevails when we worship God on the Lord's day. Routinely we enter the sanctuary each Sunday morning to hear the pastor preach, yet our minds will retain his message for only a few days. As statistics show, during a given Sunday we retain only 30 percent of the sermon the pastor preaches that day. This percentage dwindles to less than 5 percent by the last day of that same week.

In the Old and New Testaments, however, we are told to treasure God's Word.

The psalmist rejoices in that Word and confides to God, "I have hidden your word in my heart that I might not sin against you" (Ps. 119:11). And Jesus exhorts the churches in Thyatira and Philadelphia with these words: "Only hold on to what you have until I come" (Rev. 2:25; with variation, 3:11).

Greek Words, Phrases, and Constructions in 17–18

Verse 17

μνήσθητε—the aorist passive imperative of the deponent verb μιμνήσκομαι (I remember) takes an object (τῶν ῥημάτων, the words) in the genitive case. The use of the aorist instead of the present tense sharpens the command to remember these apostolic words.

προειρημένων—as a compound from πρό (before) and the defunct form ῥέω (I say), this perfect passive participle shows action that occurred in the past but has lasting effect for the present.

Verse 18

ἔλεγον—note the use of the imperfect tense to indicate repeated action in the past.

τῶν ἀσεβειῶν—although the plural *godlessnesses* is cumbersome in English, in Greek these words (definite article and noun) are emphatic at the end of the sentence. They are also descriptive because the plural form summarizes the words and deeds of the godless men (see vv. 4, 8, 13, 15, 16).

B. Avoid Heretics
19

Here is Jude's last word on the errorists who are bent on dividing and destroying the church. Throughout his epistle Jude has not called these men false teachers, but in this verse he designates them "the ones who cause a division."[75] They do the opposite of those who are building each other up in respect to the Christian faith.

19. These are the men who divide you, who follow mere natural instincts and do not have the Spirit.

Precisely what are these godless men doing in the Christian community? Jude says that they are busy drawing boundaries for the purpose of separating Christians from the fellowship of believers. They are "*making divisions* or *separations*" in the church.[76] Obviously, their purpose is to create schisms and factions, which is the common practice of people who proclaim heresies.

Some scholars assert that Jude employs key words in Greek that were important within the heretical movement called Gnosticism. The Gnostics of the second century taught that a division existed between the physical

---

75. Bauer, p. 90.
76. Thayer, p. 61.

and the spiritual realm. The physical was the lower realm and the spiritual the higher. In this higher realm were two categories of people, the psychic and the spiritual. Christians belonged to the psychic class, but Gnostics to the spiritual category. The Gnostics were spirit-filled people who, free from moral obligations, assumed a position far superior to that of the psychic Christians.[77]

However, the objection to this explanation is that although we know these key words were employed in second-century Gnostic teaching, we have no evidence that Gnosticism was an issue one hundred years earlier when Jude wrote his epistle. Perhaps we can say that the heretics in Jude's day were forerunners of the movement which in the second century became known as Gnosticism. "It is safer to interpret Jude's words in their own context."[78]

Jude characterizes the heretics as persons who created divisions in the church. Apparently they claimed to have the Spirit and to be morally free in respect to their behavior. Most likely they indicated that the Christians lacked this gift. Jude, however, turns the matter around and states that the heretics "follow mere natural instincts and do not have the Spirit." These people are apostates. In a few words Jude has put the godless men in their place. They have no part in the church, for they lack the Spirit of God.

Greek Words, Phrases, and Constructions in 19

οὗτοι—describing the apostates in the major part of his letter, Jude resorts to frequent use of this demonstrative pronoun (see vv. 8, 10, 12, 16).

ἀποδιορίζοντες—from ἀπό (away from), διά (through), and ὅρος (limit), this compound present active participle appears only here in the New Testament. It means "making separations."

C. Persevere and Pray
20–21

The last few verses of his letter Jude devotes to the initial readers. In contrast with the lengthy discourse about the wickedness of the apostates, the final remarks to the believers are brief. In a series of four commands Jude tells them to cultivate the familiar Christian virtues of faith, prayer, love, and hope. Moreover, in these two verses Jude refers to the Trinity: God, Jesus Christ, and the Holy Spirit.

---

77. Consult Werner de Boor, *Der Zweite Brief des Petrus und der Brief des Judas*, in *Die Briefe des Petrus und der Brief des Judas*, Wuppertaler Studienbibel (Wuppertal: Brockhaus, 1976), pp. 283–84. Also see Kelly, *Peter and Jude*, pp. 284–85.

78. Bauckham, *Jude, 2 Peter*, p. 106.

20. But you, dear friends, build yourselves up in your most holy faith and pray in the Holy Spirit.

a. "Dear friends." Once again (see v. 17) Jude contrasts the readers with the heretics, and now with pastoral care he addresses them as "dear friends," that is, beloved by God (v. 1) and by Jude himself. After depicting the destructive life of the unbelievers, he states how believers ought to live positively. The first command is:

b. "Build yourselves up in your most holy faith." While the godless men enter the Christian community to bring division, Jude commands the readers to build each other spiritually and thus strengthen the unity of the church. Jude writes an apostolic command, for he puts in his own words Paul's description of the pastor's role: "To prepare God's people for works of service, so that the body of Christ may be built up" (Eph. 4:12; also see Col. 2:7; I Thess. 5:11). Jude instructs his readers: "You must continue to build yourselves up on the foundation of your most holy faith." He illustrates his message with a reference to the building trade: build on a foundation.

What is that foundation on which the believers must construct their spiritual house? Faith! This is the first virtue in the series of four Jude lists in this verse and the next (v. 21). He has returned to the subject *faith* with which he began his epistle: "Dear friends, . . . I felt I had to write and urge you to contend for the faith that was once for all entrusted to the saints" (v. 3). Hence he begins and ends his letter with the subject *faith*. This faith is the body of Christian doctrines which the apostles taught (see Acts 2:42). The reference here is not to subjective faith, the personal trust the believer places in Jesus Christ, but rather to objective faith (Christian beliefs), which is the foundation for the body of Christ.

Notice how verses 3 and 20 complement each other. At the beginning of his letter, Jude urges the readers to contend for the faith "that was once for all entrusted to the saints" (v. 3). And in verse 20 he exhorts the believers to build themselves up in the "most holy faith." This faith is a gift of God that is entrusted to Christians and is described in superlative form as "most holy." This faith which originates with God is perfect, pure, and incomparable. Believers should put forth every effort to fortify their brothers and sisters with this precious gift which they together possess. By continuing to strengthen each other, they achieve unity and purpose "to become the one holy community of the Lord."[79] In their task, however, they do not stand alone as the body of Christ. Jude lists the second of four virtues (faith, prayer, love, and hope) and commands the believers to pray.

c. "Pray in the Holy Spirit." Together Christians must pray continually in the Spirit to show their complete dependence upon God. Jude's wording is similar to that of Paul, who writes, "And pray in the Spirit on all occasions with all kinds of prayers and requests" (Eph. 6:18) to oppose the spiritual

---

79. Jürgen Goetzmann, *NIDNTT*, vol. 2, p. 253.

attacks of Satan. Jude presents the apostolic teaching, known among the early Christians, to pray continually (see I Thess. 5:17). He exhorts the believers: "Keep on praying, for you possess the Spirit." The Spirit takes our feeble prayers and perfects and presents them to God the Father. As Paul tells the church, "The Spirit himself intercedes for us with groans that words cannot express" (Rom. 8:26).

21. Keep yourselves in God's love as you wait for the mercy of our Lord Jesus Christ to bring you to eternal life.

d. "Keep yourselves in God's love." Of the four Christian virtues enumerated in this passage, Jude introduces the third, namely, love. Amid the uncertainties, difficulties, and temptations that surround the believers, Jude admonishes them to keep themselves within the circle of God's love and literally to stay in that sphere. Christians are recipients of this love when they strive to do God's will by loving him with heart, soul, and mind and by loving their neighbor as themselves (see Matt. 22:37–39).

The phrase *the love of God* can mean either God's love for man or man's love for God. Even though the choice is difficult to make, the context seems to favor God's love for man. As Jude states in the salutation in verse 1, the readers "are loved by God the Father" (also compare John 15:9–10; I John 2:5). God comes to man and surrounds him with divine love; in response man comes to God with human love.

e. "As you wait for the mercy of our Lord Jesus Christ." This is the fourth Christian virtue Jude introduces: hope. Granted that the word itself is not in the text, we know that the context clearly expresses the idea. To hope and to wait eagerly are twin concepts to which the text, in effect, testifies. The text literally says: "As you are waiting with anticipation." For instance, this expression also is used to describe our expectation of the resurrection (Acts 24:15), the prospect of eternal glory (Titus 2:13), and servants who await the return of their master (Luke 12:36).[80]

A Christian waits with eager expectation for the day of judgment in which Christ's mercy will acquit him. In other words, the text calls attention to the judgment day when all believers will experience "the mercy of our Lord Jesus Christ," but all the wicked will receive their just reward. Notice that Jude once again (see v. 17) refers to Jesus as "our Lord Jesus Christ." That is, the believers who acknowledge him as their Lord and Savior know that he grants them eternal life.

f. "To bring you to eternal life." In this last phrase Jude summarizes the work of the Trinity (God the Father, the Holy Spirit, and the Lord Jesus Christ) and the result of four Christian virtues (faith, prayer, love, and hope). Believers have everlasting fellowship with God when they experience the fullness of eternal life in his presence.[81]

---

80. Consult Walter Grundmann, *TDNT,* vol. 2, p. 58.
81. Refer to Henry Alford, *Alford's Greek Testament: An Exegetical and Critical Commentary,* 5th ed., 4 vols. (1875; Grand Rapids: Guardian, 1976), vol. 4, pt. 2, p. 541.

D. Show Mercy
22–23

With two verses that contain additional admonitions, Jude concludes his brief epistle. He designates mercy the overriding characteristic that Christians must show to their fellow men. Thus he writes,

22. Be merciful to those who doubt; 23. snatch others from the fire and save them; to others show mercy, mixed with fear—hating even the clothing stained by corrupted flesh.

What is the believer's response to the mercy of Jesus Christ which he awaits with anticipation? He responds by showing mercy to those whose hearts are filled with doubt. He wants mercy to be his hallmark. In words attributed to Stephen Grellet, he says:

> I expect to pass through this world but once; any good thing therefore that I can do, or any kindness that I can show to my fellow-creature, let me do it now; let me not defer or neglect it, for I shall not pass this way again.

a. "Be merciful to those who doubt." The New English Bible has a lucid and striking translation: "There are some doubting souls who need your pity." Jude is alerting the readers to the danger some weak Christians face when they are confronted by the apostates (compare II Peter 2:18). Whenever these people begin to doubt Christian teachings, reassure them by giving them help and understanding. Avoid any form of criticism, but show mercy and love to those who waver.

b. "Snatch others from the fire and save them." After informing the readers about the first class of people, the doubters, Jude acquaints them with another group. These people are being scorched by the fire of sin. Jude has borrowed the imagery from the Old Testament. God says to Israel, "You were like a burning stick snatched from the fire" (Amos 4:11). And God says the same thing about the high priest Joshua, who stands with the accuser Satan before God (Zech. 3:2). The image of fire relates to imminent destruction that is about to engulf those who are weak in faith and are being burned by sin. In their case, time is precious. Christians must save them by snatching them out of the fire. The question in this text is not whether man has the power to save others. We know that only God has the power to save man. What, then, is the meaning? John Calvin gives a clear explanation: "The word to *save*, is transferred to men, not that they are the authors, but [they are] the ministers of salvation."[82]

c. "To others show mercy, mixed with fear." Jude repeats the word *mercy* (see v. 22), but now he is not interested in the two groups of spiritually weak Christians who are doubters or in danger of being destroyed. Here he refers to a third class of people who persist in sin. Pity these people, coun-

---

82. Calvin, *The Epistle of Jude*, p. 449.

sels Jude, and "be kind [to them] with great caution" (JB). That is, be wary of sin so that it does not entrap you. What should be the Christian's reaction to sin? This is the answer:

d. "Hating even the clothing stained by corrupted flesh." The imagery recalls the high priest Joshua, who "was dressed in filthy clothes as he stood before the angel. The angel said to those who were standing before him, 'Take off his filthy clothes' " (Zech. 3:3–4). As Joshua's garments symbolized sin, so clothing that is "stained by corrupted flesh" represents iniquity. In brief, Jude resorts to the use of a metaphor. Jesus also uses this imagery when he addresses the church in Sardis: "Yet you have a few people in Sardis who have not soiled their clothes" (Rev. 3:4).

What is Jude trying to communicate? The picture is of undergarments that are soiled by discharges of the body. Jude wants the readers to feel intense aversion, even to the point of hatred, especially when they think about clothes that belong to someone else. Jude is saying to the readers, "Avoid all contact with sin so that it does not contaminate you. In fact, hate sin as you would loathe filthy undergarments stained by human excretions."

Textual Variations in 22–23

The Greek text in verses 22 and 23 presents many difficulties that have given rise to various translations. Apart from minor variations, the verses present either three or two categories of people. The reading in the New International Version depicts three groups of people: those who doubt; others who are snatched from the fire; and others who receive pity.[83]

Many translations reduce these categories to two: "on some have compassion," "but others save with fear" (NKJV).[84] In view of Jude's penchant for presenting his material in groups of three (e.g., vv. 1, 2, 11), many scholars believe that the triple arrangement of the passage is original.[85]

Apart from the question whether the passage mentions two or three classes of people, individual variants also cause translation difficulties. Two variations in the reading of verse 22 go back to differences in the Greek text: "And convince some, who doubt" (RSV); "And on some have compassion, making a distinction" (NKJV).

The first of these has the verb *convince* as a well-attested reading in Greek manuscripts. Without doubt it suits the meaning of the sentence, because Christians ought to convince a doubter that the gospel message is true. Conversely, if the Greek of this verb is a variation caused by an ancient scribe who wanted to avoid repetition of the verb *be merciful* (vv. 22 and 23),

---

83. Also see RSV, NASB, GNB, MLB, NAB, JB.
84. Compare KJV, NEB, SEB.
85. Consult Metzger, *Textual Commentary*, p. 726.

then we are inclined to assume that this repetitous reading is original indeed.

Before we accept this argument, however, we must consider still another Greek witness. The earliest known Greek manuscript of Jude, a papyrus document (P[72]) dating from the third century, has the shortest text of all the witnesses: "Snatch some from the fire, but on those who dispute [doubt] have mercy with fear."[86] In other words, this manuscript deletes verse 22 altogether. If we apply the general rule of textual criticism that the shorter reading deserves preference, the papyrus document may be correct. But even though this reading has merit, we must face the question whether the scribe considered verse 22 redundant and accordingly deleted it. Mainly because of this unanswered question, modern translators have not adopted this shorter reading.

Next, in the sentence, "And on some have compassion, *making a distinction*," the italicized clause is poorly attested. "[The] reading is obviously a secondary development, introduced by copyists in order to conform the [Greek] participle to the nominative case in agreement with the following two participles ["snatching" and "hating"] in verse 23."[87] Moreover, the clause itself ("making a distinction") is difficult to explain.

Last, the prepositional phrase *with fear* is placed either in the first clause of verse 23 after the verb *save* or after the second clause modifying the verb *show mercy*. The phrase should be placed in the second clause of verse 23. There it serves as an introduction to and explanation of the last part of the text, "hating even the clothing stained by corrupted flesh."

The textual variations in this passage are too complex to expect unanimity on every point. When the text itself is not clear, we ought to avoid being dogmatic and should be willing to examine and discuss all the points of view pertaining to the variants.

Greek Words, Phrases, and Constructions in 22–23

Verse 22

οὕς μέν—this is the third time that Jude employs the triple form μέν, δέ, δέ to achieve literary balance (see vv. 8, 10).

Verse 23

ἀπό—instead of the usual form ὑπό, the preposition ἀπό denotes not only agency but also causal origin.

χιτῶνα—in contrast with ἱμάτιον (outer garment), this word is used for "a garment worn next to the skin, and by both sexes."[88]

---

86. Bauckham, *Jude, 2 Peter*, pp. 108–11, 115. Also consult J. N. Birdsall, "The Text of Jude in P[72]," *JTS* 14, 2 (1963): 394–99; C. D. Osburn, "The Text of Jude 22–23," *ZNW* 63 (1972): 139–44.

87. Metzger, *Textual Commentary*, p. 726.

88. Bauer, p. 882.

24 To him who is able to keep you from falling and to present you before his glorious presence without fault and with great joy— 25 to the only God our Savior be glory, majesty, power and authority, through Jesus Christ our Lord, before all ages, now and forevermore! Amen.

VII. Doxology
24–25

In a beautiful ascription of praise the writer turns to God. Jude begins his epistle by attributing love and protection to God the Father and Jesus Christ. He concludes his letter by praising God and Jesus Christ for protecting the believers and presenting them in the presence of God. In this doxology, the church of all ages and places puts its trust and confidence in God alone.

24. To him who is able to keep you from falling and to present you before his glorious presence without fault and with great joy— 25. to the only God our Savior be glory, majesty, power and authority, through Jesus Christ our Lord before all ages, now and forevermore! Amen.

This doxology may have been sung in the early Christian church. These two verses provide literary balance and cadence that lend themselves to antiphonal singing. For instance, note the two main verbs in verse 24 (to keep and to present) with two qualifiers (fault and joy); the two names with appositions in verse 25 (God our Savior, and Jesus Christ our Lord), the four attributes (glory, majesty, power, authority) and the triple reference to past time, the present, and the future ("before all ages, now and forevermore"). The conclusion to this balanced doxology is the word *amen*.

a. "To him who is able to keep you from falling." The person to whom this paean of praise is directed is God our Savior. Although the believers observe the apostasy of heretics, they know that God is able to protect his own and keep their salvation intact. Compare the jubilant statement of Paul, "I . . . am convinced that he is able to guard what I have entrusted to him for that day" (II Tim. 1:12b).[89]

Fully aware of the danger of falling into temptation and being attacked by sin, Jude tells the Christians to put their trust in almighty God. He says, "[God] is able to keep you." God is able to guard his own people as "the apple of his eye" (Deut. 32:10), for they are his precious possession. The verb *to keep* in verse 24 means "providing protection from external attack." Hence God protected righteous Noah and his family from the raging waters of the flood (II Peter 2:5), yet Noah had to build the ark. Consequently,

---

89. The phrase *to him who is able* also occurs in other doxologies (Rom. 16:25; Eph. 3:20; and see II Cor. 9:8).

the believer knows that as God provides the means for defense against any assault, so he must use these means to protect himself.[90]

In his letter Jude teaches the twofold doctrine of God's protecting care and man's responsibility. He assures the believers that God is able to keep them from falling (v. 24), and tells them to keep themselves in God's love (v. 21). He confirms that God will present them without fault in glory (v. 24), yet they must build themselves up in the faith (v. 20).[91]

b. "Keep you from falling." Literally the text reads, "keep you from being tripped." The reference is not to a sure-footed horse that keeps itself from stumbling. Rather, the text describes believers who are kept by God himself from stumbling into sin and thus from falling away from him. Jude, then, is speaking about falling away spiritually, as is evident from the next clause: God presents the believers without fault in his glorious presence. God is active in the work of saving his own people.

c. "To present you before his glorious presence without fault and with great joy." We are unable to enter heaven on our own account, but God who is rich in mercy protects us from falling away and causes us to enter heaven's glory. Through the work of Jesus Christ, God presents us blameless in his glorious presence.[92] Peter uses the words *without blemish* when he describes Christ as a lamb without defect (I Peter 1:19). God not only cleanses us from sin, but also grants his people unceasing joy. That is, heaven is filled with the continuous rejoicing of saints and angels (compare Luke 15:5, 10; Rev. 19:7). Because of their redemption, Christians are filled not with terror but with joy when they enter the presence of God.

d. "To the only God our Savior." Here is the second part of Jude's exquisite doxology.[93] Jude ends his epistle by ascribing glory to God alone; compare the well-known Latin motto *Soli Deo Gloria* (to God alone be the glory). The adjective *only* ("alone") is commonly used in doxologies (Rom. 16:27; I Tim. 1:17; 6:15, 16) and reflects Israel's creed, "Hear, O Israel: The LORD our God, the LORD is one" (Deut. 6:4).

Granted that the New Testament writers apply the term *Savior* to Jesus, in several passages they mention that God is our Savior.[94] This ascription is common in the Old Testament, especially in the Psalms and the prophetical books. God is the Savior of his people; in the fullness of time he sent his Son

---

90. Thayer, p. 622. Also see Lawlor, *The Epistle of Jude*, p. 137.

91. Consult Guthrie, *New Testament Theology*, p. 638.

92. The concept *blameless* appears frequently in the New Testament (e.g., Eph. 1:4; 5:27; Phil. 2:15; Col. 1:22).

93. Some translations have the reading *to the only* wise *God* (emphasis added), which is a variation that has been influenced by Rom. 16:27. In view of the support of influential Greek manuscripts, translators prefer the shorter reading.

94. The term *Savior* appears twenty-four times in the New Testament, sixteen of which are applied to Christ and eight to God (Luke 1:47; I Tim. 1:1; 2:3; 4:10; Titus 1:3; 2:10; 3:4; Jude 25). Refer to Johannes Schneider and Colin Brown, *NIDNTT*, vol. 3, pp. 219–21.

to redeem them from sin. Through Jesus Christ we are redeemed from sin and guilt and translated to glory (see Col. 1:12–14).

e. "[To him] be glory, majesty, power and authority." In his doxology Jude lists four divine attributes. To God belongs everlasting glory, for it is essential to his being. Glory is commonly ascribed to him in doxologies (except for I Tim. 6:16; I Peter 5:11). Ascribing glory to God, however, is merely acknowledging an essential aspect of his being, for in essence God is glory. On earth Christ's followers reflect the glory of God in word and deed. But when they enter heaven, believers are glorified and share in God's glory (see, e.g., Rom. 8:30).

The expression *majesty* applies only to God the Father. It occurs three times in the New Testament (twice in the Epistle to the Hebrews, where it is used instead of the name of God [1:3; 8:1], and once here). In postapostolic literature the term also refers to God.[95]

In the New Testament the last two attributes, power and authority, are virtually synonymous. The word *power* appears in doxologies and refers to God and to Christ (I Tim. 6:16 ["might," NIV]; I Peter 4:11; 5:11; Rev. 1:6; 5:13). And the term *authority* occurs in Jesus' majestic utterance: "All authority in heaven and on earth has been given to me" (Matt. 28:18). Thus, God the Father gave his Son Jesus Christ all authority (see John 5:27; Rev. 12:10).

f. "Through Jesus Christ our Lord." This is the fourth time in his epistle that Jude names Jesus Christ "our Lord" (vv. 4, 17, 21, 25). In the Greek, the previously mentioned phrase follows the words "to the only God our Savior." We can give glory, majesty, power, and authority to God only through our Lord Jesus Christ. Conversely, the proximity of this clause to the word *savior* should not be overlooked. The translators of the New International Version place the clause near the end of the doxology to connect it with the last phrase.

g. "Before all ages, now and forevermore! Amen." In a few words Jude describes the totality of time pertaining to the past, the present, and the future. With our finite minds we are unable to comprehend eternity and accordingly must express ourselves in generalities. The writer of Hebrews uses common terms when he describes time in relation to Jesus. He says, "Jesus Christ is the same yesterday and today and forever" (13:8).

Jude ends this outstanding doxology with a resounding "amen." May everyone concur and say, "So be it." Following Jewish custom, Christians normally end their doxologies with the concluding *amen*.

Greek Words, Phrases, and Constructions in 24

φυλάξαι—this is the constative aorist active infinitive of φυλάσσω (I guard, protect). "This use of the aorist contemplates the action in its entirety."[96]

---

95. E.g., see the many references in I Clem. (20:12; 27:4; 36:2; 58:1; 61:3; 64; 65:2).
96. Dana and Mantey, *Manual Grammar*, p. 196.

ἀπταίστους—the verbal adjective expresses the passive voice together with the negative ἀ (not to be tripped).

ἀγαλλιάσει—the dative of ἀγαλλίασις (exultation) denotes manner. The -σις ending of the noun signifies process.

Summary of the Epistle of Jude

Jude writes a letter to strengthen the readers in their faith and to warn them not to be misled by apostates who in life and doctrine try to lead them astray. After identifying himself, he greets the recipients and pronounces a blessing of mercy, peace, and love.

In a personal manner, Jude says that he had planned to write a letter about the doctrine of salvation and to urge the recipients to contend for the faith, that is, the gospel. However, he changes his mind because of the presence of immoral men who have infiltrated the Christian community. Jude reminds the believers of three Old Testament examples that illustrate divine judgment: the unbelieving Israelites in the desert, the rebellious angels who left their positions of authority, and the immoral men of Sodom and Gomorrah.

Jude calls the infiltrators "dreamers" who engage in immorality, rebellion, and slander. He cites the incident of the archangel Michael, who refrained from bringing an accusation against Satan. These ungodly men follow the way of Cain, Balaam, and Korah. They are blemishes in the company of Christians. Relying on a prophecy of Enoch, Jude describes the coming of the Lord with his myriads of angels. The Lord will judge the ungodly according to their words and deeds.

The readers know about the coming of the scoffers, for the apostles have given them instructions. Jude urges the believers to strengthen one another in the faith and to wait prayerfully for the realization of eternal life. He exhorts them to show mercy to doubters, to save others from destruction, and to be wary of sin's contamination. He concludes his epistle with a splendid doxology to God.

Select Bibliography

Commentaries

Aalders, Gerhard Charles. *Genesis*. Translated by William Heynen. Bible Student's Commentary series. 2 vols. Vol. 2. Grand Rapids: Zondervan, 1981.

Alford, Henry. *Alford's Greek Testament: An Exegetical and Critical Commentary*. 4 vols. 5th ed. Vol. 4, pt. 2. 1875. Grand Rapids: Guardian, 1976.

Barnett, A. E. "The Second Epistle of Peter." *The Interpreter's Bible*. Vol. 12. New York and Nashville: Abingdon, 1957.

Bauckham, Richard J. *Jude, 1, 2 Peter*. Word Commentary series. Vol. 50. Waco: Word, 1983.

Beare, Francis Wright. *The First Epistle of Peter: The Greek Text with Introduction and Notes*. 2d ed. Oxford: Blackwell, 1961.

Bengel, John Albert. *Gnomon of the New Testament*. Edited by Andrew R. Fausset. Translated by William Fletcher. 5 vols. 7th ed. Vol. 5. Edinburgh: T. and T. Clark, 1877.

Best, Ernest. *I Peter*. New Century Bible series. London: Oliphants, 1971.

Bigg, Charles. *A Critical and Exegetical Commentary on the Epistles of St. Peter and St. Jude*. International Critical Commentary series. 1901. Edinburgh: T. and T. Clark, 1961.

Blum, Edwin A. *Jude*. In *Hebrews-Revelation*, vol. 12 of *The Expositor's Bible Commentary*. Edited by Frank E. Gaebelein. 12 vols. Grand Rapids: Zondervan, 1981.

————. *1, 2 Peter*. In *Hebrews-Revelation*, vol. 12 of *The Expositor's Bible Commentary*. Edited by Frank E. Gaebelein. 12 vols. Grand Rapids: Zondervan, 1981.

Boobyer, G. H. "II Peter." *Peake's Commentary on the Bible*. Edited by M. Black and H. H. Rowley. London: Nelson, 1962.

Calvin, John. *Commentaries on the Catholic Epistles: The Epistle of Jude; The First Epistle of Peter; The Second Epistle of Peter*. Edited and translated by John Owen. Grand Rapids: Eerdmans, 1948.

Cranfield, C. E. B. *I and II Peter and Jude: Introduction and Commentary*. Torch Bible Commentaries series. London: SCM, 1960.

de Boor, Werner. *Der Zweite Brief des Petrus und der Brief des Judas*. In *Die Briefe des Petrus und der Brief des Judas*. Wuppertaler Studienbibel. Wuppertal: Brockhaus, 1976.

Fitzmyer, Joseph A. *The First Epistle of Peter*. In *The Jerome Biblical Commentary*. Edited by Raymond E. Brown, Joseph A. Fitzmyer, and Roland E. Murphy. 2 vols. Vol. 2. Englewood Cliffs, N.J.: Prentice-Hall, 1968.

Select Bibliography

Goppelt, Leonhard. *Der Erste Petrusbrief*. Kritisch-Exegetischer Kommentar über das Neuen Testament. Edited by Ferdinand Hahn. 8th ed. Vol. 12/1. Göttingen: Vandenhoeck und Ruprecht, 1978.

Green, Michael. *The Second Epistle General of Peter, and the General Epistle of Jude: An Introduction and Commentary*. Tyndale New Testament Commentaries. Grand Rapids: Eerdmans, 1968.

Greijdanus, S. *De Brieven van de Apostelen Petrus en Johannes, en de Brief van Judas*. Kommentaar op het Nieuwe Testament series. Amsterdam: Van Bottenburg, 1929.

Hiebert, D. Edmond. *First Peter: An Expositional Commentary*. Chicago: Moody, 1984.

Hendriksen, William. *Colossians and Philemon*. New Testament Commentary series. Grand Rapids: Baker, 1964.

————. *The Gospel of John*. 2 vols. in 1. New Testament Commentary series. Grand Rapids: Baker, 1954.

————. *Romans*. New Testament Commentary series. Grand Rapids: Baker, 1980.

Holmer, Uwe. *Der Erste Brief des Petrus*. In *Die Briefe des Petrus und der Brief des Judas*. Wuppertaler Studienbibel. Wuppertal: Brockhaus, 1976.

Hort, F. J. A. *The First Epistle of St. Peter*. London: Macmillan, 1898; Minneapolis: Klock and Klock, 1976.

James, M. R. *The Second Epistle General of Peter and the General Epistle of Jude*. Cambridge: Cambridge University Press, 1912.

Johnstone, R. *The First Epistle of Peter*. Edinburgh: T. and T. Clark, 1888.

Kelly, J. N. D. *A Commentary on the Epistles of Peter and Jude*. Thornapple Commentaries series. 1969. Grand Rapids: Baker, 1981.

Lawlor, George Lawrence. *Translation and Exposition of the Epistle of Jude*. International Library of Philosophy and Theology series. Nutley, N.J.: Presbyterian and Reformed, 1972.

Leaney, A. R. C. *The Letters of Peter and Jude*. Cambridge Bible Commentaries. Cambridge: Cambridge University Press, 1967.

Lenski, R. C. H. *The Interpretation of the Epistles of St. Peter, St. John, and St. Jude*. Columbus: Wartburg, 1945.

Luther, Martin. *The Catholic Epistles*. Vol. 30 of *Luther's Works*. Edited by Jaroslav Pelikan and Walter A. Hansen. St. Louis: Concordia, 1967.

Mayor, Joseph B. *The Epistle of St. Jude and the Second Epistle of St. Peter: Greek Text with Introduction and Notes*. 1907. Grand Rapids: Baker, 1965.

Moffatt, James. *The General Epistles: James, Peter, and Judas*. Moffatt New Testament Commentary. London: Hodder and Stoughton, 1928.

Mounce, Robert H. *A Living Hope: A Commentary on 1 and 2 Peter*. Grand Rapids: Eerdmans, 1982.

Plummer, A. *The General Epistles of St. James and St. Jude*. London: Hodder and Stoughton, 1891.

Plumptre, E. H. *The General Epistles of St. Peter and St. Jude*. Cambridge: Cambridge University Press, 1892.

Reicke, Bo. *The Epistles of James, Peter, and Jude*. The Anchor Bible. Vol. 37. New York: Doubleday, 1964.

Schelkle, Karl Hermann. *Die Petrusbriefe, Der Judasbrief*. Herders Theologischer Kommentar zum Neuen Testament series. 5th rev. ed. Vol. 13/2. Freiburg: Herder, 1980.

Select Bibliography

Schrage, W. *Die "katholischen" Briefe: Die Briefe des Jakobus, Petrus, Johannes, und Judas*. Translated by H. Balz and W. Schrage. Neuen Testament Deutsch 10. 11th ed. Göttingen: Vandenhoeck und Ruprecht, 1973.

Selwyn, E. G. *The First Epistle of St. Peter: The Greek Text with Introduction, Notes, and Essays*. London: Macmillan, 1946.

Senior, D. *1 and 2 Peter*. New Testament Message 20. Dublin: Veritas Publications, 1980.

Sidebottom, E. M. *James, Jude, and 2 Peter*. Century Bible series. London: Nelson, 1967.

Stibbs, Alan M. *The First Epistle General of Peter*. Tyndale New Testament Commentaries series. Grand Rapids: Eerdmans, 1960.

Wand, J. W. C. *The General Epistles of St. Peter and St. Jude*. Westminster Commentaries series. London: Methuen, 1934.

Windisch, Hans, and Herbert Preisker. *Die Katholischen Briefe*. Lietzmann's *Handbuch zum Neuen Testament*. 3d ed. Tübingen: Mohr, 1951.

Wolff, Richard. *A Commentary on the Epistle of Jude*. Grand Rapids: Zondervan, 1960.

Studies

Abrahams, Israel. *Studies in Pharisaism and the Gospels*. 2d series. 1924. New York: Ktav, 1967.

Bammel, Ernst. "The Commands in I Peter ii.17." *New Testament Studies* 11 (1965): 279–81.

Bauckham, Richard J. "The Delay of the Parousia." *Tyndale Bulletin* 31 (1980): 3–36.

Bauer, J. B. "Aut maleficus aut alieni speculator (1 Petr 4, 15)." *Biblische Zeitschrift* 22 (1978): 109–15.

Bavinck, Herman. *Gereformeerde Dogmatiek*. 4 vols. Vol. 2. Kampen: Kok, 1928.

Berkhof, Louis. *Systematic Theology*. 2d rev. ed. Grand Rapids: Eerdmans, 1941.

Best, Ernest. "1 Peter and the Gospel Tradition." *New Testament Studies* 16 (1969/70): 95–113.

———. "1 Peter 2:4–10—A Reconsideration." *Novum Testamentum* 11 (1969): 270–93.

———. "Spiritual Sacrifice. General Priesthood in the New Testament." *Interpretation* 14 (1960): 273–99.

Birdsall, J. N. "The Text of Jude in P[72]." *Journal of Theological Studies* 14, 2 (1963): 394–99.

Boobyer, G. H. "The Verbs in Jude 11." *New Testament Studies* 5 (1958): 45–47.

Brooks, O. S. "I Peter 3:21—The Clue to the Literary Structure of the Epistle." *Novum Testamentum* 16 (1974): 290–305.

Brown, J. P. "Synoptic Parallels in the Epistles and Form-History." *New Testament Studies* 10 (1963/64): 27–48.

Cavallin, H. C. E. "The False Teachers of 2 Pt as Pseudo-Prophets." *Novum Testamentum* 21 (1979): 263–70.

Charles, R. H., ed. *The Apocrypha and Pseudepigrapha of the Old Testament*. 2 vols. 1913. Oxford: Clarendon, 1977.

Charlesworth, James H., ed. *The Old Testament Pseudepigrapha*. 2 vols. Garden City, N.Y.: Doubleday, 1983.

Combrink, H. J. B. "The Structure of 1 Peter." *Neotestamentica* 9 (1975): 34–63.

Cranfield, C. E. B. "The Interpretation of 1 Peter 3:19 and 4:16." *Expository Times* 62 (1957/58): 369–72.

Cross, F. L. *I Peter, A Paschal Liturgy.* London: Mowbray, 1970.

Dalton, William Joseph. *Christ's Proclamation to the Spirits: A Study of I Peter 3:18–4:16.* Analecta Biblica 23. Rome: Pontifical Biblical Institute, 1964.

DeRidder, Richard R. *The Dispersion of the People of God.* Kampen: Kok, 1971.

de Ru, G. "De Authenticiteit van II Petrus." *Nederlands Theologisch Tijdschrift* 24 (1969–70): 1–12.

Dillenberger, J., ed. *Martin Luther: Selections from His Writings.* Garden City, N.Y.: Doubleday, 1961.

Dunham, Duane A. "An Exegetical Study of 2 Peter 2:18–22." *Bibliotheca Sacra* 140 (1983): 40–54.

Elliott, John Hall. *The Elect and the Holy.* Supplements to *Novum Testamentum.* Vol. 12. Leiden: Brill, 1966.

———. "Peter, Silvanus and Mark in 1 Peter and Acts: Sociological Exegetical Perspectives on a Petrine Group in Rome." *Wort in der Zeit: Neutestamentliche Studien.* Karl Heinrich Rengstorf Festschrift. Edited by W. Haubeck and M. Bachmann. Leiden: Brill, 1980, pp. 250–67.

Epstein, I., ed. *The Babylonian Talmud.* 35 vols. London: Soncino Press, 1935–52.

Eusebius. *Ecclesiastical History.* Loeb Classical Library series. London: Heinemann; New York: Putnam, 1966–76.

Eybers, I. H. "Aspects of the Background of the Letter of Jude." *Neotestamentica* 9 (1975): 113–23.

Feinberg, John S. "I Peter 3:18–20, Ancient Mythology, and the Intermediate State." *Westminster Theological Journal* 48 (1986): 303–36.

Foh, Susan T. *Women and the Word of God: A Response to Biblical Feminism.* Nutley, N.J.: Presbyterian and Reformed, 1979.

Gundry, Robert H. " 'Verba Christi' in I Peter: Their Implications Concerning the Authorship of I Peter and the Authenticity of the Gospel Tradition." *New Testament Studies* 13 (1966–67): 336–50.

Guthrie, Donald. *New Testament Introduction.* Rev. ed. Downers Grove: Inter-Varsity, 1971.

———. *New Testament Theology.* Downers Grove: Inter-Varsity, 1981.

Hemer, C. J. "The Address of I Peter." *Expository Times* 89 (1978): 239–43.

Hennecke, E., W. Schneemelcher, and R. Wilson, eds. *New Testament Apocrypha.* 2 vols. London: Lutterworth, 1963, 1965.

Hiebert, D. Edmond. "The Prophetic Foundation for the Christian Life: An Exposition of 2 Peter 1:19–21." *Bibliotheca Sacra* 141 (1984): 158–68.

Hurley, James B. *Man and Woman in Biblical Perspective.* Grand Rapids: Zondervan, 1981.

Isaac, E. *I (Ethiopic Apocalypse of) Enoch.* In *The Old Testament Pseudepigrapha.* Edited by James H. Charlesworth. 2 vols. Vol. 1. Garden City, N.Y.: Doubleday, 1983.

Käsemann, Ernst. "An Apologia for Primitive Christian Eschatology." In *Essays on New Testament Themes.* Studies in Biblical Theology, no. 41. London: SCM, 1964.

Kümmel, Werner Georg. *Introduction to the New Testament.* Translated by A. J. Mattill, Jr. 14th ed. Nashville and New York: Abingdon, 1966.

———. *Introduction to the New Testament.* Translated by H. C. Kee. 2d ed. London: SCM, 1975.

Select Bibliography

Ladd, George E. *A Theology of the New Testament*. Grand Rapids: Eerdmans, 1974.

Leaney, A. R. C. "1 Peter and the Passover: An Interpretation." *New Testament Studies* 10 (1963/64): 238–51.

Longenecker, Richard N. "Ancient Amanuenses and the Pauline Epistles." In *New Dimensions in New Testament Study*. Edited by Richard N. Longenecker and Merrill C. Tenney. Grand Rapids: Zondervan, 1974.

Luther, Martin. "Sermons on the Epistle of St. Jude." In *The Catholic Epistles*, vol. 30 of *Luther's Works*. Edited by Jaroslav Pelikan and Walter A. Hansen. St. Louis: Concordia, 1967.

McKelvey, R. J. "Christ the Cornerstone." *New Testament Studies* 8 (1961–62): 352–59.

Martin, Ralph P. *The Acts, the Letters, the Apocalypse*. Vol. 2 of *New Testament Foundations: A Guide for Christian Students*. 2 vols. Grand Rapids: Eerdmans, 1978.

Michaels, J. Ramsey. "Eschatology in I Peter iii.17." *New Testament Studies* 13 (1967): 401.

Murray, John. *Redemption: Accomplished and Applied*. Grand Rapids: Eerdmans, 1955.

Neyrey, J. H. "The Apologetic Use of the Transfiguration in 2 Peter." *Journal of Biblical Literature* 99 (1980): 407–31.

Osborne, Thomas P. "Guide Lines for Christian Suffering: A Source-Critical and Theological Study of 1 Peter 2, 21–25." *Biblica* 64 (1983): 381–408.

Osburn, C. D. "The Text of Jude 22–23." *Zeitschrift für die Neutestamentliche Wissenschaft* 63 (1972): 139–44.

Priest, J. *Testament of Moses*. In *The Old Testament Pseudepigrapha*. Edited by James H. Charlesworth. 2 vols. Vol. 1. Garden City, N.Y.: Doubleday, 1983.

Ramsey, J. R. "Eschatology in 1 Peter 3:17." *New Testament Studies* 13 (1966/67): 394–401.

Rees, P. S. *Triumphant in Trouble: Studies in 1 Peter*. Westwood, N.J.: Revell, 1962.

Reicke, Bo. *The Disobedient Spirits and Christian Baptism: A Study of I Peter III.19 and Its Context*. Copenhagen: Munksgaard, 1946.

Roberts, Alexander, and James Donaldson, eds. *The Apostolic Fathers*, vol. 1 of *The Ante-Nicene Fathers*. 1885. Grand Rapids: Eerdmans, 1962.

Robertson, P. E. "Is 1 Peter a Sermon?" *Theological Educator* 13 (1982): 35–41.

Robinson, J. A. T. *Redating the New Testament*. London: SCM; Philadelphia: Westminster, 1976.

Rowston, D. J. "The Most Neglected Book in the New Testament." *New Testament Studies* 21, 4 (1975): 554–63.

Spitta, Friedrich. *Christi Predigt und die Geister (I Petr. 3, 19ff.): Ein Beitrag zur neuetestamentischen Theologie*. Göttingen: Vandenhoeck und Ruprecht, 1890.

Sylva, Dennis. "Translating and Interpreting 1 Peter 3:2." *Biblical Translator* 34 (1983): 147.

Taylor, Vincent. *Jesus and His Sacrifice*. London: Macmillan, 1937.

Thornton, T. C. G. "I Peter, a Paschal Liturgy?" *Journal of Theological Studies* 12 (1961): 14–26.

Toon, Peter. *The Right of Private Judgment*. Portland, Ore.: Western Conservative Baptist Seminary, 1975.

Van Gemeren, Willem A. "The Sons of God in Genesis 6:1–4." *Westminster Theological Journal* 43 (1981): 320–48.

van Unnik, W. C. "The Teaching of Good Works in I Peter." *New Testament Studies* 1 (1954–55): 92–110.

Zahn, Theodor. *Introduction to the New Testament.* Translated by M. W. Jacobus et al. 3 vols. Vol. 2. Edinburgh: T. and T. Clark, 1909.

Tools

Aland, Kurt, et al., eds. *The Greek New Testament.* 3d ed. New York: United Bible Societies, 1975.

Bauckham, Richard J. "2 Peter: A Supplementary Bibliography." *Journal of the Evangelical Theological Society* 25 (1982): 91–94.

Bauer, Walter, W. F. Arndt, F. W. Gingrich, and F. W. Danker. *A Greek-English Lexicon of the New Testament and Other Early Christian Literature.* 2d ed. Chicago: University of Chicago Press, 1978.

Berkhof, Louis. *Introductory Volume to Systematic Theology.* Grand Rapids: Eerdmans, 1932.

Blass, Friedrich, and Albert Debrunner. *A Greek Grammar of the New Testament.* Translated and revised by Robert Funk. Chicago: University of Chicago Press, 1961.

Bromiley, Geoffrey W., ed. *The International Standard Bible Encyclopedia.* Rev. ed. 4 vols. Grand Rapids: Eerdmans, 1979–.

Brown, Colin, ed. *New International Dictionary of New Testament Theology.* 3 vols. Grand Rapids: Zondervan, 1975–78.

Dana, H. E., and Julius R. Mantey. *A Manual Grammar of the Greek New Testament.* 1927. New York: Macmillan, 1967.

Dodd, C. H. *The Parables of the Kingdom.* 1935. Rev. ed., New York: Charles Scribner's Sons, 1961.

Elwell, Walter A., ed. *Evangelical Dictionary of Theology.* Grand Rapids: Baker, 1984.

Farstad, Arthur L., and Zane C. Hodges. *The Greek New Testament According to the Majority Text.* Nashville and New York: Nelson, 1982.

Hanna, Robert. *A Grammatical Aid to the Greek New Testament.* Grand Rapids: Baker, 1983.

Hupper, William G. "Additions to 'A 2 Peter Bibliography.'" *Journal of the Evangelical Theological Society* 23 (1980): 65–66.

Josephus, Flavius. *Antiquities.* Loeb Classical Library series. London: Heinemann; New York: Putnam, 1966–76.

———. *Wars of the Jews.* Loeb Classical Library series. London: Heinemann; New York: Putnam, 1966–76.

Kittel, Gerhard, and Gerhard Friedrich, eds. *Theological Dictionary of the New Testament.* Translated by Geoffrey W. Bromiley. 10 vols. Grand Rapids: Eerdmans, 1964–76.

Merk, Augustinus. *Novum Testamentum.* 9th ed. Rome: Pontifical Biblical Institute, 1964.

Metzger, Bruce M. *A Textual Commentary on the Greek New Testament.* 3d corrected ed. London and New York: United Bible Societies, 1975.

Moule, C. F. D. *An Idiom-Book of New Testament Greek.* 2d ed. Cambridge: Cambridge University Press, 1960.

Moulton, J. H., and G. Milligan. *The Vocabulary of the Greek Testament Illustrated from the Papyri and Other Non-Literary Sources.* 3 vols. London: Hodder and Stoughton, 1929.

Moulton, J. H., et al. *A Grammar of New Testament Greek.* 4 vols. Edinburgh: T. and T. Clark, 1908–76.

Select Bibliography

Nestle, Eberhard, and Kurt Aland, rev. *Novum Testamentum Graece*. 26th ed. Stuttgart: Deutsche Bibelstiftung, 1981.

Robertson, A. T. *A Grammar of the Greek New Testament in the Light of Historical Research*. Nashville: Broadman, 1934.

Snyder, John. "A 2 Peter Bibliography." *Journal of the Evangelical Theological Society* 22 (1979): 265–67.

Strack, H. L., and P. Billerbeck. *Kommentar zum Neuen Testament aus Talmud und Midrasch*. 5 vols. München: Beck, 1922–28.

Thayer, Joseph H. *A Greek-English Lexicon of the New Testament*. New York, Cincinnati, and Chicago: American Book Company, 1889.

Trench, R. C. *Synonyms of the New Testament*. 1854. Grand Rapids: Eerdmans, 1953.

Index of Authors

422

Index of Authors

Index of Scripture

426

438

439

Extrabiblical References